LANDLORDING

Dedication

This book is dedicated to the scrupulous landlady in my life. Ivy, that's you.

Acknowledgements

I would like to acknowledge the following good people for their help in one way or another: Robert Armentrout, Denise Berger, Bob Bochemuehl, Maynard Briggs, Bob Bruss, Nelly Bunn, Norma D'Andrea, Wallace Darling, James Doherty, Bud Ekstrom, Ron English, Dan Faller, Fred Felder, Robert France, Herb Frank, Ruth Furey, Dave Glubetich, Al Good, Vernon Graves, David Halbrook, Scotty Herd, Larry Hughes, Tom Javorina, Robert Jones, John Koczan, Delwyn Levno, Carl Lindh, Marion Mahnken, Charles Manning, Robin Maydeck, Oliver McClory, Margaret Miglia, Rita Moore, Connie Nakano, David Patton, Carol Pladsen, Richard Randolph, Jack Reed, Daniel Robinson, Dario Robinson, Nancy Robinson, Christina Salamo, Corinne Schultz, Ira Serkes, Jo Stender, Suzanne Stevenson, Jeffrey Taylor, Joel Vuylsteke, Paul Warren, Suzanne Wehausen, David Williams, Nancy Williams, Jay Wilson, Jim Woollen, and the hundreds of landlords and landladies who've endured my landlording classes with many suggestions and few complaints.

Without their help, this book wouldn't be in the shape it's in.

The Usual Caveat

This publication is designed to provide accurate and authoritative information in regard to the subject matter covered. It is sold with the understanding that the publisher is not engaged in rendering legal or accounting service. If legal advice or other expert assistance is required, the services of a competent professional person should be sought.

— From a declaration of principles jointly adopted by a committee of the American Bar Association and a committee of publishers and associations.

LANDLORDING

A Handymanual for Scrupulous Landlords and Landladies Who Do It Themselves

written by
LEIGH ROBINSON

illustrated by
**DAVID PATTON, NANCY ROBINSON,
JAN BROWN, and CHRISTINA SALAMO**

published by

**P.O. BOX 1639
EL CERRITO, CA 94530-4639**
landlording.com; expresspublishing.com

FIRST EDITION	September, 1975
SECOND EDITION	May, 1976
Revised	February, 1977
Revised	March, 1978
Reprinted	September, 1978
Reprinted	November, 1978
Revised	June, 1979
THIRD EDITION	March, 1980
Revised	October, 1980
Revised	October, 1981
Revised	February, 1983
Reprinted	January, 1984
Reprinted	August, 1984
Reprinted	January, 1985
Reprinted	May, 1985
FOURTH EDITION	January, 1986
Revised	July, 1986
Revised	April, 1987
Revised	February, 1988
FIFTH EDITION	October, 1988
Revised	April, 1989
Revised	February, 1990
Revised	February, 1991
SIXTH EDITION	February, 1992
Revised	November, 1992
Revised	October, 1993
SEVENTH EDITION	July, 1994
Revised	February, 1995
Revised	February, 1996
EIGHTH EDITION	December, 1997
Revised	January, 1999
Reprinted	September, 2000
NINTH EDITION	September, 2001
Revised	February, 2003
Revised	May, 2004
Revised	October, 2005
TENTH EDITION	November, 2006
ELEVENTH EDITION	July, 2010

COPYRIGHT ©1975, 1976, 1977, 1978, 1979, 1980, 1981, 1983, 1986, 1987, 1988, 1989, 1990, 1991, 1992, 1993, 1994, 1995, 1996, 1997, 1999, 2001, 2003, 2004, 2005, 2006, 2010 by Leigh Robinson

LIBRARY OF CONGRESS CONTROL NUMBER: 2010929149

ISBN: 978-0-9329-5633-0

COVER DESIGN by David Patton

COMPOSED ON A MACINTOSH® USING ADOBE PAGEMAKER®

PRINTED IN THE U.S.A.

The LANDLORDING SERIES™, of which this is BOOK ONE, and the LANDLORDING CHARACTER™, who appears on the front cover and elsewhere in this book, are trademarks of ExPress and Leigh Robinson.

Prefaces

Preface to the First Edition (1975)

After I bought my first rental property, I soon learned how little practical information there was to help landlords and landladies through the many tribulations they face day after day after day. So, I took "Landlording" at Hard Knocks College. The tuition was dear, but I learned what I needed to survive.

This book was written to be the text for the course at good old HKC. If you study it carefully, you should be able to make a good grade.

As a landlord who does in fact teach school and who also does all of the bookkeeping chores, some of the maintenance, some of the repairs, and some of the managing of thirty-five rental units, I have indeed spent many years at HKC, but I have had little uninterrupted time to write. These pages bear the marks of many interruptions to fix cold heaters, broken windows, leaky faucets, leaky roofs, dead electrical outlets, wet-bottom water heaters, and so on and so on. Sympathize, if you will, dear landlord or landlady. No one else will.

Preface to the Third Edition (1980)

Since *Landlording* first appeared in 1975, I have learned much more about the residential income property management business from my tenants, my students at dozens of University of California Extension seminars, and from readers of the first two editions who have kindly taken the time to write.

This new edition incorporates those suggestions made so generously, as well as some new ideas which have occurred to me spontaneously over the past four years. In addition, that information in the earlier editions which was specific to California has been deleted, so that barring certain local laws and regulations, this edition may be used anywhere in the U.S.

The old evictions chapter has been replaced by a new one on getting rid of problem tenants, both because the old one contained information useful only in California and because there are other good ways to "evict" people which you should know about and which you should try as your first resort, good ways landlords and landladies can use anywhere. That old evictions chapter, by the way, is still available, but in a new guise. It has been expanded and now appears separately under the title, *The Eviction Book for California*.

There are other changes in this edition which are equally important. Some, such as the discussion of whether or not you should do a task yourself, have resulted from an increase in the size of my own landlording business. Those 35 rental units my wife and I used to have in 1975 have become 244. With that many tenants to look after, there's no way we can handle everything ourselves. We have had, therefore, to learn more about hiring people to work for us—managers, painters, bookkeepers, gardeners, maintenance helpers, and others. In the process, we learned, surprisingly enough, that some work in this business, no matter how few or how many units you may have, is not worth doing yourself. In fact, doing it yourself may be costing you money rather than making or saving you money.

Other changes in this edition, such as the much expanded chapter on getting good tenants and the new chapter on keeping good tenants, have resulted from a continuing search for methods which work successfully for many people under varying conditions.

One change suggested by a female reader, re-titling the book *Landladying*, I have politely rejected. Someone else will have to write that book.

Incidentally, you will notice that various product brand names and suppliers' addresses appear in this book, and you may wonder whether these companies pay for the plugs. The answer is no. Having had first-hand experience with each of these products and companies and having been thoroughly satisfied, I am pleased to recommend them to you along with their names and addresses so you won't have to waste the time hunting for them that I did. If you choose to use any product or company mentioned here and you are dissatisfied for any reason, please write me in care of ExPress stating the nature of your complaint, and I will investigate. Likewise, if you know of any outstanding company or product related to this business which would be of use to other landlords and landladies throughout the U.S., please let me know, and I will consider including it in a later edition.

I hope you find this new edition of *Landlording* useful.

Preface to the Fourth Edition (1986)

A little more than five years ago I last revised and updated *Landlording* from cover to cover. Since then, I've acquired more properties, dealt with more tenants, encountered more problems, made more mistakes, met more people in the business, listened to more battle stories, given more seminars, attended more seminars, heard from more readers, and read more books and articles on the subject. As a result, I have learned still more about how to survive and succeed at landlording.

Much has happened during that time in the world at large to change how we ought to go about this business, too. New laws and new interpretations of old laws have compelled us to make certain changes. Microcomputers have entered our lives in force and abundance. And a wealth of new ideas and materials have appeared on the scene.

With so much having happened all 'round since the third edition appeared, I have felt obliged to produce a completely new edition of *Landlording*.

In this "new and improved" fourth edition, I have retained the best of the rest of the earlier three editions, generally in an expanded form. I have split two old chapters into four, added six new chapters, and dropped two old ones.

Dropped were the two chapters with maintenance and tool information, including information on subjects such as repairing sheetrock holes, locksmithing, using a ceiling access plate, and exterminating abominable pests. One of these days, all of that and much more will appear in a new book.

Added were six chapters on subjects which I hope you'll find of interest: managing the rental house, coping with legal matters, participating in the Section 8 subsidized housing program, fattening the bottom line, counting your assets, and using a computer.

Split were the two old chapters, "Taking Over & Keeping Good Tenants" and "Insurance & Security." Each of these subjects cried out for separate treatment and more space, so I gave it to them.

Although I have been experimenting with singing eviction notices, I haven't quite succeeded in perfecting them yet. I am still trying, but I've been having some problems setting them to the right music, finding the right key, getting them to stand up in court, hogtying tenants so they'll hear the entire message out, and subduing bystanders' laughter. If you think of any ways to solve these persistent problems, please let me know.

Singing eviction notices may not appear here, but a dozen new graphic rent reminders do. I have no conclusive, scientific proof that they work 76.893% of the time. All I can say for sure is that they work pretty well most of the time and that they aren't carcinogenic. I'm as unbiased as a pathologist working on cancer research for a tobacco company when I make that statement, of course. Give them a try sometime and see whether you agree that they can be effective.

Besides the graphic rent reminders, there are lots of other new illustrations here. I hope you enjoy them and this new edition and that you go about landlording with a broad smile on your face. It's the only way!

Preface to the Fifth Edition (1988)

This edition marks a milestone in the happy life of *Landlording*. Born in 1975, it's a teenager now, and I am pleased to report that it has reached this important stage in its life without bursting out in pimples or tripping over its own gawky prose.

Still, I have wanted to make some changes before sending it out into the world again, and this fifth edition has afforded me the perfect opportunity to dress it up, add a chapter, redesign all of the old forms, create several new ones, and fiddle more with the text. I think that it's a better book than it was, and I hope that you will agree.

Preface to the Sixth Edition (1992)

We're in the nineties now, and we cannot manage rental property as if we were landlords in the seventies, or even the eighties.

The business of landlording keeps changing, and so must this book change if it is to be of any use to the troops in the trenches. Some of these changes in our business have resulted from legislation and lawsuits. Some of them have resulted from the availability of new products and technology. Some are for the better. Some are for the worse.

We cannot ignore what's happening around us because we are, after all, businesspeople. We are subject to more scrutiny than ordinary citizens, and we are subject to more laws. Ignore what's happening, and sooner or later we will come to grief.

This sixth edition of *Landlording* is no more of a lawbook than previous editions. It does not purport to take into consideration every landlord-tenant law enacted around the country. Nor is it particularly exhaustive. It remains the words of one person who tries to keep abreast of what's happening in the business, who tries to gather together the ideas and suggestions of many knowledgeable people, and who tries to make some sense of it all.

This is a bigger book than ever. It has more forms, more drawings, and more good ideas. I hope that it will help you become a more successful landlord, a landlord of the nineties.

Preface to the Seventh Edition (1994)

While reviewing the sixth edition of this book prior to reprinting it, I decided that too much had happened in the world of landlording over the past two years for me not to do a new edition. Just think, two years ago Sears was still the king of the catalog merchandisers, and I was still

saying in SOURCES & RESOURCES that you had to be a time traveler or a refugee from the second or third world if you hadn't heard of the Sears Catalog. As you know, the unthinkable happened. Sears stopped publishing the big catalog.

Of course, that change alone wouldn't have been sufficient justification for a new edition. It's merely an illustration of the changes going on in our world, changes which seem to be accelerating year after year.

Today, because of all these changes, being a scrupulous landlord requires more than an attitude of fairness. It requires information, hard work, and vigilance. This new edition should give you some of the information you need to be a scrupulous landlord at the end of the 20th century. You will have to work hard and be vigilant on your own.

Long may you prosper!

Preface to the Eighth Edition (1997)

What has happened over the past three years to warrant another edition of *Landlording?* Plenty!

When the last edition of *Landlording* came out three years ago, few people had heard of the internet, and fewer still were using it. Nowadays "everybody" has heard of it, and many are using it. You might be able to use the internet yourself in landlording. You'll find some practical suggestions for doing so in this new edition.

You'll also find some new topics scattered here and there throughout the book's twenty-one chapters. One I'd like to draw your attention to is "itemizing rents." I've become a believer in itemizing rents because it has helped me pass along certain of my increased expenses much sooner than I otherwise could have. Maybe you will become a believer, too, after reading something about this timely and important topic.

As always, *Landlording* contains lots of forms designed to lessen the burden of being a landlord. Among them are four new ones, one of which can save you much time and grief because it serves to weed out unqualified applicants before they ever submit their applications to you. It's called "Rental Application Instructions." It intimidates applicants who have something to hide. It informs applicants who have nothing to hide. Take a good look at it and try it the next time you have a vacancy.

Besides having more information and more forms, this new edition has a whole new look. It's the book's first real design overhaul in years, and it's supposed to make everything more readable. I hope that you find this new edition of *Landlording* both readable and useful.

Preface to the Ninth Edition (2001)

This ninth edition of *Landlording*, the first of the new century, is the first to use a two-column format. It's more readable than the single-column format used in earlier editions, even more readable than the narrowed single-column format used in the eighth edition.

Readers familiar with the eighth edition may have noticed that this edition has fewer pages. These fewer pages resulted from having less white space on a page and slightly smaller type, not from having fewer illustrations, fewer forms, or less text. There are no fewer nor any more illustrations in this edition, but there are more forms and more text than in any previous edition. I want you to get your money's worth.

Preface to the Tenth Edition (2006)

The ninth edition of *Landlording* came out four days before the audacious attacks on the World Trade Center.

Five years on, the world is less stable than ever, but the world of landlording is much the same as ever except for the benefits it derives from the steady advancement of technology.

The 21st century landlord can no longer afford to do business without a cellphone, a digital camera, and a computer with high-speed internet access. That's a given. This tenth edition takes technological advancements into account, but it also continues to include certain old-fashioned landlording methods for the Luddites among us.

It includes five new forms, too. All of them should help you in one way or another. One of them should help you qualify applicants more objectively. One of them should help you dodge the mold and radon bullets. One of them should help you confirm a move-out. One of them should help you establish tenants' rent payments with certainty. One of them should help you avoid tenant alteration troubles.

Help is not on the way. Help is here.

Preface to the Eleventh Edition (2010)

As the internet becomes increasingly important to the way we live and do business, we landlords must embrace it or suffer the consequences. Neglect the internet, and you'll be paying more in expenses and having more vacancies, both of which affect a rental property's bottom line and its market value.

This new edition builds upon the information about the internet included in previous editions of *Landlording* and should help you take advantage of what's now available to you through the internet.

Also, you'll find information here about renting to lodgers, something becoming all the more common nowadays as the housing market undergoes an unwonted shakeup. People who never thought they would become landlords are becoming landlords as they rent out a room or two in their own homes to complete strangers who never thought they would become lodgers. These newbie landlords need a somewhat different landlording roadmap to follow to help them negotiate their way along the best, most trouble-free routes to success. Here's that roadmap.

Table of Contents

Introduction

Of all the people in the world, who's more detested than the landlord? After all, he raises rents whenever he pleases, he ignores tenant complaints, he keeps at least one cockroach colony in every rental dwelling, he loves the fresh air which broken windows provide, he welcomes rodents of all kinds to make their nests in his rental properties, he takes no pity on tenants who suffer misfortunes, he drives unfortunates from their homes, he sneers when others laugh, he laughs when others sneer, he dallies with divorcees, he drives an ostentatious Cadillac car, he runs over stray dogs and cats and blames them for not running fast enough to get out of his way, he wears a big black cape, and he smokes smelly cigars.

And if that landlord happens to be a landlady—well, then, everybody knows what she's like! She's got a schnoz longer than Pinocchio's, larger than a wicked witch's, and she puts it into every tenant's business. Her ears rival Dumbo's, and they're ever on the alert to learn the latest gossip. She's privy to Big Brother's personal findings on everyone, and she blabs them everywhere. She's devised ways to pinch her pennies that Scrooge never dreamed of, and while there may not be snakes growing in her hair, big pink rollers sure do.

You're a landlord or a landlady, aren't you? Don't these descriptions sound just like you? What did you say? They're not a bit like you?

Well then, you must be a scrupulous landlord or landlady. Wonderful! Wonderful! Thank heavens we found one another! You're pretty difficult to recognize, you know. You're not at all like the characters described above, those odd legendary creatures. You look and act like a normal human being who just happens to be involved in the landlording business.

Being quite normal yourself, you have probably wondered how the landlords of this world ever got such terrible reputations in the first place and why they get so little sympathy from most people today, no matter what the situation, no matter who's at fault.

They got such bad reputations deservedly years ago because they were largely unfettered by laws (what laws there were, were of their own making) and could easily take advantage of their tenants, and so some did, arbitrarily controlling their tenants' lives like petty dictators. They were feared for the power they wielded and naturally they were hated, becoming folklore villains who were always portrayed as being insensitive, cruel, thoughtless, heartless, and greedy to an extreme.

Although they have been stripped of most of their power, landlords are hardly liked even today because they provide an essential service (who likes the water and power companies?), and they continue in ill repute (tarts are in ill repute, too, of course, but at least they're frequently portrayed as having hearts of gold) because they make such good news stories when they try creative remedies to extricate themselves from seemingly impossible situations.

What kind of a story do you think the news media made out of the landlord who chopped down the outside stairway to his deadbeat tenant's second-story duplex apartment or the landlady who poisoned her tenant's mongrel pooch which she and the tenant had been feuding over for months? Nobody cared that this landlord and landlady were really good people at heart who had been driven temporarily crazy when they committed these foolish acts. They committed the acts and thus they unwittingly succeeded in perpetuating the old folklore-villain stereotypes.

Don't be suckered into believing these old stereotypes. They're wrong, terribly wrong. Most landlords today are just like you, decent human beings who happen to own some rental property

13

which they'd rather rent out than leave vacant. It is true that they're more skeptical, more practical, more resourceful, more imaginative, more circumspect, and more intelligent than the average Tom, Dick, and Harriet, but it's not true that they're any greedier, uglier, smellier, or stingier.

What happens when Dick and Harriet sell their house for whatever the market will bear and get twice what they paid for it? Are they considered greedy? Are they called price gougers? Heck no! They're considered smart.

All right, then, what happens when Lester Landlord rents out his apartment for whatever the market will bear? He's not called smart. He's called greedy. He's an "A-Number- One Rent Gouger," a scourge of society! Try sorting that one out! The "greed" charge is a bum rap, and don't you forget it!

You cannot charge more for anything than someone is willing to pay for it. That's how "the market" works, and it applies to rents just the same as it applies to anything else which is bought and sold, from rice to garlic, from flashlights to computers, from gasoline to automobiles, from stocks to bonds.

If you don't believe me, go ahead and try some industrial-strength rent gouging. Raise your rents 100% and see what happens. At first you'll be vilified. That's for sure. Then your tenants will look around for somewhere else better and cheaper to live. If they find it, they'll move and you'll be left with vacancies. Then you'll have to adjust your rents to market levels or despair of ever getting anybody else to rent from you. If they can't find a cheaper place, they'll grumble and stay.

Market forces determine what your rents are. You don't. You can be way under market, but you can't be way over. You can be a rent slouch, but you can't be a rent gouger, that is, not unless you want to have lots of vacancies.

I have met many a rent slouch in my day. They're the landlords who never have any vacancies. They have "waiting lists," and they brag about how long their waiting lists are. Now, think for a moment about why they have those waiting lists of people who can't wait to move in.

Rent slouches have waiting lists because their rents are too low. Tenants-in-waiting know that the rent is a deal. That's why they're on the list. They could tell the rent slouch a thing or two, but why should they? They want to take advantage of the deal themselves.

As for rent gougers, I have to admit that I have yet to encounter one personally. I keep looking, though, and I know exactly what I'm looking for, but there must not be many of them out there. I have to assume that they exist because I read about them in the newspaper now and then.

I read about one who surfaced after the big fire in the Oakland (California) hills back in 1991. At an estimated damage of $2 billion, it was the worst urban disaster in U.S. history. The fellow had wanted something like $1,600 per month for his rental before the fire and then he raised the rent to $2,500 after the fire. The columnist who wrote about this rent gouger wanted all the world to know that such terrible landlords exist. Tsk, tsk, tsk!

What the columnist failed to mention was that this landlord still had a vacancy three months after the fire. He may have tried to be a rent gouger, but he wasn't being very successful at it. The market taught him a lesson. He couldn't charge more in rent than the market would bear. He wound up with a vacancy, a vacancy which lasted and lasted, even during a tight rental market, because his rent was too high.

Rent gougers, wherever they are, are not successful landlords. They don't understand the nature of the business they're in. They think they can do whatever they please. They can't. Bigger forces hold sway.

Okay, you know the landlording stereotypes. Who doesn't? What should you do about them?

Don't overreact to them. That's what. Don't say to yourself that you're going to be different from your money-grubbing counterparts, that you're going to win your tenants' hearts by becoming friends with them and giving them cheap rents. You won't succeed, I can assure you. They won't think you're kind. They'll think you're foolish. They'll think you have an I.Q. equal to the outside temperature on a cool day. What's more, you'll be costing yourself more money than you think.

Don't go out and buy yourself a hairshirt because you want to atone for the sins of being a landlord. There aren't any.

Don't be ashamed to admit that you're a landlord when people ask you the second question they have on their minds upon meeting you socially. Be proud of yourself for doing something so smart and for doing it so well.

Don't be apologetic about this role you're playing in our society. It's not merely important, it's absolutely essential. Be pleased with yourself that you're providing an essential service. You have people depending on you for a roof over their heads. You're giving them that roof. You're keeping them warm and dry. You may be the butt of jokes and you may get worse press than serial killers, but so what? Regardless of what some people may say or think, nobody provides rental housing better than does the private-enterprising landlord like yourself. Nobody but nobody out there does it better.

Ask yourself what the state of housing in general would be like in this country if you and others like you weren't around to provide rental housing. There'd be a whole lot more people living with outdoor plumbing than there are now; that's for sure. People would be living in tents, lean-to's, mud huts, caves, cars, and cardboard shanty towns on a permanent basis. Anybody lucky enough to obtain conventional housing in an ugly government-provided high rise apartment block would jam two, three, and four generations into it. Each room would become a multiple-family dwelling in itself. Families would be

sleeping in shifts. People would be waiting years to get even remotely habitable accommodations.

Take a look at studies of the much distorted administrative-command housing system of the former Soviet Union, the system in place there from 1927 until 1990. Take a look at *National Geographic* photographs showing what life is like today in the Third World. Well, that's how people would be living in this country except for you.

Americans wouldn't be happy living that way, you say? Perhaps you're right. Perhaps they would be out there clamoring to that solver of all society's problems, government, to do something about the country's wretched housing conditions. Perhaps government would try to provide residential rental housing for one and all. So how do you think the government would fare as the country's landlord?

Well, we happen to have some way of knowing because the President's Private Sector Survey on Cost Control, otherwise known as the Grace Commission, reported some time ago that the federal government as landlord employs seventeen times the people and spends almost fourteen times as much money on total management costs as a private company. Can you imagine spending that much more on management costs than you already do? I can't either. The government can do it. The government can find all kinds of ways to be inefficient. It wrote the book on inefficiency.

What kind of shape would rental housing be in if the federal government were the sole provider? That's some question to consider! First of all, you know that there wouldn't be enough housing to go around. Young couples would have to live with their parents for years until a vacancy became available somewhere, maybe a hundred miles from where they worked. Yet, with all this demand, when somebody moved or died, the unit would remain vacant for six months until it could be made ready for new occupants, any of the hundreds of people on the waiting list. Of course, nobody would be allowed to have two rental dwellings in two different cities where they do business, nobody except high government officials, that is. Nobody would be allowed to live alone either.

The federal government would probably have a full-time manager for every fourplex, and those managers would probably be so busy doing their paperwork that they wouldn't have time to fix a faucet themselves. No, I forgot. That wouldn't be the main reason. It would be their 616-page job description which would keep them from repairing a faucet. Management people don't do "maintenance" work, not even minor repairs. So they'd call upon an $86-an-hour approved plumber who'd either replace the leaky faucet with an approved $350 model or fix the old one with $55 worth of approved parts.

Where would the money come from to pay for seventeen times the people and fourteen times the overall management costs? Oh, from the usual sources, a billion from here and a billion from there. Borrow more, tax more, print more. That's how it's done, and that's how it would be done without you.

Do you know how much the federal government spent on its White House "rental" complex during the eight years of the Reagan administration? $44,600,000! $9,472,100 of that went just to renovate the presidential guest house. The work was undertaken after a gas leak developed at the house and a chandelier fell to the floor in the bedroom reserved for heads of state. Sounds as if the place had a little deferred maintenance, wouldn't you say?

How about state governments? What kind of a job are they doing? The State of California did a great job looking after the elaborate new governor's mansion approved for construction when Ronald Reagan was governor. Once the place was built, it was kept in perfect shape. The only trouble was that it never had a tenant. What was the problem? When it was finally ready for occupancy, the governor then in office didn't want to live there. So what happened to it? Did they rent it out to somebody else? Are you kidding? It was vacant for more than ten years before it was put up for sale. They didn't have to worry about loan payments and property taxes, so why should they worry about generating rental income? What a luxury that would be! Owning rental property and not having to rent it out, not having to deal with tenants! Boy, oh boy! But that's not really landlording, is it? That's not providing anyone with housing.

How about local governments? How do they fare? Well, the City of San Francisco with its 6,000 units in 43 developments scattered throughout the city is by far the biggest residential landlord in San Francisco. Are the city-owned rental dwellings kept up? Are the tenants happy? Are the costs

kept under control? No, no, and no! Resounding noes!

A federal audit revealed that the San Francisco Housing Authority was failing to collect $42,504 in damage charges and $239,000 in rent every year. Its total *monthly* deficit was around $180,000, and "nobody" on the scene seemed to be aware of it. Can you imagine that? Losing $180,000 every month and nobody knowing a thing about it? I can imagine how that much negative cash flow might be possible for a time in some privately operated housing projects with loans to service and high vacancy factors during fill-up periods, but these places had no loans to service and no vacancy factors to worry about.

This deficit was no temporary matter either, because the housing authority owed millions of dollars in overdue utility bills to the Pacific Gas & Electric Company alone. How many private landlords could get away with that? The housing authority was receiving almost half of its $24 million annual operating budget from the U.S. Department of Housing and Urban Development (HUD), and yet it was still $5 million in the hole!

What's more astonishing, though, is that the city's public housing projects weren't even being properly maintained. According to HUD's regional administrator, the San Francisco Housing Authority was "failing to adequately maintain its housing units in a decent, safe and sanitary condition." The enormous monthly deficits were resulting in housing which was actually going downhill!

Finally, the housing authority hired a new director to straighten out the mess. The last thing I heard he was being praised for reducing the turnover time from 125 days to 21! That's a considerable improvement, to be sure, but can you imagine taking an average of three weeks to redecorate every time you have a vacancy? Me neither.

Remember that famous photograph showing a huge St. Louis public housing building being blown to smithereens in 1972 when it was structurally sound and still had lots of good years left in it? Something similar occurred in my home town, except that the building there was only twenty-four units and it was only five years old. Private-enterprising landlords had nothing to do with these projects. Perhaps they should have.

Oh, and here's one for the books. When residents who were living in Oakland's public housing projects began raising their voices in unison to complain about the poor maintenance there, the housing administrators hired a *consultant*. Consultants don't do maintenance, do they? Have you ever hired a consultant to take care of your maintenance problems? No, neither have I. We take care of our rental properties' maintenance problems ourselves, or we hire maintenance people to take care of them for us. Who needs a consultant for this kind of work? Apparently, public housing administrators do.

So much for the government as landlord. Are we mom-and-pop operations any better at land-lording than these faceless, feckless, wasteful government operations? How can we not be? We are so much closer to the problems. We act quickly. We show understanding. We keep our costs in check. We provide our "customers" with what they want in a place to live for a price they're willing to pay. We are truly free enterprise at work.

Not only are we free enterprise at work, we are, for the most part, true mom-and-pop businesses. Landlording is not the oil business. The sky doesn't darken with Lear jets around the country when politicians meet to discuss rental housing legislation in Washington or Tallahassee, Sacramento or Austin, Albany or Springfield. No, all in all, we're strictly coach-class in our political activities.

People go about lamenting the passing of the corner grocery store and the family farm, but they don't seem to realize that the landlords in this country are in the same category. We're small-time operators, too, and we're being driven out of business as well. What's driving us out of business, however, is not big-time operators coming in and taking over. It's excessive legislation spawned by do-gooders who still believe in those old stereotypes. They still believe that tenants are noble and landlords are greedy. They still believe that government could do a better job of housing people. They still believe in the fairy godmother, Robin Hood, deficit spending, and the resolution of any kind of problem in time for the 11 o'clock news, too. They don't understand that tinkering with the rental housing business makes it less competitive and that less competition creates poorer housing at a higher price to society.

What they do understand is a sobbing welfare mother and her half dozen waifs being evicted in front of a TV camera on Christmas Eve. That news item and others like it provide them with further verification of our terrible reputation. That's what we landlords are supposed to be doing on Christmas Eve, isn't it?

Sure, we've got a past. Sure, we've got a terrible reputation. The fact that precious few of us live up to that reputation doesn't matter very much, though.

Part of the problem is that most people know full well what it's like to be a tenant, but they have never experienced the problems and frustrations of being a landlord.

Never have they been hit or cursed or threatened or cheated or robbed or bullied by an unscrupulous tenant. They cannot know the mental anguish and anxiety of waiting out an eviction week after week while some devil-may-care tenant who's being evicted for nonpayment of rent uses free legal aid to contest the eviction, hammers holes in the walls, puts out cigarettes on the carpets, burns the linoleum, plays music late and loud, and hurls insults at all the neighbors. Most people cannot possibly know what it's like to deal with that unscrupulous tenant and to feel so helpless, so wronged.

Another part of the problem is that people love to have a scapegoat, someone to blame for every housing problem imaginable. We're that "someone." We're it.

Don't get too upset about being a scapegoat.

Don't bother starting a local chapter of the Landlord Anti-Defamation League (LADL). Just expect to be hissed and booed now and then. Retaliate by thinking bad thoughts about the unscrupulous people who make the landlording business tougher than it ought to be.

If only the unscrupulous tenants would get together with the unscrupulous landlords of the world to do business with each other, rent to each other and rent from each other! That would solve most of the problems the rest of us poor folk have in this business. Unfortunately, since that's about as likely to happen as our ever again being able to buy gasoline for thirty cents a gallon, gold for thirty-five dollars an ounce, or rooms for six bucks at Motel 6, we have little choice but to seek help.

To help the scrupulous tenant deal with un-scrupulous landlords, there are pamphlets, books, hot lines, tenant action groups, government-provided legal aid, and publicly funded housing organizations. The scrupulous tenant is hardly alone. Helping hands abound.

We scrupulous landlords, on the other hand, seem to be so totally alone when we have to deal with an unscrupulous tenant who's doing us wrong. Nothing is free to us. We are expected to have unlimited funds available for legal counsel and representation and for management, repairs, and services. We shouldn't need any help from outside sources.

Well, we do. You know it and I know it. This book is intended for scrupulous landlords who want to do well by themselves and by their tenants but need some help to do just that. I hope it provides you with the help you're looking for.

1
Do-It-Yourself Landlording

When Sad Sack Landlord decided to sell his fourplex and learned what it was worth, he was not pleased. "$152,000? Holy buckets!" he exclaimed. "That's almost eighteen thousand dollars less than what I paid for the place seven years ago!"

"It may be, but you've had some mighty rough tenants in here. You've got vacancy problems that won't quit, and there's so much deferred maintenance now that you just can't get any more for it. Whoever buys it is going to have to spend some major money to fix up the inside and the outside of the building."

Sound familiar? I hope not. "Deferred maintenance" is a euphemism for gross neglect in real estate jargon. Those dilatory property owners who ignore their tenants, neglect maintenance, and do slipshod repairs on their property suffer more losses than they realize. They can't get good tenants, they can't get good rents, and they can't get a good price when they sell. Their buildings are depreciating not only on paper at tax time, they're depreciating in value every month.

Anyone who neglects a business, any business, deserves to lose money at it, and people do lose money at landlording, for it's nothing if it's not a business, a business involving some very serious money.

Ah, but you don't have to lose money in this business so long as you take some time to learn the ropes. Here's a look at some of those ropes, together with something of an overview of this very funny business which people from all walks of life can succeed in, even you!

Understanding the Business

Landlording is a funny business, to be sure. It requires one to know at least the rudiments of the skills of an accountant, appliance repairer, arbitrator, architect, attorney, banker, bill collector, bookkeeper, buyer, carpenter, carpet layer, color consultant, computer whiz, contractor, counselor, custodian, diplomat, drapery hanger, electrician, financial analyst, garbage collector, gardener, glazier, insurance agent, interior decorator, landscape architect, lobbyist, locksmith, painter, pest controller, plumber, psychologist, real estate agent, roofer, salesperson, secretary, sleuth, social worker, trucker, vinyl tile layer, wallpaper hanger, and webmaster.

In addition, the landlord must have some business savvy, a heap of common sense, and equanimity by the boatload. A sense of humor, though not absolutely required, sure helps.

Breathes there a person with all these skills and all these attributes?

Hardly! The only people I know who have every bit as much equanimity as this landlording business requires have body temperatures considerably below 98.6° Fahrenheit (37° C.), and equanimity is their only attribute. They have none of the other attributes nor any of the skills. They reside permanently in cemeteries.

The only people I know who have all the skills and common sense this business requires are purely fictional. Even if they did exist, these James Bonds and Wonder Women, they wouldn't have any time for a pursuit so mundane as landlording. They'd be out of town most of the time, spending their days and nights saving the world from villainy.

Where does this leave us real-world landlords who are very much alive and bent on providing decent housing to decent people at decent prices in anticipation of making a decent profit? It leaves us with lots to learn and lots to do.

No wonder so many people neglect their rental properties and fail at landlording! They're overwhelmed by what's required of them in terms of skills, attributes, and time. Make no mistake! Landlording is not simply an investment as it is often regarded by the uninitiated, one you sink your money into and forget all about. No, it's a business, a tough business. You have to work at it. You have to know so much. You have to be so self-sufficient, and you have to understand people so well, too.

You even have to understand that you are an imperfect landlord dealing with imperfect tenants and that you will make mistakes, mistakes which, I can only hope, will not sour you on the business forever. "We should be careful to get out of an experience only the wisdom that is in it –and stop there; lest we be like the cat that sits down on a hot stove lid. She will never sit down on a hot stove lid again–and that is well, but also she will never sit down on a cold one anymore," wrote Mark Twain in *Following the Equator.* You will sit on more than one hot seat in this business. Don't abandon the business altogether because of them.

We have to be like those old inflatable punch-me clown toys. Remember them? About three feet tall with sand in their shoes and air in their bodies, they'd always bounce back whenever somebody tried to knock 'em flat. One moment they'd be down, the next moment they'd be back for more punishment.

We have to bounce back when we're flattened, too, that is, when we fail to check out an applicant thoroughly or fail to mollify an irate tenant or fail to raise the rent on a "friend" or fail to repair a roof properly or fail to confront a tenant about a mysteriously appearing bulldog. All of us fail at landlording a little bit in one way or another. We can't help it, but we shouldn't let it worry us so long as we learn from our failures and keep them from overwhelming us. After we have failed, we just have to get up off the floor, dust ourselves off, remind ourselves for the thousandth time that landlording is a business which must be operated like any other business, and then

we must doggedly continue, resolving not to make the same mistakes again.

Do-it-yourself landlording is surely more mistake-prone than the ordinary homeowner variety of do-it-yourselfing, and it differs also because you as the landlord must repair and maintain your property promptly and professionally. You have contracted with your tenants to provide them with habitable accommodations. That's what the business is all about. You cannot leave messy, unfinished, or neglected jobs if you wish to continue landlording successfully. That might work all right at home, but tenants won't stand for it, nor should they. After all, if they are paying full price for habitable shelter, they have every right to expect full service for their money.

On the other hand, being businesslike when you're handling the maintenance and repairs on your property yourself requires that you do the work as quickly and as well as you can and then leave. Tenants have a knack for finding just one more little job for you to do if you linger, and you can waste precious time fixing the little things they should be fixing themselves. If you don't have any business there, stay away. Otherwise you tend to develop personal relationships which will hinder your making wise business decisions. Being there too much and getting too involved with your tenants is almost as bad for your business as neglecting the place entirely.

Being businesslike doesn't mean that you have to be callous and tyrannical. Don't be. Let your common sense guide you. Be flexible when a situation calls for flexibility.

If a tenant gives you a six-day notice that he's moving after having been there only two months, and he asks you whether he can get his deposit back in spite of his agreement to give you thirty days' notice, tell him you'll accommodate him so long as he leaves the place clean. Agree to give him back a generous portion of his deposit, even though you may legally be entitled to keep every dollar, and if he does leave the place clean, pay up. That deposit refund he knows he doesn't deserve is a powerful incentive for him to leave everything in good shape.

If you stubbornly refuse to return any of his deposits, he might take out his frustration on your rental property's windows, doors, and walls. You know that you don't want a mess on your hands because you know how much messes cost to clean up. By returning more of his deposit than you have to, you will ensure that he doesn't leave you with a mess, and you will be creating the good will that you need to succeed. He will want to rent from you again if the need arises, and he will tell others that they should rent from you, too, because you treated him fairly.

Yes, landlording is a funny business, but through many trials, many errors, much tribulation, and much work, you can make it into a good business, one which will be very good for you and to you.

Joining with Other Landlords

Joining with other landlords through membership in a rental housing association is good business. These organizations offer a wide range of services and benefits to the small-timer as well as to the big-timer.

Besides distributing a publication, holding periodic meetings, sponsoring seminars, supplying readily available and current landlording information over the phone, providing access to credit bureau information on applicants, and in some cases maintaining websites with listings of available rentals, associations advise their members of pending legislation and support lobbying efforts so that not every new landlord-tenant law favors tenants.

If all this doesn't seem to you to be worth the basic membership fee of around $100 (the fee varies according to the number of units you have), then consider the advantage of meeting people who can keep you current on rents and vacancy factors in your area, people who will listen sympathetically to your woeful tales of landlording despair because the same thing happened to them only last week, people who can understand the lack of balance in media stories about landlords,

and people who know what choice rental properties are coming on the market even before they're listed. A hundred dollars a year is a small price to pay for all that.

If you don't know of a rental housing association in your area, go online and search "rental housing association [your town and state]." No luck? Then try one of these information sources for landlords: Mr. Landlord (mrlandlord.com), Rental Housing On Line (rhol.org), or Landlord Association (landlordassociation.org).

One other source which may be helpful is the National Apartment Association (naahq.org), but do note that the NAA lists only its affiliate organizations, and not every rental housing association in the country is an affiliate.

Once you find a local association, go to their meetings. Don't assume that because you own only one rental house or one fourplex you'll be out of place there. You won't be. You'll find people just like you at their meetings, people who are eager to share what they know about the business with you.

Finding Discounts

As a landlord do-it-yourselfer, you use more supplies than the average homeowner do-it-yourselfer does, and suppliers know that you do.

Your local independent hardware store may give you charge-account privileges and a discount to boot. Ask. Some offer charge accounts; some offer discounts to their best customers; some don't do either. You have to ask to find out.

Many hardware store owners will special-order for you those items which they don't stock regularly, items such as glass-fronted fire extinguisher boxes, apartment house mailboxes, and locksmithing supplies.

My local hardware store owner even gave me a portable, hand-cranked Keil key-cutting machine which he found covered in cobwebs in a back room. It has proven to be a big timesaver, cutting my umbilical cord to the local locksmith. (Unfortunately, these handy little machines are no longer in production, so don't expect to find a new one somewhere.)

Other firms are anxious to do business with you, too. Let them know who you are and what your requirements are. Sears has a commercial sales department (contractsales.sears.com) which offers rental property owners special discounts on certain merchandise, like coin-operated laundry machines and other appliances. Home Depot, the nationwide chain of big box stores selling hardware and lumber, offers commercial accounts to landlords. Lowe's, too, has a commercial desk offering special services for rental property owners.

Check your rental housing association's vendor list and the ads in its publication for those firms which specifically solicit business from landlords. They understand the nature of your business and give you the service and discounts you deserve as a volume buyer.

Don't forget the internet and catalog vendors which cater to commercial customers, vendors such as HD Supply (formerly Maintenance Warehouse) and Grainger. They have big, useful catalogs and websites (hdsupplysolutions.com and grainger.com). Grainger has stores throughout the country where you may pick up what you need immediately instead of having to wait for a delivery truck to bring it to you.

You'll find more of these internet and catalog vendors listed in SOURCES & RESOURCES.

Cultivating Business Contacts

There are certain business people in your community who are in a position to help you run a successful landlording business, and you should strive to cultivate personal contacts with them whenever you can. You may have to shop around awhile before you find trustworthy people in these relevant business pursuits, people who suit you and who know their businesses well, but once you find good contacts and you come to know each of them personally, you'll find that they will go out of their way to assist you with service, advice, equipment, and supplies. Remember that your relationship should be mutually beneficial. You are in a position to help your contacts by recommending their services to the other landlords you know, and you should.

At one level, you should seek out and nurture business contacts with an accountant, an attorney, a banker, an insurance agent, a loan broker, a real estate agent, and a social worker, each of whom has some special expertise directly related to your making or losing substantial sums of money in landlording. These people can help you with their advice and with their specific and knowledgeable answers to your many questions in their fields.

At another level, you should seek out an appliance repairer, a computer whiz, a floor covering installer, a hardware store owner, a painter, a plumber, a process server, and a roofer. While these contacts may save you money with their advice, they benefit you chiefly by coming to your aid with their labor, materials, and supplies when you need immediate solutions to your pressing problems.

How well should you know these people?

You should know them at least well enough so that you could reach them on the telephone and be greeted familiarly, and then you could pose a question involving their field of expertise, expecting them to give you a direct answer, perhaps free of charge, perhaps not.

Be good to these people. Take them out to breakfast or lunch now and then, send them "thank you" notes when they do something you appreciate, send them a personalized Christmas card, patronize them, and, of course, pay them promptly when you owe them money. You might think about throwing a party once a year during the summer, when nobody else is throwing a party, and inviting all of them to come and enjoy themselves at your expense. Even if they don't come, they'll know that you care enough about them to invite them to attend your party.

If you elect to expand your business at all, you will come to rely upon these people more and more, and they will become a kind of advisory board for you, absolutely essential to your success in landlording.

In addition, and surely as important as any of the business people whose acquaintanceship you should be cultivating, is that contact you should make with another landlord who either owns as much rental property as you do or has owned rental property longer than you have and is willing to compare notes about matters of local concern to landlords.

You are in a position to help each other psychologically and physically more than you may ever imagine at first. Consider just the benefit you'd get out of knowing someone trustworthy and capable whom you could call upon to look after your properties when you take sick or go out of town. The two of you could form your own "rental-property-sitting co-op" so you'd know that your properties were well looked after when you're unable to look after them yourself. That alone is reason enough to cultivate a relationship with another landlord, isn't it? You aren't competitors so much as you're fellow business-people engaged in the same occupation.

Handling the Bucks

Keeping a separate checking account for your landlording transactions is a good business practice. Some landlords go even further and open a separate account for every building they own (if their rentals are single-family dwellings, they have one account for all), and then they use that account as their only "bookkeeping system," funneling all of each building's income and expenses through the account, a simple but workable approach.

Whatever you do, open at least one checking account specifically for your rental property business, whether you own only one rental house or whether you own more rental houses and apartments than you can count. Then itemize your deposits and checks carefully so you can handle your bookkeeping chores more easily later and so you can satisfy the first request made by every IRS auditor should you be unlucky enough to have your tax return audited. An IRS auditor wants to see that your landlording expenses are being kept separate from your personal expenses. Mixing the two is a "no-no" because the auditor knows that if you do, you'll be more tempted to claim certain personal expenses as business expenses, like that trip you took to Hawaii "to look at a condo for sale" or that dining room table you bought "to have more room for handling your landlording paperwork."

Before you visit a bank to open your landlording account, select the name you want to use for it. This name has nothing to do with how you hold title to the property, how you write rental agreements, what name the property bears on the sign out front, who is authorized to sign checks, or what street the building is on. It's only the name which your tenants will use as the payee for their checks and money orders.

Presumably to prevent someone else in the area from using the same name you have selected, banks require that everyone opening an account under a business name, one which does not include the owner's real name, must file a fictitious name statement, a process involving a filing fee and legal advertising.

Whereas your business name would be a valuable asset to you if you were operating the "Playtime Tavern" or the "Capri Motel," it's hardly important in the rental property business, except for the large complexes which have their names featured in advertising. Even then, nobody else would want to confuse people in the area with a second "Sun Garden Apartments" if you were already using that name. Nobody else would be likely to adopt it except through an oversight.

Since your business name itself is really unimportant, you might as well circumvent the folderol of filing a fictitious name statement by opening your account under your own name and having your checks imprinted in bold letters with your surname followed by the word "PROPERTIES." If your name were Lester Landlord, for example, then your tenants could make their checks and money orders payable to "LANDLORD PROPERTIES," and you could distinguish between the accounts you open for different buildings, if you wanted to, by simply calling them "LANDLORD PROPERTIES ONE," "LANDLORD PROPERTIES TWO," and so on sequentially.

If you want to open an account under a fictitious name like "Sun Garden Apartments," expect to encounter a banker who will insist that you file a fictitious name statement. If you do not wish to go to all the trouble of filing, however, and you want to use the name "Sun Garden Apartments" as payee, merely open the account under the name "Lester Landlord's (use your own name here) Sun Garden Apartments," and you may accept checks made out simply to "Sun Garden Apartments." That's really all you care about anyway, isn't it? You want to get the rent checks deposited into an account that you can write checks on, an account which is easily distinguishable from your personal account and carries a name easy enough for your tenants to remember when they're preparing their rent checks or money orders every month.

Before we leave the subject of fictitious names, you should know that you must file a fictitious name statement if you plan to use a fictitious name as the lessor on your rental agreements because you cannot take a tenant to court if you neglected to file the statement and a fictitious name appears on the tenant's rental agreement instead of the owner's name. Neither using a fictitious name on the sign attached to the front of the building nor accepting checks made out to the name of the building, matters. The name on the rental agreement is what matters.

Courts will allow you to file a fictitious name statement when you file a legal complaint, but you cannot proceed with the complaint until the fictitious name statement procedure has run its course, and that will definitely delay your lawsuit, something you will find awfully frustrating when you're trying to evict a tenant legally and quickly.

Once you decide upon the name you want for your landlording bank account, you will want to familiarize yourself with the bewildering array of checking and savings accounts available nowadays. Don't expect your financial institution to open an account for you which will necessarily be the best for your situation. Financial institutions make their profit by obtaining your money at the lowest possible rate (they like it free if they can get it; did you know that when Swiss banks are overwhelmed with deposits, they not only stop paying interest, they actually *charge* interest on new deposits?) and lending it out at the highest possible rate. Ask about the options available. Look out for yourself.

The checking account you open for your landlording monies should be categorized by the bank as a business account, not a personal account, because banks close the books on business accounts at the end of every month to help businesses keep their financial books in order. Banks close the books on personal accounts throughout the month, which is no problem for people who merely want to know where their monies went and want to balance their checkbooks periodically, but it is a problem for people who must follow "generally accepted accounting principles" for their businesses in addition to balancing their business checkbooks.

(Third parties, such as lenders to whom you are applying for a loan, have every right to expect that you are keeping your books according to the standards known as "generally accepted accounting principles," meaning that you are keeping them free from bias and inconsistency and not "cooking" them so as to make your financial statement look better than it really is.)

Your business checking account should bear maximum interest with the minimum of minimum balances (you should make yourself keenly aware of this minimum balance so you don't start incurring the dreaded fees charged to accounts which fall below the minimum). It should allow you to write without charge as many checks as you'll reasonably need each month. It should provide printed checks at a minimum charge or let you use checks from a check printer you find online. It should make your deposits available to you for check-writing soon after you make the deposits rather than preventing you from using the funds until your tenants' checks have cleared their accounts. It should charge reasonable fees for stop-payments, and it should have some kind of overdraft protection so your own checks don't start bouncing after you deposit several of your tenants' rubber checks.

In addition to keeping at least one separate checking account for your landlording monies to flow through, you may want to open a savings account as your "escrow account" for refundable deposits only. These monies are not taxable when you receive them and should be distinguished as separate from your other landlording income, all of which is taxable. These deposits still belong to your tenants, not to you. Separating them will make them readily available when you need to use them or return them. Separating them will also help to remind you to pay interest periodically if you are compelled to do so by law in your area or if you are inclined to do so as a good-faith gesture.

Sums designated as last month's rent belong to you, not to your tenants. They are taxable as soon as you receive them, and they should not be kept in the same savings account as your tenants' refundable deposits. All rents, whether paid in advance or in arrears, whether they be first month's or last month's or any month's in-between, are designated as rent and nothing else and should be deposited into your regular property checking account for operations use.

Circulating Business Cards

After you have opened the bank accounts you need for your rental property, get yourself some business cards. "Business cards for landlords you say? Ridiculous! What a waste of money!"

Although you might scoff at the idea initially, consider some of the many uses for business cards in your do-it-yourself landlording business before you reject the idea completely—

✔ Use them as your "open sesame" for access to many "Wholesale Only" suppliers of appliance parts, plumbing parts, electrical parts, and the like. These suppliers may refuse to sell to the general public, but they will sell to you if they think you have a legitimate business, and yours, landlord, is as legitimate a business as any and more legitimate than some.

✔ Pass cards out to your tenants for handy reference when they need to contact you (designating yourself as owner, manager, or partner on your business cards lends credibility to your adopted landlording role; see "Should You Own Up to Being the Owner?" in chapter 13).

✔ At rental housing association meetings, pass your cards out to other owners. You never can tell what might come of the contacts. They might call you when they need to consult with somebody about rents, or they might give you a call when they're thinking about selling their buildings directly to another landlord.

✔ When those good business contacts you're cultivating hand you their business cards, hand them each one of yours in return. Then they'll understand that you do know one of the first things about running a business.

Besides being useful, business cards are one of the least expensive landlording purchases you will ever make. Local printers will print you up an adequate supply for a pittance (even though you're tempted by the small incremental cost of a greater number, order the minimum; telephone area code changes, email address changes, and changes in other relevant data occur just often enough to make such cards obsolete rather quickly). Office-supply stores, mail-order firms, and printing companies with websites (enter "business card printing" to search for them) will print up a sufficient supply for a pittance as well. GotPrint.com and VistaPrint.com are two printing companies with websites which enable you to design a business card online using any of their many templates, which include stock photographs for use as colorful backgrounds.

You may even print your own business cards using your computer, a word processing program, your printer, and the business card blanks designed for this purpose and carried by office supply stores. Each sheet yields ten cards. Use up all ten cards, and print yourself another ten, perhaps with slightly different information.

When you're ordering or printing cards for yourself, print some for your manager if you have one. Personalized business cards show managers that you have confidence in their professionalism and their permanence and are always much

appreciated.

Here are some samples of what your business cards might look like. Notice that they include a website address and an email address. Yours should, too.

---

123 Neat Street
Littletown, CA 91111
(510) 123-4567
lesterlandlord@yahoo.com

LANDLORD PROPERTIES
landlordpropertieslittletown.com

LESTER LANDLORD
Partner

DANDY PROPERTIES
dandypropertieslittletown.com

LESLIE LANDLADY
Manager

453 Sweet Street   *(510) 123-6789*
Littletown, CA 91111   *leslielandlady@yahoo.com*

Making Good Use of the Telephone

Alexander Graham Bell wouldn't recognize what we call telephones today, nor would he believe all the things that today's phones can do, whether they're landline phones, basic cell phones, smartphones, VoIP (voice-over-internet protocol) phones, or satellite phones.

Manufacturers keep making them smaller, more stylish, and more functional, and carriers keep offering more and better service at lower prices, all because the competition is so fierce. Ma Bell no longer has a monopoly on the phone business, and we're the beneficiaries of the resulting competition among today's manufacturers and carriers.

You needn't buy the latest phone and subscribe to the most comprehensive phone service available to be a successful landlord, but you do need to make good use of the telephone to save yourself time and money.

Now, I know some people who seem perfectly normal in other ways, but they have an irrational fear of talking on the telephone. They have no fear of flying, public speaking, darkness, high places, or their mother-in-law's raw-fish dinners, but they will not initiate a telephone call or take a phone call for any reason. You, landlord, cannot afford such a phobia. The telephone is one of the tools you must learn to use both effectively and routinely in order to be an efficient landlord. It's as necessary to your business as a garlic press is to an Italian chef.

Here are some suggestions which might help you use the telephone more effectively and more routinely in your landlording business—

✔ Maintain a separate phone number for your landlording calls, and set it up with call forwarding so your landlording calls will go to whatever phone number you designate. You could make your cell phone your primary landlording number, but think twice before you do because you could lose your cell phone or forget to charge it or be out of cell phone range and as a result lose all phone contact with your business until your cell phone service is restored. With a landline number as your primary landlording number, you needn't worry if your cell phone goes dead or missing. You merely forward your calls to another accessible phone or else use your landline and its answering machine to take your landlording calls.

A separate landlording number will help keep your private affairs separate from your business affairs (by answering it, "[YourName] Properties," you'll sound more professional) and simplify your business-call recordkeeping because it will save you from having to prorate your bills and from having to keep track of every business call you make on your personal number. If you make all of your business calls on the landlording line, you can expense the entire bill without having to spend time poring over it.

✔ At a minimum, get a basic cell phone and remember to take it with you whenever you're out and about. Even a basic cell phone will let you run your landlording business from almost anywhere, whether it's your dentist's waiting room, the neighborhood dress shop, the driving range, or the corner Starbucks.

While limited in features compared to smartphones, a basic cell phone may be all the mobile phone you need. They're much, much cheaper than smartphones and still offer basic telephone functionality.

The cheapest of the basic cell phone plans is a pay-as-you-go (prepaid) plan from carriers you may never have heard of, carriers which sell over the internet and in stores like Target and Wal-Mart. Net10 (net10.com) is a good example. Net10 sells basic cell phones over the internet for $20 to $60, which amounts to nothing or next to nothing because they all come bundled with $30 of prepaid talk time (300 nationwide minutes, good for sixty days following activation). Net10 requires no credit card information and no long-term commitment, that is, no contract, and the monthly minimum to keep the phone activated is only $15 if you buy two or more months at a time. That's $30 for sixty days *and* 300 nationwide anytime minutes. Unused minutes roll over to the next payment cycle, and additional minutes in increments of 200 cost ten cents per minute. The cell phone's display shows the number of minutes currently available and the date when the cell phone's account is due for recharging. Cancellation fees? There are none.

The major cell phone carriers, AT&T, Sprint, T-Mobile, and Verizon, all offer basic plans, too, both pay-as-you go and standard. Their standard plans include deeply discounted cell phones but come with strings attached, chief of which is their long-term contract. Beware!

Because calling plans and rates keep changing all the time, review yours as a matter of course at the end of your first contract period and regularly thereafter. Your cell phone carrier won't automatically give you the best current rates which they advertise to attract new customers. Once they have you as a customer, they think you won't care how much you're paying for their service and that you won't compare rates. Compare their rates, and go with another carrier if you find a better deal.

Remember, your cell phone number is yours to keep. You can have it transferred from one carrier to another.

✔ Get a smartphone if you feel the need to stay connected with the world. Smartphones like the iPhone, Blackberry, Palm Pre, Motorola Droid, and Nexus One are expensive to buy and expensive to keep in service, but they're more than phones. They're computers every bit as powerful as many desktops. They're also personal digital assistants (PDA's), still cameras, camcorders, global positioning systems (GPS's), music players, game machines, alarm clocks, flashlights, calculators, WI-FI devices, radios, televisions, and whatnots. Become accustomed to using one and you'll be hooked. You can't live without it.

Can't live without checking your email every few minutes. Get a smartphone. Can't live without microblogging (social networking). Get a smartphone. Can't live without having a search engine at your thumbtips? Get a smartphone. Can't live without checking your computerized appointment calendar whenever you want? Get a smartphone. Can't live without accessing your contact database from anywhere? Get a smartphone. Can't live without keeping tabs on the stock market in real time? Get a smartphone. Can't live without having the latest cool gadget? Get a smartphone.

Remember, smartphones are small. Smallness is good for making them easily portable. It's bad for making them easily lost or stolen. So, synchronize your smartphone with your primary computer regularly and you won't lose all the precious and sensitive data you stored on it should it ever go missing.

✔ Look into getting a digital phone system, AKA internet phone or VoIP phone, for your home office. They cost less per month than a conventional landline, come loaded with features which normally cost extra, and enable you to select an out-of-area phone number if you think it would be of advantage to you.

✔ Keep all of your tenants' phone numbers handy—their home numbers, their work numbers, and their cell phone numbers. Because many tenants nowadays have unlisted numbers which no operator or directory could possibly provide, as well as cell phone numbers which they themselves cannot remember, having the numbers handy will save you from having to make a personal visit to inform tenants of minor, but necessary, matters, such as an anticipated utility shutdown the next day.

✔ Even though telephone directories are going the way of daily newspapers because of the internet, they're still with us and still useful to some degree. Whenever you use the Yellow Pages to shop for a product or service, make relevant notes right in the book itself next to the listings of those firms you've called so you'll have some clues to follow the next time you're searching for that same product or service. Don't be afraid to write in the book. It's yours. Nobody will whack you on the knuckles for writing in it.

✔ Get a toll-free number and use it together with your landlording number whenever you advertise a vacancy. Nobody balks at calling a toll-free number, whereas some people do balk when they have to make a toll call on a telephone which has a limited free-calling area.

Once upon a time, I bought a fourplex owned by a fellow who had moved twelve miles away from his rental property, out of the local calling area. Only one of the units was occupied when I bought it. Three tenants happened to move out at the same time, and the poor fellow was trying desperately to rent the three vacant units without success. He advertised them in the paper and put a sign outside, but he just couldn't get people to call his new number. It was a toll call. He practically begged me to buy the building and then he practically gave it to me when I did buy it because he couldn't fill it himself.

All I had to do was put my local phone number on the for-rent sign, and I had plenty of prospects calling for information. I filled the place within ten days. I figure that his not having a toll-free number for people to call cost that seller a quarter of the value of the property!

Toll-free numbers are inexpensive nowadays. $2 per month and 5¢ per minute is common. Compare AT&T, MCI, NACI, Sprint, and Phone People. They all offer toll-free numbers.

You should know that a toll-free number does not require an additional incoming phone line. Calls coming into your toll-free number go to whatever number you designate to your carrier.

You should also know that if you were to order a toll-free number today, you wouldn't get an 800 number. They're all gone. The only way to get one is to find somebody who isn't using theirs and will assign it to you (selling toll-free numbers is illegal). Instead of getting an 800 number, you'd get another number in the toll-free series, 888, 877, or 866 (855, 844, 833, and 822 are reserved for future use as toll-free numbers). Because some people don't know that numbers other than 800 are toll-free, you should put "toll-free" in front of your toll-free 888, 877, or 866 phone number on whatever signage or advertising you use.

Whenever you face a landlording task which involves communication, ask yourself first whether you can take care of it with a phone call before you crank up your old Ford truck to make a personal visit or get out your old Smith-Corona typewriter to write a letter.

Using the Internet

Dot-com companies may come and go, and the stocks of the survivors may be more of a crapshoot than a real crapshoot in Vegas, but the internet is here to stay. It's a boon in many ways to many people in many walks of life. It's definitely a boon to landlords. No, it's many "boons" to landlords.

It's a boon for advertising vacancies and reaching prospects far beyond the reach of your local newspaper.

It's a boon for enabling prospects to see what a rental dwelling looks like without your having to show it to them personally.

It's a boon for checking market rents.

It's a boon for checking applicants' credit histories and eviction records quickly and conveniently at any time of the day or night.

It's a boon for tracking the whereabouts of tenants who skip out owing you money.

It's a boon for finding the latest landlord-tenant laws for your city, county, and state.

It's a boon for learning the latest about federal housing laws and federal housing programs.

It's a boon for communicating with tenants, managers, and other landlords at everybody's convenience.

It's a boon for researching the best products to do a job.

It's a boon for locating and ordering tools, equipment, parts, and supplies, including those which would otherwise be hard to find.

Use it for these tasks, and you'll be saving yourself time and money. You'll know that you're charging the right rent because you checked the rents for other dwellings similar to yours. You'll know that you're buying the right toilet because you checked plumbers' comments about the various brands and models. You'll know that you rented to the right applicants because you checked them out thoroughly. You'll know that you have a better handle on your business than ever before because you're using the many boons of the internet to help you with your business.

Organizing Everything

There are many sources of discouragement in this landlording business, many of which you can do absolutely nothing about, but there is one source of discouragement which you can do something about, and that is disorganization.

Disorganized landlords make the job much more difficult than it already is, and consequently, they become needlessly discouraged time and time again because they cannot find what they're looking for in the chaos of their stacks and piles.

There are tenant records to keep organized as well as receipts, insurance policies, building records, checks, keys, supplies, tools, and spare parts, and you cannot have a memory sufficient to locate all of them when you need them. You have to get them organized or you will fail miserably in this business.

You will find a number of hints and forms in this book to help you get organized. Use them, adapt them to fit your needs, and you will succeed in making your job easier and surely far less discouraging.

Don't make this business any harder than it already is. Get organized. Stay organized.

If you need some help, hire a professional organizer, also known as a "clutter buster." These professionals can help you put order in your surroundings so you will be able to do more in less time, in other words, become a more efficient landlord. Use the website of the National Association of Professional Organizers (napo.net) to locate an organizer near you.

Continuing Your Education

If you own no rental property at all right now, you are wise ("Wise people learn by others' mistakes; fools, by their own."–Old proverb), not because you own no rental property, but because you're taking the time to educate yourself before you do own rental property. Few first-time landlords ever have the street smarts or the knowledge necessary to handle the many problems they will encounter in this business sooner or later. Some cope well and thrive. Some give up after the first setback and sell. Some capitulate and commit hari-kari. Most of us just muddle through.

There's no reason for you to repeat the same mistakes others have made so many times before and to pay a high price for making those mistakes again because now there's an abundance of information available in books, on tapes, in periodicals, in classes, in seminars, and on the internet. Learn all you can from these sources.

Hard Knocks College no longer has a monopoly on rental property management education. Adult schools, community colleges, university extensions, and rental housing associations all offer sessions for landlords who want to know more about this business they find themselves in.

If such sessions are not available where you live, ask for them. The people who schedule these sessions try to accommodate local needs, but they sometimes overlook the need for rental property management courses entirely because they have no familiarity with the business themselves. If nobody requests these courses, there won't be any.

New owners obviously profit from attending these sessions, but experienced owners profit from continuing their education, too. Remember, you are dealing with large sums of money in this business and you cannot afford to be complacent or uninformed. Times change, things change, and laws change, and you need to reassess your business operations all the time, picking up one good idea here and another there, and you can do that best by continuing your education both formally and informally. Continuing education offers you the opportunity to spend a little and save a lot.

Wearing Proper Attire

Not every rental property has them–busybodies who thrive on buttonholing the manager or owner and babbling on interminably. If you do have such tenants, however, you know they can be more of a nuisance than hemorrhoidal tissues. They're usually model tenants otherwise and you hate to offend them, but you also hate to waste your precious time lending them your ears for very long.

Take courage. You can avoid gossipmongers by wearing overalls that are all speckled with paint whenever you set foot on your rental property. You may have just showered or awakened from your afternoon nap, but they won't think so. Those overalls are your uniform, and they clothe you with a certain busy-worker mystique. They give you license to do what you came to do and then leave without having to make or listen to small talk.

Maintaining Your Image

As a landlord, you are always in the crosshairs, targeted by some ignorant ninny or other as one of the banes of society. Be on your guard. What you do, what you say, and how you look, all of these things affect the way your tenants see and react to you.

If you really must have a Cadillac SUV or a Mercedes roadster or a Jaguar sedan, don't drive it anywhere near your rental properties. Your tenants know for a fact that you paid for it in cash with their rent money. You didn't earn the money to pay for it. You got the money from them.

No matter how warranted a rent increase is, if your tenants think you are a wealthy and uncaring owner, they will resent the increase and resent you, too. Give them no cause to resent you.

Don't tell your tenants about your country club activities or your tours around the world. Don't show them your gold Rolex watch, your two-carat diamond solitaire ring, or your jet helicopter. Sure, you've worked hard for these trappings of success, but you should save displaying them for the gatherings with your in-laws.

Keep a low profile around your tenants. Drive your oldest vehicle to your rental properties. Make your tenants think that you need this month's rent money to pay this month's mortgage payment and the property's various other expenses, whether you do or you don't.

The image you maintain around your tenants should be as neutral as possible. It shouldn't call attention to you as a miser or a profligate. It should be the image of the average Jill or Joe struggling to make ends meet. It should be one suitably matched to your tenants.

Prioritizing Your Work and Keeping Sane

Don't expect spontaneous remission to remedy many of your tenants' complaints for repairs, but do give it a try sometime by prescribing the tardy treatment for certain piddlin' problems. Since no one has yet found a way to fix a leaky roof over the telephone, you must make a visit for that kind of thing and you should make it soon after you're notified, but if the problem's of a lesser magnitude, you should reassure the tenant with a gentle voice that everything will be taken care of in due time and then jot down the job on your list of priorities. Don't rush over to your properties for every little thing. You'll soon need a new spouse and an expensive shrink if you do. Accumulate the little repair jobs until they warrant a fixit visit themselves or until you need to go there for some other reason. You'll be surprised how often the little problems will have taken care of themselves in the interim.

Just because you don't leap up immediately to respond to every tenant's complaint doesn't mean that you should discourage your tenants from reporting the little maintenance problems they notice. On the contrary, you should be encouraging them to report these problems because you will pay dearly for postponing repairs on your rental property too long.

Linoleum which is just beginning to pull loose at a seam is so much easier and cheaper to repair as soon as it becomes apparent than it is when a piece has torn away and been lost. A water leak under a kitchen sink will eventually cause wood decay in the cabinetry if it's neglected, decay which the termite inspector's keen eyes won't overlook when he comes to inspect the place for a buyer. A small roof leak can cause ceiling damage the likes of which can bust your budget.

Use your good common sense to determine when you should make a visit to your property and when you should stay away.

Equating Your Time with Money

Remember that all of your landlording expenses are tax-deductible as business expenses and that there will be times when you'll have to pay more than you think you should for something you need in a hurry. There will be times when you have no choice but to call for professional help because you lack the expertise or the tools to do a job, because you're fed up and shouldn't do it, or because you simply don't have the time to do it. Call for the help and think of the bill as a business expense. That's what it is. Don't get frustrated because you couldn't do it yourself and save the cost of having somebody else do it.

You can't always do everything yourself. I repeat. *You can't always do everything yourself.*

You're not the ordinary do-it-yourselfer, remember. You don't have their kind of time to case creation for what you want to buy at the price you want to pay. Let ordinary do-it-yourselfers boast about how they spent long hours scrounging to find something and then got it for a song. Good for them! You have no time for that. You have a business to tend to, a business in which time translates into money, your money.

Monitoring Turnover Rates and Equating Downtime with Money

On average, 45% of all rental dwellings in the U.S. turn over every year, and the downtime for turnovers averages eighteen days. These averages include professionally managed properties as well as owner-managed properties. As a do-it-your-self landlord managing your own rental proper-ties, you should keep these averages in mind and use them as benchmarks for your own operations to see how you measure up.

Keep in mind that this average turnover rate of 45% translates into tenancies which last a little longer than two years, 2.2 years or 811 days to be exact (365 days per year divided by .45). In comparison, a turnover rate of 100% per year translates into tenancies which last exactly one year (365 days per year divided by 1.00).

Keep in mind that a downtime of eighteen days translates into a loss of rent equal to 2.22%, based upon one turnover per dwelling every 811 days (18 days of downtime divided by 811 days of occupancy). That's the equivalent of losing one day of rent for every forty-five days of occupancy (811 days of occupancy divided by 18 days of downtime).

Another way to calculate the cost of eighteen days of downtime for every turnover is to divide one month's rent by thirty (yields the daily rent) and multiply that times eighteen. If the rent is $750 per month, one day's rent is $25, and a downtime of eighteen days reduces your rental income by $450 (18 days times $25 per day) ev-ery 811 days. That's for one dwelling only. For four dwellings, a downtime of eighteen days re-duces your rental income by $1,800 every 811 days or $810 every 365 days.

Of course, we're assuming here that the turn-over rate is 45%. If it were 100% and the down-time were still eighteen days, then the reduction in rental income for a dwelling with a rent of $750 per month would be $450 every 365 days for a single dwelling and $1,800 for four dwell-ings. That's equivalent to losing one day of rent for every twenty days of occupancy.

Any way you look at equating a dwelling's downtime with money, you can see that there's serious money involved here, your money.

There's no doubt as to whether a shorter downtime is better than a longer one. It is. A longer downtime reduces your income. A shorter downtime increases your income.

You can shorten your downtime between ten-ancies by being quick about everything required to prepare a dwelling for occupancy and by be-ing quick about getting good tenants. Using the suggestions in this book for being quick, you should be able to beat the average. Concentrate on shortening your downtime every time you have a vacancy. Be nimble, be quick, and you'll beat the eighteen-day average. After all, that av-erage includes properties managed by people who don't own them. You as a do-it-yourself land-lord, you who care about your property more than anyone else, you who will work 24/7 when you have to, you will beat the average.

Beating the downtime average of eighteen days is one thing; beating the turnover average of 45% is quite another. There is some doubt as to what is the optimum turnover rate. Is a turnover rate of 20%, which means the tenants stay five years, better than a turnover rate of 45%? How about a turnover rate of 100%, which means they stay a year, or one of 200%, which means they stay six months? Are they any better than 45%? There is no simple answer to each of these questions, not if your objective is to maximize your landlording income.

There is a simple answer if your objective is to minimize your landlording troubles, that is, if you want to put your landlording business on "auto-matic pilot" as much as possible and distance yourself from it so you can spend more time on other things you enjoy more. That simple an-swer is this. Strive for a lower turnover rate. It will minimize your landlording troubles. If you have a turnover rate approaching zero, if your tenants only move from your rental dwellings to the cemetery, then you're seldom troubled with turnovers and all the associated work involved, but you're also charging too little in rent, for you need do little else to reduce your turnover rate other than to keep your rents low.

On the other hand, if you want to maximize your landlording income, you will experience a higher turnover rate, somewhere between 45% and 100%. In other words, your tenants will stay an average of one to a little more than two years. Some might stay longer than that, and some might stay shorter than that. If one tenant stays four years and another stays four months, the turnover rate for those two tenancies averages out to 45%.

A turnover rate in the 45%-to-100% range in-dicates that you are charging market or near-mar-ket rents, that you are providing your tenants with the services they want, and that you are maxi-mizing your income.

Remember, these figures are only benchmarks, nothing more. Use them to get an idea about how you're performing as a do-it-yourself landlord compared to everybody else in the business.

Ignoring Tenant "Chaff Clouds"

Landlording do-it-yourselfers tend to be more patient, understanding, helpful, and credulous than their professional counterparts who work for the corporate owners of large apartment complexes. Landlording do-it-yourselfers know their tenants and are known by them. They develop a personal relationship with their tenants. They will give their tenants one chance, two chances, even three or four chances to shape up before they begin eviction proceedings, and when they do, they feel as if they themselves have failed somehow, not their tenants.

There's no reason you have to lose your humanity when you become a landlord. You should be patient, understanding, and helpful, but you should not be credulous, especially not when you are dealing with applicants or new tenants. You don't know them, and you don't know what they're capable of.

When a fighter pilot is trying to confuse an enemy missile headed straight for him, he releases a chaff cloud from the rear of his aircraft to make the missile veer away or detonate out of harm's way.

Some tenants know this technique well and know how to use it to their benefit. They release their chaff clouds whenever they feel the need to confuse a landlord. Their chaff consists of half truths and whole lies which work well to make credulous landlords veer away from the target.

Don't you be credulous. Be on the lookout for these tenant chaff clouds. Try to recognize them for what they are. Try your best to ignore them and head straight for your target.

In every case, you can best ignore tenant chaff clouds by following your standard operating procedures, whether it's a procedure for getting good tenants, for collecting all the move-in monies, for collecting rents promptly, or for enforcing the rental agreement.

Let's say that some well-dressed, well-mannered applicants want you to rent to them right away before you have a chance to check out their application. They show you a stack of greenbacks which equal more than the amount you require for them to move in. They tell you that they're new to the area and need a place to rent for the long term. They need it right now, today. What do you do?

Take your eyes off that stack of greenbacks for starters, and remain calm. Tell these people that you do not rent to anybody without checking them out. That's your standard operating procedure, and you can't deviate from it. Tell them that you will check them out and give them an answer within hours, whatever number of hours allows you enough time, 6, 12, or 24. If they say they'll have to find some other landlord who will let them move in immediately without checking them out, tell them to go ahead. Tell them that a landlord who doesn't check rental applications is a landlord who has tenant problems or will have tenant problems, and those tenant problems will affect them as good tenants. If they want to rent from such a landlord, that's their business. Be firm.

Let's say that some applicants tell you after you have approved them to move in that they don't have all the money required because their son was in a car accident out of state and they had to wire him some money. They ask you whether you'll allow them to move in if they pay you the first month's rent now and promise to pay the deposit over the next three months. What do you do?

Tell them you're sorry that their son was in a car accident, especially now when their own lives are in turmoil during the process of finding a new place to live and then moving into it. Tell them you're also sorry that you cannot allow them to move in without paying all of their move-in monies up-front. That's your standard operating procedure, and you can't deviate from it. Tell them that you will hold the dwelling for them if they give you the money to hold it but that you cannot let them move in until they have paid everything required to move in, both the rent and the deposit. Be firm.

Let's say that some other applicants whom you have approved to move in now want to move in a few things so they can save the upcoming rent on their storage unit. They're still living elsewhere for another two weeks while you're completing some remodeling. They have paid you nothing other than the small sum they gave you to check out their application. What do you do?

Tell them that you can appreciate their wanting to save money on their storage unit. Tell them that you would be happy to let them move their things from the storage unit to the rental dwelling's storage area or garage, provided that they pay you everything required to take possession, even though their rent won't start until the move-in date you have agreed upon. That's your standard operating procedure, and you can't deviate from it. Be firm.

Let's say that some tenants who moved in a little more than a month ago are a week behind on their rent and they have made no effort to contact you about it. You contact them, and they say that they are really stressed out. The husband just lost his job. The wife broke her arm. The son was thrown out of school for smoking pot on campus, and the thirteen-year-old daughter ran off with her twenty-one-year-old boyfriend. They say that they'll pay you their rent as soon as they can.

Tell them you know that "bad things happen to good people" and you know that they are good people, but something even worse is going to happen to them if they don't pay you their rent money now. They're going to be evicted for nonpayment of rent, and they're going to have an eviction on their tenancy history and on their credit report for a long time to come. Give them the notice to pay rent or quit which you brought along with you already filled out. Tell them that giving them the notice is part of your standard operating procedure when people haven't paid their rent on time and you can't deviate from it. Be firm.

Let's say that some tenants who just moved in are keeping two dogs in their dwelling when they have an agreement to keep only one. A neighboring tenant informs you about the two dogs because barking duets have been interfering with her afternoon nap. You approach the tenants and they admit that they have a second dog, but they say that it's not theirs. It's there only temporarily. They're looking after it for a friend who has gone abroad. As soon as the friend returns, they say, the second dog will go. When you ask them about the friend's return, they become elusive and can't give you an exact date.

Tell them that they have an agreement for one dog and one dog only. The second dog will have to go within seven days or else they will have to go themselves along with both dogs. Tell them that you are giving them a written notice about this breach of their contract and that it will re-

main in their tenant file. Tell them that giving them the notice is part of your standard operating procedure. Be firm.

Enough of these stories! You get the picture, don't you? In each story, the applicants or tenants release chaff clouds to convince you that you ought to veer away from your target, that you ought to let them take possession before you've checked them out thoroughly or collected all the move-in monies normally required, that you ought to let them pay their rent whenever they can, and that you ought to let them break their rental agreement for an indefinite period.

You know the consequences of renting to someone whose credit and tenancy history you haven't checked, especially if they're trying to entice you to rent to them by flashing a stack of greenbacks.

You know the consequences of letting new tenants move in just a few of their things or everything they own without paying you all of the move-in monies you normally require.

You know the consequences of letting tenants get behind on their rent, no matter how compelling is their story, no matter how sincere are their promises.

You know the consequences of letting tenants break their rental agreement and keep an extra pet, no matter whose pet it is, no matter how well behaved they say it is, no matter how soon they say it will go.

You know these consequences instinctively. You don't want to know them intimately. Listen to your instincts. Don't be confused by tenant chaff clouds. Don't be credulous. Stick with your standard operating procedures. Be firm.

Learn to ignore tenant chaff clouds and you will go a long way in the landlording business.

Noting Store Hours

That portion of your spare time given over to maintaining your rental properties hardly coincides with normal business hours. Most likely you work at your properties in the evening, at night, in the morning, and on weekends.

Because these times are on the fringes of most stores' normal hours, you have undoubtedly experienced the frustration of scurrying off to the paint store at 6:15 on a Sunday evening to buy that last can of paint you need to complete redecorating a dwelling which a new tenant wants to move into the very next day, but when you arrive, you find that the paint store closed at six. What's all the more frustrating is that you could have been there before six had you known when it closed.

How can you avoid a repetition of this frustrating situation? The next time you go on one of your buying errands, write down the hours for each store you visit and keep their hours in that wallet, purse, or glove compartment which usually accompanies you on your landlording tours of duty. If you use a smartphone, enter the hours there in a database. One quick glance at this information will tell you which store is still open at 9:12 on a Tuesday night when you need to buy the parts to replace a useless toilet valve that came apart in your hands.

You will spare yourself more spare time for plotting rent raises and smoking noxious cigars if you aren't waiting around for stores to open in the morning or you aren't driving wildly about town looking for any supplier who's open late at night.

Doing It Your Way

Some people prefer their toilet paper to roll off the front of the roll, some prefer it to roll off the back, and I'm sure there are those who prefer no roll at all. They like their toilet paper in separate sheets. No one way is "right."

Likewise, there is no right or wrong way to do every little thing in landlording. You have to decide what's right for you, what you're comfortable with, and what works for your tenants, and then continue in that direction. There are many ways to collect rents promptly, for example, and though I do give more than one way in the chapter on rents, I don't give them all. In truth, I'm sure that I don't know them all.

Use what you read in this book as starting points for developing your own ways of doing things. Don't suppose that there are no other ways to do them. There are. Be creative. Find your own way. You'll enjoy landlording much more if you do.

Taking Your Front-Row Seat at a Long-Running Comedy

Do-it-yourself landlording isn't all cleaning up other people's messes, coaxing space heaters to work on Christmas Eve, painting wall after wall the same ivory white, chasing elusive deadbeats for their rent, taking nuisance calls in the middle of the night, doing battle with uncooperative tenants who flaunt the rules, and studying the latest landlord-tenant laws.

No, it's not.

It's a front-row seat at a long-running human comedy. There are humorous things happening all around you, landlord. Take the time to recognize and enjoy them.

Chuckle to yourself when your tenant tells you that he couldn't pay his rent because he had to pay his girlfriend's rent or she was going to be evicted. Chuckle to yourself when you're looking into the eyes of a tenant who, with a straight face, is making up some pretty imaginative reasons why there just happens to be a St. Bernard in his no-pets apartment when you come by unannounced to check on the smoke detectors. Chuckle to yourself when your very worst tenant, the one who has told you where to go more than once, tells you to get rid of his neighbor right away because the neighbor has been smoking pot.

Don't work all the time with your head hanging down, muttering to yourself, "Woe is me! Nobody ever appreciates what I do for them. Everybody tries to take advantage of me. I work such long hours while everybody else seems to be having all the fun."

Look for the humor that there is in this business. It's there, and it will provide you with the comic relief you sometimes need as you plug away doing the nasty work which comes with the territory, landlording territory.

Some Last Words

Some of the things you have to do in landlording may be tough to do. No scrupulous landlord ever said this business was easy, but if you practice sound business methods, use your common sense, keep a level head, learn enough skills to do some things yourself, and know enough to call for help when you need it, you won't find your property declining in value. It will actually be increasing in value, making money for you while you sleep. Indeed it will!

Haven't you always wanted to make money while you sleep? Haven't you always wanted to buy the mixed nuts without the peanuts and not give the purchase a second thought? Landlord, you can! Just keep minding your landlording business, and in time it will pay better dividends than you ever expected.

2
Taking Over
As the New Owner

Let's eavesdrop on some new owners as they're sharing their initial landlording experiences and impressions with anyone who will listen.

"Here I am paying for the privilege of being these people's landlord. The rent they pay me doesn't cover nearly all of my expenses, and still they expect me to hotfoot it over there day or night to unplug the toilet which they stopped up. Hear what I'm saying? Their kids stop up the toilet with a full roll of toilet paper, and I'm supposed to go running over there, unplug the thing, and clean up the whole stinkin' mess which is all over the floor. What kind of a business have I gotten myself into anyway?"

"I felt like maybe I'd died and gone to hell! My phone never stops ringing. There's always somebody calling me with their problems. They're unhappy about this. They're unhappy about that, and they want me to do something right now to make them happy. Trouble is, I can't make them happy, no matter what I do. I've tried. My, how I've tried!"

"My landlording bloopers that first week were enough to start a whole new TV series."

"I felt as lonely as a flatulent sheep dog."

"I could almost see my hair turning gray when I had to serve eviction papers on my tatooed muscleman doper tenant. I think he's the real reason the previous owner sold me the building so cheap. Until he and his motorcycle gang are out of there, I'm keeping a low profile and keeping protection handy. Know what I mean?"

"Never before had anybody called me up at 3 o'clock in the morning demanding that I come right over and kill a monster cockroach which was darting about in their kitchen."

"I never realized before just how many tenants are street lawyers. Why, they know the chapter and verse of every landlord-tenant law there is and every court decision, too! What is it with these tenants? Don't they have anything else to do with their lives?"

Yep, becoming a landlord, taking over as the new owner of a rental property, can be pretty traumatic for some people. At the very least, it's an eye-opener for all but the thickest skinned. You may find yourself wondering what ever possessed you to get involved in this crazy business in the first place. Take heart; it's not all that bad, and there's a lot you can do to get things running smoothly right off the bat.

Let's say that you have just acquired some residential income property and you are anxious to get started fulfilling your role as the new owner. You have already bought a copy of *Landlording*, a most commendable beginning. You have joined your local rental housing association and have bombarded all the people there with your questions. You have secured a copy of the applicable housing codes from the powers that be and have familiarized yourself with the basic services and amenities which you must provide by law. You have notified the appropriate utility companies about the property's change in ownership so that all the master-metered bills will be sent directly to you. You have decided already how you're going to be doing the banking and bill-paying for the property. You have decided to handle the off-site management yourself and are looking over the existing tenants for somebody to assume certain on-site management responsibilities. You have thought about the building and about what needs to be done there, having made several inspections before you ever bought the place, and you have lined up some workers to help you take care of the property's obvious deficiencies.

You're certainly on the right track, but because the former owner kept such abominable records, you have no information whatsoever about the tenants you inherited, and, what's more, they have

September 16, XXXX

Dear *Ms. Melander*,

   You probably know already that the building where you live has
changed hands. Because tenants usually feel some apprehension
every time such a changeover occurs, we would like to take this
opportunity to clear the air by letting you know just what you can
expect in the future about a few things.

   DEPOSITS...One special concern you must have is your deposits.
We are concerned, too, and we want to make absolutely certain that
all of your deposits are credited to you. To avoid any
misunderstandings about your deposits and other matters related to
your living here, we would like you to answer the questions on the
sheet attached. They are questions which you should be able to
answer quickly from memory or by referring to information readily
available to you. Please do so as soon as possible and return
your answers to us in the envelope provided.

   PAYMENT BY CHECK OR MONEY ORDER...Since it is unwise for anyone
to keep or carry cash around in quantities, we request that you
pay your rent by check or money order (made payable to us exactly
as underlined below). You will be protected and so will we.

   PROMPT PAYMENT...You are expected to pay your rent within three
days after the due date. For example, rent due on the first must
be paid by the fourth at the very latest. If you anticipate being
late beyond that for any reason whatsoever, please let us know
beforehand. If you don't, we will assume that you are
deliberately avoiding payment, and we will immediately serve you
with the notice which starts eviction proceedings.

   MAINTENANCE...We expect you to pay your rent promptly, and you
can expect us to respond promptly to maintenance problems.
Sometime within the next week, we will visit you to inspect for
any building maintenance work that should be taken care of. You
can help by starting now to make a list of such work which you
notice around the house.

   RENTAL AGREEMENT...We will also stop by soon to explain to you
the standard rental agreement we use, and we will leave you with a
copy of your own.

   We are reasonable people and we will try anything within reason
to make living here enjoyable for you, but naturally we need your
cooperation. If we have it, we will get along well together and
we can all take pride in this place that you call home.

                                    Sincerely,

                                    Margaret Miglia, Manager
                                    DANDY PROPERTIES (123-4567)
                                    400 Busy Ave., Goodloc, CA 09777

none about you. They're now wondering what to do with their rent monies, whom to call about their cockroaches, when the rent's going up, what's happened to their deposits, and how soon they're going to get the new carpets promised to them last Christmas by the previous owner's property manager.

Making Contact—The Letter

The very next thing you should do is communicate with them, for communication is the lifeblood of this business. Send them a letter or, better still, for establishing good rapport with them all the more quickly, take a letter around to each of them and meet these people who are now your tenants. They want to put a face on you, landlord. They want to know what they're up against. Are you an ogre? Are you a pushover? How big are your horns? Do you smile? How do you dress? What do you drive? What kind of a creature are you? They want to know. Consider this an opportunity to let them have a good look at you and judge for themselves what kind of a person you are while you have a good look at them and judge for yourself what kind of people they are.

Advise them in the letter that the building has indeed changed hands, just as they suspected, and that you are now looking after it as the owner or one of the owners or the manager (determine now whether you intend to stop the buck or pass it—see chapter 13). Give them your name, address, landlording phone number, and email address so they will know how they can contact you when necessary. Allay their fears about their deposits, inform them about your rent collection procedure, tell them you do want to hear about their maintenance problems, and mention that you expect to come calling soon with a rental agreement.

The letter given here includes all of these elements and more, and like the other forms shown in the text, you will find a full-size copy ready for your use in the FORMS section in the back of this book. You may photocopy the letter as is, or you may enter the text into your word processor and adapt it to fit your own circumstances. If you do plan to use the letter as is, make sure you intend to follow through with all that you are promising to do in it, visiting your new tenants within a week or two to check for maintenance problems, and so forth. Don't say you're going to do something unless you can do it and will do it,

especially not now, not when people you've never done business with before are looking at you with a "show-me" eye. Prove yourself to be a person of your word and not a flim-flammer.

Gathering Tenant Information

Besides telling your new tenants about their building's new management, you need to gather some information about them as well. Along with your first letter to them, provide them with a Tenant Information form and include a stamped, self-addressed envelope for its return. This information is intended to take the place of most of what you would already have in your files on those tenants you select yourself, information you'd normally collect using the Rental Application and Condition & Inventory Checksheet forms.

Neither the application nor the checksheet is appropriate to use when you inherit tenants whom you know nothing about, for then you are merely trying to establish some basic facts about them and their tenancy. The Tenant Information form is designed for gathering the information needed in this particular situation.

Give your new tenants two weeks to return the Tenant Information form to you. Then, whether they have returned it or not, arrange to meet with them face to face to discuss your policies and go over the written rental agreement you intend to use. Or, if you prefer, combine your visit to do a maintenance check with your visit to gather tenant information and review the rental agreement. There's no good reason to separate them.

Some tenants are inclined to be stubborn and secretive when asked to reveal anything at all about themselves which they consider to be none of your business. Like some primitive people who are afraid to be photographed lest their inner spirit be robbed of them, they imagine that you are snooping into their private lives so you can lay them bare to some big-brother intelligence gathering agency.

To counteract this paranoia, try to be as delicate and inoffensive as possible if they don't volunteer to provide you with the information themselves. Be neither offensive nor defensive about gathering it. After all, there are sound, logical reasons why you need every bit of it, so you may want to stress that their own best interests are being served by their divulging the information to you.

Tenant Information:

Your Name __Nelly Bunn__

Your Address __452 Summit, Apt. 206__

Your Home Phone __555-0912__   Cell Phone __555-6720__

Your Email Address __NELLY452@BMAIL.COM__

Your Soc. Sec. No. __555-55-5555__ Driver's License __MONTANA 2987676__

Who lives with you? (Include ages of children, please) __Nobody.__

_____

What pet(s) do you have? __3 small dogs__

Do you have a waterbed? __No__

What vehicle(s) do you have? Make(s) __Toyota__ License(s) __442A701__

Where do you work? (Company name) __Sears__

What is your phone number at work? __555-7575__

Where does your co-tenant work? (Company name) __N/A__

What is your co-tenant's phone number at work? __N/A__

When did you move in? __March 1, XXXX__

What is your current rent per month? __$650__

What date is your rent paid up to right now? __September 30, XXXX__

When is your rent due each month? __1st__

What refundable deposits have you paid? Keys $ __5-__ Security $ __1,250-__

   Cleaning $ __150-__   Other (please explain) $ __∅__

   When you moved in, you paid your first month's rent. Did you also

   then pay your last month's rent? __NO__ If so, how much did you

   pay? $ __NA__ Does what you paid as last month's rent now equal

   your current rent? __NA__

Which of the following furnishings in your dwelling belong to the

   owners of the building? (Please give room locations where

   appropriate.)

   Carpets __Living room, hall, bedroom__ Drapes _____

   Shades __Kitchen and bath__   Blinds _____

   Stove __Kitchen__   Refrigerator __Kitchen__

   Other appliances? (Please list) _____

   Other furniture? (Please list) _____

Do you have a rental agreement or lease in writing? __Yes__

   If so, what is the date of the latest one? __March 1, XXXX__

In case of an emergency, what friend or relative should we contact?

   Name __Martha Price__   Phone Number __555-0011__

Date __9/18/XX__   Your Signature __Nelly Bunn__

If you have to, explain why you need to know each of the items on the Tenant Information form.

You need to know their home, cell, and work phone numbers in case there's an emergency and you need to get in touch with them in a big hurry. Let's say that a neighbor notices somebody prowling around their dwelling and calls you about it or else their smoke alarm starts wailing and nobody seems to be home. Your having their phone numbers available at those times will save them and you much grief later. If they say they have an unlisted number and prefer not to give it out, tell them that you will take every reasonable precaution to keep their number from falling into anybody else's hands.

You need to know their email address, too, in case you can't get in touch with them by phone.

You need to know their Social Security and driver's license numbers so you can verify their tenancy information for the businesses and credit reporting agencies which sometimes call you as the landlord when tenants are applying for credit.

You need to know who lives with them so you will be able to keep unauthorized people from entering their dwelling. For example, you need to know what you ought to do if a complete stranger asks you to let her in, someone who says she lives there and forgot her key. Does she really live there? Should you let her in?

Emphasize especially the concern you have about determining precise sums and dates, both of which you need to establish now in order to prevent misunderstandings later. You need to know exactly how much they paid in deposits to the previous owner so you will know exactly how much to set aside for them when they move out. You also need to know whether they paid their last month's rent and if so, how much they paid.

Tell them that the previous owner provided you with a set of figures before you bought the property but that you need to verify them against the tenants' own figures.

If they just won't cooperate with you in providing the information, there's nothing you can do to force them, and you shouldn't bother getting upset about the matter yourself or making them upset by saying unkind words or threatening them. Retreat. Let them be. Consider them to be ignorant, foolish, mentally unbalanced, generally uncooperative, or any combination of these possibilities. Then rely on others to supply the information. Use the deposit figures provided by the previous owner, and ask him what else he knows about the tenants. Tracking down the few facts needed to complete the Tenant Information form from other sources is certainly possible. It's just more time-consuming than getting the information directly from the tenants.

Remember that part of your effort to communicate with your new tenants involves proving yourself to be a reasonable human being. Don't allow yourself to be drawn into an argument. Don't talk about other tenants. Don't talk about yourself unless you're asked, and even then be brief. Find out what's on these new tenants' minds, what's troubling them. Let them talk if they want to, and listen carefully to what they have to say. Look them in the eye, be concerned, be polite, and be more ready to smile than a Miss America contestant at a press conference.

Coming to Terms
Using Your Rental Agreement

Before you ever bought your rental property, you should have found out what kind of agreements or leases the previous owner was using, but if you didn't, during your first tenant visit you will want to establish what governs your relationship with your new tenants. Ask to see a copy of their rental agreement, if any. You may be flabbergasted when they actually produce one whereas the previous owner couldn't find one to pass along to you.

To get a copy for your files, give the tenants a dollar or two and ask them to make you a copy. Don't ask them to give you their copy so you may take it to a copy shop or to your home or office unless they can accompany you there because they may become suspicious that you won't return it. Don't give them cause to be suspicious. By giving them a little money to make a copy, surely more than it will cost them to copy the agreement at a copy shop, you will have them thinking that you're trustworthy rather than suspect, generous rather than parsimonious, someone who will be a better landlord than the "scoundrel" who was their previous landlord.

When you inherit tenants, the agreement they had with the previous owner governs your business relationship with them. The agreement may be a current lease, an expired lease which has become a month-to-month agreement, a written month-to-month agreement, a written agreement for some period less than a month, or even a verbal agreement.

No matter which one of these agreement types governs your relationship, it governs you and your tenants for a certain period of time. More than likely, this period of time coincides with the rent payment schedule. If the tenants pay their rent on a weekly basis, they're probably on a weekly contract. If they pay their rent on a fortnightly basis, they're probably on a bi-weekly contract. If they pay their rent on a monthly basis, they're probably on a monthly contract or on a lease.

If they have a fixed-term lease, like it or not, you're bound by its terms, whatever the terms happen to be, and for whatever period it covers, six months, one year, or even more. Do take a close look at the lease to see what it says, if anything, about the sale of the dwelling. It may allow you as the new owner to boot the tenants out and take possession upon notice of thirty, sixty, or ninety days, should you be so inclined.

In any case, you cannot shove a new agreement at your new tenants and tell them that they have to sign it right away and abide by it from that day forward. You have to give them notice. That's only right, and what's more, it's their due.

You may give them your Rental Agreement any time you want to, of course, but you cannot enforce it until they have signed it and have had some period of time to get accustomed to it. How much time must you give them? Barring any especially restrictive local ordinances, before you can change the terms of their existing periodic-term (month-to-month, week-to-week) contract, you have to give them the same amount of time as the term of their existing contract. When tenants have an existing contract covering a period shorter than a month, you ought to give them thirty days' notice of a change anyway. That's only fair. When they have only a verbal agreement and nothing in writing, give them thirty days, too. In fact, to be fair, you ought to give thirty days to everyone except those who are on leases. Give lease holders a contract at least thirty days before their lease expires so it will take effect the very day the lease actually does expire.

You have every right to expect tenants who are on leases to sign a new lease when their old one expires. If they want to continue their tenancy and don't want to sign a new lease, then they have no lease at all. They become month-to-month tenants, that is, if you accept any rent from them, and you may treat them the same as you treat any other month-to-month tenants.

Spend some time with each tenant you inherit and explain the terms of your Rental Agreement just as you explained the Tenant Information form to them. Listen to their objections and make adjustments if warranted.

Some may object mightily to everything in the agreement and refuse to sign. What do you do about these contrary tenants? Can you have an enforceable written contract signed by only one of the two parties involved?

In most cases involving contract conditions, when the tenant already occupies the premises, you certainly can change the contract conditions yourself without their signature. If they won't sign, explain to them that you will then simply go ahead and prepare a Notice of Change in Terms of Tenancy and attach it to a copy of the Rental Agreement you intend to use. This notice is very much like the one you use to increase rents. Their signature is not required for a notice of this sort to take effect in thirty days. It takes effect regardless.

By refusing to sign, they gain absolutely nothing. They label themselves uncooperative. That's all. Tell them that you would like to have their cooperation in your mutual business dealings but that you will go ahead and manage the property your way, which you feel is quite a reasonable way, whether you get their cooperation or not.

Naturally, the conditions in your new agreement must be legal, but they should be sensible, too. You can't make your inherited tenants tolerate elephants upstairs or rats underfoot any more than you can make any other tenants tolerate such things. You can set quiet hours, require them to pay their rent by a certain day of the month, stipulate that they pay their rent by check, money order, or electronic funds transfer, limit the premises to personal use, make them responsible for drain stoppages which they themselves cause, designate certain parking areas for residents and guests, restrict motor vehicle repairs, and make other similar conditions.

If your new conditions are much different from the ones under which your inherited tenants have been living, especially if you try to initiate a no-pets policy when the tenants already have pets, understand that you will have a fight on your hands, a fight you cannot win because it will be aggravating to you and to the tenants, and it may wind up costing you more than you ever thought it would. People simply will not give up a pet without a fight. Pets are family members.

Rather than trying to get existing tenants to give up their pets, you might be wise to adopt a no-pets policy for all new tenants and a policy of no-new-pets for existing tenants. After all, the old pets have probably already done as much damage as they're going to do both in and around the building. Be reasonable. Try to think through the consequences of your new conditions. Ask yourself how you would react if you were the tenant and your new landlord were imposing these same conditions upon you.

Consider asking a tenant whom you have come to know better than any of the others to give you his reactions to the agreement you want to use. Listen to him. Question him. Discuss his ideas with him and with your "partner." Thank him for his input with a little gift, a plant or a pound of candy.

Once you determine that your agreement is reasonable for this particular property, be resolute about imposing it upon your new tenants. This may be your first test as the new owner. Be firm. Stand up to your tenants now, and they will be easier to deal with later. They will respect you.

Handling Tenants' Deposits

The only time I've ever been hauled into court for failing to return a tenant's deposit was when I acquired a small property and hadn't received any of the deposits from the previous owner. He claimed that he didn't have any deposits. That owner always collected $50 upfront as a cleaning deposit and never returned any of it to his departing tenants. Though he called it a "deposit," he really thought of the money as a cleaning "fee." He assumed that none of his tenants would leave their places clean enough to get a deposit back anyway, so he gave his manager the money as compensation for cleaning the apartments before the tenants moved in. The tenant who was suing me had assumed in the absence of a written agreement that the $50 was a cleaning deposit, not a fee. He left his apartment clean and, as far as I was concerned, he did deserve to get the money back, but because I had never received it from him or from the previous owner, I didn't think that I was the one to return it.

Don't get caught in a squeeze like this. If possible, get all the tenants' deposits sorted out and credited to you at closing. In order to do it the

[Every state sets its own time frame for this notice. If you don't know your state's time frame, call your local rental housing association, check the landlord-tenant laws on your state's website, or check the landlord-tenant law summary in the guest subject area of rhol.org.]

Notice of Change in Terms of Tenancy

TO   Suzanne Stevenson   , Tenant in Possession

12 Apollo Avenue

Big City, CA 09501

YOU ARE HEREBY NOTIFIED that the terms of tenancy under which you occupy the above-described premises are to be changed.

Effective _____ May 3 _____, XXXX, there will be the following changes:

the terms of the RENTAL AGREEMENT attached, which you have refused to sign, shall take precedence over any written or verbal agreement which you may have had with a previous owner.

Dated this __1st__ day of _____ April _____, XXXX.

Julius Caesar
Owner/Manager

This Notice was served by the Owner/Manager in the following manner (check those which apply):

(X) by personal delivery to the tenant,
( ) by leaving a copy with someone on the premises other than the tenant,
( ) by mailing,
( ) by posting.

right way, you should know precisely what the seller *and* the tenants believe those deposits to be before you ever take over. Then you'll be able to take care of any discrepancies while you still owe the seller money. You won't have to take him to court later to collect.

Besides worrying about whether they're actually receiving the correct deposit amounts, new owners frequently worry about whether the deposits they do receive from the previous owner are enough to compensate them for future difficulties. Worry about it if you want to. Just don't do anything about it. Don't even consider raising your tenants' inadequate deposits at this time or at any other time unless you want to precipitate a mass revolt. Most tenants will simply refuse to give you more deposit money. Then what do you do? Evict them? Take them to small claims court? Yell and scream at them? Threaten to raise their rents to unconscionable levels? Forget it. You'll look toothless and inept trying to collect higher deposits, and you'll spend too much energy trying. Don't undermine your position as a no-nonsense landlord by attempting to accomplish that which none but a Mafia capo with hired guns at his side could accomplish.

Raising the Rent

You'll find a few words about the "right" and "wrong" times to raise rents in chapter 6. Read those words when you have the opportunity. All you need to know now is that one of the right times to raise rents is when you acquire a new property, not necessarily the very day you acquire a new property, mind you, but certainly within a month.

I recommend that you do not raise the rent immediately upon taking possession. You have enough else to do. If you feel that a raise is definitely warranted when you take over, wait several weeks until you have begun to establish yourself and have become better acquainted with the situation you've acquired or until you're ready with your new rental agreements, whichever comes first. That's the right time to raise the rents when you acquire a new property.

If the previous owner raised the rents to realistic levels within the previous twelve months, and the rents now are only slightly below market, make your rent raise coincide with the anniversary date of that last rent raise. Under normal conditions, raising rents any more frequently than once a year causes tenants too many anxieties.

If you know that the rents are too low, though, regardless of when they were last raised, don't wait any longer than a month to raise them. Not only will you be losing income by delaying the increase, but your tenants will come to think of you as so soft in the financial head that you would probably "pay interest on borrowed time." Don't miss this perfect opportunity to increase the property's income.

What's the right amount to raise the rent when you acquire a new property? That depends entirely upon the market. There is no rule of thumb. How much you raise it should not be limited to percentages or to amounts.

I can tell you this much. I once raised an inherited tenant's rent by a whopping 50% when I bought a property. I gave him sixty days advance notice, and he neither screamed, "RENT GOUGER, RENT GOUGER!" nor did he move. He knew that he had been enjoying a good deal from the previous owner and that I was well justified in raising his rent 50%. After that, I gave him rent increases every year to keep pace with the market, and he stayed there for years.

Sorting Out the Keys

At the same time you're sorting out the paperwork for your newly acquired rental property, take the time to sort out its keys as well. A handful of keys given to you by the previous owner may be so mixed up that they're worse than useless when you're trying to find a particular key to open a particular lock. They're a detriment, especially if you're in a hurry.

Almost anything may have happened to mix them up. Tenants may have changed their own locks and neglected to give the previous owners a key to their new ones. A maintenance person may have mislabeled some keys. A set of locks that were installed at one place may now be installed at another, and the installer may have neglected to change the labels on the landlord's keys. Some locks may have been misplaced. Some may have malfunctioned and been discarded. Others may have been lost for good.

Take all the keys you have for the property with you when you make your maintenance rounds and try to match each unit up with the right key. If you can't make a proper match, ask to borrow the tenant's key for a few minutes so you can have a copy made, and then try the copy

Notice of Intention to Enter

TO ___Mayme Frank_____ , Tenant in Possession
___730 Delta St., Apt.3_____
___Dumps, CA   09007_____

YOU ARE HEREBY NOTIFIED that at or about __10:00__ (a.m.) (~~p.m.~~)
on _____May 17_____ , __xxxx__ , the Owner, Manager, Owner's
agent, or Owner's employees intend to enter the premises
identified above which you hold and occupy. They should need to
stay approximately __ONE__ hour(s).

The purpose for entry is as follows:
___TO REPLACE ELECTRIC OVEN ELEMENT_____

_____

You are not required to be on the premises to provide access.
Whoever comes to enter will first knock and after determining that
no one is available to answer, will enter using a passkey.

If the lock has been changed without proper notice and you
have not given management a duplicate key, a locksmith will be
called upon to open the door and rekey the locks. Your account
will be charged for these services, and you will be provided with
a new key.

This is intended to be a reasonable notice of at least twenty-
four (24) hours.

This Notice was personally served by the Owner/Manager at the
following time: __6:15__ (~~a.m.~~) (p.m.) and date: __May 15, xxxx__ .

_____Pauline Felder_____
Owner/Manager

when you return to make sure that it works.

Because some tenants insist on being the only ones with keys to their rental dwellings, you may have to approach the matter of obtaining copies with strong resolution. If they are insistent, tell them that they have no right to withhold keys from you, that you, in fact, have every right to have copies of all the keys for all the locks restricting entry to the premises no matter who installed them. Tell them that you recognize they have a right to privacy and that you have no intention of violating that right. Tell them that you will use a passkey only when you are legally entitled to do so, and that is in four well-defined situations—

1) In order to take care of an emergency;

2) In order to make repairs after giving advance notice of 24 hours as required in most jurisdictions;

3) In order to make repairs after obtaining the consent of the tenants; or

4) In order to show the property to prospective tenants or buyers after giving appropriate advance notice.

Show them a copy of the Notice of Intention to Enter form if you plan to use it to advise tenants when and why you intend to enter their dwelling. Tell them that you want to be reasonable and cooperative and that you expect them to be the same.

After this explanation, most people realize that you are being reasonable and they will cooperate. If they flatly refuse, explain calmly that you will have to charge them for locksmithing services in case you have to change their locks under any circumstance entitling you to enter their dwelling legally. Don't fight them. Don't take it upon yourself to change their locks in retaliation. Merely treat them coolly from then on.

Handling the Last Month's Rent

For the various reasons given in chapter 6, I recommend that you do not collect a last month's rent when tenants move in, but you may acquire a property where the previous owners have followed a policy of collecting it from every new tenant. Their having collected it may present a problem for you now, and then again it may not.

So long as the last month's rent as turned over to you by the previous owners is the equivalent of the current rent, there is no problem, but a problem arises should you inherit a tenant whose last month's rent has never been increased to the current level. Why? Tenants generally assume that the last month's rent which they originally paid when they moved in ought to suffice as the last month's rent when they actually move out. They're wrong, of course.

Let's say that when they moved in they paid $600 for their first month's rent and another $600 for their last month's rent. Let's say that they stay six years, and during that time their monthly rent has increased to $925. When they give notice that they're going to move, they may think that their last month's rent has been paid in full with the $600 which they paid as "last month's rent" when they moved in. Wrong, wrong, wrong! They actually owe you an extra $325, and you should take the time to explain the facts to them when they give notice that they're planning to move.

If they're adamant about not paying the extra amount they owe you, you're going to be out the money yourself unless you can find their new address and you want to go to the trouble of taking them to small claims court. There's no time to pursue any other remedy.

You never would have had to consider a legal remedy like small claims court had the former owners been aware of what they were doing. With each rent raise, they should have increased the amount earmarked as the tenant's last month's rent to the amount of the current rent. Then there would have been no confusion over whether the full last month's rent had been paid or not.

Whenever you take over as a new owner and encounter this situation, you might want to give your new tenants a choice so as to avoid needless conflict. Tell them that they may increase their last month's rent to the equivalent of the current rent or they may convert their last month's rent into a deposit, augmenting the other sums already designated as such. The first choice would require them to part with some funds right away. The second would not. Either choice would eliminate the confusion which is sure to arise later unless the situation is dealt with now.

No matter what you decide to do, no matter what choice your tenants make, be sure that you spell out in writing everything that you've decided. Don't wait until the tenants are ready to move before trying to sort everything out. Anticipate the problem and deal with it now.

Some Last Words

Make the transition of ownership as smooth as possible by showing your human side, while at the same time you are giving every indication that you are businesslike and reasonable and that you sincerely want to improve the management and maintenance of the property.

3
Advertising

You don't know them yet and they don't know you yet, but out there somewhere are some very nice people searching for a suitable place to live and a nice landlord like you. They may have put up a posting on Craigslist under "housing wanted" (check the postings). They may have tacked up fliers in public places (look around). They may be pumping their friends for information (keep your ears open). They may have placed an ad in the "Rentals Wanted" column of your community newspaper (look there). They may even be out pounding on doors in the neighborhood where they want to live (open up).

Of course, they may not be doing any of these things because they may not be so enterprising or because they may be able to find vacancies aplenty without having to take any such initiatives. Since you cannot count on being found so easily by every good prospective tenant who's in the market for a place to live, you may have to take the initiative yourself when you have a rental dwelling available or coming available. You may have to spread the word out there to reach those nice people you want to have as your new tenants. In other words, you may have to advertise your rental property vacancy.

There are lots of ways to advertise a rental property vacancy. You might put the word out to your tenants, friends, and acquaintances that you have a place available for rent. You might let people know with a posting on Craigslist, a sign on the premises, a 3"x5" card on a community bulletin board, a card on a bulletin board at a local business, a card on a bulletin board at a nearby church, an item in the employee newsletter where you work, a flier circulated locally, a listing at a college or company housing office, an ad in a community newspaper, or a listing with a real estate agent.

You might try any one or any combination of these methods, but first, whatever you do, stop and take a good look at the exterior appearance of your building. Here's why.

No matter how professional, how costly, how comprehensive, or how artful is your advertising campaign, you will never get your place rented to those desirable tenants who are out there looking for you if they are repulsed by the exterior of your rental property. Any rental dwelling's foremost "advertisement" is a well-kept, neatly painted exterior which looks so inviting to good prospective tenants that they will want to take the time to inspect the inside. That's a lesson I had to learn from experience at the College of Hard Knocks. It's a lesson I will never forget.

Once upon a time, shortly after my wife and I purchased a fixer-upper sixplex with two vacancies, we prepared one of the vacant apartments for rent, advertised it in the local newspaper, and found that we couldn't get a single good prospect to stop by and inspect the interior of the apartment itself, even after the people called and promised to show up at an appointed hour. We would notice cars slowing down and necks craning, and then off they'd go, roaring down the street before we could run out there, flag them down, and convince them to stop and have a look inside. What a disappointment! We had redecorated this one apartment beautifully, and we were already working on the second, but because the exterior of the building looked so shabby and because everyone who responded to our newspaper ad saw that shabby exterior first, no one except the truly undiscriminating would venture further.

Faced with the dismal prospect of renting only to leather-faced transients chugging through the neighborhood in their battered Ford station wagons which appeared to levitate on clouds of exhaust smoke and were crammed with screaming

47

kids and their barking bulldogs, while towing utility trailers piled high with distressed furniture, we reacted in a hurry. We fixed up the exterior. We hadn't planned to do anything to the exterior of the building quite so soon, but as soon as we did, the quality of our prospects improved dramatically.

People do judge a rental dwelling by its exterior. Why shouldn't they? They intend to live there and invite their friends to visit them there, and they want themselves to be identified with a building which projects the kind of image they have of themselves.

A building with a well-kept exterior advertises to one and all that the living is better there than it could ever be in a dilapidated building. It shows that the owners have been careful to select good tenants, that the maintenance is being well taken care of, and that everyone living there takes pride in the property.

Remember, whenever you have a vacancy and you're trying to interest prospective tenants to rent the place by using any number of the many advertising methods to spread the word, you will no doubt attract all kinds of prospective tenants through your advertising, but you will never attract good tenants unless you give your building what real estate people call "curb appeal," that is, an attractive appearance on the outside which creates a good first impression.

Got that? Good! Now let's consider straightaway what you should be doing to stay out of trouble when you're advertising a vacancy.

Advertising for Trouble

You are hoping that your rental advertising will attract the attention of good people who are looking for a place to rent. Unfortunately, good people who are looking for a place to rent aren't the only ones likely to be attracted by your advertising. People who want to determine whether you're practicing any kind of illegal discrimination in your advertising or in your tenant selection process are likely to be attracted as well.

These people have no intention of renting from you. They do have every intention of making you suffer dearly if they can prove that you are practicing any illegal discrimination in word or deed. They may work for a fair housing agency, or they may work for themselves and earn their living by bringing discrimination claims against landlords. In either case, they are looking for tell-tale signs that you are discriminating illegally. They are looking for anything you might say in your advertising which shows that you won't rent to children or to American Indians or Jehovah's Witnesses or the handicapped or any other protected group. They are also looking for telltale signs that you favor a certain classification of people in any of the protected groups.

If they conclude that you are discriminating illegally, they will file a claim against you with the U.S. Department of Housing and Urban Development (HUD) or some other government agency and demand that you pay them some money to settle it. If you refuse to pay and they refuse to drop their claim, they will get all the free investigative and legal assistance they need to help them prove their case. You will have to hire assistance and pay for it out of your own pocket, and if the claimants can prove that you were indeed discriminating, you will have to pay the claim and the penalties out of your own pocket as well. Your insurance company won't help you at all unless you purchased a policy specifically written to protect you from discrimination claims.

Because your advertising is the first indicator of your rental policies and because it is the first thing to attract the "discrimination police" and the "discrimination opportunists," be very careful what you say when you advertise a vacancy and be very careful how you say it.

A statement in your advertising like this— "adult nonsmoker preferred"—would be advertising for trouble. The word "adult" would be taken as evidence that you are discriminating against children. Children, remember, are in a protected category. The word "nonsmoker" is all right to use in your advertising because smokers are not in a protected category.

Stating that your rental dwelling is—"close to Jewish synagogue"—would be advertising for trouble regardless of whether you meant merely to help people determine the dwelling's location with the synagogue reference. Some people would say that your use of the words "Jewish synagogue" in your advertising shows that you prefer Jews over Roman Catholics, Moslems, Buddhists, fundamentalist Christians, Mormons, and Jehovah's Witnesses. Religion, you see, is a protected category.

Stating—"single men only need apply"— would be advertising for big trouble. It signals that you are discriminating in two protected categories, gender and marital status.

Be careful in your advertising. Be very careful in your advertising. Do not suppose that you will be able to fend off any discrimination-in-advertising claim brought against you because you made some innocent blunder and didn't know any better. Government agencies charged with the responsibility of enforcing fair housing laws presume that you know what you're doing because you're in the landlording business and that what you're doing is by design. As far as they're concerned, that's a given. They are deadly serious in their efforts to root out illegal discrimination in housing, and they will not absolve you of any wrongdoing merely because you say that you were confused or uninformed or careless and that you would never think of discriminating illegally and that you will never do again what you did unknowingly to get yourself into trouble.

Forget the good excuses. Forget the pleading on bended knees. It won't do you any good. If your advertising signaled some kind of illegal discrimination on your part and you were accused of discriminating illegally, you will have to pay the consequences.

You can avoid trouble in your advertising by concentrating on the dwelling itself. Describe it in some detail, trumpeting its features and amenities in colorful, but not loaded, terms.

Make no mention of the dwelling's physical limitations which might be construed as an ill-concealed effort to discriminate against people who have a certain handicap and cannot live in a place with those limitations. Make no mention of its proximity to a certain landmark, such as an ethnic restaurant or a mosque, which might be construed as your preference toward tenants who have a special interest in that landmark.

Make no mention of your tenant preferences. You may prefer tenants of a certain age, but don't say so. You may prefer tenants of one sex or another, but don't say so. You may prefer tenants who work in a certain occupation, but don't say so. You may prefer tenants who are married over those who are "living together," but don't say so. You may prefer English-speaking tenants over those who speak only Spanish, but don't say so.

Make no reference whatsoever to the breed of tenant you're looking for. Let everyone understand that you're looking for good tenants. Let everyone understand that you're looking for tenants who are clean, who have some regard for their neighbors, who have a good track record as tenants, who have the wherewithal to pay the rent, and who pay their rent on time. That's all.

Still have questions about fair housing laws? You'll find straight answers and more, including states' fair housing extensions, on Craiglist's website at "craigslist.org/about/FHA."

Play your advertising straight, and you'll stay out of trouble.

With this caution out of the way, let's go on to what people normally think of nowadays when they think of advertising vacant rental properties.

Advertising Methods

Here are the advertising methods do-it-yourself landlords use most commonly today, together with some of the advantages and disadvantages of each, and a listing of the various factors affecting the decision to choose one method over another, all of which may assist you first in selecting the best advertising methods for your own rental property and then in making them work well for you.

■ **Word of Mouth**—Existing tenants in your multiple-family dwellings have as much of an interest in whom you select to be their new neighbors as you do, no, they have more. That rental building of yours may be your investment and your business, but, after all, it's their home twenty-four hours a day, seven days a week, and you can't blame them for wanting to have compatible neighbors.

No matter who they are, what they do for a living, where they live, or how they live, above all, your tenants want to feel safe and secure where they live, and they hope that you will select new neighbors for them who will bolster their safety and security, not jeopardize it. They might even hope that their new neighbors would be pleasant and accommodating people, ready with the loan of a tool, a cup of milk, or a bottle of beer when asked.

Because of this common interest in securing good new tenants that you and your existing tenants share (neighbors around a rented single-family dwelling share this same common interest), you are wise to advise them of any impending vacancy as soon as you know about it, and, if warranted, even to offer them a finder's fee of, say, fifty or a hundred dollars for their efforts in helping you find good new tenants.

Whenever possible, include all of your tenants in your word-of-mouth advertising campaign so that none of them can accuse you of favoritism or discrimination. Much as you might want to exclude your marginal tenants, remember that they are precisely the ones who will try to find some reason to trouble you with a frivolous lawsuit. Don't give them cause. Besides, they seldom respond to these offers anyway, so you have more to lose by excluding them than you do by including them

If you do elect to offer a finder's fee, avoid any misunderstanding over your obligation to pay by insisting that the finders accompany those whom they have interested in the place on the first visit or, at the very least, that they call you and give you the person's name before the first visit. You don't want a tenant claiming a finder's fee unless that tenant was directly responsible for the prospect.

Besides approaching those who, because of where they live, will be most affected by the selection of the new tenants, approach others who meet and talk with the public in the course of doing business in the area, people such as Avon ladies, barbers, beauticians, clergy, corner grocers, insurance agents, mail carriers, neighborhood pharmacists, self-storage staff, service station managers, truck rental dealers, motel desk clerks, and apartment house managers. They all hold positions conducive to passing the word along.

Whenever you enlist anyone in your word-of-mouth advertising campaign, apprise them of at least these relevant facts about your vacancy—amount of rent, size of unit, number of bedrooms, size of building, location, and availability, and then give them your business card so they'll know how to get in touch with you when they do find someone.

You may want to consider preparing an informal flier to augment what you're telling people about the vacancy. They might have occasion to pass it along to somebody who's interested. It needn't be anything fancy. Something on a half sheet of paper in your neatest handwriting would do fine. In fact, I have found that something which looks informal works better than something formal because people tend to think that the place hasn't been exposed much and that they could be the first person to see it.

No matter who the referral is, even if it's a relative of someone you know well, don't be swayed by the source of the referral. Judge applicants on their own merits, and, by all means, complete the full procedure outlined in the next chapter, "Getting Good Tenants." Sometimes the friends and relatives of finders are not up to your standards for tenants at that particular property, and you may be the only one discriminating enough to understand why you shouldn't rent to them. Make that decision the same way you would make it concerning anyone else who applies to rent from you.

Now, what are the advantages and disadvantages of this kind of advertising?

> *Advantages*—inexpensive, targeted, usable anywhere for any kind of rental.
> *Disadvantages*—uncertain, inclined to be slow, time-consuming, awkward if you have to refuse unqualified prospects.

■ **The Sign**—You might be surprised by how many people there are who will pick an area where they want to live and then scout that area for vacancies. Believe it or not, more than half of all tenants do it this way, and some of them don't even wait for signs to appear before knocking on doors. When they see any indication that someone is moving, they begin making inquiries about the dwelling's availability. These super-sleuths aren't always looking for moving vans and rental trucks, though. Most people who are searching around a neighborhood for places to rent are looking for a "For Rent" sign.

The "For Rent" sign you use reveals to the public something about the kind of business you're running and should be consistent with the exterior image of your rental building. A crude, hand-lettered sign indicates a penny-pinching operation run by amateurs, and whereas such a sign will do all the advertising you'll ever need during periods of high occupancy, when everyone becomes a super-sleuth, it's just not good enough during periods when you're competing with everyone else for good tenants.

There's no reason to skimp on a custom sign purchase, no matter what the vacancy factor in your area happens to be, because a sign is a one-time expense, and that one-time expense is quite reasonable, especially now that sign makers no longer have to be skilled painters to make good-looking signs. Anybody who has a personal computer with a sign-making software program and a computer-controlled vinyl cutter can make a sign today both quickly and cheaply.

A professionally produced sign cost me the same as two tanks of fuel for my Ford pickup truck and has lasted for years. It's a two-sided 20"x30" sign in three contrasting colors on a tan-painted 5/8" exterior-plywood "blank," and it's designed to hang at any of my buildings from a yardarm positioned at right angles to the street so that people passing in either direction can see it readily (the hardware used to attach the sign consists of eye bolts, clevis hooks, and harness snaps). The "1" in the "1 BDR APT" is on the board itself because some of my apartments happen to be one-bedroom units, but you may cover this number over with another number by attaching it directly to the board itself with one bolt or two Velcro® strips. If necessary, you could add a similar provision for changing "unfurnished" to "furnished." The telephone number on the sign is my own rental properties number, so prospects may call me directly if the manager is unavailable at the site.

Create your own sign design to look as good as your rental units and say whatever you require, and then hire someone to make it for you. You'll like the image this combination projects and so will your discriminating tenants.

Because a sign maker may require a few days to make a custom sign, order yours before you need it so it'll be ready for use when a vacancy arises and you really need it.

Whereas a sign makes good sense for advertising multi-family dwellings, it may not make any sense at all for single-family dwellings. Children will sometimes mess with the sign. Squatters and vandals will sometimes have their way with the vacant house. Interested parties will sometimes bother the occupants. Moreover, because single-family dwellings tend to be in quiet residential neighborhoods, there may be so little traffic driving by the sign that it won't attract a single person who's interested.

To minimize these problems, use a sign on the premises of a rental house only while the soon-to-be-vacant house is still occupied. Locate it out near the street where it's easily visible. Make it similar to a "property for sale" sign in size, appearance, mounting, and height, and include the wording, "Do not disturb occupants," at the bottom of the sign.

These measures will help make the sign work to attract interest without jeopardizing the condition of the house or the departing tenants' peace and quiet.

Advantages—inexpensive, orthodox, immediate.

Disadvantages—dependent on traffic exposure, inviting to troublemakers when used at vacant single-family dwellings.

■ **Bulletin Boards**—Just as general stores used to provide community forums around their pickle and cracker barrels years ago, many supermarkets and some other stores provide community bulletin boards as a service to their customers, but the exposure, and hence the efficacy, of bulletin board advertising varies widely. Some boards are prominently located within busy stores where customers can't miss them, while others are almost hidden from view by stacks of merchandise and rarely ever seen. Some boards are well organized and well maintained by the management, and others are just a jumble of fliers, business cards, 3"x5" announcements, coming-events posters, and small lost-and-found items. For best results, select the busiest boards within the trading area surrounding your rental. Ask your tenants where these boards are if you don't shop much in the area yourself.

To make your bulletin board rental ad most effective on any bulletin board, whether it be a

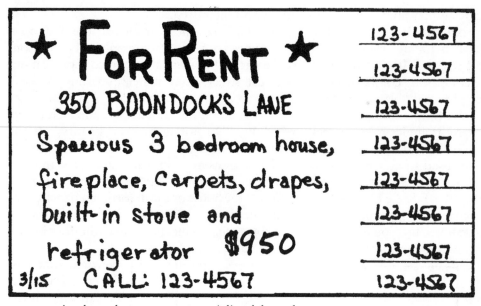

community board or a more specialized board such as one where you work or where others work (schools, fire departments, bus "barns," county offices, and the like generally have their own bulletin boards for employees and will gladly post your ad if you mail or take it to them) or where people worship in the vicinity of the rental dwelling, take the time to prepare it carefully. Use a 3"x5" card with a large "FOR RENT" at the top; describe it well enough to answer the obvious questions; add color or a simple eye-catching design to make it stand out; and date it. Because you are advertising something perishable, a vacancy, the date is important to anyone who is out looking for a rental and happens to see your ad. Therefore, you should try to replace the card every week with one bearing a more current date.

One danger with this kind of advertising is that without your knowing it, your card may simply disappear into the hands of someone who is interested in responding but has forgotten to bring paper and pencil. To accommodate these people, you might make a few cuts in one side of the card and put your telephone number on each removable tab so the entire card won't be removed, just bits of it.

Advantages—inexpensive, localized.

Disadvantages—time-consuming to prepare and post, limited in exposure.

■ **Fliers**—Fliers are a time-honored advertising method for a variety of things, and today with computers, photocopying, and "instant" printing all readily available, you can prepare professional-looking fliers faster and cheaper than ever

before, but preparing them isn't everything. You have to distribute them as well. Aye, there's the rub! You have to make certain that they reach the kind of people you're looking for.

Also, when you do put them out there before the public, try to keep your flier distribution from cheapening the image of your rental dwelling. Avoid hiring kids to pass them out on street corners so that people who have no interest in a rental dwelling won't be littering the streets with them. Avoid plastering them "everywhere." Tack just one or two onto a telephone pole next to where commuters line up to take public transportation. Don't cover the pole with them, and don't put one on every pole on an entire block. That's tacky. That's overkill.

Use your fliers to extend and reinforce your word-of-mouth advertising campaign within the community. Give some to the local business people you patronize and ask them to display the fliers by their cash registers or in their store windows. Give some away as reminders to people you know who appear interested either for themselves or for others. Post some on those bulletin boards which allow fliers. You'll be reaching the public you want to reach in ways which won't turn them off.

When you distribute fliers, keep a list of their locations so that when you do rent your dwelling, you will know exactly where to go to retrieve them. If you leave them hanging about for more than a few weeks, people will begin to wonder why somebody hasn't rented the dwelling yet?

Advantages—relatively inexpensive, localized.

Disadvantages—time-consuming to prepare, distribute, and retrieve; suitable primarily for less expensive rentals; dependent upon your personality and contacts.

■ **Housing Offices**—Many college campuses and military installations, as well as large public and private employers, maintain their own housing offices to assist their students and staff in finding local housing. These offices are subsidized and hence charge neither the renters nor the landlords who use the service.

Once you decide upon which of these local housing offices you wish to use, you may use them repeatedly by simply making a phone call or accessing their website, but do remember to cancel your listing as soon as you come to terms with a new tenant, so the housing office can keep its records up to date.

> *Advantages*—inexpensive, targeted, simple to use.
>
> *Disadvantages*—slow and inefficient at times.

■ **Internet**—With so many people now using the internet to search for information, goods, services, people, properties, and pleasure, advertising dollars are moving more and more to the internet from television, the print media, and the Yellow Pages. Google's and Yahoo's incomes are going up and up, while income such as the phone company's from its Yellow Page advertising is going down.

Landlords couldn't have asked for a better way to advertise their vacancies than internet advertising. It's inexpensive. It's immediate. It's easy to use. It's comprehensive. It's targeted.

What's more, unlike any other advertising medium, internet advertising is accessible from anywhere in the world. Newlyweds who are relocating from Toulouse, France, to St. Louis, Missouri, where you own a duplex and have a two-bedroom unit for rent, can learn about it and communicate with you about it before they ever leave French soil. That couldn't have happened before the internet.

You may use the internet to advertise a vacancy in a number of ways. Here are three possibilities you should know something about—

1) Listing your vacancy on one of the sites set up to carry classified advertising of all kinds;

2) Listing your vacancy on one of the sites focused primarily on rental housing;

3) Listing your vacancy on your own website. Let's look at each of these in turn.

1) Many websites carry classified advertising, including ads for rental housing. Some, like Yahoo, charge for the service, but the giant in the business, Craigslist, does not. As of now, Craigslist charges only for job postings in certain big U.S. cities, for brokered apartment rental postings in New York City, and for adult and therapeutic services postings wherever they are in the U.S.

No rental property owner can afford to ignore Craigslist. It is unique in all the world. It is one of the most popular sites in all the world, and it is one of the most egalitarian sites in all the world.

Want to use Craigslist to find a soulmate? Cost? Nothing.

Want to use Craigslist to sell that rusty VW bus in your driveway? Cost? Nothing.

Want to use Craigslist to rent a house for your weeklong Hawaiian vacation? Cost? Nothing.

Want to use Craigslist to let the world know you have an apartment for rent in Taos? Cost? Nothing.

Want to use Craigslist to let the world know you have a house for rent in Ft. Lauderdale? Cost? Nothing.

What's the catch? Nothing. There is none.

Check it out. It's an "online community" with a presence in all fifty states, plus the District of Columbia and the major U.S. territories, and in foreign countries from Argentina to Vietnam.

Drill down to as local an area as you can find in Craigslist by clicking on your state, territory, or country first. If there are localized areas, they will appear in a list, and you may choose which one you want to access for postings. If there are no localized areas, the name of the state, territory, or country will appear at the top of the list of categories, and you may choose which postings category you want to search through.

Click on "Montana," for example, and you'll find a list of towns and cities in the state, each of which has local postings. Click on "Rhode Island," and you'll find that every posting is a local posting.

Look through the "apts/housing" postings in your local area to see what other postings look like and what other landlords are charging for rentals similar to yours.

Then make up your own posting for a vacancy. What do you have to lose? After all, it costs you nothing. It's completely free. Did I mention that it's free?

Within fifteen minutes after you upload the posting for your rental and without your ever having to pay anything to anyone or talk to a Craigslist representative who wants to sell you something you don't want, you will see your rental property on the list in the applicable classification where anybody with access to the internet anywhere in the world will be able to see it, and you may start getting responses immediately.

To use Craigslist most effectively, do the following—

• Include four digital photos of your rental (some users won't even look at an ad unless it has photos, and they can tell from the list of postings whether it has photos or not; it will have "pic" after the posting's one-line title).

• Include the rental's address so users can pinpoint it on a Google or Yahoo map.

• Include your phone number.

• Include a link to your website, if you have one, where interested parties may find more information about your rental property.

• Anonymize your email address by using a Craigslist-assigned address (automatically forwards email responses to you and thwarts spammers who harvest email addresses).

• Note how long the posting will remain on Craigslist (varies according to locale) before it disappears.

• Cancel the posting every so often and resubmit it so it will be on the latest lists.

• Apply for a Craigslist account (it's free) so you can retrieve and repost your expired postings.

• Have somebody proofread your posting for errors in spelling and errors in information.

There are other sites with classified listings likely to be frequented by potential renters looking for a place to live. To find them, run searches on "classifieds [your town]" and "[apartments] [houses] for rent in [your town]."

Once you understand how these sites work and how they charge, check to see how many listings they have in your area for your type of property. Avoid using those which have no listings in your area for your type of property and those which fail to suggest listings in nearby communities.

Note that some daily newspapers, wary of losing their classified advertising, which is a major source of their advertising revenue, have developed their own classified advertising websites where they list the ads currently running in their newspapers. If you place a classified ad in their newspaper, you will get a listing on the newspaper's website for little or nothing extra.

2) Many websites focus primarily or exclusively on rental housing listings. Here are several of them: "apartments.com," "forrent.com,"

"rentals.com," and "rentalhousehunter.com." Pay them and others (run a search on "rental housing listings [your town]" to find the sites) a visit to see how they work and see whether you might benefit from using them yourself. Each of them works differently and charges differently.

Again, I urge you not to use any commercial website to advertise your rental property unless it has listings in your area for your type of property. You don't want to be paying to be the only rental house in your town listed on a website which purports to attract tenants who are looking for a house in your town. The mere fact that your house is the only listing is a good indication that the website is not attracting the eyes of tenants who are likely to rent your house.

3) Many landlords today create their own websites to give their rental properties more exposure whenever they have a vacancy. You should do likewise.

Creating a website of your own to advertise a vacant rental house may seem like a waste of time at first, but when you consider all that you can say and show about a house or apartment on your own site, you begin to see the possibilities.

Besides, creating a website is not nearly as difficult as it used to be when you had to know how to use cryptic HTML codes to do anything at all yourself or else you had to hire an expensive web designer to create a site for you.

Now, if you know how to use a word processor, you can create web pages using a basic web authoring program like WebEasy on Windows computers or iWeb on Macs. These programs and others like them all come with a slew of professionally designed templates you may use to jumpstart creating a website yourself.

Another option for creating a website yourself are the web authoring programs provided by website hosts such as "123ehost.com," "godaddy.com," and "justhost.com" as a part of their many services included with their primary service, web hosting.

Just because you have a website on the internet, though, doesn't mean that millions of people will flock to see it or even that the one tenant you're looking for will see it. You could spend all kinds of time building a beautiful site with your rental property's floor plan, photos, video, map location, neighborhood information, description, availability, and viewing times and still never attract anybody to it. Nobody would know it's there.

Don't worry. Your site doesn't have to attract people on its own. It might attract some people, of course, if you index it properly with the web search engines (check out the possibilities for "search engine optimization"), but it doesn't have to be both a stand-alone advertisement *and* a repository of information to supplement the notice of its availability elsewhere. It ought to be a repository of information primarily, a site which all the rest of your advertising could point to with just a link to its web address, so that anybody who is interested could find more information, enough to help them determine whether they should arrange to see the dwelling themselves.

In addition to advertising a vacancy, your website can help prospects prequalify themselves because it can include your prequalification questions and even a copy of your rental application, so that by the time the prospects first contact you, they already have a clue about what you're looking for in a tenant and you don't have to waste time telling them about your policies regarding move-in monies, credit, prior evictions, pets, maximum tenant count, and smoking.

Try one or all of these possibilities to see which one works best for you, and keep looking for other good advertising possibilities on the web as well. It's changing every day.

By the way, when you're choosing a website address, also known as a "universal resource locator" (URL), give some thought to the following three factors and then search "whois" to see whether it's available—

1) Brevity–Choose a short URL so it will fit easily into the space available in your other advertising.

2) Mnemonics–Choose a URL which is easy to remember.

3) Universality–Choose a URL which you can use for the properties you have now and for those you acquire in the future.

> *Advantages*—available to people anywhere, anytime; inexpensive.
> *Disadvantages*—available only to people who have access to the web.

■ **Classified Ads**—Classified ads in large-circulation daily newspapers used to be the primary advertising vehicle for rental properties, but they aren't any longer. They've taken a back seat to internet advertising. That's bad news for the large-circulation dailies and one of the reasons

why they're disappearing, but it's good news for us landlords because internet advertising costs little or nothing and has a much greater reach than classified ads in the large-circulation dailies.

Incidentally, in his book, *The Vanishing Newspaper*, Philip Meyer, a professor emeritus of journalism, estimates that newspapers as we know them in America will disappear by the year 2043!

Classifieds ads for rental properties have not disappeared from newspapers altogether. In fact, classified ads in small-circulation newspapers, that is, community newspapers, special-interest newspapers, shoppers, and free tabloids, continue to be popular because these newspapers target local readers, produce good results, reach the Luddites among us who haven't yet let a computer into their lives, and are inexpensive for advertisers.

Because the ads in these newspapers are inexpensive, you can afford to run a more detailed ad in one of them than you ever could in an expensive large-circulation daily newspaper, and you needn't try to cram your ad into just a few words to save on cost.

Whereas you might have wanted to create an ad like the one shown here for a large-circulation

6 RMS RIV VU. 123-4567.

newspaper with as few words and lines as possible in order to save on cost, you wouldn't want to create such an ad for a small-circulation newspaper, even if the newspaper did allow single-line ads, because their classified advertising sections tend to be poorly classified. They wouldn't have a classification for unfurnished apartments in Boyle Heights or partly furnished houses in North Dover, for example. They're likely to lump all of their ads for rental housing under a single heading, "For Rent," so you need to come up with an informative first line to let the reader know what kind of a rental you have available and where it's located.

The ad shown here, which is designed for

QUIET 3-BR HOUSE, NORTH DOVER. Carpets, stove, refrigerator, drapes, garage. $1250. 123-4567. ourprops.com

placement in a community newspaper with a three-line minimum and only a single classification for every kind of rental housing, answers readers' primary questions in its very first line.

These are their primary questions—Where is the rental? How many bedrooms does it have?

What kind of rental housing is it? Is it an apartment, a house, a tree house, a townhouse, a geodesic dome, a yurt, a teepee, an Earthship, a cave, a trailer, a motorhome, or a mobilehome?

The ad goes on to answer the rest of the primary questions readers have when they're looking for a place to rent.

These are the rest of their primary questions—How much is the rent? Does the place come with kitchen appliances? Is it carpeted? Is there covered and secure parking for my vehicle? How can I find out more?

Put an ad like this in your community newspaper's classifieds, and prospective tenants won't be bothering you both day and night with phone calls wanting to know the answers to these questions before they decide whether to have a look at your rental house.

If you want to bulk up your ad with even more verbiage about your available rental, you might want to include the following in addition to what is already included in the three-line ad used as an example here, that is, if they apply—laundry hookups, carport, off-street parking, fireplace, dining room, utilities, pets, yard, storage, and pool.

Include the size of the building only if it's favorable. Smaller sizes, four or fewer units in the same complex, are the most favorable (some people prefer the community feeling of smaller buildings over the institutional feeling of larger ones).

These other items to include are marginal, depending upon the rental and the area—water, garbage, air conditioning, hardwood floors, lawn, flower garden, vegetable garden, solar panels, and steam heat.

Include the address only if you feel comfortable that making it public won't jeopardize the dwelling's security.

Before you place your classified ad in any newspaper, consider the following factors which affect its effectiveness—column rank, appealing words, and ad copy deadlines.

As for column rank, determine how your newspaper arranges its ads so readers will see yours near the beginning of the ads for rental housing, not near the end.

If your newspaper arranges its ads randomly or by date of insertion, there's nothing you can do to put yours near the beginning of all similar ads, but if your newspaper arranges them alpha-

betically, and that's easy to determine, you will want to make sure that your initial word begins with one of the first letters in the alphabet or with a number so it will appear among the first of the listings. How about "A-1" or "3-Bedroom"?

As for appealing words, try to include one or two somewhere in your ad's first line. Think of your ad as a billboard which must catch the reader's eye immediately or be missed completely, and you'll understand the importance of its initial words. Since you can't include a picture of the place in your ad, the descriptive words you use must conjure up the most appealing picture possible. Words like "sparkling," "just painted," "quiet," "superclean," "cozy," "superbig," and "quaint" all create positive, pleasant pictures in readers' minds. Those words may be enough to entice readers to pursue looking more closely at your available rental.

Should you feel uninspired in coming up with good appealing words yourself, scan the rental ads in several newspapers, make note of the words that appeal to you, and use them in your own advertising. Remember, you're not trying to win a prize for creativity in advertising. You're merely trying to fill your vacancies. Don't be afraid to appropriate other people's good ideas and incorporate them in your own ads.

You don't have to think like a Madison Avenue copywriter to write effective ads for rental properties. You're not trying to sell ten million sticks of still another underarm deodorant. The people who are looking for you have a definite need for housing. All you have to do is direct their attention your way so they will read the ad, become interested, and respond.

As for ad copy deadlines, recognize how important they are to you when you have a rental available and that rental is costing you money every day it's vacant. Be certain you know your newspaper's deadline for ad copy, and make it if you can. If you miss it, launch an aggressive advertising campaign using other media while you're waiting for the newspaper's next ad copy deadline.

For greater advertising "punch" when you have several units for rent at one time and you want to attract all the attention you can get, you may want to increase your advertising budget (think of the increase in terms of its cost per vacant unit rather than as a lump sum; that way you can compare it to your advertising cost when you have only one unit for rent) and devise an ad which will stand out from the rest, one which will draw readers' attention with its cleverness or graphics or both. Large apartment complexes hire advertising agencies to design their ads. You needn't. Look at their ads and come up with your own ideas. Here are several such ads with punch—

```
■■■■■■■■■■■■■■■■■
CLOSET LOVER?
You'll LOVE our big, walk-in
closets and our big rooms. You'll
also LOVE our other amenities—
• Wall-to-wall carpet •
• Laundry hookups •
• Dishwasher, disposal •
• Patio •
1-2 Bedrooms
$895-1195
556 Flint Road
www.beeskneesapts.com
888-8888
■■■■■■■■■■■■■■■■■
```

```
★ ★ ★ ★ ★ ★ ★ ★ ★ ★ ★ ★ ★ ★ ★
CAR OPTIONAL
CLOSE TO EVERYTHING
Walk to shopping, markets, bank,
cinemas, gym, bus, & airport bus
Well-behaved pet OK
2 bedrooms, 2 baths
Ceiling fans, decorator wallpaper
Central heating, air conditioning
$995
 Open house, Fri., 4-6; Sat., 1-3
77 Avon Avenue
www.sweetapts.com
888-8888
★ ★ ★ ★ ★ ★ ★ ★ ★ ★ ★ ★ ★ ★ ★
```

Once you have devised a well-worded ad that suits you and yields a good response, make a copy and keep it on file so you can use it over and over again or at least have a model to follow, and you won't have to waste time making up a new one from scratch every time you advertise.

When your ad first appears in the newspaper, check it out yourself to verify that it's in the proper classification and that it's worded exactly the way you want it to be. Ad takers do make mistakes, you know, and you might find that you're waiting around for calls that never come because your ad was misclassified or had an incorrect telephone number.

After you have verified that the ad is correct and you're still not getting any calls, reassess the ad's other factors and consider making adjustments.

>*Advantages*—well-exposed, simple, timesaving, orthodox.
>
>*Disadvantages*—deadline dependent, costly.

■ **Real Estate Agents**—Not every real estate agent will help you find a renter, but those who will generally promote themselves as providing a "real estate rental service." The range of services they provide in this context varies widely from merely advertising your vacancy in their window free of charge to advertising it actively to fully managing the property, including advertising the vacancy, showing it, and screening the prospective tenants.

Seldom do real estate agents make any money by providing these services. Mostly they are just trying to build a dedicated and obligated clientele who will bring them more lucrative business later when old properties are disposed of and new properties are acquired.

Agree in advance on the exact services your agent will provide, including the kinds of advertising to be used, and agree upon the charges for those services as well. You should have to pay only if your agent secures a renter and only if that renter stays at least six months. Shorter tenancies should entitle you to more services without additional charge. Get the arrangement down on paper.

>*Advantages*—based on commission (no results, no payment), helpful to absentee owners living out of the area.
>
>*Disadvantages*—obligating, expensive in comparison to other kinds of rental advertising.

Advertising Factors

Aware as you are about the advertising methods commonly available to landlords today and about the various advantages and disadvantages of each, you might wonder which are the best methods for advertising a vacancy at your own rental property.

Should you break with tradition and advertise it with a 30-second spot on the six o'clock news? The answer to that question is an obvious "no" because your rental doesn't need that much exposure and because you'd have to sell, or at least mortgage, the property to pay for the ad, but the answer isn't so obvious if you're considering which of the eight methods you should use to advertise the rental house you own next door to where you live or a vacancy at the four-unit apartment house you own in a community an hour's drive from where you live.

Numerous factors affect your advertising decisions. Here are fourteen of them:

■ **Number of Units**—Is the rental dwelling a house, or is it in a fourplex or a twenty-five unit complex?

Use on-site signs at multiple-family dwellings for maximum exposure, but avoid using them at single-family dwellings unless the old tenants are still in possession and agree to cooperate or unless you live nearby and can keep an eye on the place. As a rental house owner, you do not want people trampling the petunias to get a peek in the windows, and you definitely do not want vandals or squatters to suspect that the house may be empty. No matter how many units there are in your rental dwelling's building, put the word out to all the neighbors that you have a vacancy now or will have a vacancy on such-and-such a date and that you are looking for good people to fill that vacancy.

■ **Location**—Is it in a high-, medium-, or low-traffic location, that is, Main Street, Middle Road, or Boondocks Lane?

Rely upon on-site signs more at high- and medium-traffic locations than at low-traffic locations. If enough people pass by your rental property regularly, a sign might be all the advertising you'll ever need.

■ **Amount of Rent**—Does it rent for a song or an aria, $395 or $3,950?

Pull out all the stops to advertise an expensive rental because you stand to lose so much more every day the place is vacant and because it has a much smaller number of potential renters to reach than the $395-a-month rental dwelling has.

■ **Rental's Availability**—Is the rental vacant and available now or have your tenants just informed you at Christmas time that they'll be moving by Easter?

Before your rental becomes vacant, try the least expensive advertising methods. If they fail to attract the kind of tenants you're looking for, supplement them with other methods.

■ **Areawide Vacancy Factor**—Are vacant rental dwellings scarce or are they in ample supply?

The appearance of outward-bound furniture will suffice for "advertising" during scarcities, while searchlights and sideshows may be insufficient during high-vacancy periods. Prepare to spend more on advertising and be more creative when the areawide vacancy factor increases.

If a major employer leaves the area and tumbleweeds begin to litter the streets, you may need to change more than your advertising. You may need to change your tenant profile. A changeover to allowing pet owners and their pets, encouraging nudists and their pool parties, and welcoming motorcyclists and their entourages to inhabit your rental property might save you. "Balderdash!" you say. "Ridiculous!" you exclaim. No, these tactics are not ridiculous. They really do work. You might even consider advertising in whatever your local communities of pet owners, nudists, and motorcyclists read. You won't find many other landlords advertising there.

■ **Distance from Management**—Are you managing a rental property seventy miles from where you live or do you live in the building?

Find a local contact, perhaps another tenant, a real estate agent, or a next-door neighbor, to take phone calls and show your rental if you live some distance from the property. People tend to be wary about dialing a number with an unfamiliar area code unless they have no other choice or unless they have an unlimited calling plan. Consider getting your own toll-free number with calls directed to your home or cell phone.

■ **Effort**—How much effort do you wish to devote to your advertising campaign?

Very little or whatever it takes? Remember that advertising using newspaper classified ads, Craigslist and other web classifieds, signs, real estate agents, and housing offices all take less effort than full-scale word-of-mouth, bulletin-board, and handbill advertising campaigns.

■ **Time of Year**—Is there a seasonal nature to

rental accommodations in the area?

Vacation and student rentals have obvious seasons, but surprisingly enough, so do other rental properties. The two most active periods for long-term rentals are around the beginning of summer as identified by the Memorial Day holiday and again around the end of summer as identified by the Labor Day holiday. People like to be settled in by then. Advertise during these periods with the less expensive kinds of advertising and add the more expensive kinds only in the final week before Memorial Day or Labor Day.

■ **Targeted Clientele**—Are you looking for little old ladies with Harleys, students with Moog synthesizers, newlyweds with round waterbeds, municipal bus drivers with tabbies, Mother Hubbards with umpteen urchins, or nerds with hoards of computer hardware?

To reach a particular clientele, target them by making contact through certain people, certain housing offices, certain bulletin boards, certain community newspapers, or certain websites.

Many senior centers, businesses, churches, synagogues, and union halls have bulletin boards and periodicals. Advertise there to target the type of tenant you prefer.

If you prefer to rent to college students, list with the housing offices at the nearby colleges, and you'll have students aplenty inquiring about your vacancies in late August and early September. You're targeting them.

WORDS OF CAUTION—Never state in your advertising that you're looking for tenants in a particular category because a statement to that effect may be considered illegal discrimination in tenant selection, and you don't want to be accused of that. Merely get the word out to the people you prefer as tenants by carefully selecting the places where you advertise and not by stating your tenant preferences in your advertising itself.

■ **Local Exposure**—Should your advertising reach out to millions of people wherever they happen to be?

The landlording business is a local business. Its customers are people who want to put their roots down in a particular place. To reach those potential customers, you may need to expose your rental vacancy to lots of people, especially if it's an expensive rental, but you needn't bother exposing it to the many people who are within hundreds of miles of the property. Expose it to those people who are within tens of miles of the property, and rest assured that anybody beyond that geographical area who is interested in moving to where you own rental property will consult local sources after deciding where they plan to locate.

You'll notice that Craigslist breaks down its listings by location. Its listings are local. Your advertising should be local, too. People with internet access anywhere in the world can access these local listings merely by switching their Craigslist location no matter where their physical location happens to be.

■ **Advertising Availability**—Are housing offices, bulletin boards, and real estate agents who list rentals all available in your rental's area?

Make some effort to discover all the locally available advertising sources and use those which suit your needs.

■ **Advertising Cost**—How much are you willing to spend? Nothing or whatever it takes?

Take full advantage of all the free and inexpensive advertising available to you—word-of-mouth, bulletin boards, handbills, signs, Craigslist, and housing offices, but weigh the cost of avoiding the more expensive advertising with the loss of rent you sustain so long as your rental remains unoccupied.

■ **Previous Experience**—Have you had good experience previously with a local newspaper shopper, a sign planted in the front lawn of your rental house, a particular bulletin board, Craigslist, or a cooperative real estate agent?

Conduct your own advertising survey by asking those who inquire about your rental how they learned about it, and then continue using whatever works for you. Whenever you notice that the effectiveness of your old reliable methods is diminishing, try others.

■ **Orthodoxy**—Are rental housing seekers accustomed to responding to this particular advertising method?

Advertise in ways and places that rental seekers expect you to use so they'll be looking for you there. Whereas skywriting, TV spots, searchlights, and helium air balloons will undoubtedly yield some results, the eight methods mentioned in this chapter are more orthodox and will yield more results per dollar than unorthodox methods ever will.

There's nothing wrong with using unorthodox methods, of course, so long as they pay off. One landlady who caters to pets and pet owners advertises her vacancies in the "Pets for Sale" classifieds. She begins her ads with the words "Pets and Pet Owners Wanted." That's not a very orthodox way to advertise, but she claims it works because pet owners read those ads, and it costs no more than placing an ad in the usual "For Rent" classification.

An Application of the Fourteen Factors

Applying the fourteen factors to your own particular vacancy, you might construct a scenario something like this.

If your available rental is a three-bedroom house located on Middle Road in Cleveland, Ohio, if it rents for $950 and is one of several similar houses for rent in the area, if you want to spend less than $100 on advertising, if your calendar reads "July," if you live next door to this rental house of yours, if the house is now ready for occupancy, if you have little time yourself to spend on spreading the word, and if you know your way around the internet, then you would be wise to use two advertising methods first, a "For Rent" sign on the property and a posting on Craigslist. The sign is cheap. The posting is free.

If you haven't rented the house in five days, put a classified ad in your local community newspaper and opt to put it on the newspaper's website as well.

If there are no nibbles, reconsider very carefully the rent that you're advertising and re-word the posting and the ad to expand on the best features of the house, but be prepared to have a vacancy for a few weeks until the market becomes especially active again around Labor Day.

Some Last Words

Whichever method of advertising you prefer, whichever you use, be sure you keep word about the availability of your rental dwelling before the public, for if nobody knows it's vacant, you can't possibly rent it. It might as well be off the market altogether. You're not collecting any rent while those fixed expenses of yours continue unabated. Hustle the place. Lace up your black patent leather shoes, wax your mustache, slick down your hair, practice your business card tricks, shell out a few bucks, and get the place rented.

Remember—somewhere out there are some very nice people searching for a suitable place to live and a nice landlord like you. Go all out to help them find you.

4
Getting
Good Tenants

Vacancy times are times which try landlords. They're working times, loss-of-revenue times, doubtful times, and if you're a small-time landlord whose every vacancy represents a high percentage of all your rentals, you are likely to be especially anxious to get that vacant rental filled.

Be anxious, but don't be hasty. You want a smooth operation, one which won't continue to be trying when there's no vacancy at all.

The most important factor of all in the smooth operation of rental properties is getting good tenants. If you become adept at this, all your landlording troubles will be little ones, and you may skip the whole of chapter 9, "Dealing With Problem Tenants." How lucky you are, getting to skip a whole chapter! How shrewd you are, knowing enough to "evict" bad applicants in the first place, before they ever have a chance to become your problem tenants! You practice prevention when you should. Good for you! A few minutes of prevention now are worth many hours of cure later.

No matter what procedure you follow for selecting tenants, so long as it's legally nondiscriminatory and it's working well for you, keep at it. No one can argue with success. But if you have reason to doubt your tenant selection procedure, consider making some modifications until you hit upon a successful combination which does work well for you. This chapter may give you some ideas.

The Ten Steps

Just as anyone can pick a horse to bet on in a race, anyone can pick a tenant, but picking winners ain't easy. It requires diligence and patience, as well as a little luck and some good intuition. Fortunately, though, the odds are better for picking good tenants than they are for picking winning horses, and the odds improve geometrically if you follow these ten steps which are arranged here more or less chronologically—

1) Prepare the dwelling for occupancy.
2) Prequalify the prospects.
3) Show the dwelling.
4) Accept and scrutinize applications.
5) Check references and qualify the applicants.
6) Visit the applicants' current home.
7) Review your rules, requirements, and policies, and satisfy the various disclosure requirements.
8) Fill out and sign the rental agreement.
9) Request all monies or a hefty deposit.
10) Create a written and a photographic record of the dwelling's condition, contents, and tenants.

You may skip every one of these steps except the seventh (the required disclosures) and the ninth (the payment) if you're remiss about your business, and you might actually get good tenants. Who knows? You just might get lucky! You just might beat the odds, but you might as well be buying a used car from Slick Tawker down at Kurt's Kar Korner without so much as starting the engine or kicking the tires. Sooner or later you'll get a lemon for a tenant, and then you'll learn in the hardest way possible that getting rid of a lemon tenant is considerably more difficult than getting rid of a lemon automobile.

You can always donate a lemon automobile to a charity, find some sucker to take it off your hands, sell it to a junkyard for parts, park it where it's sure to be stolen, bury it somewhere, shove it off a cliff, give it to an art school so they can transform it into a work of "art," or charge a buck to let people take a mighty sledgehammer swing at it. The list is endless, and after your lemon car is gone, you can forget all about your car troubles.

Ah, but you cannot dispose of lemon tenants so easily. You can't even get some cheap satisfaction out of pummeling them or, at the very least, depriving them of electricity and running water, much as you'd like to. Once you get lemon tenants, you're stuck with them for some time to come, and when you finally do succeed in getting rid of them, they're likely to leave some sour evidence behind just so you won't forget them.

Cull out the lemons from among your applicants. Follow the ten steps religiously, steps which any landlord can follow, including you, and you'll never rent to them. Leave the lemon tenants for those unscrupulous landlords you hear and read about. They deserve each other.

These ten steps are hardly what one might call difficult, but they do require time and attention, some of them more than others. Take the time and give them the attention they require, for when you consider the dreadful alternatives to getting good tenants, the time and the attention spent on all ten steps are well spent indeed.

After any of the seven initial steps, you might choose to reject the prospective tenants, and you shouldn't be afraid to do so. You *are not* obligated to rent an available rental dwelling to the first person who expresses an interest in renting it. You *are* obligated to rent an available rental to the first person who expresses an interest in renting it *and* also qualifies according to your legally nondiscriminatory standards. There's a big difference. Read on.

You're looking for a good tenant, right? Right! So keep on looking until you are satisfied that you have found an applicant who will be a good tenant for your building. Maybe the first person who wants to rent from you and has the means to rent from you will be a good tenant, and then again maybe not. You never know straightaway. You have to dig through the information available to you to make that determination.

Just remember that nobody can force you to rent to a particular person, not the government, not the applicant's mother, not the mayor of your town, and not the applicant's motorcycle gang. You get to make the selection yourself, and in doing so, you must be very, very discriminating, legally discriminating, of course.

Exercising Discrimination

Be as discriminating as you can be in making your selection, but by all means, do not be discriminating about race, color, national origin, religion, sex, disability, and family status (includes individuals or families with children under 18 years of age and pregnant women). Such discrimination is illegal throughout the United States. That's federal law.

To find answers to your questions about federal anti-discrimination laws, go to the website of the U.S. Department of Housing and Urban Development (HUD). It's hud.gov. There you'll find many links to web pages with relevant information about federal and state landlord-tenant laws in general and housing anti-discrimination laws in particular. To ask questions of a HUD employee directly, call (202) 708-1112.

In addition to the federal anti-discrimination criteria we all must follow, some states have laws prohibiting discrimination on the basis of marital status, sexual orientation, source of income (occupation), personal appearance, political affiliation, place of residence, place of business, matriculation (student status), and family responsibilities. Then there are states which have less specific, but more encompassing, anti-discrimination laws prohibiting discrimination in rental housing unless it is based on legitimate business grounds. To find answers to your questions about your state's anti-discrimination laws, go to "craigslist.org/about/FHA."

What is left that you may be discriminating

about? Quite a bit, believe it or not. You may still be discriminating about the tenant's ability to pay, willingness to pay, past record as a tenant, pets, waterbeds, number of vehicles, type of vehicles (you may not discriminate against motorcyclists, but noisy motorcycles are another matter), recommendations, number of co-tenants (even though you may not discriminate against children, you may still limit the number of people you will allow to occupy the premises), honesty, attitude (use care with this one; I measure their attitude by whether they laugh, or at least smile, at my stupid jokes), smoking or drinking habits, permanence, noisiness, cleanliness, and the like. In other words, you may be discriminating about any number of things which will affect your business relationship with your tenants.

Although in the states with the strictest anti-discrimination laws, you may not refuse to rent a two-bedroom apartment to an applicant on the grounds that she is a lesbian who collects welfare, wears black leather hotpants and frizzy pink wigs, solicits tricks at the local tavern, lives with her incorrigible five-year-old son and a succession of painted ladyloves, and is an anarchistic student twenty-one years old, you may refuse to rent to her if she smokes cigars, and you rent only to nonsmokers.

That's the equivalent of the government's pursuing an underworld character for tax evasion when they don't have enough evidence to nail him on any other charge, even though they know full well that he's running illegal gambling, prostitution, toxic-waste-disposal, drug, and money-laundering operations. Refusing to rent to someone who's undesirable on many counts only because she smokes cigars is perfectly legal, and it's perfectly just. There is a legitimate business reason for doing so. Furthermore, you'd have to be totally indifferent to the matter if you couldn't find some reason to refuse to rent to her.

Don't despair about anti-discrimination laws. They mean well. A great many people have been unfairly discriminated against in finding housing only because they were old or HIV-positive or Mormon or black or female or Irish or Jewish or divorced. The laws merely declare that those are no longer valid reasons by themselves to refuse to rent to someone. You may not discriminate arbitrarily. That's all. You should always be able to find a valid legal reason not to rent to someone you consider objectionable. Set your own

standards well within the law, and then set about getting good tenants you can work with.

Your standards for a particular two-bedroom rental in a fourplex might look like these—

> *Gross income*—three times rent
> *Income stability*—at least six months with same source of income
> *Assets*—five times rent (bank account and automobile equity)
> *Credit*—established, nothing negative; FICO score of 620 or better
> *Credit cards*—one major card
> *Checking account*—established
> *Rent punctuality*—prompt, never late
> *Pets*—none
> *Waterbed*—one queen-size OK
> *Vehicles*—one auto, no motorcycles louder than an auto
> *Former landlords' recommendations*—good
> *Personal recommendations*—one available (preferably local)
> *Number of tenants*—maximum of four
> *Attitude*—cooperative
> *Smoking*—no
> *Drinking*—moderation (maximum of two drinks daily)
> *Illegal drug usage*—none on record
> *Permanence*—at least six months in each of last two residences
> *Cleanliness*—average
> *Interest in the dwelling*—average to high (willing to pay more in rent than asked)

Whatever your standards are, put them in writing so you can prove to anybody that you do not discriminate illegally. You discriminate legally according to your own well-conceived and equally applied standards. You treat everybody the same way.

Naturally, some of the standards you use are relative to a given dwelling, some are relative to you, some are relative to a particular state or county or municipality, and some are relative to commonly accepted rules of thumb. Be reasonable in determining your standards because if they are overly restrictive, you may well find that no one who wants to live in your rental can possibly qualify. For most standards, you will have to determine yourself what is reasonable and what is overly restrictive (see chapter 13 for ideas about accepting pets and waterbeds), but there are some rules of thumb you might want to follow. One of them concerns gross income.

For gross income, the commonly accepted rule of thumb is *three times rent*, though some landlords have seen fit to reduce that even further. If an applicant's gross income is less, then you must reject him outright unless you have adopted a policy which you apply to every applicant equally that you will accept applicants whose gross income is less than your standard so long as they come with sterling recommendations from two previous landlords or they come up with a larger deposit, say, an additional $200 (be careful when asking for a larger deposit because you must not exceed the maximum deposit permitted under your state's laws governing deposits; for unfurnished units, it's likely to be two times the monthly rent; for furnished units, three times).

You may also adopt a gross-income policy requiring that *every* adult occupant have a gross income equal to three times the rent. After all, tenants' living arrangements, whether sanctified by marriage or not, may break up, and you, dear landlord, may get stuck with the one tenant who has no income and can't pay the rent. (You don't have to be this restrictive if you don't wish to be, but you may be this restrictive if you do wish to be.)

Note that if you choose to separate the income of two adults who volunteer the information that they're unmarried, then you must separate the income of couples who volunteer the information that they're married. Likewise, if you combine the income of married couples, you must combine the income of unmarried couples. Apply your standards to one and all alike. That's what anti-discrimination laws require you to do.

Regarding occupancy standards, there used to be a rule of thumb. It was *one fewer than the number of rooms*. A studio or efficiency dwelling (two

rooms) would accommodate one occupant; one bedroom (three rooms), two occupants; two bedrooms (four rooms), three to four occupants; and three bedrooms (five rooms), four to five occupants. Were you to apply that rule of thumb to rentals in most states today, you could be accused of illegal discrimination for your two- and three-bedroom units.

Today there are federal, and in some cases, more restrictive state standards, and you must comply with them. You have no choice. Federal occupancy standards say that you must allow up to two people per bedroom in your rentals. This translates as follows— studio or efficiency dwelling (no bedrooms), one occupant; one bedroom, two occupants; two bedrooms, four occupants; three bedrooms, six occupants; and four bedrooms, eight occupants.

In other words, you must not discriminate against applicants on the basis of the number of people in their living group so long as they do not exceed two people per bedroom. You may rent to a family of three who want to rent a two-bedroom house if you want to, but everything being equal otherwise, you must not give them any preference over a family of four who also want to rent the house. You must treat them exactly the same.

Some states modify the federal occupancy standards somewhat by increasing them slightly. They say that you must allow two people per bedroom plus an additional one. This translates as follows— studio or efficiency dwelling (no bedrooms), one occupant; one bedroom, three occupants; two bedrooms, five occupants; three bedrooms, seven occupants; and four bedrooms, nine occupants

Some landlords fudge on the numbers by decreasing them. Don't, at least not arbitrarily. Decrease them only if you have good reason, say, because your three-bedroom rental house's septic system is sized for only four people and you can prove that additional people would severely strain the system, or because the rooms are small and the fire codes dictate that only three people can safely occupy the house on a square-footage basis. Those are good reasons for decreasing the numbers.

What does all this hullabaloo about discrimination mean to you? It means simply that you cannot be discriminating in certain prejudice-oriented ways when you're selecting tenants, but you can be, and you should be, discriminating in a great many other ways, business-oriented ways, if you wish to protect your property and make it a good investment.

The truth is that you have to be discriminating when you're selecting tenants because you will find that some people are completely incapable of selecting their own living accommodations prudently themselves. They think that a family of five, soon to be six, one dog, one cat, and a pet crocodile will fit comfortably into one of your one-bedroom apartments. You have to instruct them in the folly of their thinking.

The Ten Steps Amplified

Now let's take a closer look at how you can be discriminating in selecting tenants. Let's examine individually each of the ten steps for getting good tenants.

1) Prepare the dwelling for occupancy.

This first step in getting good tenants would appear to be totally unrelated to the overall task, but it is, in fact, just as important to getting good tenants as their payment of rent is to their staying on as tenants.

Your job at this point is to fix up, paint up, clean up, and dress up your rental dwelling to make it attractive enough so that a good prospect will want to rent it from you for the rent you want to charge. You will always attract the best tenants and get the most rent from that dwelling which shows well and smells good. (Give vacating tenants an incentive to clean well and hope that they do, but don't bank on it.)

Even so, don't become overly concerned about sanitation or perfection when you are preparing a dwelling for occupancy. Remember that you are appealing primarily to the senses of sight and smell. In this context, clean the appliances, stove hood, and cabinets (under the sink, too) both inside and out. Remove all nonadhesive shelf paper. Clean the showers, tubs, toilets, sinks, mirrors, and medicine cabinets (inside as well). Dust the ceilings (for cobwebs), the baseboards, window sills, blinds, and closet shelving. Wash the kitchen and bathroom walls, and spot-clean the walls in other rooms. Dry-clean the draperies. Wash the light fixtures and windows inside and out. Vacuum and deep-clean the carpets. Scrub and wax the floors. Sweep the entry, patio, storage enclosure, and garage. Remove all personal belongings of the previous tenants (including clothes hangers and cleaning supplies). Finally, dispose of all trash.

One landlady I know who takes this business very seriously took her preparation cues from hotels and motels. She asked herself how they manage to make their rooms appear clean every day when they can't possibly clean every square inch of those rooms every day. She noticed that motels spend extra effort in the bathroom, wrapping the glasses, supplying new bars of soap, sanitizing the toilet bowl, wrapping a paper band around the seat, folding the next sheet on the toilet paper roll carefully, and sometimes providing shower caps and shampoo. Now she prepares her rentals in somewhat the same fashion. She bought a supply of those paper bands, and she wraps one around each toilet seat after it's been thoroughly cleaned. She leaves a new dispenser of liquid soap at the sink, and she puts an unwrapped roll of toilet paper in the paper holder. Needless to say, the people who look at her vacancies are impressed. Then, on the day her new tenants move in, she leaves a small box of chocolate-covered mints on the kitchen counter with a welcome note.

Do a good job of cleaning overall, but do not do such a good job that you get calluses on your knees from crawling all over the floors scrubbing them laboriously and polishing them to a mirrorlike finish. Do not work your fingers to the bone by scrubbing the tile grout with a toothbrush. That's wasted effort.

Remember this one very important truism about each of your rentals—

You, landlord, are not going to live there.

Remind yourself. Remind your partner. Say it out loud now and again while you're cleaning, "I am not going to live here." Do not give way to excessive cleaning. Clean your rentals well, but don't try to clean them any better than a house-

APPLICANT QUALIFIER

Name _Richard Renter_   Date/Time _5-1-XXXX_

Dwelling _453 Sweet St., Littletown, CA_

Disqualifiers
Any ONE of the following conditions automatically disqualifies the applicant.

1) Applicant has failed to provide essential information, that is, information about current or previous tenancies, employment, identification (drivers license or Social Security Number), or finances.
2) Applicant has falsified essential information.
3) Applicant was evicted through court action within the previous 24 months.
4) Applicant has gross income less than three times the prospective rent.
5) Applicant cannot pay all move-in monies prior to move-in.
6) Applicant is not prepared to move in when unit is available or not prepared to pay rent as of that date.
7) Applicant has no verifiable source of income.
8) Applicant has been convicted of a felony which is drug-related, violent, or sexual in nature.
9) Applicant and fellow residents exceed the maximum number of people legally permitted to occupy the dwelling.
10) Applicant refuses to sign notice and release agreement regarding mold and radon.
11) Applicant's current dwelling fails scrutiny during inspection visit.
12) CONDITIONAL: Applicant smokes (if dwelling is non-smoking).
13) CONDITIONAL: Applicant has a dog or cat (if pets are forbidden).
14) CONDITIONAL: Applicant has a waterbed (if waterbeds are forbidden).
15) CONDITIONAL: Applicant has too many vehicles (if parking is limited).

Qualifiers
Give ZERO points if no choice applies in a category.
Numbers in parentheses are points suggested for that choice.

∅ ADEQUACY OF INCOME
Applicant has gross income 21-100% higher than three times the monthly rent. (20)
Applicant and others in the household have gross income 21-100% higher than three times the monthly rent. (15)
Applicant has gross income 10-20% higher than three times the monthly rent. (15)
Applicant and others in the household have gross income 10-20% higher than three times the monthly rent. (10)

15 STABILITY OF INCOME
Applicant has had same sources of income for two years or more. (20)
Applicant has had same sources of income for one to two years. (15)
Applicant has had same sources of income for less than one year. (10)

15 CREDIT STANDING
Applicant has a FICO score of 690 or greater. (20)
Applicant has a FICO score of 620 to 689. (15)
Applicant has a FICO score of 560 to 619. (10)
Applicant has a FICO score below 560. (5)
Applicant has no credit information available. (0)

∅ BANKRUPTCY (Previous 48 Months)
Applicant has never declared bankruptcy. (0)
Applicant has declared bankruptcy due primarily to divorce or medical expenses. (-5)
Applicant has declared bankruptcy for reasons other than divorce or medical expenses. (-15)

keeper would clean a room in a two-star motel.

Your new tenants may be as fastidious about housekeeping as Felix Unger is in *The Odd Couple*, and if they are, they will probably clean everything again themselves anyway. Your thorough housecleaning efforts are a waste of time and energy in that case, and they're definitely a waste if your new tenant is an Oscar Madison.

In addition to preparing the place for occupancy by cleaning, perfume it as well. No, not with Chanel No. 5. That's for people, not dwellings. Perfume the place by cleaning the kitchen and bathroom with a lemon or pine-oil scented cleaner. Or use a commercial air freshener to make the place smell of honeysuckle, limes, or new-mown hay. Or make it smell of grandma's fresh-baked delights by heating two tablespoons of imitation vanilla extract on the stove. Or allow the new paint odor to dominate the air. Any *one* of these smelly procedures is sufficient to make the place smell clean and fresh. Be wary about mixing them.

The sense of smell is very important. Those who study such things say that smell revives memories more than any of our other senses. Remember the wonderful aroma of homemade cookies and all the pleasant memories that go along with them? Who doesn't! Well, those boutique cookie shops which have become successful in shopping malls across the country are trading on those very memories and, of course, on your weakened sales resistance once your salivary glands start reacting to the fresh-baked-cookie aromas. That's how they snag you as a customer. Good odors conjure up pleasant memories and help to sell products.

Likewise, they can help you rent residences. If prospective tenants are charmed by agreeable odors of one kind or another, they become more willing to pay good rent for a place. You know what new cars smell like, don't you? Can you imagine someone ordering a new car to be delivered without that new car smell? Give your vacant rental dwelling a fresh, clean, pleasing odor, too.

2) Prequalify the prospects.

Begin learning whether prospects are qualified to rent from you when you make your first contact with them. You simply cannot assume that everybody who inquires about your vacancy is qualified, and you don't want to waste their time or yours if they aren't.

You begin learning whether they're qualified in this second step. Based upon your tenant standards, whatever they happen to be, it consists of certain determinations which you can make rather quickly, even over the telephone. It will save you untold time, gasoline, shoe leather, and grief. This step serves to eliminate those people who are interested in renting from you but fail to qualify. Here you are prequalifying them before you ever take the time to show them the rental or have them fill out an application, so you won't be exasperated to learn late in the process that they really didn't qualify to rent from you in the first place.

You can't very well determine at this stage whether someone will qualify according to all of your tenant standards. That questioning would be much too tedious to go into right now, and besides, it wouldn't yield useful information anyway (certain things you must observe in people, not ask about; can you imagine asking callers straightaway about their cleanliness?), but you can certainly select a few important items and prequalify callers with them, devising questions suitable for getting truthful answers.

To avoid wasted time, wasted effort, and possible embarrassment later, prequalify prospects when you first speak with them by making these eight determinations about them and their circumstances—

1) When they are ready to move in;
2) Whether they have enough money to move in;
3) Whether they have good credit;
4) Whether they have ever been evicted or asked to move out;
5) Whether the number of people who intend to live there falls within your limits;
6) Whether they smoke;
7) Whether they have pets; and
8) Whether they have a waterbed.

If the prospects are not ready to move in yet and your dwelling is ready for immediate occupancy, look for someone else. If you require $1,735 to move in and they have only $400 to commit right now, why keep talking to them? Look further. If they admit to having bad credit, tell them they'll have to rent elsewhere. If they admit to having been evicted before, thank them for being honest and tell them you aren't in the business of rehabilitating problem tenants. If they

Applicant Qualifier (Page 2)

10 RENT PAYMENT HISTORY (Previous 24 Months)
    Applicant has never been late in paying rent. (10)
    Applicant has never been more than five days late in paying rent. (0)
    Applicant has received one or more notices to pay rent or quit and has paid the rent
       within the time limit and satisfied the late payment consequences. (-10)
    Applicant habitually pays late within ten days after the due date. (-10)

15 EVICTION HISTORY (Previous 24 Months)
    Applicant has never been evicted or been given a "notice to comply" for any reason.
       (15)
    Applicant received a "notice to comply" for a reason other than nonpayment and
       complied fully. (-5)
    Applicant received a notice to pay rent or quit, vacated voluntarily in the time
       allowed, and paid landlord the entire amount owed. (-5)
    Applicant received a notice to pay rent or quit, vacated voluntarily in the time
       allowed, but did not pay landlord the amount owed. (-15)

10 RENTAL HISTORY
    Applicant has lived in the same dwelling for the past 24 months. (15)
    Applicant has lived in two different dwellings in the past 24 months. (10)
    Applicant has lived in more than two different dwellings in the past 24 months. (5)
    Applicant lives with roommates and is a responsible party on the rental agreement.
       (5)
    Applicant lives with roommates and is not a responsible party on the rental
       agreement. (0)
    Applicant has never lived away from home before. (0)

20 LANDLORD RECOMMENDATIONS
    Previous landlord would rent to the applicant again. (20)
    Previous landlord is unavailable. Current landlord would rent to the applicant
       again. (5)
    Neither previous nor current landlord is available to give a recommendation. (0)
    Applicant has no previous tenancy. (0)
    Previous landlord would not rent to the applicant again. (-15)
    Previous landlord is unavailable. Current landlord would not rent to the applicant
       again. (-20)

10 RENT COMPARISON
    Current rent is equal to, or greater than, prospective rent (10).
    Current rent is 10% below prospective rent (5).
    Current rent is 11-20% below prospective rent (0).
    Current rent is more than 20% below prospective rent (-10).

___ CO-SIGNER (Make-Up Points)
    Applicant agrees to secure a co-signer who has a FICO score of 700 or greater and
      owns local real estate. (10)

___ ADDITIONAL DEPOSIT (Make-Up Points)
    Applicant agrees to put up an additional deposit equal to one-half of the
      prospective rent. (10)

Total   Points

95 TOTAL POINTS (90 or more is acceptable; 80 to 89 is marginal; below 80 is
    unacceptable.)

are a family of four, and you're looking for a maximum of three people, tell them so. If they smoke, and you don't want smoke to permeate the place, tell them you don't rent to smokers. If they have a cat and a canary, and you don't take pets, say the magic words, "Sorry, we don't take pets!" If they have a huge heart-shaped waterbed for themselves and a twin-sized waterbed for their four-year old, and you have decided against allowing any liquid-filled furniture in this house you inherited from your favorite uncle, well, then, that's that.

Unless you have a lie detector handy, though, establishing the truth regarding these particulars may take some doing. Certain people will tell you exactly what they think you want to hear. They will tell you that they're ready to move in now, but they can wait until you're ready for them to move in. They have $2,000 in cash to cover all of their move-in costs. They have spotless credit. They have never been late with their rent and have never been evicted. They have been married for eleven years and have no children. They do not smoke. They have no pets and no water-filled furniture. Also, they will tell you with a smile in their voice, "We're friendly, cooperative, tolerant, neighborly religious people who sing in the choir and live by the Golden Rule." That's what they may say, but where does the truth lie? Who knows?

How do you get at the truth? At this stage, without being omniscient, all you can do is phrase your questions whenever possible in such a way that you give few clues to the answers you're looking for.

Because people seldom dissemble in answering questions about their readiness to move, their ability to pay the move-in costs, and their credit, you can be pretty direct about the first three questions. State whether the place is available now or will be in two weeks, and ask whether the prospects' moving plans might coincide with that time frame. State flatly what sum you require to be paid before they move in so much as a bag of groceries or a toothbrush, and ask them whether this is within their means right now. Tell them you run a credit check on every applicant, and ask them whether theirs is decent.

The next four questions are the ones which generally involve the most deceit—tenant history, number of people, smoking, and pets. These are the ones to be most wary about.

To learn something approaching the truth about their tenant history, simply ask the prospects disarmingly what kind of recommendations their current and previous landlords will give them when you call.

Then ask them how many people will be living with them. Do not say, "We allow only three people to live in this rental. How many people will be living with you?" That approach will surely elicit this response, "There are only three of us."

After establishing that the prospects fall within your definition of acceptable numbers, ask them point blank, "Does anyone in your household smoke?"

Likewise, ask them, "How many pets do you have?" Don't reveal your policies on smoking and pets before asking the questions, of course, or you will likely be able to predict their answers. Reveal your policies only after you hear their answers.

Finally, now that you have prequalified the prospects on seven counts, and they pass, ask whether they plan to keep any water filled furniture in the place they want to rent from you. Again, reveal your policy only after you hear their answer.

With all of these matters settled to your mutual satisfaction, invite them to take a look at the place. They're prequalified.

As you continue with the next steps, you may at any time elect to quantify the information you learn about the prospects in order to keep yourself focused during the go-no-go decision-making process. The Applicant Qualifier form shown here does just that. It first lists the conditions which would disqualify the applicants, and then it assigns points for their standing in the categories relevant to their being good tenants. Adjust the points to reflect what's most important to you in a tenant and then be as consistent as you can be in scoring every applicant who's interested in renting from you.

Do not show this form to applicants. It's for your use only. Should an applicant happen to see it and disagree with your scoring, you'll have a fight on your hands which could drag you straight into the bailiwick of the discrimination police, where you're assumed to be guilty before you ever open your mouth. If you show it to anybody, show it to the discrimination police once they nab you, if you think it would be useful as proof that you are not discriminating illegally.

Rental Application for (address) 456 Sweet Street

Name Richard Renter   Home Phone 555-1975   Cell Phone 334-1975

Email Address RENTERMAN@YAHOO.COM   Social Security No. 432-10-6789   Driver License No. A0989677

Present Address 1510 Morton Ave

How long at this address? 10 mos. Rent $640— Reason for moving want to be closer to work

Owner/Manager Muretta Norby   Phone 555-3210

Previous Address 1 Bunn Circle, Apt. 105

How long at this address? 2 yrs. Rent $480— Reason for moving got married; apt. too small

Owner/Manager Betty Hardison, owner   Phone 555-1001

Name of every person to live with you, even if only temporarily:

Rose Renter

Any pets? NO Describe —   Waterbed? Yes

Present Employer Bi-Lift Elevator Systems   Phone 123-4440

How long with this employer? 2½ yrs. Supervisor George Judge   Phone 123-4444

Previous Employer Upstate Lifts   Phone (200) 111-2160

How long with this employer? 6 yrs. Supervisor Herb Frank   Phone (200) 111-2160

Current Gross Income Per Month (before deductions) $2150—

Sources and amounts of other income (other than present employment income above):

None

Amount of alimony and/or child support you receive $ None or pay $ None

Savings Account: Bank Safe Savings Branch Downtown Account No. (Last 4 Digits) ..0011

Checking Account: Bank Big Bank Branch Main Account No. (Last 4 Digits) ..586-3

Major Credit Card Visa (Last 4 Digits) ...3509 Balance Owed ∅ Monthly Pmt. ∅

Credit Reference A-Z Furniture Account No. (Last 4 Digits) R-346 Balance Owed 650— Monthly Pmt. 85—

Credit Reference — Account No. (Last 4 Digits) — Balance Owed — Monthly Pmt. —

(Use back to explain any "yes" answers to questions below.) HAVE YOU..ever filed bankruptcy? NO ever been evicted? NO ever been convicted of a felony? NO

Vehicle(s) Make(s) VW Model(s) Golf Year(s) 1999 License(s) ZZZ0013

Personal Reference Delwyn Levno Address 101 Beaver, Littletown Phone 555-1933

Contact in Emergency Glenda Renter Address 400-15TH St., Honest, CA Phone (200)185-3061

I declare that the statements above are true and correct. I authorize verification of my references and credit as they relate to my tenancy and to future rent collections.

Date 1/6/XXXX Signed Richard Renter

Verified: SSN ✓ DL/ID ✓ CurTenancy ✓ Prev ✓ Credit ✓ Inc ✓ PersRefs ✓ By db

3) Show the dwelling.

This step requires no special talents or skills. It's straightforward. Anybody can do it, but you should be aware of a number of ideas you could use to make showing the dwelling less time-consuming, less troublesome, and more productive.

✔ After you have prequalified those who phone and express an interest in renting your available dwelling, ask them whether they have any questions and answer their questions while you still have them on the phone. Explain exactly where the rental is located so they aren't unpleasantly surprised by the neighborhood if it's not quite what they expected. Also, give them clearly understandable directions so they won't get lost while making their way there.

✔ If you're one of those much maligned absentee landlords who rents out a house or an apartment complex which is located at some distance from where you live or work, you'll want to minimize making trips there. Do so by encouraging people to drive by the building first and then call back for an appointment to see the inside, or do so by holding an "open house" for showing your vacancy at designated hours (should be one to two hours long) which are convenient for most people. Tell those whom you have prequalified just when you intend to hold this open house and then make certain that someone is there to show the place. You will save yourself many wasted trips and hours of waiting around for a specific caller who may or may not even bother to show up.

✔ Holding an open house so that many prospects can tour your rental at the same time is a real convenience to the absentee landlord, but it has another advantage which even the landlord who lives on the premises should bear in mind. It tends to stimulate greater interest. When several people show up and express an interest in renting a particular place, each one feels all the more interested just because someone else wants it. The open house creates a kind of "auction atmosphere" which stirs the bidders' blood and puts you, the "auctioneer," in command. You needn't negotiate rent and conditions, as some crafty tenants would have you do. You are in a position to dictate rent and conditions. You are in a position to be courted. You may even have somebody tell you they like the place so much that they'll pay more for it than what you're asking.

✔ If you make separate appointments to show the dwelling to callers, you will want to minimize no-shows. You don't want to waste your time traveling to an appointment, only to find that nobody shows up when they're supposed to show up. You'll go a long way to minimizing no-shows if you do the following—1) get the callers' names and cellphone numbers; 2) give them your cellphone number; 3) tell them to call you on your cellphone as soon as they start their trip to meet you at the dwelling; and 4) tell them you won't even start out to meet them at the dwelling until they call you.

✔ Never rent out a dwelling sight unseen. Some prospective tenants will tell you over the phone that they want to rent your place without even looking at it. If they're that eager, don't insist that they see it, but don't rent it to them either. Something's sure to be suspect if they're that undiscriminating.

✔ Never rent to any person sight unseen. Be wary of the prospective tenant who does not appear in person but is being represented by somebody else, say, a social worker, parent, friend, or minister. The prospective tenant could be a soon-to-be-released felon or a mental incompetent who might be a real danger to your other tenants and to you. Insist that the prospective tenant appear in person. After all, should this person become your tenant, you will have to deal with him in person then. That pleasant social worker or minister isn't going to be available all the time as a go-between to make sure that everything goes smoothly during the tenancy.

✔ If you have a dwelling coming up for rent in a multi-family building and you know the dwelling is in such poor condition that it won't show well, don't show it. Instead, show another one which is similar and is occupied by a clean, cooperative tenant. Before you do, however, be absolutely certain that the prospects are well qualified and very interested in renting from you. In other words, you should feel reasonably certain that the prospects are not really well-dressed burglars casing the joint.

✔ If possible, accompany your prospects on their tour of the premises rather than handing them the keys and telling them to look the place over by themselves. Consider the showing an opportunity to talk with the prospects and size them up. If you can't accompany them on their tour,

RENTAL APPLICATION INSTRUCTIONS

We appreciate your interest in the rental dwelling we currently have available. Because we want to rent this dwelling to people who are considerate of their neighbors, clean in their living habits, capable of paying the rent, and prompt in paying their bills, we use a rental application to help us determine whether our applicants meet these qualifications.

In order for you to rent from us, you must complete a rental application. We want you to know how to complete the application we use, and we also want you to know what our company does with your application.

When filling out the application, put something in every blank, even if you have to put "None" or "N.A." in some blanks. Try to write so that your entries fit in the spaces provided. If they don't, continue them on the back side. Take your time and look up any information called for on the application which you're at all uncertain about. Don't guess.

Make sure that you read the declaration just above the signature line and agree to it before you sign your name to the application. It states that the information on your application is true and correct, and it authorizes us to verify your references and your credit as they relate to your tenancy now and to your paying rent in the future.

When you have completed your application, read it over carefully to make sure that it is accurate, complete, and legible. Look especially for misspellings and transposed numbers.

Once we receive your application, we verify as much of it as we can. If you look at the last line on the application itself, you will notice all of the things we verify. We verify your Social Security number (SSN), your driver's license (DL) or personal identification number (ID), your current tenancy (CurTenancy), your previous tenancy (Prev), your credit (Credit), your income (Inc), and your personal references (PersRefs). When we have verified each of these items, we put a check mark next to its abbreviation.

We verify this information in a variety of ways. We look at your Social Security card or some other evidence of your Social Security number. We look at your actual driver's license or some other official picture identification which you use whenever you cash a check. We call your current landlord or manager to ask whether the information you put on your application is correct about how long you've been at your current address, how much you've been paying in rent, and why you are moving. Then we call your previous landlord or manager and ask the same questions about your previous tenancy.

At the same time that we order a credit report, we also order an eviction report and a bad check report. The credit report tells us whether you pay your bills on time. The eviction report tells us whether you have ever been evicted and why. The bad check report tells us whether you write bad checks.

Next, we call whoever can verify your source of income to determine how much you generally receive from that source every month and how long you have been receiving it.

Finally, we call your personal references to verify that they know you and that we have their correct addresses and phone numbers so that we can contact them should anything happen to you.

That's the procedure we follow when we check applications.

Now, if you suspect we might discover a "skeleton in your closet" when we check your application and you want to tell us about it before we go to all the trouble of checking you out, please feel free to do so. We'd be glad to talk with you about it. Otherwise, we will expect no surprises when we're checking you out and hope that we will soon be doing business together as landlord and tenant.

take precautions about getting the key back promptly. Look at the Property Viewing & Keys Agreement in chapter 10 and consider using it. It's designed specifically for the absentee landlord who allows prospects to take self-guided tours of vacant rental houses.

✔ Ask every prospect to produce a government-issued ID before you show a dwelling. Log the ID on a list and lock the list and the ID up somewhere (in your office if it's on the premises, or else in your car) during the showing. Return it after you show the dwelling. This precaution assures you of the prospect's correct identity right from the start, and it serves as notice that the prospect must behave in order to get his license back. He won't have anonymity to protect him if he robs you or does you bodily harm.

✔ If you have any reason at all to suspect that a prospect is more interested in robbing or assaulting you than in seeing the vacancy you have available, do not show the dwelling by yourself alone. Wait until somebody is available to accompany you. At the very least, carry some sort of personal protection device such as pepper spray which irritates the eyes and burns the skin of an attacker when triggered or a personal alarm which sounds an ear piercing noise when triggered, and be prepared to use it.

✔ Do not "steer" prospects to a particular dwelling when you have several available. You might think that the young family of four who answered your ad for a three-bedroom apartment should not be shown the two-bedroom you also have available because it shares a common wall with two quiet spinsters, but you ought to show it to them anyway. You can be accused of discriminating against families if you don't show it to them and you do show it to a childless couple who come for a tour of your vacancies right after the young family leaves.

✔ When you show prospects through any dwelling, you'll want to make a little sales pitch. Point out all the features of the place, including the special features of the building and the neighborhood. Be honest, though. Don't say it's quiet in the evening when, in fact, right next door there's a fundamentalist church which rattles and rolls to loud gospel music every Tuesday, Friday, and Sunday night. If you ignore the drawbacks, you may have to contend all over again with an-

other vacancy very soon. The prospective tenants have a right to know what the place is really like at all hours, and you should tell them. Of course, you may want to speak of the drawbacks as if they were advantages: "One thing I really like about this place is the great gospel music they play next door three evenings a week. It's such a joyful sound, don't you think?"

✔ The first impressions you have of prospects when you're showing them around may tell you all you need to know to reject them outright, but you don't want to alienate them by telling them right now. Do what small claims court judges do when they don't want to anger a losing party in court. Take the matter "under submission." This simply means that to avoid fistfights in the corridors, the judge will render his decision at a later time even though he may already have made the decision.

✔ Offer rental applications and instructions for completing the applications to all who look at the place, and tell them that you check the applications thoroughly. Applications are your best defense against discrimination lawsuits because they show that you are methodical rather than arbitrary in tenant selection.

4) Accept and scrutinize applications.

Your rental application should be simple to read, simple to follow, brief, and yet thorough. You don't need applicants' entire life histories to help you decide whether to rent to them. You might satisfy your idle curiosity by reading those life histories, but they likely wouldn't be any more useful to you in determining whether you ought to rent to somebody than would the information contained in a simple one-page application.

The application you use should have sections with information on the applicant's current and previous tenancies, current and previous jobs, fellow occupants, pets, financial status, credit references, vehicles, Social Security number, and driver's license. If this information is complete, you will have plenty to consider and check in the next step.

Should an applicant balk about giving you his Social Security number because he's afraid it will fall into the wrong hands and result in his identity being stolen, explain that you cannot check his credit without it. Giving it to you is mandatory because the rental application is an application for credit as much as it is an application for a

Deposit Receipt & Agreement

RECEIVED FROM ___*Richard Renter*___ , Applicant,

the sum of ___*Two hundred fifty dollars*___ $ _*250*_

for the purpose of verifying information submitted on the application and for holding the rental dwelling commonly known as

___*456 Sweet Street*___

until ___*January 10, XXXX*___ or such earlier time as the undersigned Owner/Manager is able to complete a verification of the information submitted on Applicant's rental application.

This dwelling will be rented to the Applicant provided that:
1) The Applicant's rental application and credit history satisfy the Owner/Manager;
2) Within 24 hours of being approved, the Applicant signs the rental agreement offered by the Owner/Manager, a copy of which the Applicant has received, read, and approved; and
3) Within 24 hours of being approved, the Applicant pays all of the sums necessary to move in.

Should the Applicant be approved to rent this dwelling and meet all three conditions above, all monies received will be refunded except for the sum of $___*30*___ , used to process Applicant's rental application, here itemized as follows:
1) Cost to obtain credit report, eviction report, and/or other screening reports $ ___*20*___
2) Cost to process and verify information (time and associated costs) $ ___*10*___

Should the Applicant be approved to rent this dwelling and not do so, none of the monies received will be refunded.

Should the Applicant not be approved to rent this dwelling, the Owner/Manager will refund all monies received except for the sum used to process Applicant's rental application (itemized above).

Date: ___*January 7, XXXX*___   ___*Leslie Landlady*___
                                                      Owner/Manager

Time: ___*1 PM*___   ___*Richard Renter*___
                                           Applicant

_____
                                           Applicant

rental dwelling, and it requires a credit check. Explain that you know about the importance of keeping personal data from falling into the wrong hands and that you take seriously your responsibility of protecting it. Say that you protect it by keeping rental applications with the other important documents you have in your possession and that there's no reason for him to worry about any adverse consequences of giving it to you.

Notice that among other things, the application I use asks for the name of a person to contact in an emergency. This information is of no real use now, when you're still trying to decide whether an applicant would make a good tenant. Yet, it may prove to be vital later when the applicant has become your tenant and he disappears without a trace, as some are wont to do, fails to show up to pay rent, or dies on the property. Such things do happen, you know, and you ought to be prepared for them if they do.

Along with the rental application, you may want to give applicants a sheet of instructions which tells them how to fill out the application and what you do with the information once they submit it. The form I use for this purpose includes a paragraph which puts dishonest applicants on full alert that you check applications thoroughly and do not look kindly on any attempt to lie or cover up negative information. It asks applicants to reveal any negative information in advance of your checking out their application so you may discuss whether it is important enough to disqualify them from renting the dwelling you have available.

Dishonest applicants are betting that you won't check their applications, that you'll be so charmed by their broad smiles and winning ways when you first meet them that you will rent to them without bothering to check them out. They're betting that you're a trusting simpleton, that you will take them at face value and rent to them simply because they seem like such nice people.

Trust me. You cannot afford to take that bet. It's too risky.

It's not the least bit risky for you to ask all of your applicants to be upfront with you about the skeletons in their closets. Ask them and see what happens. If they say nothing about skeletons, go ahead and check them out. If they say something and it's enough to disqualify them, you needn't bother checking them out. You've saved yourself both time and money.

To save yourself from being accused of ignoring the federal law prohibiting landlords from refusing to rent to someone on the basis of familial status, ask every adult who intends to occupy your rental dwelling to fill out an application. Husbands and wives should fill out separate applications, and adult roommates, regardless of their relationship to one another, should each fill out an application as well.

Do get an application from the live-in boyfriend or girlfriend, and check it out. You never know when the primary tenant might get itchy feet, move out, and leave you with somebody you know nothing about and wouldn't have rented to in the first place. You'll use a good many more applications this way, but you'll be well protected against accusations of unfair discrimination and you'll have plenty of good information for later reference.

Some landlords require applicants to submit deposits along with their rental applications. Some don't. In the old days, when I didn't have to prove to anybody how fair I was in selecting my tenants, I used to be among the latter. Now I'm among the former. I do require applicants to submit deposits along with their rental applications because deposits separate the shoppers and the testers from the serious applicants, and they help me prove that I treat everybody the same way.

You don't want to bother checking out anybody except those who are serious about renting from you, and there's only one way to tell the difference. Require them to put up a deposit with their application.

A deposit implies an agreement between you and the applicants, and this agreement may be either exclusive or nonexclusive. Tell the applicants which it is. Before you accept a deposit, tell the applicants whether you will be accepting several deposits on the same vacant dwelling (nonexclusive) or only one (exclusive). Be consistent with everybody who is interested enough to put up a deposit. Let them know whether you're asking for their deposit because you're serious about them in particular or whether you're asking for it to help defray the cost of checking their application along with others before you decide which applicants best qualify to rent the dwelling.

Whatever you do when you take deposits with applications, make your agreement more than implied. Make it explicit. Put it in writing. Give the

Credit Check & Screening Receipt

RECEIVED FROM _____*Richard Renter*_____, Applicant,

the sum of _____*thirty dollars*_____ $ *30⁰⁰*

for the purpose of verifying the information submitted on the
application to rent that dwelling commonly known as

_____*456 Sweet Street*_____.

Sum received will be used as follows:
   1) Cost to obtain credit report, eviction $ *20⁰⁰*
       report, and/or other screening reports

   2) Cost to process and verify information $ *10⁰⁰*
       (time and associated costs)

It is understood that this sum received is in no way to be considered
a deposit to hold the dwelling. The Owner/Manager may take other
applications to rent the dwelling and indeed may already have done
so.

The sum received is refundable only if the owner/manager selects
another applicant to rent the dwelling BEFORE checking Applicant's
credit history. Otherwise, this sum is entirely non-refundable.

Date: _____*January 6, xxxx*_____   *Leslie Landlady*
Time: _____*5 P.M.*_____   Owner/Manager

                         Richard Renter
                            Applicant

                            Applicant

applicants a receipt which explains exactly what their deposit means. There are two receipt forms given here. Use the one which best approximates your understanding with the applicants.

The one entitled "Deposit Receipt & Agreement" is an exclusive commitment to hold the dwelling off the market and to rent it to these particular applicants so long as three conditions are met—1) the application and credit history satisfy the landlord; 2) the applicants sign the rental agreement within 24 hours of being approved; and 3) the applicants pay all move-in monies within 24 hours of being approved.

The one entitled "Credit Check & Screening Receipt" is a nonexclusive understanding. It requires only a small sum of money, and it makes clear that you are not committing to hold the dwelling off the market for these particular applicants. You are merely taking their money to verify the information on the application, and you may be working with other applicants simultaneously.

If there's limited interest in your vacancy and you're trying to snag those applicants who have made a good first impression on you, you'll want to use the "Deposit Receipt & Agreement" and ask for the equivalent of at least three days' rent to hold the place. If there's lots of interest in your vacancy and you want the freedom to choose the best of those who are interested in renting it, you'll want to use the "Credit Check & Screening Receipt" and ask for $30 or thereabouts to pay for your costs in checking the application (be aware that your state may have a law setting a maximum amount you may keep for running a credit check, whether you rent to the applicant or not).

As for filling out the rental applications, you have the option of asking the applicants the questions verbally and writing their answers on the applications yourself, or you may let the applicants do it all by themselves. Both options have advantages. Asking the questions verbally gives you the opportunity to ask certain pertinent questions which don't appear on the application, open-ended questions which allow them to reveal something about themselves. On the other hand, letting them fill out the application saves you time and gives you some idea how neat and thorough they are.

When you have the completed applications in hand, look them over quickly for legibility and completion. Look to see whether the application gives you enough data to check out the applicants using the tenant screening services available to you, services which can provide you with their credit report, their eviction records, their criminal background, their lawsuit involvement, and their sex offender status.

Like it or not, privacy is a thing of the past now that the internet has invaded our world. We may not like it when anybody can discover things about us which we would prefer to keep private, but we ought to like it very much when we can discover things about applicants which we never could before and which can help us determine whether we ought to rent to them.

But we can access none of this information unless we have enough data to identify the applicants with certainty to begin with

You can't even begin to check out a Judy who lives on Lee Lane in Peach Creek if you don't have Judy's phone number or her last name or her exact address or her Social Security number.

Make sure that the applications are signed, too. Applicants' signatures authorize you to conduct credit checks. Without those signatures, you're invading the applicants' right to credit privacy if you begin snooping into their credit bureau information, and you may be fined for doing so. Remember that credit bureaus keep track of everyone who inquires about someone's credit. You will be found out if you make unauthorized inquiries. Do not make them.

Tell the applicants once more that you're going to be checking them out thoroughly. You're going to be calling their landlords and their employers, and you're going to be running a credit check, ordering an eviction report, and inquiring about their bad checks. Ask them again whether there's anything negative which might show up when you're checking them out because now would be the time for them to give you their side of the story. You'd be surprised how many negative things some people will volunteer to tell you about themselves which you never would have uncovered in your snooping. Make careful note of this information on the back of their application, and take it into consideration when you make your decisions. You may find from what they tell you about themselves that you don't need to check them out any further because they have eliminated themselves from consideration.

Then ask to see their driver's licenses and credit cards for identification. Write down their date of birth as it appears on their driver's license. You will need it to run a credit check. Ask non-driving applicants for some other form of "official" identification with their picture on it, such as a passport, military ID, or other government agency ID card. Compare the pictures on the identification with the faces you see before you, and say something kind or droll about the likenesses if you can. Compare the numbers on the identification and credit cards with those given

on the applications to verify the information as given. Then compare the address on the identification or license with the address on the application. Do likewise with the signatures. If these things don't match up, ask why they don't. You have no way of knowing otherwise whether the person whose name and references are listed on the application is the same person who wishes to rent from you.

While you have the driver's license or other identification available, make a photocopy and keep the photocopy together with the application. You may find that there's more information on the license which you need later and don't have available to you anymore.

Remember that whenever you rent out a dwelling, you are entrusting a valuable piece of property to a stranger. You must know whether that stranger is a proper stranger. You must know what that stranger's true identity is. Car rental agencies ask for identification before they will rent you an automobile. Merchants ask for identification before they will cash a five-dollar check. Yet your rental property is many times more valuable than an automobile or a check for a paltry sum. Shouldn't you at least check your applicant's I.D.? You stand to lose plenty if you rent to an unscrupulous tenant, not to mention all the grief and aggravation you could suffer. Be cautious. Check the applicant's identification for certain.

If, for one reason or another, you fail to check an applicant's identification while you are looking the application over initially, don't despair. You can still check it when you visit the applicant's home. As for me, I prefer to check it at the first opportunity because I don't want to waste any more time than I have to if an applicant proves to be impersonating someone else, such as a friend or a relative who has impeccable credit and references.

Unless you already know more about the applicants than what's on their applications, look at each application as if you were trying to collect a court judgment. If applicants have no job, no automobile, and no bank accounts to attach, then how will you be able to get any money out of them if they stop paying you their rent and you have to evict them in court? Some applicants may be rejected at this step without your having to do any further checking. You can "evict" now at the lowest possible cost. (On the back of every rejected applicant's application, jot down the reasons for your decision and keep the application on file for at least three years as proof of your fairness in tenant selection.)

Not only is the information on applications essential to the selection process, but also because you have more information to base your selection on than just the obvious things such as sex, race, or color, the chances of your being considered culpable of illegal discrimination on the basis of these criteria are substantially reduced.

Face it. You are less vulnerable to charges of illegal discrimination if you solicit applications than if you do not. Without applications, you have little information to base your decision on, and the deciding factors may more easily be construed as illegally discriminatory.

Once you have scrutinized the applications to check for internal inconsistencies and obvious disqualifying factors as measured by your tenant standards, you should act promptly. Other landlords are looking for good tenants, too, and your prospects may be filling out applications for more than one dwelling.

5) Check references and qualify the applicants.

Note the very last line on the Rental Application provided here. It's a verification checklist for you and for whoever else may be checking applications for you. It's there so you will know what has been checked and what hasn't. Use it.

Some tenant applicants know that because many landlords fail to check the information on rental applications, they can get away with a lie here and there. Are you surprised? You're not? Good, then you should be able to hold your own in this business.

Yes, people do lie on rental applications, but nobody has ever gone to jail for lying on a rental application. Nobody has ever even had to pay a fine for lying on a rental application. It's not a capital offense. It's not even a misdemeanor. So what do applicants have to lose by being "creative" when they fill out their rental applications? Nothing, absolutely nothing. Neither a jail term nor a fine awaits them if you discover they're lying. They don't even get a slap on the wrist. They just move on and try to dupe some other unsuspecting landlord.

The burden of discovery rests upon you. You have to separate the truth from the falsehoods, and you get no special reward for your efforts when you do discover that an application is full of lies. You merely get to sigh in relief that you didn't rent to somebody who might have been a terrible tenant.

Be suspicious about the information given on *every* rental application submitted to you. Tenants who have had problems with their landlords in the past are not going to disclose those problems on their rental applications. They're not going to give an honest reason why they're moving from their present address. They're not going to admit that they have ever been evicted. They know full well that you won't rent to them if they tell you the truth about themselves. So, they fabricate. They lie. They dare you to prove them wrong. They force you to dig for the truth. Sometimes you need only scratch the surface, and you'll discover something which causes you to have second thoughts about them. One phone call might be enough. Sometimes you have to dig deep to get at anything which can help you make your decision. Ten phone calls might not be enough. Keep digging. You have too much to lose by renting to just anybody.

Start your checking with tenancy references. If they give you any serious doubts, you needn't bother checking further. No matter how good their employment and credit references are, if the applicants have defied their previous landlord and sneaked in a dog or refused to pay late fees when they were late with their rent, you don't want 'em.

■ **Tenancy References**—Call the current landlord to learn whatever you can about the applicants' tenancy, but be careful, very careful, about two things—whether you are speaking to the real landlord or an impersonator and whether the landlord is telling you the truth or telling you what he knows you want to hear in order to get rid of his bad tenants.

Fellow Landlord:

_____Dennis Lee_____ has applied to rent from us and has identified you as a current or former landlord or rental property manager having first-hand experience with him/her as a tenant.

We are trying to determine what this person was like when living at ___7 Leeway Lane, Horace___ as your tenant and would appreciate your answering the following questions about him/her:

How long was this person your tenant?
Less than six months [ ] Six months to a year [ ]
One to two years [ ] More than two years [X]

When did this tenant move out? __7-31-XX__

How much was the rent when he/she moved out? $__630-__

How many other people were living with this tenant?
None [ ] One [X] Two [ ] Three [ ] Four [ ] Five [ ] Six [ ]

Did the tenant have any pets?
Yes [X] No [ ] If so, what kind? __Dog__

How many times did the tenant fail to pay the rent on time?
Once [X] Twice [ ] Three times [ ] More than three times [ ]

Did you ever have to serve the tenant with a notice to pay rent or quit? Yes [ ] No [X]

Did you ever have to serve the tenant with any other notice?
Yes [ ] No [X] If so, what kind? _____

Was this tenant reasonably quiet? Yes [X] No [ ]

Was this tenant reasonably clean? Yes [X] No [ ]

Did the tenant give enough notice that he/she was moving?
Yes [X] No [ ]

Did the tenant leave the premises clean and undamaged?
Yes [X] No [ ]

If you withheld any of the tenant's cleaning/security deposit, why did you withhold it? ___N/A___

Did the tenant leave owing you any money?
Yes [ ] No [X] If so, how much? $_____

On a scale of one to ten, with ten being the most cooperative and zero being the least cooperative, how would you rate this tenant in terms of his/her cooperating with you?
(10) 9 8 7 6 5 4 3 2 1 (Circle only one number.)

If you had the opportunity, would you rent to this tenant again?
Yes [X] No [ ]

Thank you very much for answering these questions.

Sincerely,
Maya Ward

Since impersonating a landlord over the phone is relatively easy, you might be talking to a person other than the applicants' real landlord, so you need to be a bit cagey at first. Say something like this when you call to check the reference: "Hello, I'm Lester Landlord, a landlord in Littletown. Richard and Mary Renter have given you as a reference on an application they made to rent a house from me. Can you tell me how you came to know them?" Don't say, "Richard and Mary Renter have listed you as their landlord on their rental application, and I'm calling to find out what kind of tenants they've been for you." There's a big difference in the two approaches, a crucial difference.

You do not want the person answering the phone to know what his role is supposed to be. In the first approach, you give him no clues. You ask how he knows the applicants. That's all. The real landlord will say straightaway that he is the applicants' landlord. The role-player who's been primed to trick the inquiring landlord won't know whether he's supposed to pretend to be a friend, a neighbor, a landlord, or an employer. If you give him a clue, then the role-player will know what role he's supposed to be playing.

Should you still have doubts about whether you're talking to the applicants' real landlord or a phony, tell the person who answers the phone and claims to be the landlord that the rent is substantially higher or lower than what's given on the rental application and ask for a verification. The real landlord will know right away what the correct rent is. A phony won't.

Once you feel reasonably confident that you are talking with Richard and Mary Renter's honest-to-goodness landlord, try to learn the answers to the following questions—

How long have they lived there?
How many people are there in the household?
Do they have any pets?
Do they bother the neighbors?
Are they quiet?
Are they clean?
Are they cooperative?
Are they demanding?
How much rent are they paying?
How many times have they been late with their rent?
Why are they moving?
Did they give proper notice that they would be moving?

Have there been any particular problems with them?

The final question, the key question, you should ask a landlord is whether he would rent to these tenants again if he were given the opportunity.

Honest answers to all of these questions will give you some good clues as to whether you want Richard and Mary Renter to be your tenants, but a yes-or-no answer to the key question will tell you everything.

Besides the pitfall of the phony landlord routine, one other pitfall you might encounter when asking an applicant's current landlord to say a few words about a departing tenant is that the current landlord may be so anxious for the tenants to move that they may be recommended to you even if they are being evicted. Be especially wary, therefore, of glowing recommendations made by the current landlord, and weigh them cautiously against whatever else you have learned about the applicants. Compare the reasons for moving given by the tenants on their applications with the reason given by the current landlord, and if there's even a hint of a discrepancy in their stories, check with their previous landlord.

More than likely, some time has elapsed since the applicants rented from their "previous landlord," and you might not be able to contact that person. He might have gone out of the business, moved away, kept poor records, forgotten all about his previous tenants, lost his memory, or died in the interim. But if you can contact the previous landlord, do. That person no longer has any interest in whether the tenants stay or move and would be the best one to give you an unbiased appraisal.

Approach the previous landlord warily, just as warily as you approached the present landlord, that is, until you feel certain that you are speaking with the indisputable previous landlord. With the information given on the Rental Application as a starter, find out whether it's correct. Then ask the same questions you asked the current landlord.

Sometimes you may not be able to contact the applicants' present or previous landlords at all by phone. You'll want to try contacting them somehow, perhaps by email or fax. To get your responses most quickly, email the "Fellow Landlord" form to the landlord, asking for a prompt response. As a last resort, send the form to the

Employment Verification

TO: EMPLOYER   ___Bi-Lift___
           ___100 Walter Avenue___
           ___Littletown, Calif.___
RE: EMPLOYEE   ___Richard Renter___

We are in the process of checking out a rental application submitted by the person named above as "EMPLOYEE."

This person claims to be working for you currently as a ___operator___ earning $___2,150___ per ___month___. This person also claims to have started working for you as of ___2½ years ago___.

Because time is a factor in our approving this employee to rent from us, we would appreciate your PHONING us as soon as possible with a verification of this information. Our telephone number is ___123-6789___, and we are generally available at the following times: ___8AM - 6PM___.

If you cannot phone us, please complete the section below and mail this entire letter back to us at your earliest convenience.

Thank you.   Signed   ___Leslie Landlady___
                Address ___453 Sweet Street___
                         ___Littletown, Ca. 09090___

- -

The above information is correct with the following exceptions:

_____ (if none, write "none.")

Is this employment part-time? _____ or full-time? _____

Is this employment temporary? _____ or permanent? _____

INFORMATION PROVIDED BY

Name_____ Title_____ Date_____

landlord by Priority Mail, and ask that it by faxed back or mailed back as soon as possible.

Sorry to say, because we landlords are so afraid of being sued, you may encounter some who are reluctant to talk about their tenants at all. In those cases, be as sweet as you can be, and tell them that you aren't asking for a good or a bad recommendation. You're not asking for opinions. You're merely asking for a verification of information of the "name, rank, and serial number" variety. The least they can do is verify the information which the tenants have supplied on their application. Even the most lawsuit-shy landlord should verify for you how much the tenants' rent is, how long they've lived there, and whether they gave proper notice. That's straightforward stuff which doesn't require any interpretation and shouldn't drag anybody into "lawsuitland."

Still, you ought to try to drag an answer out of them for the key question, whether they would rent to these tenants again. The answer to this question sums up everything you need to know about the tenants' conduct as tenants. Landlords can answer with a simple "yes" or "no," and they may give you a clear answer without even thinking. You know they know the answer, but they may not know how to answer.

If they answer with a clear "yes," they mean "yes." More than likely, they won't answer with a clear "no" because they're afraid of repercussions. If they mean "no," they're likely to equivocate by saying they'd rather not answer, and you may as well take that response as a "no." It certainly isn't a "yes."

■ **Employment References**—After checking into the applicants' current and previous tenancies and finding nothing negative, you will want to know something about their employment. You will want to know how much each applicant earns, how long he has been employed, whether the work is part-time or full-time, and whether it is temporary or permanent. This information will help you determine whether the applicants can afford to pay the rent month after month.

First, try to obtain this information by making a phone call, being just as wary about some trickery as you were when calling the landlord. Check the internet or a telephone book for the employer's phone number and try calling that number rather than the one given on the application. The number on the application might ring at the employer's all right, but it might be a di-rect line to one of the applicant's friends who works there. It might be a complete phony, too. Be wary if the "employer" answers with a "hello" rather than with a business name.

When you get through to somebody at the employer who has the information you're looking for, you might say something like this, "Hello, my name is Lester Landlord. I'm a landlord in Littletown. Richard Renter, who says he works for you, has made an application to rent a house from me, and I'd like very much to verify some information about him so I can qualify him and his wife to move in as soon as possible."

In effect, you are saying that your inquiry will benefit the employee and that you are only trying to verify some information you already have. Smaller firms will agree to this reasonable request readily because they know their people individually and want to help their employees obtain housing. Larger firms may switch you around until you reach somebody with authority, and you may have to repeat your speech from the top, but they will generally verify the information you give them as well.

Continue by saying, "Richard Renter says he has been working there for a year and three months. Is that about right?" If they answer in the affirmative, say, "He has indicated that he earns a gross income of $1,855 per month. Is that about right?" Phrasing your questions in this way, so they may be answered either affirmatively or negatively, relieves employers of the anxiety they sometimes feel about divulging information they shouldn't.

Sometimes you may get nowhere with a large employer which has restrictive policies about divulging employee information over the phone. Go in another direction. Stop trying to search through the normal channels for personnel information. Try the applicant's immediate supervisor. Immediate supervisors likely have no policies about discussing personnel matters. They tend to be frank in talking about their staff so long as you approach them in the right way.

If you can't seem to get much information out of anyone over the telephone, ask the applicant to get a letter signed by his employer verifying the information you need, or send the company an Employment Verification form letter such as the one shown here and request the information in writing. To be taken seriously and to ensure a prompt reply, send it with a self-addressed,

Request for Verification of Deposit

Instructions: Landlord—Complete items 1 through 7. Have applicant(s) complete item 8. Forward directly to depository named in item 1.
Depository—Please complete items 9 through 15 and return DIRECTLY to landlord named in item 2.

Part I—Request

1. To (Name and Address of Depository)	2. From (Name and Address of Landlord)
Big Bank 501 Main St. Littletown, CA 09090	Leslie Landlady 453 Sweet St. Littletown, CA 09090

3. Signature of Landlord/Manager	4. Title	5. Date
Leslie Landlady	landlady	1/07/xx

6. INFORMATION TO BE VERIFIED

Type of Account	Account in Name of	Account Number	Balance
Checking	Richard Renter	V04309586	$ $ $ 2,285⁰⁰/xx $

To Depository: I/We have applied to rent a dwelling and stated in the rental application that the balance on deposit with you is as shown above. You are authorized to verify this information and to supply the landlord identified above with the information requested in items 9 through 12. Your response is solely a matter of courtesy for which no responsibility is attached to your institution or any of your officers.

7. Name and Address of Applicant(s)	8. Signature of Applicant(s)
Richard Renter 1510 Zebra St. Littletown, CA 09090	Richard Renter

To Be Completed by Depository

Part II–Verification of Depository

9. Deposit Accounts of Applicant(s)

Type of Account	Account Number	Current Balance	Average Balance for Previous Two Months	Date Opened
		$	$	
		$	$	
		$	$	
		$	$	

10. Bank Card Accounts of Applicant(s)

Type of Bank Card	Account Number	Current Balance	Average Monthly Payment	Expiration Date
		$	$	
		$	$	

11. Loans Outstanding to Applicant(s)

Loan Number	Date of Loan	Original Amount	Current Balance	Installments		Secured by	No. Late Pmts.
		$	$	$	per		
		$	$	$	per		

12. Please include any additional information which may be of assistance in determination of credit worthiness. (Please include information on loans paid-in-full in item 11 above.)

13. Signature of Depository	14. Title	15. Date

The confidentiality of the information you have furnished will be preserved except where disclosure of this information is required by applicable law. The form is to be transmitted directly to the landlord and is not to be transmitted through the applicant(s) or any other party.

stamped envelope.

To verify the income of applicants who are self-employed, you will want to see their personal income tax returns for the past two years. Examine them for authenticity first. Look at the second page and note who prepared the return. I tend to give a little more credence to those prepared by someone other than the taxpayer only because the taxpayer who does his own can easily prepare two returns, one to submit to the IRS and another to submit to lenders and others who want to verify income. Next, check the income section. Is at least some of it from dividends and interest, showing that the applicant has set aside a little money for a rainy day? Is the income enough to afford the rent?

In addition, you will want to see some bank statements of the self-employed person's operations account, not the personal account. Ask for statements covering the past six months or at the very least, the past three months. Look at the average balances and the deposits. How consistent are they? How high are they? Is there enough money available to pay the rent?

■ **Other Income**—Should the applicant derive income from sources other than ordinary employment, say, from Social Security, pension funds, welfare, alimony, child support, inheritance, investments, unemployment, disability, scholarships, school loans, or relatives, you will want to verify the source, the amount, and the continuity of the source as best you can. Ask to see whatever records the applicant has to substantiate the amounts shown on the application.

■ **Credit References**—Regarding credit information, you have four choices:

1) Choice one is to make no inquiries at all, relying solely on the applicant's self-reporting of his credit history and on the tenancy, employment, and other income references already obtained to provide good clues about his ability and willingness to meet the financial obligations incurred in renting from you.

2) Choice two is to check directly with some or all of the credit references listed on the application. Finance companies and merchants with customer charge accounts will usually give you the information you need over the phone, but banks will not release any information unless authorized to do so by the customer, and even then, getting it may take a few days. To get this information, use the Request for Verification of Deposit form shown here. It must be signed by the applicant-customer first, then by you. Fill in as much of the information as possible in items 6 and 7, especially the account numbers. Send or take it to the bank with a self-addressed, stamped envelope, and they will return it directly to you by mail unless the people at the tenants' bank know you and will return it to you in person.

You may, of course, do a "quick-and-dirty" financial resources investigation by calling the bank and inquiring whether a fictitious check for a certain sum of money would clear the applicant's checking account.

3) Choice three is to request a full credit report on the applicant. These reports generally take from several seconds to several hours to obtain and can reveal information on bad debt collections that you wouldn't otherwise uncover. They're available with or without credit bureau risk scoring.

Credit bureau risk scoring originated as a scientific approach to interpreting credit data, virtually eliminating the personal bias which a human might apply when interpreting the data. The scoring system developed by Fair, Isaac, commonly known as FICO®, is by far the most popular credit scoring system.

A FICO score tells a creditor how likely someone is to pay bills on time. It weighs a combination of five factors to come up with a score. Those factors are payment history, amounts owed, length of credit history, new credit, and types of credit use. FICO scores range from a low of 300 to a high of 850. An "A" score ranges from 690 to 850; a "B" score, from 620-689; a "C" score, from 560-619; and a below-average score, from 300 to 559.

Credit unions want a score of 570 or better; banks and credit card companies want a score of

CREDIT BUREAU RISK SCORING		
Score	Percentage of Population	Delinquency Rate (%)
800-850	11	1
750-799	29	2
700-749	20	5
650-699	16	15
600-649	11	31
550-599	7	51
500-549	5	71
300-499	1	87

620 or better. As a landlord, you might decide that you want a score of 560 or better for your apartment house at a marginal location and a score of 650 or better for your rental house at an upscale location.

Examine the table on the previous page, and you'll notice that people with scores between 550 and 599 have a delinquency rate of 51%. They're just as likely to pay a debt as not. That's not exactly good credit, and if I were a lender, I'd be reluctant to lend them a dollar out of fear that they'd repay only 49 cents. You might be reluctant to rent to certain people in this category, too, unless you discover that they are never delinquent in their rent. Through inquiry, you might discover that they always pay their rent on time before they pay any of their other bills. Their FICO score might be low, but that needn't concern you if they have a good record of paying their rent on time.

FICO scores aren't everything for landlords. They are a point of departure, a good one. If the scores are high, you needn't worry about whether the applicants will pay. They have demonstrated that they will. If the scores are low, you need to find out why. You need to discover how important the applicants' payment of rent is to them. That's how you ought to use FICO scores.

FICO scores add approximately $3 to the cost of a credit report and enable you to be just as objective as a banker in analyzing credit data. Without scores, you need to spend more time analyzing the data and may be accused of being too subjective. Of course, you would be.

You may obtain credit reports through many different sources.

Regional rental housing associations—Every association belongs to a credit reporting agency and provides its members with credit reports at a nominal charge.

Online landlord organizations—Every online landlord organization offers its members credit reports among its other benefits. Take your pick. Listed alphabetically, here are five to look at: American Apartment Owners Association (american-apartment-owners-association.org); Landlord Association (landlordassociation.org); Mr. Landlord (mrlandlord.com); National Association of Independent Landlords (nail-usa.com); and Rental Housing On Line (RHOL.org).

Online services—Use an internet search engine and search on "tenant credit reports" or "tenant screening" as key words. You will find all kinds of companies listed under those key words. Go to their websites and compare their prices for credit reports.

4) Choice four is to ask the applicant to order a copy of his credit report himself and make it available to you. He's entitled to a free one once every year through annualcreditreport.com (877.322.8228), the only authorized source of free credit reports under federal law. If he has already used the service during the previous twelve months, he may order a report directly from one of the big-three credit reporting agencies for a small fee. Here are their particulars: Equifax (equifax.com), 800.685.1111; Experian (experian.com), 888.397.3742; and TransUnion (transunion. com), 800.888.4213. The report the applicant shows you should be as recent as possible, no more than two months old at most, and it should be the original. Do not accept a copy unless you can also see the original. Someone may have doctored it to eliminate negative references.

How much credit information you should obtain on applicants depends on the amount of rent involved, the percentage of their income that will be paid out in rent, and the difference between the old and new rents. If the new rent is high or if it's equal to more than 30% of the applicant's gross monthly income (rent, together with monthly credit obligations, should total around 50% of gross income) or if it represents a considerable increase over what they have been paying, you should check the credit thoroughly.

There's a lot of information available, but you have to spend money or time to obtain it, and only you can determine how much information would be helpful to you in making your decision whether to rent to someone. All the information available to you on applicants is merely a supplement to your good judgment. You alone must decide whether they will make good tenants based upon your standards.

By the way, if you ever reject applicants because of a negative credit report, you must provide them with the information they need to secure a copy of their report. They will probably want to see it for themselves to check it for accuracy. They're entitled to a free copy of whatever report caused them to be denied credit, so long as they apply for it within sixty days of their having been denied. You are denying them credit when you refuse to rent to them because of the information in their report. For this purpose, use the form shown at the end of this chapter.

■ **Analysis of Applicants' Finances**—Analyze carefully the finances of those applicants you are serious about before committing to rent to them, and you will have fewer collection problems later because you will know in advance whether they can afford to pay you their rent. You want tenants who are able to pay their rent comfortably month after month after month, tenants who have sufficient income and know something about handling money.

Some applicants never analyze their finances for themselves. Either they don't know how, they aren't interested, or they don't want to know. They know little more about their finances than how much cash they have in their wallets and purses. You ought to do it for them and for yourself. Appearances can be deceiving. How much they earn and how much debt they have isn't everything. There's more to be concerned about in determining whether they can really afford to pay the rent on the dwelling they want to rent from you.

A young couple earning $5,316 per month gross and making a $623 car payment and a $420 MasterCard payment, while they're both working and trying to raise two small children, cannot afford to rent a dwelling from you at $1,500 per month, even though they would appear to qualify easily based upon the rule-of-thumb multipliers for rent and gross income. The truth is that this family, for all its income, has one foot on a financial banana peel atop a house of cards and you'd be remiss in renting a dwelling to them for $1,500 per month when they can comfortably afford to pay only $998. If they make one little slip, their house of cards comes tumbling down, and you don't want to be in it with them when it does.

You can analyze your applicants' finances by spending a few minutes completing the Financial Qualifier form shown on the next page. Its end result is how much they have available every month to pay their rent. Here's what you do (all figures are monthly)—

✔ Itemize their total gross income from verifiable sources, including wages, Social Security, pension, alimony, child support, interest, dividends, and anything else they receive on a regular basis.

✔ Deduct 20% of their total gross income for state and federal taxes. If your state is one of the few without income taxes, deduct 17%.

✔ Deduct the regular monthly payments they make on their credit card debts.

✔ Deduct the payments they make on their vehicles.

✔ Deduct whatever other payments they make to banks and finance companies. Look at both their application and their credit report for information about these debts.

✔ Deduct vehicle expenses (insurance, repairs, maintenance, and fuel) equal to $100 per vehicle if currently financed or $75 if owned outright. Deduct an extra $30 if they happen to fall into a high-risk category. Ask them.

✔ Deduct a sum for gas and electricity which you have determined is an average in your area for this size dwelling. Call your local utility company for figures if you have trouble coming up with figures yourself. They'll help you. They keep track of such things.

✔ Deduct $25 for landline phone service and $40 for each cellphone.

✔ Deduct the basic rate for cable television service and $40 for high-speed internet access.

✔ Deduct $140 per person for food.

✔ Deduct $80 per person for health care if not covered by an employer. Deduct $20 per person if covered by an employer.

✔ Deduct $450 per child for full-day child care. Deduct $200 per child for after-school child care.

✔ Deduct $35 per dog, $25 per cat, for food and veterinary care.

✔ Deduct $200 per adult and $100 per child for miscellaneous expenses such as clothing, entertainment, etc.

✔ Credit them with 5% of their savings as being available to pay their monthly bills.

✔ Whatever is left over is what they can afford to pay you in rent.

Can the applicants afford to pay the rent on the dwelling they want to rent from you? Let's hope so.

If the Financial Qualifier raises any doubts in

FINANCIAL QUALIFIER
(all figures monthly)

APPLICANT NAME	Sanders
Number of Adults	2
Ages of Children	3, 6
Adults all work?	Y
Health plan through work?	Y
Child care?	Y
Pets?	cat

G R O S S   V E R I F I A B L E   I N C O M E

	(amounts)	(notes)
Wages	3266	
Wages	2038	
Wages		
Wages		
Social Security		
Pension		
Alimony		
Child Support		
Interest	12	
Dividends		
Other		
TOTAL INCOME	5316 (+)	

E X P E N S E S   &   D E D U C T I O N S

	(amounts)	(notes)
Income Taxes	1103	20% if state inc tax; 17% if none
Credit Card Payments	180	
Vehicle Payments	623	
Loan Payments	420	
Vehicle Expenses	100	$100/fin; $75/not; add $30 hi risk
Gas & Electricity	80	check local utility for sq ft avg
Telephone	25	ask re avg bill; otherwise $25
Cable TV	32	
Food	560	$140/person
Health Care	100	$85/person wo paid plan; $25 with
Alimony		
Child Care	650	$450/child full day; $200 partial
Child Support		
Pet Care	25	$35/dog; $25/cat
Other	600	$200/adult; $100/child
TOTAL EXPENSES & DEDUCTIONS	4498 (-)	

SAVINGS ACCOUNT BALANCE _____ 3600 add 5% bal to "available for rent"

AVAILABLE FOR RENT _____ 818 (=) ADJUSTED _____ 998
(total income minus total expenses & deductions)

your mind, talk with the applicants. Show them your findings. Listen to what they have to say about how they spend their income. Don't try to suggest how they might spend less on such-and-such so they'd have more to spend on rent. You're not a financial counselor. You're a financial analyst. You are interested only in whether the figures you have come up with are reasonably accurate. If the applicants say that they don't subscribe to cable TV, remove that item. If they say they spend a minimal $15 per month for telephone service, change that item. If they say that a grandmother takes care of their two kids during the day free of charge, remove that item. You want their financial picture to be accurate. Sure, you might see how they could trim their expenses. Keep mum about it. These people's spending habits aren't going to change just because you have some good ideas for changing them. They have to want to change their spending habits.

■ **Eviction Search**—Computer databases being so easy and inexpensive to maintain and use nowadays once the data has been gathered and entered, more and more companies have come to specialize in providing landlords with information about tenants who have been evicted. They search through court records for this information on a daily basis so it is current, and they report evictions which have been filed and evictions which have been concluded. Some such companies combine this information with a more extensive tenant history solicited from landlords in the area. It can be very, very useful information indeed.

Avail yourself of this information. You may find that your local rental housing association has already contracted with an eviction search service and that they can order you an eviction search at the same time they order you a credit report. Tell them to order both for you, by all means, especially if you are the least bit suspicious abut the applicants.

If you need to find an eviction search service on your own, try the internet. Go to one of the search engines and enter the key words "eviction search service." You'll get a lengthy list to select from. Choose the most promising of the listings and go to their websites, looking for one which covers your area, offers speedy service, delivers its findings in a convenient form, and charges reasonable fees.

When you find one which meets your criteria, contact them and ask whether they will do a trial search for you before you pay them their account setup fee. Run a check on a tenant you know who should set off all the warning whistles, and see what kind of information they come up with. If you're satisfied with the results, sign up for the service and use it every time you check the backgrounds of your applicants.

■ **Criminal Search**—Just as eviction records are readily available, so, too, are criminal and sex offender records (usually combined). You may want to order a criminal search on every applicant as a matter of course, especially if you're renting to families with children.

■ **Tenant Screening Packages**—If you want more information on applicants than a credit report and an eviction report when you're making a "rent or no rent" decision, order up an entire screening package. You'll find that a package is cheaper than separate searches.

An entire screening package available from a an internet screening service (they do require signup fees and an onsite facility inspection) like advantagetenant.com costs around $26 and consists of a credit report, a FICO score, a bankruptcy report, a collections report, an eviction report, Social Security number verification, a statewide criminal report, a sex offender search, and a Patriot Act terrorist search.

■ **Evaluation of Applicants' Qualifications**—By now you know more about the applicants than most of their close friends do. You have tenancy information, employment information, other income information, asset information, credit information, eviction information, personal information, and background information. You need to evaluate this information you have gathered to determine whether these particular applicants would make good tenants for this particular rental dwelling, whether they would be round pegs in a square hole or round pegs in a round hole.

What do you look for? You look for *wincers*, items which cause you to wince and wonder whether you ought to accept these applicants as your tenants.

Remember, nobody this side of heaven is perfect. You're not looking for just one wincer, unless it alone is egregious enough to disqualify the applicants, you're looking for a number of them. You're creating a profile.

Here are the wincers you should look for—

Personal information (from application, conversation, personal visit to the applicant's current home, and personal observation)

Incomplete application

Sloppy application

No telephone

No driver's license or other "official" identification

Poor hygiene and grooming

Expectations of a big lawsuit payoff

Excessive anxiety about moving in right away

Careless handling of a cigarette

Tenancy information

Current housing–relatives or friends

Current housing–motel or van

Little or no information about previous landlords

Repeated moves

History of late payments

No notice of intent to vacate

Attempt to apply security deposit to last month's rent

Employment/Income information

No job

New job

Frequent job changes

Insufficient income

No income documentation

Asset information

No savings account

No checking account

Bad checks

Insufficient move-in monies

No car

Car dented, broken down, or abused

Credit information

No credit history

Low credit score

No credit cards

Credit cards with high balances

Bill collections

Retail accounts with high balances

Numerous inquiries into their credit history

History of late payments

Recent bankruptcy or foreclosure

Car loan arrearages

Car repossession

Home foreclosure

Eviction information

Move demanded by previous landlord

Defendant in an eviction

Eviction judgment on record

Background information

Violent crime on criminal record

Sex offense

Numerous traffic violations

Social Security number falsification

Has nothing you know about these applicants so far started you wincing? Good, good! Maybe, just maybe, they're the good tenants you're looking for.

■ **An Aside**—The screwups, bad actors, deadbeats, and scofflaws of this world who make terrible tenants and who account for fewer than 6% of all tenants, have reveled in playing their "Dupe the Landlord" game for years. They would find some landlord somewhere to rent to them without checking their references, and then they would proceed to make that landlord's life miserable, paying their rent in promises all the while they were destroying the property and staying put until the very last moment when an officer of the law arrived on their doorstep to remove them from the premises.

Only recently has the game's playing field been cleared and leveled. The bulldozer responsible for making this change in the playing field is the enormous database of personal information which agencies gather daily and make readily and cheaply available to those making decisions about granting credit to borrowers and entrusting rental property to tenants.

No longer can terrible tenants hide their wicked ways so easily as they once did. They leave crumbs behind every time they fail to pay a bill, every time they pass a bad check, every time they declare bankruptcy, every time they get arrested, every time they change jobs, and every time they become evicted. Put together, those crumbs take shape and tell you what you need to know when you're deciding whether to entrust your property to them.

As a landlord with a signed rental application, you have legitimate access to that information, and you should use it when checking out applicants unless you have a very good reason not to.

More and more landlords are using the bulldozer on the playing field and are winning at "Dupe the Landlord." A bulldozer may seem to be a heavy-handed approach to weeding out terrible tenants and winning the game. It isn't. It's only fair play. Besides, it works. I know it works. I know because the self-storage managers in my area have told me that the obviously recognizable terrible tenants of rental dwellings are leaving their worldly goods in storage longer and longer between moves.

■ **Handling A Special Situation**—Every so often you will want to check the references of applicants who look outstanding both on paper and in person, but because it's a holiday weekend at the end of the month and you can't complete a proper screening, you're stymied. The information you need to make your decision is simply unavailable for a few days. What might you do? Here are four possibilities—

1) Who says you can't complete a proper screening on a holiday weekend? You can, that is, you can if you're already set up to use an internet screening service. Computers generate screening services' reports, and their computers work 24/7/365. You place your order on their website, and before you can say "Rumplestiltskin," it's ready. You don't need to ask a human in Dallas, Dublin, or Delhi to generate it for you.

If you're already using an internet screening service and you encounter this special situation, you'd be stymied only if you need to follow up on the screening reports and the people you need to contact are unavailable.

2) If you're not already using an internet screening service and you have no way to check the applicants' credit history and background over a holiday weekend, tell them they'll have to wait until you can check their references as you normally do. Apologize that you're unable to check their references immediately, but assure them that you will check everything as soon as the holiday weekend is over.

The advantage of this option is that you run little risk of renting to the professional deadbeats who will try to rush you into renting to them before you can check them out. They know you won't rent to them if you do take the time to check them out

The disadvantage of this option is that you risk losing good tenants who will likely continue looking around until they find another suitable place which they can rent without having to wait for clearance. Take the risk rather than risk renting to somebody you wouldn't have rented to had you known more about them.

3) There's a price you pay for using this option, but it's a well defined price and the technique provides protection against renting to deadbeats.

Tell the applicants to find accommodations for the entire weekend if necessary and tell them you will deduct, say, $70 from their first month's rent for every night they have to sleep at a motel, provided, of course, that their references do check out and that you do rent to them. If you have to pay for two or three nights' lodging in order to secure good tenants, the expense is money well spent compared to the loss you would sustain if you had to evict problem tenants.

4) The fourth option is a little more creative and requires some special shrewdness to carry off, but it is almost as cautious as the others, and it usually settles the matter quite sufficiently. Ask the applicants to show you their latest rent receipts and their latest payroll stubs. If current, a rent receipt will verify an applicant's tenancy, and a payroll stub will verify employment and wages.

Since few people carry these two items around with them and since the rent receipt could be forged pretty easily if the applicants were to leave your sight after you have made the request, refrain from requesting the rent receipt unless you are visiting the applicants at their current residence in the next step. A payroll stub, on the other hand, is more difficult to forge, so have no qualms about asking to see one when you first decide to try this option. If the applicants claim to have stubs at home, tell them you'll meet them there shortly.

When you arrive, ask to see both their payroll stubs and rent receipts. With the latest rent receipt in hand, check whether the rent is current, whether the address for the rental property is the same as the address shown on their application, and whether the manager who signed the receipt has the same name as the one given on their application. Note the Social Security number shown on the payroll stub and verify that it's the same one given on the application.

Also, check the year-to-date total wages to determine how much the applicants have been making. Year-to-date wages yield a more complete picture of their employment history than the amount paid for any given pay period. Seasonal workers might be making large sums for a few months during the year and nothing at other times. Calculate how much they are making per

Co-Signer Agreement Dated _June 19, XXXX_
(Addendum to Rental Agreement)

This agreement is attached to and forms a part of the Rental Agreement dated ___6/19/XX___ between ___Vernon Graves___, Owners, and ___Dana Levno___, Tenants.

My name is ___Ellen Levno___.

I have completed a Rental Application for the express purpose of enabling the Owners to check my credit. I have no intention of occupying the dwelling referred to in the Rental Agreement above.

I have read the Rental Agreement, and I promise to guarantee the Tenants' compliance with the financial obligations of this Agreement.

I understand that I may be required to pay for rent, cleaning charges, or damage assessments in such amounts as are incurred by the Tenants under the terms of this Agreement if, and only if, the Tenants themselves fail to pay.

I also understand that this Co-Signer Agreement will remain in force throughout the entire term of the Tenants' tenancy, even if their tenancy is extended and/or changed in its terms.

I am paying the sum of ten dollars ($10) as a consideration of acceptance of this Co-Signer Agreement by all parties concerned.

_____
                    Co-Signer

_____
            Accepted by Owner/Manager

Page __6__ of __6__

month, and determine from that whether they can afford to pay the monthly rent. You want to insure that there is a steady income stream, for rent comes due month after month. You know that. They may not be thinking about it.

■ **Handling Another Special Situation**—Your rental applicants may have good credit, poor credit, or no credit established at all. You'll want to eliminate those with poor credit, of course, but you may want to consider renting to those who have never established credit before.

Let's say that your applicant is a twenty-one-year-old registered nurse who's always lived at home before and has just taken a new job in the area. She hasn't had the time or the opportunity to build a tenancy, employment, or credit record yet. Should you refuse to rent to her for lack of credit references? You may, certainly, but you may be wise to consider renting to her if everything else checks out satisfactorily, and you feel inclined to give her a chance to prove herself. For your own peace of mind, however, you could request that she secure a co-signer, someone who already has an established credit rating which you could check by having the co-signer fill out a separate rental application.

Be as careful in checking the co-signer's credit as you were with the applicant's. If everything checks out satisfactorily, ask the co-signer to sign a Co-Signer Agreement in your presence when you complete the tenant's rental agreement. Completing both agreements either simultaneously or nearly simultaneously will avoid legal hassles later, but if you cannot complete the Co-Signer Agreement and have it signed along with the rental agreement, have it completed before. It should not follow the rental agreement because the rental agreement is dependent upon it.

Try to get a co-signer who lives and owns real estate in the area rather than one who lives elsewhere. You may have to contact that person at some time. You may even have to sue that person at some time. You don't need the aggravation you'd have to endure in trying to collect money from someone who lives out of the area.

With this additional agreement in hand, you reduce the risk involved in renting to someone who lacks established credit. If the tenant turns out to be a deadbeat, you have someone of substance to pursue.

6) Visit the applicants' current home.

If everything about the applicants checks out satisfactorily so far, call them on the phone and arrange to visit them shortly at the place where they are currently living.

Much as you might like to show up without letting them know you're coming, you'll find that calling them first will insure that they'll be at home when you arrive and save you a wasted trip if they're not at home. You are not trying to catch them completely off guard, only slightly off guard. You might want to invent an appropriate pretext for the visit, perhaps that you need to review their application with them or that you need more information about the credit and personal references given on their application, but the main reason for this visit is to see how the applicants live and to meet all those who will become your tenants.

Taking a look at where the applicants live now is like looking at the parents of a person you're planning to marry. The mother is a preview of what the daughter will look like in twenty-five years. The father is a preview of what the son will look like in twenty-five years. The place where the applicants live now is a preview of what your rental dwelling will look like in six months. You don't need a crystal ball to look into the future.

Disclosure of Information on Lead-Based Paint and/or Lead-Based Paint Hazards

Lead Warning Statement

Housing built before 1978 may contain lead-based paint. Lead from paint, paint chips, and dust can pose health hazards if not managed properly. Lead exposure is especially harmful to young children and pregnant women. Before renting pre-1978 housing, lessors must disclose the presence of known lead-based paint and/or lead-based paint hazards in the dwelling. Lessees must also receive a federally approved pamphlet on lead poisoning prevention.

Lessor's Disclosure

(a) Presence of lead-based paint and/or lead-based paint hazards (check (i) or (ii) below):

(i) _____ Known lead-based paint and/or lead-based paint hazards are present in the housing (explain).

_____

(ii) __X__ Lessor has no knowledge of lead-based paint and/or lead-based paint hazards in the housing.

(b) Records and reports available to the lessor (check (i) or (ii) below):

(i) _____ Lessor has provided the lessee with all available records and reports pertaining to lead-based paint and/or lead-based paint hazards in the housing (list documents below).

_____

(ii) __X__ Lessor has no reports or records pertaining to lead-based paint and/or lead-based paint hazards in the housing.

Lessee's Acknowledgment (initial)

(c) _____ Lessee has received copies of all information listed above.

(d) *HL BL* Lessee has received the pamphlet *Protect Your Family from Lead in Your Home.*

Agent's Acknowledgment (initial)

(e) _____ Agent has informed the lessor of the lessor's obligations under 42 U.S.C. 4852(d) and is aware of his/her responsibility to ensure compliance.

Certification of Accuracy

The following parties have reviewed the information above and certify, to the best of their knowledge, that the information they have provided is true and accurate.

Lester Landlord 7/25/xx		
Lessor	Date	
Harold Link 7/25/xx	Lessor Bella Link 7/25/xx	
Lessee Date	Lessee Date	
_____	_____	
Agent Date	Agent Date	

All you need to do is visit the applicants' current home, and you'll see the future of your rental property with these applicants as its tenants.

If the applicants presently live too far away for you to make a visit, you may have to skip this step, but do so reluctantly.

On your arrival, say a few pleasantries and then begin asking questions such as these: "I see here that you work at Dario's Pizza Parlor. What are your hours there? Do you receive any commissions in addition to your regular salary? How long have you been banking at Midtown Bank? Is Cash Kramer still the manager there? Did you attend school in this area? How long have you lived around here? What keeps you living in this area?" and so on.

While you're conversing, strain your peripheral vision so hard that you'll need peripheral-vision glasses on your temples some day. Look around for various indications of how well these prospective tenants care for the place where they currently live. Is there a half-assembled motorcycle in the living room? How many holes are there in the walls and doors? Are there burns in the carpets? What shape is their furniture in? How's the housekeeping? How closely does this place resemble the dwelling they wish to rent from you? The closer the resemblance, the better they will be as your tenants.

Also, look and listen for pets and people likely to make the move with the household. You might expect that the springer spaniel asleep on the sofa will make the move. If he doesn't appear on the application, ask why he doesn't. If they say they're planning to get rid of old Rufus, make a note of their answer and judge for yourself whether they're telling the truth.

If you hear two kids raising Cain somewhere out of sight and it appears to be the kind of dispute that siblings usually have, you can assume that these offspring will both be accompanying the adult applicants in the move. If only one kid appears on the application, inquire into the matter.

If the adults say they're trying to get a former spouse to take one of the kids, ask for more information. Ask what can they tell you about custody. Ask where the former spouse lives. Ask whether you might contact the former spouse, and if so, how you might make the contact. Ask when they expect the former spouse to take the kid. If you can, ask the kids why they're moving

and compare their answer with the one given on the application.

At some time during your visit, if you haven't done so before, say that you'd like to see the applicants' driver's licenses, or another form of identification bearing their photographs, and some major credit cards so you can verify the numbers. When you have them in hand, check to see whether the numbers and the signatures match those shown on the applications, note the full names (including middle names), and record the birth dates.

If you have any doubts about the applicants after this interview, say only that you want to check the applications further and leave, but if everything meets with your approval, proceed at once with the next three steps.

7) **Review your rules, requirements, and policies, and satisfy the various disclosure requirements.**

Before you finally commit yourself to accept any applicants as your tenants, review your rules, requirements, and policies with them in order to avoid possible ambiguities and prevent later misunderstandings (your rules ought to be in writing; see chapter 22 for suggestions). Remember that at this time, while you are talking with the tenants before they move in, you can get them to agree more readily to strict terms than you can at any later time.

Discuss your rules, requirements, and policies regarding the following: deposits, rent collections, rent payment, first month's rent, last month's rent, guests, smoking, parties, quiet hours, parking, utilities, garbage, pets, waterbeds, hanging things on the walls, changing locks, painting, maintenance, emergencies, window breakage, drain stoppages, lockouts, and renters' insurance. Add to this list any other special considerations which may apply to your situation such as pool hours and whether the pool is heated. Be candid. You want your new tenants to have realistic expectations about living there.

Indicate that you are especially concerned that they keep the dwelling clean, that they be relatively quiet, and that they pay their rent promptly. Tell them that you are quick to evict tenants who do not abide by the rules and ask them whether they think they can live there in your rental under those circumstances. If they agree, and you believe them, commit yourself to rent the place to them.

Notice and Release Agreement--Mold and Radon

Property Address: ___456 Sweet St., Littletown, CA___

Mold is a general term for the visible growth of fungus, whether it is
plainly visible or whether it is visible only when barriers like building
components, such as walls, or furnishings, such as carpets, are removed.

Radon is an invisible, odorless, radioactive gas.

**TENANTS ARE HEREBY NOTIFIED, AND UNDERSTAND, THAT CERTAIN MOLDS AND
RADON HAVE THE POTENTIAL TO CAUSE SERIOUS HEALTH PROBLEMS.**

**TENANTS ARE ENCOURAGED TO OBTAIN THE SERVICES OF A QUALIFIED AND
EXPERIENCED PROFESSIONAL TO CONDUCT INSPECTIONS AND TESTS REGARDING
MOLD AND RADON PRIOR TO THEIR COMMITTING TO RENT.**

Tenants acknowledge and accept that the property described above is being
offered for rent with no representations as to its condition regarding mold
or radon. The owners of the property have no knowledge of mold or radon in,
on, or around the property other than the following:

_____*none known*_____.

Tenants represent and warrant that they have not relied on the accuracy or
completeness of any representations that have been made by the owners as to
the presence of mold or radon and that the tenants have not relied on the
owners' failure to provide information regarding the presence or effects of
any mold or radon found on the property.

Tenants are hereby notified and agree that they are solely responsible for
any required remediation and/or resulting damages, including, but not limited
to, any effects on health, due to mold or radon in, on, or around the
property.

In consideration of the rental of the property to the undersigned tenants,
they do hereby release, indemnify, hold harmless and forever discharge the
owners of the property from any and all claims, liabilities, or causes of
action of any kind that the tenants may have now or at any time in the future
against the owners from the presence of mold or radon in, on, or around the
property.

Tenants have been given the opportunity to review this release agreement with
their attorney or other advisors of their own choosing, and hereby
acknowledge reading and understanding this release. Tenants also understand
that the promises, representations, and warranties made in this release are a
material inducement for the owners to enter into the agreement to rent the
property to tenants.

Date: ___5-1-XXXX___

Richard Renter   *Rose Renter*
Tenant's Signature   Tenant's Signature

RICHARD RENTER   ROSE RENTER
Tenant's Printed Name   Tenant's Printed Name

Before you go any further in renting to these tenants, however, you *must* satisfy the mandatory federal lead-based paint regulations which apply to dwellings built prior to 1978, and you should discuss the subjects of mold and radon with them and get them to sign a notice and release agreement.

To satisfy the lead-based paint regulations, you *must* disclose whatever you know about lead-based paint in the dwelling, you *must* give the tenants a sixteen-page EPA (Environmental Protection Agency) pamphlet entitled "Protect Your Family from Lead in Your Home" (available from many sources, including HUD's website (hud.gov) and EPA's website (epa.gov), and both you and the tenants *must* sign a statement entitled "Disclosure of Information on Lead-Based Paint and/or Lead-Based Paint Hazards."

Because mold and radon have become such contentious issues, you should discuss the subjects (see chapter 18 for discussions of both) with them and get them to sign the Notice and Release Agreement–Mold and Radon. Not only does a discussion of the subjects let the tenants know that you are aware of the dangers of mold and radon and that you want to protect them from those dangers, but the notice/agreement will give you a leg to stand on if you find yourself hauled into court for supposedly failing to protect the tenants from those dangers.

8) Fill out and sign the rental agreement.

Now put in writing most of what you have already agreed upon verbally. Use a simply worded rental agreement (see chapter 5 for a more comprehensive agreement than the one shown here), one which most tenants can easily understand. In fact, you should use agreements written not only so they can be understood, but also so they cannot be misunderstood.

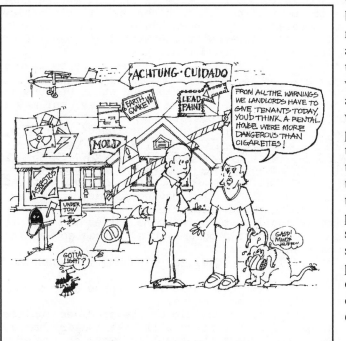

Explain every bit of your agreement to your new tenants, word for word. Give them blank copies and read everything to them as you are filling in the blanks. Many adults cannot read, and many others won't read anything thrust at them for their signatures. They'll simply sign. Because the rental agreement is so important to your future relationship with these people, read it to them now in order to avoid misunderstandings later.

If you decide to give tenants a discount or a rebate for paying on time instead of adding a late charge when they're late, explain that the monthly rental figure used in the agreement is higher than what you advertised because this gross rent includes an amount, usually between $10 and $20, which is granted as a discount or rebate when the rent is paid on or before the late date. Tell them you advertise the net rent because that's what most people pay. Make sure they understand this rent policy before you continue (see discussion in chapter 6).

If you know that the laws and courts in your area will permit you to charge new tenants something, anything, to cover some of your costs in servicing new tenants, then consider charging a higher first month's rent. Now is the time to discuss the matter with the new tenants. Explain that the first month's rent is higher than the usual rent because it is supposed to cover some of the many costs connected with a new tenancy, costs such as cleaning the carpets and drapes (tell them they won't have to clean the carpets or drapes or wax the floors when they move out; tell them that move-in costs are borne by those who cause them, new tenants; otherwise the rents would have to be higher for everyone), advertising, showing the dwelling, checking credit, and changing locks. Tell them that the difference

Rental Agreement

Dated January 15, XXXX

(Month-to-Month)

Agreement between Lester Landlord , Owners,
and RICHARD and ROSE L. RENTER , Tenants, for a dwelling
located at 456 Sweet Street, LITTLETOWN, CALIFORNIA .
Tenants agree to rent this dwelling on a month-to-month basis for $ 778 per
month, payable in advance on the 1ST day of every calendar month to Owners
or their Agent*, X X X X X , whose address is
453 Sweet Street, Littletown, CA 09090 .
When rent is paid on or before the 4th day of the calendar month, Owners
will give Tenants a (discount) (rebate) of $ 20 .

The first month's rent for this dwelling is $ 880 .

The security/cleaning deposit on this dwelling is $ 1,000 . It is
refundable if Tenants leave the dwelling reasonably clean and undamaged.

Tenants will give 15 days' notice in writing before they move and will
be responsible for paying rent through the end of this notice period or until
another tenant approved by the Owners has moved in, whichever comes first.

Owners will refund all deposits due within 7 days after Tenants have
moved out completely and returned their keys.

Only the following 2 persons and Ø pets are to live in this dwelling:
RICHARD and ROSE RENTER .
Without Owners' prior written permission, no other persons may live there,
and no other pets may stay there, even temporarily, nor may the dwelling be
sublet or used for business purposes.

Use of the following is included in the rent: CARPETS, DRAPES, SHADES
and STOVE. REFIGERATOR on TEMPORARY LOAN.

Remarks: WATER and GARBAGE PAID BY OWNERS. TENANTS PAY
ALL OTHER UTILITIES. PARKING IN SPACE #2. OCCUPANCY CONTINGENT
TENANTS AGREE TO THE FOLLOWING: UPON EXISTING TENANTS VACATING THE PREMISES.

1) to accept the dwelling "as is," having already inspected it.
2) to keep yards and garbage areas clean.
3) to keep from making loud or bothersome noises and disturbances and to
   play music and broadcast programs at all times so as not to disturb other
   people's peace and quiet.
4) not to paint or alter the dwelling without first getting Owners' written
   permission.
5) to park their motor vehicle in assigned space and to keep that space
   clean of oil drippings and grease.
6) not to repair their motor vehicle on the premises (unless it is in an
   enclosed garage) if such repairs will take longer than a single day.
7) to allow Owners to inspect the dwelling, work on it, or show it to
   prospective tenants at any and all reasonable times.
8) ~~not to keep any liquid-filled furniture in this dwelling.~~ RR XX
9) to pay rent by check or money order made out to Owners. (Checks must be
   good when paid or applicable late-payment consequences will apply.)
10) to pay for repairs of all damage, including drain stoppages, they or
    their guests have caused.
11) to pay for any windows broken in their dwelling while they live there.

Violation of any part of this Agreement or nonpayment of rent when due
shall be cause for eviction under applicable code sections. The prevailing
party (shall) (~~shall not~~) recover reasonable legal services fees involved.

Tenants hereby acknowledge that they have read this Agreement, understand
it, agree to it, and have been given a copy.

Owner Lester Landlord , Tenant Richard Renter

*By_____ Tenant Rose Renter

*Person authorized to accept legal service on Owners' behalf

Pg 1 of 3

between the first month's rent and the rent for succeeding months is in no way to be considered a deposit. It is not a deposit. It represents an all-inclusive charge to new tenants only for the services which they alone require.

I should mention here as an aside that landlords and tenants have done battle for years over move-in costs. Landlords have always maintained that new tenants should pay for the extra costs involved in a change of tenancy, and tenants have always maintained that these costs are nothing more than the ordinary costs of doing business, and as such, they should be absorbed into the regular rent. Personally, I feel that tenants who stay put should not be subsidizing those who don't. Tenants who come and go are more expensive to deal with, and consequently, they should pay something more. In times past, some landlords have collected this "something more" in devious ways, most notably by withholding deposits, and tenants have screamed loudly enough so that laws to curb these devious ways are now on the books in many jurisdictions.

The best way I have found to charge new tenants something more to offset move-in costs is to charge a higher first month's rent, just as tool rental yards charge one hourly rate for the first four hours and another hourly rate for the balance of a twenty-four-hour period. If you explain your reasons to your tenants at the outset of their tenancy, there won't be any confusion about refundability later. It won't be an issue.

You should know, however, that some California tenants have challenged the legality of charging a higher first month's rent, arguing through some pretty tortuous reasoning that the extra rent is in reality a deposit and therefore refundable. Rather than come under legal attack as a landlord doing business in California, a state with laws and courts which favor tenants in too many ways, I decided reluctantly to stop charging a higher first month's rent. You will have to decide for yourself whether you can use it in the area where you do business. Either put a higher sum in the rental agreement's blank for first month's rent and explain why you're doing it, or put the regular month's rent in the blank. The decision is yours.

Next, explain what your policy is regarding deposits, that you lump all deposits together so that any of the money might be used for damages, extraordinary cleaning costs, unpaid rent,

or other accrued and unpaid charges. Tell them that you make no distinction as to what is a cleaning deposit, what is a security deposit, and what is a key deposit. Tell them that you will give them their deposits back after they move out so long as they leave the place reasonably clean and undamaged and give proper notice and furthermore, that you *want* to give them their money back because you'd rather do that than have to clean up after them and have to chase after them for their rent. Tell them that you're fair about returning deposits, and if appropriate, tell them to check with the departing tenants if they don't believe you. Also tell them whether you will be paying them interest on their deposits and if so, when. In some areas it's mandatory; in others, it's voluntary.

Tell them how much notice they should give you before they plan to vacate. Thirty days is most common, but I use fifteen because that's all the time I really need to prepare for a vacancy, and fifteen days is much more realistic for tenants. It has another important side benefit for you as well, one which I'll explain in step nine.

Ask for the names of all persons and pets who will be living in the dwelling, and write them into the agreement by name. Explain that nobody else may live there without your written permission, even temporarily. Tell them that their "guests" become tenants after two weeks (in some areas, laws may set the guest limit for a longer period, up to one month, and may allow any one person to be a guest twice in one year; check the applicable law for your area) and will have to be approved and added to the agreement at a slight increase in rent. Tell them what your pet policy is (see "Should You Accept Pets?" in chapter 13). If it's a no-pets policy, tell them exactly what you mean by "no pets." Point out the words "even temporarily" in the contract. Tell them that those words mean what they say. You do not allow pet-sitting for even five minutes.

List briefly the appliances and furnishings which are included in the rent and indicate whether any of them are on "loan" (see "Should You Furnish the Major Kitchen Appliances?" in chapter 13). Explain that you and they together will make a complete on-site survey of the dwelling using the Condition & Inventory Checksheet as a record.

Explain which utilities you pay for and which parking space or garage the tenants may use, and

Availability of Information Regarding Registered Sex Offenders

(Addendum to Rental Agreement)

This disclosure is attached to and forms a part of the Rental Agreement dated ___9-26-XX___ between ___Vernon Graves___, Owners, and ___Richard Renter___, Tenants.

The following text applies in California only:
Notice: Pursuant to Section 290.46 of the Penal Code, information about specified registered sex offenders is made available to the public via an Internet Web site maintained by the Department of Justice at www.meganslaw.ca.gov. Depending on an offender's criminal history, this information will include either the address at which the offender resides or the community of residence and ZIP Code in which he or she resides.

The following text applies in states other than California:
Notice: The state justice department, sheriff's departments, police departments serving jurisdictions of 200,000 or more and many other local law enforcement authorities maintain for public access a data base of the locations of persons required to register pursuant to "Megan's Law" or a similar statute. The data base is updated on a regular basis and is a source of information about the presence of these individuals in any neighborhood. Contact the state justice department to determine whether it also maintains a telephone service through which inquiries about individuals may be made.

The following acknowledge that the Owner or Owner's Agent whose signature appears below has provided a copy of this Rental Agreement Addendum to the Tenant(s) whose signature(s) appear(s) below.

Date___9/26/XX___ Tenant ___Richard Renter___

Date_____ Tenant _____

Date___9-26-XX___ Owner or Manager___Leslie Landlady___

PAGE 4 of 4

indicate this information under "Remarks."

Also, if the rental is still being occupied, stipulate here that the agreement is contingent upon the other tenants vacating the premises (see "Two Tenants—One Rental Dwelling" in chapter 22).

Review once more the other requirements in the agreement just as you did in step seven. Remind them that they are responsible for any drain or sewer blockages which they themselves cause. Tell them that you don't use their drains and you aren't going to unclog their drains or pay to have them unclogged unless the tenants can prove to your satisfaction that the *building* was at fault. Remind them that they are responsible for any windows broken in their rental dwelling regardless of who breaks them, and remind them that they shouldn't expect you to provide lockout service 24 hours a day free of charge. Explain that the regulations will be strictly enforced and that after fair warning, you will evict them for any violations.

Read in chapter 5 about the pros and cons of asking for legal services (attorney) fees, and decide whether to put the word "not" in the blank to indicate that you do not want the prevailing party to recover reasonable fees or whether to put a horizontal line in the blank to indicate the opposite.

If applicable, complete roommate, pet, cosigner, and waterbed agreements, and an addendum disclosing the availability, per Megan's Law, of information regarding registered sex offenders.

Finally, sign the Rental Agreement yourself and have the tenants sign. Give them a copy and keep one for your records.

9) Request all monies or a hefty deposit.

Think back for a moment to step two, "Prequalify the Prospects," and remember two of the questions you asked then to determine the following—when the prospects would be ready to move in and whether they would have the money necessary to move in. If their answers to these questions satisfied you then and if they were truthful answers, you'll be able to conclude this initial phase of your rental relationship with relative ease.

At this point you have a signed agreement in hand and you have taken the dwelling off the market. So, as far as you are concerned, the place is now rented and the rent should begin today or tomorrow, but if the tenants cannot move in for a week or so, you might consider splitting the rent with them for this short period as a goodwill gesture. For example, if you come to terms with them on Monday, March 10th, and they can't move in until Wednesday, March 19th, you might begin their rent with March 14th. Whatever you do, though, don't split rents for more than two weeks, don't do it if the tenants are going to be moving in immediately, and don't do it at all around the first of the month. Above all, don't come to terms with prospective tenants, tie up the place for a week or two while they are preparing to move, and then begin the rent from the day they actually move in. That's not a goodwill gesture at all. That's a foolish gesture, for you suffer the full loss of rents due to circumstances which are beyond your control. It's their problem that they can't move in, not yours. You're ready for them to move in now. Share the loss, if you're inclined to, but don't assume it all yourself.

If you and the Richard Renters agree that their rent should begin March 14th, then their rental period for that first month is March 14th through April 13th. Since you probably want their rent to be due on the first (see chapter 6 about the advisability of having rents due on the first) of the month, prorate their rent the second month, not the first. Request the full month's rent when they move in as a full commitment from them and a kind of insurance for you.

On April 1st, collect rent to cover the period April 14th through April 30th. Make a point of telling them that the prorated rent for the balance of April is due on the first of April, not on the fourteenth, the same as it would be if they owed rent for the entire month. Keep them a full month ahead during this crucial early period of tenancy when you are just getting to know them and you don't know yet how dependable they are.

Be careful when you prorate rent. You can cheat yourself quite easily doing proration calculations. Consider the period of April 14th through April 30th, for example; is it 16 days or is it 17? It may appear to be 16 because the difference between 30 and 14 is 16, as every sixth grader knows, but it's not. It's not because this period includes both the 14th *and* the 30th, as well as the days in between. To calculate the number of days correctly, you have to subtract 14 from 30 and add one. If that doesn't make much sense to

Agreement to Hold Dwelling Off the Market

RECEIVED FROM ___Marion Mahnken___, Approved Applicant,
the sum of ___nine hundred dollars ————___ $___900—___.

$___300—___ of this sum is <u>nonrefundable</u>. It shall be used for the purpose of holding off the market the rental dwelling commonly known as

___1100 Staples Ave., Apt. 716___

for the period from ___8/26/xx___ through ___9/05/xx___ only.

$___600—___ of this sum is <u>refundable</u> if approved applicant does not move in. If applicant moves in, it shall be applied to move-in monies.

The applicant whose name appears above has been approved to rent the dwelling identified above but for one reason or another cannot take possession now.

The applicant has read and approved the rental agreement but has not paid all of the sums required to move in. The applicant has no right to receive keys or take possession of the dwelling until all of the sums required to take possession have been paid in full.

The owner/manager retains possession of the dwelling under this agreement and is obligated to safeguard it and maintain its condition so that it does not deteriorate during the term of this agreement. If it is materially damaged, applicant shall receive a refund of all monies paid.

At least twenty-four hours prior to the termination of this agreement, the applicant must notify the owner/manager of his/her intentions to take possession or not take possession of the dwelling. Notice must be made in writing and delivered to the owner/manager during normal business hours (9am-5pm) at the owner/manager's address shown below.

Should the applicant fail to notify the owner/manager of his/her intentions to take possession as outlined above, owner/manager will put the dwelling back on the market upon the termination of this agreement.

Should the applicant take possession of the dwelling prior to the termination of this agreement, the applicant will be credited as having paid rent through the termination date of this agreement, and this agreement will then be superseded by the rental agreement.

Should the applicant not take possession of the dwelling prior to or upon the expiration of this agreement, the owner/manager will keep the entire nonrefundable sum paid as consideration for having held the rental dwelling off the market for the time period specified above and will refund the applicant's refundable sum within forty-eight hours.

8/26/xx 10:30 A.M.	Marion Mahnken
Date/Time	Approved Applicant--Name / Signature
	657-11th St., #108 555-1937
	Address / Phone
8/26/xx 10:30 Am	Suzie Que - Manager
Date/Time	Owner/Manager--Name / Signature
	1100 Staples Ave. #201 555-1109
	Address / Phone

you, count the days on your fingers and toes, and you'll see that 17 is correct. Once you know the correct number, divide the monthly rent by the total number of days in the month and multiply that figure, which is the rent per day, by the number of days the tenants are going to be occupying the premises. Tell them what this amount is even before they move in so they will know how much to set aside to pay you on the first of the following month.

As for advance money, you should request as much as you can get from new tenants. How much is enough? Whatever the market will bear and the laws will allow. Some local laws restrict advance money for unfurnished dwellings to the equivalent of three months' rent and for furnished dwellings to four months' rent. That should be sufficient. All told, that would work out to the first month's rent and combined deposits for security, cleaning, pets, waterbed, and keys equal to two months' rent.

Unless the laws in your area specify exactly what you are allowed to collect in the categories of first month's rent, last month's rent, and combined deposits, do not require any last month's rent at all. Instead, add an equivalent amount to the deposits. Make the deposits larger because you can use them to offset repairs, cleaning, or rent, whereas whatever sum is designated as last month's rent must be used for last month's rent and nothing else.

Last month's rent also must be reported immediately as income, whereas deposits are not considered income until they are used. They're limbo monies.

There is, of course, always the problem of tenants who want to use all or part of their deposits for last month's rent, and there's not much you can do about it except to require high deposits in the beginning and stress that these deposits are *not* to be considered last month's rent. So long as you hold a deposit significantly higher than their last month's rent, you won't have too much cause for concern if tenants try to apply their deposits to the last month's rent.

Another solution to this problem is to require less than thirty days' notice to vacate. If you require only a fifteen-day notice, the tenants' rental period and the notice period do not coincide, and tenants are less likely to think about using their deposits for rent. In most cases, when they do decide to give notice, they will already have

paid their last month's rent two weeks before and won't be tempted to use their deposits for rent.

Much as you'd like to get the equivalent of three months' rent before tenants move in, you can't always get it, so you should have a minimum, too. The minimum amount to request before letting tenants move in under a month-to-month agreement, no matter which day of the month they do so, is the sum of the first month's rent, a security/cleaning deposit equal to one month's rent minus $25, and a two-dollar deposit for each key. Consider that the minimum.

In bygone days when anybody could buy a new tract house for no money down, I used to request less than this minimum in order to be competitive, but I wound up losing too much to unscrupulous tenants. That's Lesson Number 206 at Hard Knocks College—*Require plenty of upfront money.* For some strange reason, the greater the deposit, the more tenants will do to get it back. Hmm! Imagine that!

The more advance money you require, the better you're protected, but the harder becomes the search for new tenants who have a large advance sum.

To help you decide how much to require, inquire into the prevailing practice in your rental area and then follow suit.

No matter how much or how little you require, you will find that some people won't have on hand all the money they need to move in.

If they cannot pay you all the rent and deposits immediately, accept a minimum of half a month's rent, and use a form like the Agreement to Hold Dwelling Off the Market to establish without a doubt what your relationship is at this point and how their monies are to be used.

Make no mistakes here. Mistakes here can be very costly and very regrettable. People who have been approved to rent from you and have given you only a portion of their move-in monies are not your tenants yet until you give them possession, and you should not give them possession until they have paid all of their move-in monies. Just by giving them the keys, you are giving them possession and the rights of tenancy. *Do not give them the keys until they have paid you all of their move-in monies.*

If you do give them possession before they pay all of their move-in monies and if things go awry at the very beginning of your landlord-tenant relationship, you will have to evict them, and

Condition & Inventory Checksheet

Tenants: RICHARD and ROSE RENTER   Dated: JAN. 15, XXXX

Address: 456 Sweet St., Littletown

Date Moved In: 1/15/XX   Notice Given: _____   Moved Out: _____

Abbreviations:

Air Cond, AC	Clean, Cl	Drape, Drp	Hood, Hd	OK, OK	Table, Tbl
Bed, Bd	Cracked, Cr	Dryer, Dry	Just Painted, JP	Poor, P	Tile, Tl
Broken, Brk	Curtain, Ctn	Fair, F	Lamp, Lmp	Refrigerator, Rf	Venet'n Blind, VB
Carpet, Cpt	Dinette, Din	Good, G	Lightbulb, LtB	Shade, Sh	Washer, Wsh
Chair, Ch	Dishwasher, Dsh	Heater, Htr	Linoleum, Lino	Sofa, Sfa	Waxed, Wxd
Chest, Chst	Disposer, Dsp	Hole, H	Nightstand, Ntst	Stove, Stv	Wood, Wd

Circle rooms; enter abbreviations	Walls, Doors cond.	chgs.	Floors cond.	chgs.	Windows cond.	chgs.	Lt. Fixtures cond.	chgs.	Inventory: Appliances, Furniture Item	cond.	chgs.
(Living Rm)	OK		CL. Cpt.		wind-cr scrn-OK DRP-OK		θ		θ		
Dining Rm											
(Kitchen)	OK				scrn-OK sh-G		L+B OK		STV, Hd Ref (on loan)	Cl. Cl.	
(Bath 1)	JP				scrn-OK sh-G		Lt B OK				
Bath 2											
(Bedroom 1)	OK				Scrn-OK Drp.-cl		L+B OK		θ		
Bedroom 2											
Bedroom 3											
Other											
Itemized Charges											

TOTAL ITEMIZED CHARGES _____

Other Charges Not Itemized
(Dirty garage, etc.
Explained on Backside) _____

Deduction for Improper Notice _____

Deduction for Missing Keys _____

TOTAL DEDUCTIONS _____

TOTAL DEPOSITS $850

minus (-) TOTAL DEDUCTIONS _____

equals (=) DEPOSIT REFUND
or (Amount Owed) _____

[X] Tenants acknowledge that the smoke detector was tested in their presence and found to be in working order and that its operation was explained to them. Tenants agree to test the detector at least every other week and to report any problems to Owners in writing. If the detector is battery operated, Tenants agree to replace the battery as necessary with a new ALKALINE battery (unless applicable laws require otherwise).

Tenants hereby acknowledge that they have read this Checksheet, agree that the condition and contents of the above-mentioned rental dwelling are without exception as represented herein, understand that they are liable for any damage done to this dwelling as outlined in their Lease or Rental Agreement, and have received a copy of this Checksheet.

Lester Landlord
Owner

_____
BY Person authorized to represent Owners

Richard Renter
Tenant
Rose Renter
Tenant

pg 2 of 3

you will be poorer by hundreds, if not thousands, of dollars. An eviction is a painful procedure, and you want to avoid it whenever possible, especially at this juncture when it's so easily avoidable.

The Agreement to Hold Dwelling Off the Market form refers to these people who don't have all of their move-in monies as "approved applicants," and that's what they are. They are not tenants. It states exactly how long a time they have to come up with the balance of their move-in monies. It states exactly what you will do with the monies if they do come up with the balance. It states exactly what you will do with the monies if they don't come up with the balance. It states exactly when and how they need to notify you of their intention to take possession. It states exactly what you will do if they do not notify you of their intention to take possession.

Use this agreement to avoid confusion whenever you accept monies from approved applicants to hold a rental dwelling off the market. Confusion occurs because tenants tend to think that their monies are a deposit, a refundable deposit. If they do not come up with the balance or if they change their mind and decide not to rent from you, they want you to return their deposit, not just some of it, all of it. Likewise, if they do come up with the balance of the move-in monies and do take possession, they want you to apply all that they paid you initially to their rent and deposits beginning with the very day when they take possession. They don't expect to compensate you for the days you held the dwelling off the market for them and them alone.

Don't be bamboozled! Don't cheat yourself!

Monies which approved applicants give you to hold a rental dwelling off the market are not rent, and they are not a deposit. Neither are they refundable. Those monies compensate you for the rent you would have received had a paying tenant been occupying the dwelling. When you're holding a rental dwelling off the market, you cannot rent it, even for a day, to someone else, and you should not lose income because the approved applicants cannot take possession. That's their problem, and you shouldn't be losing income because of a problem of theirs. You should be charging them for every day you hold the dwelling off the market. The Agreement to Hold Dwelling Off the Market form will help explain the charges before they become an issue of dispute.

When accepting monies to hold a dwelling off the market, go ahead and accept a personal or business check so long as you have enough time to verify that the check has cleared the bank before the approved applicants pay the balance of the money and receive possession.

When accepting move-in monies in full, *never* accept a personal or business check unless you withhold possession until the check actually clears. The check must be at least as good as the greenbacks the government prints before you issue keys.

Otherwise, insist that move-in monies be in the form of greenbacks, gold coins, silver bars, money orders, or cashier's checks.

Under no circumstances should you issue keys so they can move in a "few things." Every last cent of the move-in monies you have agreed upon must be paid first. I repeat. Every last cent of the move-in monies you have agreed upon must be paid first.

Too many landlords get burned by allowing tenants to move in some belongings without their having paid the full amount owed. Once they're in, the tenants pay not a cent more and have to be evicted. Don't get burned with this little ruse.

Be sure to issue a receipt for whatever money they pay. If you don't have a receipt book with you, use the back of the Rental Agreement to write up an itemized receipt, making at least an original and one copy.

10) Create a written and photographic record of the dwelling's condition, contents, and tenants.

"The palest ink is better than the most retentive memory," states an old Chinese proverb. Because you and your nice new tenants will surely differ in your recollections of the rental dwelling as it was when they moved in compared with its condition when they finally do move out, you should have a record of its condition and contents to protect both yourself and them. That record ought to be written, to be sure. It also ought to be photographic, perhaps even videographic.

To make a good photographic record, take at least four inside shots of the areas which tend to show the most damage, and *include the new tenants somewhere in these shots.*

There are three reasons why you should include the new tenants in these shots. First, you should have a photo of them somewhere in your files so you will know how to identify them to a

Date: _____10 / 21 / xx_____

To: _Bourne A. Luzer_____

We appreciate your applying to rent a dwelling from us. We regret to inform you that you will need to continue looking for a place to live somewhere else for the following reasons:

CIRCUMSTANCES

[ ] Dwelling rented to previously approved applicant

[ ] Unsigned application   [ ] Incomplete application

[ ] Discrepancies on application

CREDIT REPORT (If items here are checked, see attachment.)

[ ] Credit not verifiable   [ ] Bankruptcy filed

[ ] Judgments, garnishments, liens   [X] Slow pay

[ ] Account(s) sent for collection   [ ] Low credit score

INCOME/ASSETS

[ ] Income not verifiable   [ ] Insufficient income

[ ] Assets not verifiable   [ ] Insufficient assets

EMPLOYMENT HISTORY

[ ] Employment not verifiable   [X] Unsteady employment

[ ] Temporary employment

TENANCY HISTORY

[ ] Tenancy not verifiable   [ ] Eviction on record

[X] Late payments   [ ] Insufficient funds checks

[ ] Agreement violation(s)   [ ] Lack of cooperation

PERSONAL REFERENCES

[X] References not verifiable   [ ] Negative reference

OTHER REASONS

_____

Your application will remain in our files for a minimum of two years. If you would like to discuss it or our reasons above, please contact us for an appointment.

We wish you good luck in finding an even better place to live.

Sincerely,

Padre D. Clark

process server should you ever have to take them to court. Second, you should have a photo of them to discourage gang activity. Gang members do not want any photographic record linking them to the place where they live. They do not want to be so easily identified to the police. Third, you should have some proof that the photographs of the dwelling were taken right before the tenants moved in. Nothing else you can do will fix these photographs as firmly in time as including the tenants themselves in the photographs. Nobody can dispute later exactly when the photographs were taken. They were taken *before* the tenants moved in, and they showed the fine condition of the dwelling at that time.

If you don't have a digital camera yet, get one and use it for these shots so you know right away what they look like and can keep snapping shot after shot until you are satisfied that you have enough of a photographic record to prove to anybody what the dwelling looked like before the tenants moved in.

To make a good videographic record, turn your camera on and start out by saying into the microphone, "Here we are on such-and-such a date doing a walk-through at such-and-such an address. This rental dwelling will soon be occupied by the so-and-so's whom you can see over there." Pan *slowly* across every bit of the dwelling from room to room while talking into the microphone yourself about what you're looking at and remarking about the condition of the place. You might even ask the new tenants to make some comments about the condition of the place. Their own words will go far to prove to any judge or jury what the place really looked like before the tenants move in, should the matter ever come into dispute.

So much for the pictorial record.

To make a good written record, complete the Condition & Inventory Checksheet. To fill it out properly, show the tenants the smoke alarm paragraph, take them to where the smoke alarm is located, demonstrate how it works, and get them to initial the paragraph to indicate that they know how to look after it. Then go through each room of the dwelling with the tenants, circle the applicable rooms, and fill in the "condition" and "item" columns with the appropriate abbreviations. Do not put anything in the "charges" columns. They're for you to fill in after the tenants have moved out. Now add up the security/clean-

ing, pet, waterbed, and key deposits and write down that sum as the total deposits. Date the checksheet, sign it yourself, and have the tenants sign it as well. Keep the original and a copy and give them a copy.

Later, when the tenants have moved out and are demanding their deposits back, take the original and your copy and make a comparison inspection of the dwelling, marking the charges for broken shades, dirty carpets, etc. (see chapter 8).

Now that you and your new tenants have signed the Rental Agreement, filled out the Condition & Inventory Checksheet, and settled all of your accounts, you should issue keys and change the mailbox label. Both of you are completely committed to one another, having created that special landlord-tenant relationship.

Even after you have completed all ten steps with Richard Renter and have created that special relationship, you and he will still be conjuring up strange mental images of one another, but you will have done all you can do to assure yourself of getting a good tenant. Give him a chance to prove that he is what he seems to be, at the same time you're proving to him that you are what you seem to be.

Rejecting Applicants

Rejecting those applicants whom you believe would be poor tenants for one reason or another is a corollary to this whole process of getting good tenants. Rejection is hard for some people to take, and it is still harder for others to give. Some landlords rent to the first person who expresses an interest in renting their place because they just can't say "no." That kind of timidity you can ill afford. You have to get used to saying "no" in this business every so often, and one of the most important times you'll ever say it is when you refuse to rent to an applicant.

The trick is to say "no" in a kindly way. If you have more than one applicant for a vacancy and the first among them qualified according to all of your standards and also decided to take the place, saying "no" to the others is relatively easy, for you are merely informing the unsuccessful applicants that you have rented the place to somebody else.

In that case, you might call them one by one and say something like this, "Hello, Gulley Jimson, I just wanted to let you know that somebody else rented the house on Sixth Street that

Date: ___8/29/xx___

To: ___Danni De Faltz___

Your application to rent from us has been rejected either partly or solely because of information provided by the following sources:

CREDIT REPORT

[X] Equifax Credit Information Service, P. O. Box 740241, Atlanta, GA 30374-2041; 800.685.1111

[ ] Experian Consumer Assistance, P. O. Box 949, Allen, TX 75002; 800.682.7654

[ ] Trans Union Consumer Relations, P. O. Box 1000, 2 Baldwin Place, Chester, PA 19022; 800.888.4213

[ ] _____

COURT RECORDS REPORT

[ ] American Tenant Screen, 131 N. Narberth Ave., Narberth, PA 19072; 610.664.2323

[ ] _____

BAD CHECK REPORT

[ ] Telecheck Services, P.O. Box 4513, Houston, TX 77210-4513; 800.366.2425

[ ] _____

The federal Fair Credit Reporting Act requires us to reveal the source of whatever credit reports figured in the decision to reject you as an applicant. Please note that the agencies checked above only provided information about you. They did not make the decision, nor can they explain the decision.

Under federal law, you have the right to obtain a free copy of your credit report within sixty days from the date when we inquired about your credit. That was ___8___/___28___/___XX___.

To secure the report, you must provide the following: your full name, your complete mailing address, your residential address if different from your mailing address, your daytime phone number, your employer's name, your Social Security number, your driver's license number and the state where issued (bad checks only), and the name of the company which rejected you. Our company name is ___Madre and Padre Rentals___.

If you believe your report is inaccurate or incomplete, you may contact the agency to dispute its accuracy and insert a 100-word consumer statement of explanation. Assistance is available at the credit reporting agency to help you with the statement.

You may have additional rights under the credit reporting or consumer protection laws of your state. To find out what they are, you may contact your state or local consumer protection agency or the office of your state attorney general. See the government listings in the white pages of your telephone book.

Sincerely,

Padre D. Clark

you were interested in. We had four applications for it, and I sure do wish we'd had four places to rent because all four applicants would have made fine tenants, but unfortunately we had only the one vacancy and we could accommodate only one tenant. We'll certainly keep your application on file in case something else comes up, and we'd like to wish you good luck in finding something else even better suited to your needs. How do you want us to return the deposit you gave us with your application?" This kind of rejection sounds sympathetic enough to be acceptable to practically anybody. It's inoffensive and it's entirely plausible. It works well.

If your dwelling has not been rented, however, such a rejection would be both foolish and risky. Never say a place has been rented unless it actually has been rented. Never say it has been rented in order to dissuade a persistent inquirer or anyone else, for that matter. Such a simpleminded ploy will only cause you trouble. Even when you are not actually discriminating against someone illegally, this falsehood, if discovered, could be construed to be a sign of blatant discrimination, and it could be all the evidence needed by those who thrive on suing unsuspecting landlords for discrimination.

Be more cautious than that. Even when you have yet to find a suitable tenant and you are being pestered for acceptance by undesirable applicants, don't ever resort to saying the place has been rented just to get them off your back. Stall if need be. Say that you turned the applications over to a tenant-screening service and that they are a little slow at times in notifying you of the results. It's not the best approach, but it will suffice for a few days while you pray for good acceptable applicants to come along so you can rent to them and then use the kindly rejection approach on the others.

"Dear Mr. Burns:
 I've got some good news and some bad news for you. The bad news is that you didn't get the apartment you wanted to rent from us on Elm Street, so we're returning your deposit. The good news is that you won yourself $25 for submitting 'The Most Unbelievable Application of the Month'...."

Sometimes the best approach is one which is honest, direct, and timely. It may not appear to be kindly on the surface, but it is, because it deflates the applicants' high hopes for your rental early on so they can realistically assess their prospects and won't waste any more time waiting to hear from you.

Tell the applicants by phone, if possible, that you're sorry they just don't fit your tenant guidelines and that they should begin looking further for housing. They may take the news well, ask you a question or two about other places for rent, say thanks, and say goodbye. If they don't, be as polite as you can be while they argue their case, recount their sad story, bang the receiver in your ear, or string together a few profanities. Don't budge from your decision, no matter what they do or say. You know you don't want them to be your tenants because they don't fit your standards.

Another good direct approach is rejection by letter with the reason or reasons clearly identified. For that, there's a form you may use consisting of seven sections and any number of reasons with checkboxes next to them. As soon as you know that you won't be renting to a particular applicant, complete the form, include whatever deposit monies you must return, make a copy for your records, and send everything off to the applicant.

No matter how you inform the applicants about their having been rejected, you must comply with the federal Fair Credit Reporting Act regulations if one of the reasons for rejecting them was a negative credit report. Check the Federal Trade Commission's (FTC) website (ftc.gov) for the regulations and various examples.

To comply with the regulations, you should

not give or show the rejected applicants the report itself, and you should not show or discuss it with anyone else, either. You should give the applicants the name of the credit reporting agency you used and give them information about how to contact the agency, so they can obtain a complimentary copy of the report within the next sixty days.

The form on page 108, which the FTC refers to as an "adverse action notice," will suffice for compliance with the regulations. It tells the applicants something about their rights, whom to contact and when, and how they can go about adding their own one-hundred-word statement of explanation to their credit report.

Rejecting applicants who want to rent from you is no pleasant task, but it's a very necessary task, one you cannot ignore. Grit your teeth and get it over with. Endure the few unpleasantries right now that your rejection of them might cause, and you won't have to cope with them later as unsuitable tenants.

Some Last Words

This whole process of getting good tenants without rubbing somebody the wrong way, without running afoul of some law or other, without getting sued, without getting cheated, and without getting stuck with the wrong tenants is challenging, even daunting.

It's minefield territory.

Some people would rather put up their hands and surrender than face this minefield and the dire consequences which can result from a single misstep. Such people are not landlord material. They surrender much too easily.

You who are landlord material, you who do not surrender too easily, you can traverse this minefield and get good tenants time and time again. You will learn quickly where to step and where not to step.

Even so, you cannot become complacent about getting good tenants. The minefield is always dangerous. Step through it cautiously.

5 Searching For the Right Rental Agreement

Some poor souls keep searching for the Fountain of Youth as long as they live. You'll be searching for the "right" rental agreement as long as you're in this business. Laws change, practices change, locales change, times change, technology changes, the business climate changes, your property mix changes, and your tenant mix changes. You have to adapt your business practices to these changes or suffer the consequences, whatever they may be.

The rental agreement you use is at the very core of your business. You must feel comfortable with it. You must feel that it covers everything you want it to cover, and you must feel sure that it's as legal as it can be in the very community where you do business.

The Kitchen Sink Agreement

The single-page rental agreement introduced in chapter 4 does not include the proverbial kitchen sink. Nope, it is simple and understandable, and it includes only the essentials needed to formalize a landlord-tenant relationship involving a residence. It is much better than a verbal agreement. That's for sure, but it is not nearly as good as a comprehensive umpteen-page agreement drafted for your particular rental property by an attorney familiar with all the pertinent laws and practices in the locale where the property happens to be. Naturally, such an agreement would include the kitchen sink and maybe a bathroom sink and tub as well.

The trouble with most lengthy agreements, however, be they custom-made or "standard" forms, is that they tend to be repetitive and incomprehensible. They're so full of legal jargon that they don't make much sense to the parties they're supposed to make sense to, and they're so lengthy that you can't possibly review them word for word with new tenants unless you spend half a day pouring over them together. Try reading over a multi-page, small-print agreement with a new tenant sometime, and you'll barely be able to keep from stifling yawns and rolling your eyes as you read all the "wherefores," "whereases," and "hereinafters."

Long agreements aren't necessarily bad, especially not when they're well thought out and well organized. Incomprehensible agreements, on the other hand, are bad. Don't use any agreement, long or short, unless you understand it yourself and are able to explain it to your tenants as you read it over with them. Anything else, especially if it has lots of fine print, may seem sneaky to them, whether it is or not. (One landlady I know goes to all the trouble of writing her rental agreements out by hand. She claims that her tenants trust handwritten documents more than those which are typed or printed, and she feels that her tenants' trust is more important than anything else.)

A rental agreement must communicate the particulars of what you and your tenants have agreed upon, and it must be legally enforceable. That's all. It needn't repeat every last detail of the applicable landlord-tenant laws as some agreements do, and it needn't be written so that only someone with a law degree can understand it.

If you feel somehow vulnerable unless you use a rental agreement lengthy enough to cover almost everything in your landlord-tenant relationships, that is, unless it includes the proverbial kitchen sink, get a long-form agreement from your local rental housing association, or if there is no association in your area, get one from your state rental housing association. You can be sure that their agreement has been reviewed by attorneys who are intimately familiar with the applicable landlord-tenant laws and that it will include every essential element plus a whole lot more. But don't stop there. Read it over carefully. If it doesn't make perfect sense to you, translate it yourself into a more meaningful document so that you understand it well enough to be able to help your tenants understand it also.

Another good cover-all-bases agreement is available from Professional Publishing, which now makes its property management forms available through TrueForms (trueforms.com). Go to their website, click on "Property Management" under "Individual Forms (Adobe® PDF format)," and you will see a list of Professional Publishing's property management forms. Click on any form to see a pdf of that form with the word "DRAFT" written across it. If you like the form, you may purchase it in a usable version.

No matter what agreement you use, keep checking it all the time for legality. Landlord-tenant laws do change.

One thing doesn't change and won't change in this country so long as democracy is alive. That one thing is people's rights. No matter what you write into an agreement, you cannot take people's rights from them.

As you know, slavery is against the law in this country. Were someone to agree voluntarily to become your slave and were you to draw up a slavery agreement which your slave then signed without any coercion whatsoever on your part, you could not enforce that agreement through any court in the land. When your "slave" wants out of his shackles, you'd better let him go. Don't try to argue that the shackles are foam padded. He has an inalienable right to liberty. That's a right he cannot sign away under any circumstances.

So, too, your tenants cannot sign away their rights even if they wanted to. Your agreement should not include any provision which deprives them of the rights guaranteed to them by the laws of the land, such as their right to privacy, their right to a habitable dwelling, their right to quiet enjoyment, their right to minimum notice periods, their right to have children living with them, their right to sue for injuries, their right to a prompt return of their deposits, and their right to keep a service animal. Such clauses would be unenforceable and may cause a judge to look askance at your entire agreement.

Keep unenforceable clauses, needless repetition, and legal obfuscation out of your agreement. Keep your agreement reasonable so that you and your tenants can live with it contentedly throughout your relationship.

Good Clauses

Good clauses help to protect you from litigious tenants who are bent upon using legal ruses to clobber you in court. One such clause in the kitchen sink agreement concerns the arbiter (judge or jury) who sits in judgment should you and your tenants ever have a dispute which goes to trial.

GO AHEAD... SHOW ME WHERE MY LEASE SAYS I CAN'T HAVE ANY SNAKES!!!

Juries, as we all know, tend to favor tenants in their judgments, while judges tend to be impartial. You want to insure that a judge will hear and decide upon the settlement of your dispute and not a jury with some members who tend to be sympathetic toward all tenants and antipathetic toward all landlords.

The "Trial by Judge" clause near the end of the kitchen sink agreement is the good clause which rules out a jury trial if you and your tenants initial it.

Ah, but some state supreme courts have ruled that waiving a jury trial *prior* to a dispute is unconstitutional and unenforceable. They declare that only *after* a dispute arises may the two parties to the dispute agree to accept a bench trial (trial by judge), not before.

Because the clause has not been found wanting in every state, however, it remains in the kitchen sink agreement. Leave it untouched, strike it, or initial it as you please.

The question then arises whether the entire agreement is invalid because of this one clause. Does it invalidate the entire agreement?

No, it doesn't, not when the agreement includes a good clause specifically addressing this situation. It's called a *savings or severability clause*, and here it is: "Illegal Provisions Not Affecting Legal Provisions—Whatever item in this Agreement is found to be contrary to any local, state, or federal law shall be considered null and void, just as if it had never appeared in the Agreement, and it shall not affect the validity of any other item in the Agreement."

That's one good clause to include in a rental agreement. There are a number of others as well.

Here's one: "Non-Waiver—Should Owners waive their right to enforce any breach of this Agreement, that waiver shall be considered temporary and not a continuing waiver of any later breach. Although Owners may know when accepting rent that Tenants are violating one or more of this Agreement's conditions, Owners in accepting the rent are in no way waiving their right to enforce the breach. Owners shall not have waived their rights to enforce any breach unless they agree to a waiver in writing."

A *non-waiver clause* such as this keeps the entire agreement enforceable even though the landlord has chosen to accept rent while knowing full well that the tenants are violating some provision in the agreement.

Should you twice accept rent from a tenant after the late date, for example, and fail to require payment of a late fee, you would still have the right to require payment of a late fee according to the rental agreement if you decided that the tenant was taking advantage of you when he paid his rent late for the third time, and you then decided to make him pay a late fee.

Here's another good clause: "Entire Agreement—As written, this Agreement and its attachments constitute the entire agreement between the Tenants and Owners and supersede any previous agreements or understandings. The Tenants and Owners have made no further promises of any kind to one another, nor have they reached any other understandings, either verbal or written. Only a written document signed by both the Tenants and Owners can amend this Agreement."

This *merger and integration clause* keeps both tenants and owners from claiming that the other party made promises outside of the agreement.

Mediation and arbitration clauses, which

sometimes appear in rental agreements, may be good, or they may be bad.

They're good when they speed up the resolution of disputes and reduce the cost. They're bad when they do just the opposite.

Some college housing offices require mediation and arbitration clauses in the rental agreements of landlords who use their services because they have mediators and arbitrators identified and readily available to handle disputes. Such clauses under those circumstances make perfect sense. They do speed up the resolution of disputes and reduce the cost.

Mediation and arbitration clauses, which, by the way, must be agreed upon and initialed by both parties to be valid, can prolong the resolution of disputes and increase the cost of resolution when mediation or arbitration must be used prior to or instead of going to court.

Some jurisdictions have landlord-tenant courts, which are designed to be efficient and inexpensive, and some jurisdictions have rules giving unlawful detainers (evictions) precedence over other civil court cases. Use these advantages when they're available to you, and don't stymie yourself with clauses which force you to mediate or arbitrate. Instead, leave mediation and arbitration clauses out of your rental agreement, and give yourself the freedom to decide on a case-by-case basis whether you ought to use mediation or arbitration.

My "Two-in-One" Kitchen Sink Agreement

Have you taken a good look at a new stepladder lately? Stepladders are plastered with as many stickers as a hippie van's bumper. They all warn ladder buyers to be careful. Here's a sample. "Do not stand on the top step or the bucket shelf." "Do not climb on the back section of the ladder." "Do not place the ladder in front of a door opening toward the ladder." "Maintain a firm hold on the ladder." "Lock the spreaders before use." "Keep metal ladders away from live electrical circuits." There are more of these stickers on the ladder I'm quoting from, but I'm not going to quote them all. I'm sure you get the picture.

You might ask yourself why all of these warnings have to spoil the appearance of your new ladder when they're so obvious. Doesn't every fool know that it's foolish to place a ladder in front of a door which might swing open and knock the ladder over? Doesn't every fool know enough not to stand on the bucket shelf? Doesn't every fool know that a metal ladder could shock the life out of him if it's touching a live wire?

You know the reason for these superfluous warnings, don't you? Sure. Lawsuits. Lawsuits have forced the manufacturers to plaster warnings all over their ladders. Some fool *did* stand on the bucket shelf. After he fell and became a paraplegic, he sued, claiming that the ladder manufacturer should have warned him about standing on the bucket shelf. He settled for $7 million. That lawsuit and others like it added these various self-evident warnings to the ladders we buy today.

Now, you know that a ladder is pretty straightforward compared to a rental property, and I hope that the day never arrives when we landlords are forced to plaster the walls of our rental properties with warning stickers such as these: "Do not touch light switch when in contact with water." "Keep stray fingers away from door jamb when closing door." "Keep head out of oven when gas is on and pilot light is off." "Enter and exit dwelling through doors only, not windows." "Keep hands out of garbage disposer at all times, especially when grinding garbage." "Sweep up and dispose of broken window glass to prevent accidental cuts." "Unscrew light bulbs from their sockets by turning them counterclockwise." "Cover ears when smoke alarm sounds to avoid loss of hearing." "Remove obstruction from toilet bowl when water overflows." "Close doors and windows to maintain inside temperature."

If ladder manufacturers can come up with twenty warnings, we should be able to come up with at least a thousand. Wouldn't you say? True enough. Thank heavens we don't have to. Not yet anyway. But in these litigious times we may need to come up with a rental agreement which covers more than just the basics of the landlord-tenant relationship, an agreement which circumscribes as many potential problem areas as possible.

One apartment tenant sued his landlord because the landlord had moved the garbage dumpster from one part of the property to another, where the garbage truck could get to it more easily. The tenant sued, claiming that the dumpster in its new location was obstructing his view and that he wouldn't have rented the apartment had he known that the dumpster might be moved. The judge looked at the rental agreement and let the landlord tell his side of the story, and

then he ruled in favor of the tenant because the landlord had failed to include a paragraph in the rental agreement which specifically reserved him the right to place objects outside the building wherever he wanted to place them.

That landlord must have wished that he had paid more attention to his rental agreement. You can be sure that he does now.

What a rental agreement says is important, you know. You'll know just how important it is when somebody hauls you into court on what you thought was some insignificant matter and clobbers you there because you were guilty of a minor oversight.

Although I still use the shorter agreement for many of my rentals, I finally gave in and drafted a longer agreement for those properties which tend to have tenants who are more prone to "question authority" and sue when they feel wronged.

My agreement is short on the legalese and long on the vernacular. It's not a perfect agreement, not by any means. It's a work in progress, and I'll be changing it as long as I'm in this landlording business. I call it my "two-in-one kitchen sink agreement." It's "two-in-one" because it serves as either a month-to-month agreement or a fixed-term agreement, and it's a "kitchen sinker" because it includes both practical considerations and boilerplate.

It may or may not be a good agreement for you to use. That's for you to decide. Some of it may be illegal where you do business. Some of it may be overly restrictive as far as you are concerned. Some of it may not apply. Some of the things which are really important to you may have been overlooked. That's all right. If you want to make changes, make them. If you want to use this agreement as a source of material to help you draft your own agreement, go ahead. Just make sure that you know what's in any agreement you adopt as your own, regardless of its sources, and try your best to be circumspect when you contemplate the consequences of including or not including a certain clause.

As written, this agreement will work for either fixed-term or month-to-month tenancies. It will work for single-family dwellings or multiple-family dwellings. It will work no matter how you handle late rent payments (see chapter 6 for a discussion of the various prompt-payment policies), no matter how you handle lockouts (see chapter 13 for a discussion of lockouts), no matter how you decide to handle the legal services

Rental Agreement

Dated: *October 17, xxxx*

Agreement between Owners: *Delwin and Muretta Levno*
and Tenants: *James and Ann Phelan*
for a dwelling located at: *730 Beaver Avenue, Sunny, OR 08100*

[Initial ONE of the boxes below to indicate whether this Agreement is month-to-month or fixed term.]

☑ **Month-to-Month Agreement**—Tenants agree to rent this dwelling on a month-to-month basis beginning *November 1, xxxx* .

☐ **Fixed-Term Agreement (Lease)**—Tenants agree to lease this dwelling for a fixed term of _____, beginning _____ and ending _____.
Upon expiration, this Agreement shall become a month-to-month agreement AUTOMATICALLY, UNLESS either Tenants or Owners notify the other party in writing at least thirty days prior to expiration that they do not wish this Agreement to continue on any basis.

Rent—Tenants agree to rent this dwelling for $ *850* per *MONTH* , payable in advance. The first month's rent is $ *900* .

Rent Due/Late Consequences—Rent is due on the *1ST* . It is late on the *5TH* . Owners expect to RECEIVE the rent BEFORE the late date. Should exceptional circumstances prevent prompt payment, *Tenant will pay a late fee of $20* .

Returned Checks—If, FOR ANY REASON, a check used by Tenants to pay Owners is returned without having been paid, Tenants will pay a returned check charge of $ *15* AND take whatever other consequences there might be in making a late payment. After the second time that a Tenants' check is returned, Tenants must thereafter secure a cashier's check or money order for payment of rent.

Form of Payment—Tenants agree to pay rent in the form of a personal check, a cashier's check, or a money order made out to *LEVNO PROPERTIES* .

Rent Payment Procedure—Tenants agree to pay their rent in the following way: *in person to manager*

Deposits—Tenants agree to deposit with the Owners the sum of $ *1,100* , payable before they occupy the premises. Owners may withhold from these deposits only what is reasonably necessary to cover the following tenant defaults: 1) damages to the dwelling; 2) certain cleaning costs following Tenants' departure; and 3) unpaid rent and various other accrued and unpaid charges. Tenants may not apply any part of these deposits to their last month's rent.

Refund of Tenants' Deposits—Within *7* days after Tenants have moved out completely, Owners shall provide a written accounting of the disposition of the Tenants' deposits and shall at the same time return all deposits remaining.

Utilities/Services—Tenants agree to pay all utilities and services with the exception of the following which Owners agree to pay: *water and garbage*

Occupants—In addition to the Tenants mentioned above, only the following persons may live in this dwelling: *X   X   X   X   X   X   X   X*
No one else may live there, even temporarily, without Owners' prior written permission.

Guests—Tenants may house any single guest for a maximum period of fourteen days every six months or for whatever other period of time the law allows. Provided that they maintain a separate residence, nurses or maids required to care for Tenants during an illness are excepted from this provision.

Subletting and Assignment—Tenants shall not sublet the entire premises or any part of the premises, nor shall they assign this Agreement to anyone else without first obtaining the Owners' written permission. Owners shall not withhold permission unreasonably.

Rental Agreement—Page 1 of *5*

Pets—Tenants have received permission to house the following pet(s) on the premises: X X X X X X X X
Tenants may house no other pet of any kind on the premises, even temporarily, without first obtaining Owners' written permission. "Pets" includes, but is not limited to, both warm- and cold-blooded animals, such as dogs, cats, fish, hamsters, rats, birds, snakes, lizards, and insects. "Pets" does not include animals trained to serve the handicapped, such as seeing-eye dogs, hearing dogs, or service dogs. These animals may be housed on the premises so long as they are in the direct service of those they were trained to serve and so long as Owners are notified in advance in writing of the circumstances.

Liquid-filled Furniture—Tenants agree not to keep any liquid-filled furniture in this dwelling without first obtaining Owners' written permission.

Vehicles—Tenants agree to park their vehicles in assigned spaces and to keep those spaces clean of oil drippings. Tenants agree to keep no more than __2__ vehicle(s) on the premises. Vehicle(s) must be both operable and currently licensed. Tenants agree to advise their visitors about parking and to take responsibility for where their visitors park. Only those motorcycles which have exhaust muffling comparable to that of a passenger car are allowed. Only those self-propelled recreational vehicles which are used for regular personal transportation are allowed. Tenants agree not to park boats, recreational trailers, utility trailers, and the like on the premises without first obtaining Owners' written permission. Tenants agree not to repair their vehicle(s) on the premises if such repairs will take longer than a single day unless the vehicle is kept in an enclosed garage.

Appliances—Although the following appliances are presently in the dwelling: STOVE AND REFRIGERATOR
the use of these appliances is not included in the rent. If Tenants wish to use these appliances, they agree to assume all responsibility for care and maintenance. If Tenants wish to use their own appliances, they may request that the owner's appliances be removed from the premises.

Tenant Inspection—Tenants have inspected the dwelling and its contents and agree that they are in satisfactory order, as are the electrical, plumbing, and heating systems.

Notification of Serious Building Problems—Tenants agree to notify the Owners immediately upon first discovering any signs of serious building problems such as a crack in the foundation, a tilting porch, a crack in the plaster or stucco, moisture in the ceiling, buckling sheetrock or siding, a leaky roof, a spongy floor, a leaky water heater, or termite activity.

Reasonable Time for Repairs—Upon being notified by Tenants that there is some building defect which is hazardous to life, health, or safety, Owners shall undertake repairs as soon as possible. Should there be a delay of more than seventy-two (72) hours in making the repairs, due to a difficulty in scheduling the work or obtaining parts or for any other reason beyond the Owners' control, Owners agree to keep Tenants informed about the progress of the work.

Windows—Except for those windows which are noted in writing as being cracked or broken when Tenants move in, Tenants agree to be responsible for any windows which become cracked or broken in their dwelling while they live there. Tenants may repair the windows themselves if they can do the work in a professional manner. Otherwise, they may hire a glazier or submit a maintenance request to Owners. If they submit a maintenance request, Owners will charge them no more for the work than the least expensive written bid for the work which Tenants can obtain.

Drain Stoppages—As of the date of this Agreement, Owners warrant that the dwelling's sewage drains are in good working order and that they will accept the normal household waste for which they were designed. They will not accept things such as paper diapers, sanitary napkins, tampons, children's toys, wads of toilet paper, balls of hair, grease, oil, table scraps, clothing, rags, sand, dirt, rocks, or newspapers. Tenants agree to pay for clearing the drains of any and all stoppages except those which the plumber who is called to clear the stoppage will attest in writing were caused by defective plumbing, tree roots, or acts of God.

Trash—Tenants agree to dispose of their ordinary household trash by placing it into a receptacle for periodic collection. They agree to dispose of their extraordinary household trash, such as Christmas trees, damaged furniture, broken appliances, and the like, by compacting it so that it will fit inside their trash receptacle or by hauling it to the dump themselves or by paying someone else to haul it away.

Outside Placement—Owners reserve the right to place trash receptacles, portable storage units, and the like wherever convenient on the premises. Owners further reserve the right to construct property improvements above or below the ground anywhere on the premises so long as they conform to all building codes.

Damage—Tenants agree to pay for repairs of all damage which they or their guests have caused.

Locks—Tenants agree that they will not change the locks on any door or mailbox without first obtaining Owners' written permission. Having obtained permission, they agree to pay for changing the locks themselves and to provide the Owners with one duplicate key per lock.

Lockouts—Should Tenants lock themselves out of their dwelling and be unable to gain access through their own resources, they may call upon a professional locksmith or the manager to let them in. In either case, they are responsible for payment of the charges and/or damages involved. Management charges a fee of $15 for providing this service between the hours of 8 a.m. and 6 p.m., Monday through Saturday, excepting holidays, and a fee of $25 at other times. This fee is due and payable when the service is provided.

Landscaping—[*This paragraph applies only if it is initialed by both parties.*] Tenants agree to maintain the existing landscaping by watering, weeding, fertilizing, mowing, and shaping it as necessary.

Alterations, Decorations, and Repairs—Except as provided by law, Tenants agree not to alter or decorate their dwelling without first obtaining Owners' written permission. Decorations include painting and wallpapering. Further, Tenants agree not to repair their dwelling or anything belonging to the Owners without first obtaining Owners' written permission unless such repairs cost less than one hundred dollars ($100), and Tenants agree to pay for them. Tenants shall hold Owners harmless for any mechanics liens or proceedings which Tenants cause. When approved by Owners, Tenants' plans for alterations and decorations shall bear a determination regarding ownership. If Tenants are able to convince Owners that Tenants can remove the alterations or decorations and restore that part of their dwelling to its original condition, then Owners may grant Tenants the right to remove them. Otherwise, any alterations or decorations made by Tenants become the property of Owners when Tenants vacate.

Painting—Owners reserve the right to determine when the dwelling will be painted unless there is any law to the contrary.

Access—Owners recognize that Tenants have a right to privacy and wish to observe that right scrupulously. At certain times, however, Owners, their employees, or agents may have to gain access to the Tenants' dwelling for purposes of showing it to prospective Tenants, purchasers, lenders, or others or for repairs, inspection, or maintenance. When seeking access under ordinary circumstances, Owners will schedule entry between the hours of 8 a.m. and 8 p.m., Monday through Saturday, excepting holidays, and Owners will provide Tenants reasonable notice of twenty-four hours, or less than twenty-four hours notice with Tenants' concurrence. In emergencies, there will be no notice.

Peace and Quiet—Tenants are entitled to the quiet enjoyment of their own dwelling, and their neighbors are entitled to the same. Tenants agree that they will refrain from making loud noises and disturbances, that they will keep down the volume of their music and broadcast programs at all times so as not to disturb other people's peace and quiet, and that they will not install wind chimes.

Telephone—If and when Tenants install a telephone in their dwelling, they will furnish Owners with the number within five calendar days. When divulging the number, Tenants shall advise Owners whether the number is listed or unlisted. If it is unlisted, Owners agree to take reasonable precautions to keep it from falling into the hands of third parties.

Prolonged Absences—Tenants agree that they will notify Owners whenever they plan to be absent from their dwelling for more than ten days.

Business Use—Tenants agree to use this dwelling as their personal residence. They agree to conduct no business on the premises without first obtaining Owners' written permission.

Lawful Use—Tenants agree that they will not themselves engage in any illegal activities on the premises nor will they allow others to engage in any illegal activities on the premises insofar as they have the power to stop such activities.

Insurance—Owners have obtained insurance to cover fire damage to the building itself and liability insurance to cover certain personal injuries occurring as a result of property defects or owner negligence. Owners' insurance does not cover Tenants' possessions or Tenants' negligence. Tenants shall obtain a Tenants' insurance policy to cover damage to or loss of their own possessions, as well as losses resulting from their negligence. Tenants agree to show Owners evidence of such a policy within one month from the date of this Agreement.

Insurance Considerations—Tenants agree that they will do nothing to the premises nor keep anything on the premises which will result in an increase in the Owners' insurance policy or an endangering of the premises. Neither will they allow anyone else to do so.

Fire or Casualty Damage—During any time when the dwelling cannot be used because of fire or casualty damage, Tenants are not responsible for payment of rent. Should a portion of the dwelling become unusable due to fire or casualty damage, Tenants are not responsible for payment of rent on that portion. In either case, Owners reserve the right to decide whether the dwelling is usable and what portions are usable. Owners are not responsible for repairing or replacing any improvements made by Tenants if those improvements are damaged. Should the fire or casualty damage have been caused by Tenants' own action or neglect, they shall have not be relieved of the responsibility for payment of rent, and they shall also bear the full responsibility for repair of the damage.

Rules and Regulations—Owners' existing rules and regulations, if any, shall be signed by Tenants, attached to this Agreement, and incorporated into it. Owners may adopt other rules and regulations at a later time provided that they have a legitimate purpose, not modify Tenants' rights substantially, and not become effective without notice of at least two (2) weeks.

Service of Process—Every Tenant who signs this Agreement agrees to be the agent of the other Tenants and occupants of this dwelling and is both authorized and required to accept, on behalf of the other Tenants and occupants, service of summons and other notices relative to the tenancy.

Identity of Manager—The person who is responsible for managing this dwelling and is authorized to accept legal service on Owners' behalf is BEVERLY HAVENS whose address is 728 BEAVER AVENUE, SUNNY, OR 08100, PHONE 123-4567.

Changes in Terms of Tenancy—[*This paragraph applies only when this Agreement is or has become a month-to-month agreement.*] Owners shall advise Tenants of any changes in terms of tenancy with advance notice of at least 30 days. Changes may include notices of termination, rent adjustments, or other reasonable changes in the terms of this Agreement.

Notice of Intention to Vacate—[*This paragraph applies only when this Agreement is or has become a month-to-month agreement.*] When Tenants have decided to vacate the premises, they will give Owners written notice of their intentions at least 15 days prior to their departure, and they will give an exact date when they expect to be moved out completely.

Holding Over—If Tenants remain on the premises following the date of their termination of tenancy, they are "holding over" and become liable for "rental damages" equaling one/thirtieth of the amount of their then current monthly rent for every day they hold over.

Possession—Owners shall endeavor to deliver possession to Tenants by the commencement date of this Agreement. Should Owners be unable to do so, they shall not be held liable for any damages Tenants suffer as a consequence, nor shall this Agreement be considered void unless Owners are unable to deliver possession within ten (10) days following the commencement date. Tenants' responsibility to pay rent shall begin when they receive possession.

Sale of the Dwelling—If Owners sell this dwelling or otherwise transfer its Ownership to another party, they shall have the right to terminate this Agreement by giving Tenants written notice of at least sixty days, notwithstanding any conflicting occupancy rights Tenants might have under a fixed-term agreement. Should Tenants have conflicting occupancy rights guaranteed them by law, however, those legal rights shall prevail.

Illegal Provisions Not Affecting Legal Provisions—Whatever item in this Agreement is found to be contrary to any local, state, or federal law shall be considered null and void, just as if it had never appeared in the Agreement, and it shall not affect the validity of any other item in the Agreement.

Non-Waiver—Should either Owners or Tenants waive their rights to enforce any breach of this Agreement, that waiver shall be considered temporary and not a continuing waiver of any later breach. Although Owners may know when accepting rent that Tenants are violating one or more of this Agreement's conditions, Owners in accepting the rent are in no way waiving their rights to enforce the breach. Neither Owners nor Tenants shall have waived their rights to enforce any breach unless they agree to a waiver in writing.

References in Wording—Plural references made to the parties involved in this Agreement may also be singular, and singular references may be plural. These references also apply to Owners' and Tenants' heirs, executors, administrators, or successors, as the case may be.

Application Part of Agreement—The rental application Tenants submitted to rent this dwelling forms a part of this Agreement. Falsified information on the application shall be considered a breach of this Agreement.

Entire Agreement—As written, this Agreement constitutes the entire agreement between the Tenants and Owners. They have made no further promises of any kind to one another, nor have they reached any other understandings, either verbal or written.

Consequences—Violation of any part of this Agreement or nonpayment of rent when due shall be cause for eviction under appropriate sections of the applicable code.

DL JP AP

Trial by Judge—[*This paragraph applies only if it is initialed by both parties.*] Should any aspect of this Agreement or tenancy be litigated in civil court, Owners and Tenants agree to waive their rights to a trial by jury and have the matter tried by a judge.

DL JP AP

Legal Service's Fees—If either party to this Agreement shall bring a cause of action against the other party for enforcement of the Agreement, the prevailing party [*cross out the alternative which does not apply and initial the beginning of this paragraph*] (shall) (~~shall not~~) recover reasonable legal service's fees involved.

Other— NONE

Acknowledgment—Tenants hereby acknowledge that they have read this Agreement, understand it, agree to it, and have been given a copy.

Owner: *Delwin Levno*

BY Person authorized to represent Owners: *Beverly Havens*

Tenant: *James Phelan*

Tenant: *Ann Phelan*

Rental Agreement—Page 5 of 5

fees question (that comes later in this chapter).

This is a very versatile agreement, so versatile that you could overlook one of the opportunities it gives you to make choices. For example, if you were to decide to charge a set late fee of $20, you'd need to cross out the other alternatives in the late fees paragraph and cross out the discounts/rebates paragraph altogether. If you were to decide to use the rebate policy, you'd need to cross out the late fees paragraph altogether and cross out the word "discount" where it appears in the discounts/rebates paragraph.

Should any paragraph contradict your policy on guests, appliances, pets, liquid-filled furniture, or anything else, you could merely strike it out, initial it, and have the other parties do the same. If you felt compelled to include your own policy in these matters, whatever it might be, you could insert it wherever there's enough blank space.

Note that the agreement's total page count is determined by the addition of other agreements, such as a Co-Signer Agreement or a Pet Agreement. The total number of all these pages goes in the blank at the bottom of each page of the Rental Agreement and the addendum agreements.

All in all, this agreement does not have as many teeth as some I've seen. It has only enough to nip wayward tenants and keep them in line. What's most important is that it shouldn't have any teeth which will come back to bite you. Them's the worst kind.

Examine this "kitchen-sink" agreement and decide for yourself whether you could use all or any part of it.

Two Unresolved Questions

There are two questions which keep coming up whenever we landlords are searching for the right rental agreement.

One is the hoary question of whether the agreement should be month-to-month or fixed-term (lease). The other is a newer question, whether we ought to request that the loser in a lawsuit pay the winner's legal services fees. The second question is not quite so pressing, that is, it isn't quite so pressing unless you happen to be affected. Then it can be more pressing than a bloated bladder before the intermission at a Wagnerian opera.

Here are some of the rationales used in formulating answers to these questions.

■ **Should you use month-to-month agreements or leases?**—You'll notice that there are only two choices given in the question above—month-to-month agreements and leases. In truth, there are four choices—oral month-to-month agreements, written month-to-month agreements, oral leases (leases for any period longer than a year must be written), and written leases, but oral month-to-month agreements and oral leases, while they may be binding, are seldom used anymore because people don't trust their memories or each other as much as they once did. Forget about making oral contracts (after all, some people nowadays even put their nuptial agreements in writing to remind their spouses of certain obligations), and you'll avoid the many misunderstandings caused by people's foggy recollections of what they agreed upon initially. Consider only whether you should use a written month-to-month agreement or a written lease, and keep in mind the difference between the two.

Basically, the difference is a simple one, but it is an exceedingly important one. Month-to-month agreements cover time periods which are indefinite, whereas leases cover a definite and longer fixed term (generally a year for residential property). Although they may contain rent escalation and thirty-day termination clauses, in which case they are essentially month-to-month agreements anyway, leases bind both parties to the terms of the agreement so that neither party may make any changes until the lease expires or unless one party breaks it.

Lease breaking occurs every day and you don't have to think too much about the matter to figure out who usually breaks them. Tenants do. In theory, if tenants move before their lease expires and they do not have whatever your state or community defines as a good cause for breaking their lease legally (a "good cause" might be entering active duty with the U.S. military or taking employment in another community or losing the main source of income used to pay rent), then they are responsible for paying the rent covering the entire lease period, so long as you have been unsuccessful in a reasonable effort to find new tenants at the best rent possible. In practice, however, even if you do make a reasonable effort to re-rent the place and find nobody to rent it, you would have a difficult time collecting all the rent owing on the lease unless the tenants had sufficient assets, and even then you'd probably have to sue them every month in separate small claims actions to recover.

Leases are like those treaties which the English so naively signed with Germany during the late '30s. They bound the English, just as leases bind landlords, while the Germans did exactly as they pleased, impudently enjoying the limitations they had placed upon their foolish adversaries. The Germans had nothing to lose, and neither do most tenants. The Germans were too powerful for any agreement to matter. Most tenants are too poor.

Leases bind only those who have some assets and want to be bound. Tenants generally have little to lose by breaking a lease, but woe be unto you, landlord, if you should ever try to break a lease! That "Clark Kent of consumerism," Ralph Charell, in his book, *How I Turn Ordinary Complaints into Thousands of Dollars*, boasts of collecting a $25,000 payoff from his landlords for dispossessing him before his lease was up, and his was a lease which new owners inherited.

Remember that any and all rental agreements, leases included, which are in effect at the time of a property transfer become the responsibility of the new owners to uphold, that is, unless there is a distinct provision to the contrary.

Covering extended periods of time as they do, leases can affect the transfer of property substantially if the new owner wants to assume possession of the dwelling or change the terms of the agreement. If you are renting out a house, for example, on a one-year lease which has four months to run, and you have found a buyer who wants to move in upon close of escrow, you may lose the sale entirely unless you can somehow convince your buyer to wait four months or you can convince your renters to move before their lease expires.

All of these considerations appear to reflect so negatively on leases that you may wonder why any landlord would ever use one. There are a few circumstances, precious few, where leases might prove favorable to the landlord, and even then they should be limited to periods of a year or less (except for commercial properties, which vary according to area and market conditions).

Those circumstances include student rentals (to assure year-round occupancy), luxury rentals (to encourage tenant improvements), established tenancies (to ease good, long-term tenants' fears), high vacancy areas (to offer security from rent increases as an incentive), Section 8 subsidized housing (to participate in the program at all), rental houses (to promote greater tenant commitment, but only if you feel certain that you won't be selling the house during the lease period), and commercial properties (to facilitate business cost projections and encourage stability and improvements).

Unless you can conceive of some obvious advantage to you for using leases, use written month-to-month rental agreements instead, and you'll stay out of some of the trouble leases can cause.

■ **Should you ask for any attorney's or legal services fees in your rental agreement?**—Before considering possible answers to this question, we should differentiate between "attorney's fees" and "legal services fees."

"Attorney's fees" is a narrowly defined term restricted to the fees charged by an attorney, and only an attorney, for services rendered, whereas "legal services fees" is a more broadly defined term which includes attorney's fees as well as the fees charged by anyone else who is rendering "legal" services, such as the secretarial service you might use to prepare your eviction paperwork. What's more, courts are interpreting "legal services fees" even more broadly and awarding landlords something for their own time spent in representing themselves whenever they win a contractual dispute with their tenants. There's no way that you could possibly be awarded anything for your time if you were asking only for attorney's fees in your rental agreement.

If you are going to put anything in your rental agreements about such fees, don't limit them to the fees charged by attorneys. Go beyond attorney's fees. Use the term "legal services fees" instead.

Now let's consider whether you should ask for any of these fees at all.

As a matter of course, most rental agreements include a provision which awards attorney's or legal services fees to the prevailing party in litigation between the landlord and tenant. Without such a provision, a landlord who wins a contractual claim cannot recoup these fees.

Not being able to recoup the fees sounds like an unpleasant prospect. Doesn't it? Ah, but what happens if your tenant wins a long, drawn-out suit claiming that you failed to maintain his rental house adequately and that's why he hasn't been paying you any rent for six entire months?

Here's what would happen. You'd lose all or most of the rent for six months. You'd have to pay your own costs and legal services fees, and you'd have to pay thousands of dollars for your tenant's costs and legal services fees as well. You'd be triple-penalized for losing, and it wouldn't matter one whit that you knew full well the tenant was lying in court. His prevailing in court would entitle him to the fees because of that provision in your rental agreement.

You cannot know exactly how this provision or the lack of it is going to affect you at some time in the future. An attorney who's advising you on your rental agreement isn't going to know for sure either. Only in retrospect will you ever know whether you made the right decision.

You should certainly think about the matter, though, and here are some of the points you should consider.

Do not ask in your agreement that legal services fees be awarded to the prevailing party if—

- The kind of tenant you generally rent to is "judgment proof" anyway, that is, he wouldn't have the money to pay you if you did get a court judgment against him.
- Your tenants generally use legal-aid attorneys to represent them.
- The courts in your area tend to favor tenants in their decisions.

Do ask in your agreement that legal services fees be awarded to the prevailing party if—

- Your tenants tend to have the wherewithal to pay a judgment.
- The courts in your area appear to be relatively impartial in landlord-tenant cases.
- You are confident that you will be the prevailing party forty-nine times out of fifty.

After thinking about these various points, review your rental agreement and see that it reflects your thinking on awarding legal services fees.

Some Last Words

As you search for *your* right rental agreement, keep your eyes and ears open wide for ideas wherever you are, whatever you're up to. Keep your Swiss Army scissors at the ready to cut out whatever pertinent newspaper articles you chance upon. Unsheathe your Swiss Army pen to write down whatever ideas you come across. Be prepared to make changes to your agreements as needs arise.

Remember, you're dealing with people and a society in a constant state of flux. Recognize that you aren't going to find the right rental agreement for all time, so you might as well enjoy the search.

This much is certain. When one of those clauses that you were shrewd enough to include in your agreement helps you win a case in court, you'll feel the same immediate relief you feel when the full-grown St. Bernard you're petting decides to lift his paw off your foot.

6
Rents, Rents, Rents

Sometime, somewhere, two tenants were talking with one another, and the following conversation took place. I'd be willing to bet my biggest and best pipe wrench on it.

"What do you think our landlady does with all the rent money we pay her?"

"Oh, I suppose she buys designer clothes, expensive jewelry, spa treatments, Parisian cosmetics, and other stuff we couldn't afford, and she goes on cruises every summer, 'love-boat' cruises, I think somebody told me. She must buy a new luxury car every year or two as well. She just doesn't drive it around here. The rest of it she probably stashes under her mattress or deposits into a Swiss bank account. She's a rich lady to be owning this building. That's for sure!"

Many tenants believe that you pocket either their entire rent payment or a substantial portion of it. They cannot understand what else you might be doing with it. They are completely oblivious of loan payments, property tax bills, garbage bills, utility bills, gardening bills, maintenance bills, repair bills, advertising bills, insurance bills, legal bills, bookkeeping bills, special assessments, and replacement reserves, not to mention vacancy losses and management costs.

They regard rent as a kind of legal extortion, a fee levied upon the deserving poor by the idle rich, and thus, some of them feel completely justified in spearheading or joining efforts to enact rent control to deprive you of the freedom to charge whatever rent the market will bear, or else, if they can't stir up enough support for rent control, they feel completely justified in trying various shenanigans to deprive you of their rent money.

Short of turning over the property completely to your tenants and letting them try to pay all the bills themselves out of what rent they are able to collect from one another, you may find that convincing them that their rent money pays bills directly related to their tenancy is just as hard as convincing them that their daily lottery ticket is a sucker's bet. Old, preconceived notions about landlords and rents are deep-rooted indeed and they die hard.

Try educating your tenants little by little whenever you have the opportunity. Sometime when you're collecting their rent, ask them what they think the rent money goes for, and be prepared for some astonishing answers. Most tenants haven't a clue what you do with their rent money.

Of course, you might not know yourself exactly what percentage of every rent check goes to pay utilities, what to insurance, and so on, and you should certainly calculate those percentages (use expenses for the previous tax year and include as an expense at least 5% of the income to represent your own time contribution for overall off-site property management) before you ever broach the subject to your tenants.

On an average, the percentages are as follows for multiple-family dwellings purchased with a 25% down payment—insurance, maintenance, repairs, and utilities, 25%; property taxes, 25%; mortgage interest, 35%; debt retirement, 2%; vacancy factor, 5%; overall property management, 5%; and cash flow, 3%.

Once you calculate your own percentages, you may be astonished by how little of your tenants' rent money you get to pocket (positive cash flow) or by how much you have to contribute (negative cash flow) to keep a roof over their heads. Like any teacher preparing a class lesson, you may learn more about the money side of the landlording business while preparing to teach your tenants something on the subject than you ever knew before.

Don't be too hopeful that your students will learn their lessons, however, for you have some very reluctant learners. Neither these informal discussions nor formal disclosures with copious explanations will enlighten your tenants about their rent so thoroughly that they will volunteer to pay their "fair share" of the expenses. Dream on! But through such attempts, you *might* find them a *little* more understanding about rent collection, rent raises, and rent control, all topics of this chapter.

Itemizing Rents

Before we proceed to the major rent topics, let's consider a minor one, although it's a topic which can have major consequences nowadays when a landlord's costs for certain essentials change unexpectedly overnight.

Let's say that you have just raised your monthly rents $23 across the board. You're mighty pleased with yourself because you have weathered the usual tenant complaints about an increase in the rent, your rents are more than keeping pace with your costs, your vacancies are manageable, and you're showing some healthy positive cash flow at last. You're beginning to think that buying this rental property you bought several years ago was a stroke of genius. Your spouse and even your teenagers are showing you a little more respect. You're expecting most of the rent increase to add to your cash flow. Your money worries appear to be vanishing. Life is good. Landlording is wonderful. All is right with the world.

Then comes your sewer bill and with it a notice that the rates are going up $17 per dwelling within the next sixty days. Your spirits sink. There goes most of your rent increase, right down the drain. What should you do about the situation? Should you go back to your tenants and give them another rent increase, this time for $17? No, no, don't do that. They wouldn't understand. They would blame you for everything wrong in their lives, everything wrong in the world. They expect you to take the additional rent they're paying you as a result of the rent increase and use it to pay for all of the higher costs you'll be facing over the next year, no matter what those costs are and no matter how much they happen to be.

Your tenants will think that you don't know what you're doing if you raise their rent twice in quick succession. They would be saying to themselves, and likely to you directly, that you should have known the sewer rates were going up. That's your job as landlord to keep track of your ex-

penses and anticipate increases in certain ones. Why should they as tenants have to pay you still more rent because you made a mistake and miscalculated your expenses? Huh? Why?

Although I resisted adopting the obvious solution to this problem for many years, I have come to be a believer. Not only does it make good sense, it works.

The solution I'm referring to here is itemizing rents. You determine a base rent and then you add your actual costs for certain basic items such as water, sewer, garbage, and special assessment districts (fire, ambulance, street lighting, storm drainage, libraries, and whatever else your local politicians decide they need to add onto your property tax bill to generate more revenue). When these costs go up, you pass the increase along to your tenants right away. When these costs go down, you pass the decrease along to your tenants right away.

I must admit that I resisted itemizing rents for a long time because I had become completely conditioned to making my rents all-inclusive. I wanted to keep everything simple and keep my expenses as much of a secret from my tenants as possible. Itemizing rents would only complicate my paperwork and confuse my tenants, or so I thought, and it would reveal to them what I was paying for certain expenses. I didn't want them to know what my expenses were because I didn't want them to be doing the math. They might think that I was making too much money and start questioning what I was charging them for rent.

How wrong I was!

Yep, itemizing rents does complicate the paperwork, and it does require more of your time. You have to watch your basic expenses more carefully, and you have to give your tenants notice that their rent will be adjusted accordingly whenever there's a change. Then, you have to prepare a statement for them every month so they will know exactly how much they owe. That's the downside of itemizing rents.

The upside is that tenants don't seem to be any more interested in questioning their rent when it's itemized than they are in questioning it when it's not itemized. They seem to understand better why their rent is changing and to accept the changes as inevitable, even though the changes may occur more frequently than otherwise. In addition, they seem to like the possibility that they will see a decrease in their total rent if any of the itemized charges should decrease, even though decreases rarely occur.

Besides the primary advantage you realize in itemizing rents, being able to pass along increases in the costs you cannot control for the essentials your tenants cannot do without, you will also find that you can deflect your tenants' displeasure over the increases. They can't blame you for the increases. They can blame city hall, and they will. They can understand much better how increased costs affect them directly, and they will stand with you when you and other property owners challenge those increased costs in public forums.

To begin itemizing your rents, calculate exactly how much the things you currently include in the rent, but want to itemize, are costing you per unit per month.

Let's say that you have a fourplex with rents of $875 per unit per month, and the rents include water, sewer, and garbage service. Your water bill has averaged $41 per month over the past year; your garbage bill is $47 per month; your sewer bill is $216 per quarter; and your street lighting assessment is $12.36 per quarter. These figures translate into monthly per-unit figures of $10.25 for water, $11.75 for garbage, $13.50 for sewer, and $1.03 for street lighting. These are the figures you would use for your initial setup. Add them all together and you get $48.89. Deduct them from your lump-sum rent and you get a base rent of $826.11.

Advise your tenants in a Notice of Change in Terms of Tenancy that their total monthly rent consists of a base rent of $826.11, plus so much for each of the itemized charges. Advise them that their base rent will change no more frequently than once a year but that the other charges may fluctuate at any time according to your actual costs. Advise them further that you will give them proper notice that their total rent is going up or down whenever one of the itemized charges changes.

Be sure you refer in your notice to the sum of the base rent and the itemized charges as "the rent," "the gross rent," or "the total rent" because you want to be able to use that total figure as "rent" in any legal paperwork you may have to file to evict the tenants at some future date. You don't want to have to itemize it in your legal paperwork. Itemization only confuses court clerks and judges.

You may have noticed that most of the itemized costs above are flat-rate charges, all except water, which may or may not be a flat-rate charge if it's provided by a utility company (if it's well water you're providing your tenants, don't itemize it because its cost is too difficult to calculate). More than likely, water is the one item which fluctuates every month, and you may wonder how you can itemize it if the property is master metered, that is, unless you install a separate meter for every unit. All you're doing here is taking a twelve-month average as your initial cost for water, and you're going to change that figure only if the water *rate* changes. You would not change it according to the tenants' usage. If the rate goes up, you'd take the percentage of the increase and add that to whatever sum you calculated as the initial cost for water. That's all.

If you choose to itemize your rents, do not play games with the figures when you're advertising a vacancy. Advertise the total of what you're charging for everything, the base rent plus the various other basic items you're itemizing. Do not advertise the base rent alone and then tell the applicants when they're about to sign the rental agreement that they will have to pay extra for basic items which they must have in order to live there. That approach, every bit as shady as a "bait-and-switch," will cause them to question your way of doing business from the git-go. It's underhanded, and it's bad business.

Give this itemizing-rents procedure some thought. Test it on paper for a property to see whether it would make a difference. Then decide whether you ought to implement it.

In certain circumstances, it can make a big difference in your income. At one of my larger properties, it bumped my income up by $1,400 per month when my costs increased unexpectedly by that amount and I couldn't otherwise have passed along those costs in the form of an ordinary rent increase for eight more months. Let's see now. Multiply eight times $1,400. That amounts to $11,200 of additional income over an eight-month period! Wow, that's real money!

I'm a believer, a true believer.

Collecting Rents

You may have trained your tenants to pay you their rent a week or more before it's due. If so, skip this section and the next. You don't need to know anything more about collecting rents. You

RENT PAYMENT DETAILS

These rent payment details apply to the tenancy formalized in the Rental Agreement dated __2/26/xxxx__ between __JOE & MICHELE FLETCHER__, Owners, and __MARGARET HARE & JOHN PRINGLE__, Tenants, who occupy the rental dwelling located at __1632 MYRTLE CT, JIMTOWN__.

Rent Payment Dates: Due date __FIRST__; late date __FOURTH__

Prompt Payment Policy
[X] Fee of $ __32__ charged when payment NOT RECEIVED by LATE DATE
[ ] Discount of $_____ given when payment RECEIVED by LATE DATE
[ ] Rebate of $_____ given when payment RECEIVED by LATE DATE

Rent Statement Delivery
[ ] Statement mailed to address above or to this alternative address _____
[X] Statement sent to Tenants' email address below
[ ] Statement faxed to Tenants' fax number below
[ ] Statement not provided
[ ] Other _____

Rent Collection
Rent payment shall be made in the following way:
[ ] Delivered to Owner's office or office of Owner's Agent
[ ] Picked up by Owner or Owner's Agent at Tenants' dwelling
[ ] Mailed to Owner's office
[X] Electronic transfer from Tenants' account
[ ] Electronic transfer via payment processor _____
[ ] Other _____

Rent Payment
Rent payment shall be made in the following form:
[ ] Cash [ ] Personal check [ ] Money order [ ] Cashiers check
[X] Electronic funds transfer to Owner's account (nine-digit routing number) __106678901__

Rent Receipt Delivery
Owners shall acknowledge receipt of payment in the following way(s):
[ ] Receipt held for pickup at _____
[ ] Receipt mailed to address above or to this alternative address _____
[X] Receipt sent to Tenants' email address below
[ ] Receipt faxed to Tenants' fax number below
[ ] Receipt not provided
[ ] Other _____

Notice of Nonpayment of Rent
Owners shall notify Tenants of missed rent due date as follows:
[X] Notice sent to Tenants' email address below (courtesy) __ON THIRD__
[ ] Notice mailed to address above (courtesy)
[X] Notice delivered to Tenants (begins eviction proceedings) __ON FIFTH__

Best ways to contact Tenants (priority number in brackets)
[X] Email __MHARE@TMAIL.NET__
[X] Cell phone __555-789-2777__   [ ] Home phone _____
[ ] Work phone _____   [ ] Fax number _____

Best ways to contact Owner (priority number in brackets)
[X] Email __FLETCH@CMAIL.COM__
[ ] Cell phone _____   [ ] Home phone _____
[X] Office phone __555-777-6543__   [ ] Fax number _____

We acknowledge a familiarity with the rent payment details given above.

__2/26/XX__
Date

__Margaret Hare__
Tenant(s)

__2/26/XX__
Date

__Michele Fletcher__
Owner

should be giving lessons to the rest of us. Everyone else, read on.

Collecting rents on time requires persistence, consistency, and firmness. You can't expect tenants to pay you their rent promptly if you aren't making a concerted effort to collect it from them promptly, or if they're confused about when and where and how to pay it, or if you let them pay it late once or twice without saying so much as a word about the consequences of paying late.

Be persistent. You earn that rent money, and you shouldn't be the least bit timid about collecting it. Keep after those tenants who haven't paid up. Be aggressive. Hound them until they pay.

Be consistent. Rent collection is so important to landlording that you must learn to drop everything else when rents come due so you can pursue rent collection in the same way month after month, year after year.

Be firm. Convince your tenants that their rent money is your top priority and that you won't be swayed by their sob stories or tolerate their feeble excuses.

Remember that paying rent is just as unsatisfying to tenants as paying property taxes is to you. Neither rent nor taxes pay for anything that the payer didn't already have before, or so it would seem. Few would pay if they didn't believe that they would be penalized somehow for failing to pay.

You have to establish yourself from the very beginning as intolerant of nonsense, a landlord who expects the rent to be paid promptly, no matter what. When it isn't, you become a force to contend with, a menacing someone who knows how to evict tenants in short order and will.

Some tenants think they can get away with not paying their landlord more easily than they can get away with not paying their dentist, cellphone company, cable TV provider, furniture store, dress shop, credit card company, finance company, oil company, insurance company, and even their gym. Who then gets paid last, if at all? You, that's who! Why? You're not firm enough when you should be.

Be like the family dog that is faithful and loving except when someone tries to take away his food. Then he growls and bites. There's no reason why you can't be considerate to your tenants in all things except where rents are concerned. Then you have to be menacing. After all, you

and your properties live on rent money just as dogs live on Alpo.

Make not paying rent to you more difficult for your tenants than not paying anyone else. Explain precisely what your policy is regarding rent collection. Tell them before you ever rent to them that their rent is due on the first, it is *late* on the fifth, and if it's not paid by the fourth, you'll be visiting them in person on the fifth to give them just three days to pack up and leave. Talk tough. Be tough when you collect rents. You won't be understood otherwise.

Besides persistence, consistency, and firmness, collecting rents on time requires a reasonable, lucid, and strict rent collection policy more than anything else, a policy which should include a mutually agreed upon collection procedure, a specified form of payment, statements when called for, written receipts, a set due date, a set late date, and either a certain penalty for late payment or an incentive to pay on time.

The Rent Payment Details form shown on the opposite page clarifies every detail related to the payment of rent so that tenants and landlord alike know what to expect of one another when rent time rolls around. It's an informal agreement which the tenants and landlord need to fill out together because each of them contributes different bits of information.

■ **Collection Procedures**—Which collection procedure you use will depend upon what kind of tenants you have, where you live in relation to the units, how many units you have, how much you want to be involved, whether you have an on-site manager, and whether both you and your tenants trust the electronic banking system.

Some landlords prefer to have tenants visit them or the manager to pay the rent in person, some collect it by mail, some actually go themselves to their tenants' dwellings to collect the rents in person, some appoint an on-site rent collector, some arrange electronic transfers, and some arrange for a third party to handle the transfer of the rent money out of the tenant's bank account into the landlord's. There are merits to each of these procedures.

The first collection procedure, having your tenants come to you or to your manager, if either of you lives or has an office close by, is surely the most common procedure. It's personalized and it's reasonably efficient, but it may make you feel confined to one place while you wait for tenants to come to you.

To eliminate the feeling of confinement, install a secure mail slot where the tenants can put their rent checks when neither you nor your manager is available. Some tenants will use any excuse they can think of for not paying their rent promptly, and one of those excuses is that nobody was available to collect their rent when they came to pay it. A secure mail slot alternative puts an end to that excuse.

The second procedure, collecting rent by mail, is a time-honored way to collect rent, especially for single-family dwellings, and there's a good reason why it has lasted so long. It's easy and efficient for both landlords and tenants.

To make it especially easy for your tenants, send them a statement and a self-addressed, stamped envelope on the 18th of every month and ask them to send you by return mail a check, postdated the first, to pay their next month's rent. Then, when the first rolls around, you will already have their check in hand, and neither you nor your tenants need worry about whether it will reach you on time.

IF YOU DON'T PAY YOUR RENT, I'LL DO SOMETHING DRASTIC!!

I'LL PAY!! I'LL PAY!!

What's more, you don't have to waste time going to each tenant's dwelling or waiting around for the tenant to come to you. You don't have to listen to the latest gossip about the neighbors, and you don't have to listen to the inevitable complaints. It's quick and it's easy, but it's also impersonal, and it separates you from your source of income to a point where you risk losing touch with your property and your tenants.

Despite some very real disadvantages to the third procedure, its inefficiency and its placement of the burden for the transaction on you, there are real advantages to collecting rents on the tenant's doorstep or inside the tenant's dwelling itself. It's as personalized as possible. It shows that you care enough to take the time to visit your property. It shows that rent collection is important to you. It lets you know straightaway whether a tenant is going to be late and, if so, what the tenant's excuse for late payment is. It also allows you more freedom of movement because you don't have to wait around for anybody to come to you. You're going to them.

The fourth procedure you might think about trying if you happen to be an absentee owner with no manager on the premises of a reasonably small multiple-family building involves selecting the most senior tenants you have in the building and giving them, say, $5 for every rent they collect, including their own.

Many seniors like the responsibility. They like to feel useful, and they appreciate the opportunity to earn a little extra income. They're also more conscientious in their rounds than you would ever be. The other tenants are less likely to give the usual excuses for being late with their rent to one of their neighbors, especially when that neighbor is a senior and is something of an authority figure who "must be obeyed." You save yourself from having to make repeated trips over to the property and having to spend time dealing with many people separately, too. At $5 per unit, the collection at a six-plex would cost you a mere $30 a month. That's money well spent.

Be certain that you have workers' compensation insurance if you use this procedure. A senior who falls and breaks a hip or an arm while collecting rents for you would most definitely qualify for compensation.

For years you could wire money via Western Union from one place on the globe to another. You still can, but now you can do pretty much the same thing yourself with electronic bank transfers, the fifth collection procedure.

Transferring funds from one bank account to

another electronically is a free service and one of the most efficient ways for tenants to pay rent. It's convenient for them and for you. All they need is your bank account's nine-digit routing number, and they can deposit their rent money directly into your account from their account automatically every month on a certain date, or else they can deposit it into your account when they're reviewing and paying their bills every month.

To accept your tenants' rent payments using electronic banking, you should have a separate landlording bank account at a bank which has a user-friendly website, so you can quickly check for deposits made into the account whenever you like, 3 P.M. or 3 A.M.

The sixth collection procedure, payment processing, requires some faith, yours and your tenant's. It also requires a tenant bank account, a landlording bank account, and a payment processor.

Here's how it works. With the tenant's permission, the landlord arranges with a payment processor to withdraw the rent electronically from the tenant's bank account and deposit it into the landlord's bank account on one or more days every month. The processor sends a bill and a reminder to the tenant and advises the landlord when the rent has been paid.

Payment processing is best set up over the internet using the processor's website, but it can also be set up by phone.

Search "rent collection service" on the internet, and you'll find a number of such companies to select from.

If you're inclined to try a payment processor, be careful. These companies are handling your tenants' money and your money, thousands upon thousands of dollars. They're not regulated as banks are, and they may be located anywhere in the world. Even though they show a U.S. address as their headquarters, they could be operating out of one of the scam capitals of the world, Russia or Nigeria.

Can you trust them to handle your rent payments without disappearing suddenly with the money? Other people's money is mighty tempting when it flows through the hands of the many Ponzis and Madoffs of this world. What recourse would you have if they did abscond with your funds? None, I warrant. Keep these questions in mind when you're thinking about using a payment processor.

If you keep in touch with your tenants at other times and in other ways, then by all means, have your tenants mail their rent to you or arrange electronic payment, but if rent collection day is the only chance you have all month to see your property, then maybe you'd better collect the rent on the premises. You might see something there that should be remedied soon, and you might see it while it still can be remedied easily, before it becomes an aggravating or expensive matter.

No matter which collection procedure you decide upon, you should be absolutely certain that your tenants understand how you expect to collect their rent. You don't want them to be waiting around for you to knock on their door to collect it when you're expecting them to mail you a check.

■ **Form of Payment**—You want to be absolutely certain that every cent of the rent money paid to you will reach your bank, don't you? Of course you do! You're not in this business for the fun of it. Who is? All right, then. Make sure that you collect your rent promptly and that what you do collect goes directly into your bank account as soon as possible.

Because cash can disappear much too easily on its way to the bank, don't accept it. Stipulate in your rental agreement or in a special notice of change in terms of tenancy (use a notice if you don't want to redraw rental agreements for existing tenants) or else in the less formal Rent Payment Details form, that tenants who pay in person or by mail are to make all of their rent payments by check or money order, not in cash.

If you have no agreement or understanding with your tenants about accepting cash for rent, you must accept cash when it's offered because it is, after all, legal tender, but it comes with two big drawbacks—bulkiness, which makes it difficult to conceal in large quantities, and attractiveness, which makes it irresistible to muggers, who like nothing better than easy prey.

Inevitably, if you accept cash, some of your tenants will pay you with wads of bills that would choke a hippo, and you'd have to do whatever you could to conceal those bulky wads. You could wind up looking like a dope dealer carrying an attache case full of cash around with you at rent collection time except that you wouldn't have any bodyguards to protect you. You'd be worried sick that a low-life might figure out what was in your attache case, target you, and snatch all of your

Landlady Properties
453 Sweet Street
Littletown, CA 09090
800-555-1212

STATEMENT

Date: August 21, XXXX

Mailing Address:
Dorothy Mae Mahoney
456 Sweet Street
Littletown, CA 09090

Unit Address:
456 Sweet Street
Littletown, CA 09090

Tenant: SS1DM   **Name:** Dorothy Mae Mahoney
Unit: SS1   **Property:** SS   Sweet Street

Our records show that your rent is current through August 31, XXXX.

Your next payment should amount to the following:

Stmt Date	ID	Category	Qty	Price	Amt Due
8/21/XXXX	4101	Rent		872.50	872.50
8/21/XXXX	4221	Garbage		16.00	16.00
				Total Balance Due	$888.50

Your rental payments are due on the 1st of every month. To avoid the consequences of paying late, please pay promptly.

Please make your payment payable to Landlady Properties.

Please report any leaky faucets or toilets. We'll fix them promptly!

rents for the month.

Save yourself that worry. Don't accept cash. Require tenants who pay in person or by mail to pay by check or money order.

Besides checks and money orders, there are other "safe" forms for the payment of rent you might want to consider—electronic transfers using direct deposits, electronic transfers using online banking, electronic transfers using a payment processor, and credit cards.

To arrange for electronic transfers using direct deposits, you must get an authorization letter signed by the tenant which you then send off to the tenant's bank. The bank will contact the tenant to verify the authorization before starting to make the transfers, but once that's done, the tenant's bank will transfer the rent money like clockwork from the tenant's bank account into yours according to the schedule you and the tenant have agreed upon, and there's no charge to you or the tenant.

Neither is there a charge for electronic transfers made online from the tenant's bank account to yours. The tenant and you would have to agree to online-banking rent payments, and the tenant would have to set everything up, but it's a simple matter for anybody who's used to online banking.

Charges do apply to electronic transfers arranged through payment processors, but you may find their extra services, such as billing and notification, worth the small cost.

As for charging rents to the tenant's Visa or MasterCard, it's a natural extension of our society's habit of charging everything now and paying for it later.

The main drawbacks to this form of payment, as far as you are concerned, are twofold—you must establish yourself as a credit card "merchant," and you must pay a fee for accepting payment by credit card.

You didn't think the Visa and MasterCard people offered their services for nothing, did you? They don't. They take a percentage of every dollar charged. Out of $650 in rent charged to a tenant's card, they would take 2 or 3%, depending upon the volume of funds you run through your account. You would net $630 to $637.

You have to weigh those drawbacks against the advantage of accepting credit cards, the primary advantage for you being that you could count on prompt and certain payment. The only

circumstance which would keep you from getting paid would be where a tenant has exceeded the card's limit. You could find that out easily enough, of course, by calling the credit card company. They know and they will tell you immediately when you inquire as a merchant.

The primary advantages to tenants in paying by credit card are 1) knowing that their rent would never be late, that is, if they opt to give you the right to charge their credit card automatically every month and 2) knowing that paying their rent this way would help them accumulate certain benefits, such as airline miles if they have an airline-affiliated card.

■ **Statements**—Many businesses send their charge account customers monthly statements. These statements serve two purposes—they inform the customer of the account balance and the expected payment, and they remind the customer to pay promptly.

Except for some landlords who handle their rent collections by mail, landlords generally don't send statements to their tenants. "Why bother?" the frugal landlord says, "Statements would just be a waste of my time and money. I'd have to prepare them, stuff them into envelopes, stamp the envelopes, and put them in the mail. My tenants pay the same amount of rent to me month after month anyway. Why should I go to all the trouble of billing them?"

There's some logic to that point of view, to be sure. If your tenants do pay promptly and if they're paying the same amount every month throughout the year, you needn't go to the trouble of billing them, but if they don't pay promptly and don't pay the same amount every month and you think that sending them statements might remind them how much rent they owe and when they need to pay it, try sending them statements ten days before their rent due date. See what happens. Those statements may get them to pay more promptly.

At one of my properties which has an on-site manager who collects the rent in her office, we discovered that a third more of our tenants were paying their rent prior to the due date after she started sending them statements every month. Statements yielded good results in that case, and they do to this day.

On the opposite page is a sample of a statement created by a rental property management program. It creates statements from the data in

Landlady Properties
453 Sweet Street
Littletown, CA 09090
800-555-1212

RECEIPT
RENT PAYMENT

Receipt Number: 5

Date: August 22, XXXX

Mailing Address:

Dorothy Mahoney
456 Sweet Street
Littletown, CA 09090

Unit Address:

456 Sweet Street
Littletown, CA 09090

Tenant ID: SS1DM **Name:** Dorothy Mahoney	
Unit: SS1 **Property:** SS Sweet Street	

Received From: Dorothy Mae Mahoney $888.50

Eight Hundred Eighty-Eight and 50/100 Dollars

Paid By Check: $888.50 **Check Number:** 5896

Cash: $0.00 **Money Order:** $0.00 **Other:** $0.00

ID	Category	Qty	Price	Owed	Amt Paid	Bal Due
4101	Rent		872.50	872.50	872.50	0.00
4221	Garbage		16.00	16.00	16.00	0.00
				TOTALS	$888.50	0.00

Date Rent Paid From: September 1, XXXX **Through:** September 30, XXXX

Thank you for paying the full amount owed.

Please let us know if there is anything we can do for you!

Received by: *Leslie Landlady*
LL

its files either on a tenant-by-tenant basis or on a property-by-property basis. You may do the same thing using a spreadsheet, a word processing program, or a database program with a template you create yourself, or you may do them the old-fashioned way, by hand.

■ **Receipts**—Since you want to keep good rental income records which brook no argument, take the precaution of receipting all rents. The negligible expense and trouble involved in writing receipts for every rent payment collected, even for those paid electronically or by check or money order, have paid off for me more than once when I've had to come up with proof of something or other related to a tenant's payment.

Neither you nor your tenants should have to rely upon your memories to remember dates, amounts paid, and rental periods. Put them in writing. Write a receipt every time you collect rent, and you won't have to clutter your memory with still more dates and numbers.

Take note of the following—There's no substitute for an original receipt as proof of payment, an original receipt written on paper and signed by the person who can acknowledge receipt of the funds.

Pegboard System

Where once there was only one kind of rent receipt available, the handwritten receipt-book receipt, now there are four. There's the handwritten receipt-book receipt. There's the handwritten pegboard-system receipt. There's the computer-program-generated receipt, and there's the web-based receipt.

■ **Receipts (Handwritten Receipt-Book)**—Most landlords begin their careers using a receipt book for their rent receipts because the setup time is minimal. It consists of nothing more than a rent receipt book purchased at an office supply store.

The best book to purchase has four tearout carbonless receipts on a single page, with each receipt numbered and each set of receipts consisting of an original and two copies.

You can get away with an original and one copy if you're the only one who's writing the receipts, but if someone else is writing receipts, you'll want all of them to be in triplicate, an original and two copies (one copy for the tenants, one for the person who collects the rent, and one for you).

Minimal setup time is one big advantage of the rent receipt book, but so is its portability. You can easily take a book with you when you collect rents on tenants' doorsteps, and you can write a receipt when the rent money changes hands instead of having to wait until you return to your office to write the receipt.

There's still one more advantage of the rent receipt book, and that is its cost. It's the cheapest of any method for receipting rents. Even the fanciest and biggest rent receipt book costs only a few dollars.

■ **Receipts (Handwritten Pegboard System)**—While pegboard systems are less portable than receipt books, take more time to set up, and are more expensive, they have more features.

Pegboard systems, sometimes called "shingle systems" because the receipts resemble overlapping shingles, have three paper parts—receipts, receipt journals, and tenant ledgers—as well as a special board which has little pegs along its left side to help keep the journals and receipts aligned. When you write a receipt, you insert the tenant's ledger between the receipt itself and the journal. Then everything you write on the top line of the receipt will transfer via carbon to both the tenant's ledger and the journal.

You'll have a receipt to give the tenant. You'll

have a record of the tenant's payment on the tenant ledger, where all of this tenant's other payments appear. You'll also have a record of the payment on the receipt journal, which lists chronologically all payments made by all tenants.

By sorting the tenant ledgers according to those tenants who have paid and those who haven't, you can tell immediately who hasn't paid and take steps to remind them of their oversight. By glancing at the journals, you can tell how much has been collected over any given period, and you'll know how much you should have on hand to deposit as well as how much you should have deposited at other times.

Depending upon how many units you write receipts for every month, you might want to use a new receipt journal for every bank deposit or for every month's receipts rather than filling each journal full of entries and then filing it away. If someone other than you collects the rents, have the rent collector make two journals by putting a sheet of carbon paper between them. One is for the rent collector, and one is for the owner.

BUT, HERBIE, YOU NEVER SAID ANYTHING LAST MONTH WHEN I DIDN'T PAY YOU THE RENT. I DIDN'T THINK IT WAS IMPORTANT....

RENT DUE!

COLLECT RENT PROMPTLY!

If writing receipts by hand is more to your liking than writing them by computer, you should adopt a pegboard system as soon as you find yourself hiring people to work for you, for then you will be more in need of a thorough and foolproof recordkeeping system, and it is all of that.

Whichever type of handwritten receipt you use, make sure that each receipt is numbered sequentially. Unique numbers imprinted on the receipts help keep everybody honest. Lax owners sometimes discover that managers are keeping receipt books of their own which resemble the owners' receipt books, and they are writing receipts for monies paid by tenants but never turned over to the owners. Don't tempt your managers. Use a

system which makes cheating difficult. "Difficult" is the proper word here. No matter what system you use for receipting rents, you will find that cheating is possible. All you can do is minimize the opportunities.

By the way, Peachtree Business Products (pbp1.com), which appears under "Suppliers" in the SOURCES & RESOURCES section of this book, carries rent receipt pegboard systems among many other products for landlords. Many office supply stores sell them as well, either from stock or by special order.

■ **Receipts (Computer-Generated)**—Computer programs designed specifically for rental property management will generate numbered rent receipts and print them out on blank paper, too. They do everything a pegboard rent receipt system does and more.

They produce a variety of tenant, property, and delinquency reports using the data entered on the receipts, even in some cases producing delinquency letters and pay-or-quit notices based upon that same data.

In other words, they put the receipt data to greater use than receipt-only systems do. They leverage the data. They can tell the landlord at any given time who's late with the rent, and they can create pay-or-quit notices for those tenants.

■ **Receipts (Web-Based)**—With the widespread use of the internet have come more uses than anybody could ever have imagined a few years ago. One of those uses is the payment and tracking of rents online. Search the phrase "online rent payment," and you will find any number of web-based rent payment services which will provide you and the tenant with a receipt for the payments they collect. Such convenience!

Using a web-based rent payment service is certainly convenient, but it's also risky business because your rent monies could disappear into an unscrupulous operator's bank account one day, and you would have little recourse for retrieving it. Weigh the risks and the advantages of using such a service before you decide to use one.

■ **Due Date**—You may have noticed I mentioned before that rent ought to be due on the first. My rents all are, at least they are initially. Why the first? There are several good reasons.

Rents traditionally are due on the first. Tenants are in the habit of paying on the first. They associate the first of the month with bill paying and rent payments, and consequently they are more likely to remember to pay without having to be prompted. Busy as you are, you remember, too, when rents are due on the first. You can identify and handle the delinquencies more readily if the rents are all due at the same time instead of trying to remember which day of the month each tenant's rent comes due.

Once I bought a 41-unit residential income property which had rents due throughout the month. This interminable series of rent due dates confused the tenants as much as it did the manager and me.

The manager and I put our heads together and decided that we should try changing a quarter of the tenants' due dates to the first of the month and see what happened. We were delighted by what happened. Collections immediately became easier, and delinquencies declined. The tenants remembered to pay, and we remembered to collect. A month later, every tenant's rent at that property was due on the first.

■ **Other Due Dates and Frequencies**—Sometimes tenants cannot pay you their rent on the first because the first doesn't coincide with the day when they get paid. Should you accommodate them? By all means you should, but you might also want to charge them a little extra for this privilege so that it's worth your while to make the exception.

If they happen to be paid weekly or biweekly or semimonthly, you might even consider collecting their rent more frequently than once a month to insure that you get their rent money before they have a chance to spend it on something else, but in exchange for this accommodation you should definitely charge them more. How much more? Anywhere from $5 to $50 per month.

Some landlords accommodate their tenants who get paid every other week by allowing them to pay the equivalent of half a month's rent every time they get paid. Do the math, and you'll discover that the tenants are actually paying an extra month's rent every year. That's an extra 8.3% they're paying for the convenience of paying their rent when they themselves get paid. It's not a deal I would agree to if I were a tenant, but then I don't pay a commission to have my checks cashed at a check cashing store, either. I use a bank.

Should you encounter a tenant who wants to pay you half a month's rent every other week, instead of one month's rent every month, put the payment amounts and the payment frequency in writing as an addendum to the rental agreement or redraw the whole rental agreement to reflect this payment arrangement.

■ **Late Date**—Just as important as a realistic due date for rents is a realistic late date. This is the day when you first consider rents delinquent and start assessing penalties. I believe in giving my tenants several days of grace to get their rent to me, considering their rent late only if it hasn't been paid by the fourth of the month. If it's paid on the fifth or thereafter, they're late, and they know they have to face the penalty. Why? There are two good reasons, one somewhat legal and one very practical.

In some jurisdictions, there's a law on the books requiring that a rent due date must be a banking day, that is, a weekday when the banks are open. According to the thinking behind the law, tenants must have an opportunity to visit their bank in person to cash a check, buy a money order, or withdraw funds to pay the rent. If the rent due date falls on a Saturday, Sunday, or holiday, days when they cannot get to their bank, you may not consider their rent late until the day following the next available banking day.

Yes, I know that many banks are now open Saturdays and that every bank has an ATM for dispensing cash, but these laws won't change anytime soon. After all, many states still have obsolete laws on their books. There are laws banning housewives from hiding dirt under their rugs, laws banning pet owners from exposing their pets to cigar smoke, laws banning marble and domino games on Sunday, and laws banning motorists from driving with uncaged bears in their cars.

Under current landlord-tenant laws in many

[Every state sets its own time frame for this notice. If you don't know your state's time frame, call your local rental housing association, check the landlord-tenant laws on your state's website, or check the landlord-tenant law summary in the guest subject area of rhol.org.]

Notice to Pay Rent or Quit

TO: __CHESTER & CATHY CAREFREE__

and all other tenants in possession of the premises described as:
__460 SWEET STREET, LITTLETOWN, CA 09090__

PLEASE TAKE NOTICE that the rent is now due and payable on the above-described premises which you currently hold and occupy.

Your rental account is delinquent in the amount itemized as follows:

Rental Period: __MARCH 1 THROUGH MARCH 31, XXXX__ Rent due $ __650.00__

less partial payment of $ __Ø__

equals TOTAL BALANCE DUE of $ __650.00__

YOU ARE HEREBY REQUIRED to pay said rent in full within __3__ days or to remove from and deliver up possession of the above-described premises, or legal proceedings will be instituted against you to recover possession of said premises, to declare the forfeiture of the Lease or Rental Agreement under which you occupy said premises and to recover rents and damages, together with court costs and attorney's fees, according to the terms of your Lease or Rental Agreement.

RENT MUST BE PAID IN FULL AND IN PERSON TO THE FOLLOWING PERSON OR ENTITY:

Name __LANDLADY PROPERTIES__ Phone __800·555-1212__

Address where rent is to be paid __453 SWEET STREET, LITTLETOWN, CA 09090__

Usual days and times for payment of rent __M-F 5-8P; SAT. 9A - NOON__
Please phone in advance to make sure that someone will be available to accept payment.

OTHER REQUIRED WORDING, IF ANY:
```
If your tenancy terminates pursuant to this notice, you have the
right to request an initial inspection of your unit and be present
during the inspection. This is to allow you the opportunity to
correct any deficiencies in the unit in order to avoid deduction
from the security deposit, if any. Please contact your manager at
the phone number above to request an initial inspection which will
occur more than 48 hours after service of this notice.
```
Dated: __MARCH 5, XXXX__   *Leslie Landlady*
                                    Owner/Manager

PROOF OF SERVICE (Complete this proof of service only AFTER tenants have been served.)
   I, the undersigned, being at least 18 years of age, declare under penalty of perjury that I served the above notice, of which this is a true copy, on the above-mentioned tenant(s) in possession in the manner(s) indicated below (NOTE: Methods two and three below may also require mailing):

☒ On __MARCH 5, XXXX__, I handed the notice to the tenant(s).

☐ On _____, after attempting personal service, I handed the notice to a person of suitable age and discretion at the residence/business of the tenant(s).

☐ On _____, after attempting service in both manners indicated above, I posted the notice in a conspicuous place at the residence of the tenant(s).

☐ On _____, I sent a true copy of the notice in a sealed envelope via ☐ first-class ☐ certified ☐ registered mail with U.S.P.S. postage fully prepaid, addressed to the tenant(s) at his/her/their place of residence.

Executed on __MARCH 5, XXXX__, at the City of __LITTLETOWN__,
County of __SADDLEBACK__, State of __CALIFORNIA__.

                    Served by *Leslie Landlady*

places, if the rent due date falls on the Saturday of a three-day weekend, the rent may be paid on the following Tuesday without penalty, and it is not considered late until Wednesday. Now if that Saturday were the first, and the first were your normal rent due date, that Tuesday would be the fourth of the month. Four days would be the longest possible legal period of time that tenants would ever have in which to pay their rent without incurring a penalty.

So, in order to be entirely consistent, I use this same grace period throughout the year—*four days*. There are no exceptions.

In practice, this grace period works well. You no longer have to listen to those hackneyed excuses tenants concoct for not having paid their rent on or before the first. You know and they know that if they haven't paid their rent by the fourth, there's either a significant excuse or there's a conscious attempt to avoid paying altogether. You save innumerable phone calls and trips on the second or third or fourth of the month to inquire about the rent, and you can feel entirely justified collecting more from a tenant who's missed the due date by at least four days.

While I was still requiring tenants to pay by the first of the month, I would feel guilty about charging a late-paying tenant $20 more if that tenant were only a day or two late. Sometimes I'd just tell the tenant to forget it, or I'd allow some tenants to get away without paying the additional sum and say nothing about it because I knew that collecting it from them would be well nigh impossible anyway. Such inconsistency in my collections made the whole process too subjective, and it made me uneasy. On the one hand, I wanted to be reasonable when somebody's paycheck got held up, and on the other hand, I wanted to be tough and collect rents promptly when due. I couldn't be both reasonable and tough, not when I was trying to enforce a policy which enticed me to make exceptions to the rule. My first-of-the-month late date became as well enforced as a big city's panhandling ordinance.

Changing my definition of lateness and adopting a policy that the tenants and I could live with, a policy which brooks no exceptions, made all the difference. It works! Try it. You'll see.

■ **Prompt-Payment Policies**—To encourage your tenants to pay their rent on time, you need a prompt-payment policy. There are four such policies that I'm aware of. Choose the one which best fits your circumstances, and then write it into your rental agreement. That's all you have to do. Lacking some landlord bashing ordinance or another in the area where your rental property is located, you don't need to follow the dictates of a higher authority in selecting a policy, at least not yet. You get to decide for yourself which one you want to use.

The first prompt-payment policy is the late fee policy. The second is the discounted rent policy. The third is the rebate policy, and the fourth is the timely eviction policy. Let's take a look at each of them in turn.

The late fee policy has been around at least since some delinquent tenant first told his landlord, "Your check has been dispatched via Pony Express. It'll get there sometime soon unless it gets there sometime later. Sooner or later you'll get your money. You don't need to have a cow about it." Late fees penalize tenants for paying late. They're in the same no-nonsense category as library fines, parking tickets, income tax penalties, loan payment late charges, and property tax delinquency assessments, and they're hated just as much. They're downers. Nobody likes paying them, but everybody understands why they're necessary, so long as they apply to everybody else. They're for the other forgetful dingalings and no-good scofflaws. Right?

Late fees carry negative connotations, and you should be sensitive to those connotations because of the stereotypical image of the landlord as a "money grubber." Do your part to shed that stereotype. Show that you're not a money grubber, that the purpose of your prompt-payment policy is simply to get the rents in on time so you can pay your bills.

In addition, you have to understand that tenants sometimes become so upset about being assessed late fees that they will seek vengeance, especially if they learn that you are enforcing your late fee policy selectively. Make them too upset at you, and they might punch another hole in a wall or else sue you for discrimination or for charging excessive late fees.

If you're writing a late fee into your rental agreement, make sure that it's a reasonable one. It should be coercive rather than punitive. It should serve to compel tenants to pay their rent on time. It should not serve to generate additional revenue. Some judges have ruled that late

Payment Pledge

Dear Landlord/Landlady:

On or before _OCTOBER 15, XXXX_ , I promise to pay you
$_1,600 —_ for rent and other charges now owing on the dwelling
which I rent from you located at _1001 SWIFT ST., APT #4_ .

I expect to be receiving sufficient funds to pay you from the
following sources:

Name	Address	Phone	Amount Expected
AID CREDIT UNION,	306 Willow Ave.,	555-1337	$1,600 —

Should you wish to, you have my authorization to verify these
sources.

If I fail to honor this pledge, I understand that I will be
evicted and that this pledge will be used against me as evidence
of my bad faith in paying what I owe.

_X_ I acknowledge receipt of a Notice to Pay Rent or Quit as
required by law to begin eviction proceedings. I understand that
the Notice may show a balance owed which is different from that
given above because a Notice to Pay Rent or Quit can demand only
delinquent rent. I also understand that the period mentioned in
this Notice is being extended to the date given above, at which
time I promise to pay you what I owe. If I fail to pay on or
before that date, you have the right to continue the legal
eviction procedure against me without having to serve me another
Notice to Pay Rent or Quit. I have already been served. I am
being given the extra time to pay only as a courtesy and only this
once.

Signed _John Hancock_

Dated _OCTOBER 8, XXXX_

fees must not exceed the damages you sustain when tenants pay late, whatever those damages happen to be. You shouldn't get into trouble for charging excessive late fees if you keep them in the $20 to $50 range, depending upon the amount of rent involved.

If you want to be daring, you could calculate each unit's share of the property and charge as your late fee that proportion of the late fee your lender charges you when you're late with your loan payment. You could justify doing so by arguing that you face that penalty when the tenant hasn't paid his rent and you need his rent money to make your loan payment.

Here's an example. Let's say you own a duplex. Your loan payment is $1,200 per month, and your late fee on the loan is $120. Each tenant's rent is $900, $600 of which goes to the loan payment. Use half of the lender's late fee, or $60, as the late fee on the rent because that's the "damage" you sustain when the duplex tenant pays late and you can't make your loan payment.

A variation on the standard late fee imposed on the very day rent becomes late is the imposition of an additional late fee which accumulates every day the rent is late. This daily fee, which ought to be a reasonable dollar or two per day, begins accumulating after the initial late fee is imposed and keeps accumulating until the tenants pay in full.

I would advise you not to use this policy because the "bookkeeping" becomes confusing, especially if the tenants make partial payments or are more than a month in arrears, and because judges tend to look upon daily late fees as Shylockian and may treat you unsympathetically in court when you are otherwise reasonable in your policies and fair in administering them.

The second prompt-payment policy has been around at least since some clever merchant devised the idea of discounting, that is, selling merchandise below its so-called "regular" price. Who wouldn't like to get a discount on rent of all things if one were offered? Yep, people love a bargain. They don't seem to care when you tell them that the advertised rent is what they pay if they pay on time and get the prompt-payment discount. The gross rent as written in their rental agreement may be $50 higher, but they hear only the word "discount," and they hear you say that if they pay their rent on time, you will give them a $50 discount off the gross rent. In other words,

they pay the net advertised rent. Such a deal!

Discounting rents by a small amount won't get you into any trouble. Discounting rents by a large amount may get you into trouble, and a troublesome tenant may take you to court claiming that it's nothing more than a ruse to circumvent the laws governing rental property late fees. I know of nothing in landlord-tenant law specifically about a discounted rent policy, so its validation depends upon whether a judge sees it as a ruse for collecting a late fee and decides to apply late-fee laws to your discounted rent.

Does discounting rents work? You bet it does!

It does have a drawback. It's self-administered, that is, tenants get to take the discount themselves. They will pay you whatever rent they feel they owe you, and that's the discounted rent, naturally. So you may have to remind them of the terms of your agreement whenever they're late, and you may have to play tough to make sure that they pay you the gross, non-discounted rent when they owe it to you.

The third policy has been around ever since the 19th century, when large companies introduced rebates to undercut competition from smaller companies. Except for one important difference, the rebate policy for rent is just like the discount policy for rent. Instead of tenants' determining for themselves whether they qualify to take their discount every month, you determine whether they qualify for their rebate. They send you the same amount of rent money every month, no matter what, and you send them a rebate check so long as they have complied with the terms of their rental agreement. As sole arbiter of whether they qualify, you get to exercise better control over the situation.

There's a price you pay for taking control, however. You have to take the time to make out and return those rebate checks. If that doesn't scare you off, you can be sure that your tenants will love you for giving them a rent rebate every month. They'll think you're a year-round Santa Claus.

A good variation on this rebate policy involves your sending out a statement every month and including on that statement a credit for the rebate the tenants earned by paying their previous month's rent on time.

The fourth prompt-payment policy has been around at least since the tenants of the Garden of Eden left their first home under duress. Because Adam and Eve failed to comply with the terms of their rental agreement, their Landlord evicted them. He wasted no time. He accepted no excuses. He gave no written notice. He showed them the way out and shut the gate behind them.

You may not do the same. You must give your late tenants a "pay or quit" notice first, and then you must follow the eviction procedure your jurisdiction prescribes. What is most important about following this no-nonsense, zero-tolerance prompt-payment policy is that it must be completed in a timely manner.

Timely evictions require careful attention, much persistence, and a good working knowledge of your jurisdiction's legal procedure for forcing nonpaying tenants to move out. Show your tenants that you know how to evict them when they don't pay, and they'll get the message. Don't get discouraged. The message may take a while to get through.

Late fees and timely evictions are the "stick" approach to encouraging tenants to pay promptly as compared to the "carrot" approach of the other two policies. As any parent knows, some kids respond better to the stick and some respond better to the carrot. The trouble is that you don't know which policy works best with your tenants until you try it, and these policies, once set, aren't something you want to change every so often just to give them all a try with the same tenants. So, when choosing a policy, consider the circumstances carefully, and then try the one you think would work best. Don't change it for a particular set of tenants unless you feel you have to. Experiment with different properties and different tenants. Eventually you'll hit upon an effective policy which you and your tenants can live with.

Your prompt-payment policy is supposed to get your tenants to pay their rent promptly, but it won't work at all unless you make it work, unless you make your tenants understand that they have to pay their rent on time or face real consequences, one monetary, the other, bothersome. Not only are they going to have to pay more when they're late, they're going to be bothered. You are going to be after them to pay. You're going to be bothering them, and you're going to bother them in the extreme by turning them out on the streets if they don't pay.

■ **Late Rents**—Collecting rents requires an effective, pragmatic rental policy with teeth in it

and someone to carry it out who is both firm and quick to act. You are in business and you should mean business when you are collecting rents.

Always treat late rents with gravity, but also treat late payers with understanding, depending upon your past experience with them as tenants. Sometimes the unexpected will cause even the most diligent of tenants to pay a few days late, and they will advise you voluntarily in advance just why they expect to be late and when they will have the money to pay. Such tenants deserve your patience while they cope with a calamity in their lives or a disruption in their income, and you would do well to accommodate them if you believe their explanation and if you believe that their rent will be forthcoming when they say it will be.

If, however, by the third day after the rent due date, normally the fourth of the month, the tenants have neither paid you their rent nor informed you that the rent will be delayed for some good reason or another, you should make plans to visit them the very next day to deliver a Notice to Pay Rent or Quit. Listen to their explanation sympathetically. If appropriate, talk with them about rental assistance programs available. Then have them make a definite commitment to pay on or before a certain date, not over two weeks hence for the best of tenants and within just a few days for those doubtful ones. Tell them that they will give you no choice but to begin eviction proceedings if they do not pay by the promised date. Have the notice already filled out so you can hand it to them before you leave, and tell them, "We give everybody one of these notices if the rent isn't paid by the fourth of the month, regardless of who it is. We treat everybody the same way."

In addition to serving the tenants with a Notice to Pay Rent or Quit, you might want to consider using another form, the Payment Pledge, shown on a previous page. This form serves several important purposes. By asking the tenants to reveal the source of their anticipated funds and by committing them in writing to a particular payment date, it forces them to think twice about making you a hollow promise to pay at some vague time in the future. It also acts as a kind of receipt for the notice. With their signatures on the pledge, the tenants acknowledge that they have received their Notice to Pay Rent or Quit. They won't be able to appear in court and claim that they never received any notice, not when you have their signatures on the pledge.

Giving them the notice on the fifth strengthens your case should you have to go to court later because you would have waited a reasonable period of time before giving the notice and you would have waited longer than required by law before filing the court papers. You would not appear hasty to the court, but more importantly, you would already have begun your court case.

If you fail to give the tenants a notice on the fifth, and they don't pay on the appointed day, you'll have to deliver the notice on the appointed day or the day after, and you'll have to wait the required number of days following service of the notice before you can file your papers with the court. That wastes precious days; whereas, if you deliver the notice on the fifth and the tenants don't pay on the appointed day, you can go right ahead if you wish and file your court papers that very same day because you have already served the notice and you should already have waited the required number of days.

What's that? Did I hear you say that you'd rather not give your delinquent tenants a Notice to Pay Rent or Quit the very first time they're late with their rent? Okay. That's somewhat understandable. Although a whack on the side of the head in the form of an "official" notice, along with the threat of a full-scale eviction, may be the only thing sufficient to motivate some ten-

ants to pay, others may be motivated better through a tap on their funny bone in the form of a lighthearted rent reminder.

Displayed here are two of the twelve reminders in the FORMS section. All of them are different, and all of them are designed to remind tenants in a half-humorous, half-serious way that their rent hasn't been paid yet and that you are going to do something about it unless they pay up.

Use these reminders sparingly, and vary them. Because each particular one loses its impact if used a second time, don't give the same one twice to the same tenants. Better tenants shouldn't need reminding that often anyway.

A dozen reminders should be enough to last a tenancy's lifetime.

Remember that these reminders do not take the place of a Notice to Pay Rent or Quit as far as legal eviction proceedings go. They're just a human-to-human approach intended to keep your relationship with your tenants from becoming too adversarial. They're a friendly nudge. That's all.

The sample reminders shown here are much reduced versions of those available in the back of this book. The full-scale versions are sized to accommodate copying on either half- or full-sized sheets of paper. Select the one you want, copy it, insert the appropriate names, deliver it, and expect to get your rent money with a smile.

■ **Partial Rent**—Sometimes your tenants won't have all of their rent. They will offer to pay part of it and promise to pay the balance before the month is out. If they do, hesitate a little just to be dramatic, and then take the money. Tell them you prefer not to accept part of their rent but that you will do it this time under the circumstances, provided they understand that they must pay the balance within a specified time frame or suffer the consequences of late payment, whatever those consequences are.

Much as I dislike the extra bother involved in collecting partial rent, I would rather get some of their rent money than risk getting none at all.

Whenever you accept partial rent, give the tenants a receipt which does not cover a specific rental period. Just identify the payment as "on account." The second receipt you write, the one for the balance, should include the rental period covered by both payments. Trying to calculate exactly how many days in a 31-day month are covered by 56% of the rent money is too confusing. Don't even bother.

> WHAT DO YOU MEAN "PAY UP OR GET ON DOWN THE ROAD"? I THOUGHT YOU WERE COOL.

> I'M NOT COOL. I'M YOUR NO-NONSENSE LANDLADY. YOU PAY, YOU STAY. YOU NO PAY, YOU NO STAY.

> BORN TO BE A LANDLADY

■ **Receipts for Past-Due Rents**—Writing receipts for past-due rents can be every bit as confusing as writing them for partial rents. Just remember that you should *never* write a receipt for a current rental period if your tenants are in arrears for an earlier period. All rent monies should apply first to the earlier period, and only after it has been paid in full should the monies apply to the current rental period.

Here's the reason why you must be especially careful when writing receipts for past-due rents.

Suppose some tenants are one month behind in their rent and you sue them for nonpayment. Suppose also that on the first of July they paid June's rent, but you gave them a receipt showing that they paid rent for the month of July.

Later, when you are suing them for nonpayment of rent and you're in court to prove your case, the tenants produce the receipt you wrote for the current month of July and tell the judge they lost the receipt for June. The judge will have to assume that they're telling the truth because you can't prove conclusively that they didn't pay for June. Your not having a copy of their June rent receipt doesn't prove anything. It's only what you have in your possession that counts. How can you prove that you don't have something? How can you prove that their June rent receipt never existed? You can't. Your stating under oath that they didn't pay for June doesn't prove anything, either. It's your word against theirs. So, the judge has to base his decision on the existence of their July rent receipt. It suddenly becomes important because it proves that they paid for July, and if they paid for July, then they probably paid for June. They win. You lose. You lose a month's rent, and you lose your court case, too. Not only do you have to begin your court case from the beginning if you want to evict the tenants, you have to endure the shame of having lost a battle on a battleground you ought to know better than your tenants.

Losing an entire month's rent because of a seemingly meaningless oversight can be hard to swallow, can't it? I repeat—*Never write a rent receipt for a current rental period if the tenant is in arrears for an earlier period.*

■ **Ramifications of Late Payment**—When tenants do get behind on their rent, the chances are good that they're behind on their other bills as well, and they'll be shaping up a list of payment priorities mentally or on paper. See that yours is on top. Pressure them. Become a physical and psychological presence in their lives.

Credit experts rank most people's priorities for paying their bills in descending order as follows:

1) Rent/Mortgage
2) Utilities
3) Telephone
4) Car payments
5) Insurance
6) Taxes
7) Heating fuel
8) Cleaning/Laundry
9) Schools
10) Doctors
11) Dentists
12) Club dues

Surprising, isn't it? You're right up there on the top of most people's bill priority list. Even so, remember that landlords are fair game to some nefarious people. They think there's nothing wrong with trying to beat you out of the rent money. They think that they can string you along with one promise after another and that you'll be so beguiled by their ruses that you will neither collect rent from them nor evict them for a long time to come.

What do you wish to allow your tenants to get away with? It's up to you. I have seen a middle-aged schoolmarm, 4 feet 10 inches tall and all of 90 pounds, keep supposedly incorrigible, hyperactive high school boys under her complete control even though they were more than twice her size. Another teacher, marveling at the situation, asked one of the boys why he never misbehaved in Miss Cheever's class. The boy replied, "Oh, she doesn't allow it." You cannot allow your tenants to pay late. If you do, you'll be the one who "pays" in the long run. Don't allow it!

If tenants don't have one month's rent when it's due, they're certainly not going to have two months' rent in thirty days. The longer they stay without paying, the harder it is for them to pay and the less desire they have to pay. Staying without paying becomes easier and easier. Why should they pay for time they have already spent under your roof? By allowing them to stay there rent free, you are only postponing the inevitable.

Don't think you're doing your tenants a favor by allowing them to stay there rent free. You aren't. You're spoiling them. You're leading them to believe that they don't have to be responsible for their debts.

Don't think your act of kindness in allowing them to stay there rent free is going to win you the tenants' undying love and sincere appreciation. It won't. They will think of you as a dupe and a weakling.

What's more, they see a big delinquent rent bill as your problem, not theirs. You caused them to owe you all that rent money. You allowed it to happen.

Yes, you read that right.

Tenants who owe their landlord months and months of back rent don't blame themselves for their not having paid what they owe. They blame their landlord for allowing them not to pay. They blame their landlord for not trying to collect and for not evicting them in a timely manner. That's the reason why they owe their landlord all that rent money. It's not their fault. It's their landlord's fault. Their landlord should have known that they could never pay multiple months of back rent in a lump sum. It's their dummy landlord's fault that they owe him so much money, and now he must take the consequences and suffer the loss.

Such thinking is much like that of the son who murdered his mother and father and asked the court for mercy because he was an orphan. Such thinking is ridiculous and self-serving, but it's the kind of twisted thinking you can expect from tenants who do everything possible to avoid paying their rent.

In all my experience as a landlord, I have never been pleased with myself when I have allowed any tenant to stay more than fifteen days beyond a missed rent due date. Dealing with these delinquencies has always cost me extra money, extra time, and extra aggravation. Even so-called safe risks, teachers, preachers, police officers, apartment managers (yes, even them), and college student body presidents, have moved out owing me money when I have permitted them to get more than fifteen days behind. I have collected lots of promises and a sheaf of sob-story letters from such people. In a very few cases I did manage to collect the past-due rent in full, but it always required a lot of my time, and I had to become a bill collector to do it.

Bill collectors charge creditors 50% of whatever they are able to collect. They know how much time and effort such work requires. You aren't charging enough rent to include bill collection among your many services, and you really do become a bill collector when you have to scurry around collecting late rents. Your rents should be paid promptly and voluntarily. Each collection should require no more than ten minutes of your time per month. That's all. That's enough.

Remember, too, that tenants who aren't paying you their rent are actually stealing from you. They might as well be picking your pocket or snatching your purse, but the law doesn't quite see it that way. The law gives you no immediate recourse. You can't call the cops for help. You have to rely upon your own self to get them to pay up or move out, and if you do something drastic, you're the one who'll be in trouble, just like a homeowner who harms a burglar with a booby trap. Only after you have resorted to a legal eviction procedure can you get the law behind you to settle the matter.

Collecting your rents swiftly and doggedly on a scheduled basis will prevent evictions for nonpayment of rent more than anything else you can do. Your tenants will know full well what they can expect of you. They may test you once, but they won't test you again. It's too costly. If they have to, they will borrow the money from someone else to pay their rent rather than risk your wrath and risk being evicted.

Lowering Rents

"Are you crazy? Lowering rents is un-American! It's Communistic with a capital 'C'! It's ludicrous! It's idiotic! It's ruinous! Why, everybody knows rents are supposed to go up year after year, not down!

"Did the soft drink bottlers raise their prices when sugar skyrocketed some years ago? You bet your sweet closet auger they did. Did they lower their prices when sugar prices plummeted? Not on your paint-spattered spectacles they didn't. Well, I won't lower my rents either! I don't care if everybody else in this town has lowered their rents. I'm not gonna follow 'em and lower mine.

"I need to charge higher rents, not lower rents. My costs are going up and up and up. Have you seen what a gallon of paint costs nowadays? It's up two bucks a gallon since the last time I had a vacancy. Have you seen what they're charging now for water and sewer compared to last year? They're both up almost 50%! I'd leave my places

vacant before I'd even consider lowering my rents."

This subject tends to animate those landlords who come from either or both of the following two schools of thought—those who think their costs should determine their rents and those who think they have a sacred duty to the "landlording cause" to raise rents whenever they can.

Forget such thinking.

Whether we like it or not, landlording is a competitive business subject to the free-market economy. Rents are just like any other commodity in the marketplace. The law of supply and demand determines what they will be. When the supply goes up and the demand remains the same, rents come down. When the demand goes up and the supply remains the same, rents go up. Students learn that simple lesson in Econ 101, and you as a landlord ought to recognize it and incorporate it into your business thinking.

When a developer builds a new housing tract close to where your vacant rental house is, and investors snap up those tract houses and start renting them out for a hundred dollars less than what you expect to charge for your older and smaller rental house, you've got a problem, a big problem. Either you lower your rent accordingly, or you'd better become accustomed to having a vacancy on your hands for a long time to come. The same holds true when the overbuilding of apartment houses or the departure of a big employer increases the vacancy factor in an area.

Some landlords respond to an area-wide vacancy increase by offering certain incentives, all with the express purpose of attracting warm bodies to occupy their rentals and increase their occupancy rates. The three most common incentives are these—reduction in move-in costs, premiums like television sets and microwave ovens, and "free" rent.

The one thing they'd never consider is lowering their rents. Too bad!

Let's stop to consider the costs and implications of the three incentives they like to use and compare those incentives to the one they ought to use, lowering rents.

Let's say that a standard 2-bedroom unfurnished apartment in our Sampletown is going for $800, and let's say, too, that each one of the incentives being tried by different landlords is reasonably successful in attracting tenants.

Reducing move-in costs to the bare minimum

of one month's rent and nothing more, the first of our incentives, is certain to increase the potential number of people who want to rent our property. In particular, it will attract the kind of people who lack the good sense needed to put money aside for contingencies. They can't afford to put up the normal deposit because they have no savings. You have to believe that such people are likely to be less responsible than tenants who have some savings.

So, what happens when you rent to some of these likely irresponsible hand-to-mouth tenants?

Here's what happens. You collect one month's rent before they move in. That's good. That's income, and we all like income, but at the end of their first month, they have possession of your apartment unit, which is worth $100,000, and you have nothing of theirs. You have no prepaid rent, no security deposit, and no cleaning deposit, nothing to insure that they will live up to their obligations to you as tenants.

If they choose to stay there until they're evicted and if they tear the place apart, which they might conceivably do, you're going to lose a bundle. You may even wind up giving them cash out of your own pocket as a bribe to get them to move. If that works and they do move out, you could still have a devastated apartment on your hands.

Crazy, eh? First you give them an incentive to move in, and then you give them an incentive to move out.

Eliminating deposits to attract tenants is reckless. It's risky business, and you as a landlord ought to avoid taking such risks because you have too much to lose if things go wrong, and things do go wrong when you're taking big risks.

What can you possibly hope to gain by filling a rental property with tenants who haven't complied with the time-honored requirement made of tenants, that they put up a deposit in case there's a problem later? Eliminating deposits is an invitation to trouble, big trouble, for it puts you at the tenants' mercy. They can leave their rental dwelling in any condition they want and at any time they want, and there wouldn't be a thing you could do about it. The monetary cost to you of this incentive is an unknown as are the worry and the pain, both of which are psychological costs to you.

My advice is this—*Do not eliminate or even reduce your move-in costs in order to attract tenants.*

How about the second alternative which some owners seem to love, the free TV or microwave oven? This one may work, but don't forget. It's going to cost you cash money up front. Nobody who moves in to get a free television set is going to wait a day, let alone a year, for the payoff. They want their payoff now, and what do you do when the tenants give notice after three months that they're leaving? Ask for the merchandise back? What do you do when they decide to move out at the end of a year so they can get a new bedroom set offered as a move-in premium at another apartment complex? Do you offer to match the premium they expect to get for moving elsewhere?

My advice on offering premiums in order to attract tenants is this—*Don't.*

How about offering a month's "free" rent as an incentive? After all, everybody perks up when they hear the word "free." Everybody likes something for nothing. Free rent should attract tenants the way free love attracts shore-leave sailors. Yes, it does, but the trouble is that neither the tenants nor the sailors tend to stay around very long, and good long-term tenants are the name of the game in rental housing, aren't they?

Then there's always the question about which month should be free. Should it be the first? the second? the sixth? the twelfth? And again, what do you do when tenants move out immediately after they get their free month? Should those who stay longer than twelve months get an extra month's rent free, too? You know they'll want it.

Another problem with free rent is that it interferes with the smooth flow of your property's income. You could have some months with no income, some with minimal income, and some with normal income.

Appraisers don't like to see spikes and see-saws in a property's income. They like to see consistent income, and so do the lenders who examine your books to determine whether your property qualifies as sufficient collateral for that new loan you want to put on it.

My advice on free rent is this—*Don't open the store every Monday and give away the product.*

All right, how about lowering the rent? Lowering your rent $25 below everybody else's will bring you all the applicants you could wish for. It will cost you $25 per month, and that's $300 spread out evenly over a year's time, *but* it will likely gain you tenants who will still be around after a year, at which time you would be reassessing Sampletown's vacancy situation and resetting the rent higher or lower.

My advice on lowering rents is this—*If you feel you have to do something in order to be competitive and keep your occupancy rate up, then, by all means, lower your rents. It can actually increase your income.*

If lowering rents makes sense as a way to be competitive, you have to wonder why there's any resistance to it. The answer isn't hard to find. Owners of multiple-family rental properties are reluctant to lower their rents because they think they're lowering the value of their property. In spite of the disconnect between rents and property values today, rents still do affect the value of a multiple-family rental property somewhat.

A seven-times-gross property would be worth $2,100 less if the rent on only one unit were reduced $25 per month (25x12x7). A ten-times-gross property would be worth $3,000 less (25x12x10).

Consequently, many owners in high-vacancy areas prefer to concede anything other than rent. They think of the cost of lowered rent in terms of property devaluation rather than annual rent loss. They'd rather give away a $300 TV set or a month's rent to preserve the illusion that their property is worth thousands more. Such people are merely deceiving themselves and hoping to deceive others into thinking that their property is worth more than it is.

Don't deceive yourself into thinking that you can prop up the value of your property by charging a new tenant at least as much rent as you were charging a previous tenant, not when the market has changed and the demand for a rental dwelling like yours has declined. You have to go with the market. You have no choice. You have to lower your rent to fill your vacancies.

Do not hesitate. Do it.

Setting Rents

If your rental property is in a rent-controlled area, you don't have to worry about setting your rents. The rent control authority does the job for you, but you do need to keep the authority honest. You do need to check their numbers to make certain that they're allowing you to charge as much rent as the regulations allow you to charge.

If your rental property is not in a rent-con-trolled area, you need to set your rents yourself. No, that's not right. You need to determine what the market is for vacant dwellings such as yours and set your rents accordingly.

Setting rents used to be a simple matter because rents used to be tied closely to property values. The rule of thumb for an unfurnished house or duplex provided that the monthly rent should equal one percent of its fair market value. A $50,000 house, for example, would rent for $500 a month, and the tenant would pay for all the utilities and handle the minor repairs. For multiple-family dwellings larger than duplexes, the rule of thumb provided that the sum of the monthly rents would approximate 1.2% of the value of the property, a figure which is the reverse of the common yardstick that the value of ordinary multiple units in ordinary neighborhoods should equal seven times their annual gross rents. Each apartment in a $60,000 fourplex, then, would normally have rented for $180 per month.

Those old rules of thumb pretty much guaranteed owners a decent cash flow return on the investment.

Today, they no longer apply as they once did, for property values have swung wildly up and down while rents have merely crawled up or down. Today, a $100,000 house may rent for any sum of money, from $500 to $1,200, from one-half of one percent of the property value to 1.2%, and a multiple-family dwelling may rent for as little as one-half of one percent to as much as 1.4% of its value.

Property values do bear some relationship to the rents you might set for a multiple-family dwelling but no relationship at all to the rents you might set for a single-family dwelling. Supply and demand set property values in the sales marketplace, and supply and demand set rents in the rental marketplace, but they are two different marketplaces.

Just as you cannot simply peg your rent to the value of your property, you cannot add up what you are paying for utilities, maintenance, repairs, financing, bookkeeping, taxes, and management, and then add a percentage for your profit and say that you're going to rent your property for that sum of money. That's not the way the business works. Nobody guarantees a landlord anything these days, least of all a profit. Rents no longer guarantee owners a cash-flow return, and setting them is no longer a simple calculation using percentages and multipliers.

Since the residential real estate market, which is measured in property values, and the rental housing market, which is measured in rents, have diverged appreciably over the years so that they are no longer bound together by time-honored rules of thumb for setting rents, you must look to the rental housing market itself when you set rents today. In other words, with rents no longer contingent upon the value of your property or upon your costs for holding and maintaining the property, you have to familiarize yourself with what people are willing to pay for living quarters like those you have available for rent, and then set your rents at a level sure to attract good applicants.

You can't expect to get $1,000 a month for your $100,000 house if other owners are renting similar houses for $850, and some of them are going begging. You might have to ask $800 to get a good tenant. Then again, if houses like yours are renting for $1,200 a month and there are none available for rent when yours becomes available, you might find good tenants right away who are willing to pay $1,400 a month.

Whether we like it or not, the rental property business is no monopoly. It's private enterprise in action, and wherever there's private enterprise in action, there's a free marketplace. Some foolish landlords might think they have a monopoly. They might think they can set their rents as high as they want and then tell people, "Take it or leave it." They're wrong, and the marketplace will tell them they're wrong. People will "leave it" if they can rent the same thing elsewhere for less, and the foolish landlords are left with vacancies which produce zero revenue and zero profit until they come to their senses and set their rents at realistic levels according to the market.

People aren't fools with their rent money. They're price-sensitive. They try to figure out the market by looking at the various rental dwellings available when they themselves are in the market. They shop around.

Tenants look for the best buys in rents just as shoppers look for the best buys in automobiles, gasoline, corn flakes, orange juice, and bacon. What dictates the prices of these items? The market does, the market of supply and demand.

When Florida has a freeze and juice oranges suffer, the price of orange juice increases because the supply has decreased. The price increases until people stop paying it, until they say to themselves that they can do without orange juice at such high prices. They wait, maybe they substitute tomato or apple juice, until the price of orange juice comes down. That's the free market at work.

When oil crews descended *en masse* upon the small Montana community where my wife grew up, the demand for rental housing outstripped the community's supply, and rents increased overnight until the oil crews balked and started living in their cars and motorhomes. Seeing an opportunity to cash in on the boom, one enterprising rancher leveled a few acres, built a trailer park, and took care of some of the demand for housing. Local contractors built a number of apartment houses and took care of more of the demand. Finally, when everybody was accommodated, rents stabilized. They fluctuated across a narrow range until the crews left *en masse* several years later. When that happened, the demand plummeted and rents did, too, because the supply remained high when the demand became low. That's the free market at work.

Keep in mind that this free market for rental dwellings is a disorderly market because rental dwellings do not have the uniformity of commodities like corn and crude oil and orange juice or securities like stocks and bonds. Commodities and securities have orderly markets because they are uniform. You can ascertain the price of one share of IBM or one bushel of corn delivered in Chicago just by checking them online or by making a simple phone call. One share of IBM is the same as any other share, and one bushel of corn delivered in Chicago is the same as any other bushel delivered in Chicago. Not so with rental dwellings! They're all different. As a result, there's no one source you can call, no one place you can look, to ascertain the market price for your rental dwelling.

Even units in the same building will rent for different prices because they're different. Some might have views of a park. Some might have views of an air shaft. Some might have desirable corner locations which get lots of sun. Some might have less desirable locations along a corridor which never gets any sun. Some might have special amenities such as larger closets or remodeled kitchens. Some might not have been touched since they were built immediately after WWII.

Consider these differences when setting your

rents. Set the rent higher for desirable sunny units with a view and lower for dingy units looking out onto an air shaft even though they're exactly the same otherwise. Desirability translates into demand in the disorderly market for rentals, and demand translates into higher rent.

To determine what the rents ought to be for your rentals, you have to do a little work to learn approximately what the market prices are, the same kind of work that tenants are doing who are in the market for a rental dwelling like yours. They're out shopping.

Now comes another key element in this whole discussion about the rental dwelling market, something you should remember whenever you're setting your rents. The market in rental dwellings is not a market in *all* rental dwellings. It's a market in *vacant* rental dwellings. They alone are your competition. They alone are available for rent. They alone are *on* the market for people who are *in* the market to rent a dwelling. You needn't concern yourself with the rents being charged for occupied dwellings. Those places are no longer available to the public. They are currently off the market and can't be rented by anybody at any price. Only when they come back on the market do they become your competition. Then they become vacancies, and they again become the "supply" in the supply-and-demand equation.

Whenever I think about how supply-and-demand affects rents, I think about the housewife who goes to the market to ask the butcher for a five-pound, cross-rib roast. He shows her a beautiful one, well-marbled and well-trimmed, and as he puts it on his scale, he says, "Let's see, at $3.99 a pound, that'll be $16.95." She looks at him wide-eyed and exclaims, "$3.99 a pound! Mr. Crump down the street sells me his cross-rib roasts, which are just as nice as this, for $2.69 a pound."

So the butcher asks, "Then why don't you go down the street and buy one from Mr. Crump?"

"I'd like to, but he doesn't have any!"

To that, the butcher responds, "Well, if I didn't have any, I'd sell 'em for $2.69, too!"

The housewife couldn't buy the roast at $2.69 a pound because nobody had them available at that price. They were all sold out. She had to buy what was available or go without, and she chose to pay the $3.99 price.

Prospective tenants can compete with each other only for available rental dwellings. They might have some friends who are renting a two-bedroom house for $650, and they might think that they can get a similar one for $650, but if all the two-bedroom houses now on the market are renting for upwards of $725, that's what the prospective tenants are going to have to pay unless they can convince an anxious landlord, who currently has a vacancy and is worried about making his loan payment and paying his property taxes, to lower his rent. They might indeed be able to convince a landlord to lower his rent by pointing out how much rent their friends are paying, that is, unless the landlord understands that he shouldn't be trying to match the rents of occupied houses. The rents being paid for occupied houses were set in a previous market, not the current market, and they should not concern him. His vacant rental house is in the current market.

More out of curiosity than for direct help in setting the rent for your vacant dwelling, you may want to check the rental data available on the internet. Rentometer.com and zilpy.com are two of a number of websites which provide rental market data for landlords and tenants alike to use as benchmarks when they're curious about rents.

As benchmarks, this rental market data is good to keep in mind, but it's no substitute for neighborhood knowledge, which is more specific and more current. Also, because it's weighted more toward occupied units, this data does not reflect what's happening in the market for vacant units right now, today, and you should not rely upon it exclusively when setting your rents.

To set your rents at current market levels, you need to learn what your competition is asking in rent for vacant dwellings which are comparable to yours in location, size, condition, amenities, and upkeep. You can find that information easily on the websites of rental property management companies operating in your city. To find them, search on the words "rental property management companies [your city]." This information is as current as any because every listing represents a vacant rental dwelling.

To go further, you may want to visit the listings to see whether they are, in fact, comparable to your vacant rental. You may want to ask other members of your rental housing association what they think the rent ought to be for a dwelling such as yours. You may want to ask the same question of other owners you know and of the local housing authority which administers the Section 8 Housing Program. You may want to check HUD's fair market rents for your area available on their website at huduser.org/portal/datasets/fmr.html. You may want to check Craigslist for vacant properties in the area and drive by them.

Still unsure about the market rent for your rental dwelling? Try this.

Check the ads for rental properties similar to yours in a community newspaper which is several weeks old or on Craigslist (Craigslist organizes its listings by date, so finding an old listing is easy). Contact several of the advertisers and ask if their dwellings are still for rent. If they are, you know the rents are too high. If they have already been rented, the rents are either too low or about right.

When you have done your homework, you will know what constitutes a competitive rent for your dwelling, and you won't have to wonder after it's rented whether you could have charged more.

Remember that when you set any rent, you are virtually fixing it at one level for a twelve-month period. Treat this process as seriously as the serious business it is.

Remember also that setting the rent too low is the biggest mistake you can make when you're setting rents. Don't be afraid to set your rent high, because anyone who looks at the place will tell you if the rent really is too high, whereas they won't say a word if it's too low. If no potential renter offers an opinion and you're wondering what they think about the rent you've decided to charge, ask them. You can easily lower the rent any time you want, but you can't always raise it so easily.

By the way, there's another method you might want to try when setting the rent for a particular unit. It's not for the faint of heart because it's a little unorthodox and contains an element of risk. It also requires a little extra work.

The method is holding an auction. Auctions are as legitimate a marketplace as there is, and so long as enough people who might be interested in the auction items know about the auction, the sales prices will be market prices.

Surely you've heard of the phenomenal success of eBay, the website where sellers come to auction off everything from soup bowls to nutcrackers, from yesterday's computers to today's software, from Japanese automobiles to Florida real estate. These auctions work because the website is well organized and because anyone anywhere with access to the internet can participate. With so many people, dealers and end users alike, aware of the items for sale, sales prices reach levels higher than they would were the auctions held only for a limited audience, that is, for those who are able to attend in person.

Whereas you could try conducting an internet auction for your vacant rental, it may not yield the best results. It may not yield the best results because the "merchandise" you're selling has two significant limitations. It's rooted in place, and it's rooted in time. You can't package it up and send it off to Timbuktu, nor can you hold it off the market for the "buyer" who wants it six months from now. The buyer must have an immediate need for the unit and must want to live there in particular rather than anywhere else on the planet.

An internet auction would expose the unit to many people, that's true, but that's of no advantage when only a very small number of those people would be interested, and some people who would definitely be interested in renting it don't use the internet and would never know about the auction. You want anybody and everybody who might be interested to know. You also want them all to see the unit before they bid on it. An internet auction, eBay style, would limit the rental unit's exposure and unnecessarily complicate the renting process.

You could organize a live auction, just as Sotheby's and Christie's do when they organize formal auctions for collectibles, but such auctions would be impractical for rental dwellings. They take too much time to arrange. By the time you could arrange a well-publicized auction to attract a gathering of potential renters, your property would have been vacant a month or more, and the prospects who were looking at rentals when you first had your vacancy would already have found a place to rent. They wouldn't want to wait around for you to hold an auction and not know until then whether they were going to get the place. Time in landlording is too important to waste. Whereas you would know that your auction helped you determine the market rent for your rental dwelling, you'd have had to sacrifice too much to get it.

The best auction alternative for rental properties is a silent auction, one held during an open house or for some short (two days at most), specified period. You would start the bidding at the lowest price you're willing to take and invite those who have seen the place to submit a higher bid along with their applications. Before closing the bidding, you would contact all bidders, apprise them of the highest current bid, and give them the opportunity to raise their bids one last time. Then you would take the highest bid, check out the highest bidder's application, and, upon approval, rent to that person.

A silent auction leaves no doubt as to what the market is for your rental, at least as long as you have advertised the place in the right ways to attract enough interest, but because it takes some extra time and involves some uncertainty for the bidders, you stand to lose good tenants who want to conclude their search quickly and move in quickly. You also stand to lose good tenants who simply don't want to participate in something as unorthodox as a bidding process when they're in the market for a rental unit. In addition, you stand to lose face if nobody bids and you have to lower the lowest price you're willing to take, something which your current tenants will learn about soon enough, and then they will pressure you to lower all of your rents. Those are the risks you take in conducting a silent auction.

Try a silent auction if you're in a hot rental market and tenants are beating down your doors to have a look at your vacancies. There's no better way to determine market-level rents at the very moment when you have a vacancy available.

Don't try a silent auction if you're in a cold rental market and cannot expect enough interest in your rental unit to attract more than a few applicants. Any auction under those circumstances would be a futile exercise.

Raising Rents

If you are at all like most landlords, you dislike rent raises more than any other aspect of this business because of the tenant dissatisfaction and resentment they frequently cause. In spite of what you see in the media, statistics show that landlords have a real aversion to raising rents, for not only have rents failed to keep pace with percentage increases in property values over the years, they haven't even kept pace with the consumer price index. In other words, no matter what people in general think about rent levels, no matter how shrill their cries for rent control, landlords have actually been both lax and restrained in raising rents.

There's no good reason for you to stop disliking rent raises, but you should come to accept them as a necessary element in the conduct of your own landlording business, an element made absolutely necessary by the impact of inflation on your expenses. Since your very business survival depends upon your being able to meet these increased expenses with increased revenues, you have no choice but to raise rents or go out of business.

You must expect that any raise may expose you to charges of profiteering and may precipitate a whole host of tenant complaints, but you must learn to cope with these problems unless you have some perverse desire to subsidize your tenants, in effect, for the dubious privilege of serving them as their landlord or unless you wish to invest your money and time in a business venture which only loses money. You are in this business to make a profit, aren't you? It certainly is not worth the worry, the risk, the trouble, the time, the sweat, and the dollar investment otherwise.

To have the desired effect, raising rents requires a policy as carefully outlined as your rent collection policy, one calculated to minimize tenant dissatisfaction and resentment. Rent raises under this policy should occasion neither a mass revolt nor a mass exodus of your tenants because they should come to understand that your rent raises are fair and, therefore, acceptable.

This policy should involve six elements—careful preparation, proper timing, extended lead time, reasonable increments, amicable notices, and personal contact.

■ **Careful Preparation**—Careful preparation for rent raises consists of much more than merely preparing the notices to change terms of tenancy. That's the most visible, most mandatory part of the preparation, but it's really the smallest part and the least time-consuming, too. Actually, careful preparation should continue year-round. As soon as you give one increase, you should already be preparing for the next one.

Here's what you ought to be doing to prepare—

✔ Prepare by keeping up with your bookkeeping every month so you know how much your expenses are and how high you need to raise the rents in order to operate profitably and also so you can refer to your expenses knowledgeably whenever you discuss with your tenants your reasons for raising the rent.

✔ Prepare by keeping track of market conditions in your area so you know what current rents are for other similar rentals.

✔ Prepare by beginning a rumor that the rent will increase to a level higher than what you anticipate, so the tenants are relieved when they learn later how small the increase was in comparison to what they had expected.

✔ Prepare by telling your tenants exactly when they can expect the rent to increase.

✔ Prepare by charging new tenants the rents you're planning to charge when you do raise rents so that when the rents are raised for everyone else to those market levels, or close to them, you can tell your old tenants that new tenants have already been paying the higher rents (because good, long-term tenants are hard to find and cost you far less in many ways than do short-term tenants, give them special consideration when you're raising rents, and keep their rents a few dollars below market levels).

THAT ABOUT DOES IT, SYBIL... YOUR OLD KITCHEN FAUCET WAS SO WORN OUT I HAD TO PUT IN A NEW ONE. IT SHOULD LAST A LONG TIME!

I SURE APPRECIATE ALL THE WORK YOU DO AROUND HERE, LARRY... YOU MAKE THIS A PLEASANT PLACE TO LIVE.

I ALMOST FORGOT. WE'RE GOING TO HAVE TO RAISE YOUR RENT $12⁰⁰. WE HATE TO DO IT BUT WE JUST HAVEN'T BEEN MEETING OUR EXPENSES LATELY.

WHAT?! @#* YOU EXPECT ME TO PAY $12⁰⁰ MORE FOR THIS DUMP?!

WHY DO THEY CALL HER SYBIL?

With such preparation, you will forestall most of the arguments tenants are inclined to use when they're trying to prove that your rent increase was unfair and irresponsible.

■ **Proper Timing**—The proper time to raise rents is always when tenants are expecting an increase. More than at any other time, they expect increases when there is a change in ownership, so give them an increase then if one is justifiable, but take a week or two first to become acquainted with the property and determine whether an increase is, in fact, justifiable.

Once when I was new to the business of landlording and reluctant to raise rents at all, I waited twenty months after buying a building before making a well-warranted $20 increase across the board, which amounted to 12% of the rent at that time. As soon as she received her notice, one irate tenant called me to complain. She said that she had expected me to raise the rents when I bought the building almost two years before, but coming when it did, the increase was a complete surprise to her and therefore totally unfair. How do you argue with reasoning like that? You don't. Clearly, I had done things wrong even though I hadn't done her wrong. I had assumed that an impersonal increase notice and all that elapsed time since their last increase would be sufficient for the tenants to accept a new rent raise unquestioningly. Of course, that wasn't sufficient because the tenants simply were not expecting an increase right then. I had failed to condition them with careful preparation, and I hadn't timed the increase properly.

Take my advice and raise your rents when tenants expect increases, and condition them to expect increases like clockwork one year after the rents were last raised.

Following this policy, you might want to stagger your rent increases throughout the year by scheduling them to coincide with the anniversary of each tenant's arrival. In doing so, you spread whatever repercussions there might be to your rent increase. Dealing with a few disgruntled tenants is easier than dealing with lots of them.

If possible, time your rent increases to coincide with some improvements you are making to the property so the tenants will believe they are getting something more for their money and will complain less at having to pay more.

Proper timing refers to the cycle of increases and to tenant conditioning, and it also refers to the actual moment when the official written rent

[Every state sets its own time frame for this notice. If you don't know your state's time frame, call your local rental housing association, check the landlord-tenant laws on your state's website, or check the landlord-tenant law summary in the guest subject area of rhol.org.]

Notice of Change
in Terms of Tenancy
(Rent)

TO _Sam and Barbara Brooks_ , Tenant in Possession
 3104 Dogwood Drive
 Big Town, CA 09601

YOU ARE HEREBY NOTIFIED that the terms of tenancy under which you occupy the above-described premises are to be changed.

Effective _____ _August_ _____, _XXXX_ , your rent will be increased by _#22_ per month, from _#650_ per month to _#672_ * per month, payable in advance.

Dated this _2nd_ day of _____ _June_ _____, _XXXX_ .

Fred Felder, Manager
Owner/Manager

This Notice was served by the Owner/Manager in the following manner (check those which apply):

(X) by personal delivery to the tenant,
( ) by leaving a copy with someone on the premises other than the tenant,
( ) by mailing,
( ) by posting.

* When rent is paid on or before the third day following the rent due date, you may take a $20 discount.

Sorry, Sam & Barbara! I hate doing this but our increased expenses are getting the better of us.

increase notice will reach the tenants.

Now I have to admit that I haven't come to any conclusion yet as to what is the best time of the day to deliver rent increase notices. I'm still studying that one, but I do believe that I know the best time of the month to deliver them. The best time of the month to deliver rent increase notices is right after tenants have paid their rent, when they have put rent out of their minds for another month and it's no longer a matter of immediate concern.

■ **Extended Lead Time**—Normally, any changes in terms of tenancy, including rent increases, require a lead time equal to the rental period. Tenants who rent on a monthly basis are supposed to get thirty-day notices. Tenants who rent on a weekly basis are supposed to get seven-day notices.

This isn't enough lead time for rent increase notices. I recommend *doubling* the lead time for rent increase notices. Sound ridiculous? It isn't ridiculous in the least. It's a sound business strategy. Here's why.

Upon receiving a thirty-day notice that their rent is going up, some tenants have a knee-jerk reaction and immediately give notice that they're going to move. They know that they're supposed to give you thirty days notice (unless you follow my advice and stipulate in their rental agreement that they need give you only fifteen days notice), and they feel that they have to register a quick protest to your notice. Your notice is a threat to them, and they feel certain that they can find a better place to live for less. Even when they discover that they can't find a better place to live for less, they may feel too proud to approach you about canceling their notice of intention to move. As a consequence, you could wind up losing some good tenants by not giving them an extended lead time.

Your tenants will appreciate a sixty-day notice. They will feel far less threatened when you give them that much time to consider their alternatives. They will have a whole month to look around before they have to give notice that they intend to move if indeed they do decide to move. The strategy lessens the tension and wins as much of their cooperation as you can possibly expect at this time.

Time heals all wounds. Time also lessens the impact of rent increase notices.

I first learned how effective this extended lead time could be when I bought a new property and decided to raise one tenant's rent 50% in order to bring it up to something approaching market levels. The tenant, of course, was irate about the whopping increase. I explained to him that he had been enjoying especially cheap rent for a long time under the old owners but that I couldn't afford to let him stay there at such a low rent. I told him, "You probably don't know how cheap your rent's been because you haven't had to look at places for rent for a long time. I tell you what. I'll give you a full sixty days before your rent goes up. You can look around for forty-five days to see whether you can beat the value you're getting here at the increased rent. If you can, give me just fifteen days notice that you're going to be moving, and I'll be happy."

He did some looking and quickly became convinced that he couldn't beat the rent he would be paying when the rent increase took effect. He didn't move out. Nope, he didn't move a thing. What's more, he actually thanked me for giving him the extra time to look around. I had raised his rent 50%, and here he was thanking me!

Be aware that in some parts of the country legislators have been looking closely at how little time tenants have to vacate when they're faced with a move precipitated by a rent increase. Finding a new dwelling and moving into it requires more than a month, say the legislators, so landlords ought to give tenants an extra month to move and give the tenants this extra month at the lower rent.

If you elect to give your tenants thirty days notice of a rent increase rather than sixty, you may be disappointed. You may be required to give them sixty. Check to see whether your legislators have granted your tenants what amounts to the extra lead time should they decide to move as a result of a rent increase. If you elect to give your tenants sixty days notice, you should already be in compliance with any such law.

■ **More Acceptable Numbers**—Having carefully prepared for the increase, you will know what rents are reasonable for your rentals and you will also then know approximately how much the raise should be.

Because you have to take many factors into consideration when you calculate any rent increase and because your final figure will usually be the result of numerous compromises, you may want to select an increment which is psychologically more acceptable to your tenants. The more acceptable numbers are those which are not multiples of five. $12, for example, is better than $10, and $18 is better than $15. Such figures lead tenants to believe that their increases have been carefully calculated to match actual increases in operating expenses rather than to include still more arbitrary profit for the owners, rounded up, of course, to the nearest $5.

■ **Reasonable Increments**—You are taking a calculated risk of creating vacancies with any rent increase you give, but that risk increases somewhat if the rent increase exceeds either 10% or the consumer price index, whichever is greater. If you have timidly lagged behind the marketplace and you now have to raise your rents higher than those guidelines to approach a reasonable rent schedule, you may want to do so even knowing full well that some tenants are going to vacate. Wish them well, and then don't get yourself into the same bind again.

Raise your rents on an annual basis from then on.

■ **Amicable Notices**—Besides preparing carefully, timing properly, coming up with acceptable numbers, and calculating reasonable increments, you should announce your raises officially in writing using honest, sympathetic notices. The notice itself is the culmination of all your work, and it should reflect the great care you have put into all the preparation thus far. The notice should soften the blow with some reasons for the raise and an expression of your personal concern about the possible hardships the increase might cause.

Use a cold, impersonal legal notice like the Notice of Change in Terms of Tenancy if you want, but add to it your own personal message. Mention the tenant by first name in a handwritten aside and apologize for the increase, saying that you are trying to maintain the tenant's dwelling as best you can, but that it is impossible to do so unless you raise rents.

Or you might want to prepare your own complete notice using personal wording like this—"As you know, we are living in inflationary times, and even though I do my best to keep costs down, there's no way I can reduce the expenses of this building back to what they were a year ago. I have absorbed these increases as long as I could, but now I am forced to increase your rent by $____, or ____%, from $____ per month to

$____ per month, effective ____, 20____."

Remember that if you use any rental agreement or lease form which has a discount provision, the increase should be based on the gross or non-discounted rental figure and not on the discounted amount that you are accustomed to collecting when the tenant pays on time. You might want to remind the tenant of this situation by stating it directly on the notice, asterisking the rental figures and explaining below as follows: "*When rent is paid on or before the third day following the rent due date, you may take a $XX discount."

Remember also that if you or a previous landlord collected your tenants' last month's rent when they moved in, the sum you originally collected won't be sufficient to cover the increased rent which will be in effect during their last month of tenancy. To avoid misunderstandings later, advise them that they must pay the increase for that last month's rent as soon as the new rent becomes effective. Otherwise you will have a difficult time collecting the difference between what they paid as last month's rent when they moved in and what the rent happens to be when they move out. Their having paid their last month's rent when they moved in does not entitle them to get their last month's rent at that lower amount. They owe you the difference, and you should collect it whenever you raise the rent.

■ **Personal Contact**—You may deliver a rent increase in person or by mail, but personal delivery is preferable because it provides an opportunity to discuss the reasons for the increase with your tenants on a personal level.

If you can't serve it personally, send them the notice, and post one on their door, too. You must rest assured that they have received at least the minimum time required by law for such notices, and your sending them a copy by first-class mail won't give you that assurance unless you give the notice plenty of time to reach them.

Should you suspect that your tenants might deny on a stack of Bibles that they ever received their notice, have somebody else deliver it. Then you will have a third party's word for verification. Accompany the third party if you like.

Controlling Rents

Can you imagine any politician proposing wage controls without price controls (trade unions might bicker among themselves about some matters, but this would unite them like iron filings on a magnet)?

Can you imagine any politician proposing ceilings on the prices which homeowners are allowed to sell their single-family dwellings for (homeowners would take up their Saturday-night specials to defend their right to sell their castles at fair market value)?

Both are such absurd proposals that any politicians espousing them today would be stripped of their offices and whisked off to asylums to babble with the other lunatics.

Yet, how many politicians are there who seriously propose rent control as the solution to rising rents, a scheme every bit as illogical as controlling wages without controlling prices and as utterly ridiculous as putting a ceiling on the price of houses? In effect, rent control does both. It limits landlords' "wages" without affecting their expenses, and it artificially limits the value of their rental property.

That's what I call "landlord bashing."

Politicians who support rent control don't see it that way, and they don't see themselves as fascists either. They see themselves as Robin Hoods, championing the cause of impoverished, victimized renters in the interminable and righteous struggle against the porky, wealthy landlords of this world. Them's you and me, remember. They hear the caterwauling of their tenant constituents lamenting the hardships of living on a fixed income and decide that the simplest way to appease these people is to limit the obscene profits flowing unabated into the pockets of the money-grubbing property owners. You and me again.

Although do-gooder politicians are only greasing the squeaky wheels in their communities when they act to control rents and are ignoring the long-term ramifications of what they are doing, they are in truth attempting to silence those noisy tenants the only way they can, with a specious solution to a large and complex problem.

The problem we all face, tenants, politicians, and rental property owners alike, is not constantly increasing rents, and the solution to constantly increasing rents is not rent control. The real problems are a shortage of housing and an increase in the many expenses involved in landlording, from toilet parts to garbage collection rates. The only real solutions are to build more housing, control inflation, and subsidize the housing of those who are truly poor. Obviously these are formidable solutions, ones which local politicians cannot effect easily, inexpensively, or quickly, if at all.

Rent control, on the other hand, is easy to enact and relatively inexpensive to administer, and it provides politicians' vociferous tenant constituents immediate relief. So what if it does exacerbate the real problems? So what if it does victimize those who own rental property? So what if it does favor all tenants regardless of their financial need? It appeases the people with the votes. Therefore, it is an ideal political solution for harassed politicians struggling to cope with what appears to be a local problem they feel they can handle, and it is a solution which is off-budget and unseen. Why not? It offers something for nothing. It appeals to people's greed.

Whenever it becomes an issue in your area, you would be wise to become involved in the political process which will determine whether rent control will be adopted, and if so, what form it will take. Any talk of rent control should bring you to your feet before rent control itself brings you to your knees. Support the political efforts of your rental housing association. Attend hearings. Drum up the support of homeowners and other landlords to oppose rent control.

Ask the reference librarian at your local library to help you find some of the many studies on the subject. Use the search words "rent control drawbacks" to search the internet for articles and books on the subject. Contact the Pacific Legal Foundation (see SOURCES & RESOURCES), which has been fighting rent control in the courts for years and years and has had some notable victories.

Write letters to your politicians and to the editor of your local newspaper citing certain rent control case studies and outlining your own views relative to the local situation. If, at last, you sense that some form of rent control is inevitable, become involved with the shaping of the measure so that it will be easier to live with. Face the fact that we live in a world which is more consumer-oriented than ever before, and expect that you will have to give a little.

Odious as rent control sounds to us landlords, conjuring up images of abandoned properties and unjustifiable bankruptcy, it may be written as a compromise to everyone involved. Tenants fear quantum leaps in their rents, increases of 30% and 50% a year, and you can hardly blame them. Landlords fear being forced to maintain rents at certain base levels *ad infinitum* and eventually losing their buildings. But some form of rent control might assuage both those fears.

Would you balk, for example, at rent control which would apply only to buildings with six or more units and would allow owners to pass through all increased expenses and prorations of improvements, as well as to increase rents by 10% per year? That wouldn't be hard to live with, would it? Well, that is rent control just as much as is a measure which requires you to roll back your rents to what they were twelve months ago and then keep them there forever. Compromises are possible, even desirable at times, in order for everyone involved to save face and prosper.

Finally, if rent control is adopted in any area where you own rental property, take the time to learn all you can about it. Are certain sizes of rental dwellings exempt from controls? Under what circumstances may you raise rents? What procedures are there for grievances? How are evictions affected by the controls?

The rent control regulations and the bureaucrats who administer them will answer these and other pertinent questions you might have. Become more familiar with the regulations than your tenants are. Be cooperative with the authorities, work within the law, and seek to change it whenever possible.

Don't panic. Don't give up. Don't sell. Shrewd owners study such predicaments thoroughly and learn how to profit from them. There's usually a way.

As for investing any more of your money in properties located in rent control areas, I wouldn't and don't. Invest it elsewhere. You don't need a "partner" who's telling you what you can and cannot do while looking over your shoulder all the time, assuming no responsibility, and contributing absolutely nothing toward providing better rental housing at a reasonable cost.

Some Last Words

Rents are the lifeblood of the landlording business. Setting them, raising them, lowering them, and collecting them are subjects you must know well if you're going to succeed. Return here now and then to reread this chapter so you will be ever mindful of these subjects.

By all means, remember that your raising rents doesn't suddenly metamorphose you into a greedy, unscrupulous monster of a landlord. Rather, it means that you are a good business person who understands the nature of the business you find yourself in. You understand that you can lose money in this business if you want to, just as you can lose money in any other business, and that no one will care, least of all your tenants. You understand that no one is going to nominate you for the "Landlord of the Year Award" just because you leave your rents low, nor is anyone going to tell you that your rents are too low.

When was the last time one of your tenants told you the rent was too low and offered to pay more? Don't wait for it to happen. It won't. Tenants who offer to pay higher rents are as rare as one-armed violinists. Just because they don't volunteer to pay more, however, doesn't mean that the dwellings they occupy aren't worth more rent and that they can't pay more.

You are the only one to judge what is the right rent based upon market conditions, and you alone must take the initiative necessary to raise your rents. Set up a schedule for raising rents. Mark the dates on your calendar. Then do it.

7
Keeping Good Tenants

Although some high fallutin landlords like to think of themselves as privileged aristocrats, while at the same time they think of their tenants as peons, people born to be kicked around, they are utterly wrong in that persuasion, just as wrong as those arrogant tenants are who think of landlords as their natural-born enemies.

You, landlord, are a businessperson. Your tenants are your *customers*. Never forget that. Your tenants are your customers. They're not peons. They're not people to be ignored, stepped on, or kicked around. They're customers, and they're not merely one-time, single-purchase customers, either. They're repeat customers, loyal customers, the very best customers any businessperson could hope to have. Month after month, they pay you good money to occupy the shelter you own and maintain.

When was the last time you heard the businessperson's credo, "The customer is always wrong"? No, I've never heard it either. Yet that's the way some landlords treat their very best customers. They act as if their tenants are always wrong. They act as if they would be better off having no tenants at all. Bunk, balderdash, bull, and baloney! There's no doubt that we would be better off without certain tenants—the sneaks, the complainers, the deadbeats, the gossips, the noisemakers, the pigs, the agitators, the rebels, the thieves, the screwups, the egotists, the blowhards, and the crazies—but that doesn't mean we'd be better off having no tenants at all. No, we wouldn't, not by a moon shot!

We landlords need tenants just as tenants need us. We are mutually dependent.

The Importance of Tenants

Tenants are important to this business. In fact, they are crucial to this business. Perhaps you've never stopped to consider just how crucial your tenants really are. Let me explain.

You probably already know from your reading about real estate that there are four ways in which you as an investor can make money in the residential income property business.

First, there's *appreciation*, also known as *capital gain* (as a result of the natural inflation caused by the government's 'round-the-clock printing of paper money or the forced appreciation caused by your having improved the property somehow, your property should be worth more when you sell it than when you bought it).

Second, there's *equity buildup* (your loan principal decreases every time you make an amortized loan payment, and as a consequence, your equity in the property increases).

Third, there's *tax shelter*, sometimes called *depreciation* (at tax time you deduct a portion of your property's improvements and consider them paper losses to offset your income).

And fourth, there's *cash flow*, that is, positive cash flow (this is the money left over from rental income after you've paid all the bills).

Although one or several of these four ways might be more significant than others for a certain property, all of them are important to the overall business we are in.

Of these four ways, however, only one of them will keep working for you regardless of how you treat your tenants. Only one of them will work for you if you neglect tenant matters to the point where tenants stop paying you their rent and start tearing the building apart, window by window, door by door, wall by wall, toilet by toilet. That one way is tax shelter.

Sometime after you first acquire a residential income property, you or your accountant will set up a depreciation schedule for the building, and each year you will depreciate it for tax purposes, using whichever method of depreciation is most advantageous to you. You will continue depreciating the building on paper regardless of whether the building is shipshape or dilapidated, occupied or vacant. Its condition makes no difference whatsoever. As far as tax shelter is concerned, tenants are as unimportant to an owner as bag ladies are to a fashion designer.

Ah, but things are very different for the other three ways we landlords make money with rental property—appreciation, equity buildup, and cash flow. In order for appreciation to work for you, you and your tenants together have to keep their dwellings livable, even attractive, so the property will increase in value. In order for you to pay off your loan every month and take advantage of equity buildup, your tenants have to keep paying you their rent so you can make those loan payments. And if you are ever to have any cash flow, it will have to come from your tenants. They are the ones who pay you the money that pays the bills and accumulates in your wallet, purse, or bank account.

Can you afford to cut yourself off from three of the four ways to make money in residential income property? If you can, then go ahead and neglect your tenants all you want. That's your prerogative. But you should be asking yourself why in the world you're in this business anyway. You really ought to be enjoying yourself clipping your bond coupons, fondling your gold coins, debating which Rolex to wear, driving around in your Rolls, showing off your Picassos, admiring your diamonds, wearing your designer clothes, and taking cruises throughout the sunny climes of the world. You ought to think about getting out of the landlording business altogether or at least delegating the management of your property to someone else who has more landlording savvy than you have. You're giving the rest of us a bad name.

If, on the other hand, you cannot afford to cut yourself off from three of the four ways to make money in residential income property, you

should, by all means, not neglect your tenants. You cannot really succeed in this business if you do unless, perhaps, you decide to invest in that one kind of residential income property where tenant problems are minimized, cemeteries. Those tenants you could neglect. They don't complain. They don't plug toilets, break windows, mark up walls, burn holes in the carpets, hold noisy parties, fight with one another, or refuse to pay their rent. No matter what you do, you'd have them for keeps, forever and ever, and you could concentrate most of your energies on keeping the property itself in tip-top condition.

Come to think of it, running a cemetery isn't the only way to avoid tenant problems entirely and keep your rental property in tip-top condition. You could simply not rent it out at all just as the state of California did for years with its governor's mansion. Keep the place empty. You'd have no tenants to worry about, none whatsoever. You could get along perfectly well without tenants, couldn't you? Who couldn't? So, why not let your building age and weather gracefully without subjecting it to all that tenant abuse and without subjecting yourself to all those tenant problems? Sound interesting? It is, except that without any tenants at all you'd lose out on one of the most time-honored and most important ways to make money in this entire business. You wouldn't have any positive cash flow. There would be cash flow all right, but it would be flowing in the wrong direction. It would be negative cash flow, flowing out of your bank account and into the property instead of out of the property and into your bank account. Of course, you would get the old standby, tax shelter, and you might get some appreciation, but not as much as you'd be getting if you had good tenants occupying your property. Buyers would question the value of a residential property which houses nobody. "What's wrong with the place?" they would ask. "Is it haunted?" Haunted properties don't command good prices in the marketplace. Buyers for such properties are limited. Well, what about equity buildup? You'd get some, naturally, but because the loan payments would be coming entirely out of your own funds every month, the equity buildup couldn't be considered a way to make money. You'd merely be robbing Peter to pay Pauline, taking money from one of your bank accounts and putting it into another. That'll never make you wealthy.

All things considered, then, renting to good tenants and keeping them content enough to stay right where they are for a very long time is surely the best way to run a landlording business. You need those tenants and they need you.

Besides, good tenants also help to determine the value of every rental property you can possibly imagine, that is, with one exception, the house or duplex which buyers want to occupy themselves. Even in that case, although the buyers may want to displace the tenants and don't care two fig leaves about rental values, they'll pay more if good tenants have been keeping the property in good condition.

Prospective buyers who have no intention of displacing existing tenants will always pay more for a rental property which already has good long-term tenants living there, tenants who pay their rent on time, respect the property of others, and respect other people as well. Such tenants are prime assets. You cannot get along without them. Treat them well, these good customers of yours, for they are laying your golden eggs.

How to Keep Good Tenants

Recognizing that good tenants are indeed important to you and that losing them will cost you hundreds, if not thousands, of dollars, you are wise to consider various ways to keep your tenants living right where they are for as long as you possibly can, while you're still charging them market or near-market rents.

You can increase your chances of keeping your good tenants longer by being friendly with all of them, though friends with none, by being reasonable at all times, and by making an extra effort to please them at certain times.

Take note of the following specific things you can do to keep your good tenants longer—

■ **Change or rekey locks upon move-in—** When tenants first move in, make a big production of changing or rekeying the door locks right before their eyes and impress upon them that nobody has keys to their locks other than you and them (see chapter 18 for hints on changing and rekeying locks; usually the best time to do the job is when you're reviewing the Condition & Inventory Checksheet).

■ **Change or rekey locks when requested—** Continue to provide your tenants with that same sense of security during their tenancy that you gave them when they moved in. Change or rekey their locks whenever they request a change for what they regard as a good reason. Here are some good reasons—they have lost their keys and have looked everywhere for them, their car was stolen with their keys inside, their home was burglarized, or a roommate has moved out and hasn't given the keys to the remaining roommates. (NOTE: Because you are responsible to each tenant who has signed your rental agreement, you may not change or rekey the locks to exclude any one of them. If you do, you will have to provide access to that person later anyway so long as his or her name appears on the agreement. Before you go to the trouble of changing or rekeying the locks, therefore, advise the remaining tenants of this responsibility you have. Of course, if the excluded tenant has not signed the agreement or if the remaining tenants can show you a restraining order, you have no responsibility to provide access to the excluded tenant.)

■ **Give a maintenance guarantee—**Give your tenants some extra assurance that you will take care of maintenance problems promptly. Give them a written guarantee that you will take care of maintenance problems within a reasonable period of time or else you will stop charging them rent.

Sound pretty radical? At first, it may sound radical, but it's not, not really. Well, maybe it would sound radical to some landlords, those who promise their tenants anything and everything and then never perform, but for the rest of us, for us scrupulous landlords, it's not at all radical. It makes good sense, and it's a good way to keep good tenants.

As landlords in America, we have a responsibility to provide our tenants with dwellings which are livable according to modern American stan-

TIMELY
MAINTENANCE
GUARANTEE

The management responsible for maintaining the dwelling located at the address given below hereby guarantees to repair any defects discovered in the dwelling which are hazardous to life, health, or safety within seventy-two hours (three days) following notification by the tenants who occupy the dwelling. Tenants' notice may be either verbal or written, but it must be *acknowledged* in writing by someone whom management has authorized to accept such notice.

Should management fail to repair the defects, either temporarily or permanently, within seventy-two hours (three days), tenants shall be relieved of the responsibility for paying rent for every day or portion thereof during which the defects go unrepaired following the initial seventy-two-hour (three-day) period allotted for completing this work in a timely manner. Tenants' responsibility for paying rent shall begin again once the defects have been repaired.

To receive the benefit of any rent abatement owed to them under this guarantee, tenants must be current in their rent payments and must pay their next rent in full when due. Whatever rent abatement is owed will then be paid to them in the form of a rebate within forty-eight hours following receipt of their rent payment.

This guarantee applies only to those defects which are the responsibility of management to maintain as mandated by law and/or as outlined in the applicable lease or rental agreement.

This guarantee does not apply when a portion of the dwelling becomes uninhabitable as a result of flooding, fire, earthquake, or an act of God, and the tenants choose to remain in residence during reconstruction. In such cases, management and tenants will negotiate a fair rent covering the reconstruction period.

This guarantee shall remain in effect so long as there is a valid lease or rental agreement between the parties below covering the dwelling located at the address given below.

Dated __2/2/xx__ Address __999 Charm Lane__

Tenants __CAMERON MITCHELL__

Owner/Manager __Lester Landlord__

dards. These dwellings must have heat, water, sewage, and power, and they must keep out the wind, the rain, and the vermin. When our dwellings cannot provide these basic amenities, we shouldn't be charging any rent at all because we aren't providing our tenants with what we agreed to provide them in the first place.

Remember, we are supposed to be providing our tenants with more than just an address, more than just four walls and a roof. We are supposed to be providing them with a place to live, a place where they won't have to do battle with the elements when they're indoors, a place where they can take care of their bodily needs safely and comfortably.

The Timely Maintenance Guarantee commits to writing what we landlords are supposed to be doing anyway, maintaining our rental dwellings, except that it goes two steps further. It gives time limits, and it gives consequences.

Under the terms of the Timely Maintenance Guarantee, should you fail to fix an inoperable water heater, a leaky roof, a broken entrance lock, or some other significant defect within seventy-two hours following notification of the problem, your tenants will start getting a rent abatement. In other words, your income as a landlord will be cut off if you fail to do your job.

Tenants love this guarantee. Good tenants love it all the more. It's something which puts smiles on their faces because it offers them "satisfaction guaranteed or their money back," something they're not accustomed to getting when doing business with ordinary landlords, certainly not something they're used to getting in writing.

Under normal circumstances, when good tenants can't get their landlord to keep things in good repair, they will start looking around for another place to live rather than fight to get satisfaction. But they know as well as anyone else that moving costs money, and they don't want to have to move just because they can't get their landlord to maintain their property properly.

Under the terms of the Timely Maintenance Guarantee, they don't have to worry about whether their landlord will maintain their property properly. They know that it will be maintained, or the landlord is going to suffer. They also know that they shouldn't have to fight their landlord to take advantage of this guarantee. After all, their landlord was the one who offered it to them in the first place. If he had no intention of standing behind the guarantee, he never would have taken the initiative himself and given it to them.

This guarantee, then, is a goodwill, public-relations gesture from you to your good tenants, something which can gain you an edge in doing business without really costing you anything. What's more, it's a stimulus for you to get necessary maintenance work completed quickly.

In the lingo of game theory, the Timely Maintenance Guarantee is strictly "win-win." Good landlords win when they use it, and good tenants do, too. Nobody loses.

■ **Provide free WiFi**—Many places where people linger, such as coffee shops, hotels, and airports, provide WiFi (a wireless network for internet access). Even entire towns are being set up to provide WiFi. Some of these wireless networks are free to users, and some require users to pay by credit card.

The cost to set up a multi-family building for WiFi is minimal, as are the monthly access charges paid to the telephone or cable company, and yet free WiFi access has a great perceived value.

As a rental property owner, you should let the tenants at your smaller properties provide their own internet access because the cost per unit is high and would require higher rent. Consider providing it as an extra amenity in multiple-family buildings with five units or more.

Not only will you keep your good tenants longer by providing free internet access, you will attract more good tenants to rent from you.

■ **Make portable heaters and coolers available for emergencies**—Whereas the Timely Maintenance Guarantee gives you seventy-two hours to make either a temporary or a permanent repair, sometimes you should respond even faster. Recognize as certainties that the heaters at your rental properties will malfunction only on the coldest Sunday of the year and that the air conditioners will malfunction only on the hottest holiday. Naturally, there will be neither the parts nor the repair people available to fix the heating or cooling equipment right away, and your tenants may think that you are somehow to blame for the delay. Keep your "cool." Anticipate that such problems will occur regardless of how good your preventive maintenance is, and prepare for them.

Buy a good portable electric heater which the building's electric circuitry can reasonably accom-

Maintenance Request

Tenant _Jerome Peters_
Unit _1012 Park Street_
Home Phone _244-4444_   Work _246-8888_
Date of Request _10/12/xx_ Time _5:15pm_
Maintenance Request _Toilet loose in master bathroom_

Permission to Enter _OK_
Best Time _anytime_
Request Submitted By _Jerome Peters_

Work Order

Work Order No _XX-101_ Status _Complete_
Work Authorized By _JJ_
Date Work Attempted _10.13.XX_ Time Begun _9:15A_ Ended _9:45A_
Date Work Completed _____ Time Begun _____ Ended _____
Work Completed _Toilet bowl itself was securely bolted to the floor. Seat hinge was broken. Replaced entire seat._

Materials Used _Toilet seat._

COST	
Labor	Ø
Materials	12.32
Services	Ø
TOTAL	12.32

Percentage of Work
Charged to Tenant _0%_
Work Performed By _JJ_

Tenant Notice

We entered your dwelling today for necessary repairs, maintenance, and/or inspections.
The work is _complete_

Incomplete work, if any, resulted from a lack of the following:

☐ tools. ☐ parts. ☐ time. ☐ assistance.
We expect to return on or about _____

Thank you for your cooperation.
Date _10.13.XX_   _Jennifer James_

modate, and lend it to your freezing tenants until their broken heater can be repaired. Likewise, buy a portable cooler or a large-bladed box fan and lend it to your sweating tenants until their air conditioner is back in service.

Another alternative is a portable air conditioner, many of which will heat or cool a room or two. They're a little heavy and a little pricey, but they're very versatile, very compact, and very easy to set up and use. Tenants love them.

Such thoughtfulness will convince your tenants that you do care about whether they're freezing or sweating when their heat pump, swamp cooler, air conditioner, or heater fails, and that you are attempting seriously to remedy the problem.

■ **Make a plumber's helper and a garbage disposer wrench available**—Make available to your tenants both a plumber's helper (plunger) and a garbage disposer wrench. They're so low on most thieves' requisition lists and they're so inexpensive that you needn't worry much about whether they'll disappear from an accessible location. They're handy, easy-to-use tools, and their availability to your tenants may save you a few maintenance trips when a toilet clogs or a garbage disposer stops working.

■ **Memorize their names**—Memorize all of your tenants' names, as well as the names of their pets and kids, and try to remember a few specific things about each of them which you might use later in conversation. Everyone responds better to the personal touch, and what's more personal than a name?

■ **Listen to your tenants**—Give two ears to your tenants when they come to you with their concerns. Unless they're talking while you've got your head under their sink, look them straight in the right eye and concentrate on what they're saying. To show them you've been listening, ask them questions every so often and express agreement.

Always let them do more talking than you do. Take time to listen to the bores as well as everybody else. After a while you'll know which tenants have the sense to limit their own chatter themselves and which ones you'll have to limit. If you've been reasonably patient in listening to your tenants all along, they will listen to you more readily when you come to them with your concerns.

■ **Encourage the use of the Maintenance Request form**—Give your tenants a blank Maintenance Request form and encourage them to use it whenever they have a routine maintenance problem. Explain to them that the form is actually a three-in-one form. It's a maintenance request, a work order, and a tenant notice. When they submit it, they need to complete only the upper section. The maintenance person will then do the work and return the form to them with details about what was done.

■ **Hire tenants**—Whenever possible, hire tenants to work for you, doing such things as cleaning, yardwork, and painting. Tenants appreciate the opportunity to pick up a little extra money without having to travel any distance from their home, and they take more pride in the place where they live if they have contributed some of their own labor to make it look more attractive. My best groundskeepers have always been tenants who lived on the premises. My best vandalism deterrents have always been those troublesome teenager tenants I've hired to do odd jobs for me (be advised that teenagers working for you do require supervision and that you must have workers' compensation insurance for everybody you hire).

■ **Help tenants find housing assistance**—Become familiar with the various kinds of rental housing assistance available through public agencies and other charitable organizations. Help your tenants who might qualify for this assistance to apply for it and run the bureaucratic maze to get it. Many tenants who should be getting assistance are totally unaware that it exists or are too timid or too proud to apply. There may be some tenants you'll encounter who cannot read or write well enough to fill out even the simplest of the necessary forms and are too embarrassed to admit their deficiency. Your help could make the difference between their remaining as your good tenants and their moving to less expensive and less desirable quarters.

■ **Pay interest on deposits**—Sometime during the holiday season, send your tenants holiday greetings, express your gratitude for their having been your good tenants for whatever length of time they have lived there, and enclose a check which equals the bank interest earned during the year by their security/cleaning deposits. Some jurisdictions have laws on their books requiring

For Your Information:

<u>Important Numbers</u>

Police_____911_____   Telephone Co. 555-1000

Fire_____911_____   Gas Co._____555-2000

Ambulance_____911_____   Electric Co.__555-3000

Paramedic_____911_____   Water Co.____555-4000

Doctor_____911_____   Manager_____555-0413

The best time to contact the manager is 8AM-6PM Mon-Fri.

In an emergency, when you cannot get hold of the manager, call

_____555-0240_____.

<u>Helpful Hints</u>

1) A fire extinguisher is located under kitchen sink.
Use short bursts aimed at the base of the fire. Never use water on
a grease fire; either use the extinguisher provided or throw
baking soda on it.

2) The main electrical shutoff for your dwelling is located
_____JUST OUTSIDE BACK DOOR_____.
Check there to see whether a fuse has blown (have an extra on
hand) or a circuit breaker has tripped. Restore service by
replacing any fuse which appears to be blown (use one with the
same number on it) or by flipping the circuit breaker switch back
and forth once.

3) The main gas shutoff for your dwelling is located
_____N.E. CORNER OF BUILDING_____,
but there may be an individual valve on the line supplying each
appliance as well. Shut off the gas by turning the valve 90
degrees, that is, so it crosses the direction of the supply line.

4) The main water shutoff for your dwelling is located
_____JUST OUTSIDE BACK DOOR_____,
but you may be able to shut off the water to an individual faucet
by turning off the supply valve below your sink or toilet (not
your tub or shower). If hot water is leaking anywhere, shut off
the valve on top of the hot water heater.

5) Whenever you defrost the refrigerator, turn it off or set
the control knob to defrost. Place a pan to catch the water and
empty it when necessary. Do not try to break up the ice with any
implement like a knife or an ice pick. Let it melt on its own or
speed it up by placing a pot of hot water in the freezing
compartment. Dry the floor thoroughly when you have finished.

FOR YOUR INFORMATION - Page 2

6) Whenever you use the garbage disposer, if you have one, feed garbage in gradually along with lots of cold water, and let the water run for half a minute after you turn off the switch. Use the disposer only for those things which are edible, but don't put either cooking oil or grease down it; put them and everything else except toxic liquids in the trash. Keep metal objects out of the sink while using the disposer and turn off the switch immediately if you hear any loud metallic noises. Do not put your hand into the disposer (use tongs to retrieve objects) and do not use any chemical drain openers. If the disposer stops running on its own and you haven't heard it make any strange noises, something may have gotten stuck. Try turning the blades with a disposer wrench. Then push the reset button. After you have tried all this and you find that it still doesn't work, call the manager.

7) Whenever you want to dispose of any liquids which aren't edible, please see the manager. Many liquids are toxic and should not be put down the drain or into the trash. They must be disposed of carefully so they will not contaminate the soil or the water supply in this area. Included in this list of hazardous household wastes are the following: oven cleaners, ammonia-based cleaners, drain cleaners, floor wax, furniture polish, deodorizers, spot removers, medicines, paint, thinners, paint removers, wood preservatives, art supplies, photographic chemicals, antifreeze, car waxes, crankcase oil, fuels, radiator flushes, rust inhibitors, engine cleaners, insect sprays, weed killers, and swimming pool chemicals.

8) Whenever water rises in the toilet bowl, do not try flushing the toilet again. The bowl can hold just one tank of water at a time. More water from the tank will only cause the bowl to flow over. Use a plunger first, and then try flushing it again. Do not try to flush feminine napkins or paper diapers down the toilet. They may disappear from the toilet bowl, but that's no guarantee they'll clear the sewer pipes completely. They could require a plumber's visit, and that'll cost you money.

9) Whenever you have showered or bathed, please take a moment to mop up the excess water on the bathroom floor. A dry floor is a safe floor.

10) Whenever you want to hang anything from, or stick anything to, the walls or ceilings in your dwelling, please ask the manager to explain how to do it acceptably.

11) Whenever you want to remove the screens from your windows, please ask the manager how to do it properly. Some screens have to be removed from the inside and some from the outside. The manager will show you how.

COMPLAINT

We understand that every so often you may have a complaint which you want to make known to the management. We want to hear about it so we can take care of it or if we already know about it, so we can tell you what we're doing about it. Please use this form to register your complaint with us.

Type of complaint: [ ]   Against management

                          [X]   Against another tenant

                          [ ]   Regarding general conditions

If your complaint is against a particular person, please give that person's name and address.

Name _Anne Noyance_

Address _251 Grace Avenue_

Give details about the incident, complaint, or problem (include date, time, and place as applicable):

Noise is always coming from her apartment. I can hear her tv when I am trying to sleep. She also puts her garbage in my garbage can.

What action do you suggest that management should take?

Tell her to stop playing the TV so loud and to stop putting her garbage in my can.

Please note that management cannot promise complete confidentiality if this complaint is raised against another tenant.

Submitted by _Heidi Tidi_   Date _November 11, xxxx_

* *

Received by _Charles DeRege_   Date _11-11-xx_

Action taken _Arranging for a meeting of both tenants, to be held before Thanksgiving, to discuss the complaint_ owners to pay interest on tenants' deposits. In those places, your payment is no more than compliance with the law rather than a goodwill gesture.

When the payment is made voluntarily, however, you will find that it makes a pleasing and long-lasting impression on the recipients. Remember, too, that the interest on an $800 deposit at 4% is only $32, and that $32 will pay a bigger dividend when paid to your tenants than it would if it were to remain in your own bank account.

■ **Send greeting cards**—Remember your tenants' special days with greeting cards. People in service businesses have known for years the public relations value of sending personal greetings to their customers on special occasions. You'll find that your tenants like to be remembered by their landlord.

■ **Feed your mourning tenants**—Order a catered platter of food or some other token of your concern delivered to those tenants who are mourning the death of a loved one they have been living with. Times of death are awkward times. They're also times when hordes of people suddenly descend upon the survivors with their condolences. Hungry people they are, too. A platter of food materializing out of nowhere is always welcomed, and you will find yourself welcomed later when you pay a visit to express your sympathy once again and learn how the death will affect the survivor's tenancy.

■ **Use good tenants to find other good tenants**—Include your good tenants in your efforts to secure other good tenants. Enlist them in your word-of-mouth advertising campaign (see chapter 3), for they have as much of an interest in who their new neighbors will be as you do. Generally they welcome the opportunity to participate in the search for new tenants and make a conscientious effort to find good ones.

■ **Provide useful written information**—Provide your tenants with useful written information for coping with some of life's little emergencies and for doing various things around their home. On previous pages is a two-page form which you may use for this very purpose. It has space for your name (as manager) and telephone number along with other important telephone numbers, numbers which should all be readily available in one place.

There's also space you may use to indicate where the utility shutoffs are and how to shut them off, and there are some suggestions for coping with such problems as plugged toilets and ice-jammed refrigerators. Many times you will assume that your tenants understand how to use, say, a garbage disposer or a fire extinguisher when, in truth, they don't have a clue because nobody has ever taken the time to explain how to use one to them before and they themselves are too embarrassed to ask.

Whether you make this information part of your move-in procedure or distribute it later is up to you.

■ **Provide a tenant Complaint form**—Provide your tenants with a tenant Complaint form and encourage them to use it. One of the worst things that can happen to a conscientious landlord is to lose good tenants over a matter which could have been corrected had the landlord known about it in time to do something about it.

Some good tenants are too timid to say a single word about those things which irritate them until after they have moved out or made irrevocable arrangements to move. Sometimes even then they don't say anything, and you never do learn the real reason why they moved.

Sometimes the source of their frustration surfaces quite fortuitously when you happen to be talking with them about their future while they're moving their things into a rental truck parked in the driveway. Once you learn the real reason they're moving, you want to whack yourself on the side of the head for not having made an effort to find out why they decided to move when you could have done something about it and kept the good tenants.

Time and time again, good tenants will move because of problem tenants who live nearby and are causing them grief. Yet they don't complain about the matter. They move. Had their landlord known, he could have told them what was happening with the problem tenants. Perhaps they were being evicted for nonpayment of rent or for some other cause and would be gone in a matter of days. Had the good tenants known, they might have stayed put.

You want to know when things are going right around your rental properties, and you need to know when things are going wrong. You need to know so you can make adjustments as necessary. This tenant Complaint form is the communications device which will put you "in the know." It makes complaining easy for your tenants who have a complaint. They don't have to sit down and compose a letter, worrying about form and content. They merely fill in the blanks. It's all content, and it's as easy to use as painting by numbers.

Now look at the form itself and notice how its nine basic elements fit together to make a whole. All of the nine elements except one are either neutral or else they encourage the tenant to submit the complaint. That one element is the caveat that management cannot promise complete confidentiality if the complaint is raised against another tenant. Like it or not, you need to include this caveat to protect yourself from grief should there be an unfortunate incident between the tenants involved. The incident may not even be related to the complaint, but if it is, you can be sure that it will be considered as such and that you will be targeted as a cause of the incident for having revealed the source of the complaint. You should try your best to protect the confidentiality of the person who submitted the complaint, but you may not succeed, especially because the person who is the target of the complaint will probably figure out who made the complaint anyway.

The only other form elements of note here are those beneath the line of asterisks. They're for the landlord to complete—the one, an acknowledgment of receipt; the other, a description of action taken. Both are especially important in case there should be any litigation. The acknowledgment shows that you actually received the complaint. The description of action taken shows how you responded. A litigious tenant bent on proving that you are an irresponsible landlord could produce a bundle of tenant complaints and claim that you had failed to do anything about them, but if you hadn't at least acknowledged receipt, you could argue that you never received them. Problem tenants can and will twist anything to their advantage.

When a tenant submits a written complaint, sign it and make a copy for the tenant. After you take action and complete the description of the "Action taken" section, make another copy and give it to the tenant. You'll have a paper trail and so will the tenant.

■ **Redecorate occupied units**—Offer to redecorate your good tenants' dwelling if it hasn't been done in years and the place is beginning to look shabby. All too frequently good tenants feel compelled to move because their landlord expects them to tolerate living in a dwelling which needs new linoleum in the bathroom, paint in the living room, drapes in the bedroom, and carpeting in the hallway. When they decide not to tolerate such conditions any longer and they move to a dwelling which has been completely redecorated by a new landlord, their former landlord is forced not only to redecorate but to lose rent while the place is vacant and then to bear the expense and suffer through the process of finding new tenants who may or may not be as good as the old ones.

That former landlord would actually have saved money by redecorating to keep the good old tenants instead of redecorating to attract good new ones.

You cannot afford to be oblivious to the condition of your occupied rentals any more than you can afford to be oblivious to the condition of your vacant rentals.

Some Last Words

You may be a greedy, myopic, misanthropic landlord if you want to be, one who pooh-poohs any act of cooperation or kindheartedness, but your tenants will move out more frequently than will those of benevolent, circumspect landlords who value their good tenants and cater to them whenever possible, while still being formidable enough, when need be, not to permit any tenant to kick sand in their faces.

Remember that as a landlord you are managing both buildings and people. Buildings are easy. Any simpleton can manage them. People are not so easy. They require management with care, loving care mixed with caring discipline.

8
Helping Tenants Move Out

Tenants come and tenants go with some degree of frequency. Every year throughout the United States, almost half of all the tenants who live in unfurnished rentals will move on to other quarters. When you happen to be the landlord whose tenants are moving out, you have certain responsibilities which you should be aware of and be prepared to carry out.

You know pretty well what those responsibilities are when tenants move in, and you probably pay close attention to them then, but chances are good that you know only superficially what your responsibilities are when tenants move out and that you pay them little attention.

Except in the most perfunctory ways, we landlords tend to neglect helping tenants move out because we are disappointed that they're moving and regard it as a desertion of sorts. Moreover, their moving is overshadowed by our simultaneous preparation for new tenants, something we consider much more important to our business.

While the pitfalls you face when tenants move in may be more momentous than those you face when they move out, pitfalls do exist when they move out, pitfalls which can cause you unnecessary aggravation and cost you plenty in terms of wasted time, energy, and money.

Ask a sampling of small claims court judges about the landlord-tenant cases they hear most frequently, and they will tell you that almost all such cases involve disputes which arise over what occurs at the conclusion of the landlord-tenant relationship, when the tenants move out and somebody feels cheated. Sometimes the landlord will feel cheated and bring the case into court. Sometimes the tenants will feel cheated and file suit, but almost always the cases are related to the tenants' moving out.

Many things can happen at move-out time to cause a dispute serious enough to wind up in court.

Either the deposits aren't refunded as they should have been, or the deposits aren't sufficient to cover the charges owed for damages and cleaning, or there are misunderstandings about the condition of the dwelling when the tenants moved in as compared to its condition when they moved out, or there are misunderstandings about the meanings of the expressions "reasonably clean and undamaged" and "normal wear and tear," or there are misunderstandings about how much the landlord charged to repair a hole in the wall and replace a missing light fixture, or there are misunderstandings about the ownership of certain contents of the dwelling, or there are misunderstandings about whether the deposits may be used for last month's rent.

That's altogether too much misunderstanding, if you ask me, and even though it cannot all be avoided, most of it can be avoided so long as you know what steps to take to avoid it and so long as you follow those steps as best you can.

Ten Measures for Avoiding Move-Out Misunderstandings

The ten measures given here for avoiding move-out misunderstandings require a little extra preparation, a few extra forms, and some extra effort in communication, but they work. They work well.

Follow them, and they will make your landlording life a little bit easier.

1) Prepare at move-in time for the move out.
2) Provide a written Notice of Intention to Vacate form for your tenants to fill out, sign, and give to you when they decide to move.
3) Advise your departing tenants what they can do to get their deposits back.
4) Establish what constitutes actually "moving out," and settle upon how the keys will be returned.

169

Rental Agreement

Dated **January 15, XXXX**

(Month-to-Month)

Agreement between **Lester Landlord**, Owners,
and **RICHARD and ROSE L. RENTER**, Tenants, for a dwelling
located at **456 Sweet Street, LITTLETOWN, CALIFORNIA**.
Tenants agree to rent this dwelling on a month-to-month basis for $ **778** per
month, payable in advance on the **1ST** day of every calendar month to Owners
or their Agent*, **X X X X X X**, whose address is
453 Sweet Street, Littletown, CA 09090.
When rent is paid on or before the **4th** day of the calendar month, Owners
will give Tenants a (discount) (rebate) of $ **20**.

The first month's rent for this dwelling is $ **880**.
The security/cleaning deposit on this dwelling is $ **1,000**. It is
refundable if Tenants leave the dwelling reasonably clean and undamaged.
Tenants will give **15** days' notice in writing before they move and will
be responsible for paying rent through the end of this notice period or until
another tenant approved by the Owners has moved in, whichever comes first.
Owners will refund all deposits due within **7** days after Tenants have
moved out completely and returned their keys.

without Owners' prior written permission, no other persons may live there,
and no other pets may stay there, even temporarily, nor may the dwelling be
sublet or used for business purposes.
Use of the following is included in the rent: **CARPETS, DRAPES, SHADES
and STOVE. REFIGERATOR on TEMPORARY LOAN.**
Remarks: **WATER and GARBAGE PAID BY OWNERS. TENANTS PAY
ALL OTHER UTILITIES. PARKING IN SPACE #2. OCCUPANCY CONTINGENT**
TENANTS AGREE TO THE FOLLOWING: UPON EXISTING TENANTS VACATING THE

Rent Payment Procedure—Tenants agree to pay their rent in the following way:
in person to manager

Deposits—Tenants agree to deposit with the Owners the sum of $ **1,100**, payable before they occupy
the premises. Owners may withhold from these deposits only what is reasonably necessary to cover the
following tenant defaults: 1) damages to the dwelling; 2) certain cleaning costs following Tenants' departure;
and 3) unpaid rent and various other accrued and unpaid charges. Tenants may not apply any part of these
deposits to their last month's rent.

Refund of Tenants' Deposits—Within **7** days after Tenants have moved out completely, Owners
shall provide a written accounting of the disposition of the Tenants' deposits and shall at the same time return
all deposits remaining.

Occupants—In addition to the Tenants mentioned above, only the following persons may live in this dwelling:
X   X   X   X   X   X   X   X
No one else may live there, even temporarily, without Owners' prior written permission.

Guests—Tenants may house any single guest for a maximum period of fourteen days every six months or
for whatever other period of time the law allows. Provided that they maintain a separate residence, nurses or
maids required to care for Tenants during an illness are excepted from this provision.

Subletting and Assignment—Tenants shall not sublet the entire premises or any part of the premises, nor
shall they assign this Agreement to anyone else without first obtaining the Owners' written permission.
Owners shall not withhold permission unreasonably.

Rental Agreement—Page 1 of **5**

5) Give the tenants your "list prices" for move-out charges.

6) Recognize the difference between "normal wear and tear" caused by ordinary comings and goings and "damage" caused by carelessness, abuse, mysterious disappearance, thievery, accident, rules violation, or special request.

7) Inspect the dwelling and itemize its various deficiencies.

8) Calculate the charges fairly.

9) Get the keys and document the move-out, including the stuff left behind.

10) Return the deposits promptly, but not too promptly.

These ten measures don't sound so very difficult, do they? They're not. You probably know enough already to be doing many of them automatically. Still, let's look at each of them more closely. The more you know about move-out misunderstandings, the more you'll be able to avoid them.

1) Prepare at move-in time for the move out.
Avoid this kind of misunderstanding:

"Mrs. Lilliput, we're going to be moving to Houston next Tuesday, and we'd like to use our deposits to pay for the balance of the rent we still owe you from last month, plus whatever else we'll owe you when we leave. That'll just about balance everything out, won't it?"

"I can't believe what you're saying, Mr. Runfree! You give me five days' notice that you're moving and you want me to apply your deposits to the rent? I can't do that. You're supposed to get your deposits back after I've inspected your place and found it to be reasonably clean and undamaged. Right now you owe me $65 on last month's rent, and since you're giving notice today, legally you owe rent for a full one month from today as well."

"Oh, don't you worry your pretty little head about it, Mrs. Lilliput. We'll leave everything spic 'n' span. You'd be refunding our money anyway. We'll even be saving you the postage you'd have to pay to send the refund to us at our new address."

When your tenants first moved in, you were already preparing for them to move out, whether you ever thought about their moving out at some future time or not. You stipulated how much notice they should give when advising you that they were going to be moving. You asked for proper notice in writing. You inspected the dwelling with the tenants before they took possession, and you noted its condition and inventoried its contents in writing. You collected adequate deposits, and you informed the tenants that those deposits were not to be considered last month's rent. You did each of these things for one very good reason—to avoid misunderstandings when the tenants were about to move out.

Should you fail to establish these things at the very beginning of your relationship, you will have to expect misunderstandings later, for you cannot expect tenants to know what they should and should not do when they move out unless you inform them at the first opportunity and remind them at every later opportunity.

Unless you tell them otherwise, isn't it logical for them to assume that their deposits should cover their final rent payment, especially if the two are identical sums? Isn't it logical for them to expect to receive all of their deposits back as soon as they move out so long as they clean up after themselves? Why should they have to wait two or three weeks? Why should they have to wait even one single day? And why should they have to give you any notice at all? You'll only re-rent their place the very next day anyway, won't you? Ain't nothin' to this landlording business but cashin' checks!

Discuss the end-game rules with tenants before you ever rent to them, and put those rules in writing in terms which cannot be misunderstood. That done, move-out time will be no trouble at all.

2) Provide a written Notice of Intention to Vacate form for your tenants to fill out, sign, and give to you when they decide to move.
Avoid this kind of misunderstanding:

"Hello, Lester? This is Raymond Renter. I just called to let you know we're all moved out and we'd like to get our deposits back."

"That's news to me, Raymond. You never gave me any notice."

"Come on, man! I did, too! Don't you remember last month when I told you we were planning to move before school started? Isn't that notice enough?"

"No way! I remember when you told me you might be moving sometime soon, but you never said exactly when you'd be moving. How was I to know you'd be out today?"

Notice of Intention to Vacate

TO: __LESTER LANDLORD__

FROM: __RICHARD and ROSE RENTER__

Dated __9/13/XX__

Please be advised that on __SEPTEMBER 30, XXXX__ we intend to move from our residence at __456 SWEET ST, LITTLETOWN__.

We understand that our Rental Agreement calls for __15__ days' notice before we move and that this is __17__ days' notice. We understand that we are responsible for paying rent through the end of the notice period called for in the rental agreement or until another tenant approved by the management has moved in, whichever comes first.

We understand that our deposits will be refunded within __7__ days after we have moved out completely and returned our keys to the management, so long as we leave our dwelling reasonably clean and undamaged.

Reasons for leaving: __We bought a duplex!__

Forwarding address: __1610 Igloo Ave., Littletown__

In accordance with our Rental Agreement, we agree to allow the management to show our dwelling to prospective tenants at any and all reasonable times.

Tenant __Richard Renter__

Tenant __Rose Renter__

Received by __Lester Landlord__

Date __9/13/XX__

The primary reason for requiring written notice from your vacating tenants is to tie them down to a specific moveout date so you can start making preparations to re-rent the dwelling to someone else without delay. Written notice is always better than verbal notice because it's definite and it's incontestable evidence in those cases which wind up in court with the tenant claiming one thing and the landlord claiming quite another.

Some tenants will take the time to compose a thoughtful letter of their own to advise you dutifully of their plans to move out. Accept it so long as it includes the following three necessary elements: anticipated moveout date, the address of the place they're renting from you, and the signatures of those who signed the rental agreement. But because few people either learn or remember how to communicate anything in writing anymore, you should be prepared to provide a ready-made form for your tenants to complete in order to make your written notice requirement easier for them to satisfy. When they give you verbal notice, supply them with one of your forms and ask them to fill it out then and there if possible.

If you don't have a form handy when they give you verbal notice, use a blank sheet of paper and write down as much of the verbiage as you can remember, making certain that it includes the three necessary particulars. Then have them sign it. You want to tie them down to a specific moveout date as soon as possible following their verbal notice so you won't have to bother chasing them down with the form later.

The form provided here includes space for the necessary information plus space for the tenants to indicate why they are leaving, information which might prove useful to you in case there's something you might do to get them to stay, should you be so inclined. It's also information which may enable you to improve your landlording operations in general.

3) Advise your departing tenants what they can do to get their deposits back.

Avoid this kind of misunderstanding:

"What do you mean you're going to deduct $75 from my deposit? The place is spotless! I spent $15 on cleaning supplies and $5 on washing and drying the draperies, and I cleaned in there myself for at least six hours! I scrubbed the kitchen and bathroom floors on my hands and knees. They were never that clean when I moved in. I found a good spot remover for the carpet and removed some spots that were there when I moved in. I cleaned the oven so it shines like new. Why, you could rent the place to Martha Stewart, and she wouldn't have to do a thing before moving in!

"I admit that on the whole the apartment's clean, but just look at those drapes! They were new only last year, and now they look so threadbare that I wouldn't even wear them to a toga party! You weren't supposed to wash them. They have to be dry cleaned."

"Well, how was I supposed to know they needed to be dry-cleaned? You never told me what to do. I thought they would come clean in one of those commercial washers down at the laundromat. You gotta admit I tried."

"You tried. I can see that, but you ruined the drapes, and I just have to charge you something for the replacements.

Some of the conditions you impose on your tenants for the return of their deposits are necessarily subjective and open to interpretation. You may have explained what those conditions were

September 13, XXXX

Dear **Margaret and Charlie,**

Moving time is always a busy time, and you will have lots of things on your mind now that you have given notice you are moving. One of those things undoubtedly is how to get your deposits back promptly. In your case, they amount to $ **1,250** .

Contrary to what some tenants believe, we WANT to return your deposits, and we WILL return them to you so long as you leave your place "reasonably clean and undamaged." That's what your rental agreement says and that's what we will do. You're probably wondering, however, what "reasonably clean and undamaged" means, so we'd like to tell you how we interpret it and tell you also what you should do to get your deposits back.

"Reasonably clean" to us means as clean as you would leave your dwelling if you knew your best friend or your favorite aunt were going to move in after you. To get it that clean, we expect you to clean the appliances, stove hood, and cabinets (under sinks, too) both inside and out; remove all non-adhesive shelf paper; use an appropriate cleanser on the showers, tubs, toilets, sinks, mirrors, and medicine cabinets (inside as well); dust the ceilings (for cobwebs), baseboards, window sills, and closet shelving; wash the kitchen and bathroom walls and spot-clean the walls in the other rooms; wash the light fixtures and windows inside and out; vacuum the floors; scrub the floor tile or linoleum; sweep the entry, patio, storage enclosure, and garage; remove all personal belongings (including clothes hangers and cleaning supplies); and dispose of all trash. PLEASE DO NOT CLEAN THE DRAPERIES, SHAMPOO THE CARPETS, OR WAX THE FLOORS. We prefer to do those cleaning chores ourselves, and we will not deduct anything from your deposits for our doing them.

"Reasonably undamaged" to us means that items which we have supplied should not be missing (including light bulbs) or broken; that there should be no new burns, cracks, chips, or holes in the dwelling or its furnishings; and that the paint on the walls should be sufficient to last at least two years from the time they were last painted. PLEASE DO NOT REMOVE ANYTHING YOU HAVE ATTACHED TO THE WALLS OR CEILING WITHOUT FIRST TALKING TO US, and please try to avoid nicking the paint in the halls and doorways as you move things out.

Please note that until you have returned your keys, you have not "officially" moved out, and you are still liable for paying rent. Make sure that you give us your keys as soon as you move out.

After you have moved out, we would like to inspect your dwelling with you to check it for cleanliness and damage. We will refund all deposits owed to you within seven days thereafter.

We expect you to have moved out completely by **September 30, XXXX** Because we are making arrangements for new tenants to move in after you move, we would appreciate hearing from you immediately if your moving plans should change.

We hope your moving goes smoothly, and we wish you happiness in your new home.

Sincerely,

Hate to lose you!

Leslie Landlady

way back when the tenants first moved in, but since time tends to muddle recollections and since the tenants were hardly thinking then about moving out now, you should review your conditions once more when they are thinking much more specifically about moving out and are more concerned about getting their deposits back.

Discuss your conditions with them in person or send them a letter like the one shown here outlining the conditions, or, better yet, do both. Whatever you do, remind them of the amount of their deposit which is at stake and convince them that you will refund it promptly. They want as much of their deposit back as they can get. You can't blame them. You would, too.

If they refuse to believe that you are a scrupulous landlord who returns deposits, give them the name of somebody who moved out recently and received his deposits back. Tell them to contact that person to learn what kind of treatment they can expect to receive from you when they move out.

Even if you are legally entitled to keep all or most of their deposits because they have accumulated lots of late charges during their tenancy and have adamantly refused to pay them or because they have already failed to meet certain of your move-out conditions, you should still establish some refundable amount which you will pay them no matter what, provided that they return the place to you reasonably clean and undamaged. Give them an incentive to do just that. Don't try to squeeze a few extra dollars out of them at move-out time. That's not in your interest. Bend over backwards, reach into your pocket, and give them a handful of dollars after they move out. You don't want them to avenge themselves on your property because you failed to be reasonable.

As for cleaning the place, you know that tenants will seldom clean the draperies, shampoo the carpets, wax the floors, or remove their wall and ceiling attachments to your satisfaction, so you should give them precise instructions for performing these jobs or tell them not to bother at all. Well-meaning tenants may attempt a job and bungle it so badly that you will have to spend extra time and money setting things right, and the tenants, for their part, will expect a full refund regardless of the extra work they have caused you or the extra expense they have cost you. That kind of situation frustrates everyone involved and can easily be avoided through good communication before they move out.

4) Establish what constitutes actually "moving out," and settle upon how the keys will be returned.

Avoid this kind of misunderstanding:

"When we moved out on the last day of the month, we cleaned and cleaned and left everything spotless. We left the keys inside the apartment where anybody could find them and locked all the doors behind us. That's what we always do when we vacate a motel room.

"The next thing we know, we get our deposit back minus two days' rent. That's not fair!"

"You did do an excellent job of cleaning. I'll grant you that, but I never got your keys back until the second day of the month because I was expecting you to bring them over to me. Vacating a motel room where you've spent a night or two and vacating an apartment where you've lived for an entire year are two very different events. Each has different procedures. You ought to know that technically you haven't moved out until you've returned the keys.

"It was just by chance that I happened to go over to your old apartment on the second day of the month to ask you when you would have everything moved out. That's when I learned from your former neighbors that you had already moved out and left the keys behind. You should have told me that's what you were going to do with the keys. I'd have gone over there earlier, and I wouldn't have had to charge you for those two extra days."

"You didn't say anything to us about what you wanted us to do with the keys. How were we supposed to know?"

Just as your handing the keys over to the tenants when they moved in symbolized your transferring possession to them, their returning the keys to you after they have vacated the premises symbolizes their transferring possession back to you. This transferring of the keys is more than symbolic, however. It constitutes the final step in the termination of the tenancy. Upon returning the keys, the tenants have "officially" moved out.

Inform them of the importance of returning the keys both in the move-out letter and verbally. Tell them that they will be charged extra rent if they move out completely and keep the keys because the keys give them access to the dwelling and essentially leave them still in possession.

Move-Out Charges

Here's what we charge for most of the things we have to do when tenants move out and leave their dwelling in need of something or other. Please note that these charges are averages. Sometimes the actual charges are higher; sometimes they're lower. But most of the time they are exactly as shown. We give allowances for normal wear and tear, of course, and for the length of time something has been in use. Replacement charges include parts and labor.

Cleaning

Clean refrigerator	20.—
Clean stove top	10.—
Clean oven	30.—
Clean stove hood	20.—
Clean kitchen cabinets	20.—
Clean kitchen floor	35.—
Clean tub/shower and surround	15.—
Clean toilet and sink	15.—
Clean bathroom cabinets & floor	20.—
Vacuum throughout dwelling	40.—
Clean greasy parking space	20.—

Flooring

Remove carpet stains	80.—
Deodorize carpet	85.—
Repair carpet	75.—
Repair hardwood floor	90.—
Refinish hardwood floor	580.—
Repair linoleum	45.—
Replace kitchen linoleum	375.—
Replace bathroom linoleum	225.—
Repair floor tile	30.—
Replace kitchen floor tile	250.—
Replace bathroom floor tile	150.—

Walls

Remove mildew and treat surface	12.—
Cover crayon marks	35.—
Repair hole in wall	45.—
Remove wallpaper	135.—
Repaint (per wall/ceiling)	15.—

Doors

Repair hole in hollow-core door	45.—
Repair forced door damage	65.—
Replace door (inside)	125.—
Replace door (outside)	225.—
Replace sliding glass door (sgl)	150.—
Replace sliding glass door (dbl)	250.—
Rescreen sliding door screen	25.—
Replace sliding door screen	45.—

Electrical

Replace light bulb	1.50
Replace light fixture globe	12.—
Replace light fixture	45.—
Replace electrical outlet/switch	5.—
Replace electrical cover plate	1.50

Plumbing

Replace kitchen faucet	50.—
Replace bathroom faucet	45.—
Replace faucet handle	7.50
Replace faucet aerator	3.50
Replace shower head	12.—
Replace toilet tank lid	15.—
Replace toilet	130.—
Replace garbage disposer	80.—

Locks

Replace key (door or mailbox)	2.—
Replace cylindrical doorlock	25.—
Replace passage doorlock	15.—
Replace deadbolt lock	25.—
Replace mailbox lock	6.50

Windows & Window Coverings

Replace window pane (sgl)	75.—
Replace window pane (dbl)	125.—
Replace Venetian blind	75.—
Replace window shade	15.—
Replace drapery rod	25.—
Replace drapery (sill length)	75.—
Replace drapery (floor length)	150.—
Rescreen window screen	10.—
Replace window screen	18.—

Miscellaneous

Replace refrigerator shelf	25.—
Paint refrigerator	75.—
Replace stove/oven knob	6.—
Repair ceramic tile	85.—
Replace ceramic tile countertop	450.—
Repair plastic countertop	35.—
Replace plastic countertop	275.—
Replace cutting board	15.—
Replace mirror	45.—
Replace medicine cabinet	75.—
Replace towel bar	12.—
Replace shower curtain rod	15.—
Replace shower/tub enclosure	150.—
Repair porcelain	135.—
Replace thermostat	60.—
Recharge fire extinguisher	20.—
Replace fire extinguisher	30.—
Fumigate for fleas	125.—
Remove junk and debris	55.—

Settle upon a convenient time and place for the transfer of the keys. Try to combine the transfer with the move-out inspection if possible, but if you can't, just make sure that both you and the tenants understand precisely where and when the transfer is going to take place. There's nothing wrong with letting the tenants leave the keys on the kitchen counter or with somebody on the premises when they depart, so long as you know that you can expect to find the keys there. Tenants who are moving are frequently in a hurry and don't want to wait around for somebody to show up. Neither you nor they have the time to be playing "hide and seek" when you're transferring the keys.

5) Give the tenants your "list prices" for move-out charges.

Avoid this kind of misunderstanding:

"Hey, Edith, this accounting of my security deposit sure is outrageous. It says right here that you kept $20 to clean the refrigerator and $24 to pay for two missing towel bars in the bathroom and $12 to pay for eight burned-out lightbulbs and $45 to repair a hole in the wall. That's a lot of money for those things."

"Those things cost a lot of money nowadays, Mr. Joad. We're not living back in the Great Depression, you know."

"I know that. It's just that if I'd've known how much you were going to charge me for all these things, I'd have seen to 'em myself. I could've gone down to Wal-Mart and bought a perfectly good chrome towel bar for $6.99. You charged me $12 for the replacement you put in there, and it's no better than the one I'd have bought. That's highway robbery!"

"Call it whatever you want. I think those charges are fair and reasonable. They're what I had to pay, and I have the receipts to prove it."

"Not in my book they're not fair! I'm gonna see you in court!"

Business establishments as diverse as dry cleaners, auto repair shops, legal offices, and dental clinics all have list prices for the various routine services they offer. When you bring a lady's two-piece suit to a dry cleaners, for example, the person at the counter will consult a price list and tell you immediately how much you'll have to pay to have it cleaned and pressed. When you take your Ford pickup truck to a shop for an alternator replacement, the mechanic will consult a price list

and tell you how much the job will cost. When you ask an attorney how much an uncontested eviction will cost, you'll learn the "list price." When your dentist schedules a visit with the dental hygienist for a cleaning, you will receive a quote for the service if you want one. In each of these cases, you find out in advance exactly how much the work will cost, provided, of course, that there are no complications.

Why not do the same thing with your routine move-out charges? Let your tenants know in advance of their moving just how much your move-out charges really are. If they know what charges they face at move-out time, they'll be less argumentative when you start deducting certain sums from their deposit. They'll be expecting to pay $45 for repairing a hole in the wall, $75 for repainting the refrigerator, and $30 for replacing a missing fire extinguisher.

Try it and see what happens.

Itemize the many things you might have to do to a place when tenants move out, and assign a dollar figure to each (use the form shown here with the prices shown here if you can live with these numbers; if you can't live with these numbers, enter other prices in the blanks which reflect more accurately the labor and parts costs prevalent in your area). Then give these "list prices" to your tenants when they first rent from you and again later when they give you notice that they're moving (the prices may have changed during a long tenancy), and you'll detect a difference in their attitude when you give them an accounting of their deposits. They'll be less defiant, and you won't have to be so defensive about your charges.

Be aware that even though you have a well-defined, realistic, and comprehensive price list for move-out charges, your tenants may still haul you into court to dispute those prices. They may dispute your charging them anything at all to clean the greasy stove and foul-smelling refrigerator they left behind.

Be aware that a judge may disregard your price list, too, especially if you did the work yourself. Judges respond better to actual costs incurred rather than to approximations. If you hired somebody to do the work for you and you have receipts to show for the labor and materials, you have a much better chance of convincing a judge that the departing tenants should pay you those sums than you will if you merely point to your

"WEAR AND TEAR" OR "DAMAGES"?

"Normal wear and tear" caused by ordinary comings and goings	"Damage" caused by carelessness, abuse, thievery, mysterious disappearance, accident, rules violation, or special request
Well-worn keys	Missing keys
"Sticky" key	Key broken off inside lock
Balky door lock	Door lock replaced by tenant without management's permission
Depressurized fire extinguisher with unbroken seal	Depressurized fire extinguisher with broken seal (not used to put out fire)
Worn pattern in plastic countertop	Burn in plastic countertop
Rust stain under sink faucet	Sink discolored by clothing dye
Loose, inoperable faucet handle	Missing faucet handle
Rusty refrigerator shelf	Missing refrigerator shelf
Discolored ceramic tile	Painted ceramic tile
Loose grout around ceramic tile	Chipped or cracked ceramic tile
Carpet seam unraveling	Carpet burn
Threadbare carpet in hallway	Rust marks on carpet from indoor plant container
Scuffing on wooden floor	Gouge in wooden floor
Linoleum with the back showing through	Tear in linoleum
Wobbly toilet	Broken toilet tank lid
Rusty shower curtain rod	Kinked shower curtain rod
Rust stain under bathtub spout	Chip in bathtub enamel
Tracks on doorjamb where door rubs	Hole in hollow-core door
Door off its hinges and stored in garage	Missing door
Plant hanger left in ceiling	Two-inch-diameter hole in ceiling
Stain on ceiling caused by leaky roof	Stain on ceiling caused by popping champagne or beer bottles
Cracked paint	Crayon marks on wall
Chipped paint (minor)	Walls painted by tenant in dark color necessitating repainting
Pleasing, professional tenant wallpapering	Amateurish tenant wallpapering
Mildew around shower or tub	Mildew where tenant kept aquarium
Urine odor around toilet	Urine odor in carpet
Discolored light fixture globe	Missing light fixture globe
Odd-wattage lightbulbs which work	Burned out or missing lightbulbs
Light fixture installed by tenant which fits its location	Light fixture installed by tenant which must be replaced
Window cracked by settling or high wind	Window cracked by movers
Faded shade	Torn shade
Paint-blistered Venetian blinds	Venetian blinds with bent slats
Sun-damaged drapes	Pet-damaged drapes
Drapery rod which won't close properly	Drapery rod with missing parts
Dirty window screen	Missing, bent, or torn window screen
Ants inside after rain storm	Fleas left behind by tenant's pet
Scrawny landscaping which was sparingly watered due to drought conditions	Neglected landscaping which must be replaced with similar plantings
Grease stains on parking space	Caked grease on parking space

price list and tell the judge that you charged the tenant exactly what was on the price list, no more and no less.

6) Recognize the difference between "normal wear and tear" caused by ordinary comings and goings and "damage" caused by carelessness, abuse, mysterious disappearance, thievery, accident, rules violation, or special request.

Avoid this kind of misunderstanding:

"Lonnie, I'm afraid I'm going to have to take something out of your security deposit to get this fire extinguisher recharged. The gauge says it's completely discharged. I know it was fully charged when you moved in, and I know you didn't use it on any fire. Somebody in your household must have been playing around with it."

"Let me see it. You're right, Mr. Sims, it is discharged, but nobody in my family ever touched this extinguisher. It must have become discharged all on its own."

"How can you be so sure?"

"Well, take a look at the seal. It's still there, see, right where it's always been. If the seal were broken, then I ought to have to pay to get the extinguisher recharged. Since it's not broken, I shouldn't have to pay. It lost its charge on its own."

"Okay, so the seal is still there, and maybe nobody in your household played around with it, but somebody's got to pay to have the extinguisher recharged or replaced, and I can't see why I should be the one to pay. I always charge tenants whenever they move out and I find that their fire extinguisher is discharged."

"That's not right. As you can see with your own eyes, I didn't do anything to it. The seal is still there. I shouldn't have to pay for something I didn't damage."

"Hmm. Well, let me think about this situation for a while, and I'll get back to you."

Look at the two lists on the opposite page. They show the sometimes subtle differences between "wear and tear" and "damage," things you shouldn't charge your tenants for and things you should. Note that sometimes the results are identical, such as the discharged fire extinguishers and the cracked windows, but the causes are different. The *causes* of a particular condition determine who's responsible for paying the bill in some cases.

In other cases, the *extent* of the "damage"

determines who's responsible. A plant hanger left in the ceiling is "wear and tear," but if the tenant rips out the hanger and leaves a hole of some consequence, then it becomes "damage."

In still other cases, the presence or absence of an item determines whether you consider the matter "wear and tear" or "damage." Take a faucet handle, for example. If the handle were so loose and corroded that it couldn't turn the faucet on or off, it would be "wear and tear," but if the same handle were missing, it would be "damage." Missing handles cannot be fixed, whereas there's always a chance that a corroded handle can be. Anything which is supposed to be in the dwelling but turns up missing is "damage."

You might want to advise your tenants how you distinguish between "wear and tear" and "damage," so they will come to understand that you're not being entirely arbitrary when you calculate how much you're withholding from their deposits. You might even want to give them a copy of the lists so they can judge for themselves whether you're correct in your assessments.

As for that discharged fire extinguisher with its seal still intact, the landlord should take responsibility for having it recharged and for paying the bill. The tenant didn't cause the extinguisher to discharge. Its gasket failed and allowed the gas inside to escape.

7) Inspect the dwelling and itemize its deficiencies.

Avoid this kind of misunderstanding:

"That oven was much dirtier when I moved in. I hardly even used it."

"I know it was clean when you moved in, Marge Renter, because I remember cleaning it myself. It was a 'two-cans-of-Easy-Off' job, and it took me half a day to make it sparkle after the previous tenants moved out."

"Well, I cleaned it after I moved out, too. I know that much, and I say you aren't going to charge me for a dirty oven! I'll take you to court! You can't prove anything anyway. It's your word against mine."

If you can possibly arrange for the vacating tenants to accompany you when you inspect their dwelling to determine deposit refunds, do so. You can then explain precisely what is wrong with the place, and you can give them the choice of correcting those deficiencies themselves or paying for the corrections.

Condition & Inventory Checksheet

Tenants: RICHARD and ROSE RENTER   Dated: JAN·15, XXXX
Address: 456 SWEET ST., LITTLETOWN
Date Moved In: 1/15/XX   Notice Given: _____   Moved Out: _____

Abbreviations:

Air Cond, AC	Clean, Cl	Drape, Drp	Hood, Hd	OK, OK	Table, Tbl
Bed, Bd	Cracked, Cr	Dryer, Dry	Just Painted, JP	Poor, P	Tile, Tl
Broken, Brk	Curtain, Ctn	Fair, F	Lamp, Lmp	Refrigerator, Rf	Venet'n Blind, VB
Carpet, Cpt	Dinette, Din	Good, G	Lightbulb, LtB	Shade, Sh	Washer, Wsh
Chair, Ch	Dishwasher, Dsh	Heater, Htr	Linoleum, Lino	Sofa, Sfa	Waxed, Wxd
Chest, Chst	Disposer, Dsp	Hole, H	Nightstand, Ntst	Stove, Stv	Wood, Wd

Circle rooms; enter abbreviations	Walls, Doors		Floors		Windows		Lt. Fixtures		Inventory: Appliances, Furniture		
	cond.	chgs.	cond.	chgs.	cond.	chgs.	cond.	chgs.	Item	cond.	chgs.
(Living Rm)	OK		Cl Cpt.		wind-Cr scrn-ok Drp-ok		⊖		⊖		
Dining Rm											
(Kitchen)	OK				scrn-ok sh-G	scrn mending 1800	L+B ok		STV, Hd Ref (on loan)	CL CL	
(Bath 1)	JP										
Bath 2											
(Bedroom 1)	OK	hole in wall 45.00	CL. cpt		scrn-ok Drp-cl		L+B ok		⊖		
Bedroom 2											
Bedroom 3											
Other											
Itemized Charges	45		⊖		18		∅				∅

TOTAL ITEMIZED CHARGES $63.00

Other Charges Not Itemized
(Dirty garage, etc.
Explained on Backside) _____
Deduction for Improper Notice _____
Deduction for Missing Keys 2.00
TOTAL DEDUCTIONS $65.00

TOTAL DEPOSITS $850
minus (-) TOTAL DEDUCTIONS 65
equals (=) DEPOSIT REFUND $785
or (Amount Owed) _____

☑ Tenants acknowledge that the smoke detector was tested in their presence and found to be in working order and that its operation was explained to them. Tenants agree to test the detector at least every other week and to report any problems to Owners in writing. If the detector is battery operated, Tenants agree to replace the battery as necessary with a new ALKALINE battery (unless applicable laws require otherwise).

Tenants hereby acknowledge that they have read this Checksheet, agree that the condition and contents of the above-mentioned rental dwelling are without exception as represented herein, understand that they are liable for any damage done to this dwelling as outlined in their Lease or Rental Agreement, and have received a copy of this Checksheet.

Lester Landlord
Owner

_____
BY Person authorized to represent Owners

Richard Renter
Tenant
Rose Renter
Tenant

pg 2 of 3

Tenants' conceptions of what their dwellings looked like when they moved in are as likely to be mistaken as yours, but from quite the opposite perspective. That's why a proper move-out inspection requires a record of a prior inspection attested to by the tenants. If one is lacking, there is no standard for comparison.

Did the vacating tenants put twelve burns in the carpet or only seven? Did they break the toilet tank lid or did their predecessors do it? Were the lightbulbs working in every fixture when they moved in or were the bulbs mostly burned out? Was the kitchen floor really new when they moved in?

To prove whether the current tenants are at fault, take whatever records you made of the place before the tenants moved in—written, photographic, and videographic—and compare them with what you see now.

Although clear photographic and videographic records are important, sometimes even crucial, when you have to prove your case to a skeptical judge, they aren't as important as a written record when you have to account for a dwelling's deficiencies to tenants. Consider photographic and videographic records as evidence to supplement what appears in your written record.

Your written record should be something like the Condition & Inventory Checksheet. It should have been filled out in triplicate before the tenants moved in, one copy for the tenants to keep, and two for you to use now at move-out time. Retrieve those same two sheets from your files and itemize in duplicate all the various deficiencies you notice this time around during your tour of inspection, from holes in the screens to holes in the walls. Then you can make direct line-by-line comparisons of the place's previous condition with its current condition, and you can ana-

lyze the discrepancies. If you have to refresh the tenants' memories as to its previous condition, show them whatever visual records you have.

8) Calculate the charges fairly.

Avoid this kind of misunderstanding:

"How come you kept $350 out of my deposit for cleaning?"

"You didn't leave the place clean."

"I suppose you're right, but that's still an awful lot to charge me for just a little cleaning. I don't think it's fair."

"We had to do more than a little cleaning, Buster. You're no housekeeper. The stove and refrigerator were a mess, and the bathroom looked like it hadn't been cleaned since we cleaned it ourselves before you moved in two years ago. You're lucky we didn't charge you any more than we did. We had to go through your place with every cleaning product known to soap opera fans. Two of us spent a whole day in there working. We broke our fingernails and sucked more dust into our lungs in that one day than my vacuum sucks out of my house in a whole year. That's how bad your place was. Anybody cleaning up after you oughta get hazard pay."

"All right, all right, I get your drift. All the same, $350 is too much to charge anybody for cleaning something as small as a one-bedroom apartment."

Having itemized the rental's deficiencies, you can begin calculating approximately how much to charge the departing tenants to restore their dwelling to its original splendor, minus normal wear and tear, of course. These calculations ought to be based upon some list of charges as suggested in step 4, but lacking such a list, you should be as realistic as you can be in your estimates. Household lightbulbs don't cost $2 apiece, and

MOVE-OUT CONFIRMATION

We confirm that we have moved out of the dwelling located at the following address:

1301 Honey Ave., apt. 108, Littletown, California

We have returned our keys to the owner/manager and have returned possession to the owner/manager as of this date.

KEYS

[ ]   To the best of our knowledge, there are no keys to the dwelling in anyone's possession other than those keys we have returned.

[X]   We will retrieve the _1_ duplicate keys which are now in the possession of _Grandmother, Ellen Dove_ and give them to the owner/manager within _7_ days.

ITEMS LEFT BEHIND

[ ]   We have left no items of value to us on the premises.

[X]   We have left certain items of no value to us on the premises and authorize management to dispose of them and charge us for doing so.

[ ]   We have left certain items of value to us on the premises and will return to pick them up by _____ after arranging a pickup time with management at least twenty-four hours in advance of pickup. If we do not return to pick them up by this date, we authorize management to dispose of them and charge us for doing so.

[ ]   We have left certain items of value to us on the premises and will return to pick them up by _____ after arranging a pickup time with management at least twenty-four hours in advance of pickup. If we do not return to pick them up by this date, we authorize management to move them to another location and store them for pickup and to charge us for both moving and storage. If we do not return to pick them up within _____ of the date when this acknowledgment was received by the owner/manager, we authorize management to dispose of them and charge us for doing so.

RETURN OF DEPOSIT

We understand that our deposit will be accounted for and refunded to us within _14_ days. We prefer that both the accounting and the deposit be given to us in the following way:

[X]   Held for us to pick up on or after _11/15/XX_ .
       (PLEASE NOTE: Pickup time must be arranged at least twenty-four hours in advance.)

[ ]   Sent to us at the following address _____ .

_10/31/XX 10:30A_   _Richard Renter, 331 Fox St., Littletown, CA 555-0107_
Date/Time   Tenant / New Address / Best Phone Number for Contact

_10/31/XX 10:30A_   _Rose Renter, 331 Fox St., Littletown, CA 555-1017_
Date/Time   Tenant / New Address / Best Phone Number for Contact

_10/31/XX 10:30A_   _Leslie Landlady, P.O. Box 521, Littletown, CA 555-9891_
Date/Time   Received by Owner/Manager / Address / Phone

oven cleaning, no matter how dirty the oven, shouldn't take anyone twelve hours to complete. Be reasonable.

Remember that you should charge tenants only for the useful life remaining in an item which is broken or missing, not for its full replacement cost. If tenants move out a year after they moved in and their draperies, which were already three years old when they moved in, are now missing, charge them for only a fourth, rather than all, of the cost of the replacements. Likewise, because interior paint jobs should last two years when people are moving in and out, charge for just half of a new paint job when tenants move out and leave their walls, which were painted one year before, looking like the walls in a flophouse. After all, you got three-quarters of the useful life out of those drapes and half the useful life out of that paint job before the tenants did them in.

Just as you want to be fair to tenants when you calculate the charges to be deducted from their deposits, you want to be fair to yourself.

Remember that not all the charges against tenants' deposits are necessarily for cleaning and damages to the dwelling. You may charge them for accumulated late charges which they were always refusing to pay. You may charge them for having given you too short a notice that they intended to move. You may charge them for certain utility bills which they hadn't paid when they moved out and which you must now pay.

Be especially wary of tenants' unpaid utility bills, whichever ones they paid directly themselves. In most areas, utility companies hold the landlord accountable for the bills tenants leave behind, especially water, sewage, and garbage bills. Just assume that you are liable. Ask your tenants for proof that they have paid their closing bills so you're not hit with those bills yourself as a big surprise sometime after you have returned the deposits and have no hope of getting the tenants to reimburse you.

9) Get the keys and document the move-out, including the stuff left behind.

Avoid this kind of misunderstanding:

"What do you mean, you threw away the keys? You 'throw away the keys' only when you imprison a mass murderer, an al Qaeda terrorist, a foreign spy, a drug lord, an underworld kingpin, or a crooked politician, not when you vacate an apartment."

"Come on, I know that you always change the locks whenever a new tenant moves in. That's a well-known fact around here. I never thought you'd want my old keys. I never thought they'd be important to you. How was I to know?"

"How could you not know? When you gave notice that you were moving, I told you that I wanted to get the keys back. I also told you that returning the keys to me was the sign I needed from you that you'd moved out."

"If you did tell me that, I must've forgotten, but I can tell you something I didn't forget when I moved, two boxes I left in the back bedroom closet. What did you do with them?"

"What do you think I did with them? I threw them in the dumpster, and the garbage truck took them away on Thursday. I assumed they contained junk or else you wouldn't have left them behind."

"How could you do such a thing without consulting me? In one of those boxes you threw away was my butterfly collection that I've been working on ever since I was ten, and in the other box was my mother's wedding dress. It had great sentimental value to me. I left both of them behind because I wanted to be extra-careful when I moved them. I didn't want to take them away in the moving truck with all the rest of my stuff. I came back in my car to get them, and I couldn't believe that they were gone! I'm devastated! They were priceless! There's no way I can ever replace them!"

Uh, oh! Here comes trouble, double trouble! The tenant should not have thrown the keys away, and the landlord should not have thrown the tenant's precious possessions away. You can visualize a small claims court dispute developing out of these misunderstandings, can't you?

Avoid them by making a special effort to get the keys and by getting a written confirmation covering the keys, the stuff left behind, the return of the deposit, and the return of possession.

Be wary of keys on the loose. They can cause you terrible trouble later, particularly in those situations which dictate the reuse of the original keys for some good reason, say, because your rental house is old and has an antiquated mortise deadlock which requires a professional locksmith to rekey at great expense.

You don't want former tenants to retain access to their dwelling after new tenants have moved in. Anything could happen, and you'd be held liable for not having taken the reasonable precaution of installing new locks, rekeying the old locks, or gathering up all of the keys from the former tenants at the very least.

Keys on the loose can sometimes even return to haunt you later when you're moving locks around as you should be. Keys used long ago at one dwelling may resurface to open a totally different dwelling when the locks are put back into service there.

No, such things don't happen often. They happen just often enough to be a worry.

Make a special effort to retrieve every key you issued to your departing tenants when they moved in so you can consider the tenants as having officially moved out and so you won't have any key problems later.

Also, ask your departing tenants to give you any duplicate keys which they or their friends may have. If there are any, make an extra effort to get them, even to the point of asking for information you can use to contact the friends so you can retrieve the keys yourself if the tenants fail to produce them.

Just as you want to get the keys back from the departing tenants so you can establish for certain that they have returned possession of their rental dwelling to you, departing tenants may want the stuff they have left behind after they have moved the bulk of their earthly goods to their new home, and you should go to great lengths to find out what they want you to do with it.

One of them may have told you what they want you to do with it, but that's not the same as putting their thinking in writing.

Besides, your two tenants' thinking on the subject may differ. She may never want to see his scruffy high school letterman's jacket again, and that's why she left it behind in a closet, while he still clings to it as a reminder of his glorious high school football career and would feel lost without it. He hates to see any of their limited closet space taken up by a discolored wedding dress nobody will ever wear again, and that's why he left it on the floor of their bedroom, while she treasures this dress which belonged to her mother, all the more so because she salvaged it from the fire which took her mother's life.

The Move-Out Confirmation form confirms their thinking and saves you from misunderstanding their intentions.

Chances are good that a move-out will go smoothly without your ever having to use a form like this. It's not as important as the rental agreement you use when tenants move in, but it's here for you to use in those circumstances which warrant its use. You decide when to use it.

10) Return the deposits promptly, but not too promptly.

Avoid this kind of misunderstanding:

Scene 1. Telephone conversation.

"Where's our deposit, Les? We just went through today's mail looking for your check, and it wasn't there. We sure could use that money now to pay some of the bills we ran up during our move. It's been five days since we moved out, you know. Isn't it about time you sent us back our deposit money?"

"I've been so busy with the preparations for my daughter's wedding that I haven't had a chance to check your apartment. Is everything all right there? Nothing's damaged?"

"Everything's perfect, just the way it was when we moved in."

"OK, I'll send you the money tomorrow."

Scene 2. Courtroom.

"But, your honor, I returned their deposit before I had a chance to check their apartment for damage. They said they needed the money, and I took them at their word that there was no damage. Later, when I did check the apartment, I found all this damage that I never expected to find. It was a surprise to me, a big surprise, because they seemed to be good tenants. As you can see from the bills here, I spent over $700 repairing things after they moved out, things they damaged while they were living in the apartment. They owe me that money."

"Mr. Landlord, you are to be commended for returning your tenants' deposit so promptly, but you should have inspected the apartment first. I can't possibly award you a judgment for $700 because when you refunded the deposit to your tenants, you acknowledged that you were accepting the condition of their dwelling and were settling all debts with them, whether you understood that or not. Be more careful next time. The law in this great state of ours allows you twenty-one days to return tenants' deposits, and you should take what you need of that time to figure out everything the tenants owe you. Don't be so hasty. Don't try to be such a nice guy. I have no choice but to rule in favor of the defendants. Next case!"

Do not return tenants' deposits until you are absolutely certain that you have added up everything you can possibly deduct from their deposits, including the late fees they refused to pay during their tenancy, their unpaid utility bills, and a charge for a pest exterminator to rid the place of their dog's fleas which emerged from hiding to attack the painter four days after the tenants vacated.

If you have already returned the deposits and you later learn that you could have deducted the late fees the tenants owed you, that they neglected to pay a $25 water bill which you as the property owner are now obligated to pay, and that their dog left a swarm of pesky fleas behind, you have no legal grounds for collection, and as a practical matter, you might as well forget it, too. They aren't going to open their purse or checkbook to compensate you.

Most laws which govern rental deposit refunds allow you a very reasonable fourteen or twenty-one days to return and account for the deposits after the tenants move out. That's being generous. Seldom should you need that much time, but there are reasons why you need at least some time before returning the deposits. Take the time. Ten days should be enough. That's only a portion of the time which is most likely coming to you anyway. Take it. Take it because you're entitled to it and you don't want to get burned.

Some tenants will pressure you to return their deposits the very day they move. Resist. Tell them simply that you will be sending them their deposit check within ten days. Tell them you need that much time to determine whether there's anything else you may have overlooked in your assessment of charges, something which just hasn't surfaced yet. If they insist upon learning what you've found so far, tell them what your preliminary assessment of charges is, and tell them that you hope you won't find anything more to de-

duct over the next few days. Tell them that you want to give them every dollar that's coming to them.

If you're using the Move-Out Confirmation form, check it to see how and where the tenants prefer to have their deposit returned, and return it and your deposit accounting to them in that way.

If you're not using the form and you have no other instructions from the tenants, mail the deposit accounting and the refund to the forwarding address they supplied earlier on their Notice of Intention to Vacate. It may be incorrect because they may have changed their moving plans since they gave you notice a month ago, so verify it if you can. If you have neither a forwarding address nor instructions for returning the deposit, mail it and the accounting to the same address where they have been living, and get a Proof of Mailing from the post office. That will keep you from being accused of failing to return the deposit in the time allowed by law.

Remember that those tenants' deposits you hold are not yours. They have been entrusted to you in good faith to insure tenants' compliance with the terms of their rental agreement. If the tenants have indeed complied and you feel certain that you have determined everything which might be deducted from their deposits, then there's no reason to keep the money any longer. Refund it promptly.

One More Thing

There is one more thing I must mention on the subject of returning deposits.

If you should determine that the tenants have exhausted their deposit monies and actually owe you money, whether you despair of ever getting them to pay you what they owe you or not, you must still give them an accounting. They have a right to know where their deposit went.

Most states' landlord-tenant laws require landlords to give an accounting to every tenant who moves out, even if the tenant happens to have been evicted.

Along with the accounting, send tenants who owe you money a bill for what they owe and give them ten days to pay it. Include a self-addressed, stamped envelope for their payment, and you may be surprised when the envelope arrives in the mail with payment in full.

Some Last Words

You'll have to forgo an acquaintance with your local small claims court judge if you follow these ten measures for fulfilling your responsibilities when tenants move out, but you'll be well compensated. You'll be saving yourself a great deal of aggravation, as well as time, energy, and money, and you'll be earning yourself a reputation as a fair landlord, too. That's good business. People will remember you for your fairness and will recommend your rentals to others, and the tenants who remain with you will feel relieved of any worry about whether they will get their own deposits back when the time comes. They will know what to expect.

9
Dealing with Problem Tenants

Problem tenants are the bane of the landlording business. They are always testing you. They're the last ones to pay and the first ones to gripe. They're the ones who paint all their interior walls and woodwork flat black, adopt stray animals and leave food out for the poor skunks and squirrels, leave their preschool kids home alone to look after one another, report you to the environmental health department when their garbage can overflows with disposable diapers which stink to the heights of heaven, pull up the new wall-to-wall carpet and dispose of it because they prefer wood floors, call the plumber to unplug their toilet and make sure that the bill gets sent to you, change their own locks and refuse to give you a key, invite their latest friends to move in with them, and part out a car in the front yard, all without saying one word to you first.

They can be noisy, contrary, destructive, malevolent, or hypocritical all at the same time or at various separate times. They enjoy their music one way, loud, especially between midnight and sunup, and they can cuss as well as any guttersnipe, but what they seem to enjoy most of all is misquoting landlord-tenant laws to their fellow tenants and to you. They especially love those incredulous looks on your face when they tell you what your legal responsibilities are as their landlord and what their rights are as your tenants.

Have you ever encountered such people? Let's hope not.

Unless you inherit them from a previous owner, you'll never have the displeasure of encountering them yourself if you practice prevention whenever possible, that is, if you select tenants carefully, enforce agreements assertively, and collect rents promptly.

Remember that in landlord-tenant relations, an ounce of prevention is worth many pounds of cure, for cures are costly, agonizing, time-consuming, crisis-oriented, and sometimes downright dangerous to life, limb, and property. Prevention methods, on the other hand, are not particularly cheap, but they are definitely not costly. They may cause dyspepsia at times, but they are hardly agonizing. They do take some time to perform, but they save much time in the long run. What's most important, though, is that they serve to eliminate crises altogether, and they never endanger anyone or anything.

Fortunately, only a small percentage of all tenants are truly problem tenants, and if you happen to be lucky, you may never encounter them at all during your landlording career, although you may encounter ordinary tenants with an inclination toward becoming problem tenants. If you do, you'd better be ready to deal with them head-on before they cause you grief.

Here are some suggestions.

Identifying Problem Tenants and Outwitting Them

The full moon isn't the only thing that makes some people difficult to deal with. Some people are difficult during every phase of the moon. They're difficult all the time. They don't know any better.

You can deal with them much better if you know their type. That's right, difficult people come in different types, and they require different responses according to their type. To learn how to identify and outwit them, read *Coping with Difficult People*. It's a gem of a book, a seminal work written by somebody who has studied the subject for a long, long time.

From reading it, you might learn that you have been using the wrong approach in dealing with a particular tenant. He's really a "Sherman Tank" type, and you should be standing up to him rather than bending over backwards to agree with him.

He senses weakness in those who agree with him, and he will take every advantage of the weak. You need to face up to him and deal with him aggressively, whether that's your style or not, so that he will ultimately come to respect you and be a good tenant.

You might learn why you shouldn't expect too much from a "Super-Agreeable" type who will promise you anything and everything but won't follow through.

Of course, this one book isn't going to turn you into a perfect judge of people and a savvy negotiator, but it will get you thinking about the many things you might do to outwit and tame problem tenants.

Giving Problem Tenants One Last Chance—Mediating

When seemingly irreconcilable marital differences arise between spouses, and these differences threaten to destroy the marriage, husband and wife generally seek guidance from a marriage counselor before filing divorce papers. If they haven't sought any counseling by the time their case gets to court, the judge will make a strong recommendation that they do.

As an impartial third party trained to deal with marital disputes, a marriage counselor listens to both sides, sorts out the issues, and initiates discussions designed to help open each spouse's eyes to the real problems as seen through the other spouse's eyes. Once both spouses understand the problems, they can begin to work on solutions. Divorce may be the solution they ultimately settle upon, but at least they will have considered others with the help of someone knowledgeable in these matters.

Divorces and evictions are somewhat similar proceedings, and just as there are impartial third parties available to help spouses settle their differences, there are impartial third parties available to help landlords and tenants settle theirs. These impartial third parties who help landlords and tenants also help other people settle their differences, people who have problems with neighbors, friends, relatives, or businesses. The problems might involve barking dogs, spite fences, loud music, short changing, shoddy merchandise, broken promises, view-obstructing trees, or anything else which might be a source of discontent.

These impartial third parties are called media-

tors. They're a kind of community Peace Corps.

Mediators come from all walks of life. Most are retired and volunteer their services through charitable organizations which coordinate the people involved, the places, and the scheduling. They receive some training in handling disputes, but it is far from a college education in mediation. The truth is that mediators don't really need a college degree in mediation. They need common sense much more, as well as a love of people, a willingness to listen, and a lifetime of good and bad experiences to draw from. As you might imagine, good landlords make good mediators. They have the "right stuff."

Like a judge, the mediator listens to both parties state their positions, but instead of rendering a verdict, he asks questions to gain more information and tries to get the parties to discuss their differences frankly and work out a solution between themselves.

A judge, you see, has the long arm of the law available to insure compliance, so he can make unilateral rulings, and the disputants must comply or else.

The mediator has neither the position nor the authority of a judge and makes no rulings himself. Because he's not hamstrung by legal procedures and courtroom mumbo jumbo, he is in a position to let the disputants "slug it out," figuratively, of course. He is more like a referee who is trying to guarantee a fair fight. He gives the disputants as much time as they need to talk about their problems one-on-one, something they can't do in court, and he relies not on any threat of force for compliance but on the disputants' perception of the fairness of "their" agreement. They make the agreement, and they feel responsible to abide by it.

Should you feel that mediation might work to help settle a dispute you're having with a problem tenant, you'll want to locate the nearest mediation center first. To find it, try any of the following—Search the internet using "mediation [your town, your state]" as your search words. Look for listings under "Mediation" in the Yellow Pages. Call either the United Way or the office of your county's public defender and ask for the whereabouts of the nearest center.

When you finally find it, inquire into the services available. Mention the nature of your problem, and be sure you ask about scheduling, charges, and the background of those who ordinarily act as mediators. You definitely don't want to have to wait more than two weeks to be heard. You don't want to be surprised to learn that you're supposed to pay more for the service than you expected, and you don't want to have some whippersnapper legal aid attorney with minimal life experiences acting as the mediator, either.

After you establish these details, contact the tenant and offer to submit your dispute to mediation. Tell him as much as you know about the mediation process yourself, and tell him that you'd like to try resolving the dispute this way if possible because you think that it would be fair to both of you.

Remember, you have to get the tenant to agree to come. You might be able to drag someone before a judge, but you cannot drag anyone before a mediator. Mediation is strictly voluntary. The mediator isn't going to issue a default judgment or a bench warrant if the tenant fails to appear.

If the tenant agrees to attend, set up the meeting, and hope that you'll be able to reach a mutually satisfactory agreement.

At the meeting, be prepared to convince the tenant of the merits of your case, and be as reasonable as you can be in understanding the tenant's point of view. Negotiate if you have to, but emphasize why you maintain the position you do. Say that you, after all, have to look after the concerns and welfare of a number of people, not just yourself or this tenant, and that you aren't on some kind of a power trip. You're just trying to be realistic. The tenant has to behave in a certain way, or you can't tolerate having him around any longer.

If the two of you can reach an agreement, put it in writing. You might each want to write down what you've agreed upon and sign it. Then you give your tenant a copy of what you've written, and he gives you a copy of what he's written.

Give the tenant a chance to abide by the agreement, but don't waste any time in evicting him if he doesn't.

Getting Problem Tenants Out; It's an Easy Choice—Them or You

When you recognize that you have problem tenants who do not respond to your best efforts to deal with them fairly and you know for certain that mediation won't work, you cannot think in terms of prevention any more. You have to think in terms of cures. You have no choice really. Either you get rid of them or you'd better begin preparing yourself for complaints from the neighbors, deterioration of your property, departures of your good tenants, your bankruptcy, your capitulation, or all five. Humor these problem tenants no longer, ignore them no longer, pacify them no longer. Marshal your forces, steel your will, and think in terms of getting them out.

You can get them out, you know, and while you're at it, be mindful of the following—

✔ Be more interested in getting recalcitrant problem tenants out than in teaching them a lesson. No matter what their IQ happens to be, they simply do not learn life's lessons easily.

✔ Be pragmatic and businesslike with nonpaying tenants rather than feeling wronged and challenged. You will either lose the challenge or pay a big price to win. Suppress your feelings. Contain your ego. This is purely a business matter.

✔ Make a big effort to stop losing rent money as soon as possible instead of relying solely on the certainty of an eviction to cut your losses later. Be relentless. Hound those tenants to get them to move today rather than tomorrow.

✔ Heed the adage, "Spare the evictions, spoil the tenants," but recognize that "evictions" can mean alternative eviction methods as well as the conventional ones which use the judicial system full-strength.

Considering the Legal Alternatives to Eviction

You can always hope that a Notice to Pay Rent or Quit (used when tenants are in arrears), a Notice to Perform Covenant (used when tenants break their rental agreement), or a Notice to Terminate Tenancy (used when you wish to terminate a rental agreement for any reason at all; check its legality in your jurisdiction) will precipitate the response you desire, but don't bet any big money on it.

Like all consumers nowadays, tenants are better informed than ever before, and many know that you simply cannot legally put them out on the street in just a couple of days. Consequently, they tend to linger beyond the period specified in the notice, and you then seemingly have only

Agreement to Vacate   Dated June 15, xxxx

Agreement between JAY AND LINDA WILSON _____, Tenants,
who occupy a dwelling located at 101 PARROTT AVE, DOWNTOWN, IL
and DENNIS LEE _____, Owners, who are the
owners of this dwelling.

Tenants acknowledge that no one other than those listed above currently
occupies the dwelling.

Tenants occupy this dwelling under a rental agreement dated 12/1/xxxx .
This agreement is (X) month to month; ( ) a lease expiring _____.

The current rent for this dwelling is $ 932.xx . The current late fee
is $ 20.xx .

As of this date, tenants have paid rent through the following date:
 4/30/xx . They owe owners a total of $ 1,864.xx , itemized as follows:
 RENT FOR MAY AND JUNE _____.

Tenants agree that they have no excuses or defenses for failing to pay
what they owe.

Tenants agree to vacate the dwelling on or before 6/20/xx
at 7 pm/am.

If tenants DO vacate as agreed above, owners agree to the following:

(1) to apply the tenants' security/cleaning deposit to the amount owed
and to waive the balance of any amount owed; any excess remaining from the
security/cleaning deposit after the full amount owed has been paid in full
shall be returned to the tenants after they have moved out completely,
provided that they leave the dwelling reasonably clean and undamaged;

(2) to release tenants of any further obligation to pay rent under the
lease (if any);

(3) to make no report to any credit reporting agency regarding tenants'
credit;

(4) to make no report to any eviction reporting agency regarding tenants'
tenancy.

If tenants DO NOT vacate as agreed above, this agreement shall be null
and void, and owners may begin eviction proceedings immediately.

Tenants agree to keep this agreement confidential between the parties
involved. If tenants fail to keep this agreement confidential, this agreement
shall be null and void.

Owner _Dennis Lee_____   Tenant _Jay Wilson_____

By _____   Tenant _Linda Wilson_____

one alternative—a full-scale eviction.

Even if you handle an eviction yourself the legal way, it will cost you somewhere between $150 and $500 in out-of-pocket expenses for filing and process-serving fees, not to mention what the lost rent will amount to. Also, you'll have to spend time preparing the paperwork and more time presenting the papers to the court. Finally, when it's all over with, after you have painstakingly followed every single obligatory legal step, from serving the proper notice to accompanying the sheriff or marshal as they put the widows and orphans out on the street, you begin to realize that you and your tenants have been duped because all of you have wound up losers in one way or another.

Take heart. There are other perfectly legal alternatives you might try when you want to get problem tenants out without ever going to court, alternatives which might seem to be unreliable at first because they follow neither a clear-cut procedure nor a precise timetable and, in addition, require a somewhat artful approach. Some might even say that they require a bit of chicanery. Maybe they do. Still, they usually work surprisingly well, and, what's more, they don't make losers of everyone involved. These other alternatives you might try are talking, bribery, intimidation, and throwing a temper tantrum. On third thought, forget the last one. It's legal all right, but generally it's not very effective. Let's consider just the first three: talking, bribery, and intimidation.

Remember that with any of these methods you are trying essentially to convince your tenants that it is more advantageous for them to leave than to stay put. After all, if it *is* more advantageous for them to stay put, they will do exactly that. Wouldn't you?

■ Talking

All right, how do you convince tenants to vacate merely by talking to them?

You go to their dwelling. Do not summon them to yours like some pompous potentate, and do not talk with them by telephone except to arrange a meeting. Make sure when you arrive that the decision-maker of the group is there. Ask them to explain first of all what has happened, why they have broken their agreement with you, and give them plenty of time to answer without interrupting them. Listen to them. Listen to them intently. Show them how serious you are about what they have to say by taking notes, whether they're saying anything noteworthy or not, and, when you aren't taking notes, by making steady eye contact.

Then say, "Let me see whether I understand you. You are saying blah, blah, blah. Is that about right?" Only after you can state their position in a way acceptable to them should you go ahead and state your own.

With that done, outline the situation matter-of-factly as you understand it and suggest some alternatives. Ask them what they would do if they were in your shoes. If they offer up some unacceptable solution, tell them quite frankly why it wouldn't work and pose your own. Try to be understanding and try to reach an agreement that allows them to save face. Give a little, take a little, all the time being both reasonable and business-like.

If you can reach an agreement, formalize it in writing. A written agreement will be most helpful to you if the tenants do not vacate when promised and you have to evict them through court action. You will have something signed by the tenants to prove certain facts to the court and also prove that you were trying to be reasonable. Otherwise, the tenants may deny ever having agreed to anything, and you won't be able to prove that they had agreed to anything. You don't want to get yourself into a their-word-against-yours argument.

You'll want to put the agreement in writing immediately so that both of you can review it before you sign it and so that the tenants won't have time to reconsider. Come prepared with paper and pen, with paper and typewriter, or with a laptop and printer.

If the tenants agree to vacate, you may want to use the Agreement to Vacate form shown here. It establishes exactly who is living in the dwelling so they can't say later that you failed to serve everybody with eviction papers and therefore you can't evict anybody. It establishes the particulars about the rental agreement and the tenancy, including the agreement's type and date, the current rent, the late payment consequences, the date through which their rent has been paid, the amount owed, and an itemization of what is owed. It further establishes that the tenants have no excuses or defenses for not paying what they owe and that they will vacate the dwelling by a specific time and date.

In exchange for the tenants' agreeing to vacate and for keeping the agreement confidential, the owner agrees to apply the security/cleaning deposit to what the tenants owe, release the tenants from further rent obligations, and forego reporting the tenants to credit bureaus and eviction reporting services. In other words, the tenants would be leaving with a clean slate so they could get on with their lives somewhere else.

Considering that such an agreement could save you court costs, legal services fees, more lost rent, and lots of aggravation, it's a pretty good deal, especially if your chances of collecting a court judgment against the tenants are slim to none.

If you simply cannot reach an agreement which you consider fair, tell them you are left with no alternative but to evict them through the courts. Tell them you are loathe to go to that extreme because they will then be identified in public records as having been evicted, and it will be all the more difficult thenceforth for them to rent anywhere. Tell them that eviction reporting services, which search court records for the names of people who have been evicted, will identify them and make the information widely known.

Even their credit rating will suffer because credit bureaus include court judgments in their credit reports, and lest they think that they'll be able to avoid paying whatever they owe you after they've been evicted, tell them that a bill collector will begin hounding them to collect the judgment because you have a standing agreement with a certain collection agency to turn over all judgments to them for collection.

In addition, they will never again be able to answer honestly on rental applications that they have not been evicted.

After stating these consequences candidly, see if the tenants still persist in being unreasonable. If so, depart and say, "I'm disappointed that you have left me no choice. I had very much hoped we could work something out." Don't get into an argument with them. Don't leave in a huff. Just go.

Your success or failure in using this maneuver will depend upon the kind of relationship you have already developed with your tenants, as well as upon your skills of persuasion. Tailor the appeal to the people you are dealing with. Above all, be polite, but also be firm. Don't antagonize them. Don't call them names or impugn their ancestry. You may believe strongly in your heart of hearts that they are doing you wrong, but remember that your doing them wrong will only make you feel better. It won't help matters in the least. In fact, it will only make matters worse, much worse. So resist all of your basic urges to "punch them out." Keep your head. Swallow your pride. Keep the dialogue open-ended. If you cut off the dialogue, your impending lawsuit to evict them will be all the more difficult to pursue. You want the tenants to be available to be served with court papers as the case progresses. You don't want to alienate them so much that they will fight you at every step, avoiding service and delaying your case in any way they can.

Talking can work well for some landlords. I know one who successfully persuaded a motorcycle gang leader and his savage-looking retinue to vacate a house they had rented under false pretenses. That's right, he did it with talk. Well, not entirely. Here's what happened.

One evening the landlord brought over a case of beer (their brand) and cannily convinced them that he was entirely sympathetic with their wanting to remain but that he was being harassed so much by the neighbors who were telephoning at all hours to tattle about what was happening at his rental house that he was falling asleep at work and was in danger of losing his job. He apologized about asking them to move out, but he said that he just couldn't see any other way to end the neighbors' wee-hour phone calls. The gang moved out the following weekend. When the neighbors called to report that the motorcyclists were actually moving their things out, he rushed right over there with two more cases of their favorite beer and gave them his heartfelt thanks. They left the place spotless. Of course, talk alone didn't do the trick. The beer helped.

For more suggestions on how to settle landlord-tenant disputes by talking, read the classic little book called *Getting to Yes*. It resulted from years of systematic study into how people reach agreement in negotiations. It includes a full discussion of positional bargaining and negotiation jujitsu, as well as some specific examples of landlord-tenant negotiations. Read the whole book if you have the time. If you don't, read just the seven-page analytical table of contents in the back of the book. It summarizes everything you need to know.

Perhaps you have already tried talking your tenants into leaving, or you feel that your talking to them just wouldn't work. Well, how about bribery?

■ Bribery

Some people gasp and then start whispering at the mere mention of the "B" word, as if it were illegal or somehow wrong. In some situations it may be both, but not here. Here it's a motivating factor, nothing more. It's a motivating factor because it appeals to one very basic human instinct, greed, an instinct which problem tenants seem to be so richly endowed with. The more your bribe excites their greed instinct, the faster they'll react.

Besides being fast-acting, bribery can be inexpensive or even free. That's right! It might cost you absolutely nothing! If you required a big enough deposit from your tenants before they moved in, you would, if you were to act quickly, have money enough available from their deposit to pay the tenants for leaving. This possibility that they might stop paying you their rent was one of the reasons for requiring a deposit in the first place, wasn't it?

Obviously, should you succeed in suing to evict them, the money judgment, including court costs, would be subtracted from their deposit, and they could expect to receive little or no money back. In fact, they'd probably owe you some money. An offer to return what's left of their deposit after you deduct something for the rent they owe you might be enough to get them moving, and it wouldn't cost you anything!

Calculate approximately how much a full-scale eviction and the rent lost during the eviction would cost you, especially if you hire an attorney to handle the case, before you make your offer, and you'll likely find that a bribe will cost you far less. Even if you do have to sweeten the offer somewhat out of your own pocket because

you have delayed so long that there's only a paltry deposit balance remaining of, say, less than $100 (few tenants will move for less), you will come out way ahead by bribing them to leave, and so will they.

Greed triumphs again! Oh, who cares? Each of you wins, wouldn't you say? Your tenants get a few bucks, and you get your rental property back. You go away happy. They go away happy. Given the circumstances, what could be better than that?

There are some good variations on the bribery gambit, too. You might offer to store the tenants' goods in one of your unused garages or pay the rent on a self-storage unit for a few months. The tenants would then be free to stay with friends or relatives until they are able to get back on their feet, and you'd have a dwelling available for a paying customer.

You might offer to arrange and pay for a rental truck and a small crew to move the tenants' possessions anywhere within fifty miles or so.

You might cut a $100 bill in half right before the tenants' eyes, give them half, and keep half yourself until they have moved out completely on or before a designated date, or you might leave the entire $100 bill with a trusted neutral party who has instructions to give it to the tenants if they move by a certain date. This ploy is pretty dramatic for most tenants who can't come up with their rent money. It's dramatic enough to work, and it also circumvents many tenants' natural skepticism about whether you will pay off or not. Naturally, you should never pay off until you have verified that they have, in fact, vacated.

You might offer to buy the tenants' television, stereo, appliances, furniture, and computer if they have fallen on hard times. This would unburden them enough so the move would be easier and so they would have the funds needed to pay their other persistent creditors.

Before consummating your purchase, determine whether they're still making payments on the items you intend to buy from them. If you have reason to believe the items are collateral for a consumer loan, ask the tenants for written permission to run a credit check. It will tell you what you want to know. If you think that the items have been fully paid for, ask for a bill of sale.

Be creative. Be practical. Bribe your tenants to leave if the numbers make sense. You'll be free of them sooner rather than later.

■ Intimidation

Another maneuver which is perfectly legal and often prompts tenants to vacate without your having to resort to the courts is intimidation. No, I don't mean hiring goons or gorillas to scare your tenants out. I mean hiring a sheriff, marshal, or constable to scare them out. How? Have a law-enforcement officer serve your notices.

Sure, you can serve the notices yourself, but you're too familiar a face. You're simply not intimidating enough. You cannot possibly impress your tenants enough about the gravity of the matter as much as can an armed and uniformed law-enforcement officer who's handing them a notice signed by you stipulating that they have a fixed number of days to clear out. That is most intimidating to most people. They simply do not want to get mixed up with the law if they can help it, and they will sometimes mistake your notice for one from a court which actually sets a firm date for their eviction. It all seems so official and imperative. That's precisely the impression you want to give them.

For $50 or so you may be able to arrange to have your notice served by the law-enforcement officer who customarily serves legal process papers in your area (check into the availability of this service; some law enforcement agencies provide it; some don't). The on-duty officer will understandably take a few days longer to get around to serving the notice than you would if you were to handle the service yourself, but official service is more effective in getting action out of most tenants, and the nominal delay may be worth the results.

There's a variation on this method. You simply hire an off-duty law-enforcement officer directly. In many jurisdictions, officers may wear their uniforms while off duty and act as process servers. Inquire whether officers moonlight doing this in your area. If you can find someone who performs this service, your notices will be served all the more promptly than they would be if you have to work through a bureaucracy to enlist an officer's services.

In those situations involving tenants who are breaking their rental agreement, you may find that you can intimidate them and gather evidence to build a case against them all at the same time. Here's how. Take a video of whatever the tenants are doing to break their agreement, and do it openly. You want them to see you in the act of recording their loud music, taping their vicious threats, documenting their messy yard, or photographing their prohibited pet. Do everything possible to arouse their interest in what you are doing, and once you have it, tell them that you are gathering evidence for the court case you are preparing against them. You may find them more cooperative after that, and then again you may not, but even if this activity does not serve to intimidate them into changing their hellish ways, you still would have managed to gather some pretty incriminating evidence to introduce into court should you have to go to the mat with your case.

Recognizing Which Alternatives Are Illegal

In some respects, we're fortunate that there are laws to keep us landlords from acting rashly when we're trying to force problem tenants to move out. After being frustrated repeatedly, some of us might be driven to near distraction and feel compelled to take the law into our own hands. We might lock tenants out, toss them out, turn off their utilities, barge in and take their belongings, poison their animals, threaten them with bodily harm, harass them mercilessly, or even damage the dwelling we own so as to render it uninhabitable.

Why do laws keep us from carrying out such "perfectly reasonable acts"? These acts disturb the peace. That's why. They enrage tenants and endanger the lives and limbs of everyone concerned, yours too, to say nothing of the possible property damage they could cause.

People get hurt when they're being tossed out on their ears without due process. People become infuriated when their belongings are peremptorily confiscated. People become incensed when someone locks them out of their homes. They strike back blindly. Tempers flare. Problems grow out of all proportion, and the police have to be called in to quell the disturbances. Right behind the police, of course, are the media mongers, ready to broadcast to the world how mean and hateful landlords are.

Avoid illegal self-help eviction methods. They may seem suitable and reasonable. They're not. They're tempting, but they can cause you more harm than good. The penalties can be extremely severe, resulting in horrendous fines and even imprisonment. Some jurisdictions fine headstrong landlords $100 *per day* for every day tenants remain in their dwellings with the utilities shut off. Fines of $15,000 and more in these cases are not unheard of, and naturally, there's no rent accruing during such times.

The electric company can shut off the electricity if customers aren't paying their bills. You can't. You can't deprive tenants of electricity or any other utility if they stop paying their rent, not even when the utilities are included in the rent. You have to swallow the losses until you finally evict the tenants legally.

That's not fair, you say. No, it's not fair. Neither life nor landlording is fair, but we have to live with the laws governing our business whether we think they're fair or not.

All right then, what may you *not* do on your own initiative to force problem tenants out?

- You may not lock them out or lock them in.
- You may not toss them out on their ears and throw their belongings after them.
- You may not turn off their water, electricity, or gas.
- You may not clog their sewers intentionally.
- You may not take their belongings.
- You may not petnap their Fido or give arsenic to their Felix.
- You may not threaten to break their kneecaps or their skulls.
- You may not disturb their peace and quiet in order to make life there so unpleasant that they'll move.
- You may not remove a door, a window, a staircase, a toilet, a water heater, or even a faucet, nor may you do anything else to violate their "warranty of habitability."

These eviction methods are illegal, all of them. They can get you into big trouble and cost you big bucks.

Yet, I know of some landlords who do resort to such methods when they believe the circumstances are right for quasi-illegal self-help methods to work, that is, when they anticipate no complications. Generally they're street-wise people dealing with other street-wise people, people who don't use the courts to settle their disagreements anyway. The secret to using self-help methods successfully, they say, is to keep a low profile, know exactly what you're doing, know full well the kind of tenant you're dealing with, stay utterly alert, and be a convincing bluffer.

I also know of tenants who goad their landlords into taking illegal steps to evict them just so they can sue their landlords and collect big judgments.

The film *Pacific Heights* reveals the ways of a professional con man who preys on unsuspecting landlords and makes a handsome living exploiting them. Rent the video sometime, watch it, and learn from it. You'll be surprised to discover that it's actually sympathetic to landlords! Even if you happen to be watching it in the company of tenants, you'll be able to root for the landlords. They're the good guys in this film! Honest, they are!

[Every state sets its own time frame for this notice. If you don't know your state's time frame, call your local rental housing association, check the landlord-tenant laws on your state's website, or check the landlord-tenant law summary in the guest subject area of rhol.org.]

Notice to Perform Covenant

TO: HENRY & GLADYS LEVNO

and all other tenants in possession of the premises described as:

460 SWEET STREET, LITTLETOWN, CA 09090

PLEASE TAKE NOTICE that you have violated the following covenant(s) in your Lease or Rental Agreement:

TENANTS AGREE NOT TO PAINT OR ALTER THEIR DWELLING WITHOUT FIRST GETTING THE OWNERS' WRITTEN PERMISSION.

YOU ARE HEREBY REQUIRED within __3__ days to perform the aforesaid covenant(s) or to deliver up possession of the above-described premises which you currently hold and occupy.

If you fail to do so, legal proceedings will be instituted against you to recover said premises and such damages as the law allows.

This notice is intended to be a __3 —__ day notice to perform the aforesaid covenant(s). It is not intended to terminate or forfeit the Lease or Rental Agreement under which you occupy said premises. If, after legal proceedings, said premises are recovered from you, the owners will try to rent the premises for the best possible rent, giving you credit for sums received and holding you liable for any deficiencies arising during the term of your Lease or Rental Agreement.

Dated: APRIL 5, XXXX   *Lester Landlord*
                                                        Owner/Manager

---

PROOF OF SERVICE (Complete this proof of service only AFTER tenants have been served.)
   I, the undersigned, being at least 18 years of age, declare under penalty of perjury that I served the above notice, of which this is a true copy, on the above-mentioned tenant(s) in possession in the manner(s) indicated below (NOTE: Methods two and three below may also require mailing):

☒ On _APRIL 5, XXXX_ , I handed the notice to the tenant(s).

☐ On _____, after attempting personal service, I handed the notice to a person of suitable age and discretion at the residence/business of the tenant(s).

☐ On _____, after attempting service in both manners indicated above, I posted the notice in a conspicuous place at the residence of the tenant(s).

☐ On _____, I sent a true copy of the notice in a sealed envelope via ☐ first-class ☐ certified ☐ registered mail with U.S.P.S. postage fully prepaid, addressed to the tenant(s) at his/her/their place of residence.

Executed on _APRIL 5, XXXX_ , at the City of _LITTLETOWN_ ,
County of _SADDLEBACK_ , State of _CALIFORNIA_ .
                              Served by _Lester Landlord_

Taking Legal Steps

When you have tried and failed to rid yourself of problem tenants by hook or by crook, you have no alternative but to try an eviction by the book. You need legal clout to get them out.

Before you begin, however, you should know that in some jurisdictions evictions are handled in small claims courts as well as in other courts, but small claims courts have one major disadvantage. In a word, they are slow. Whenever you hear of a case involving a landlord who has been trying to evict a tenant for three months or more, chances are good that the case was filed originally in small claims court and worked its way up to a higher court.

Don't use small claims courts for your evictions. They may save you money, but they take way too much time, and time is money when you're evicting a tenant.

Every day tenants spend in your dwelling costs you money. Figure it out. A house renting for $930 a month is costing you $31 a day in lost rent, money you might as well forget about ever seeing again. Fifteen days of that rent would easily pay all of your costs in those courts which expedite evictions. If it's summary justice you want, don't go to small claims court. Go instead to whatever other court acts on such cases in your jurisdiction, be it municipal court, superior court, justice court, county court, or circuit court.

You should also know before you begin that you may represent yourself in an eviction case or you may be represented by an attorney, although you cannot represent yourself if you hold title to your rental property in the name of an entity separate from you as the owner. Corporations and limited liability companies are such entities. They require representation by an attorney.

If you can represent yourself, you may want to think about doing so. Most of the time you'll be able to handle everything yourself because evictions are little more than a formality requiring that certain forms be filled out properly and that certain time limits be observed carefully. Attorneys seldom do this work themselves anyway. They delegate it to their secretaries, and their secretaries select the appropriate form from a form collection which, by the way, you will find available in your court's law library or on the internet, and then they fill in the blanks. That's all they do, and you can surely do the same (California landlords who want to do their own evictions may

use *The Eviction Book for California*; see SOURCES & RESOURCES).

Besides, you will devote more attention to your own eviction proceedings than will attorneys who may have some 50 to 150 other cases vying for their attention. You will certainly get the tenants out sooner yourself because you have an incentive which attorneys don't. You are losing money every day a nonpaying tenant remains. Attorneys aren't. Regardless of how long an eviction action takes, attorneys will charge you the same sum for their services. In fact, if your eviction takes longer and presumably takes more of your attorney's time, he will charge you more. Yes, I know, he ought to charge you less the longer it takes, but that's not the way the system works.

Be shrewd enough, though, to recognize when you do need to engage the services of an attorney. Generally you need one when your tenants have hired an attorney themselves, when your tenants in an apartment house have organized against you, when your tenants have filed a serious written answer to your complaint or affidavit, or when there are any complications you don't understand. That's when you should hire yourself an attorney, and remember that even though you have begun an action on your own, you may always hire an attorney to assist you whenever you feel you need one as the case progresses.

Although the procedures and time limits for evictions do vary considerably from place to place, here is some information on evictions which should prove useful to you as you wend your way through the legal maze to get problem tenants out, no matter where you do business.

■ Notices

Every legal eviction must begin with a notice advising the tenants of your intentions. It must be properly filled out and properly served. The notice should include the number of days the tenants have in which to comply (minimums are set by laws governing such matters in the jurisdiction where your rental property is located), the tenants' names and the names of any other adults living there (if you don't know their names, call them "Does I through X" until you can discover who they are), the address of the rental dwelling, the amount of rent due through the current rental period (applicable only in evictions for nonpayment of rent), the period for which this rent is due, the date of the notice, and your signature.

[Every state sets its own time frame for this notice. If you don't know your state's time frame, call your local rental housing association, check the landlord-tenant laws on your state's website, or check the landlord-tenant law summary in the guest subject area of rhol.org.]

Notice to Terminate Tenancy

TO: _ANN PHELAN and MAYA WARD_

and all other tenants in possession of the premises described as:
462 SWEET STREET, LITTLETOWN, CA   09090

PLEASE TAKE NOTICE that you are hereby required within _30_ days to remove from and deliver up possession of the above-described premises, which you currently hold and occupy.

This notice is intended for the purpose of terminating the Rental Agreement by which you now hold possession of the above-described premises, and should you fail to comply, legal proceedings will be instituted against you to recover possession, to declare said Rental Agreement forfeited, and to recover rents and damages for the period of the unlawful detention.

Dated: _MARCH 31, XXXX_   _Lester Landlord_
                                                                          Owner/Manager

PROOF OF SERVICE (Complete this proof of service only AFTER tenants have been served.)
   I, the undersigned, being at least 18 years of age, declare under penalty of perjury that I served the above notice, of which this is a true copy, on the above-mentioned tenant(s) in possession in the manner(s) indicated below (NOTE: Methods two and three below may also require mailing):

☒ On _MARCH 31, XXXX_ , I handed the notice to the tenant(s).

☐ On _____, after attempting personal service, I handed the notice to a person of suitable age and discretion at the residence/business of the tenant(s).

☐ On _____, after attempting service in both manners indicated above, I posted the notice in a conspicuous place at the residence of the tenant(s).

☐ On _____, I sent a true copy of the notice in a sealed envelope via
   ☐ first-class ☐ certified ☐ registered mail with U.S.P.S. postage fully prepaid, addressed to the tenant(s) at his/her/their place of residence.

Executed on _MARCH 31, XXXX_ , at the City of _LITTLETOWN_ ,
County of _SADDLEBACK_ , State of _CALIFORNIA_ .
                              Served by _Lester Landlord_

Personal service is better than what attorneys call "nail and mail" (affixing the notice to the door and mailing a copy) because longer waiting periods apply in substituted service situations. You may serve the notice yourself if you want to, but you may be smart to have someone else serve it for you if you think you may be dealing with a perjurer. Some tenants will deny under oath that they ever received the notice, and the judge then has to weigh your word against theirs.

To circumvent this problem, you can always hire an intimidator to do the job for you, or you can serve the notice yourself along with the Payment Pledge introduced in chapter 6. That particular pledge is designed for nonpayment-of-rent situations, but by changing a few words here and there, you could use it in other situations. What's important about the pledge here, though, is that the tenant acknowledges service of the notice when signing the pledge, so the tenant would have a hard time denying in court that he ever received the notice.

■ Waiting Periods

In most jurisdictions, you may count weekends and holidays when determining the waiting periods in an eviction, but the final day for the tenants to pay the rent, vacate, or answer the complaint must be a day when the courthouse is open for business. Find out from the court clerk whether you may count weekends and holidays. If you may count them, you will save time and expedite your case.

■ Best Times to Serve

Whenever weekends and holidays count in determining waiting periods, there are certain especially good days for serving 3-day notices in order to take advantage of weekends and holidays in the count. Those best days are Sunday and Monday. Delaying service of a 3-day notice until Tuesday will, believe it or not, cost you at least five extra days in the whole process.

In those areas where weekends and holidays do not figure into the count, there are no "best" days for serving 3-day notices. They're all good.

The best time to serve a Notice to Perform Covenant or a Notice to Terminate Tenancy is always right after the rent has been paid. After being served, the tenant's will to pay rent diminishes drastically. You may actually create an eviction-for-nonpayment situation by serving the notice at a "wrong" time, although that may be a blessing in disguise because an eviction for nonpayment of rent is easier to win than an eviction for any other reason.

■ Copies

Make enough extra copies of all your eviction papers, including the notices, and you will avoid much disappointment and aggravation later. The copies needed will vary, depending upon the type of form and the number of defendants you have to serve. If you produce an original and three copies of each, you can be reasonably certain that you will have enough of every form to go around.

■ Accepting Rent

You must accept rent offered to you by someone who is responding to your Notice to Pay Rent or Quit within the period specified in your notice so long as the amount offered equals the entire amount owed. After the notice expires, you may accept the entire amount owed if you want to, but you don't have to.

Be aware that if you do accept so much as one dollar at any time following service of the notice, you will have to begin all over again from the beginning by serving another notice. For this reason, you should not accept any rent after you have spent the money to file your complaint or affidavit, unless the tenant agrees to pay the entire back rent plus your out-of-pocket filing expenses.

Should your tenant offer to pay you a substantial sum which is still only part of the total rent owed, and should you want to take it without risking the loss of your court case in the future after all the time and money you've spent to get into court, secure a formal court agreement with the tenant. Stipulate in the agreement that you may obtain a court judgment for eviction if the tenant fails to pay the balance of the rent or vacate by a certain date. In this way, you get some rent money, and you retain your priority for evicting the tenant if he doesn't pay or vacate.

■ Records

Whether or not you expect the tenant to appear in court, take with you into court all the records you possess on the tenant you're evicting. These should include whatever is applicable from the following list: rental agreement or lease, pet agreement, condition and inventory checksheet, waterbed agreement, correspondence, certified mail receipts, invoices covering repairs of damage, collection records, notices, photographs, videos, and even a chronology of the events in your deteriorating relationship.

Such records will strengthen your case much more than anything you're likely to say in court. Judges don't really want to hear you and the tenant vent your spleens. They want to see hard-and-fast evidence.

■ Bankruptcies

Bankruptcy used to be the last refuge of the deadbeat tenant whose landlord had gone to all the trouble and expense of pursuing a legal eviction. Prior to the Bankruptcy Abuse Prevention and Consumer Protection Act of 2005, which affects all fifty states, tenants who were being evicted could file bankruptcy at the very last minute and delay their eviction by a month or more. That tactic no longer works.

They can still file bankruptcy to get an "automatic stay" and stop their eviction, but they have to get it before the landlord gets a judgment against them. Once the landlord has a judgment in hand, no bankruptcy filing can stop its enforcement.

That change in the bankruptcy laws alone would have been enough to curtail the activities of the eviction delaying attorneys who were filing tenant bankruptcies willy-nilly for no other reason than to delay evictions, but there's something else in the new bankruptcy law which helps landlords. Bankruptcies are more difficult to file now and are better scrutinized, so that tenants are far less likely to file bankruptcy only to delay

an eviction, though they may still file to extricate themselves from their financial difficulties and delay their eviction at the same time.

■ Lesson

A peremptory notice to vacate eviction notice on one door of an apartment building serves as a convincing lesson to other tenants that you know how to evict and that you will evict when necessary.

Leave the notice on the door just long enough for at least one other tenant to see it and then remove it yourself. The word will spread quickly along the building grapevine to the other tenants living there. Don't leave the notice up for an extended period of time (an afternoon should suffice), however, because you don't want other owners in the area to see it. They will be wondering what's wrong with your building and will depreciate its value in their minds.

A final eviction notice on the door of a single-family dwelling serves no useful purpose after the tenants have seen it and vacated. Remove it from the door and throw it away once they have cleared out.

Some Last Words

Remember that not getting rid of problem tenants is much more aggravating than all the aggravation of actually getting rid them. Go on. Get it over with. Get rid of those problem tenants. Then get on with your business.

10
Managing the Rental House

The rental house business as described in Dave Glubetich's book, *The Monopoly Game*, Robert Allen's book, *Nothing Down*, and John Schaub's book, *Building Wealth One House at a Time*, all of which became popular at various times when house prices were skyrocketing, is a little like the Rent-A-Wreck® used car rental business which enables used car dealers to realize additional income from the cars in their inventory.

Any car sitting on a used car lot is costing the dealer money because it ties up funds which earn him zero interest, because he has to provide valuable space on his lot for displaying the car, because the car is depreciating in value as it becomes older and more outdated, and because he has to look after the car to keep it from deteriorating cosmetically and mechanically. The longer he keeps it, the more costs he incurs, so he tries to buy cars which will sell quickly and sell for considerably more than what he paid for them. Normally, his profit is the difference between what he paid for the car and what he sold it for minus his various expenses.

By renting the car out while he's trying to sell it, the used car dealer increases his income and exposes the car to potential buyers who pay him to take it out for "test drives." His expenses increase somewhat because he has to pay for oil changes and tune-ups and extra insurance and paperwork, but his income increases a lot. That's good business.

Most rental houses are waiting around to be sold, too, in most cases until their owners believe the time is right to put them up for sale. The longer the owners hold onto them, the more the holding costs accumulate. While a house is "in inventory," the owner rents it out so he doesn't have to bear all the costs of holding onto it until he finally sells it.

The rental house business varies widely from place to place around the country. You can see this variance in the ratio of market prices to market rents. If you're lucky enough to be doing business in an area where you can buy good houses for $60,000 with little effort and you can rent them out for $600 or more per month (or a similar 100:1 ratio between purchase price and monthly rent) with little effort, you have yourself a "cash cow," and you ought to be counting your blessings every month along with your cash. You have positive cash flow. You don't need to "feed" your houses. They're feeding you. That's what they're supposed to be doing.

On the other hand, if you're among those who have to pay $160,000 for each of the houses you buy, and you can't rent them out for more than $1,000 per month (a depressing 160:1 ratio), you have a "cash crocodile" on your hands. You have negative cash flow. You are paying every month for the dubious privilege of being your tenants' landlord.

To some people that may not seem like a smart thing to do, but then again it may turn out to be as smart as buying shares in Apple Computer or Google when those stocks first came to market, especially if you learn how to handle your negative-cash-flow problems adeptly and you sell the houses when there's an upswing in their market value.

Whether your rental house "business" consists of one house or one hundred, whether it's a Cowboy Bob cash-cow operation or a Crocodile Dundee cash-crocodile operation, you need to know more about how to increase its positive cash flow. Here I call the subject "handling the negative-cash-flow problem" because most owners of rental houses are wrestling with negative cash flow. Yep, they're wrestling with crocodiles. Of all the problems in rental house investing and management, that's the one most dangerous to your financial well-being, but there are some solutions to it, and there are some solutions to the other rental house management problems, too—the vacancy problems, the neighbor problem, the restrictions problem, the bookkeeping problem, the maintenance problem, and the gardening problem. Read on.

Handling the Negative Cash Flow Problem

People who, for any number of reasons, prefer to invest in single-family houses rather than multiple-family dwellings have wrestled with the negative-cash-flow problem for some time now and have come up with some pragmatic solutions worth examining. Here are ten of them, most of which are a combination of investment and management strategies—involving tenants as partners through lease-options, actually sharing the space with a number of tenants, creating a duplex from a house, renting the house out on a short-term basis, renting out the parts of a house, building more houses on the same lot or buying property with more than one house on a lot to begin with, sharing the ownership with silent partners who want to invest in real estate but don't want to be directly involved with rental property themselves, tinkering with the financing, investing in the least expensive single-family residences available, and "stealing" the house.

Let's examine each of these solutions in some detail. Perhaps there's one of them which appeals to you enough for you to want to try it, and perhaps it'll work well enough to help you transform your cash crocodiles into cash cows.

■ **Involve tenants as "partners" using a lease-option**—Many rental house tenants would like to buy a house but don't have the necessary funds to make the down payment or the necessary expertise to find a good low-money-down deal themselves. The short-term (one-to-five-year) lease-option would seem to work well in those cases for both you and them.

It's good for you because the tenants pay you a little more in rent every month, enough to cover the house's negative cash flow, and it's good for them because they get the right to buy the house at some future time for a certain fixed price or for the current appraised value plus an annual percentage increase based upon an inflation rate such as the Consumer Price Index (CPI) or for

the house's value as appraised when they decide to exercise their option In any of these cases, they would receive a credit for what they'd accumulated from having made higher monthly rental payments.

Of course, there's another benefit to using short-term lease-options. Tenants who have an option to buy tend to think of themselves more as owners than as tenants, and they tend to take better care of the property. As a result, your management headaches practically disappear.

See Robert Bruss's book, *The Smart Investors Guide to Real Estate,* for the in's and out's of lease-options. Mr. Bruss has also written about them in his report—"How to Profit from Lease-Options (Rent to Own) If You Are a Property Buyer, Seller, or Real Estate Sales Agent" (inman.com/store/columnist-reports).

I should mention here that there's a contrarian point of view about lease-options expressed by John T. Reed in his "Single-Family Lease Options" (johntreed.com). He maintains that today's typical lease-option, which credits the tenant with money toward the purchase of the property and is too seldom exercised by the tenant, has such an unclear legal standing that it should be considered more of a gamble than a sure thing.

He admits that many people continue to use lease-options today quite successfully, but he's afraid that their glory days won't last when attorneys take up the fight for the poor tenants who too frequently lose large equities when they can't exercise their options. The courts could also recharacterize lease-options as sales. If that happens, landlords would have big problems with their ownership position, their financing, their income taxes, their property taxes, their financial obligations, and their evictions.

Should you wish to use a lease-option for a certain rental house and should you still have doubts about whether you ought to be using the technique at all, read the Reed book on the subject and seek legal guidance from a local real estate attorney. Then, if you want to give the technique a try, have the attorney prepare a lease-option agreement which you and your tenants can live with or secure one from a firm specializing in preparing legal real estate documents. Professional Publishing (profpub.com) has good lease-option agreements, some state-specific and some not. They're available online through an affiliated website (trueforms.com), where you may examine the various agreements before you commit to buy.

Knowing what I know, would I use a lease-option for a rental house of my own? Yes, I would. In fact, I do. I handle them entirely myself without using an agent, and I try to structure them so that the tenant can exercise the option 90% of the time.

■ **Share the space**—In her book, *Managing Your Rental House for Increased Income: A Unique System Designed to Make More Money No Matter What Happens to the Economy*, Doreen Bierbrier explains precisely how she rents out the rooms in her rental houses to people who do not know one another initially. They're perfect strangers. She collects more rent from all of these tenants combined than she could possibly collect otherwise if she were renting to a single household.

Perhaps you shared a house or an apartment with a group of friends when you were younger. Five of you might have rented a house together with each one of you being responsible for paying an even 20% share of the rent and utilities. When one of you moved out, that left the remaining four to pay 25% shares of the rent and utilities. That's the traditional way for groups to rent and share a commodious dwelling.

Bierbrier has come up with a variation, one which has advantages for the rental house owner and for single tenants alike. She sets up what resembles a rooming house operation in each house she acquires, but she does not live on the premises. Even so, she rents out the individual rooms herself in consultation with the people who live there, and she assumes the responsibility for filling every one of the rooms herself as well. No matter how many rooms are rented out, each tenant pays a set rent every month.

Her tenants like the arrangement because they don't have to pay any more rent when there are vacancies and because they get to help select the new tenants. She likes the arrangement because she gets a higher aggregate rent and a positive cash flow while she still gets all the other benefits of rental house ownership.

Do recognize that this arrangement necessitates much more owner involvement than the normal rental house arrangement, and it works only for certain kinds of houses in certain kinds of locations.

One reader of an earlier edition of *Landlording*, tried it and rued the experience in a six-page chronicle he sent me titled "101 Reasons Not to Split a Single-Family House into Room Rentals."

Don't try it yourself without reading Bierbrier's book first. Then proceed deliberately and cautiously if you decide to give it a try.

■ **Create a duplex out of a house**—A good friend of mine fixed up the spacious trunk of his monstrous ten-year-old American car and was actually living in it during his penurious college days back in the sixties. One day another student knocked on the trunk lid and inquired about inexpensive accommodations for rent in the area. They struck up a deal. My friend rented out the trunk of his car and moved into the back seat. He had created a duplex out of a car, possibly a first in recorded history!

When that friend began investing in rental property, he specialized in creating duplexes out of houses. With minimal renovations and minimal expense, he was able to increase his cash flow in just a few years to a point where he could leave his job as a school teacher and retire at an early age on the comfortable and secure income from his rental houses. Poor guy, he never got a real baptism in rental house ownership. He never found out what negative cash flow was. All his cash flow was positive. It still is.

Creating several separate living units out of an opulent old house is nothing new. Every city with housing stock from bygone eras has its examples of such renovations, most made necessary by a change in people's lifestyles over the years. These conversions entail radical changes in the existing living areas and permanently transform the houses into multiple-family dwellings.

You wouldn't want to create a duplex out of an ordinary rental house by chopping up the interior space that way if you ever expect to capitalize on the sale of the house to an owner-occupant who will pay a high price for the home of his dreams. No, what you should be doing is creating a duplex while leaving the house itself intact as much as possible. You should be creating an additional living unit out of unused or underused space, such as a basement, a rumpus room, an attic, a garage, an outbuilding, or an expandable crawl space (houses on the sides of hills are excellent candidates for crawl-space conversions).

Good as the idea of creating a duplex out of a house may sound at first as a means of increasing cash flow, you should not go to any great expense to create a second living unit unless you can expect a good return on your investment while you own the property because the money you put into the extra living unit may not make the house worth any more when you go to sell it. Remember, house prices and rents have nothing to do with one another. They're determined in separate marketplaces. Ordinary house (single-family dwellings) buyers are seldom interested in a house's rental income, whereas apartment house buyers are always interested in a building's rental income.

If the conversion you're contemplating is as simple as installing some used kitchen appliances in a basement which already has a small bathroom and an outside entrance, and for this outlay of $500 you are able to collect an extra $500 per month in rent, obviously the conversion makes good sense. No, it makes great sense!

If the conversion you're contemplating is going to cost $12,000 and yield $500 per month in extra rent, it would be worth the outlay only if you were planning to hang onto the property for two years at least, or if you could count on the conversion adding $24,000 to the property's value.

Find several real estate agents who know property values in the area and ask them how the addition of an income unit would affect the value of your property.

So much for the financial aspects of creating a duplex out of a house. How about the legal aspects?

Often a second living unit is called an in-law apartment because owners used to create them for aging relatives who lacked either the funds or the ability to live completely on their own, and often these in-law apartments were bootlegged, that is, constructed illegally. Owners didn't want to have to deal with building inspectors and zoning ordinances. The zoning ordinances may even have prohibited such conversions altogether.

Today, however, most areas are lenient about creating independent living units in existing houses, and the units don't have to be bootlegged. They're legal. Make some anonymous inquiries before you start building yours to find out whether they're legal in your area.

Believe it or not, there's an entire book devoted to this subject, and it happens to be a good one. Called *Creating an Accessory Apartment* and written by two land-use planners, it's a must-read for anybody who's remotely interested in adding rentable self-contained space to a house (currently out of print, the book is available in libraries and from booksellers who partner with Amazon).

Keep this in mind—two self-contained living units with the same square footage as an equivalent single living unit will always yield more rent than the single unit, and more rent translates into more cash flow month after month after month.

■ **Rent the house out on a short-term basis—** Just as there is a need for rentals on a long-term basis, there is a need for rentals on a short-term basis.

Companies transfer their employees to distant locations or put them to work miles away from home and need temporary housing. People on vacation want to stay in a home away from home where they can spread out and relax and also cook for themselves rather than be cooped up in a hotel or motel room. Couples want to try living together for a time before they give up their own digs and commit themselves to a long-term relationship.

In any of these situations and the many others which create a demand for short-term rentals, tenants are willing to pay more for every day they stay in a short-term rental, from twice to five times as much as they would pay per day for a long-term stay. That's the upside of the short-term landlording business. The downside is the additional time and money required for furnishing, cleaning, maintaining, bookkeeping, advertising, communicating, scheduling, troubleshooting, and greeting the tenants upon arrival.

Short-term landlording is more of a hands-on business than long-term landlording, but it can and does pay off well, especially when the location is good, when you're renting out several such houses in close proximity to one another, and when you're using the internet to promote them inexpensively.

Before the internet first became available and later became so popular, there was no good way for a landlord in Montana to let a fly fisherman in Florida know about a house for rent by the week along the Yellowstone River, where the fly fishing can't be beat. Now there is, and getting the word out is ludicrously inexpensive, whether through a noncommercial website such as craigslist.org or through commercial websites such as vrbo.com and homeaway.com.

Those websites work especially well to get the

word out when they're combined with the landlord's own website, giving all the particulars of the short-term rental house.

Some years ago, when the internet was still in its infancy, my wife and I bought a townhouse in San Francisco. We bought it for ourselves to use but found that we used it so infrequently that we decided to rent it out by the week.

We furnished the place, printed up a brochure, created a website, secured a toll-free telephone number, promoted the property through the convention and visitors bureau, advertised it periodically in San Francisco newspapers, and rented it regularly to short-term visitors. Eventually, we sold it at a tidy profit, having also realized a profit during our ownership from renting it out on a short-term basis.

There are several books available to help you manage properties rented for the short term, and Christine Hrib-Karpinski's *How to Rent Vacation Properties by Owner: The Complete Guide to Buy, Manage, Furnish, Rent, Maintain and Advertise Your Vacation Rental Investment* is a good one to start with.

■ **Rent out the existing "parts" of a house separately**—Houses frequently come with space which tenants either don't want or don't use. In that case, the space is worth nothing to the tenants who are occupying the house, whereas it may be worth quite a bit to somebody else. So go ahead and rent it out to somebody else.

Garages are the most likely "house parts" which might be rented separately, but don't overlook other candidates such as parking spaces, storage cellars, basements, garden plots, potting sheds, greenhouses, back yards, flat roof space, decks, and yes, even swimming pools.

Plenty of people are interested in renting garages, storage cellars, basements, and garden plots. Who might be interested in renting the swimming pool of a house where they don't live? Try the next-door neighbors. To them the pool next door is always bluer than their own.

If you do decide that you can rent out the existing parts of a house separately, be sure that the house tenants are apprised of the arrangement in advance. You don't want to aggravate them and perhaps lose the primary source of your income from the property by trying to squeeze out some secondary income, and if you have always included the use of all the house parts in the tenants' rent, you should give them a rent reduction to gain their cooperation in your efforts to rent out those parts which they had considered theirs, even though they had never used those parts and never would.

Also, be aware that some communities specifically prohibit the segmenting of house parts for rental purposes. Find out whether your community has any such laws before you make commitments to anybody and act accordingly.

■ **Put more houses on the lot or buy property which already has more than one house on its lot**—When you want to increase the income from your properties while playing a good competitive game of Monopoly®, you add houses to the sets of matched properties you own.

Many times you can do the same thing in the rental housing game as well except that you don't have to wait until you've acquired a full matched set of properties. You need only one property which lends itself to such development.

Two or more houses on one lot require no more land investment than one house on that same lot. Yet each one of them adds again as much rent as the one house. Those additional houses help to generate positive cash flow.

When you're looking to buy investment houses, look for those which have lots large enough to accommodate another house or two somewhere on the property and have the proper zoning, or look for properties where several houses share the same lot already.

Also, consider putting used manufactured houses on your property to increase income. They conform to HUD building codes (all manufactured houses built on or after June 15, 1976 are in conformance), cost far less than traditional "stick-built" houses, require little time to set up and become habitable, and yield just as much income as any other housing.

A few words of caution before committing to buy a used manufactured house: Check with the local building department to make sure it's legal on the property where you want to place it; check the cost of removal from the site where it currently sits, check the cost of transportation from one site to another, and check the cost of the setup on a different site; and buy only those manufactured houses which are less than ten years old and look like traditional houses.

■ **Share the ownership with a silent partner**—People with sizable incomes sometimes want to put part of their investment monies into real estate which has good appreciation potential. Yet they're so busy doing what they do to earn their sizable incomes that they don't have time to look after any rental property. That's where you come in.

You find a property with good appreciation potential as a result of both improvements and inflation, and you make as realistic a projection as you can of the property's income, expenses, potential, and holding period.

You decide what you have to put into the property, including cash, sweat equity, and management expertise, and you decide what you want to get out of the property, given your projection. Next, you decide what you want your silent partner to put into the property and what you expect the silent partner to get out of the property, given your projection. Then you identify somebody who appears to have discretionary money for investments and appears to trust you well enough to do a business deal with you, and you approach that person with your proposal. You explain the potential risk and the potential reward of the investment as clearly as you can. You explain what you yourself expect to put into the deal and what you expect the investor to put into the deal, and you say that you need the investor to make a commitment to provide some upfront monies as well as monthly payments to cover the property's negative cash flow.

Sounds pretty good, doesn't it? Well, sometimes it is and sometimes it isn't.

Be aware that silent partners who have to continue making cash contributions to an investment month after month may decide to stop making those contributions after a while and jeopardize your own ownership position.

To keep the payments coming, make them as painless and inconspicuous as possible for your silent partner so that they never even cross the partner's radar screen and the partner never has to think about them. The best way to make them painless and inconspicuous is to set up automatic bank transfers. The second best way is to get a year's supply of postdated checks.

■ **Tinker with the financing**—The largest percentage of a rental house owner's expenditures goes to the loan payment. Reduce that loan payment, and you increase the cash flow.

There are many ways to reduce a loan payment, but unless they involve a longer term, a lower interest rate, or a partial forgiveness of the debt, they will increase the amount of the loan principal. You'll be eliminating the negative cash flow all right, but you'll be creating negative amortization. In effect, you'll be taking out a small loan every month to help with the expenses and put money into your pocket. You get positive cash flow at the expense of having to pay off a larger loan balance later.

There's nothing wrong with taking out a small loan every month so long as you understand that that's how you're creating your positive cash flow. If the value of your rental house is appreciating more than the loan principal, you'll do well. If it isn't, be prepared to suffer the consequences later.

■ **Invest in the least expensive "houses" available located on land you do not own**— Mobilehomes, known to some people as "tornado targets" and to others as trailers or manufactured housing, are the least expensive housing to build and to buy. Because they compete in the rental market with much higher priced housing stock, however, these inexpensive investments can and do command good rents. Rental mobilehomes don't have negative cash flows, not when you can buy them for $10,000 and rent them out for $200 a month. That's the equivalent of renting out a $100,000 house for $2,000 a month, and I don't know of anybody anywhere who's doing that.

The truth is that the mobilehome you can buy for $10,000 will usually rent for more than $200 a month. $300-400 a month would be about right. The extra money pays for the mobilehome park's space rent if the mobilehome happens to be located in a park; otherwise, it compensates the property owner for the use of the land where the mobilehome sits and for whatever utilities and services are provided.

Before you rush out to buy a dozen mobilehomes to start your own rental fleet, you should know that there are some drawbacks to consider. Here are three—

✔ Financing mobilehomes isn't always easy, and when money doesn't come easy, you know it's going to cost you more. Expect to pay one to five percent more to finance a mobilehome than you'd pay to finance a "stick-built" house, that is, if you can even get financing from a commercial lender. The best financing for mobilehomes is seller financing. Get it if you can, or else get the cash to buy mobilehomes from other sources, and then negotiate a quick-closing cash price from the seller.

✔ Maintaining mobilehomes tends to cost more because the least expensive models have cheap fixtures which can't take much abuse and soon require replacement. Replacement parts aren't always available at the neighborhood hardware store, either. They may have to be purchased from a mobilehome parts supply house, or else you may have to do some adapting so that readily available parts will fit.

✔ Dealing with mobilehome park management can be trying, too, especially if the management is fickle about allowing non-owner-occupied mobilehomes in the park.

Still, there are benefits to investing in mobilehomes other than the cash flow they generate. Here are three—

✔ They are mobile and can be moved when economic or political or emergency conditions warrant moving them. Apartment house owners would love to put wheels under their buildings and move them when a major employer leaves town or when local politicians enact rent control or when a natural disaster strikes.

✔ They are 100% depreciable, that is, there's no land to break out of the total cost.

✔ Because they're inexpensive, they're relatively easy to sell. After all, they're the least expensive housing available.

Interested? Get a copy of Lonnie Scruggs' book, *Deals on Wheels: How to Buy, Sell, and Finance Used Mobile Homes for Big Profits and Cash Flow*, and read it.

■ **Steal the house**—Some rental house investors spend far more of their time shopping for property than they ever spend managing it. They're as close as any real estate investors come to being real used car dealers. They try to buy at wholesale from anyone who wants to get rid of a house in a hurry at any price. They hold onto it for a while. Then they sell it for as close to the retail price as they can get.

Now if you can buy $120,000 houses for $80,000 with reasonable terms and rent them out for $850 per month, you'll have solved the negative cash flow problem all right, but you're going to be working mighty hard hunting for those deals. In spite of what the late-night hucksters of real estate "secrets" say, these deals are not available at the sales office of every new housing tract. You'll have to hunt them down, and

that in itself is work.

If stealing houses sounds to you like a good way to eliminate negative cash flow and you'd like to try it, just be sure that you don't neglect management so much that you rent your wholesale houses to people who turn you into somebody who wants to get rid of a house in a hurry at any price.

Handling the Vacancy Problems

Vacancies are more worrisome to the rental house investor than they are to the multiple-housing investor. One vacancy in a fourplex means that the building is 75% occupied, whereas one vacancy in a rental house means that the building is 0% occupied. As the owner of that rental house, you're quite aware of the income implications of not having any tenants occupying the property, and you're going to be trying whatever you can to increase the occupancy level from 0% to 100% as soon as possible, but there are some other implications, too. You need to do more than hunt for new tenants during your rental house's vacancy.

■ **Take special precautions when showing your rental house**—As a rental house owner, you are by definition an absentee owner, that is, you're not living on the premises. As a result, whenever you have to show a vacancy, you have to cover some distance to reach your rental house and show it off to prospective tenants. Dropping whatever you happen to be doing and going over there to meet people who want to look at it becomes awfully tiresome after a time, especially when they turn out to be "lookie loos." Do what any other landlords do to solve this problem. Schedule the showings at a particular time when you will open the house to any and all lookers, or else tell those who respond to your advertising to drive by the place first before you schedule a showing for their eyes only.

What else might you do to cut your involvement in showing the place to a minimum? Ask a cooperative neighbor to keep the keys and either unlock the door for anyone who wants to see the place or else take the people through. Many neighbors are delighted to help, some just to get a good look at their prospective neighbors, some just to get a courteous "thank you," and some just to earn a few extra bucks.

Lacking cooperative neighbors, you might ask those who are interested in seeing the place to

Property Viewing
& Keys Agreement

With my signature below, I hereby acknowledge receipt of the key(s) to the dwelling located at __456 SWEET ST.__ __LITTLETOWN, CA__ .

I intend to use the key(s) for the express purpose of viewing the dwelling to consider whether it is suitable for me to rent, and I will neither disturb nor remove anything found there.

As a courtesy, I will report to the owner/manager whatever appears to be amiss at the dwelling.

I have given the owner/manager, whose acknowledgment appears below, a deposit of $__20—__, and also a valuable personal item consisting of __DRIVERS LICENSE__ , both of which will be returned to me when I return the key(s).

I promise to return the key(s) by __4:00__ (~~a.m.~~) (p.m.) TODAY to the owner/manager at EITHER

        (X) the same place where I picked them up OR

        ( ) the following place _____ .

Should I fail to do so, the owner/manager is entitled to keep the deposit to pay for changing the locks on the dwelling but will return my valuable personal item to me when asked.

I understand that this agreement gives me no occupancy rights whatsoever and that I must complete a rental application if I want to be considered as an applicant to rent this dwelling.

Signed _Rose Renter_

Current Address _1510 Zebra - Littletown, CA_

Current Telephone Number _555-1988_

Date & Time _Jan. 6, xxxx   2:00 P.m._

Acknowledged by _Leslie Landlady_
                    Owner/Manager

come over to your house or place of business, pick up the housekeys, and show themselves through the house. This do-it-yourself showing may work smoothly in many situations forever, but it is somewhat risky. There's always the danger that the people won't return the keys, that they will copy the keys so they can gain access later, or that they will brazenly move into the house without your ever getting a dollar out of them. If they did move in, they wouldn't be considered trespassers either, because they had your permission to enter, so you'd have a hard time getting rid of them. You couldn't merely summon the police to remove them from the premises. You'd have to evict them. For these reasons, I do not recommend giving the keys to prospective tenants and letting them view your rental house on their own unless you take four precautions.

First, prepare and have them sign a simple agreement which outlines the conditions for your giving them the keys and allowing them to look through the house on their own. Use the one shown here if you like.

Second, request that they give you a deposit of at least $50 in cash, all of which is completely refundable when they return the keys to you as agreed.

Third, request that they leave with you one item of special value to them, something which they will surely return to retrieve. A major credit card or their driver's license would qualify. Don't take a credit card or a driver's license which has expired, of course. Look at the expiration date to make sure that it's current, and look at the item closely to be sure that it's theirs.

Fourth, give them a time limit for returning the keys. Consider approximately how much time they'll need to travel to and from the house and add about an hour to give them enough time to look around. If they haven't returned the keys within an hour after they should have, make haste to the house and change the locks.

Should you choose to give prospective tenants the keys, make sure that you change the keyed locks on the outside doors just before your new tenants move in. That way, nobody who had access to the keys during the vacancy will have easy access to the house during the tenancy, and you will protect yourself from a potentially damaging lawsuit brought by tenants who claim that your supposedly lax handling of the keys to their home enabled a criminal to get in and commit a crime there. Be cautious with keys, very cautious.

■ **Safeguard your vacant rental house**—Take special pains to see that your rental house is well looked after during any vacancy period. You want to make it attractive enough for prospective tenants to want to move there, and you want to keep it from deteriorating.

Transfer the billing for all the utilities into your own name. Having utilities available when you're maintaining, repairing, cleaning, or showing a vacant house is convenient, to say the least. It also enables you to keep up the exterior of the property properly, for you can keep the landscaping watered and the security lighting turned on. What's more, it saves potential breakdowns in gas-fired space heaters and water heaters, for they tend to be temperamental when you try to light them after a period of inactivity.

Make it look occupied. Keep the lawn mowed. Keep newspapers and advertising circulars picked up. Empty the mailbox if it's located someplace where the accumulation of mail could advertise that the place is unoccupied. Keep window coverings on the windows. Install a timer to switch on a bathroom light at night. Do everything you can to discourage the vandals, thieves, burglars, squatters, and buzzards who prey on properties which appear to be unoccupied.

■ **Be sure you're fully insured during extended vacancies**—Whenever a single-family dwelling is uninhabited, it becomes more vulnerable to the calamities which owners insure their residences against. Insurance companies know this. They know that the risks of fire, flooding from burst pipes, and vandalism all increase when there's no one around to discover such disastrous developments in their early stages and when there's no one who can act quickly to contain the damage.

They understand that their exposure to property losses is greater during vacancy periods so they are sometimes careful to exclude themselves from certain losses if a single-family dwelling is vacant for an extended period.

Check your insurance policy to be sure. Look for clauses lurking somewhere which exclude coverage during vacancies of a certain length.

If you'd rather not tax your eyes and addle your brain by reading the small print in your policy, discuss the matter with your insurance agent directly. Be frank. Don't hide a thing.

Don't ignore the possibility that your insurance policy might contain such a clause and then plead ignorance later if you should have a claim. Discuss the matter with your insurance agent in advance. That, after all, is what you're doing when you secure insurance in the first place, isn't it? You're anticipating that you might conceivably have a problem in the future.

If your policy requires you to contact your insurance agent every time you have an extended vacancy so you can buy additional insurance, then do so. Buy the added insurance whether your lender requires it or not.

Handling the Neighbor Problem

Many people go out of their way not to become involved with their neighbors. They try to remain as aloof as possible so they won't be bothered by people who are always close by. They want to preserve their privacy.

As a rental house owner, you're in a different position because you aren't around enough to bother the neighbors in person. You lack the potential to become a perpetual nuisance. The neighbors think of you differently, and you should think of them differently. Don't think of them as an annoyance. Think of them as an asset. Without the usual fears neighbors have of one another, you can become friendly with them and you should.

Go out of your way to establish a relationship with the neighbors. Knock on their doors and meet them in person. Tell them who you are and tell them a little about yourself. If they don't understand that they have a stake in your rental house, then enlighten them. Tell them that even though you don't live in the neighborhood, you are still concerned about keeping it up because the condition of the neighborhood affects your

property value, too. Tell them that you may want to enlist their help now and again when you have to pick new tenants. Be sure you give them your telephone number so they can be your "first-alert" system in case your tenants try to pull any shenanigans.

In other words, "employ" the neighbors who live around your rental house. Keep them abreast of what's happening at your end, and ask them to keep you abreast of what they see and hear is happening at their end. You need them to be your eyes and ears.

Handling the Restrictions Problem

Before you ever rent out any single-family dwelling located in a condominium complex, a planned unit development, a co-operative apartment project, or a mobilehome park, apprise yourself of every word written to govern the tenancy and conduct of anyone living there, owner or tenant. This written word might be called rules, regulations, bylaws, conditions, restrictions, or covenants. Whatever they're called, they're all "restrictions" of some sort or another.

You may sometimes get away with paying scant attention to these restrictions in a complex when you're planning to live there yourself, but when there are tenants involved, you have to pay close attention. Both you and your tenants are bound by them, and you may be held responsible for things that your tenants do against the restrictions unwittingly.

These restrictions can vary widely, too. Some mobilehome parks allow no renting of mobile-homes at all. Others have no restrictions. Some co-operative projects allow unlimited renting. Others allow renting for a limited time, but only if the renter appears before a screening committee and receives their approval. Some co-ops won't admit ex-presidents or rock stars as owners, let alone truck drivers or hairdressers as tenants. Some planned unit developments have restrictions about animals, landscaping, business uses, satellite dishes, paint colors, recreational facilities, and the like, any of which might affect your tenants. You can't know what's allowed and what's not allowed unless you take the time to read up on these things.

Having become familiar with the restrictions yourself, you must inform prospective tenants of their responsibilities to the development, the park, or the homeowners' association. They cannot be held responsible unless they're informed. You'll be the one held responsible instead, and that can become quite frustrating because you'll have to take the blame and pay the bills for someone else's transgressions.

By the way, always inform the "powers that be" in one of these restricted living environments that you have tenants occupying your dwelling. They may need to know in order to extend recreational or parking privileges or somesuch to your tenants.

Handling the Bookkeeping Problem

What is the rental house owner's bookkeeping problem? It's this. The owner's bookkeeping system needs to generate an income and expense report for each rental house separately and another report for all of the owner's rental houses together.

All right then, why should the owner accomplish both of these tasks and how can he accomplish them most easily?

Here's the simple answer to the question about why you should generate a separate income and expense report for each one of your rental houses. A separate report enables you to determine exactly how well each house is performing as an investment, and it helps you decide whether to keep or dispose of a particular one.

Here's the simple answer to the question about why you should generate an income and expense report for all of your rental houses together. A combined report shows the full picture of your rental house investment business, and it makes tax preparation easier.

Finally, here's the simple answer to the question about how you can accomplish both of these

tasks most easily. Open only one checking account for all of your rental houses, and use any of the popular check writing software programs to write your checks. Every time you write a check, identify the property associated with each of the expenditures, and you can then generate separate income and expense reports for each house as well as a report for all of the houses put together.

Handling the Maintenance Problem

Rental house tenants expect less maintenance service than apartment house tenants, and they will do more things for themselves without bothering the owner. You can encourage them even more in that direction by offering either some sort of ownership participation arrangement like the lease-option already mentioned or some sort of remunerative arrangement like a discount on their rent.

Some owners give their tenants a flat $50 rent discount every month so long as the tenants take care of all the minor maintenance and repairs ("minor" to them means less than $100), pay their rent promptly, don't call the owner unless there's a major problem, and tend to all the gardening themselves. In a sense, those owners are hiring their tenants to manage the property in the same way a property management company would. It's a good idea, but it has the same primary drawback that hiring a property management company has. It distances the owner. To make it work right, you should require a large enough deposit when the tenants move in so that any maintenance they defer during their tenancy will cost them, not you, when they move out.

Handling the Gardening Problems

Did you know that there's a cult on this planet which sincerely believes that lawn mowing causes grass to suffer pain? Well, there is. Tell your tenants that you have a list of all known members of this cult and that unless you can find their names on the list, they'd better keep their grass mowed or you'll be forced to hire a gardening service and raise their rent to pay for it.

That's one way to handle one of the gardening problems you might encounter at a rental house. Consider other ways to handle other gardening problems.

Consider using a discounted rent policy as a

blanket solution for handling any and all gardening problems. As mentioned previously, a discounted rent policy is a solution used to handle maintenance problems. Why not use it to handle gardening problems, too?

Consider installing minimal-maintenance landscaping. You can't expect a rental house tenant to look after a rose garden. It may be beautiful to look at, but it's not a practical landscaping choice for a rental house. It's high maintenance. Study the minimal-maintenance choices available in your climate zone and try them. Even if your tenants don't have a single green thumb among them, they can take care of minimal-maintenance landscaping.

Consider providing the proper tools and supplies for your tenants to keep the landscaping weeded, trimmed, and fertilized. At least they can't then say that you're to blame for the sorry condition of the landscaping because you failed to provide them with what they need to maintain it.

Consider installing an automatic sprinkling system which will keep the landscaping watered without any effort on your tenants' part. If you're paying the water bill, they can't have much of an excuse for not watering so long as there's a sprinkling system available to do it effortlessly. If they're paying the water bill, they may try to cut back on the watering or eliminate it altogether.

Discuss with them their responsibility for watering the landscaping and offer to pay that portion of the water bill attributable to watering the landscaping per your estimate.

As a landlord investing in single-family dwellings, you're fortunate. You have gardening choices, whereas the owners of multiple-family dwellings have none. They simply supply gardening service. For them it's "master metered." They can't handle it any other way because there's no practical way to divide up the many different gardening tasks so that each tenant is responsible for looking after a certain plot of lawn or a certain few shrubs. What a headache that would be to administer!

Some Last Words

If someone driving down the street where you own a rental house can pick out that one house of yours from all the others which are themselves owner-occupied, then you're doing something wrong. You're not managing the place properly, and the value of your investment is declining. You do not want its value to be declining. You want it to be appreciating at the same rate as every other house in the neighborhood.

Keep looking for ways to instill a "pride of tenantship" in your tenants while at the same time you're putting some money into your pockets from the property.

11
Renting to Lodgers

Your spouse has died, and you're lonely for company. Your mortgage payments are so burdensome that you're living on rice and beans because you can't afford to buy hamburger for dinner. Your five-bedroom house is too big now that your kids have all flown the nest, but you don't want to move out of the house and neighborhood where you raised your family. Your grades suffered when you moved into an off-campus apartment by yourself, and you would like to have somebody to study with, somebody who has good study habits and is serious about learning.

You're thinking about renting a room to a lodger.

Renting a room to a lodger sounds like a good solution to loneliness, lack of money, excess space going to waste, and poor study habits, and it can be a good solution so long as you're careful in selecting the right lodger and you manage to get the right lodger. The right lodger can be a blessing and bring sunshine and extra income into your life. The wrong lodger can be a curse and cause you more grief than you know.

Keep in mind that renting to lodgers is more like finding a mate than finding a tenant. Whereas renting a dwelling to tenants is mostly impersonal, renting a portion of your own living quarters out to lodgers is personal, very personal. You come to know your lodgers. You come to know their friends, their likes and dislikes, their habits both good and bad, their wardrobe, their politics, their life story, their jokes, their music, even their body odors. You breathe the air they breathe. You see them every day. You see them in sickness and in health. You see them when they're flush with cash. You see them when they're stone broke. Over time you see them in enough different circumstances to know them well, perhaps even too well.

No matter how well you come to know your lodgers, you dare not become friends with them while they're renting from you. Only after they move out can you become friends. While they're renting from you and thinking of you as their friend, they're too tempted to ask you to do them favors like letting them get away with paying their rent whenever they please or not at all, and you're too tempted to give them what they ask.

You cannot become their friend, but you do have to get along with them, and you do have to be at least somewhat compatible with them in your habits. If you're a fussbudget, you don't want to share your living quarters with a slob. If you're a confirmed conservative, you don't want to share your living quarters with a confirmed liberal. If you're a born-again Christian, you don't want to share your living quarters with an argumentative atheist. If you're a teetotaler, you don't want to share your living quarters with a binge drinker. Your nerves couldn't take the endless strain of living in close proximity with somebody who thinks and acts so differently from the way you think and act. You'd go nuts, and no amount of rent you'd collect from that person would compensate you enough for being driven nuts, even temporarily.

Of course, you can't expect to find the perfect lodger, one just like yourself, one who needs no training in your ways. You have to expect incompatibilities, and you have to be ready to speak up when those incompatibilities surface and your lodger is getting on your nerves.

By the way, you should think twice about renting to lodgers at all if you have minor children living with you, especially if you work and your children are home alone at times. You could be subjecting them to physical and psychological danger should a lodger skate through your background check and turn out to be an alcoholic, a wife beater, a drug addict, a drug dealer, a gang member, a murderer, a hoodlum, a jailbird, an outlaw, a thief, a congenital liar, a bully, an exhibitionist, a sadist, a voyeur, a pimp, a sex worker, a sex offender, or a pedophile. No amount of additional income is worth that risk.

Definitions

I've been using the word "lodger" here to refer to someone who shares living quarters. You may be asking yourself how lodgers differ from roomers, boarders, roommates, renters, and tenants.

Good question! Let's look at the definitions of these words. They tell all.

"Lodger" is a word that has been around for centuries to describe someone who rents a room in another person's dwelling without obtaining exclusive possession of that room. "Roomer" is a more newly minted word with the same meaning. "Boarder" refers to someone who rents a room in another person's dwelling and gets meals there, too. "Roommate" refers to someone who shares living space with another person or persons in any sort of dwelling, from a school dormitory to a dwelling owned by one of the roommates. "Renter" is an old generic term referring to anybody who pays rent for anything, whether it's a backhoe, a party pavilion gazebo, a dwelling, an airplane hangar, a tuxedo, an apartment, or an entire amusement park. "Tenant" is an even older generic term than "renter," but its meaning is narrower. It refers to someone who rents a place to live in, to farm on, to conduct business in, to store stuff in, etc. and obtains exclusive possession.

I use the term "lodger" here when I could just as easily use the term "roomer." I use "lodger" because it's the term commonly used in laws regulating the relationship between anybody who rents a room in another person's dwelling and the person who rents out that room.

Lodger Laws

Speaking of laws, you may have noticed the word "possession" above. This word appears in laws regulating all kinds of rental property and refers to the landlord's right to enter the property. A landlord who rents to tenants delivers exclusive possession of the property to the tenants for a definite period of time in exchange for rent and cannot enter the property without proper notice or good cause. A landlord who rents to lodgers, roomers, or boarders does not deliver exclusive possession and can enter the rented rooms without notice and without good cause.

This distinction is important because most states have laws governing a lodger arrangement, and they're different from laws governing a tenant arrangement. They're simpler, more abbreviated. You as a landlord renting to lodgers don't have to go to great lengths to evict a non-paying or a troublesome lodger in those states. Legislators there understand that people sharing living quarters are living in close contact with one another and need their disputes resolved quickly before the disputes flare into life-threatening trouble.

I MUST TELL YOU THAT I'M LOOKING FOR A LODGER WHO IS A LOT LIKE ME.

"Clones, that's what they are!"

What determines whether yours is a lodger arrangement or a tenant arrangement?

The living space makes the determination, but you should be aware that the number of lodgers you have at any given time may affect your legal rights as a landlord renting to lodgers, too.

Rent to only one lodger at a time, and you needn't worry. Rent to more than one lodger at a time, and you may have to comply with more complex landlord-tenant laws.

As for the living space being the determining factor, the keywords are "share" and "possession." If you share living space with your renter and withhold possession of the renter's room, then you're renting to a lodger. If you share no living space with your renter, then you're renting to a tenant whether you withhold possession or not. Lodgers contract to occupy shared living space. They do not get possession. Tenants contract to rent private living space. They do get possession.

You might advertise for a lodger to occupy the downstairs room in your dwelling which you fixed up with its own entrance and its own bathroom but with no access to the space upstairs where you live, but you'd be wrong. The person occupying that living space would be your tenant, not your lodger, and would be entitled to all the legal protection afforded tenants.

If you recognize that you are renting to a tenant and not to a lodger, you should follow the procedures which form the basis of this book. If you recognize that you are renting to a lodger, you may follow the procedures described here so long as your state recognizes the distinction between lodgers and tenants. Your state's laws determine what you can and cannot do as a lodger-landlord.

To find those laws, use an internet search engine, make a trip to the law library at your local courthouse and ask the librarian there for help, or consult a local attorney knowledgeable about such matters.

You may find that your state has no lodger laws and that you as a lodger-landlord must follow its landlord-tenant laws. You may find, if your state does have lodger laws, that they contain certain wrinkles which affect your particular situation, such as a provision that you cannot take advantage of lodger law leniencies if you share only a sitting room and still state in your agreement that you're withholding possession of the other rooms. Even if your state gives you no leniency, read on with the understanding that you may follow most, but not all, of the procedures here for renting to lodgers.

Fortunately, as a lodger-landlord in most states, you do get some relief from complying with all of the fair housing laws. You need it when you're renting out a room in your own home. One thing you may do is advertise that you're looking for a female lodger whereas advertising that you're looking for a female tenant would violate one of the no-no's of the Federal Fair Housing Act and get you into a heap of trouble (landlords who live in the same small building as their tenants tend to get certain relief from the fair housing laws as well). You may also discriminate in any way you want when you're selecting a lodger, another no-no for the ordinary landlord. If you want to rent specifically to a male vampire from Transylvania who has one wooden leg, you're well within your rights as a lodger-landlord to do just that. Fair housing laws make exceptions for lodger arrangements because lawmakers understand that people sharing living quarters need compatibility in order for their living arrangements to work well.

Making Preparations

Okay, let's say now that you're seriously thinking about renting out a room in your dwelling to a lodger. Start making preparations. Proper preparations will make being a lodger-landlord painless, worry-free, enjoyable, profitable, and safe.

Preparing Yourself

Somebody who rents to lodgers must have certain attributes in order to succeed as this special kind of a landlord. These attributes are much more important than they are for an ordinary landlord because this is a job which cannot be delegated.

As a lodger-landlord, you cannot hire somebody else to take your place, not a friend, not a neighbor, not a property management company, nobody. An ordinary landlord can. An ordinary landlord, one who owns a rental house or an apartment house, can always delegate all or a portion of the management responsibilities to somebody else. Not the landlord who rents to lodgers. That landlord has to spend time with the lodgers day after day. They have to live together under one roof in peace and harmony.

Are you lodger-landlord material? Ask yourself as you read the following statements whether you can make them about yourself.

I trust people.

I am adaptable.

I am not argumentative.

I can see both sides of an issue.

I tolerate other points of view.

I can pretty much tell when someone is lying.

I can negotiate.

I can criticize behavior without criticizing the person.

I can say no.
I do not have mood swings.
I do not crave privacy.
I have a sense of humor.
I do not expect perfection out of myself or
     others.
I know how to share.
I keep a clean dwelling.
I do not drink to excess.
I do not use foul language.
I can control my tongue.
I am not in dire financial straits.
I am businesslike.

Just in case you paid little attention to one of the more important statements above, I'll call your attention to it. "I am not in dire financial straits." Renting to lodgers should produce supplemental money, not essential money, because the lodger-landlord who depends upon rent money for survival will become obsessed with this one aspect of the business and will tend to make poor decisions about other aspects. The money is important just as it is in any other business, but it shouldn't take precedence over everything else and cloud your decision-making.

All right now, can you honestly make most of the statements above about yourself? If you can, then there's a good chance you'll be successful as a lodger-landlord. If you can't, think twice and then a third time about becoming a lodger-landlord, for you are likely to be unsuccessful. You are likely to make yourself and your lodgers unhappy, although you may be so thick-skinned that you will succeed as a lodger-landlord so long as you rent to people who drink as much as you do, swear as much as you do, argue as much as you do, or hate housekeeping as much as you do.

Preparing Your Dwelling

Start preparing your dwelling by cleaning the outside and the inside. Get your grownup kids to move their accumulation of childhood junk into storage elsewhere so your lodger will have enough room to park his car and store his out-of-season wardrobe. A clean, uncluttered, presentable dwelling will attract the best lodgers and communicate the gist of what you expect from your lodger in terms of cleanliness and orderliness.

Move whatever valuables you have in your common rooms to your private rooms, and furnish the common rooms with items you can live

without should they disappear or become damaged.

Make sure that everything is shipshape in the lodger's room—lights, electrical outlets, heating, cooling, closet, and operable windows. If the room looks drab, paint it in warm colors. If you plan to furnish it at all, furnish it simply but fully with a double bed and a hotel-quality mattress, one or two nightstands, a desk, a bookcase, a comfortable chair, some table lamps, some colorful prints for the walls, and maybe a small fridge and microwave. Create a lockable closet with padlock eyes if possible.

Install locks, preferably touchpad electronic locks, on the entry doors to your dwelling, on the hallway door to your private rooms, and on the door to the lodger's room. They create a feeling of security for everybody. Touchpad electronic locks are preferable over keyed locks for two reasons. They enable you to change the access combination quickly yourself whenever the need arises, and they keep you and your lodger from having to mess around with keys. Because touchpad electronic locks don't use keys, you never have to worry about losing keys or having the right key with you when you want to open a lock.

If possible, install a separate locking mailbox for the lodger's mail. Designate it mailbox "B" as in "195B Pierce Street." Identify it with the address, and make your mail carrier aware of it. A separate mailbox will eliminate potential arguments over disappearing mail.

Having completed these tasks, you have prepared your dwelling sufficiently to accommodate a lodger.

Preparing the Terms

Rent, utilities, and duration of the agreement are the three most significant terms you need to decide upon before you can prepare your paperwork and begin advertising for a lodger.

First, there's the rent.

Before you begin the process of setting the rent for your room, read the "Setting Rents" section in chapter 6 of this book.

You want adequate compensation, whatever it may be, for opening your home to a lodger, and yet you know that you have to be competitive when you set your rent. You have to know how much people are willing to pay to rent a room in a dwelling such as yours. To settle upon that magic number, you can't resort to magic, as in "pick a number, any number, between $200 and $2,000." You have to check the market to find out what your magic number is.

Because no two rooms are alike, not even in the same dwelling, market comparisons are necessarily subjective, but they're your only yardstick for determining how much the rent ought to be for your room. Without spending days and days answering dozens of ads for rooms currently on the market in the vicinity of your home and visiting those rooms in person to get a clear idea about the market, you can get a rough idea about the market from reading the ads themselves.

Spend an hour or so looking for ads, reading them, and visualizing how the rooms being advertised compare with yours.

Compare them to yours using the four factors of most interest to lodgers: the location of the dwelling, the size of the room, the furnishings of the room, and the amenities.

You know the area where you live. You know the good, the not-so-good, and the bad neighborhoods. How does your neighborhood compare to the neighborhoods where the other lodger rooms are located?

How does your room compare in size?

How does it compare in furnishings?

As for amenities, most lodgers want laundry privileges as much as they want anything. They also want kitchen privileges, secure parking, high-speed internet access, premium cable television, and utilities. Which of these amenities are you including in the rent? Which are you not including?

Compare what you are offering a lodger to what others are offering, and adjust your rent accordingly. Remember, if you peg your rent too low, nobody will tell you that it's too low. If you peg it too high, everybody will tell you it's too high. Lodgers who are in the market for a room to rent know the market better than anybody.

Second, there are the utilities.

There are two good reasons to require your lodger to pay a share of the utilities. There are two good reasons not to require your lodger to pay a share of the utilities.

As for the two good reasons to require your lodger to pay a share of the utilities, the first is to encourage conservation. When the cost of anything comes out of a user's pocket, the user tends to be more frugal in using it than otherwise.

That's only human nature. The second reason is to keep the asking rent low so you appear to be competitive with other rooms available for rent.

As for the two good reasons not to require your lodger to pay a share of the utilities, the first is to keep yourself from being saddled with another bookkeeping chore. Assembling all the utility bills and then calculating the lodger's share is a chore. Make no mistake. The second is to avoid the controversy which inevitably arises when a lodger leaves for a weekend, a week, or longer and questions why he should have to pay for utilities he couldn't possibly have used.

In any case, you might want to say what you mean by "utilities." Do you mean gas, electricity, and water, the big three which most people consider utilities, or do you mean cable TV, landline phone, internet access, sewage, and garbage, too?

Third, there's the duration of the agreement.

Lodgers tend to be at loose ends, uncertain about what the future holds for them. For this reason alone, you should avoid requiring your lodger to sign a fixed-term agreement (lease) for a certain duration of time, whether it's for a year or any fraction of a year. Lodgers think of their living arrangement as temporary, subject to change at any time. They don't want to sign a fixed-term agreement, and you shouldn't make them sign one.

Besides, you'll find that if things don't work out and you decide to give your lodger a notice to vacate, everything will be straightforward. You won't have to worry about complications arising from your having signed a fixed-term agreement. There won't be any complications.

Preparing the Paperwork

The paperwork you need to prepare in order to conduct business as a lodger-landlord consists of a rental agreement and a set of house rules.

From the time you and your lodger first meet to the time you part company, you may conduct all of your lodger-landlord business verbally. For your sake and your lodger's sake, don't. Don't conduct all of your lodger-landlord business verbally, especially not when you're agreeing upon the terms of the basic arrangement you have with the lodger. Define the terms of this arrangement in writing so there won't be any misunderstandings later. A verbal rental agreement won't do that. It's legal all right, but it's unreliable. It's

Lodger Rental Agreement

Dated *January 15, XXXX*

Agreement between _Karen Lovelace_____, Landlord, and
_Maxine Peabody-Smith_____, Lodger, for a room located
at _540 Pelican Court, Oaktown, AZ_____. Lodger agrees
to rent this room on a (week-to-week) (month-to-month) basis, beginning
January 15, 20XX, for $_550_ per _month_, payable in advance on or
before the first day of every rental period to Landlord. Rent is due on the
first day of the rental period. It is late if not paid on or before the
_5th_ day of the rental period and is then subject to a late fee of $_15_.
   The security/cleaning deposit is $_275_. If Lodger leaves the room
reasonably clean and undamaged, it is refundable within _7_ days after Lodger
has moved out completely and returned the keys.
   The amount to be applied to the last rental period's rent is $_550_.
   Lodger will give _15_ days' notice in writing before he/she moves and will
be responsible for paying rent through the end of this notice period.
Use of the following is included in the rent: _laundry machines, shared_
kitchen appliances, and 10x10 vegetable garden plot
Remarks: _absolutely NO SMOKING inside house!! No pets! No parties!_

LODGER UNDERSTANDS THE FOLLOWING:
1) that state laws, if any, relating to lodgers/roomers govern this
   occupancy. If there are no such laws, landlord-tenant laws apply.
2) that Landlord does not grant possession of the room to the Lodger.
3) that Landlord may enter Lodger's room without notice or good cause.
4) that Landlord shares the use of this/these room(s) with the Lodger:
   kitchen, den, living room, laundry room
5) that Lodger may not have overnight guests without written permission.
6) that Lodger (is) (is not) responsible for periodic cleaning of the room
   he/she is renting under this agreement.
7) that Lodger is responsible for the security of his/her personal property.
8) that Lodger, whether in residence or not in residence, (is) (is not)
   responsible for paying a share of the utilities (gas, fuel oil,
   electricity, water, sewer, garbage, cable TV, and internet) as follows:
   all utilities paid

LODGER AGREES TO THE FOLLOWING:
1) to accept the Lodger's room "as is," having already inspected it.
2) not to paint or alter the room without first getting Landlord's written
   permission.
3) to keep from making loud or bothersome noises and disturbances and to
   play music and broadcast programs at all times so as not to disturb other
   people's peace and quiet.
4) to keep yards and garbage areas clean.
5) to park his/her motor vehicle in assigned space and to keep that space
   clean of oil drippings and grease.
6) not to repair his/her motor vehicle on the premises (unless it is in an
   enclosed garage) if such repairs will take longer than a single day.
7) to pay rent by check or money order made out to Landlord. (Checks must be
   good when paid or applicable late-payment consequences will apply.)
8) to show Landlord evidence of a current renters' insurance policy.
9) to pay for repairs of all damage, including drain stoppages, he/she or
   his/her guests have caused.
10) to do the following household chores: _put garbage bins out every Thursday_
   Violation of any part of this Agreement, incompatibility of the Lodger
and the Landlord as determined by the Landlord, or nonpayment of rent when
due shall be cause for eviction under applicable code sections.
   Lodger hereby acknowledges that he/she has read this Agreement,
understands it, agrees to it, and has been given a copy.

Landlord _Karen Lovelace_____   Lodger _Maxine Peabody-Smith_ subject to memory lapses and misunderstandings and can cause heaps of trouble later.

Have a look at the Lodger Rental Agreement shown here. It's similar in many ways to a standard tenancy rental agreement, but it's different in many more ways because it has to address the details of what is both a business and a personal relationship.

This Lodger Rental Agreement has four parts. The first covers the dates and monies part of the arrangement. The second covers the understandings part of the arrangement. The third covers the responsibilities part of the arrangement, and the fourth covers the warnings and acknowledgment part of the arrangement.

Noteworthy in part one, the "dates and monies" part, are the amount of the rent, the rental period (weekly or monthly), the late payment penalty terms, the amount of the deposit, the amount applied to the last rental period's rent, and what's included in the rent. Part one also has space for remarks specific to this particular lodging arrangement, remarks noteworthy in themselves.

Noteworthy in part two, the "understandings" part, are statements about the landlord's withholding of possession, the landlord's right to enter, the shared rooms, the overnight guests, and the lodger's obligations for cleaning, for safeguarding his personal property, and for paying the utility bills.

Noteworthy in part three, the "responsibilities" part, are statements about alterations, noise, general cleanliness, parking, vehicle repair, rent payment, insurance, payment for repairs, and chore expectations.

Noteworthy in part four, the "warnings and acknowledgment" part, are the grounds for eviction and a statement about the lodger's knowledge and acceptance of the agreement.

These are the basics of any lodger arrangement. They establish the terms and limits of the arrangement and help both parties understand their obligations. Your lodger needs to have them in writing. You need to have them in writing.

Whereas this single-page Lodger Rental Agreement covers the basics all right, it likely doesn't cover everything you may want to cover about the arrangement you have with your lodger. That's what house rules are for.

There are two primary reasons why you should supplement your rental agreement with a set of house rules designed to address the little things related to your lodger's behavior, that is, if you decide to have any written rules at all.

The first reason relates to the difference between rules and rental agreements. Rental agreements require signatures. They're difficult to change. Rules require no signatures. They're easy to change. Rules require only that you put them in the hands of your lodger and that you allow a period of time equal to the rent interval in order for your lodger to digest them before they take effect. By keeping your rental agreement separate from your rules, you may change them more easily as the need arises, and I can assure you that the need will arise as you become an increasingly experienced lodger-landlord.

The second reason applies to the little things related to your lodger's behavior. Little things such as food poaching and inappropriate attire can create so much friction over time that you may lose a good lodger unless you make your thoughts known about these things early. House rules are the proper avenue for you to make your thoughts known.

You may want to have rules governing guests, guest parking, parties, working at home, appropriate attire in the common rooms, smoking, foul language, political discussions, religious discussions, storage of valuables, mail distribution, internet usage, utility usage, laundry usage, kitchen usage, storage of food, pets, television viewing hours, sleeping hours, and specific cleaning responsibilities.

Scofflaw lodgers may think that rules are made to be broken. Good lodgers, the ones you choose, will abide by any reasonable house rules you draft for keeping them and you happy while you live together under one roof.

Advertising

Only after you have prepared yourself, your dwelling, your significant terms, and your paperwork are you ready to begin advertising your spare room for rent, for you may find that your advertising will attract somebody right away, somebody who is well qualified and wants to be your lodger as much as you want him to be your lodger. If you are not ready for him to move in, you may lose him to another lodger-landlord who is ready. Get ready. Then start your advertising.

You have already read that fair housing laws make certain allowances for lodger-landlords.

Here's where those allowances come into play.

Fair housing laws allow you to say in your advertising that you are looking for a lodger of a certain sex ("sex" here means "gender," not the kind that made Mae West famous, you know, the kind that makes the world go 'round). That's a little consolation you get as a lodger-landlord. Take it. Use it.

You may say that you're looking for a lodger who is a "non-smoking man." You may not say that you're looking for a lodger who is a "non-smoking Hindu man." Smoking is not a protected category, and you may always mention it in your advertising. Sex and religion are protected categories. You get a freebee for the one protected category, sex, but you don't get a freebee for the other protected category, religion, or for any other protected category.

Remember, the federally protected housing discrimination categories are race, color, religion, national origin, sex, disability, and familial status. Your state may have more. Find out, and then don't mention any of them, federal or state, in your advertising, that is, none of them except for sex.

Once you begin the selection process, that is, following your advertising efforts, you as a lodger-landlord are exempt from the fair housing laws. The protected categories lack protection when lodgers and landlords do business together and rightly so. After all, requiring a single Hindu woman to share her home with a lodger who is a single Moslem man in order to satisfy the fair housing laws makes less sense than keeping two Great Danes in a Manhattan studio apartment. It invites trouble. A single Hindu woman violates no law if she gives preference to another single Hindu woman when she selects a lodger. She is exercising her legal rights and increasing the chances that she and somebody like her will get along well as landlord and lodger.

Fortunately for you, that's all you need to know about fair housing laws to stay out of trouble when you're advertising for a lodger.

Now consider how you want to advertise. Read through chapter 3 to learn something about the whole gamut of advertising methods which landlords use to attract tenants in search of a place to live. Two of them bear mentioning here because they're the ones lodger-landlords use most. They are word-of-mouth and Craigslist. The good thing about both of these methods is their cost.

They're free, and yet they're both effective and easy to use.

Consider carefully whether you want to advertise by word-of-mouth because the word may get out to the wrong people, people who enjoy sabotaging others' business endeavors in one way or another for whatever reason. If you have no fear of that, put the word out to your friends, neighbors, and acquaintances that you're looking for a lodger and see what happens.

No matter what else you do to advertise, list your room for rent on Craigslist under "rooms/shared." Mention the terms, describe the room fully, say a few things about yourself, and include some representative photos of the inside of the room and the outside of the dwelling. Be sure to give the price and tell what it includes. Is the room furnished or unfurnished? How big is it? Will the lodger be sharing a bathroom? Are utilities included? What are the provisions for doing laundry? When will it be available to move in? Will you be doing a background check? What are the total move-in costs? Say something about storage and parking and about smoking and pets, and be sure to give the general location but not the exact address.

Whether you include your phone number or not is your call. Experiment. Use only Craigslist's coded email reply address first and see what happens. If nothing happens, add your phone number and see what happens.

Look through the other postings, and you'll get a feel for what yours ought to look like and what it ought to say.

Your advertising needs to say just enough about the parameters of your lodger arrangement and about you, the room, the dwelling, and the location to attract only those people who are looking for the room you have available. You don't want to waste your time communicating with people who are looking for a room you don't have available.

Responding to Inquiries

When you receive inquiries in answer to your advertising, you know that the people making the inquiries have already self-selected according to what you mentioned in your advertising. Mentioning "sex" alone in your advertising cuts the number in half. Go ahead now and help the respondents self-select even more before you take the time to meet them and show them your dwelling and the room you have available for rent.

To do that, get them on the phone and review your requirements and expectations, some of which you may have mentioned in your advertising. They might include items such as smoking, drinking, drugs, pet tolerance, allergies, noise levels, bedtimes, background check, and foul language, as well as what's needed for transportation, for furnishings, for move-in monies, and for haste. There will be questions, of course. Answer them, all of them except any about the exact location of your dwelling (you don't want people dropping by at inconvenient times and asking to see the room), that is, unless you don't mind receiving visitors at inconvenient times.

Then ask your prospective lodgers whether they would like to submit an application. If they say no, thank them for their time and end the call. If they say yes, email, fax, or mail them both the rental application and the rental application instructions introduced in chapter 4 and found in the FORMS section of this book. Ask them to contact you by email or phone to set up an interview once they complete the application.

This step weeds out still further those who know full well that they don't qualify to rent from you. From reading the application instructions and seeing the reference to the "skeletons in their closets," they can tell that you are knowledgeable and businesslike and that they'd have a hard time bamboozling you into renting to them. You'll never hear from them again. Good! You don't want to hear from them again. Let them rent from a risk-taking lodger-landlord who will rent to anybody.

Interviewing

You're in contact with somebody who is interested in becoming your lodger. He has completed an application and is ready to give it to you. Now you want to meet him, accept the application, interview him, and show him the room you have available.

Read section 4 in chapter 4 of this book and decide how you want to go about interviewing applicants.

If you feel the least bit apprehensive about meeting a stranger in your home alone, ask someone to join you during the interview, or else arrange to meet him in a public place and invite him to inspect the room only if you feel comfortable around him. During the interview, wherever it happens to be, ask to see the completed rental application and use it as a basis for your chat.

At the risk of being considered nosy, be nosy. You want answers to questions that will help you determine whether you and he can live together under the same roof with as little friction as possible.

You certainly want to know why the applicant wants to move into the room you have available because that information will give you a clue as to how much "baggage" the applicant is carrying and whether you'll have to live through some tense standoffs when someone irate appears on your doorstep, someone whom the applicant wronged. Listen carefully when he gives you the reasons why he's moving and jot down the names and numbers of anybody who might verify his reasons. They might not otherwise appear as references on the application.

Before you end the interview and show him the room, ask him whether he remembers the last paragraph in the Rental Application Instructions, the one about the "skeletons in his closet." No matter what he says, face him and ask directly whether he has anything to say on the subject. Let him talk. You never know what you'll learn when you ask the question. You know that you will learn whether you ought to spend the time to check the applicant further.

The last part of the interview is the fun part. It's your chance to show off the room you prepared to rent to a lodger and point out the amenities that go with it. It's your chance to make the applicant eager to live there.

Qualifying

You have the applicant's application in hand, and you have his written permission to check it. Read section 5 in chapter 4 of this book and decide how you want to go about qualifying your applicant.

Although you as a lodger-landlord may legitimately apply to use credit bureau services, you will likely use those services so infrequently that you may want to use another source for the information because becoming qualified to use them necessitates your paying an application fee and submitting to a site inspection.

Here are three other credit-report sources. Ask the applicant to provide you with his credit report from annualcreditreport.com, the only source supplying totally free credit reports. Prevail upon another landlord to order the credit report, a landlord who is already qualified to secure credit reports. Ask the applicant to use mybackgroundcheck.com to order the reports you designate and have them emailed directly to you.

If you opt to use the first source to secure only a credit report (the second and third sources can supply you with more than just credit reports), you may still use the second or third sources for reports on evictions and criminal records, or you may order these reports through mrlandlord.com.

Some lodger-landlords don't even bother with credit reports. They say they're interested in learning only what they can about the lodger's history as a tenant because some people will always pay their rent on time while they neglect their other bills when they're short of cash. They may have a spotty or even a horrible credit report but still be good tenants.

You get to decide what's important to you about each applicant, and you get to conduct as thorough a background check as you think necessary.

Don't stint on the costs here. You don't want to find out later when your lodger becomes violent or steals everything you have of value that you would have uncovered his record of wife beating or thievery had you just spent the money to order a criminal search. Any time and money you spend qualifying lodgers you have any doubt about is time and money well spent.

Committing

All right, you've checked the applicant's references and learned as much as you can about him. You're satisfied. Everything checks out. You couldn't find any skeletons in his closet. According to what you've learned, he was telling you the truth on his application and in the face-to-face interview. He has a steady job with an adequate income. He pays his rent on time. He minds his own business, and he likes the room you have available. You like him, and you want to rent to him.

As soon as you make up your mind to rent to him, contact him and tell him you'd like to meet with him to discuss the rental agreement and rules. Tell him you'd like to meet with him at the place where he currently lives at a mutually convenient time–the sooner, the better.

Go there prepared to rent to him, but refrain from making a commitment until you make your visit because you may find something amiss in his domicile that gives you second thoughts.

Once there, look around. See whether this place where he lives is consistent with everything you know about him already.

If it isn't, if you feel the least bit hesitant about renting to him, tell him quite frankly that you don't think you and he are a good match for one another and that he ought to look further for another lodger-landlord who is a better match. You needn't say anything more than that. If he asks for reasons, say it's your gut feeling. Say something about his being a good person but that you feel you'd both be unhappy living under the same roof because you're so different from one another. Say you're sorry. Then politely excuse yourself and leave.

If you still want to rent to him after seeing the place where he lives, ask him whether he still wants to rent from you. If he doesn't, don't ask questions. Thank him for his time, excuse yourself, and leave. If he does, get right down to business. Review the rental agreement and rules. Make sure that he understands them and feels that he can abide by them. Make sure that he understands both how much money he needs to give you before he can move in and also when you expect his rent to begin. Only then, after you and he come to this mutual understanding, should you commit to rent to him. Only then should you fill out the rental agreement, discuss the details about his moving in, and take his move-in monies.

Living Together

Your lodger has moved in and you no longer have as private a life as you had before. Your life is different from what it was. You're sharing it with somebody whom you selected to share it with. It's fuller, livelier, more interesting. It's something like having a "boomerang kid" under your roof except that this person is cleaning up after himself and paying his own way.

Little by little, you begin to take an interest in your lodger's life, and you find that you like the fellow even more than you thought you would. You also begin to forget your role, and there's the danger.

You cannot forget the role you're playing in your lodger's life. You're his landlord. You're not his pal. You're not his parent. You're not his banker. You're his landlord. You and he have a business arrangement. You're providing him with a place to live for a price. That's the bargain you struck with him, and you have to stick with it. You're giving him a place to live with the understanding that he will pay you the rent on time and abide by your rules all the time.

You want to be accommodating to him. You want to be fair to him, but you cannot permit him to take advantage of you. You cannot permit him to break his agreement with you or disobey the rules he agreed to obey.

If he fails to pay you the rent on time, you must talk to him about it. If he has taken to using foul language around you and it offends you, you must talk to him about it. If he brings someone home to share his bed and it offends you, you must talk to him about it. If he parks his car where it blocks the driveway, you must talk to him about it. If he fails to clean up after himself even once, you must talk to him about it. If he drinks himself silly and acts drunk around you, you must talk to him about it as soon as he sobers up.

When landlords have to be disciplinarians, they become disciplinarians. It's a difficult role to play for some people, but you cannot avoid it when it becomes necessary. You must not avoid it. You're a landlord, and you have to play the landlord role even when you find that it's a difficult role to play, even when you like the person you're disciplining and know that he may resent you for rapping him on his figurative knuckles.

"So what?" must be your response.

Shirk your landlording responsibilites, and you'll be disappointed with yourself. Follow through with them, and you'll be delighted with yourself and with your decision to become a lodger-landlord.

Terminating

Landlords who are conscientious in selecting their lodgers never have to evict. No, I shouldn't say "never." I should say "almost never." I'm referring here to evicting a lodger the legal way, that is, when a lodger-landlord wants a lodger to move out and the lodger resists. I'm not referring here to those times when a lodger "gets the message" that his lodger-landlord wants him to move out and he does or those times when a lodger and his lodger-landlord come to a mutual agreement that he needs to move out and he does.

Legal evictions vary enough from state to state that a comprehensive look at all of them could fill a book in itself. They may be completely non-judicial, that is, require no court involvement, nothing other than a properly written and properly delivered notice and, if necessary, a call to the police for assistance in the physical removal of the lodger who refuses to leave as directed and has thus become a trespasser. They may be completely judicial, following a precise and cumbersome legal procedure culminating in a judgment and the physical removal of the lodger by an officer of the law if necessary.

You should never have to evict one of your lodgers if you watch for signs of brewing trouble and address it early in your role as disciplinarian.

Ah, but if discipline fails and the lodger persists in misbehaving, confront him in as friendly a manner as you can, not as an exasperated parent might talk to a wayward teenager but as a patient parent might talk to that teenager. You might want to start out with some remarks about how much you have enjoyed living with the lodger, proceed to an account of what's bugging you about the lodger now, continue by saying you think the lodger needs to move out, and then ask the lodger, "Don't you agree?" or "What would you do if you were in my shoes?" Listen to what he has to say, and either agree to it or ask, "How soon can you move out?"

If he says he'll be out by such-and-such a date, draft a quick agreement to that effect and have him sign it. You may need it later if he doesn't perform as promised.

If you want him to move and he doesn't want to, you'll need to explain to him that the rental agreement you both signed gives you the right to make him move. The length of time he has to move varies according to the circumstances. It's the same as it is for ordinary tenancies. It's shorter if he's delinquent in paying his rent. It's longer if he's incompatible. To prove your point, show him the rental agreement and give him an appropriate notice which you can draft yourself following the format of the notices in this book.

Once you decide that the lodger has to move, you want him to move soon, very soon. You won't want to be around him, and he won't want to be around you. Be civil to him, tell him how much of his deposit and last month's rent monies you will give him after he moves out, and help him move if you can, while at the same time you prepare to advertise for your next lodger who will surely be perfect in every way.

Some Last Words

Marriages and lodger arrangements both bring people together to live under one roof. Some people are so afraid that they'll select the wrong person with whom to share their roof that they never share it with anybody. Too bad for them! Don't you be afraid of selecting the wrong person to be your lodger, for the chances are good that you'll select the right person, better even than your chances for selecting the right person to be your spouse.

If marriages were to begin with a gut feeling, a background check, and an eyes-wide-open evaluation as lodger arrangements do, and not primarily with body chemistry as most do, chances are good that they would last longer and be as happy as most lodger arrangements.

Begin each of your lodger selections with a good gut feeling about the applicant, supplement it with a thorough background check, keep your eyes wide open throughout the evaluation process, and you'll end up with a lodger you won't want to lose. You'll be happy with the arrangement and so will your lodger.

12
Legal Matters

You may have thought that window screens were merely supposed to keep out pesky mosquitoes, horse flies, gnats, and moths. After all, screens are pretty flimsy things, especially the fiberglass variety with the aluminum frames used so widely today. They could hardly be expected to challenge a charging elephant, a sharp-clawed pussy cat, a wily cat burglar, or even an errant baseball. Could they? Nah, anybody with even a lick of common sense could see that.

Don't be so naive. In these days of the "Twinkies Defense," the McDonald's hot coffee case, and the convoluted legal machinations performed in front of TV cameras for all to see, when some people get away with hot-blooded murder in spite of all the facts marshalled against them, common sense doesn't count for very much.

Every time you go to court, you check your handgun and your common sense in at the courtroom door.

Some time ago, a jury decided that window screens were supposed to keep out rapists. That's right! A fiberglass netting less than a thirty-second of an inch thick was supposed to have been sufficient to keep out a man with rape on his mind. There's no need for you to shake your head in disbelief. You read that right.

Because the screen was missing on the very window through which the rapist had gained entry and because the landlord had failed to replace it, the landlord was negligent and was held accountable for the rape. The landlord was to blame for the tenant's misfortune. The landlord had to pay the tenant's claim.

Was the landlord really and truly to blame for what happened? Not in my book he wasn't. Obviously, somebody else was to blame, but that person wasn't available for prosecution and if he had been available, he wouldn't have had the assets or the insurance to compensate the victim.

The landlord was quite capable of compensating the victim, and what's more, the landlord was available. So the landlord became the target of the lawsuit, and the tenant's attorney concocted an argument sufficient to convince the jury in this case that the rape would not have occurred had the landlord replaced the missing screen. That's quite a stretch, don't you think?

People today have been led to believe that there is no such thing as an accident or a misfortune which is nobody's fault. There has to be somebody at fault, somebody to blame, somebody with the means to pay up, even if that person is only a teeny weeny bit at fault.

People no longer harbor dreams of striking it rich in the gold or oil fields or in the dot-com companies. That's the stuff of movies like "Gold Rush," starring Charlie Chaplin, and "Giant," starring James Dean. It's the stuff of real life, too, as in "google.com," which began its dot-com ascent with its public stock offering in 2004 at $85. That's all the stuff of yesterday.

Today all people need do is watch the nightly news and they see ordinary Janes and Joes striking it rich by winning either a big lawsuit or a big lottery jackpot. The media trumpet these wins across the land. People watch and read about them and dream of making their own fortunes this new-fashioned way. You can hardly blame them for trying to seize their share of the winnings, especially when it costs virtually nothing to get into the game and it's so easy to play.

Unfortunately, there is another side to those dreams of gaining wealth through litigation, and that is the nightmare of losing wealth through litigation. You, landlord, are among those people who have to worry about losing their wealth through litigation. You are a target. You are especially vulnerable to lawsuits because you have what some attorneys call "deep purses" and others call "deep pockets." Presumably these purses and pockets contain plenty of money to pay off the injured party and, of course, all the attorneys involved. You have to take special precautions to protect yourself and your assets from lawsuits.

To us landlords, a lawsuit is like a breath of stale air. Lawsuits are stultifying, time-consuming, costly, tedious, and unnerving. Except in eviction matters, you aren't going to win anything from your tenants in a courtroom. Don't go there. Don't bother trying. Tenants have little or nothing that you can hope to win from them anyway. Most of them are "judgment-proof." They don't have the resources to pay a judgment which goes against them. Yet, they'll bring discrimination suits, liability suits, habitability suits, contract suits, statute violation suits, wrongful eviction suits, security deposit suits, sexual harassment suits, class-action suits, and just plain old nuisance suits against you time and time again because they think you have plenty to lose and they have plenty to gain. They're right, of course.

You're at a double disadvantage in a courtroom as a defendant because you have assets to lose and you have that persistent stereotype of the greedy landlord to contend with. As if that's not bad enough, you're also going to have to spend time and money defending yourself, and you're going to be worrying yourself sick about the uncertainty of it all. Those are not pleasant prospects.

Since you cannot hope to gain any advantage over your tenants in court, you can hope only to keep yourself from being taken full advantage of, nothing more.

Taking Measures to Reduce Legal Difficulties

Short of throwing up your hands and letting your tenants help themselves to your assets, there are some measures you can take to reduce your overall legal difficulties and to keep yourself from being taken full advantage of.

■ **Be nice**—We hear about medical malpractice settlements being common and running into the millions, and we think that all physicians are vulnerable, no matter how good they happen to be. Not so, or at least not so according to Malcolm Gladwell. In his book, *Blink*, he says that patients almost exclusively sue physicians who lack what we might call a good bedside manner, physicians who spend little time with their patients and are not "nice" to them.

Shoddy medical work is not the determining factor in whether a patient will file a malpractice lawsuit against a physician. The determining factor is the physician's attitude.

Think about how you treat your tenants. Are you "nice" to them? Do you treat them like human beings or like walking rent checks?

Treat them like human beings. Ask them questions about themselves and their families now and then. You may be amazed by how less litigious they become. They don't want to sue somebody who's nice to them.

■ **Become aware of the laws relevant to landlording in that part of the country where your rental properties are located**—Lawmakers at the federal, state, and local levels have long been busy passing law after law to help keep society running smoothly and peacefully, and they haven't neglected landlording.

There are laws at the federal level, including the Fair Housing Act (sets antidiscrimination standards); the Occupational Safety and Health Act (commonly known as OSHA, this act sets standards for safety on the job); the Fair Credit Reporting Act (sets standards for credit information and availability); the Soldiers' and Sailors' Civil Relief Act (sets special leasing provisions for military personnel); and the Truth-in-Advertising Act (sets advertising standards).

There are laws at the state level which govern tenancies at every stage, from the creation of the tenancy through the duration, termination, and even the aftermath. State laws tell you what your rights and responsibilities as a rental property owner are and what your tenants' rights and responsibilities are. They outline the proper procedures for evictions. They expand upon the federal antidiscrimination standards. They go into contracts, deposits, notices, employer/employee relationships, liens, vehicle towing, maintenance, subletting, abandonment, bad checks, retaliation, health matters, and safety concerns. In short, state laws cover almost every conceivable aspect of landlording.

There are laws at the local (county and municipal) level, too, which affect what you do as a landlord. They generally add further restrictions to federal and state laws and can be the most hobbling of all. Some zealously pro-tenant communities have virtually doomed their stock of rental housing by making landlording practically a criminal activity.

You can know how these laws will affect you only if you have a look at them, admittedly no easy task for somebody who has never opened a law book before. Let's take a look at one of these laws ourselves.

Here are some important words in the Fair Housing Act, the law of the land about housing discrimination. Check them out for clarity—

Sec. 803. [42 U.S.C. 3603] (b) Nothing in section 804 of this title (other than subsection (c) shall apply to —

(1) any single-family house sold or rented by an owner: Provided, That such private individual owner does not own more than three such single-family houses at any one time: Provided further, That in the case of the sale of any such single-family house by a private individual owner not residing in such house at the time of such sale or who was not the most recent resident of such house prior to such sale, the exemption granted by this subsection shall apply only with respect to one such sale within any twenty-four month period: Provided further, That such bona fide private individual owner does not own any interest in, nor is there owned or reserved on his behalf, under any express or voluntary agreement, title to or any right to all or a portion of the proceeds from the sale or rental of, more than three such single-family houses at any one time: Provided further, That after December 31, 1969, the sale or rental of any such single-family house shall be excepted from the application of this subchapter only if such house is sold or rented (A) without the use in any manner of the sales or rental facilities of any real estate broker, agent, or salesman, or of such facilities or services of any person in the business of selling or renting dwellings, or of any employee or agent of any such broker, agent, salesman, or person and (B) without the publication, posting or mailing, after notice, of any advertisement or written notice in violation of section 804(c) of this title; but nothing in this proviso shall prohibit the use of attorneys, escrow agents, abstractors, title companies, and other such professional assistance as necessary to perfect or transfer the title, or

(2) rooms or units in dwellings containing living quarters occupied or intended to be occupied by no more than four families living independently of each other, if the owner actually maintains and occupies one of such living quarters as his residence.

You wouldn't have to deliberate long if someone were to ask you whether mud or these words were clearer.

Most laws affecting this business appear to have been drafted by the same anonymous drudges who produce the incomprehensible instructions for income tax returns. Laws do not make for easy reading, and they are not something you want to read all the way through or commit to memory. Attorneys don't even do that. Don't you do it either. Do become generally familiar with them, though, so you will know just enough about them to be able to read specific laws whenever you have a specific question.

Where do you find these laws? Nowadays, you don't have to traipse down to your local law library to find them, although you may if you prefer. You'll find them on the internet. Do a search on the words "[your state] + codes" or "[your state] + landlord-tenant laws" and you'll find them right there on your search list. If you get a list of all the state codes, go to the property codes and to the civil proceedings codes, and look there specifically for landlord-tenant or rental property codes.

Copy the relevant codes from the internet into a word processor and store them on your computer's hard drive so you'll have them readily available whenever you want to have a look at them, or else jot down the steps you went through to find them so you'll be able to find them easily next time.

To give you some idea how ignorance of the law can affect your landlording business, consider what happened to me some years ago.

I was evicting a ne'er-do-well tenant who had stopped paying his rent. This fellow never made any effort to explain himself. He just stopped paying. What's more, he went out of his way to avoid meeting me and played hard to find. I sensed that he was digging in and was going to make every effort to extend his rent-free stay as long as he could.

I finally had him served with a summons and complaint to get his eviction moving through the courts, and he answered my complaint stating that I wasn't providing him with enough heat in his steam-heated apartment. He even quoted some law to that effect. Well, I knew nothing of any such law, so I looked it up and sure enough, there it was in black and white ten-point type. My hands trembled as I read it. The law stated that I had to provide my tenants with heat at a minimum of 60°F (15.5°C) three feet above the floor twenty-four hours a day. Yes, the law was that specific!

I knew that I was providing plenty of heat during the hours that mattered but not twenty-four hours a day. There was a timer controlling the boiler, and it shut everything down during most of the hours when everyone was at work.

After reading the law, I felt bloodied and beaten. Then I started to think about the matter further and realized that the tenant had never complained to me about the heat, nor so far as I could tell, had he ever complained to any public agency as he was supposed to do by law. Fortunately, my initial ignorance of the law didn't cause me to lose the lawsuit because the tenant had indeed made that fatal mistake. He had not registered his complaint when he should have, before the eviction began. The judge saw through the tenant's transparent ploy to gain as many days of free rent as he could possibly get, and the tenant lost.

Following that scare, though, I decided that some knowledge of the laws affecting me as a landlord was important. No, it was essential.

■ **Stay informed**—Laws are one thing. How they're interpreted is quite another. No matter how hard lawmakers try to draft unambiguous laws and enough of them to circumscribe every possible situation, there's always something they didn't think of. They're human, too. Court decisions which settle the disputes arising out of these overlooked or unclear situations affect us as much as laws do. Court decisions interpret and amplify the laws on the books and become the authority for later decisions in other courts.

Interpretation of these laws can differ markedly from state to state, from court to court, and from time to time.

In New York, there was a case regarding a landlord who refused to rent to someone for one reason only, because that person was an attorney. The attorney-applicant sued, arguing that wholesale discrimination against attorneys was illegal. The landlord responded that attorneys eat landlords for breakfast, that as a whole they are more argumentative and more likely to sue than other people; hence they are more likely to make bad tenants. Amazingly enough, the court sided with the landlord in the case, and that decision made national news (perhaps the case merely showed that attorneys are even less sympathetic figures than landlords).

As a landlord yourself, you might have thought after hearing about the New York case that you could discriminate against an applicant only because he was an attorney, counterfeiter, minister, male stripper, or ballet dancer, in other words, on the basis of occupation alone. After all, you already know that you may not discriminate on the basis of race, color, religion, sex, national origin, age, or physical handicap. That's made clear by federal law. So you might think after hearing about the New York case that you could discriminate legally according to someone's occupation because that's not one of the protected categories in the federal law or in your state or local laws. Why not? If it's not specifically prohibited, then it should be all right, eh? Maybe yes and maybe no!

The next thing you know, the California Supreme Court rules that its state's Unruh Act, which is about discrimination in business and does apply to the landlording business, must be construed to mean that discrimination is prohibited against *any* classification of people when that classification has nothing to do with the business at hand. Wow! That really changes things! Because an applicant's occupation in itself has nothing to do with whether someone will be a good or a bad tenant, landlords may not discriminate on the basis of occupation. Wages, assets, negative recommendations, and the like do have something to do with whether someone will be a good tenant. They are categories of legal discrimination, whereas occupation is not.

Had you read nothing about the California decision and had you attempted to refuse to rent to an attorney applicant on the basis of the New York decision, you could have been in trouble, depending upon the location of your property. In some jurisdictions you might have won in court; in others, you might have lost.

This is all interpretation, remember. You're not going to find a law which specifically prohibits you from discriminating against applicants by height, weight, shoe size, or handwriting, but you might find a court decision which has interpreted some other law as prohibiting you from discriminating in these ways. When you think about these as criteria for tenant selection, they sound pretty illogical anyway, don't they? To refuse to rent to an applicant on the basis of shoe size? Come on! That doesn't really have anything to do with being a good tenant, does it?

In that window-screen rape case mentioned earlier, there was no law cited which absolutely required window screens for the protection of the occupants against physical assault, for there is no such law. The plaintiff's attorney successfully created the impression that an unscreened window was an invitation to enter, and the defendant's attorney didn't argue convincingly enough that it wasn't. That's how the case was decided.

By staying informed about what's happening in the courts, you will know better what you can do to stay out of trouble yourself, and you'll make sure that all of your windows have screens. Right?

Read all the relevant, up-to-date information on rental housing that you can possibly lay your hands on. The following are good sources of legal information—daily newspapers (more to make you aware of what's happening than to provide accurate information); rental housing association periodicals (national, state, and local associations publish news of relevance to their members); various independent newsletters published specifically for the attorney who handles landlord-tenant matters and for the interested layman (see what's available at your county law library); and the internet (search on "rental housing information" or go directly to the sites listed in SOURCES AND RESOURCES).

Attend seminars which focus on the legal aspects of the rental property business. These seminars may be sponsored by rental housing associations, a particular attorney, the state bar association, or a local institution of higher learning. Some may be intended for attorneys in general practice (these are generally open to anyone interested in the subject, not just to attorneys), and some may be intended for landlords.

Seek out several people who take landlording seriously and ask them questions to clarify fuzzy matters and relieve you of any specific doubts you might have about something.

You're in a changing business which absolutely requires that you stay informed.

■ **Inspect your property and enlist others to help**—Most people consider a site inspection of their property by their own insurance company as an imposition at the very least. They think that the company is spying on them, that it's trying to find some reason to cancel their policy or increase the premium. So they're inclined not to cooperate and may even try to conceal whatever's faulty. That's not the right attitude.

First of all, remember that your insurance company is on your side. It's for you, not against you. It wants your business. It doesn't want to cancel your policy. It doesn't make any money by canceling its customers' policies. It simply doesn't want unnecessary or excessive risk. It doesn't want to pay claims which could have been avoided had somebody taken the precaution of surveying the property to search for dangerous conditions and then taken the steps necessary to remedy those conditions. That's all.

Second, any company which is concerned enough about its own exposure to send an in-

Dear **Richard and Rose Renter;**   May 01, XXXX

We want to make the place where you live as safe as it can be.
We are constantly on the lookout for anything around your home which
might prove hazardous to life, limb, or property. But hard as we
try, we cannot uncover every potential danger all by ourselves. We
need your help.

Because you are around your home much more than we are, you have
a greater opportunity to notice hazards. Please report to us
anything you notice which you think might prove hazardous to you or
anyone else. We promise that we will investigate the hazardous
condition and remedy it if we possibly can.

Please complete the bottom section of this letter and return it
to us with your next rent payment.

Thank you for your cooperation in making your home a safer place
to live.

                              Sincerely,

                              Leslie Landlady

= =

[X] We know of nothing which appears to be unsafe in or around our
home, but we will alert you whenever we do notice something.

[ ] We would like to call your attention to the following unsafe
conditions in or around our home:

_____

_____

_____

_____

We suggest that you take the following corrective action:

_____

_____

_____

_____

Signed *Richard Renter*   Dated *May 8, XXXX*

Chapter 12: Legal Matters 231

spector to look at your property is a company you want to do business with. They're trying to keep their expenses down. Lower expenses for them translate into lower premiums for you.

Third, if they don't send an inspector out, ask them to. You should know what you can do to make your property as safe as possible.

If you can't get your insurance company to send out an inspector, inspect your property yourself, especially the common areas. Look for anything which might possibly trigger a liability lawsuit. Look for exposed electrical wiring, uneven walkways, missing or broken railings, slippery floors, potholes in the parking lot, inadequate lighting, faulty locks, sharp protrusions, poorly ventilated heaters, rotted footings, loose toilet seats, inoperable smoke alarms, depressurized fire extinguishers, and the like.

By inspecting your property yourself and enlisting the aid of your insurance company to do the same, you'll find most of the obviously hazardous conditions around your property, but you're not going to find all of them, and you're not going to be giving your tenants and their attorneys second thoughts about suing you. That's why you should involve your tenants in your inspection. "Deputize" them to be on the alert at all times for hazardous conditions. Make them responsible for advising you whenever they notice something which could prove to be hazardous.

An attorney who specializes in personal injury cases and frequently represents tenants who are injured in slip-and-fall cases told me he would have a difficult time winning many of his cases if rental property owners would just send their tenants a letter every so often asking them to report hazardous conditions. Tenants would be hard pressed to argue that their landlords were negligent in maintaining the property if the tenants themselves didn't notice a particular hazard.

On the opposite page is the letter he wouldn't like you to use. Use it once a year, and follow up on it. Keep copies of your tenants' responses together with their applications, agreements, and checksheets. They're important, very important. They're part of your insurance policy against a lawsuit calamity.

■ **Do your paperwork properly and promptly**—Act as if one or more of your tenants will invariably drag you into court on some mat-

ter or other, and start building your defense in advance. Put in writing all of the understandings and transactions that you have with your tenants. Use written rental applications, written rental agreements, written pet agreements, written house rules, written condition-and-inventory checksheets, and written receipts. Make an entry in a logbook every time you respond to tenants' complaints or calls for assistance. Put your own complaints about tenants in writing instead of merely talking to the tenants. Insist that your tenants put their complaints in writing, too, and that they use a written notice to advise you that they're moving.

If your tenants turn out to be lawsuit-happy, if you have to evict them, or if they leave owing you money, this paperwork will be more essential to you than a figleaf in a nudist camp. Judges tend to be "paper slaves" themselves, and they look kindly on good documentation.

■ **Maintain your property well**—Whenever you become aware of anything on your property which might be considered unsafe, take care of it as soon as possible. No, don't fix it as soon as possible. Fix it *now*. As long as you allow a hazardous condition to continue, you are exposing your tenants to injury and yourself to lawsuits, and at the same time you could be allowing the situation to worsen. You know that you'll have to fix it sometime. Why not fix it now? Fixing it now is always less expensive than fixing it later.

■ **Use common sense**—Common sense may not count for very much in a court of law nowadays, but it still counts for something in the real world of landlording. Laws frequently acknowledge the thoughts and actions of "reasonable people," and they mention "reasonable care" again and again. These are simply other ways of saying that laws cannot cover every possible eventuality, and when something arises which they don't cover, judgment will be based on whether the people involved acted reasonably. Did they use the good common sense which reasonable people are supposed to have?

Tenant relations require you to use all the common sense you can muster. Be as reasonable as you can be when tenants are being unreasonable. Don't show anger. Don't act rashly. Don't be stubborn. People get hurt and court cases get filed when you take leave of your common sense and do something you'll regret later.

■ **Join "HALT"**—The day appears to be fast approaching when we will have no choice but to consult an attorney before we advertise a vacancy, reject an applicant, say hello to a tenant, repair a broken window, or pick up a scrap of paper. I don't look forward to that day myself, and I'm sure you don't either. To try to change this impending state of affairs, think about joining HALT. HALT stands for "Help Abolish Legal Tyranny" (see "Associations & Organizations" in SOURCES & RESOURCES). It's an organization of legal reform advocates who really believe that our justice system can be reformed.

I believe that it has to be reformed myself, and I believe that it will be reformed one of these days when people begin to realize how expensive the system is and how it benefits such a narrow spectrum of people rather than American society as a whole. Then, and only then, will reform come.

As a landlord who has been victimized by the justice system more than once, I would like to climb up on my soapbox and make two recommendations for reform. They aren't complex, and they aren't ridiculous. They're practical. They make sense. They make so much sense that other civilized countries handle legal matters just this way. We should as well.

The recommendations are these—

● *Make the losing plaintiffs pay the costs of the winning defendants.* If tenants sue you and they lose, they should have to pay what you have to pay to defend yourself. Time and time again I have been sued over something patently frivolous, and my insurer will settle rather than spend the money to put up a defense. There's a name for this dirty game which so many plaintiffs and their attorneys play with abandon. It's called extortion. I don't care whether it's legal or not. It ain't right!

● *Put time limits on lawsuits and court hearings.* Civil and criminal cases clog the courts because the attorneys involved don't care how long they take. Most attorneys are paid by the hour. The longer a case takes, the more they earn. They thrive on delays, patently ridiculous delays, which do nothing but run up the legal bills. That ain't right! By the way, do you know how much time the United States Supreme

Court allocates to each case it hears? ONE HOUR! Each side has half an hour to present its arguments. If the Supreme Court can do it...

Right now our justice system has a blank check, a check which we Americans have unwittingly written thinking that the system will somehow produce justice for all. All we have to do is make the check good. Nobody seems to keep track of what figure goes into the blank check every year. We all know that it's huge. We just don't know how huge.

We also don't quite know whether the system produces any justice. We have only a sneaking suspicion that it doesn't. We don't have any proof.

We do have HALT to thank for giving us some insights into the system and the people who run it. HALT has revived the work of Yale Law School professor, Fred Rodell, who wrote extensively about our justice system as an insider until he died in 1980. His book, *Woe Unto You, Lawyers*, published in 1939 (you may download the entire 115-page book from fredrodell.com, a website launched and maintained by HALT), is a scathing indictment of the legal profession. Rodell is as quotable as Mark Twain would have been had Twain been an attorney at odds with the profession. Here's one Rodell quote: "There are two things wrong with almost all legal writing. One is its style. The other is its content. That, I think, about covers the ground." Here's another: "In tribal times, there were the medicine men. In the Middle Ages, there were the priests. Today there are the lawyers. For every age, a group of bright boys, learned in their trade and jealous of their learning, who blend technical competence with plain and fancy hocus-pocus to make themselves masters of their fellow men. For every age, a pseudo-intellectual autocracy, guarding the tricks of its trade from the uninitiated, and running, after its own pattern, the civilization of its day."

Join HALT and have some input into where our justice system is going.

Until the system is reformed, however, you'd better come to know those attorneys who can help you with the problems which plague you now and probably will tomorrow.

■ **Identify attorneys suited to handle your particular problems**—Whenever I think about hiring an attorney, I remember the little old lady who was overheard saying, "I don't want an attorney. I want to tell the truth."

Attorneys do have to contend with a reputation as truth benders. They have been known to speak with forked tongues at times. Yet, representing clients in court in the best possible light is a small part of what they do. They can help you with their good advice, intercede for you when you seem to be getting nowhere with an adversary, review your contracts with their eagle eyes, and otherwise keep you from getting into trouble.

Like many other professionals, attorneys have specialties. One might know bankruptcies. One might know wills and trusts. One might know divorces from the husband's point of view, and another might know them from the wife's. One might know landlord-tenant law from the landlord's point of view; another from the tenant's. Find an attorney who specializes. One who doesn't specialize may be legally qualified to represent you but actually may know less about landlord-tenant matters than you do. Don't pay for that attorney's education.

You won't find attorneys who specialize in landlord-tenant law advertising on television along with the sharkskin-suited personal injury attorneys who promise to make you wealthy if you have ever suffered side effects from taking a certain prescription drug or have worked around asbestos or were injured in a traffic accident. No, you will find landlord-tenant attorneys advertising in the Yellow Pages, and that's as good a place as any to start your search for one. The attorney guide there, which follows the Yellow Pages' "attorney" classification, lists them by field of law, so you can go directly to those who specialize in landlord-tenant law instead of having to look at every attorney advertisement in the book.

Other sources for attorney references are the internet, your local rental property association, and fellow landlords. If you're looking for an attorney to handle an eviction for you, call the office of the court which handles evictions and ask for the names of the attorneys who file most of the evictions in that court.

Incidentally, HALT publishes a useful manual called *Using a Lawyer: And What to Do If Things Go Wrong*, which will help you shop for, and work with, an attorney suited to your needs.

■ **Insure yourself adequately**—No matter how conscientious you are about following the previ-

ous suggestions for preventing landlording's legal difficulties, you cannot eliminate the risk of lawsuits entirely. You cannot become a Teflon® landlord. That's why you need insurance.

There's no law requiring you to have any insurance at all except workers' compensation, and you don't need that unless you employ someone to work for you, but you could be very, very sorry that you didn't protect yourself with insurance when you get summoned into court to defend yourself on some matter or other and then have to pay an outrageous settlement for something you could not have foreseen and had no control over.

Because lawsuits are expensive and settlements are expensive, insurance is expensive, but not having it at all can turn out to be more expensive still. It can precipitate financial disaster, your financial disaster. You cannot afford that, so insure yourself adequately. See chapter 17 for some suggestions.

■ **Watch yourself when you give tenant recommendations**—We landlords are in the same quandary as employers when we're called upon to give recommendations. On the one hand, we want to *get* honest recommendations from somebody else when we're checking on an applicant and trying to decide whether to initiate a relationship. On the other hand, we're reluctant to *give* honest recommendations ourselves because we're afraid that we might be sued for saying the wrong thing.

Much as you might like the world to know what sort of a scalawag a particular tenant was when he was your tenant, you could be exposing yourself to a lawsuit by actually telling the world all of the details. If the tenant is able to convince a court that you and he merely had a personality conflict and that you in your vindictiveness had given him bad recommendations and made it impossible for him to find another place to live, he could be successful in dipping into your deep pockets.

So, what do you do?

You can't go wrong by verifying a tenant's dates of occupancy, his address, his rent, his payment history, and the circumstances of his departure when called upon to do so. Them's the facts, ma'am. That's useful information which another landlord may draw his own conclusions from in determining whether to rent to your tenant. That's not a recommendation. That's information, and so long as it's accurate, it would be difficult, if not impossible, to refute in a court of law.

Let the tenant take you to court and try to prove that you were being vindictive in supplying another landlord with information about the number of late notices you gave the tenant during his occupancy. You have copies of the notices themselves to show the court. Let the tenant take you to court and try to prove that he vacated owing you nothing. You can show the court your records to the contrary. Don't concern yourself about these possibilities. They ain't gonna happen.

Go ahead and supply a fellow landlord with information which you can prove, information which you would like to receive if you were checking out an applicant. You can't go wrong doing that.

But you can go wrong by supplying anecdotal remarks about a tenant, especially if those remarks are judgmental and detrimental. Don't say things about the tenant that you cannot prove.

If another landlord calls and presses you to reveal what you don't want to reveal about one of your departed or departing tenants, say "No comment!" That response, used widely by personalities who want to protect themselves from pesky, prying reporters, says everything and nothing at the same time.

You might even say something like this, "My attorney has advised me not to give recommendations on any of my tenants because you might sue me if I give them a good recommendation and they turn out to be bad tenants for you, and they might sue me if I give them a bad recommendation and they are able somehow to prove me wrong."

Although you really don't want to say such a thing and you certainly don't want to hear it, in these litigious times, it's an understandable statement.

Some Last Words

An acerbic old attorney once told me that there are only two kinds of landlords—those who have been sued and those who will be. That might sound pessimistic to you. It's not. It's much more realistic than you might think. You should be pessimistic about lawsuits. Resign yourself to the inevitability of your being sued for something or other sometime, and you won't get too upset when you find a process server on your doorstep, there to serve you with your tenant's formal complaint and summoning you to court.

If you're doing most of what is outlined in this book, you will be reducing your exposure to lawsuits and other legal hassles drastically. Unfortunately, you cannot eliminate them entirely, no matter what you do, no matter how careful you are, but at least you will be able to sleep well at night if you insure yourself adequately.

13
Decisions, Decisions

Solomon's decisions may have been more momentous, but they were certainly no more numerous than the decisions landlords have to make regularly. There's always some decision or other to be made, and there always seems to be so little time and help available when you have to make those decisions that you might as well be plucking daisy petals or flipping quarters to help you decide what to do.

I hope that the alternatives presented in this chapter will contribute something toward helping you make a few of those many decisions more knowledgeably, so you'll be able to improve your profitability and perhaps even begin to enjoy landlording a little. Landlording can be enjoyable, you know. Really, it can!

Should You Do "It" Yourself?

Do-it-yourself books never discuss whether you ought to consider hiring someone else to do "it" for you. Why should they? That's a subject beyond their province, and besides, they're too involved with explaining *how* you can do things yourself to discuss *whether* you ought to be doing them yourself at all. They assume that doing things yourself is more enjoyable and less expensive than hiring help, and such an assumption will generally prove correct for most do-it-yourselfers unless they botch a job so badly that they add to its complexity and have to pay that much more for professional help to fix what they botched or unless they cut off an ear or crush a toe and have to pay big medical bills.

This do-it-yourself book is different, because landlording is different. In landlording it is often good business, for a variety of reasons, *not* to do everything yourself. You can even ask yourself a few questions when you're trying to make the decision. Here are some of those questions, some obvious and some not so obvious, which take into account the special nature of this business and may help you decide whether you ought to do certain things yourself or hire them done for you.

■ **Are you able and knowledgeable enough to do it yourself?**—You know what expertise you have, and you know what you're capable of doing both physically and mentally. Can you do this job safely and well? It may necessitate climbing up the side of a two-story building on an extension ladder that sways in the wind. Are you afraid of heights? It may involve knowledge of the latest tax laws about depreciation. Have you been keeping abreast of the tax law changes? It may mean testing electrical connections with the power on. Do you know enough about electricity to avoid electrocuting yourself and shorting the circuits to the whole building?

If you suspect that you can't do the work properly or at all by yourself, hire it done.

■ **Do you want to do it yourself?**—Some jobs, like cleaning ovens, painting bedrooms, mowing lawns, and unplugging toilets, are tedious or repetitious or mundane or loathsome, and you may have no desire to do them yourself even though you know that you are able to do them.

If you simply don't want to do them yourself, hire them done.

■ **Do you need some company while you do it yourself?**—You may be knowledgeable, ready, willing, and able to do certain work all by yourself, but if you tend to work rather slowly when you work alone, consider hiring someone else to work along with you. You may find yourself becoming more productive when there's a high school or college student working alongside you because you are trying to set a good work example and also trying to compete with the student's work pace.

If you suspect that you would work better and faster working alongside someone else, hire a helper.

■ **Do you have the time to do it yourself?**—Count 'em and you'll find that there are only 168 hours in a normal week. Abnormal weeks have 168 hours, too. Even though you may at times think that you're superhuman, you still cannot cram any more hours into your weeks, whether they're normal or not, and no matter how eager you are to do everything yourself, your body demands that you spend some of those 168 hours sleeping.

If you don't have the time to do a job, hire it done.

■ **Relative to the other landlording work you have to do, how much would this job cost if you were to hire it out?**—You can figure the relative cost of a job by the type of work involved. Plumbing generally costs more than painting, and painting costs more than housecleaning. If you have a kitchen gusher on a Sunday morning, don't call the plumber and pay his $60-per-half-hour minimum for weekend work. Fix it yourself, that is, unless you figure your own time is worth more.

Sometimes the work you do yourself and the work you hire done should be determined strictly on the basis of cost so long as you are able to do both and have the time to do one or the other. Painting, gardening, yard maintenance, and housecleaning are all relatively inexpensive to hire done, whereas work such as plumbing, electrical, and appliance repair are relatively expensive.

If you have a choice, do the expensive work yourself and hire the inexpensive work out.

■ **Do you have the money to pay for hired help?**—In the beginning of your landlording career you will have more time than money and you will have to do much more work yourself whether you want to or not.

If you don't have the money available to hire work done, do it yourself.

■ **Will you lose any additional rental income by doing certain work yourself?**—Some landlords refuse to hire any help at all because they think "it costs too much" or "you can't trust workers nowadays," or they come up with some other silly reason that suits their fancy. There are plenty.

That kind of attitude often winds up costing them plenty because they haven't considered one very important factor–the rent penalty–which is the rent lost when a dwelling isn't ready to be occupied.

If preparing a vacated unit for rent will take you twenty-one days to do yourself in your spare time and the rent you may expect to get for the place is $900 per month or $30 a day, then your rent penalty for doing the work yourself is $630 (21 x $30). If, on the other hand, you hire the work done for $480 (labor only) and it takes six days, your rent penalty is only $180 (6 x $30). Adding the rent penalty to the labor costs in each case yields sums of $630 and $660, a difference of $30. In other words, you would be spending three weeks of your spare time, say, approximately 48 hours, and you would be earning all of $30 or 63¢ an hour for your efforts!

63¢ an hour! Nobody works for that kind of money nowadays. Why should you?

You may have thought you were saving $480, but you weren't. You saved a mere $30! That's chump change for someone in the landlording business who must always be looking at the bigger picture.

The advantage of hiring help would vary somewhat, of course, if there were no immediate demand for your rental, if the rent were more or less than $900, if the work took more or less than 48 hours, or if your helpers demanded more or less than $10 per hour. Be that as it may, this example serves to illustrate just how shortsighted some landlords can be when they ignore the rent penalty and try to do everything themselves only to save themselves a few bucks. Little do they realize how few are the bucks they're actually saving!

If your rent penalty approximates the cost of hiring help, then hire the help. That's using your head! That's working smart! That's looking at the bigger picture!

■ **Is the work tax-deductible?**—Every expense related to your landlording business is naturally tax-deductible. If the labor for a landlording job will cost you $200, and you're in the 28% tax bracket, you might say that the job is really costing you the equivalent of $144 ($200-($200 x 28%)) in taxable dollars.

Well, let's suppose now that you have two jobs to do, one involving exterior painting at your rental property and the other involving exterior painting at your own home. You have a $550 bid on the rental property paint job and a $450 bid for the paint job on your home, but you know you have enough time to complete only one. Which one should you do?

Do the one at home. Here's the reason. Even though it appears on the surface to cost $100 less, the paint job at home would actually cost you more if you were to hire it out because it's not tax-deductible. The home paint job would cost you $450 in pre-tax dollars and in after-tax dollars, while the rental property job, because it is tax-deductible, would cost you around $550 in pre-tax dollars but only $396 ($550-($550 x 28%)) in after-tax dollars if you happened to be in the 28% bracket.

If you must choose between doing several jobs, be sure you calculate what their tax consequences are before you decide whether to do them yourself or hire them out.

■ **Is there anyone available to do the work?**— Sometimes you will have decided to hire help, but because it's Big Game Weekend, New Year's Eve, Mardi Gras week, or the first day of elk season, there's just no one available to work for you.

If there is indeed no one available, you'll just have to groan and moan, stall until someone is available, or do it yourself. What other alternative is there?

■ **Is much travel required?**—Those rental properties you own which are located at a distance from where you live, require a certain amount of time and expense to reach, and you should calculate approximately how much time and how much money a trip there takes.

If the cost of the trip is anywhere near the cost of hiring the job done and if you have no other good reason to visit the property, pick up the phone, hire it done, and save yourself the travel expense, the time, and the bother of doing it yourself.

■ **Are your personal relationships going to suffer if you do it yourself?**—A divorced landlord once told me that no marriage could survive more than ten rental properties, be they houses or apartment buildings. His number may or may not be accurate. I can't say, but he knew from firsthand experience that his own marriage couldn't survive the fourteen rental houses and two sixplexes he and his wife had accumulated. It couldn't survive because he was trying to do everything himself.

Looking back on his own experience, he felt that ten would have been the magic number to keep his own marriage intact. Ten may be the correct number for some people, and it may be two or twenty-six for others. The number is relatively unimportant. What is important are the demands which you allow your rentals to place upon your time. Spending all your spare time and energy on your rental properties would strain any personal relationship to the breaking point and would probably strain you, too, even if you could draw your family into the business to help.

If you persist in accumulating rental properties, you must begin to hire help in order to preserve your personal relationships and your own sanity as well. Don't try to do it all yourself. You'll succeed only in becoming a lonely millionaire, sick at heart, and begrudging every alimony check you pay your former spouse.

Should You Hire a Property Management Company?

Country folk have a saying which goes, "Ain't no fertilizer like the farmer's footsteps." Landlording is no different from farming or any other business, that is, when you're referring to the relationship of the owner to the farm or the business.

The owner's presence alone makes the business more profitable.

Nobody can do the job of looking after your rental property as well as you can, absolutely nobody. You knew that, didn't you? Sure! Well, it's the truth. Nobody else cares as much about your rental property as you do because nobody else has as big a stake in it as you do.

That said, when you start swearing at your tenants more than you feel you should and you know that you want to hang onto your rental property because you're convinced that it's a sound investment, you might want to start thinking about hiring a property management company to relieve you of the headaches and get you to stop swearing so much.

Property management companies promise to take care of everything and send you a check every month so you needn't bother about anything. That they can do. In fact, property management companies can handle management on three different levels.

At the most detached level, they can handle *asset management,* which involves fact-finding and decision-making about acquiring, holding, and disposing of properties. It might be characterized as year-to-year management.

Then there's *off-site management,* which involves hiring and supervising on-site employees, contracting work out to independent vendors, purchasing the larger items, watching the expenses, paying the bills, keeping the books, and evicting problem tenants. It's pretty much month-to-month or week-to-week management.

Finally, there's *on-site management*, which involves showing vacancies, selecting tenants, purchasing the smaller items, maintaining and cleaning the property, communicating with tenants, collecting rents, and banking the deposits. That's day-to-day management.

Institutional investors, such as insurance companies and real estate investment trusts, hire property managers for all three management levels. Most individual investors handle their own asset management because it involves consequential decisions which can make or break an individual investor. It's the other two which individuals hire property management companies to handle, the off-site and the on-site management.

The charge for off-site management generally ranges from a low of 3% to a high of 10% of the gross. That's 3% for the largest complexes on up to 10% for single-family dwellings. Of course, this doesn't include the on-site manager's wages. They're extra.

A charge of 5% of the gross for looking after a twelve-unit apartment building doesn't seem exorbitant, does it? It's not. That's just what I figure I'm earning when I do my own off-site management.

Ah, but don't forget that no company is going to look after your property the way you do. That percentage of the gross may be all you're *paying* the property management company, but it may not be all their services are *costing* you.

It'll cost you extra if they create problems

which have to be remedied. It'll cost you extra if they don't shop around for good prices. It'll cost you extra if they receive kickbacks from certain service companies and suppliers. It'll cost you extra if they hire on-site managers who discriminate illegally. It'll cost you extra if they write checks for supplies and then get refunds in cash. It'll cost you extra if they collect rent for units which they report as vacant.

Temptations abound for property management companies to siphon off funds. Situations abound for them to blunder. You have to expect some dishonesty and some ineptitude whenever you hire help and especially whenever you as the owner distance yourself from their work. People from all walks of life will yield to temptation when they're tempted and will err when they're making decisions. That's the price you pay when you hire others to manage your property. Expect it.

Of course, you could get lucky. You could find a gem of a property management company, one both honest and capable, one which will relieve you of your lingering landlording headaches.

Be as careful in picking a property management company as you would be in picking a surgeon for your heart transplant or a pilot for your private jet. Select one recommended to you by more than one satisfied client who stands to gain nothing from the recommendation. Select one that is sworn by rather than sworn at.

Go ahead and hire a property management company if you are too disinterested, too busy, too distant, too exasperated, too decrepit, or too haughty to look after your rental property yourself.

As for me, I have no intention of hiring a property management company because I want control. I want to be able to hire an on-site manager

I can trust instead of having another layer of management between me and the property. I want the on-site manager to know me and feel responsible to me. I want to have my own bookkeeper handling the receipts and disbursements and the accounting reports. I want to see the bids for painting the outside of my building and for trimming the 29 palms. I want to have my finger on the property's pulse. I want to know what's going on. I want to be making the important decisions. All of this is important to me. It's important to my net worth.

Off-site management does require some of my time, but the time it takes is minimal and seldom wasted. Off-site management doesn't tie me down to a place or a time. I still have my freedom. I can manage my properties out of a golf bag. Unequivocally, I can say that being my own off-site manager yields the greatest return for the time involved than anything else I might do in managing my own rental properties.

The real time demands in property management are on the site. Hiring somebody to handle on-site management makes good sense no matter how large or how small your rental properties are because that management work does tie a person down to a place and a time. That's the management work I hire somebody to handle for me.

Why not follow my example? Plant your footsteps around your properties as their off-site manager, maintaining just the right amount of control, and watch your net worth grow and grow and grow!

Should You Own up to Being the Owner?

Shortly after I purchased my first fourplex, a friend mentioned in casual conversation that he knew a landlord who would never admit to his tenants that he was, in fact, the owner. He would call himself the manager but never, never, the owner. To someone who had just become a landlord, such a posture was inconceivable. I was proud of my new acquision and denying ownership would have been tantamount to denying the paternity of a firstborn child. Not only did I feel that I couldn't do it, I couldn't see the point of the ruse unless, perhaps, one owned tenements and didn't want to be bothered with all the attendant problems.

Years later, I came to understand the value of this polite fiction, this "buck-stops-there" approach to management, and I have come to use it with some properties successfully myself.

Invariably, something will come up that a tenant wants to do which you know you don't like, but you're on the spot, and you can't think of a good reason for refusing the request outright, so you give permission. The very next day you come up with a good reason, and you kick yourself for not having thought of it sooner, but by then the time has passed for you to do anything about it. You're stuck.

Ah, but if you're known as the "manager" or as one of the "partners," you merely say that you will have to consult the owner or your partner before you can give an answer. Then you will have the time necessary to think up a good excuse, or, if you wish, you may simply refuse the request altogether after having consulted the "owner" and not offer any excuse at all for the refusal. When asked for details, you simply say that you're awfully sorry but there's nothing you can do about the matter. You tried, but your partner couldn't be budged.

Calling yourself the manager can even work when you, the owner, live on the premises and look after everything there yourself. You are the "manager," aren't you? That's no lie.

Should You Rent It Furnished?

There is extra money to be made in renting furnished dwellings, no doubt about it, but it requires extra effort and investment, and sometimes it brings extra grief. Actually it adds yet another "business," furniture rental, to the one you're already engaged in, so it should be thought of as a sideline which has certain advantages and disadvantages all its own.

Consider these advantages and disadvantages of renting furnished dwellings—

Advantages
• More income
• Lower vacancy factor
• Increased depreciation available for tax purposes
• Less redecoration required when people move (furnished dwellings, when vacant, still look lived in and distract the eye from the walls' imperfections)
• Less wear and tear on the property caused by tenants' careless moving of their own heavy furniture and appliances

Roommate Agreement   Dated June 16, xxxx
(Addendum to Rental Agreement)

This Agreement amends, is incorporated into, and forms a part of the Rental Agreement dated 11/30/xx between Margaret Judge, Owners, and Phylis Browne, Tenants.

Tenants, also known here as "Roommates," desire to rent the premises on a "roommates arrangement." Owners agree to this arrangement under the following terms and conditions:

ROOMMATE APPROVAL AND SUBSTITUTION--Every person who wishes to become a Roommate under this Agreement, whether as an original Roommate or as a substituted Roommate, must first submit a Rental Application and be approved by Owners in writing. Owners, at their option, may require substituted Roommates to sign the existing Rental Agreement or may require an entirely new agreement to be signed by the substituted Roommates and the remaining Roommates. Upon substitution of Roommates, Owners may elect to increase the deposit.

FINANCIAL RESPONSIBILITY--Each Roommate agrees to be jointly and severally liable to the Owners for the entire rent and the entire amount of any other charges incurred under the Rental Agreement.

DEPOSITS--Roommates agree to pay deposits to Owners in the form of a single certified check or money order. Owners will hold all deposits until the entire dwelling has been vacated completely. Owners may make deposit refunds in the form of a single check made payable jointly to all Roommates with rights to the deposits. This check and the itemized accounting of deposit deductions may be sent to any one of the Roommates with rights to the deposits.

DEPARTING ROOMMATES--Roommates who move out while this Agreement is in effect continue to have financial responsibility under this Agreement unless Owners release them from this responsibility in writing or unless they are replaced by substituted Roommates approved by Owners. Upon being relieved of financial liability, departing Roommates relinquish all rights to the deposits.

MAXIMUM NUMBER OF ROOMMATES ALLOWED--Without the prior written approval of Owners, Roommates may at no time exceed 4 in number.

GUESTS--Tenants may house any single guest for a maximum period of fourteen days every six months or for whatever other period of time the law allows. Guests may at no time exceed 2 in number.

COMMUNICATIONS--Whenever Owners give a notice to one Roommate, it shall be considered as having been communicated to all Roommates. Whenever one Roommate gives a notice to the Owners, it shall be considered as having been communicated from all Roommates.

Owner *Margaret Judge*   Roommate *Lucille Melander*
By *Phylis Browne*   Roommate *Ellen Nott*
                                      Roommate *Sylvie Broerke*
Page 3 of 3

Disadvantages
- Greater investment required
- More tenant turnover
- Muscles needed for moving furniture around
- More repairs
- More maintenance (excluding redecorating)
- Increased risk of damage
- Greater theft potential
- Storage required for surplus furniture
- Added recordkeeping and bookkeeping
- Purchasing time needed (you have to select the furniture)
- Obsolescence (furniture goes out of style)

Seemingly, the disadvantages of renting furnished dwellings outweigh the advantages. They certainly outnumber the advantages. What's more important, though, in this comparison is whether you would receive adequate compensation for assuming the disadvantages, and that comes down to numbers. If the added furnishings can produce, say, a 100% return on the investment over a twelve-month period without becoming trashed during that time, then renting furnished dwellings might actually be an attractive proposition.

One landlord friend of mine has found that renting one-bedroom apartments furnished with his own sturdy homemade furniture yields him a 100% return in six months on the furniture and more than compensates him for the extra effort and investment. His turnover is slightly higher, but his vacancy factor is nil, and his cash flow is phenomenal. Renting furnished apartments has paid off handsomely for him.

If you are fully cognizant of both the advantages and disadvantages of renting furnished dwellings and if your own rentals lend themselves to being rented furnished, such as those catering to singles, armed services personnel, students, business people on assignment, or vacationers, you might try furnishing one rental as an experiment before you furnish them all. See for yourself if you like the furniture rental business and see if you can make any money at it. Then either sweep through Ikea or its equivalent on a buying spree, or call the Salvation Army and have them haul the stuff away.

If you'd rather not experiment at all, recommend to those people who come to you to rent furnished dwellings that they contact a furniture rental company (search "Furniture Renting & Leasing" in the Yellow Pages and on the internet for local companies) and rent their furniture from those who specialize in that business. The big advantage to them in renting the furniture separately from the dwelling is choice. They get to be their own decorators and choose the furniture they want to live with, instead of subjecting themselves to someone else's taste and choices.

If you happen to acquire a building which has unattractive, out-of-date, or abused furniture, and it obviously isn't adding enough income to compensate you for the trouble of looking after it, get rid of it. Don't let the frustrations of handling a furniture rental business interfere with your more important activities as a landlord.

Unless the furniture is "Antiques Roadshow material," offer to sell it to your tenants at attractive prices. If they don't want it at any price, give it to a charitable organization and take its agreed-upon value as a deduction on your income tax return.

Should You Rent to Roommates?

Nowadays you can hardly avoid renting to roommates. More and more unrelated groups of people are living together in a single household than ever before. There's no good reason why you shouldn't rent to them. In fact, you have to rent to them so long as they meet your legitimate tenant selection standards.

Because roommate living arrangements present special problems for the landlord, you need to know what the problem areas are and you need to take measures in advance to deal with them.

Basically, the problem areas all pertain to the loose nature of the roommates' relationship. When they're first looking around for a place to live, they think they're going to get along well and live together for a long, long time, but when one of them hogs the bathroom every morning and leaves dirty dishes in the kitchen sink every night, the other roommate has second thoughts about the living arrangement and moves out. The landlord is left with an inconsiderate slob who doesn't have enough income to pay the entire rent himself and a departing tenant who wants his share of the deposit back. To afford the rent, the slob finds another slob to move in with him, and soon thereafter the second slob loses his job and can't come up with his share of the rent money. The soap opera goes on and on with the landlord becoming more and more frustrated as the situation deteriorates.

You can't avoid all of the frustrations of renting to roommates by using my Roommate Agreement, but it sure helps because it addresses the seven primary problem areas—roommate approval and substitution, financial responsibility, ownership and disbursement of deposits, departing roommates, number of roommates, guests, and communications.

More than likely, these are concerns which roommates never consider before they decide to room together. Like newlyweds, they assume that the living arrangement will work out satisfactorily. If it doesn't, they'll merely come to some mutually satisfactory agreement to deal with problems as they arise.

You know that problems will inevitably arise, and you know that the roommates are going to expect you as their landlord to sort them out. You can sort them out much more readily if you begin the relationship with a written agreement.

Look at the agreement yourself to see how it addresses common problems to the benefit of everybody involved.

One thing the agreement does for your benefit as a landlord is exercise control over everyone who is allowed to move in, both original roommates and substituted roommates. You don't want to wind up housing human trash whose names you don't know after all of the original roommates have moved out. Evicting anonymous tenants can be complicated, frustrating, expensive, time-consuming, and sometimes downright ugly.

Incidentally, whenever you do approve a roommate substitution, you should amend the old rental agreement. Using an amendment, you delete the old roommate from the agreement and add the substituted roommate. The wording could be something like this: "AMENDMENT TO RENTAL AGREEMENT originally dated xx between xx and xx. As of xx date, Sam Spade is replacing John Doe in this agreement and is assuming the latter's residency rights and responsibilities. Further, John Doe is relinquishing all rights to the deposits, is no longer financially responsible for any rents or charges incurred under this agreement, and is not residing in this dwelling." This clearly worded amendment should be signed and dated by all of the roommates and by you.

Clear wording in your Roommate Agreement will help the roommates understand exactly how their relationship with you is supposed to work. Basically, the agreement says that when you as their landlord handle their deposits, rent monies, and communications, you are dealing with them as a group, not as individuals, but when they fail to live up to their financial responsibilities, you will hold them "jointly and severally liable." This legal phrase makes each of them liable for the entire amount owed by the group, and it keeps you from being dragged into their money squabbles.

All told, the Roommate Agreement makes roommates into a unitary family. They may move out one by one if they wish, but those who remain still retain the tenancy responsibilities they assumed when they moved in as a group. You needn't worry if one of them should leave in a hurry without finding a replacement. That's their problem, and you don't have to make any special rent or deposit adjustments. They have to work out those details themselves without your involvement. That's their responsibility.

Review the Roommate Agreement with all of the roommates before they move in so they know their responsibilities as soon as they assume those responsibilities.

Should You Allow Your Tenants to Sleep on Water?

We landlords tend to be pretty protective of our property. We resist anybody and anything that might pose a threat. We don't want pets. We don't want teenagers. We don't want motorcyclists. We don't want attorneys. We don't want felons. We don't want alcoholics. We don't want welfare recipients. We don't want students. We don't want musicians, and we certainly don't want people who have waterbeds. We seem ornery, suspicious, misanthropic, negative.

Yet, we become that way honestly. We start out as innocents determined to be trusting and determined to be unlike any grouchy, greedy landlord we ever knew. Then we have experiences. We learn slowly, incredulously, but we learn. After we have cleaned up the filth and repaired the damage left behind by more than one unscrupulous tenant who has vacated owing us rent, we become less trusting of people and more protective of our property. We tend to regard people and things guilty until proven innocent.

So when waterbeds first swept into faddish

favor some years ago, we landlords considered the perils of allowing one-ton water balloons to rest on the floors of our bedrooms, and we acted quickly to protect our interests. We banned them.

Inevitably, some tenants sneaked them in, and just as inevitably our worst fears were realized. Those early waterbeds stained our carpets and buckled our hardwood floors, necessitating expensive repairs. We swore never to allow them, and we wrote into our rental agreements carefully worded clauses to cover waterbeds and all future developments along the same lines. We prohibited all liquid-filled furniture, not just waterbeds.

But waterbeds are no longer a fad. They are here to stay, for there are some people who find them essential to a good night's sleep. Nor are waterbeds any longer the flimsy water bags they once were. They have become thick (they're 20 mil whereas the toughest trash bags are only 5 mil; a "mil," by the way, is 1/1000 of an inch) water containers adequately safeguarded against accidental spillage, so that today a properly designed and installed waterbed is perfectly safe for use in most rental dwellings.

They are so safe and acceptable that California landlords didn't even protest a law promoted by the waterbed industry to govern the acceptance of waterbeds in rentals throughout the state. This law applies only to buildings built since 1973, and it contains certain reasonable safeguards—the tenant must provide liability insurance, must have a quality waterbed which will put no undue strain on the building, and must install it according to accepted standards. The landlord may, in turn, increase the security deposit no more than the equivalent of half a month's rent. Sounds good to me!

In the absence of any law, what's a landlord to do? Strike that "no liquid-filled furniture" clause from the contract and let the waterbeds pour in? No!

Waterbeds are still capable of damaging your building. Flimsy waterbeds and waterbeds without either frames or liners are still in use, and they could cause you the same grief today that they caused people years ago.

So, what should you do? Above all, be protective. Either continue banning all liquid-filled furniture from your rental property (remember that you may or may not be within your rights in doing so), or else adopt a well-considered policy which will enable you to rent to tenants with waterbeds at minimal risk.

Communicate this decision, to ban waterbeds or to accept them on well-defined terms, to both prospective tenants and existing tenants. Begin when you first qualify prospective tenants by determining whether they intend to have a waterbed or not. Make no assumptions about what they will be sleeping on. Bring the matter out into the open for frank discussion, and you will virtually eliminate unauthorized waterbeds that tenants try to sneak in, beds which expose you to damages you're not protected against.

Before you ever adopt a policy to admit waterbeds, if you choose to, determine whether your building can indeed support their weight structurally. Residential buildings built to current construction standards will withstand around 60 pounds per square foot on suspended floors and can safely support most any waterbed. Poured concrete floors, of course, pose no weight limit problem at all.

If you have any doubts, first check the waterbed floor loading data readily available on the internet. Second, check with your local build-

Waterbed Agreement

Dated <u>Jan. 15, XXXX</u>

(Addendum to Rental Agreement)

This agreement is attached to and forms a part of the Rental Agreement dated <u>January 15, XXXX</u> between <u>Lester Landlord</u>, Owners, and <u>Richard Harvey and Rose L. Renter</u>, Tenants. Tenants desire to keep a waterbed described as <u>queen size</u> <u>combination foam and water</u> in the dwelling they occupy under the Rental Agreement referred to above, and because this agreement specifically prohibits keeping waterbeds without the Owners' permission, Tenants agree to the following terms and conditions in exchange for this permission:

1) Tenants agree to keep one waterbed approved by Owners for this dwelling. Waterbed shall consist of a mattress at least 20 mil thick with lap seams, a safety liner at least 8 mil, and a sturdy frame enclosure made of plywood or solid natural wood only, no particle board.

2) Tenants agree to consult with the Owners about the location of the waterbed. They agree to hire qualified professionals to install and dismantle the bed according to the manufacturer's specifications and further agree not to relocate it without the Owners' consent.

3) Tenants agree to allow Owners to inspect the waterbed installation at any and all reasonable times, and Tenants agree to remedy any problems or potential problems immediately.

4) Tenants agree to furnish Owners with a copy of a valid liability insurance policy for at least $100,000 covering this waterbed installation and agree to renew the policy as necessary for continuous coverage.

5) Tenants agree to pay immediately for any damage caused by their waterbed, and in addition, they will add $<u>50</u> to their security/cleaning deposit, any of which may be used for cleaning, repairs, or delinquent rent when Tenants vacate. This added deposit, or what remains of it when waterbed damages have been assessed, will be returned to Tenants within <u>SEVEN</u> days after they prove that they no longer keep this waterbed.

6) In consideration of the additional time, effort, costs, and risks involved in this waterbed installation, Tenants agree to pay additional rent of $<u>3.50</u>, which /includes/ ~~does not include~~ the premium for the waterbed liability insurance policy referred to in item 4.

7) Tenants agree that the Owners reserve the right to revoke this permission to keep a waterbed should the Tenants break this agreement.

Owner <u>*Lester Landlord*</u>   Tenant <u>*Richard Renter*</u>

By _____   Tenant <u>*Rose Renter*</u>

Page <u>2</u> of <u>2</u>

ing department about the floor loading limits for your building. Third, if you still have reservations, hire a structural engineering firm to determine the weight per square foot which your building can safely support. Compare that with the weight per square foot of each waterbed in question, and you will know whether your building can take the weight.

Waterbeds vary in total weight, from around 360 pounds for a twin-sized hybrid (urethane/water combination) bed to about 2,500 pounds for the large, round, all-water variety. You can estimate the total weight of any waterbed yourself by making some simple calculations. Multiply the water capacity in gallons by 8.33 pounds and then add 4% for the miscellaneous waterbed parts if it's an all-water type or 20% if it's a hybrid.

More important than total weight, though, is floor loading or weight per square foot, for these are the figures which structural engineers use to determine the stress the waterbed puts on the floor. Again, you can estimate the weight per square foot quite accurately yourself. You simply divide the total weight of the bed by the square footage of its base (unless the bed rests on a pedestal base which is smaller than the surface, the base and the surface dimensions will be exactly the same), and you come up with the weight per square foot.

As an example, let's take the most common size waterbed, the queen size (80"x60"), and we'll calculate its weight per square foot. The all-water type (9" fill) has a water capacity of 196 gallons; the hybrid, 72 gallons. 196 gallons times 8.33 pounds per gallon plus 4% equals 1,698 pounds total weight for the all-water queen-size waterbed. 72 gallons times 8.33 pounds per gallon plus 20% equals 720 pounds, total weight for the queen-size hybrid. To find the pounds per square foot for a queen-size waterbed, assuming that the base and surface dimensions are the same, multiply the length (80") times the width (60") and divide by the number of square inches in one square foot (144). That's 80"x60" or 4,800 square inches. Divided by 144, it's 35 square feet. Next, divide the weight, 1,698 pounds, by 35 and you get 48.5 pounds, which is the weight per square foot of an all-water queen-size waterbed. Divide 720 pounds by 35 and you get 20.5 pounds, which is the weight per square foot of a hybrid queen-size waterbed. That wasn't

hard, was it? You can do the same for any size waterbed.

Once the weight question is answered to your satisfaction and you know the floor loading limits for your building, you may want to consider renting to tenants who sleep on water. If so, take these seven items into consideration for each individual waterbed— specifications, components, installation, inspection, insurance, deposit, and agreement.

■ **Specifications**—Waterbeds differ considerably. Find out the size, weight, and type of each waterbed your tenants wish to install. Using these specifications, calculate whether each waterbed falls within the floor loading limits for your building. Reject those which might seem perilous to you, and suggest to the tenants that they consider lighter waterbeds.

■ **Components**—The minimum allowable components, as far as you are concerned, should be a mattress at least 20 mil thick with lap seams (preferably less than three years old so it has more flex-fatigue resistance), a safety liner at least 8 mil, and a sturdy frame. If made of wood, the frame should be at least 2"x10", the deck should be at least 1/2" thick, and neither the deck nor the pedestal should have any particleboard components (plywood or solid natural wood only).

■ **Installation**—To prevent floods and minor catastrophes when they are most likely to occur, insist that professional installers (every waterbed store has its own service department) do the installation, and insist that you be present to supervise the eventual dismantling. If, for some reason, professional help is unavailable and you feel confident enough in your own abilities, help the tenant yourself by overseeing the installation while you consult the manufacturer's printed instructions. Proper installation will validate the insurance policy and give you peace of mind.

■ **Inspection**—Make your first inspection just after the waterbed has been installed. Check its location, which should be along a load-bearing wall and away from intense heat sources. Check its problem potential, which should include feeling the frame for protrusions which might puncture the mattress. Check for water spillage from the installation, and direct the tenant to clean up any water immediately. After that, you might wish to check the waterbed periodically, say, every six months or so, for possible damage and signs of potential damage.

■ **Insurance**—Responding to popular demand, most insurance companies now include a waterbed liability provision in their renters' policies, and there's waterbed liability insurance available through agents and waterbed stores, too. The annual premium for waterbed liability coverage alone is minimal (around $35) for a policy with a $25 deductible clause and a liability limit of $100,000.

Require your tenant to secure some form of waterbed liability insurance and give you a copy of the policy. You will notice that it covers damage to the building and to the property of other tenants, but it specifically excludes fire damage; damage to buildings which do not conform to governing building codes; and damage resulting from failure to follow the manufacturer's specifications for assembling, installing, filling, emptying, locating, and maintaining the waterbed. Because these policies expire after twelve months, make certain that the tenant renews for continuous coverage.

■ **Deposit**—Require at least an extra $25 deposit from the waterbed tenant to cover the deductible should the insurance policy have to cover damages. Add this deposit to the total security/cleaning deposit so it need not be restricted in use to waterbed damages alone. That way it's available to be used for any kind of damage, for cleaning, or for rent.

■ **Agreement**—Cross out and initial the liquid-filled furniture exclusion, if any, in the rental agreement you use, and add to the agreement the terms under which you are allowing the waterbed. These terms could be included in the remarks section of the agreement; they could be written or typed on the back of the agreement and signed by all parties concerned; or they could be written as a separate agreement and referenced to the main rental agreement. Written succinctly into the remarks section, the wording might be as follows: "Tenants have one waterbed approved by Owners for this dwelling. Waterbed shall consist of mattress, liner, and frame; shall be kept insured for liability of $100,000; and shall be installed according to manufacturer's specifications."

This entire waterbed-acceptance procedure involves additional time, effort, costs, and risks which other tenants should not have to subsidize. Therefore, consider adding a nominal sum to the waterbed tenant's rent to compensate you for all this, and consider including in the sum enough to pay the premium yourself on the tenant's waterbed liability policy so you can be certain that the policy is kept current.

Waterbeds may not be what you want in your building, but if you do, and if you follow these guidelines, you will be able to rest well at night yourself no matter what you sleep on.

Should You Allow Pets?

Just as there is no federal law yet compelling you to rent to tenants with waterbeds, there's none compelling you to rent to tenants with pets, guide and signal dogs excepted, and you might be wise to exclude both waterbeds and pets from your rental property. It's your prerogative, your right, to come up with your own policy here, but in adopting a dogmatic, hidebound policy, you are excluding not just waterbeds and pets but also all of the people who go along with them, some of whom make very good tenants. By excluding pets, in fact, you are halving the number of people who qualify to rent from you, for more than half of all American households have some kind of pet. By excluding pets, you are making the task of finding good tenants that much more difficult because you have fewer people to choose from.

If finding good tenants without accepting pets is easy for you, then continue excluding pets altogether because pets undeniably do pose problems, but if you are having problems finding good tenants and if you have a building which is suitable for pets (buildings most suitable for dogs and cats are those with yards or patios and with little or no wall-to-wall carpeting), consider accepting good tenants who have good pets.

According to one university study, pet owners as a group are friendlier, richer, smarter, and more attractive than those who have no pets. Surprised? I was, too. Yet, when we think about pet owners as renters, we tend to think first about the stereotype of the inconsiderate pet owner who's never heard of pooper scoopers and doesn't believe in leashes. That's the same as people thinking first about unscrupulous landlords whenever they think about landlords. You're an example of a scrupulous landlord, aren't you? Well, there are many examples of scrupulous pet owners, too.

Scrupulous pet-owning tenants save you

PET POLICY

No pets of any kind may be harbored on the premises, even temporarily, no matter what they are and no matter who owns them.

No stray animals may be fed or kept on the premises.

If you should notice any pet or stray animal on the premises, please report the sighting and its particulars to management immediately.

PET POLICY

Subject to approval, tenants may have pets in any ONE of the following categories:
1. Caged birds (maximum of two)
2. Fish (as many as can survive happily in a fifty-five gallon, or smaller, aquarium)
3. House cats (one, spayed or neutered, at least three months old
4. Dogs (one, spayed or neutered, at least nine months old; no pugnacious breeds)
5. Other animals (permitted only on a case-by-case basis)

Tenants shall bring all prospective pets to management for approval beforehand.

Tenants shall sign a Pet Agreement covering the keeping of their pet.

Tenants shall provide proof of dog-bite insurance for their dog (at Owners' discretion).

Tenants shall neither feed nor keep any stray animals on the premises.

---

money because they tend to be more permanent residents, and they make you money because they will pay higher rent for their accommodations than will tenants without pets. My own experience with an admittedly small sample has shown that tenants with pets stay on average twice as long as those without pets and they will pay $10 to $35 more per month for a place to live where they can keep their pets. They realize that finding another place which accepts them and their pets is difficult at best and is sometimes altogether impossible, so once they move in, they tend to stay a long time and they will pay more in rent while they stay there.

Whereas some landlords think that pets never add to the value of a rental dwelling, they're thinking with blinders on. They're thinking strictly about the pets of inconsiderate owners and about the additional management and maintenance problems such pets cause. That's one way to look at the situation. There is another way.

Since pet owners will pay more rent and since higher rents translate into higher property values, pets can actually increase the value of a building. Have you ever thought about that? Twenty dollars more per month for each unit in a sixplex adds up to additional income of $1,440 per year and equals an added property value of $10,080 at only seven times the gross income. That ain't pet feed!

If you do decide to rent to pet owners, set the rent high, advertise that you accept pets, and you'll be so inundated with applicants that you'll wonder why you hadn't thought about accepting pets before.

Here's a caution. Some landlords require their pet owning tenants to pay a flat surcharge or a "nonrefundable deposit" upfront. Don't follow this practice. Upfront charges lead pet owners to believe that messes and damage caused by their pets, whatever they may be, are already paid for, so the pet owners tend to be more irresponsible in cleaning up after their pets. Charge higher rents and higher deposits (refundable, of course) instead. Higher deposits should not exceed the legal limits for all of a tenant's deposits which are set for your jurisdiction, and they should not be designated as "pet deposits" because any deposit so designated must be used only for pet damage. They may not be applied to rent, cleaning, or breakage unrelated to the pet. Designate them as deposits, plain and simple.

Now take a look at the two pet policies above. The one is completely restrictive. The other is not. It's a guide with very specific provisions describing what is allowed and what isn't.

The first policy is a classic "no pets under any circumstances" policy. The second is a "pets allowed under certain circumstances" policy which comes with a powerful "subject to approval" stipulation giving the landlord discretion to allow a docile old Beagle while refusing a domi-

Your Pet and You

Please provide us with a photograph of your pet, plus some specifics about your pet and you. This information will help us make an informed decision when we are considering both of you as tenants for our rental dwelling.

Your name _Judy Tenant_ Date _10/31/XXXX_

Description...pet's name, breed, age, weight, size (give height and length), activity level, and traits _Emily; rescued greyhound, 10 years old, 70 pounds, 30" high x 38" long; child friendly; alert; gentle_

Training...obedience school or other training (give dates, too)
Weisse Obedience School - Certificate of Successful Completion, June - October XXXX

Background...aggressiveness (ever bitten someone or exhibited aggressive behavior? if so, give particulars and indicate measures taken to curb aggressiveness since last episode)

not aggressive

Activities...exercise (give type and frequency)

Walks - 3 times a day

Health...spayed or neutered; vaccinations; health exams (give schedule); veterinarian (give name and phone number) _spayed female with all vaccinations; annual vet exams and vet visits as needed. Veterinarian: Charles Aldrich 555-1111_

Grooming...schedule of grooming; groomer (give name and phone number)
Monthly shampoo and monthly medication for fleas -- at the Petall Dog Spa — 555 9991

Care arrangements...caretaker during absences (give name and phone number)
1-3 days absence - Alice Constantin, 555-6420;
More than 3 days - Bates Pet Motel, Norman Bates, 555-6789

Commitment...duration of relationship with this pet; pet license particulars; membership in animal protection organizations such as the S.P.C.A.; willingness to put up an additional deposit _Emily has been a part of our family for more than 4 years, annual dog license, lifetime SPCA member; willing to put up a deposit._

Insurance...pet health and/or dog-bite (describe policy)

None

References...people who know your pet and you (give particulars)

Daniel McAdams (neighbor) 555-9768; Gracie Colton (friend) 555-4321 nant, aggressive young Beagle.

Whether you choose to rent to people with pets or not, you must have a pet policy. Actually you already have one whether you realize it or not, but you may not have formalized it in writing. You may have been telling your tenants all along that you do not accept pets, and they may be interpreting that to mean no fish, fowl, mammals, insects, or reptiles. Then again they may interpret it to mean that certain fish, fowl, and insects are acceptable, but not mammals or reptiles. Just what do you mean by "no pets" anyway? Would you allow someone to have twelve tropical fish in a twenty-gallon aquarium or three parakeets in a cage? They're all pets. Would they violate your policy?

Spell out what you mean when you say "no pets" or "pets OK" by putting your policy in writing and making it fair to your tenants, their pets, the neighbors, and yourself. Specify in your policy the type, age, number, and reproductive capability (if appropriate) of the pets you will accept or not accept and outline these specifications clearly. Don't bother with size or weight limitations. They don't seem to be relevant to whether a certain pet will be a nuisance around a property. The age of a pet is far more important. Older pets are more docile.

Factors such as socialization, training, supervision, humane treatment, and proper confinement all contribute to a pet's temperament, too, but because they're not readily measurable, you should arrange to interview the pet and the tenant before you allow the pet. Even a Chihuahua which has been taught to bite strangers would be too much of a nuisance to allow into a rental dwelling. An interview will tell you all you need to know when making your decision.

If you suspect that a dog might be aggressive and you still want to rent to the tenant, require the tenant to buy dog-bite insurance. Some landlords have discovered that their own liability insurance was canceled after they allowed a tenant to have an aggressive dog. Don't let that happen to you!

You have great flexibility in determining your policy and you have some flexibility in applying it, but you should be astute enough to recognize that whatever pet policy you adopt will have to apply equally to everyone in a building or at least to everyone in a very distinctly designated area. You cannot extend a privilege to some tenants and not to others. They won't stand for it. I know.

As a consequence of acquiring a fourteen-unit complex some time ago, I happened to inherit a situation involving an elderly lady who had been allowed by the previous owner to have a small house dog. It was her constant companion, her security system, her confidant, and her first love. I was averse to giving her the choice of dog or dwelling since that dog meant so much to her and since she had already lived there for fifteen years. I let her keep the dog.

Still, I was adamant about not allowing anyone else to keep a dog there because the building was being improved with new carpeting and other amenities which the wrong dog could easily ruin.

Three of the thirteen other tenants who lived there defied me by getting their own dogs. When confronted with my no-pets policy, which I had already discussed with them, all three referred to the little old lady's dog. "If she can have one, why can't we?" they asked almost in unison. Indeed, why couldn't they?

The crucial difference between them and the little old lady as far as I was concerned was that she had the dog long before I assumed ownership and before I instituted the no-pets policy. Her dog was "grandmothered" in. The other tenants couldn't have cared less how I rationalized the situation. As far as they were concerned, there was no difference whatsoever between her and them. If she were allowed a dog, then they should be as well. One of those tenants had to be evicted over this matter. The other two finally relented and gave their pets away, but they struggled hard. So did I. I had to.

By the way, if tenants ever do break your rental contract by acquiring a pet which you distinctly prohibit, you should confront them about the matter immediately and give them no more than three days to get rid of it. If you give them any more time, they will only dillydally in getting rid of the pet and become attached to it in the process, and you'll wind up having to evict them in the end. If you fail to approach them at all when you first learn about their pet, you have in effect given them your tacit approval, and you'd better be prepared to fend off your other tenants. They'll want one, too. This is another one of those little landlording problems which have a way of becoming more difficult to deal with if you procrastinate.

Pet Agreement

Dated __APRIL 6, XXXX__

(Addendum to Rental Agreement)

This agreement is attached to and forms a part of the Rental Agreement dated __1/14/XX__ between __LESLIE LANDLADY__ , Owners, and __DOROTHY MAE MAHONEY__ , Tenants.

Tenants desire to keep a pet named __" FANG "__ and described as __LHASA APSO__ in the dwelling they occupy under the Rental Agreement referred to above, and because this Agreement specifically prohibits keeping pets without the Owners' permission, Tenants agree to the following terms and conditions in exchange for this permission:

1) Tenants agree to keep their pet under control at all times.
2) Tenants agree to keep their pet restrained, but not tethered, when it is outside their dwelling.
3) Tenants agree to adhere to local ordinances, including leash and licensing requirements.
4) Tenants agree not to leave their pet unattended for any unreasonable periods.
5) Tenants agree to clean up after their pet and to dispose of their pet's waste properly and quickly.
6) Tenants agree not to leave food or water for their pet or any other animal outside their dwelling where it will attract other animals.
7) Tenants agree to keep their pet from being unnecessarily noisy or aggressive and causing any annoyance or discomfort to others and will remedy immediately any complaints made through the Owners or Manager.
8) Tenants agree to provide their pet with regular health care, to include inoculations as recommended.
9) Tenants agree to provide their pet with an identification tag.
10) Tenants agree to get rid of their pet's offspring within eight weeks of birth.
11) Tenants agree to pay immediately for any damage, loss, or expense caused by their pet, and in addition, they will add $__100—__ to their security/cleaning deposit, any of which may be used for cleaning, repairs, or delinquent rent when Tenants vacate. This added deposit, or what remains of it when pet damages have been assessed, will be returned to Tenants within __SEVEN__ days after they have proved that they no longer keep this pet.
12) Tenants agree that this Agreement applies only to the specific pet described above and that no other pet may be substituted.
13) Tenants agree to furnish Owners with a picture of their pet.
14) Tenants agree that Owners reserve the right to revoke permission to keep the pet should Tenants break this Agreement.
15) Tenants agree to purchase a dog-bite insurance policy if required by Owners and to supply Owners evidence of a current policy.

Owner __Leslie Landlady__   Tenant __Dorothy Mae Mahoney__

By _____   Tenant _____

Page __4__ of __4__

Because you never know quite how tenants will react when you approach them about a forbidden pet, consider how one savvy landlady handled tenants who claimed that they were merely sheltering a pit bull which had showed up on their porch. She bought "Bubba" for $10 and got them to agree that they wouldn't get another dog. Then she took the little bruiser off to the pound.

It worked for her. It could work for you. It's certainly worth a try.

Oh, and if you have reason to suspect that a tenant has acquired a dog on the quiet, you can find out for sure without getting a search warrant or conducting a midnight hunt. All you need is a silent dog whistle which you can buy at a pet store. Blow it outside the tenant's dwelling, and listen for dog sounds from inside. Even docile lap dogs will respond by whining or barking.

Having a pet policy which you can enforce when necessary is one thing, but finding good pet owners with good pets is another. It's a process requiring circumspection and deliberation. You will want to determine whether the owners you interview are devoted enough to their pets to care for them faithfully and whether the pets are of a type and temperament to cause you and your other tenants no grief.

Use the form, "Your Pet and You," to help you make this determination. It enables the pet owning tenant to create a "pet résumé" of sorts, covering most of the specifics about the pet and the pet owner's commitment to it.

You want to separate the casual or accidental pet owner from the committed, dedicated pet owner. This form will help you with that task.

Another way to find good pet owners with good pets is to ask questions such as "Will you rent this place if we do not allow you to keep your pet?" and "Who will be taking care of your pet in your absence?" and "Will you pay a larger refundable security/cleaning deposit of $100?" and "Can you live by our pet agreement which says the following...?" and "Who's your veterinarian?" and "Do you have pet health insurance?" and "Is your pet properly licensed?" Their answers to these questions will indicate quite clearly how important their pet is to them and how faithfully they will care for it after they move in.

The pet itself, which you ought to meet at some point before you agree to accept it, should fall within your pet policy guidelines and should be reasonably friendly, healthy, and well-behaved.

If your screening of the owners and their pet raises any doubts in your mind about their ability and willingness to respect your property, refuse to rent to them. You have every right to be discriminating in this matter, and furthermore, you should be discriminating.

Refusing applicants who have unacceptable pets or are themselves unacceptable is pretty straightforward. Refusing existing tenants who have no pets but want one is much the same, especially when you suspect that they might prove to be negligent in caring for the pet they choose. The only way to determine their attitude is to impose upon them the same set of conditions which you impose upon new tenants with pets. Caution your tenants that you will allow them to have a pet only if they discuss the matter with you in advance and only if you approve.

When they approach you, review your pet policy with them first to make sure that they understand what kinds of pets you allow. Then go over the entire Pet Agreement with them, item by item. Tell them that you treat all pet owners alike and that all of those tenants who now have pets have submitted their pets to you for approval, signed pet agreements, and increased their security/cleaning deposits. So long as your existing tenants will do likewise, they will be allowed to have a pet. Emphasize that your refusal of any particular pet has nothing to do with their tenancy but that keeping an unauthorized pet will certainly result in an eviction of both the tenants and the pet.

All of your tenants should understand that they have no right to have a pet on the premises unless you grant them the privilege under well-defined conditions. If they should fail to live up to those conditions, you will be forced to withdraw the privilege.

Should you allow pets?

Considering your building, its vacancy factor, and your own inclinations, what do you think?

The decision is yours.

Should You Furnish the Major Kitchen Appliances?

You don't always have a choice about whether to supply your tenants with stoves and refrigerators in your unfurnished rentals because sometimes the appliances are already built in and sometimes the rental market is so fiercely competitive that you have to supply them if you want to keep your rentals occupied. When you do have a choice, however, either don't furnish them at all or tell your new tenants that you no longer supply these appliances in unfurnished rentals but that you would be willing as a favor to them to supply a stove or refrigerator on loan for a few months until they get their own.

Tenants are far less likely to complain about the minor faults of their appliances when they're using a stove or refrigerator "on loan" than if you tell them that the appliances are included in their rent. Tenants fear that each time you see the appliances you'll be reminded of the loan agreement and may ask for them back, so they keep mum about the little problems.

Fiddling with a temperamental stove that bakes lopsided cakes takes far too much of your time, as does explaining why milk freezes and ice cream melts in a temperamental refrigerator. Supplying these major appliances and providing what amounts to a full maintenance contract on them in addition seldom pays off.

Should You Leave Them Plain or Fix Them Fancy?

Cosmetics people market hope. Automobile people market freedom. Clothing people market style. Wine people market status. Appliance people market convenience. Vitamin people market health.

What do you market, landlord? The blahs? Plain-Jane housing with off-white walls? How pedestrian! Shame on you! You could do better, you know, much better.

Don't get me wrong now. There's nothing wrong with renting out clean, functional dwellings with heating, cooling, electricity, carpets, drapes, and indoor plumbing, but it's just so, well,

so practical. That's all. And "practical" doesn't sell or rent for very much. Chevrolets are practical, too, but they don't sell for what Cadillacs do. People will rent your functional dwellings in tight housing markets no matter what, to be sure, but they will always pay more in any market if they believe they are getting more for their money, and you can give them more for their money without spending much more of yours.

With a little extra work and very little investment, you could be marketing the same kinds of illusions that Cadillac customers so willingly pay extra money for. What illusions? Individuality, class, style, luxury. "All that in my rental property and with very little investment? Surely you're putting me on." Not in the least. Here's how.

Put on your interior decorator hat, size up your rental dwelling from the inside out, and consider the following suggestions for what they could add to the place. Choose particular colors, patterns, and items which would add the most dazzle for your dollar. Install them. Increase the rent 5% or 10% above what you had intended to charge. Expose the place to potential tenants, and see what happens. You will be surprised.

Here are some "dazzlers" which work for me and others I know. Tailor them to the kind of property you have and the kind of tenant you want to attract.

■ **Wallpaper a wall** —Wallpaper goes in and out of fashion. No matter what's fashionable, a lot of wallpaper or a little or even none at all, you'll dazzle prospective tenants by wallpapering one prominent wall either opposite the front door or opposite the entrance to the kitchen. That wallpapered wall makes a big impression on prospective tenants as they walk in and begin visualizing themselves living there. Yet, vinyl-coated, prepasted wallpaper costs surprisingly little, is easy to apply, and is easy to care for. Watch for bargains in wallpaper remnants, but make sure you buy enough to complete the job because you may not be able to buy more later.

■ Paste a decorative paper border along the walls in a room or two—Perhaps the least expensive dazzler around and certainly the easiest to install is the decorative paper border. Paint and wallpaper stores sell these borders in rolls as narrow as three inches and as wide as eight inches. You paste them horizontally around the walls of a room at waist or ceiling height. Then you stand back and admire how much your colorful, decorative border accents whatever else is on the wall. Tenants don't need to know how little the border cost you. Don't tell them.

■ Paint some rooms with two or three attractively contrasting colors—Tenants are so used to seeing plain white walls in rental properties that they almost gasp with surprise when they come upon a dwelling which has rooms painted any other way. Select one or two of the living-area rooms in your rental dwelling, and make the walls and trim stand out with pleasing two-tone or even three-tone paint jobs. Ask your paint supplier for color suggestions, and make sure that the results look professional even if you did do the work yourself.

■ Put up a woven shade—A woven shade on any window which requires some kind of window covering anyway dazzles beholders into believing that they're getting something extra for their money, something fancy. Woven shades are fancy. They are special, and they are colorful. They can also be inexpensive. You don't have to spend a lot of money on fancy Roman shades made of wood. They're costly and no more decorative than the vinyl varieties which sell for approximately what you'd pay for ordinary window shades.

■ Hang mini-blinds in several rooms—Like woven shades, mini-blinds provide a decorator's touch to windows. Unlike woven shades, they can be adjusted precisely to compensate for outside lighting conditions. If you're combining woven shades and mini-blinds, use mini-blinds on the side of the building where the sun shines most. They're more durable when exposed every day to direct sunlight. They will let the ten-

ants make infinite adjustments for light, and they come in a full range of colors and stock sizes. Should your windows be odd sizes, either mount stock mini-blinds which are larger than the casement on the outside of the casement rather than waiting for a special order sized to fit inside the casement, or else choose some other window covering. Special orders are expensive and take more time than you're likely to have.

Be aware that some vinyl mini-blinds contain lead and that the lead will appear as a powder on the surface of those blinds which have deteriorated after much exposure to the sun. If you suspect that you have any of these blinds, replace them with new ones labeled with words like "nonlead formula" or "no lead added."

■ Put full-length mirrors on bedroom closet doors—Mirrors and smoke are so much the stuff of illusions that magicians couldn't get along without them. Forget about providing smoke illusions to dazzle your tenants. Leave them to the magicians. Stick to using mirrors instead.

Mirrors make attractive rooms look all the more attractive and also look larger. As a consequence, people like them. Because full-length, single-piece mirrors can be pricey, though, consider using mirror squares instead. They don't have quite the luxury look of single-piece mirrors, but they don't have quite the price tags either.

In addition, they have another big advantage when used in rental properties. They are both easier to install and easier to replace. Tenants who break a large mirror won't believe you when you tell them how much they'll have to pay for the replacement, whereas they'll breathe a big sigh when you tell them how little a broken mirror square or two will cost them to replace.

■ Mount a curtain-rod valance above the shower bath—A shower-bath curtain-rod valance made of 1"x6" fir or pine and painted with a simple design or covered with fancy Contact Paper® spruces up drab bathrooms as if by magic. Mounted just in front of the rod itself, the valance hides the curtain rod and lends a special illusion of warmth and luxury to the place.

■ Install a curved shower curtain rod over the shower bath—Curved shower curtain rods increase the space inside a shower bath by 25%, and they keep shower curtains from sticking to the body of the person taking a shower. They act less to dress up the inside of a bathroom than they do to create more elbow room and make showers more comfortable.

■ **Switch to oak toilet seats**—Everybody likes home furnishings made of real wood, and there's no wood better liked than oak. It's solid and durable, and it fits into almost every interior decorating scheme tenants might fancy. An oak toilet seat stands out in an otherwise sterile white-and-chrome bathroom. It's a "statement." The statement is, "Somebody here cares about the details and wants to make the surroundings especially livable."

■ **Replace a ceiling light fixture with an inexpensive ceiling fan**—Nostalgia and luxury are the trademarks of the ceiling fan, that special fixture which conjures up memories of romantic places like the Raffles Hotel in Singapore and old movies like "Casablanca." In case you haven't noticed, ceiling fans are back. People love them. Not only do they lend a special decorative touch to any room, but they do a good job of circulating warm air in winter and cool air in summer to every recess of a room. They may be harder to install than an ordinary light fixture but not all that much, and they're well worth the effort. They're charming. Everyone from Target to K-Mart and the big-box discount and hardware stores carries them.

■ **Install some distinctive lighting fixtures**—Distinctive lighting fixtures seem to add the most to kitchens and bathrooms because the fixtures there are more used than in other rooms. What people seem to like most in kitchens and baths are track lights. They're appealing, I suppose, because they have a high-tech, modern look about them, and since they can be adjusted to illuminate work areas, they have a practical value as well. Become well acquainted with the selection of lighting fixtures available through your lighting supplier, and pick up some fancy ones when they go on sale. Be especially watchful for track lights which require no special wiring, that is, those which can be wired into existing ceiling electrical boxes (avoid track lights with halogen bulbs; they're electricity hogs).

All of these dazzlers together should cost a good shopper no more than $450, and yet they have the potential to produce $50 more per month in increased rental income. Think of what that does to the value of your property. At seven times the annual gross, $50 of additional rental income increases the value by $4,200! Even for a hard-boiled capitalist like you, that's a decent return on your money, isn't it? That's better than nine times its cost!

Try these dazzlers. Be imaginative and think up others of your own. Capitalize on people's willingness to pay extra for illusions. Just make sure that whatever dazzler you try is fashionable, uncomplicated, inexpensive, easy to care for, and easy to replace. Also, make sure that you use dazzlers tastefully. Too many in one room will make it look cluttered and cheap, you know, like the inside of a movie-set bordello.

Of course, you must always keep your dazzlers in like-new condition. Shabby dazzlers make a place look even more tawdry than shabby basics. What, after all, looks worse than a millionaire's mansion which has gone to ruin? Designed to impress and delight, it only depresses. You don't want your dazzlers to depress anybody. Keep them looking like new, and replace them as soon as they start to lose their appeal or go out of style.

Should You Outfit the Laundry?

An apartment-house laundry room can be a blessing or a curse. It can pay off as handsomely as a small casino full of slot machines, or it can be simply another welfare case for you to support. Mostly there are two factors which determine whether you will "win" or "lose" in your laundry room—how much the machines are used and who owns them.

■ **Use**—All things considered, your laundry room will pay off handsomely if it's used frequently enough. Although you cannot tell for certain whether your tenants will indeed do their laundry there or how many loads they will wash every week, you can make a good educated guess based on the number of people or the number of bedrooms in the building. If you have a fourplex, for example, and you have four families living there with two children in each, you have sixteen people in all, and they will surely produce enough dirty laundry to support one coin-operated washer and one dryer. On the other hand, a fourplex tenanted by singles and couples, no matter how clean they happen to be, will not support a washer and dryer.

The rule of thumb I use to determine whether

to outfit a laundry room at all and, if so, with how many machines, is this—*Sixteen people or twelve bedrooms (even the smallest dwelling counts as one bedroom) will support one washer and one dryer.* If a building meets either of these minimums and if its laundry machines are set to charge competitive rates, the machines will produce liberal returns.

■ **Ownership**—Some landlords feel that they have better things to worry about than laundry machines and would rather let someone else handle them completely. They have that choice, and so do you if you have an apartment-house laundry room.

If you contract with a vendor to supply the machines on a lease or commission arrangement, you will be relieved of all the ownership worries. The vendor will supply, insure, and service the machines while you provide the laundry room itself, the necessary plumbing, hookups, and, of course, the utilities. The vendor will write a one- to five-year contract to assure the company a profit and then split the leavings with you.

If you supply the machines yourself, you will have to take care of the repairs and maintenance, count the coins, worry about vandalism and other calamities, see that they're insured, and you'll have to pay about twelve hundred dollars for each washer-dryer pair you buy, but you'll have the only access to the coin boxes, and you'll get to depreciate the machines over a reasonably short period of time, or, if you wish, you may elect to expense them as IRS Section 179 business equipment in the very first year.

What choice should you make? That depends.

If you are pretty clumsy or helpless about maintenance matters, if you don't think you'd enjoy the business, if you own an apartment building with fewer than sixteen occupants or twelve bedrooms, if your building is located in an area prone to break-ins and vandalism, *or* if you intend to dispose of your building within two years, don't buy your own machines. Contract with someone else to supply them.

■ **Dealing with an outside vendor**—Should you decide to have someone else supply the machines, ask other landlords to recommend trustworthy companies, and then shop around for the best available terms. They vary a lot, and I do mean *a lot*.

There are two primary contract types—straight-commission and lease-commission. Straight-commission contracts allocate a certain percentage of the gross receipts to the property owner and another percentage to the vendor, from the very first quarter to the very last. I have seen these percentages as low as 40% and as high as 75% for the property owner. That higher percentage wasn't at an enormous property with numerous machines, either. It was at a twenty-unit complex. The owner had simply done some tough bargaining, knowing that the laundry vendor business is very competitive and that there's room for negotiation.

Under a lease-commission arrangement, the vendor retains a fixed sum each month and splits the balance with the property owner, again according to some predetermined percentages, so if the machines produce only enough to cover the supplier's fixed sum, you, property owner, get nothing but lemons, oranges, and grapes. You get no cherries. Tough luck!

A straight-commission arrangement generally nets you more than a lease-commission arrangement because some money will accrue to you with each load washed, regardless of how many.

Life with a laundry room vendor isn't all cherries, I can assure you. You have to be naturally suspicious when dealing with vendors because there's more than one way that they and their employees can cheat you.

Take a look at this one clause which appears in fine print at the end of a five-year laundry equipment lease I inherited from the previous owner of a property I bought—"This lease shall be automatically renewed for the same period of time unless canceled in writing by either party at least 90 days prior to expiration by registered mail."

What's that verbiage mean? It means that if I fail to notify the vendor that I want to cancel the lease three months before it expires, I'll be stuck with it for another *five years*. Now that's what I call a cheater clause! Some wily attorney must be congratulating himself for having sneaked that one into the contract. It's entirely one-sided. The burden of canceling the contract is mine, not the vendor's, and if I'm forgetful, I could have an unwanted contract on my hands virtually forever. Read your laundry equipment lease carefully. Don't be caught without your reading specs at lease signing time, or you may be taken to the laundry, er, cleaners!

Incidentally, every laundry equipment lease I have ever seen is automatically transferred to the new owner upon change of ownership. Selling a property releases the seller from the lease but binds the buyer exactly as it did the previous owner. Whenever you're negotiating to acquire a property with leased laundry equipment, review the lease, and if you find that it has restrictive terms, make them part of your negotiations with the seller.

To make certain that buyer and seller are both well aware of the lease, some vendors will record the lease against the property in county records without your knowledge, as one did in my case. The vendor considered the lease valuable enough to record and wanted to make certain that it could not be ignored.

Consider, then, whether you are giving away something valuable when you sign a laundry equipment lease. After all, it's an exclusive right to put coin-operated laundry machines on your property for a given period of time. You might not think it's worth much when you sign the lease, but the vendor thinks differently. The vendor knows it's valuable. The vendor will protect it in every way possible, and the vendor will require you to pay the company a sum of money to break the lease before it expires if you decide you want to install your own machines.

Be wary of laundry leases. Be very wary. Read the fine print. Read the large print. Read the italics. Read the handwriting. Read the white space.

The other primary way you can be cheated when dealing with an outside vendor is through underreporting of income. If a vendor supplies you with laundry machines, the vendor also empties the coin boxes and counts the coins. The amount of income you receive depends upon how much income the vendor reports.

Remember when several large oil companies were exposed on *Sixty Minutes* for underreporting the amount of oil they were pumping from Indian lands? It ran into the millions of barrels. Trucks were loading crude oil from wellhead sites at all hours and bypassing the flow meters.

In comparison to that enormity, vendors' underreporting of laundry machine income is nickle-and-dime stuff, to be sure, but the situation is no different. The potential for underreporting income is much the same for laundry machines as it is for oil wells or a city's parking meters, for that matter. Only the amounts differ. Coins there for the taking are pretty tempting to some people, be they the vendors themselves, their employees, or your own managers.

Lest you think that those laundry coins don't amount to much, get out your calculator and multiply the cost of one coin-machine wash-and-dry times the number of loads you do every month at your home times the number of families in your apartment house. Those coins pile up into heaps of dollars!

One response to this underreporting problem by at least one vendor is the non-resettable counter. Mounted directly inside the timer access plate, it tallies each actuation of the laundry machine's coin slide. When the machines are emptied, your manager or you accompany the vendor's route collector as he empties the coin boxes, and you both take the readings from the counters so you both know how much revenue the machines have generated. It's a good idea and works well.

Another response is what's known in the trade as "verified accounting." Your manager or you are called upon to witness the collection of the coins as they're removed from the machines. After that, you witness the weighing of the coins on one of the highly sensitive, portable coin scales which give precise totals in dollars and cents of all the coins being weighed, even when they're mixed. The route collector then writes a receipt for the amount collected.

If your vendor offers neither of these verification methods, you will have to resort to a self-help method to keep from being cheated. Try one or both of these methods. The first one involves insisting that your manager or you be present when the coins are emptied, but that's not all. Because you can't know what sum of coins you're looking at unless you have some sort of quick-count method, get yourself a scale which will weigh as much as fifty pounds pretty accurately. Weigh the coins as they're emptied, write down the weights on a scratch pad, and later do the calculations to determine just how much the machines coughed up. If the coins are all quarters, as they frequently are nowadays, your calculations will be easy. If they're a mixture of quarters, dimes, and nickels, you'll have to work with the numbers a bit to come up with the right proportions, but when you do, you won't be far off.

The second method echoes one which is used by IRS agents to check the false reporting of coin laundry income at launderettes, which are so notorious for "laundering money" that they have given their name to the practice of reporting inaccurate income, in some cases overreporting the income and in others underreporting. IRS agents call the washing machine manufacturer to find out how much water one wash load takes and then examine the launderette's water bill. After allowing for a certain margin of error, say 10%, they can calculate approximately what the launderette's income ought to be and compare that with what's being reported as income.

You can do the same thing yourself even if your water in the laundry room is master metered along with the entire building's. Find out where the water line comes in to service your entire laundry room, and install a water meter right there. Yes, you as an individual may buy water meters, volt meters, watt meters, gas meters, light meters, practically any kind and size of a meter you might want. Unless it's particularly large, a water meter is reasonable priced, too. A 3/4" water meter in a quantity of one costs less than $80. When you consider how much underreporting of income you might be suffering, that's nothing. Let your vendor know that you've installed a water meter, and watch your income post an immediate increase for some strange reason. In one instance, when I'd inherited a lease from a previous owner, my laundry room income jumped $200 per month after a water meter installation.

Perhaps the most important aspect of your efforts to be treated fairly by your laundry machine vendor is the interest you show in the whole operation. Too many apartment house owners regard their laundry rooms as beneath them. The laundry room is nickels, dimes, and quarters, and they're interested only in big bucks. They don't particularly care whether the laundry room is profitable or not. When the vendor recognizes this attitude and knows he's under no scrutiny, he'll do as he pleases, but when you've gone to all the trouble of installing a water meter in the laundry supply line and/or weighing coins as the machines are emptied, and the vendor knows you've gone to these lengths, he has to treat you honestly. He's afraid not to.

If yours is a small building, you're not going to get rich from laundry proceeds even with a desirable contract. Consider the laundry room more of an amenity than a money-maker and hope that you'll be able to recover your utility costs.

If yours is a large building, your laundry room proceeds will add more than pocket change to your income. They will be a factor in the property's value. The more desirable the contract you negotiate, the more your property is worth.

■ **Going it alone**—If you are the least bit handy, if you believe you'd enjoy looking after your own coin-operated laundry machines, if you own an apartment building in an area where there's little or no vandalism, if the building has at least sixteen occupants or twelve bedrooms, *and* if you intend to keep the building for at least two years (naturally you can take the machines with you if you want to, but be sure you specify that in your property sales agreement), then, by all means install your own machines. You will be pleasantly surprised to see just how much money they can make, and soon you will understand why so many firms are in the business of supplying laundry machines on a commission basis, why they offer to paint laundry rooms for "free," why they invest in non-resettable counters, why they buy expensive coin scales for account verification, why they sponsor rental housing association events, and why they offer various inducements to managers and owners of large complexes. It can be a lucrative business.

Should you decide after due consideration to install your own laundry machines at your apartment house, you need to know something about buying laundry machines, setting rates, changing rates, getting a decent return on your investment, and counting coins.

■ **Buying coin-operated laundry machines**— As with so many other big-ticket buying decisions, when you're in the market for coin-operated laundry equipment, you need to decide upon the best brand and the best dealer.

For general brand information, consult *Consumer Reports*. It regularly tests laundry machines designed for domestic use in its own laboratories under rigorous conditions and then rates them. Coin-operated machines, one old codger many years in the business told me, have innards exactly like the domestic machines. "Only the tops are different," he said. "When my bottoms wear out, I junk 'em and put my old tops on the cheapest new domestic machines made by the same manufacturer. They last just as long as new coin-operated models." If the two are indeed that similar, then the manufacturers of good domestic machines also make good coin-operated machines.

When making your own brand decisions, visit several coin-operated laundries in your area and see what brands of machines they use. If every one in the vicinity uses General Electric equipment, then you should be able to get General Electric parts and service readily, and you might want to consider purchasing General Electric equipment for this reason alone.

In addition to merely visiting the various laundries to see what kind of equipment they have, try to talk with the owners of the laundries themselves and ask them for their opinions on the various brands.

Because so many coin-operated laundries are unattended, however, you might have to wait around for a long time before an attendant appears who could answer your questions. Don't waste your time waiting. Look around for a sign which lists the telephone number of a person to call in case of trouble. Usually that person is the owner. Call the number and ask your questions. The primary questions you should ask when inquiring about equipment brands ought to cover reliability, durability, utilities consumption, parts availability, service availability, warranty, and initial cost.

Ask also about equipment dealers because you'll want to call several dealers who sell the same machines. Prices do vary somewhat on coin-operated machines from dealer to dealer. Make sure, though, for the purposes of comparison that you are asking for quotes on the same model of machine (most companies seem to make two commercial models, one with frills and one without), the same type of coin slide (it should be fully adjustable), the same kind of warranty (the factory warranty on commercial machines may be practically nonexistent, but nonetheless, you will want to establish what it is, how long for labor and how long for parts), and the same kind of delivery (curbside delivery, delivery and uncrating, or delivery and complete installation).

Be aware that firms which consider themselves "Laundry Equipment" suppliers likely sell and lease machines. They may sneer at you when you tell them that you want to buy your own coin-operated laundry machines because their primary business may be leasing. They may try to convince you that you're making a big mistake to buy your own machines. Tell them that unless they're willing to put machines into your laundry room on a 75/25 split (75% to the property owner and 25% to the machine supplier) that you'd just as soon install your own machines. Don't be dissuaded from buying machines once you've chosen to do so.

I have been very satisfied with Speed Queen and Kenmore machines myself. They have given good service over long periods of time, and they both wash well.

Kenmore, which is a Sears brand, seems to be the low-price leader in coin-operated laundry equipment. No matter what other brands you're considering, do check the prices at Sears, but do not bother checking the prices at a regular Sears store. They may have the machines all right, but they won't have the best prices. Check the prices through the Sears Contract Sales National Appliance Operations Center (1-800-359-2000) or (contractsales.sears.com), a special department set up to handle the needs of contractors and rental property owners. The last time I checked, a set of laundry machines consisting of one washer and one gas dryer, together with the money boxes, was selling for $1,100, plus delivery.

Because coin-operated laundry machines do not come with the same guarantees as their domestic counterparts, some nervous Nellies are tempted to buy extended maintenance contracts. My own experience has shown that these contracts are priced higher than the repairs themselves cost without a contract. I don't bother with maintenance contracts. I consider them a rip-off, something you have to be sold, not something you buy.

You're better off taking your chances that the machines will not need repairs or else learning how to fix the machines yourself or sending your maintenance person off for training. Inquire when you're purchasing machines whether the dealer has maintenance manuals and maintenance classes available. Laundry machines are pretty simple to repair, but any suggestions for repairing them will surely save time and aggravation. Buy the manuals and attend the classes (they're either cheap or free). Unlike maintenance contracts, they are good value.

My biggest problem with coin-operated laundry machines couldn't be solved by any maintenance contract, that's for sure. Every so often tenants have called me to complain that the washers or dryers weren't working and I've arrived with my tools only to find that the one thing wrong with them was that I had forgotten to empty the coinboxes. So I'd "fix" the machines by emptying almost $200 from each pair. That's almost as good as hitting a jackpot in Vegas or Atlantic City!

One important consideration when you're selecting machines is whether to buy gas or electric dryers. Gas dryers are less expensive to operate almost everywhere, so if you have natural gas available, give some thought to paying the little extra that gas dryers cost initially in order to save on operating costs over the years. Before making your final decision, however, check with your local utility companies about the relative costs of operating gas and electric dryers. They'll have the current, local information you need for making your decision.

By the way, don't bother looking around for used coin-operated laundry machines unless you know their complete history or don't mind rebuilding them yourself. Used machines are available, to be sure, but they're far more trouble than they're worth because most owners simply won't part with them until they've been "through the wringer."

■ **Setting rates**—Since you with your laundry room are actually providing a convenience for your tenants rather than competing directly with coin-operated laundries nearby, you should set your machines at rates slightly higher, say, 10¢ or 25¢ higher, than the prevailing scale for local laundries. Your machines will need more repairs and wear out faster with frequent use, so you don't want to stimulate too much use by keeping the rates low. Keep them just low enough so that the machines will be used regularly, yet not so high that they won't be used often enough to justify your investment.

■ **Changing prices**—My first laundry machines had coin slides set to charge 25¢ to wash and 10¢ to dry. If I were to charge those prices today, I'd be subsidizing my tenants' laundry. As it was, I kept them much too long at those prices because the coin slides were fixed to accept only those amounts. They were not adjustable, and finding adjustable coin slides B.I. (before internet) took me a while. Adjustable slides enable you to change prices to any multiple-coin combination in minutes with only a screwdriver. These slides

may be purchased by themselves from most laundry machine suppliers and retrofitted to most existing machines. New machines come with adjustable slides nowadays as a matter of course.

When you do change prices, label the machines clearly with the new prices so users know exactly what you're charging to wash and dry a load.

■ **Getting a decent return on your investment**—Income from coin-operated laundry machines should cover your utility costs, purchase of the machines, repairs, maintenance, and a good return on your investment. The return should be very good, believe me. One of my eightplexes, all two-bedroom units, paid for its new washer and dryer and all of the overhead in just eleven months. Ever since then, those machines have simply churned out profits, never missing a beat. Over a five-year period, the return on that investment has been in excess of 95% per year, not bad for a legitimate business!

Do keep an eye on your utility costs, for they can, in certain situations, gobble up all of your profits and then some. I had one laundry room where the water heater and the dryers all operated on propane gas, and the gas bill alone each month amounted to more than the machines were grossing. I raised the prices, and that helped some, but then I hit upon the idea of shutting off the water heater entirely when I learned that the heat for hot water generally accounts for between 75% and 90% of all the energy used to wash clothes. After switching to cold-water washing only, I posted a sign to that effect, lowered the prices, and began enjoying a good return on my investment.

■ **Counting coins**—Those coins you remove from your laundry machines are all mixed up and require sorting, counting, and wrapping before being deposited in your bank account. It's a pleasant chore, counting stacks of your very own coins, one which you can do almost without thinking while you watch TV in the evening, but if you find the laundry business profitable enough to install more than one washer and dryer, you will find that counting coins becomes increasingly tedious. When that happens, buy a coin sorter for your counting house and restore some of the old pleasure to the chore.

There are coin sorters which whirl and tinkle and even tally their coins digitally, and they cost pretty pennies, too. You'd certainly need such a machine if you had a vending machine route or a casino, but you don't need the fanciest sorter available to help you count a few hundred dollars in coins every month. A simple, inexpensive sorter will handle the chore quite well.

Fortunately, there is one. It enables you to sort, count, and wrap coins quickly and accurately, and it works without having a single moving part. Gravity makes it work rather than electricity (they do have an electric "shaker" model, but I prefer the "gravity" model myself). After you feed the coins in at the top, they sort themselves by following tracks of varying widths until they wind up sorted into calibrated stacks at the bottom. Little nubs in the stacking tubes raise the 41st or 51st coin, depending on the denomination, to mark full rolls, which can then be removed, checked with the instant count verifier, and wrapped (most banks provide coin wrappers free of charge as a service to their customers).

This marvel of simplicity and utility is called the Nadex Coin Sorter and Packager, Model 607. It's available through larger stationery and business-supply stores or directly from the manufacturer, Nadex Industries, 145 Ontario St., Buffalo, NY 14207. Telephone 716-873-6600.

Should You Pay the Garbage and Utility Bills?

Landlords frequently pay the garbage and water bills themselves for their single-family rental properties rather than leaving that responsibility up to their tenants, and with good reason. Paying the garbage bill means that the garbage will positively be picked up and the property will be kept reasonably tidy. Paying the water bill means that the yard will probably be watered and the landscaping won't become parched earth. Paying both means that the tenant can offer no excuse for poor groundskeeping, and the place should look reasonably presentable when you drive by.

These arguments make sense for the house rental, but what about the apartment house which has no yard? Whenever I'm lucky enough to have separate water meters for each apartment, I require that the tenants pay their own bills. They should know what their water costs so they'll conserve more.

Garbage is another matter entirely. Personally, I prefer to pay the garbage bill for all of my rentals unless some other satisfactory precedent was established by a previous owner. Some tenants either forget to pay their bill or discontinue service altogether claiming that they would rather haul it to the dump themselves to save paying the bill, and then their cans begin to overflow and there's a constant mess for you to look after.

Control of the garbage area is always easier if you pay. If the tenants pay separate bills, there's bound to be friction caused by the invasion of one tenant's garbage can by a bag of strange garbage. That bag gets tossed aside and then begins a great garbage battle. Finally, there's more of a mess than you can cope with.

You pay and you control. Make them pay, and you'll likely be plagued by a continuous garbage war. You have better things to do with your time than participate in garbage wars.

There are ways to save on garbage bills, and you should be well aware of what they are. Garbage bills have risen dramatically because of increasingly restrictive governmental regulations on sanitary landfills. See the garbage handling alternatives at the end of chapter 16 for suggestions.

Also see the section on itemizing rents at the beginning of chapter 6 for a suggestion on how to recoup garbage bill increases when they occur rather than waiting until the next rent increase.

Should You Convert a Master-Metered Building?

As for the utilities in an apartment house, my practice is to have the tenants pay for their own so long as they're on separate meters, and if they aren't on separate meters, I try to convert their units to separate meters.

One situation which had me puzzled for a time involved a big, old fourplex with steam heat produced by one common boiler which was connected to a gas meter with dials that spun faster than a moon rocket's altimeter. I was paying the bill for that one meter myself, and with sharply rising utility rates, the bill soon rose to equal one quarter of the building's total rental income!

As if that weren't bad enough, one tenant kept complaining that he never had enough heat, and I had to turn the master thermostat up to 80 degrees (27° C) just to keep his place around 68 (20° C). Every unit but one then had to keep the windows open night and day to avoid being bathed in steam heat. Consequently, much of the heat that I was paying so dearly for was literally going out those windows.

What could I do? I knew that I couldn't raise the rents to a level where the high utility costs would be covered. That would have meant a rent increase substantially higher than market conditions permitted.

Fortunately, because each unit already had its own gas meter for its own kitchen stove and water heater, I could install new direct-vent space heaters in each unit and connect them to the individual meters already in place. I installed those heaters, and in less than twelve months, they paid for themselves in utility-bill savings, and my tenants' heating complaints evaporated into thin air that I wasn't paying to heat.

Hooray and hallelujah! Problem solved!

Tenants are more interested in lower rent, I believe, than in the inclusion of utilities, and when they have to pay their own utility bills, they conserve energy as they should.

Fortunately for me, this fourplex of mine was not a fully master-metered building. Fully master-metered buildings are dinosaurs, no longer being built today because they do not encourage utility conservation and because few owners want to speculate in gas and electricity futures. Fully master-metered buildings require more work and more money to convert than my old fourplex did, but they may be worth converting all the same.

If you happen to be stuck with one of these dinosaurs, seek out other owners who have already dealt with the problem themselves and learn what you can about their experience. Don't forget to confer with your utility company. Many offer their customers low-interest loans for energy conservation measures. Perhaps you can convince them that the conversion of your master-metered building qualifies. It ought to.

Once you know what the conversion costs are, consider how long a time you'll have to wait to get your money back. Less than three years is very good; three years is good; more than three years is questionable. Also consider whether the conversion will make the building worth more when you decide to sell it, and include that in your payback calculations, too.

Don't just sit there fretting and sweating over the bills. Do something. There's a lot you can do. Take your choice.

Should You Charge for Providing Lockout Service?

You and I know that landlording is at least a 24-hour-a-day job. Night and day we're on call with our little tool boxes just as family doctors used to be in the old days with their little black bags. We don't like to be called out in the middle of the night to repair a leaky roof or fix a balky furnace, but we go anyway because we feel responsible for providing our tenants with housing fit to live in.

When something goes awry with the building, that's one thing. We are responsible. When tenants do something foolish, that's quite another thing. We're not responsible. They are.

Yet, when tenants do something as foolish as lock themselves out, they expect us to drop everything we're doing and hurry over to let them in. They know we have a duplicate set of keys on hand, and they assume that one reason we have those keys is so that we can provide them with lockout service. They think of us as the keeper of their spare set of keys.

Nobody minds letting a tenant in when a lockout occurs at a convenient time, but all too often tenants find themselves locked out at odd hours, at times when the "keeper of the keys" is otherwise occupied or unavailable.

Here are four ways to handle lockouts—provide the service as a courtesy, charge a fee every time you let a tenant in, install a key safe, or install touchpad electronic locks.

Most landlords provide lockout service as a courtesy. There's nothing wrong with this approach if your tenants seldom call you to let them in and appreciate your efforts when you do, but if they're constantly calling you to let them in, and you're tired of being at their beck and call, change your approach.

Unless you've agreed with your tenants that their rent money covers a variety of special services like hauling off their dried-out Christmas tree, taking their extra garbage, replacing their broken windows, unclogging their sewer stoppages, and providing lockout service, you can charge them for each of these things, that is, in the absence of any law which compels you to do otherwise. Understand that you are not charging for these services in order to generate additional revenue. You are charging for these services in order to shift the burden of responsibility onto the tenants, where it belongs.

Before you begin charging them, advise them in writing of your new policy because they might be expecting you to provide lockout service free of charge and become incensed when they learn that it isn't free. The best way to advise them of your policy is to include a clause in their rental agreement. Lacking that, an ordinary letter or a Notice of Change in Terms of Tenancy will do.

For lockout service between the hours of 8 a.m. and 6 p.m., Monday through Saturday, excluding holidays, the fee might be $10. At other times, $20 would seem adequate. Don't make the fee so high that they become tempted to break in. It should be just high enough so they will feel more responsible about looking after their keys and won't be calling you immediately upon discovering that their keys are missing.

Another way to handle lockouts is to install a key safe, the modern-day equivalent of keeping a key under the doormat. A key safe resembles the lock box which real estate salespeople use when they want to provide many agents with access to many houses for sale and they don't want the hassle of duplicating and distributing keys for every one of those houses. Each agent has one master key which fits all the lock boxes in town, and inside each lock box are the keys for the house where the lock box is located.

Key safes don't have master keys. That would defeat their purpose. Key safes are for people who can't keep track of their keys. Instead of a master key, a key safe uses a combination for access, a combination which both you and the tenants know. You install the key safe in an inconspicuous place, set the combination, and after that, whenever the tenants find themselves locked out, they open the key safe with the combination and use the spare set of keys to get in.

Key safes come in two different types. There's the dial type, which opens like a school locker when you dial in three letters or numbers, and there's the pushbutton type, which opens when you push a set combination of ten buttons. I prefer the pushbutton type. They're easier and quicker to open, a big advantage for people who have poor coordination, and they're easier to change.

Key safes cost around $35 and work especially well at rental houses and small complexes where the keeper of the keys lives some distance away.

Besides solving the lockout problem, key safes relieve you of having to rendezvous with contractors who come to work on a vacant rental dwelling. You give the contractors the combination to the key safe, and they use the key inside while they're working there. When they're finished with their work, they return the key to the key safe, and you change the combination.

The fourth alternative is for you to install touchpad electronic locks on the doors. They use combinations, not keys. In the unlikely event that your tenants forget their combination, you simply give it to them over the phone. Don't you just love to fix problems over the phone?

Should You Allow Nails in Your Walls?

When you come across tenants who don't want to attach your walls to their pictures because they don't want to damage your walls, let me know, and I'll personally recommend that they be enshrined in the "Tenants' Hall of Fame." The hall still has lots of room available.

For all those other tenants, you have several decisions to make. What should you allow them to use to attach your walls to their pictures, clocks, and other lightweight stuff? Should you let them hang the heavier stuff at all, stuff like birdcages, bookcases, lamps, planters, wall systems, and bulletin boards?

First, let's consider the lightweight stuff. Remember the old days when tenants could cause their landlord to have a crying jag if they tried banging a nail into a wall and got caught? Why the concern? Because one nail in a plaster wall would sometimes cause a tiny crack which would grow into a fissure, and then chips and chunks of plaster would start falling down, and finally there would be a lath wall showing where once there had been one of plaster. Then along came some creative person who invented adhesive wall hangers, and the problem was solved. The adhesive hangers would hold light burdens without disturbing the plaster wall at all. Landlords invariably recommended them and most tenants dutifully used them, but things changed again with the advent of sheetrock, also known as plasterboard, wallboard, and gypsum board. A nail wouldn't crack the sheetrock as it would the plaster, but the adhesive wall hangers, when removed, would peel off both the paint and the paper surface of the sheetrock, leaving a broad, ugly scar underneath which was difficult to conceal.

Since both plaster and sheetrock walls are in general use, we landlords need to offer our tenants recommendations according to wall type.

Before you can make any recommendation, of course, you first must find out what kind of walls your building has. Don't be surprised if it has some walls of plaster and some of sheetrock. When older buildings are remodeled, the remodelers rarely replaster interior walls. They sheetrock 'em. Once you know what the walls are made of, you may confidently make your recommendations.

For plaster walls, recommend that your tenants use adhesive hangers wherever possible, and if they must use a nail, recommend that they drill a pilot hole first to avoid any cracking which the impact of banging too hard on a brittle wall might cause.

For sheetrock walls, recommend that your tenants use nails tapped in carefully and that they avoid using those adhesive hangers or tapes altogether. Holes left by nails in sheetrock may be filled neatly with spackling compound and do not even have to be painted in most cases.

How about the heavier stuff? Here you should think as much about the psychological aspects of the heavier stuff as you should about the damage that hanging it could possibly cause. Because tenant turnover is costly, you want your tenants to feel well rooted in your units so that, all things being equal, they will stay a long time. If they are comfortably ensconced in one of your rentals midst all of their hanging plants, their swag lamps, their wall systems, and their pet parakeets, they will likely stay a long time. Swallow hard and let them hang these things.

There is always the danger in their hanging this heavier stuff from your walls that they'll use an inadequate fastener and chunks of your walls will come tumbling down when their heavies and your walls part company, but you may avoid this danger by recommending that they first try to find a concealed stud to screw or nail into. Show them how to find a stud with one of the readily available electronic stud finders. Buy one and lend it out for this very purpose.

Attaching heavy things directly to a stud is by far the best way to hang them from either plaster or sheetrock walls, but if your tenants want to attach something to a location on a wall where there are no studs close by, recommend that they use an anchor (show them what you mean by an "anchor"; EZ Anchors® are the best) designed to support at least twice the weight of what they plan to hang.

AGREEMENT FOR TENANT ALTERATIONS

Agreement between ___Richard Renter___, Tenants,
who occupy a dwelling located at ___453 Sweet St, Littletown, CA___
and ___Leslie Landlady___, Owners, who are the
owners of this dwelling.

Owners hereby give permission for Tenants to make the following
alterations to their dwelling (identify location, describe alteration, and
indicate whether the alteration is to be removed or left behind when tenants
vacate; also indicate date when final alteration was inspected and approved):

1) Location ___Bathroom___ Alteration ___Frosted sliding glass shower doors on tub___
[ ] To be removed when Tenants vacate -- [X] To be left when Tenants vacate
Alteration inspected and approved by Owner [date, initials] ___7/20/XX (LB)___

2) Location _____ Alteration _____
[ ] To be removed when Tenants vacate -- [ ] To be left when Tenants vacate
Alteration inspected and approved by Owner [date, initials] _____

3) Location _____ Alteration _____
[ ] To be removed when Tenants vacate -- [ ] To be left when Tenants vacate
Alteration inspected and approved by Owner [date, initials] _____

   Tenants acknowledge that they are responsible for payment of all costs
incurred for alterations, including materials, labor, and permits.

   Tenants agree to hire workers, if any, who are licensed contractors and
have appropriate insurance, including workers compensation.

   If an alteration is removed when Tenants vacate, they acknowledge that
they are responsible for restoring the altered area to its original
condition.

   Tenants agree to put up a deposit of $_____ solely to insure that
they will restore their dwelling to its original condition when they vacate.

   If an alteration is to be left when Tenants vacate, they agree that it
will become the Owners' property and that they will not be reimbursed for it.

___7-12-XX___   ___Richard Renter___
Date   Tenant(s)
___7-13-XX___   ___Leslie Landlady___
Date   Owner

By all means, discuss your "hanging policy" thoroughly with your tenants before they move in because few of them will approach you for permission or advice later on. They'll just go ahead and hang things any which way they please, assuming that you don't care how they hang things because you never bothered to discuss the subject with them, but if you do discuss it with them in advance, most of them will try to follow your advice and hang their things your way.

Should You Let Tenants Make Alterations?

Some landlords oppose tenant alterations altogether. They're more concerned about keeping their rental dwellings "standard" than they are in keeping tenants in their rental dwellings. No matter what, they do not allow tenants to make alterations.

That's an understandable approach, but it's short-sighted because alterations are like roots tenants put down, roots which keep them occupying a certain rental dwelling longer than they would do otherwise.

Allowing tenants to make alterations is a better approach so long as it's handled in a way everybody understands and agrees upon beforehand.

Some tenants may think that "permission to alter" means they can knock out an inside wall to enlarge their living room, put a hole through an outside wall to install a new window, tear out a closet to put in a wet bar, and replace the hollow-core door to the master bedroom with a solid-core door to keep the kids from kicking holes in it so easily.

You may be giving them permission to make one or more of those alterations, but you must be specific when giving permission because their interpretation and yours will certainly differ unless you are as specific as you can be.

To be specific, use the form here, or else draw up an agreement of your own to be even more specific. You want to specify exactly what the alterations consist of, who's going to do the work, what's going to happen to the alterations once the tenants vacate, and whether the tenants will be compensated for whatever useful or attractive alterations they leave behind.

With these matters agreed upon, there's just one other thing you should include in any permission to alter, and that is an owner's inspec-

tion. Schedule one before the work begins so the tenant can explain the nature and extent of the contemplated alterations. You don't want to discover too late that an alteration damaged your property and will require your intervention and funds to remedy. Then schedule another one upon completion of the alterations to verify that they were done to your satisfaction.

Your decision to allow alterations or not depends upon the following factors—

- Your willingness to be flexible to please your tenants (if you're uncomfortable being flexible about allowing tenants to make alterations, don't allow alterations);
- The type of alteration the tenants want to make (if the tenants merely want to change paint colors on walls or replace a drab light fixture with a fancy one, that's one thing, but if they want to replace perfectly good floor coverings, repaint cabinets, or tear down a wall to make a living room larger and eliminate a bedroom, that's quite another);
- The appeal of the alteration to future tenants (if the alteration is peculiar and unlikely to appeal to anybody other than the tenants who want to make the alteration, think twice about allowing it);
- The tenants' sense of responsibility (if you have good reason to suspect that the tenants will not abide by the alterations agreement, deny their request to make alterations);
- The amount of the tenants' deposits (if the tenants' deposits are too meager to restore the dwelling to its original state in a worst-case scenario, you may want to ask them to increase their deposits so that you will have enough money to undo their alterations);
- The professionalism of the work (if the tenants plan to hire a contractor to do the work, you have greater assurance that the work will be done right than if they plan to do it themselves, and you might want to insist that they hire a contractor); and
- The building itself (if the building is old and unfashionable, you might want to be more willing to allow alterations which update the building than you would be if the building were newer and already had the amenities, fixtures, colors, and layouts most tenants want).

Give yourself enough time to decide whether to allow your tenants to make a certain alteration they want to make. It's a serious decision, one you should consider from every angle.

Should You Cover Those Naked Windows with Draperies, Shades, Blinds, or Bedsheets?

Yes, yes, yes, yes! Cover naked windows with something!

Every type of window covering has its place. A fancy dwelling which rents for a handsome sum should have handsome appointments, to include fine draperies, woven-wood shades, vertical slat blinds, or else wooden mini-blinds, whatever's in fashion, sometimes supplied by you and sometimes supplied by your tenants. Neither you nor your tenants want anything but the best for those dwellings.

Average rentals don't need the best window coverings, but they do need window coverings of some sort. Contract draperies are an excellent choice for average rentals. They work wonders to enhance appearances and keep tenants happy.

No matter how fancy the rental dwelling happens to be, though, don't overlook roller shades as a window covering possibility. They help to insulate. They are cheaper than drapes, longer lasting, easier to install, and easier to keep clean. They never need to be taken down for dry cleaning, they don't get threadbare, and except on sliding patio doors, both shades and drapes can coexist on the same windows at the same time.

This dual window treatment is a good one to use in average dwellings. It can be perfectly adequate while saving you money in the short run and the long run. You supply the roller shades and drapery rods yourself, and you let your tenants supply their own drapes. The initial cost is less and so is the maintenance cost. What's more, tenants who supply their own draperies tend to stay put longer than those who don't.

As for blinds, count yourself lucky if you already have Venetians in your rentals. Unless they're too dated, leave them right where they are because they should last a long time without requiring any further capital outlay. When kept cleaned and repaired by professionals (search the internet using "venetian blinds cleaning [your area]" as your search words), they cost surprisingly little to maintain.

Mini-blinds have already been mentioned as "dazzlers." They are. They have been popular with decorators for years, but they haven't always been as inexpensive, as available, or as durable as they are today. Many paint stores, department stores, hardware stores, and variety stores have ready-made sizes in stock, and because they can be mounted either inside or outside window casements, stock mini-blinds can accommodate most window sizes. That's especially convenient for you when you need a window covering right away. Just go to a nearby store, buy one, and hang it. What could be simpler? Give mini-blinds a long, hard look as a window-covering alternative which will fit well into almost any rental unit and do some dazzling. You'll find that they are more decorative, easier to clean, and easier to maintain than draperies, and they look every bit as good.

Above all, do use some kind of window covering when your rentals are vacant, yes, even if it has to be a bedsheet. The obviously vacant dwelling with naked windows is a prime target for vandals and squatters.

Should You Measure for and Install Draperies Yourself?

Any time you engage somebody to perform a service at your rental property, you can expect to pay dearly for the service.

You can measure for, and install, draperies yourself in a minimum amount of time, and you don't need to buy any special equipment to do it, so why should you pay somebody to come out to your rental property to do something you can do quickly yourself? Just take the following quick lesson before your first attempt—

• First, measure the distance across the front (face) of the installed rod or across where you want the rod installed. This measurement is called the drapery width and is always expressed first.

• Second, measure the distance from the top of the rod to one inch above the floor for floor-length draperies, or measure from the top of the rod to four inches below the window sill for apron-length draperies. This measurement is the drapery length and is always expressed second.

• Third, indicate whether the drapery is to be a panel (one-way draw opens from one side) or a pair (two-way draw opens from the middle).

Do not measure and include in your measurements either the rod projections (distance at each end between rod and wall) or the center overlap. Contract drapery shops make allowances for

ONE-WAY DRAW	
Window Opening	**Drapery Size**
5' x 6'8"	64" x 84"
6' x 6'8"	78" x 84"
8' x 6'8"	102" x 84"

TWO-WAY DRAW			
Window Opening	**Drapery Size**	**Window Opening**	**Drapery Size**
3' x 3'	42" x 44"	6' x 6'8"	78" x 84"
4' x 3'	52" x 44"	8' x 3'	102" x 44"
4' x 4'	52" x 56"	8' x 4'	102" x 56"
4' x 6'8"	54" x 84"	8' x 5'	102" x 68"
5' x 4'	64" x 56"	8' x 6'8"	102" x 84"
6' x 3'	78" x 44"	10' x 4'	126" x 56"
6' x 4'	78" x 56"	10' x 6'8"	126" x 84"
6' x 5'	78" x 68"		

them.

Do not measure an old drapery's exact dimensions and submit them for duplication. Drapery sizes, odd as it may seem, are not actual drapery measurements.

Do not add any height above the top of the rod up to a point where you think the drapery will extend.

Do not be afraid to ask whether this is the measurement method used by your drapery supplier. Whereas contract drapery suppliers do use this method, suppliers who deal with the general public may use another. To find a contract drapery supplier, search the internet using "wholesale draperies" as your search words. Yes, wholesalers will sell to you. They will likely even set you up with a charge account. (See SOURCES & RESOURCES for information on one contract drapery supplier which sells nationwide.)

If there's no drapery rod in place and you have to install one, install it so you can take advantage of the standard sizes which contract drapery shops keep in stock. Standard sizes will cost you much less and will not require you to wait those precious days while custom draperies are being manufactured to your specifications, something that is especially important when you have just finished redecorating a dwelling, have advertised it for rent, and then you learn that the draperies won't be ready for another two weeks. The bedsheets, old draperies, bedspreads, or drop cloths you'll then have to put on the windows will detract noticeably from that rental's appearance during the very time when you want it to look its best.

Shown here in two tables are the standard contract sizes (width x length), together with the common window openings they fit.

As you can calculate from these tables, the ends of the rod should normally extend three inches on either side of the window opening, and the top of the rod should be three and a half inches above the window opening. Such a rod installation will be firmly anchored in the wood of the window framing. If, because of an odd-sized window opening, you have to fudge a little to create a standard size, by all means, fudge.

Likewise, if there is a drapery rod already installed and it isn't exactly standard in length, don't despair. You can usually fit a drapery size which is an inch too big or too small without having to move the brackets. If a standard-size drapery simply cannot be fitted to your existing rod installation, move the rod brackets in or out so the standard size will fit, and use anchors as necessary.

Stay with standard sizes whenever you can.

Should You Carpet Those Floors?

Understand, first of all, that there is no such thing as a perfect floor covering for the living rooms and bedrooms in rental dwellings. Each has its disadvantages, but there is one floor covering which has fewer disadvantages and more advantages for most rentals than any other floor covering you might consider, and that one is wall-to-wall carpeting.

Besides the other attributes it has, carpeting adds tremendously to the soundproofing and income of any rental, and I can testify that it adds to the warmth and rentability as well.

After working full-time for two weeks on one apartment, installing a new kitchen counter, sink, built-in oven, and vanity, and then painting the walls and doors throughout, I thought I'd really made great changes to the place, but all that work was nothing compared to the change that the carpet installer made in only three hours.

Wowee! That apartment was transformed from stark, cold, colorless housing with bland asphalt tile on all its floors into an inviting, warm, cheerful place which someone would delight in calling home, and a "someone" did rent it promptly for a substantial sum. No wonder tenants prefer wall-to-wall carpeting and will pay more for it!

Before you buy any carpeting, think about a few important considerations to determine whether you ought to make the investment.

Consider roughly how much the carpeting will cost (draw and measure the floorplan, determine the yardage required, and multiply that by a telephone quote); consider how much additional rent you can expect to get if you add carpets (make a brief marketing survey); consider how much your income property will increase in value if you add carpets (use prevailing rules of thumb for determining the market value of income property and see whether the addition of carpets will more than offset the cost); and consider whether the condition of the present floors warrants either adding carpets or recarpeting (look them over carefully).

After you have considered those investment questions and have decided to go ahead with the carpeting, you'll still have decisions to make about areas, colors, patterns, piles, yarns, pads, prices, suppliers, and installers. Read on for some help in making these decisions.

■ **Areas**—Since one of your major concerns is the overall expense, you might save by carpeting only a portion of a unit, perhaps just a living room, because it will cost only a fraction of a "full-house" carpet installation and yet you may still tout "wall-to-wall carpet" to prospective tenants. Another possibility for savings involves laying durable sheet goods (linoleum, tile, or vinyl) by entrances (usually in a three- or four-foot square) and in hallways where traffic is heavy and the car-

pet tends to wear and spot quickly. You won't notice any savings by doing this right away, but you will in time because you won't have to replace an entire room full of carpeting to eliminate the eyesore of small worn areas.

■ **Colors**—Carpets come in all the colors God made and in some which only man could concoct, many of which you can summarily reject for rental units. No matter what color you choose, you'll manage to choose one that clashes with some tenant's taste, so don't worry too much about it. In general, avoid light and bright colors and choose those which are relatively neutral. Medium shades of gold and brown are the most neutral, but some greens and blues work well, too. Darker colors naturally show less dirt and fewer spots, while lighter colors are more cheerful and make rooms look larger. Select darker colors for rentals where you can expect kids, pets, and less responsible tenants, and use lighter colors in dwellings where you can expect sun fading and more responsible tenants.

■ **Patterns**—There may be some doubt about what carpet color is best for rental properties, but there's no doubt about what pattern of carpet is best for most rental units. Tweed is. Dirt, stains, wear areas, crumbs, toenail clippings, ashes, swatted flies, and swift cockroaches just don't show up as much on a tweed background. They blend right into its randomness. Try it.

■ **Piles**—People have "piles" and so do carpets. Carpet "pile" refers to the shape of the yarn. While the most durable carpet pile you can buy is level-loop, the most camouflaging is short shag (3/4" yarn), sometimes called "cabled plush." Both are good for use in rentals. Short shag in solid colors, and especially in tweeds, will camouflage anything that tweeds will by themselves, and what's more, it will camouflage cigarette burns as well, but it shows traffic wear more than level-loops do. A 20-ounce (face weight measures the weight of the yarn in one square yard and determines, more than any other single factor, a carpet's price) level-loop will actually outwear a 50-ounce shag. Use shag in living rooms and bedrooms which have a moderate amount of traffic and avoid using it in heavy traffic areas like hallways. Those are best covered with sheet goods in shag installations (avoid mixing carpet piles and colors within a single dwelling; it looks tacky). Because they are so tightly woven, level-loop carpets wear well and may be installed in heavy traffic areas, but they will definitely show burns. If traffic wear is your primary concern, then choose either level-loop carpeting by itself or short shag combined with sheet goods. If burns are your primary concern, choose short shag.

■ **Pads**—Remember that the pad you select is every bit as important as the carpet itself because the pad is what gives carpeting that luxurious, substantial feeling underfoot and at the same time extends a carpet's life. Use a half-inch rebonded polyurethane pad or else a polymeric pad. Avoid jute, rubber, and light polyurethane pads. Rebonded and polymeric pads are in the lower, not the lowest, price range and are well worth the money. They will last through several changes of carpet.

■ **Prices**—Don't buy expensive carpet for rentals, no matter how much more wear the salesperson says you'll get from it. It will look just as shabby as any inexpensive carpet after tenants have used and abused it for five years. When combined with a good pad, nylon carpeting which sells in the lowest third of the price range will give at least as good service as expensive carpeting.

■ **Suppliers**—Carpet sales is a very competitive business, and you can take advantage of this competition by shopping around for the best deal. You'll find that prices vary, not by a little but by a lot. When you shop, check prices at the retail carpet dealers, the contract carpet companies, and the big-box hardware stores.

Although retail dealers generally operate on a 40-60% markup (depending upon their advertising expenses and sales volume) when they're selling to homeowners, they may cut that markup in half when they know they're selling to a contractor or a landlord because they think of contractors and landlords as repeat customers. To get the best deal, identify yourself as a landlord to the salesperson and say that you're looking to buy carpet for a rental property.

Contract carpet companies generally operate on a 20-25% markup and sell primarily to high-volume buyers. To them, you as a landlord are a high-volume buyer. They will give you especially good deals when you structure a "clean deal" for them, that is, when you take your own measurements (saves them a trip), tell them exactly what you want when you examine what they have in stock (saves them time), buy their remnants and excess stock (saves them storage costs), pay cash on the barrelhead (saves them billing hassles and carrying charges), and have the carpet installed by "your own installer" (saves them employee hassles on the one part of their business where they make little or nothing). Offer them a clean deal, and you'll see how flexible they can be on price.

The big-box hardware stores like Lowe's and Home Depot carry carpet. They don't divulge their merchandise markups, but you know that it's low because they buy in such enormous quantities from the carpet mills. Their buying power is reflected in the prices they charge for the carpets they carry in stock, and that's the very carpet you should be considering for your rental property. Price it when you're shopping for carpet and compare it to what you find elsewhere.

Carpet mills offer their wares directly to landlords, too, at what appear to be bedrock-bottom prices. Before yielding to the temptation of these low prices, consider a number of factors and ask yourself why building contractors who buy a whole lot more yardage that you ever will, do not deal directly with the mills themselves.

First, there's the time problem. You have to plan your carpet purchases long in advance because there's going to be a time lag of a month or more between when you place your order and when you receive it. Second, there's the delivery problem. Mills ship via common carrier, and either you pick up the goods on their dock or you'll have to set aside a large block of time when the common carrier's local delivery truck will try to get it to you. Third, there's the off-loading problem. Carpet rolls are big and heavy, real big and real heavy. You need to have a "rhino" forklift available to handle one, to get it off the truck and move it to a convenient location. Handling it is like trying to park a Boeing 747 in your garage. It ain't easy. Fourth, there's the storage problem. Do you have the storage space needed to store full carpet rolls? If so, do you want to devote that storage space to carpet rather than renting the space out to somebody else? Fifth, there's the payment problem. Some mills require payment up-front prior to shipment. Are you ready to pay for something long in advance of when you'll be able to use it? Sixth, there's the quantity problem. When you buy from a mill, you'll have a *whole roll* of the same kind of carpet on your hands. You won't have any flexibility if it turns out to be unsatisfactory. And seventh, there's the problem of quality. Defects are an ever-present problem with new carpets. How are you going to handle them when you're dealing with a distant mill?

Get the idea?

Buying carpet directly from a mill is too much like starting another business. It creates more problems than it solves without really saving that much money. When you consider all the problems it creates, you'll likely conclude that you're better off dealing with a local supplier.

■ **Installation**—Hire your own carpet installer rather than use whoever happens to be working for your carpet supplier. You'll get better prices for the carpet alone, and you'll get consistently better installations once you identify a good installer. Many installers moonlight, and you should be able to find a good one through "services offered" classified ads or on craigslist.org under "services, carpet installer," one who will install your carpet for less than the price of the so-called "free installation" included in a package deal.

Be sure you understand who's paying for the tackless strip and the metal threshold pieces. Some installers will quote you a price per square foot which includes these items, and others will charge you for them separately later.

If you're a real diehard do-it-yourselfer, you might want to learn how to install carpet yourself by reading some instructions on the subject and then working alongside an installer on a job. It's not rocket science. Moreover, the installations you're likely to encounter in rental properties tend to be the simpler ones, and the specialized equipment you need for the work is readily available for only a small capital outlay.

Be sure you understand that installing carpet yourself puts heavy physical demands on your back and knees. You'll be lifting and dragging heavy materials. You'll be crawling around on your knees, and you'll be kicking with your knees. Protect your back and knees with proper safety and prophylactic devices.

My advice on carpet installation is this—Learn enough so that you can do the work yourself in a pinch and so that you can make repairs. Leave the big jobs and the complex jobs to the professionals. They're better conditioned to do the work.

■ **Measurements**—Take the time to measure the areas you want carpeted yourself, and learn from your carpet supplier how to translate those measurements into yardage which minimizes waste. Avoid having an installer measure for you because installers love seamless installations. They charge by the yard, not by the hour, and prefer the easiest possible installation. They don't care about waste. You're paying for that waste. They're not. If you do have an installer take measurements, ask him to show you the cuts and justify his yardage figures.

■ **Squeaks**—Before you have anyone install carpeting for you, tread splayfooted, like Charlie Chaplin playing "The Little Tramp," over every square foot of the installation area to find all the squeaks that have developed over the years by a loosening of the nails in the subflooring. Then nail the squeaks out with 2 1/2" cement-coated screw or ring nails placed strategically alongside the squeaky culprits.

Squeaky floors annoy tenants upstairs and downstairs and detract from the image of your building. Eliminate them.

Some Last Words

Hamlet, that prince of Denmark, would have made a terrible landlord. He talked too much and he couldn't make decisions. The decisions in this chapter alone would have taken him an entire stage play just to contemplate. By then, his tenants would have either left in disgust, fallen fast asleep, or taken over. You can do better. You must.

Sure, the questions in this chapter themselves are mundane—To allow pets or not to allow pets? To carpet or not to carpet? These questions are not nearly as grand or as poetic as Hamlet's "To be or not to be?" Are they? Nobody's going to write a play about real-world landlording decisions and the disturbing perplexity you go through whenever you make them, but you'll stay in this business a long, long time, and you'll prosper in it, too, so long as you can make prompt and mostly correct decisions about what will work and what won't.

Take enough time to think over the implications of your decisions, make up your mind, and then act. Sometimes you'll be right and sometimes you'll be wrong. When you're right, congratulate yourself. When you're wrong, don't chide yourself. Learn from your mistake, and make the right decision next time.

14
Hiring Help

Having decided to hire help to assist you in your landlording business (see "Should You Do It Yourself?" in chapter 13), you become a boss perhaps for the first time in your life.

Suffer no great trepidation over this new role. Simply prepare for it. You survived being called "landlord" didn't you? Surely you will survive being called "boss."

The truth is that as a landlord who hires help, you are more than just a boss supervising people. You're the personnel, accounting, payroll, legal, and administrative departments of your business all rolled into one. Sounds impressive and also a little forbidding, doesn't it? Don't worry. If you have shown yourself to be a competent landlord, you'll be a competent employer as well. It takes only some common sense, some understanding of people, and some acquaintance with certain applicable laws, practices, procedures, and forms.

These next few pages are not meant to tell you all you need to know about hiring help. That is an enormous subject in itself, and there are entire books devoted to it alone. The information provided here is intended merely to get you started in the right direction and keep you out of trouble as you face a number of responsibilities and tasks which are altogether different from the usual ones involved in do-it-yourself landlording and probably altogether different from your normal workaday world, too, unless you already happen to be self-employed and have people working for you.

You'll notice that the information in this chapter pertains more to on-site property managers than it does to the other workers you might hire. On-site property management work is different from most other work in a number of ways. It's different because it generally necessitates residency on the premises. There's both work and housing involved. It's different because on-site property managers do not work under direct supervision. There's nobody around to tell them what to do most of the time. It's also different because on-site managers need to be willing and able to work whenever the need arises. There's no telling when a drain line might plug or some tenants might drink too much and start a noisy fight, and the on-site manager has to be called into action.

As a consequence, the hiring process needs to be more thorough. You need to know more about the people you're considering for on-site property management before you hire them. You need to know whether they'd make good tenants *and* good workers. You need to know whether they have the awareness to see what needs to be done, the discipline needed to get things done whenever they need to be done, and the honesty not to steal from you when they have the opportunity.

If you're hiring other workers, that is, workers who are under your direct supervision and who are not required to live on the premises, you may still follow the procedures outlined here for hiring on-site managers. Merely modify them as necessary.

Settling the Independent Contractor-Employee Question

You have undoubtedly hired help in the past without even thinking much about it. You were hiring help when you hired a roofer to repair a leaky roof, just as you were when you called a plumber to install a new commode, but that was contractual hiring rather than employee hiring. In other words, those who did the work were not your employees. They were performing services for you while being either self-employed or employed by somebody else. You agreed to pay them a flat fee or an hourly rate, and they gave you a bill for their work. You may have blanched at their bill, but you had no hidden costs, no obligatory reports due to governmental agencies, no increased insurance burden, and no extra bookkeeping chores, all of which you would have had if the roofer or plumber had been your employee.

Because of the benefits inherent in contractual employment and because contractual employees can be expected to do good work without requiring much supervision, many landlords prefer to hire only bonded contractual help, that is, commercial gardeners, window washers, artisan house painters, professional electricians, plumbing contractors, carpet cleaning services, and the like. These landlords may pay more, but they avoid the hassles of being an employer. Besides, independent contractors generally get the work done well and quickly.

Some landlords have tried to avoid the legal obligations and paperwork involved in being employers in another way, by drawing up contracts for those they employ on a regular basis and calling these employees "independent contractors."

Years ago this stratagem worked, but it doesn't work anymore, not since the government discovered that most so-called independent contractors had joined the underground economy. They weren't reporting any income, and naturally, because they weren't reporting any income, they weren't paying any income taxes. More than anything else, this increasingly widespread evasion of taxes by workers who were being paid their full wages without any deductions being taken out, prompted a government crackdown on would-be independent contractors. Our government doesn't like to be cheated out of taxes any more than Mother Nature likes to be fooled.

You may *avoid* paying taxes as we landlords do when we take advantage of the depreciation provisions in the tax law and also when we exchange properties to avoid paying capital gains tax, but you may not *evade* paying taxes as some people do when they fail to report income.

Tax evasion is enough to get the government mad at you. It's enough to get the IRS involved in your life on a familiar, first-name basis. It's enough to get you a prison cell for a home.

As employers, we don't particularly care whether the workers we hire pay their income taxes or not. That's as much our concern as whether they say grace at the dinner table. We have other concerns when we hire people to work for us. Still, we cannot afford to overlook the government's distinction between "employee" and "independent contractor" unless we want to risk paying some punitive penalties ourselves.

When you hire an employee, don't try to convert that person into an independent contractor unless he undeniably is one. It's not worth the worry, nor is it worth the potential trouble. Bite the bullet. Yes, you are saddled with the same burdens as any other employer. Yes, you do become an income tax collector for the government, and yes, you do pay a premium for the privilege. Do it, whether you like it or not. It comes with the territory.

If you're ever wondering whether someone you hire is an employee or an independent contractor, you may apply some simple tests. Here's the primary one. If you control both *what* work is to be done and *how* it is to be done, then the person doing the work is your employee and not an independent contractor.

Other tests to determine whether workers are independent contractors are these—

- Do the workers have a business license or a contractor's license?
- Do they pay their own deductions including self- employment tax?
- Do they assume legal liability for their work?
- Do they come and go whenever they want?
- Do they qualify as specialists who work without your having to supervise them?
- Do they have a verbal or a written contract for the work being performed?
- Do they carry appropriate insurance?
- Do they provide their own tools, equipment, and materials?
- Do they work for other people?
- Do they advertise their services?
- Do they realize a profit or a loss as a result of their services?
- Do they have business cards and stationery?
- Do they bill for their work?

If the answers to these questions are mostly, if not entirely, affirmative, the workers are independent contractors, and your only responsibility is to pay them whatever they charge you for the work that you hire them to do. If not, you *must* consider them your employees, no matter what name you give them and no matter how carefully you draft a self-serving contract which both of you sign.

Whether you like it or not, the government has ruled time and time again, "An employee by any other name is still an employee."

Should someone you hire legitimately as an independent contractor turn out, unbeknownst to you, to be using the independent contractor status to evade paying taxes, you may be penalized for not having paid the employer's share of taxes for this "employee." To protect yourself from this possibility, give him an IRS 1099-MISC form (if you paid him more than $600) at the end of the calendar year. On it, give his name, his Social Security Number (SSN) or his Federal Employer Identification Number (FEIN) and how much you paid him.

Do not hire anybody to work for you in any capacity and for any length of time without first securing either a Social Security Number or a Federal Employer Identification Number so that you have the information you need to complete an IRS form if you must.

Should you ever compel an employee to be an independent contractor in order to avoid the added employer expenses and responsibilities, make no mistake. You are exposing yourself to dire consequences, especially if that worker is injured on the job or wants to begin claiming unemployment or Social Security benefits after having worked for you.

Keep in mind that on-site property managers, the helpers you are most likely to hire, are *always* considered employees no matter what ruse you use to metamorphose them into independent contractors. Therefore, you might as well resign yourself to having an extra paperwork and expense burden whenever you hire a manager.

You may get away without assuming this burden if you discount a tenant's rent a few dollars for doing yard maintenance around an apartment house or if you pay a few dollars every month to a resident who acts in your stead as, say, rent collector and resident keeper of the keys, but even then you should secure both workers' compensation and non-owned automobile insurance to protect yourself should an accident occur.

The potential liability for not having this minimal insurance when you hire help is too draconian for you to bear all by yourself. If your yard maintenance worker were to put his eye out quite by accident, you would have to pay all the medical bills and compensate him for his pain and suffering out of your own pocket. If you had workers' compensation coverage, it would pay everything. If not, you'd learn something about pain and suffering yourself. If your manager were to injure someone in a crosswalk while driving to the bank to deposit the rent money, you would be held partly responsible because the manager was on an errand for you. If you had non-owned automobile insurance, it would take care of the matter. If not, you might as well sign over your properties to the injured party.

As an employer, you assume a variety of attendant responsibilities, responsibilities which add approximately 30% to the actual wages you pay your employees, a heavy burden indeed. In other words, an employee whom you pay $10 an hour will really cost you $13.

It's no wonder, then, that landlords try to interpret certain work relationships as contractual, and it's no wonder that the government has pursued the matter doggedly to recover taxes and to protect the welfare of employees.

As for doing the burdensome paperwork involved in hiring employees, that will depend pretty much on whether you are hiring casual helpers or regular helpers and on how much money they're earning over a given period of time. If you wonder whether you ought to be doing the paperwork, call the state and federal agencies involved with collecting taxes on wages and ask them. Be frank with them and you'll stay out of trouble.

Another good source of information for would-be employers with questions about their status is the IRS website (irs.gov). Its small business section has everything from a checklist for starting a business to a virtual small business tax workshop with lessons such as "How to set up and run your business so paying taxes isn't a hassle" and "What you need to know when you run your business out of your home." The website also lists the small business tax workshops conducted regularly in every state.

Complying with Employment Laws

As an employer, you must comply with the many laws designed first to protect employees from exploitation by their employers and second to employ countless bureaucratic minions. To find out what these laws are and how they apply to you, contact your state department of employment directly. Tell them that you want to receive whatever materials they have which relate specifically to rental property management. They will supply you with the proper instructions, numbers, tables, timetables, and forms necessary for compliance.

One of the most important numbers you need to know as an employer is the minimum wage. It's more than a benchmark of wages. It's the bottom line of wages. You must pay your employees at least that amount or you're breaking the law. In some areas, the federal minimum wage is what you must pay. In other areas, the state minimum wage is what you must pay because it's higher than the federal minimum wage. In still other areas, the county or city minimum wage is what you must pay. Whichever one is the highest is what you must pay at the very least.

Because rental property management work involves odd hours and sometimes long hours, what you decide to pay a manager may not comply with the applicable minimum wage standards. Should disgruntled former managers challenge you for having compensated them with something less than their entitlements, you may be forced to pay back wages and fines, that is, unless you can produce time sheets to prove that you did pay the minimum wage or more. The burden of proof is on you as the employer.

Keeping time sheets is a chore for your managers and for you. There's no doubt about that, but those time sheets will help to keep you from running afoul of labor laws and losing a challenge over your having cheated an employee.

By the way, if you have several employees working out of one property, buy a time clock and require your employees to clock in and out so you can better verify their work hours if there's ever a dispute and you have to prove to a labor board deputy that an employee's overtime claim is fallacious. Time sheets, especially when they show the same arrival and departure times every day, may not be enough to prove that the recorded hours were the actual hours worked because the employee might say that he was coerced into recording those times and that they weren't factual, whereas a time card stamped with many different arrival times would be undeniable proof of the employee's working hours.

As for the full-time manager who earns a princely salary at or above a certain figure, you needn't bother with time sheets or time cards. That manager is exempt from the laws governing minimum hourly wages and overtime. Ask your state's department of employment for the current figure. It changes.

Setting the Pay and Defining the Job

Whenever people consider taking a job, they always have at least two questions in mind. "What's the pay?" and "What's required of me?" You should be prepared to answer both of those questions and others before you ever begin looking for help, casual or permanent, full- or part-time.

As for compensation, some landlords pay their managers a flat rate per unit per month, say, $20, and some pay a percentage of the rent collected, say, 5%, but neither of these methods for determining managerial compensation is fair to both landlord and manager because neither one reflects the actual time required to perform the tasks involved.

I know some properties where $20 per unit per month would be a windfall for the manager because the properties practically run themselves. I know others with the same number of units where it would be a pittance because there's always something for the manager to do.

Consider, for example, the difference between managing a complex occupied mostly by retirees and managing another complex occupied mostly by working families who average 1.8 children apiece. The manager of the one complex may do little more than police a cement courtyard, water a few potted plants, and write rent receipts, while the manager of the other complex may have more to do than the "old woman who lived in a shoe."

Neither a flat rate nor a percentage of the gross is fair compensation for managers.

Another, much fairer method of compensation involves paying for the work you can expect the manager to do at the property. The job might include as little as collecting rents when due, showing vacancies, and keeping the keys, or it might include all that plus pursuing late payers, checking applications, selecting tenants, banking, keeping records, doing minor maintenance and repairs, caring for the pool, cleaning, gardening, mowing the lawns, painting, and handling tenant complaints.

List the tasks you expect your managers to

perform and try to establish the amount of time you think they should be spending on those tasks during an average month. Collecting rents when due, you might figure, would average ten minutes per dwelling per month, and so on. Set the pay by multiplying an hourly rate, pegged somewhat above the minimum wage, times the anticipated number of hours you expect the managers to work. Guarantee to pay them a certain amount every month but require them to keep track of the time they spend on the job so you don't wind up underpaying them.

Review your time estimates after the managers have been on the job for a while to make sure that you haven't underestimated or overestimated the time involved.

Here are some suggestions about compensating those you hire—

✔ Inquire into local practices for compensating full- and part-time managers. Ask your rental housing association for some figures. If the association itself can't help you, its members can. Ask around.

✔ Never say that you are giving a manager "free rent." The correct expression is "rental compensation." Rent is "free" only if you are giving it away, expecting nothing in return, and if you are giving it away, you're a philanthropist, not a landlord.

✔ If you do compensate a manager by providing a residence, include the utilities only if there are no separate meters for the manager's residence. You cannot predict how much the manager's utilities will cost every month, and you wouldn't be encouraging energy conservation.

✔ If the manager's residence has no separate meters, do not estimate utility usage and charge predetermined sums for the utilities every month. That practice could get you into trouble with both the labor relations board and the public utilities commission.

✔ Pay your helpers after they have done their work, not before.

✔ Compensating part-time managers in the form of rent constitutes advance payment. Collect full rent from them every month, the same as you do from other tenants, and then pay them their wages at the end of the month. Otherwise, being human, they will tend to regard their discounted rent after a while as a birthright and not as a compensation for services.

✔ If you require managers to live on the premises in a certain unit, you should know that special tax rules apply to the portion of the managers' income attributable to the residence. There's a maximum limit as to how much you can reckon the residence is worth when you're calculating wages and trying to comply with minimum wage laws. Ask your state's department of employment for the current figure.

✔ Pay each member of a management team separately for the work each performs so that each of them will receive Social Security credits.

✔ Do not expect your employees to put forth a reasonable effort for unreasonable wages.

✔ Raise the manager's compensation every time you raise rents by the same percentage as the rent increase. Remember that the manager is on the front lines and has to take the flak whenever there's a rent increase. Give him an incentive to implement increases, maybe even to push for them.

✔ Do not give the manager so much to do that he cannot do it all adequately. If, in addition to everything else, you want your manager to paint and prepare every unit which becomes vacant, you may be saving a little money over hiring somebody else to do the work, but you may be losing a lot more money by keeping your available rentals off the market while the work is either being done or waiting to be done. Pitch in yourself or get some outside help to get those rentals ready to rent and back on the market as quickly as possible.

Establishing a Manager Profile

Recognizing that ignorant, wasteful, awkward, and careless maintenance workers and bigoted, caustic, timid, lecherous, hot-tempered, forgetful, disorganized, gossipy, and thin-skinned managers all will cost you time and money and good tenants, too, you should try to establish a profile of the ideal worker your job requires and then identify the categories of people who are most likely to fit that profile.

Managers for multiple-family dwellings, for example, should be fair, honest, reliable, used to dealing with people, intelligent, self-assured, unflappable, willing to learn, handy, helpful, thrifty, neat, clean, inquisitive, organized, modest, pleasant, and patient homebodies who can speak with an air of authority and who resemble the residents of the property they manage.

Who is most likely to fit a profile like that? Few humans I know of, but those with service-oriented backgrounds would be the most likely to fit it. Some owners go out of their way to hire school teachers as managers because teachers know how to think on their feet, are accustomed to keeping records, are used to dealing with people, are used to disciplining, have spare time during the afternoon and summer, are professional in their outlook, work without close supervision, and could use the extra money.

Some owners say that former farmers make good managers because they have good work skills and habits, are used to dealing with adversity, and tend to be honest and friendly. Other owners look for people who have any kind of a service-oriented background, such as nursing, sales, hair care, or janitorial work.

Chances are good that you'll have to compromise in your choice, so decide which of the managerial qualities already mentioned are most important for the job as you see it and which are the least important. Rank them.

While you're ranking them, don't overlook the last criterion, that the managers resemble the residents of the property they manage. It's more important than you might think. Hiring a young couple to manage a building occupied mostly by pensioners is courting trouble, just as hiring a pensioner to manage a student complex would be, or hiring a bigoted redneck to manage a black-ghetto property. Managers who resemble their tenants understand those tenants' unique problems and deal with them sensibly.

Finding Management Help

Whenever you're looking for management help, consider your existing tenants first. They already have a familiarity with the property and its occupants, and they are known to you, so you needn't be particularly apprehensive about their character. After all, you have already entrusted them with a dwelling worth $95,000, more or less, and they have not been found wanting. The chances are good that they will be equally as reliable when looking after more of the same if they have the basic managerial attributes.

Good tenants whom I have approached about becoming managers have invariably become good managers, even for as many as 113 units.

One good tenant I approached about managing an eightplex refused the job outright without offering any explanation. He simply said that he wasn't interested. I considered each of the seven other tenants for the job and decided against offering it to any of them. A week after he refused the job, I went back to this one tenant who seemed so right for the job and offered it to him again. This time I asked him why he refused the job before and asked whether he would reconsider. I learned then that he did want to look after the building all right, but that he didn't want tenants banging on his door at all hours. That was his biggest concern. We made a deal that he would be called the "caretaker" rather than the "manager" and that he would keep the keys, show the vacancies, and clean up around the building, but that tenants would send their rent payments to me directly and call me with their complaints. The arrangement worked beautifully for both of us for years, right up until I sold the property.

You might be surprised about the pool of talent that most residential income properties have, and you should not be averse to using it.

If you cannot identify one of your good tenants as a managerial candidate, advertise the position through Craigslist, the help-wanted classifieds, state employment offices, management schools' employment offices, agencies, or your rental housing association. You'll likely be besieged with applicants, for there seem to be many people who find the work agreeable.

Even though this kind of work typically doesn't pay much, it offers certain advantages which many people value—discounted housing, independence, autonomy, and a short commute.

Finding Maintenance and Repair Help

When you're looking around for maintenance and repair help, consider your tenants second on your list of prospects. Whom should you consider first? Your relatives and friends, of course. Haven't you ever heard of nepotism?

After eliminating your relatives and friends as prospects, look to your tenants for this kind of help, and only as a last resort should you have to advertise or call the local office of your state employment development department.

One good outside source too often overlooked

is the local retirement community, which might be a mobilehome park for seniors, an RV park for snowbirds, a HUD complex for low-income retirees, or even a ritzy housing development for well-to-do seniors who seem to play golf and tennis all day long. Post a notice on the community's bulletin board and see what happens.

The job might interest a healthy, skilled retiree looking for something to do, something that will make him feel useful.

Inheriting Managers

Just as you will usually inherit tenants when you acquire a multiple-family dwelling, you will also inherit managers, and you will be faced with the decision of whether to keep the old managers or find your own.

Unless there are obvious reasons to let the managers go right away, agree to keep them on for a month or two until you become familiar with the place and can make an informed decision whether to retain them on a permanent basis or let them go.

Whatever you do, don't rely solely upon the previous owner's recommendations. Those managers you're inheriting may have been duping the previous owner for years in one way or another while seeming to be the perfect managers, looking after everything and never bothering the owner with problems.

Be aware that this takeover period is the perfect time for dishonest managers to abscond with funds. They may have been using a scam which had gone undetected by the previous owner and fear that you as the new owner will find them out. So they will sometimes leave in a hurry and try to cover their tracks. Look carefully through the rental payment records of any property you acquire which already has managers. Ask plenty of questions until you understand precisely who owes what and when it is owed. If you have good reason to doubt the managers' honesty, let them go immediately.

If you decide to keep the managers, review their pay straightaway. Discuss with them the scope of the job. Calculate the time involved and determine what the job is worth to you as the new owner. You may find that, based on the actual workload, the previous owner was overpaying the managers and couldn't tell the difference because he had owned the property for such a long time free and clear and had an easily assured and gradually increasing cash flow. Consequently, he may have been reluctant to upset the situation by reviewing the managers' pay. If that's the case, you'll probably have to begin looking around for new managers. Few people will accept a decrease in pay while continuing to do the same work they've been doing all along.

On the other hand, you may find that the previous owner was underpaying the managers for the work they were doing. Even a small increase in pay may be incentive enough for them to work harder, prepare vacancies more quickly, and keep the property looking its best.

Inheriting a Property Management Company

When you acquire a building which has been managed for the previous owner by a property management company, you are under no obligation to continue using that company yourself. Even if the company has a long-term agreement to manage the property, the sale of the property nullifies the agreement. A management agreement is between an owner and a management company. It doesn't stay with the property.

Discuss the matter during the negotiations to acquire the property. Ask to see the property management agreement, and examine the termination clauses. One of them should state that the agreement terminates upon the sale of the property. If you cannot find such a clause, ask specifically about termination, and settle the matter with the seller before you take title to the property.

Prior to closing on the property, contact the property management company to advise them of your plans to keep or terminate them.

Terminating them means that you no longer wish to use their services as an off-site manager. It does not mean that you no longer wish to use the services of the on-site manager. You may terminate the property management company and still keep the on-site manager, that is, if the on-site manager is doing a good job and will work for you directly.

Discuss the matter with the on-site manager before you take title. The on-site manager may feel more of a commitment to the property management company than to the property or the new owner and may give notice if you terminate the property management company. Be prepared for that possibility.

Employment Application

>>APPLICANT<<
Name **EARL A. LACY** Home Phone **555-0222** Work Phone **555-2787**

Social Security No. **517-40-6535** Driver's License No. **2900123**

Present Address **333 DUTCH St., FUNSVILLE, NV** Own ___ Rent **✓** How long at this address? **1 YR.**

Present/Last Occupation **LABORER** Employer **UIC TECH** How long with this employer? **3 YRS.**

Reason for Leaving? **STILL EMPLOYED** Monthly Gross **1275** Name of Supervisor **JOHN TECH** May we contact? **Y** Phone **(200) 123-5500**

Previous Occupation **LABORER** Employer **SWIFT DELIVERY** How long with this employer? **1 YR.**

Reason for Leaving? **BETTER PAY** Monthly Gross **900** Name of Supervisor **Pete Swift** May we contact? **Y** Phone **(200) 333-5500**

How many years of schooling have you had? **12** Course of study **GENERAL** What languages do you speak fluently? **ENGLISH**

>>SPOUSE/PARTNER<<
Name **GLENDA LACY** Social Security No. **200-00-3000** Driver's License No. **Q375521**

Present/Last Occupation **CLERK** Employer **MM's Italian MARKET** How long with this employer? **5 YRS**

Reason for Leaving? **STILL EMPLOYED** Monthly Gross **1126** Name of Supervisor **DARIO Miglia** May we contact? **Y** Phone **(200) 345-1111**

Previous Occupation **NONE** Employer **NA** How long with this employer? **NA**

Reason for Leaving? **NA** Monthly Gross **NA** Name of Supervisor **NA** May we contact? **NA** Phone **NA**

How many years of schooling has spouse/partner had? **12** Course of study **GENERAL** What languages does spouse/partner speak fluently? **ENGLISH, SPANISH**

>>APPLICANT AND SPOUSE/PARTNER<<
What are your skills related to this job? **Plumbing, some electrical, bookkeeping**

What experience have you and your spouse/partner had related to this job? **our jobs and managing APT. House**

What tools do you and your spouse/partner have which might be useful on this job? **Electrical DRILL, SAW, hand tools**

What transportation do you and your spouse/partner have which might be useful on this job? **small PICKUP**

How many dependents do you and your spouse/partner have? **0** What do you and your spouse/partner receive monthly from pensions, alimony, etc.? **0**

What health insurance do you have? **BLUE CROSS** What do you and your spouse/partner pay monthly for debts, alimony, child support, etc.? **900.**

Are you and your spouse/partner bondable? **YES** Previous bonding? **NONE**

Savings or Checking Account Bank Name **COMFORT SAVINGS** Branch **MAIN** Account Number **0011-11-9910**

Credit Reference **SEARS** Account Number **5-500018910** Balance Owed **635** Monthly Payment **72**

Personal Reference **GEORGE JUDGE** Address **1 JAMES Rd., Bath, NV** Phone **(200) 123-5432**

Personal Reference **BRIAN NUNN** Address **77 Nuke Ct. Bath, NV** Phone **200) 123-6541**

Contact in Emergency **DAN ROBINSON** Address **207 BOXER AV, CIRCLE, NV** Phone **200) 223-6114**

Have you ever been convicted of a felony or serious misdemeanor? **NO** Will you take a drug test? **YES** When are you available for this job? **NOW**

I/we declare that the information above is true and correct, and I/we hereby authorize verification of this information and a thorough background check.

Date **5-7-XX** Signed **Earl A. Lacy**

Prequalifying

If you are considering relatives, friends, or acquaintances for a job, you have already prequalified them in your mind before you ever approach them about it, but if perfect strangers are inquiring about a job, you should take a little time to prequalify them first before going ahead with an interview. Otherwise, you'll be wasting their time and yours. At a minimum, each interview takes half an hour, so interviewing ten people will easily take a full day. That's much too much time. Unless you genuinely enjoy conducting interviews and have the time to spend doing it, there's no reason for you to spend that much time at it. Shortcut the procedure by selecting two or three prime candidates to interview.

To select them, prequalify all the respondents by requesting written resumes. Read the resumes carefully and try to imagine each of these people working for you in the job you have available. Call only the ones who appear to be the most promising. If the position involves resident management, ask them the same questions you'd ask to prequalify tenant applicants. Then ask them the same questions you'd ask of any employee applicant, questions about their experience, salary requirements, and availability. If they appear worth pursuing, set up an interview. If not, tell them you'll "get back to them" and do.

Interviewing

Arrange employment interviews at the property itself preferably. Make note of anything which might provide clues as to the people's suitability for the job. Try to determine whether they "have a drinking problem" and whether they smoke. You don't want to hire a smoker if you've been strict about keeping the building smoke-free. Note especially their promptness, overall appearance, bearing, habits, cellphone dependency, sense of humor, body odor, speech, smile, fingernails, and hands.

Outline the job first, including its responsibilities, its advantages, and its drawbacks. Tell applicants whether their living in a particular dwelling is a prerequisite for the position. Explain what the compensation is and when it's paid. Tell them whether there are raises which might be expected after a trial period, and so on.

Ask them whether the job appears attractive to them and whether they feel themselves capable of handling it. If so, proceed to ask them ques-

tions using the Employment Application as a guide, and transcribe the information yourself so you can measure their responses and let them talk freely.

In addition to the questions on the application, you might want to ask such questions as how they feel about living in close proximity to people as managers and not being able to be good friends with anybody, how they would describe themselves to a stranger, what accomplishments they are most proud of, whether they own any real property, whether they know anything about the laws governing the rental housing business, what computer software they know how to use, and why they feel they should be considered for the job.

Tell them that you are going to conduct a thorough background check, and ask whether they know of anything unflattering which might turn up in the check that they'd like to explain now. Establish good eye contact with them during the interview. Be friendly, attentive, and helpful, and encourage them to talk frankly about themselves while you take notes.

When you finish the interview, take a few minutes to show them around the property. Then make a promise to contact them within the next couple of days to inform them of your decision. Letting them know of your decision as soon as possible is only fair. Selected or not, they need to be making plans for themselves, not waiting around for you to let them know whether they got the job.

Selecting

After interviewing the applicants, you'll know whom you want to pursue further. Call the employer references directly and verify the information you have on the applicants. Ask about the circumstances surrounding their departure if they have left their previous job already, and ask quite frankly whether the employer would consider hiring them again.

Give little credence to letters of recommendation which thicken applicants' resumes. Anyone writing such a letter knows that the subject of the recommendation will see it, so it won't include anything negative. To learn what a former employer really thinks about an employee, call and ask direct questions.

After calling the employers, run a background check on the applicants, and also find out what

Management Agreement

Dated **April 20, XXXX**

Agreement between **Duke and Lady Milquetoast**, Owner, and **Earl and Glenda Lacy**, Manager, for management and maintenance of property located at **2100 Main St· Bigtown**.

Compensation for Manager shall be in the form of a lodging credit and cash payments. The lodging credit shall be $ **550·—** per **MONTH** (must not exceed credit allowed by state law). The combined rate of compensation shall equal $ **7—** per hour (must equal or exceed minimum wage). Owner may adjust the lodging credit and hourly rate upon notice to Manager.

In spite of rental property management's irregular and variable hours, Manager is responsible for planning and carrying out assigned duties so as to work no more than eight hours per day and forty hours per week. Overtime hours will be compensated provided that Manager obtains Owner's permission in advance or, in case of an emergency, provided that Owner is notified within 48 hours afterwards. Manager shall take a ten-minute break for every four hours of work and take an unpaid meal break of at least thirty minutes after every five hours of work. Manager shall record working hours on timesheets provided, one timesheet for each person, and shall submit signed timesheets at the close of each pay period to certify that the hours recorded were actually worked and that no unrecorded hours were worked. Paydays will be **Monthly, by the fifth of the month**

Other compensation shall be as follows: **hourly pay for additional tasks.**
Manager shall have days off as follows: **TUESDAYS AND WEDNESDAY**
Manager shall have vacation time as follows: **one day per month (accumulating)**
Manager shall have sick leave as follows: **one day per month (accumulating)**
Manager's duties and responsibilities shall be as follows: **clean grounds; keeps keys; collects rents; show vacancies; handle minor maintenance .**
(Either party to this Agreement may request a review of compensation, days off, vacation, sick leave, duties, responsibilities, etc. Any changes superseding the Agreement must be in writing and must be signed by all parties.)

Manager shall receipt all monies collected on the Owner's behalf and shall deposit or transfer them within **two days** of collection as follows: **Call OWNERS to report collections; make DEPOSITS to "MILQUETOAST PROPERTIES"**
Manager shall spend, or commit to spend, no more than $ **100—** on the Owner's behalf without first obtaining permission.

Manager agrees to reside on the premises of the property as an employee and not as a tenant. Manager is an at-will employee who may be terminated at any time. Either Manager or Owner may terminate this Agreement upon **SEVEN DAYS** written notice. Immediately upon termination, Manager shall surrender all keys, records, supplies, equipment, and other items related to the position and shall vacate whatever lodging Owner supplies as a condition of employment. In no event shall Manager vacate later than 72 hours following termination.

(THIS PARAGRAPH APPLIES ONLY IF INITIALED BY BOTH PARTIES. Initials: Owner **DM** ; Manager **EL GL** .) Manager and Owner agree to submit all disputes that cannot be resolved between them, except failure to vacate, to arbitration. The party seeking to arbitrate a dispute shall begin arbitration by serving a written demand to arbitrate on the other party and on the Judicial Arbitration and Mediation Services (JAMS). Arbitration costs shall be shared equally by both parties, and the costs shall be estimated in advance.

Any item in this Agreement found to be illegal, invalid, or unenforceable shall be considered null and void, and it shall not affect the validity of any other item in the Agreement.

As written, this Agreement constitutes the entire agreement between Owner and Manager. They have made no further promises of any kind to one another, nor have they reached any other understandings, either verbal or written.

Manager hereby acknowledges that he/she has read this Agreement, understands it, agrees to it voluntarily, and has been given a copy.

Owner **Duke Milquetoast**   Manager **Earl A. Lacey**

By _____   Manager **Glenda Lacy**

you can about their driving records through either your insurance company or your state's department of motor vehicles. Then, if everything appears satisfactory and you are still interested in hiring them, make an appointment to talk with them where they currently reside.

When you see where they live and how they live, you will be able to decide whether to hire them or not. If you don't like what you see, tell them you have other applicants to visit before you make your decision, and then leave. If you do like what you see, show them a blank copy of your Management Agreement and review it with them. Be certain they understand the provision in the agreement which calls for them to submit their hours of work regularly. If the job means that they will be moving into a manager's dwelling, show them a copy of the Rental Agreement and review it. Then complete both agreements, making sure that you state in the Rental Agreement that their occupancy is dependent upon their management job.

Once you have made your decision, don't continue keeping the unsuccessful applicants in limbo. Call or email them, whichever you prefer. Thank them for their interest and wish them good luck in finding an even better job.

Assessing Performance More Objectively

Because the whole process of hiring an employee is somewhat subjective, you may want to consider including a slightly more objective step in the whole process. You can, you know. Available to you as well as to large employers are assessments specifically designed to assist in employee selection.

Pre-employment assessments fell out of favor during the civil rights era because some thought the questions were racially discriminatory. Perhaps some questions back then were discriminatory. I don't know. I do know that the psychologists who create these assessments today go to great lengths to eliminate racial and cultural biases. I also know that university studies have shown that a pre-employment assessment is far and away the best predictor of success in employment. It's even better than the next best predictor, a tryout on the job.

Pre-employment assessments are not tests. They're questionnaires, and there are no right or wrong answers to the questions. The answers help to shape a personal profile which enables you to compare your applicant's profile with the profiles of others who have been successful in that particular line of work.

Now, you wouldn't think too seriously of going to all the trouble of giving one of these assessments to the applicants you're interviewing to manage a fourplex, but when you're looking for somebody to manage thirty or more units, you have a lot more to lose if you mistakenly hire inept managers. A pre-employment assessment might help you make the right decision.

There are many sources of pre-employment assessments available to you as an employer. Resource Associates (resourceassociates.com) is a good example. It has assessments for specific jobs, one of which is property management. Their assessment measures general personality dimensions, managerial dimensions, cognitive aptitude, and values.

The applicant spends approximately two hours taking the assessment online. As soon as the applicant finishes the assessment and submits it online, the employer receives an email with the results in the form of an interpretive report. The report includes a graphical display of the scores, a narrative interpretation of the cognitive aptitude scores, a display of the open-ended responses, an explanation of the applicant's strengths, an explanation of developmental concerns, and suggested interview questions for the developmental concerns. This kind of a report goes a long way toward helping an employer make an informed prediction about how well a prospective employee would do on the job.

What's the cost? $45.

Testing for Practical Knowledge

If you'd like to know what practical knowledge manager applicants have about the job, you might want to give them the "quick and dirty" test shown here. It's split into two parts, rental property management and landlording maintenance.

Here are the questions and some possible corresponding answers. You know the answers, but just in case you forgot, here they are again.

■**What Do You Know About Rental Property Management?**
1. How do you determine the market rent for a vacant apartment? *Do a market survey by*

WHAT DO YOU KNOW ABOUT RENTAL PROPERTY MANAGEMENT?

1. How do you determine the market rent for a vacant apartment?

2. If an applicant must have a gross income of three and a half times the rent, how much of an income does the applicant need in order to qualify to rent a house which rents for $1,250 per month?

3. We always collect an entire month's rent and all the deposits whenever a tenant moves in, and we prorate the rent for the second month when it comes due. Let's say that some tenants move in on the twentieth of August. Their rent is $900 and their deposits are $975. How much do you collect from them before they move in, and how much do you collect from them when their September rent comes due?

4. Give several legal reasons you might use for refusing to rent to someone.

5. Under what three circumstances may you enter a tenant's dwelling when the tenant is not at home?

6. Our rental agreement states that the rent must be paid by check or money order, not in cash. How do you respond to a late-paying tenant who offers to pay everything up in cash on a Friday afternoon?

7. What's a realistic late fee for an apartment which rents for $750 per month?

8. How do you begin an eviction for nonpayment of rent?

9. When a tenant calls to give you notice that she's moving, what should you do above all?

10. Prioritize the following tasks which need to be done before a certain vacant apartment can be re-rented: "steam" clean the carpets, dry-clean the draperies, re-key the locks, patch a doorknob hole in a bedroom wall, advertise, replace a broken window, paint the rooms which need painting.

checking the competition, that is, the current vacancies. Occupied apartments are not the competition.

2. If an applicant must have a gross income of three and a half times the rent, how much of an income does the applicant need in order to qualify to rent a house which rents for $1,250 per month? *Multiply $1,250 by 3.5; the answer is $4,375.*

3. We always collect an entire month's rent and all the deposits whenever a tenant moves in, and we prorate the rent for the second month when it comes due. Let's say that some tenants move in on the twentieth of August. Their rent is $900 and their deposits are $975. How much do you collect from them before they move in, and how much do you collect from them when their September rent comes due? *Collect $1,875 from them before they move in; collect $300 from them when their September rent comes due.*

4. Give several legal reasons you might use for refusing to rent to someone. *The applicants lied on the application; they have been evicted; they don't earn enough; they have bad credit; they have unsatisfactory recommendations from a previous landlord.*

5. Under what three circumstances may you enter a tenant's dwelling when the tenant is not at home? *You may enter with permission, upon giving 24 hours' notice, or in an emergency.*

6. Our rental agreement states that the rent must be paid by check or money order, not in cash. How do you respond to a late-paying tenant who offers to pay everything up in cash on a Friday afternoon? *Take the tenant somewhere nearby where he can buy a money order. Return with the money order in hand, and write the tenant a receipt. Tell him that he knows now where to buy a money order, and he can go there on his own next time.*

7. What's a realistic late fee for an apartment which rents for $750 per month? *Five percent of the monthly rent is realistic.*

8. How do you begin an eviction for nonpayment of rent? *Give the tenant a "Notice to Pay Rent or Quit."*

9. When a tenant calls to give you notice that she's moving, what should you do above all? *Have the tenant put her "Notice of Intention to Vacate" in writing.*

10. Prioritize the following tasks which need to be done before a certain vacant apartment can be re-rented: "steam" clean the carpets, hang the dry-cleaned draperies, re-key the locks, patch a doorknob hole in a bedroom wall, advertise, replace a broken window, paint the rooms which need painting. *If spare keys might be floating around somewhere or if the former tenants might try to move back in surreptitiously, re-key the locks straightaway. Then advertise, replace the broken window, patch the doorknob hole in the bedroom wall, paint the rooms which need painting, "steam" clean the carpets, hang the dry-cleaned draperies, and re-key the locks again if any independent service people have had a key during the make-ready interim.*

■What Do You Know About Landlording Maintenance?

1. How do you repair a toilet which cycles on and off all by itself every twenty minutes or so? *Replace the flush valve and check the valve seat. If the valve seat is corroded, install a stainless steel liner with epoxy.*

2. How do you repair a burn in a kitchen counter made of Formica® laminate? *Make the burn area level with the rest of the counter, and cover it with a glued-down cluster of ceramic tiles or a glued-down synthetic cutting board.*

3. How do you repair a four-inch hole in a hollow-core door? *Using double-sided tape, cover the hole with at least one 12-inch-square mirror tile; better still, add three more mirror tiles to make the mirrored area larger and more useful.*

4. How do you remove a bathtub spout without putting any permanent marks on it? *First, grip it with your hands as close to the wall as possible and try turning it counter-clockwise; if it won't budge, use a strap wrench.*

5. A new tenant calls to report that half of an electrical outlet doesn't work. How do you fix it? *Likely half of the outlet is wired to work all the time; the other half is wired to work with a wall switch. Tell the tenant to flip the wall switch to turn on the switchable half of the outlet.*

6. What's the difference between fuses and circuit breakers? *Fuses self-destruct when electrical current greater than their amperage rat-*

WHAT DO YOU KNOW ABOUT LANDLORDING MAINTENANCE?

1. How do you repair a toilet which cycles on and off all by itself every twenty minutes or so?

2. How do you repair a burn in a kitchen counter made of Formica® laminate?

3. How do you repair a four-inch hole in a hollow-core door?

4. How do you remove a bathtub spout without putting any permanent marks on it?

5. A new tenant calls to report that half of an electrical outlet doesn't work. How do you fix it?

6. What's the difference between fuses and circuit breakers?

7. Describe the function of each of the following: closet auger, drum auger, Teflon® tape, hack saw, saber saw.

8. What determines whether a doorknob lock is installed right-side up or upside down?

9. Where should you be sure to install a smoke detector?

10. Prioritize the following maintenance tasks: sweep the parking area, unclog a garbage disposer, replace an outside light, paint a bathroom in a vacant apartment, change locks for a tenant whose boyfriend moved out yesterday.

ing flows through them; they must be replaced. Circuit breakers trip to their off position when excess amperage flows through them; they may be reset and reused.

7. Describe the function of each of the following: closet auger, drum auger, Teflon® plumber's tape, hack saw, saber saw. *A closet auger is a short, stout snake for clearing toilets. A drum auger is a snake for clearing drains; this snake coils inside a drum when not in use. Teflon plumber's tape seals threaded pipe joints. A hack saw is a hand saw with a narrow, fine-toothed blade used for cutting metals primarily. A saber saw is an electric saw with a reciprocating blade supported on one end only so it can be used for plunge cuts.*

8. What determines whether a doorknob lock is installed right-side up or upside down? *A doorknob lock is installed correctly, right-side up, when the key inserted to open it has its keycuts pointing up.*

9. Where should you be sure to install a smoke detector? *Always install a smoke detector near the bedrooms.*

10. Prioritize the following maintenance tasks: sweep the parking area, unclog a garbage disposer, replace an outside light, paint a bathroom in a vacant apartment, change locks for a tenant whose boyfriend moved out yesterday. *Whenever possible, take care of tenant requests first, security and safety tasks second; preparation of vacant units third; and common-area maintenance last. Change locks for a tenant whose boyfriend moved out yesterday; unclog a garbage disposer; replace an outside light; paint a bathroom in a vacant apartment; sweep the parking area.*

Supervising Managers

If one of your employees were to discriminate against a prospective tenant illegally, give a tenant a black eye, fire another employee improperly, commit to having the parking lot fog-sealed by a fly-by-night crew, or even cause an automobile accident while on the way to the bank with your rent receipts, you as their employer would be held responsible. You can ill afford such problems.

Managers should save you time and worry, not cost you both. Take the time, therefore, to let your managers know how much discretionary authority they have to act on their own, how much money they can spend without asking for your approval, which suppliers and service people you prefer them to patronize, which ones you do not want them to patronize, what constitutes an emergency, what is important enough for them to call you in the middle of the night, how they should go about selecting new tenants, how you would like existing tenants to be treated, what your rent collection policy is, and how they should handle timekeeping.

After you have told them what you want them to do and how you want them to do it, let them do it. Never undermine your manager's authority either by allowing tenants to approach you behind the manager's back or by making deals without the manager's knowledge. Tenants will try to divide and conquer. Don't let them get away with it. Sometimes they will have legitimate grievances which aren't being addressed by the manager, though, so at least listen closely to what they have to say whenever they go to the trouble of contacting you directly, but then talk with the manager and either let the manager reply to them or arrange a three-way discussion. Never go to see tenants by yourself without first consulting the manager. Work *with* your managers, not *around* them.

Every time you pay a business visit to a property which you have entrusted to a manager, you'll be discussing all kinds of things about the condition and operation of the place. You'll forget most of your discussion soon after you leave and you'll confuse the rest, but you'll expect the manager to remember everything. You'll also expect the manager to do everything you told him to do by the time you return for your next business visit. When you do return, you'll wonder why the manager didn't do something you were sure the two of you had discussed, and then you'll learn that the manager doesn't remember your ever discussing it. The manager, for his part, will wonder why you didn't return with that whatchamacallit you promised you would bring.

In order to circumvent these frustrations and become more effective as a supervisor of managers, document the details of your visit on a form. The Site Visit form shown on the next page will help you focus on what's important when you visit a property. It will help you remember from visit to visit what you last discussed with the manager, and it will help you create a written history of your visits. What's more, it will give you a good

SITE VISIT

Property Name: Earl Lacy, Manager 1328 Sutter   Date: 3-28, XXXX

Needs Attention: garbage/trash area must be cleaned daily, Maybe even twice a day. One outside light in carport burned out.

Safety Concerns: Railing across from Apt. 2 is loose. Check batteries in apartments smoke detectors this month and at the same time check the smaller fire extinguishers.

Comments: Apt. 14 has been vacant too long. Find out what other similar places are going for and lower the rent if necessary.

Paperwork/Logbook: Daily entries in logbook complete - NICE WORK! Its neat and very legible.

Looks Good: Front of the building shows much improvement in apperance with new landscaping - you carried through on some good ideas! Tenants even commented on improvements.

Vacancies (circle if ready to rent): 2, (14)

Visitor's Followup: Return with latest Grainger Catalog. Look into a good supplier for durable garbage cans which aren't noisy. Get Buster a cordless phone, the smaller, the better.

Visited by: Margaret Rulli Time: 4:15-6P 1¾ hrs. Expenses: Car only excuse to mention things which need attention and things which are safety concerns, neither of which you might think is important enough to point out to your managers otherwise.

My managers have told me that they like the form. They say that they like to know what I notice when I pay them a visit because they don't look at the property the same way I do. They're too close to it, for one thing, and they recognize that they sometimes need their eyes opened. The form makes me open my eyes, too, and forces me to comment on what I see.

Fill it out in duplicate and leave one copy with the manager. Take the other copy with you and do the things under "Visitor's Followup" which you're supposed to be doing yourself after the visit. Bring your copy with you on your next visit and check to see whether the manager has completed everything under "Needs Attention" from the last visit.

Since all people like to know that their work is being appreciated, use the Site Visit form to say something about whatever looks good at the property. Show your employees that you like what they're doing for you. Praise them sincerely when they do good work, and remember them on their birthdays and during the holiday season, too.

Likewise, if they are not handling the overall job as you wish it handled, tell them the source of your dissatisfaction and give them an opportunity to improve. Document what you say to them so you'll have ammunition to use in case any of your employees accuse you of terminating them wrongly. A succession of Site Visit forms repeating items which need attention will go a long way toward proving that they're not doing their job.

Doing Payroll

Doing payroll is no simple matter because it requires more than simply calculating an employee's hours, making the payroll deductions, and writing the checks. It requires all that plus the completion and submission of quarterly data, the periodic deposits of employer and employee taxes, and the preparation of year-end forms, including W-2's.

Some employers find the task too daunting or too time-consuming and turn it over to a payroll service which handles everything for a fee.

If you prefer to hire out your payroll, even for a single employee, you will find any number of companies, from local bookkeeping services to nationwide payroll services, willing and able to do the job. Search the internet using "payroll services [your state]" as your search words, and you'll find a long list of them.

Be sure to analyze how each company charges for its services. You can always save on their fees by paying your employees less frequently. You will save by paying them monthly rather than semi-monthly or by paying them biweekly rather than weekly.

If you prefer to do your payroll yourself, go ahead. Do it. As soon as you get through the learning curve and into the routine, you might even enjoy doing it. It's not trigonometry or even algebra. It's basic math, nothing more. If you do your own income taxes, you'll find that doing your own payroll is much the same thing.

Using both the time sheets or time cards which your employees submit every pay period and the figures for deductions provided by governmental agencies, calculate your employees' gross earnings and all their necessary deductions. Write those figures in duplicate on a statement of earnings and deductions form (Rediform 4L416 is one of several available at stationery stores for this purpose) for each employee. Tear out the original and give it to the employee along with your check for the employee's net earnings. Leave the copy of the statement attached to the pad as a record of payment and then transfer those figures to the Payroll Record sheet you keep for each employee (see sample in chapter 19).

Do not deceive yourself into thinking that the employee's deductions are all you need to keep track of and pay to the government. You must contribute, too. Be sure to indicate in the "Employer FICA" column the contribution you must make as an employer. This sum, almost equal to the employee's Social Security contribution, was not reflected in the statement given to the employee, but you must keep track of it nonetheless, and you must forward it, along with the monies collected, to the various governmental agencies involved at either monthly or quarterly intervals. Failure to do so will result in a response much swifter than any made to the person who fails to file an individual income tax return. For instructions about forwarding these monies, ask the IRS and your state tax collecting agency to send you their free employer booklets.

Want to handle payroll yourself using your own

Time Sheet

ALFRED GOOD
Employee's Name

al good
Employee's Signature

450 SWEET ST.
Property

Pay Period __3/1__ to __3/15__

Date	Times		Hours	Description of Work Performed	Contract Amount
3/1	5:00 5:15 / 5:30 7:45	2½	ground keeping, rent collection	
3/2	5 6	1	"	
3/3	5:20 6:30	1⅙	" "	
3/4	5 5:15	¼	" "	
3/5	12– 1:00 / 3:00 5:00	3	" & dump run with my truck	10.00
3/6	5:15 6:00	¾	" "	
3/9	5:00 5:30	½	plumbing repair, apt. 4	
3/10	10:00 11:30	1½	court apperance-eviction #3	
3/13	6:00 7:20	1⅓	cleaning #3	

Total Hours __12__
Rate __7.00__
Hourly Gross __84.00__
Contract __10.00__
Total Gross __94.00__

Total Contract __10.00__

Approved by __Dube__   Date __3/16/XX__

computer or any computer connected to the internet? You can. In fact, you can do it easily nowadays with an online payroll service that integrates with the checkwriting software you're already using. Compare the different payroll services by searching the internet using "compare online payroll services" as your search words.

One of the best of the online payroll services is Intuit® Online Payroll. It enables you to pay your employees in any of three ways—direct deposit, handwritten checks, or computer-printed checks. It emails employees a link to their paystubs. It generates the payroll tax filings and the payroll tax deposits which you are responsible for as an employer. It even reminds you when you're supposed to run your payroll, when you're supposed to submit your tax filings, and when you're supposed to pay your payroll taxes. The monthly charge for the service isn't chickenfeed, but it's dirt-simple to set up and use, and it will save you many hours of head-scratching and pencil-licking toil. Go to the Intuit website to see it demonstrated and to try it for free.

Thwarting Thievery

Not all on-site property managers are honest. Some are downright dishonest and will create opportunities to steal from you, while some are easily tempted when opportunities present themselves.

To thwart thievery, eliminate the opportunities and watch for certain danger signs.

The primary opportunity for thievery is the handling of cash. The simple solution to eliminating this opportunity is to keep cash out of your manager's hands. Let your tenants know that they must pay by check or money order or credit card or bank transfer, never in cash, and be strict about enforcing this policy.

If there's some important reason why you must allow your manager to handle cash, make sure that the cash is deposited soon after it's received. Have the manager get two bank deposit receipts, one for the manager and one for you.

Adopt a shingle or a triple-receipt system for receipting rents, so that the manager, the tenant, and you all have a uniquely numbered record for every payment.

Instead of using a petty cash fund to pay for minor purchases, give the manager a business credit card with authorization to $100 and require the manager to use it for every business-related purchase. Examine every charge slip the manager submits before you pay it, and check periodically to make sure that the manager didn't return items later for a cash refund.

Watch for these danger signs that a manager might be stealing from you—extended vacancies (some managers will report a unit as vacant when it's actually occupied and they are pocketing the move-in monies); delayed deposits (an enterprising thief will scheme to "borrow" your funds and delay the deposit until new rent monies come in); sloppy bookkeeping (a thief will claim that his unbalanced totals were honest mistakes); a reluctance to take a vacation and leave the bookkeeping to somebody else (some managers may seem extremely conscientious; they're never absent; they're never absent because they don't want anybody else to look closely at their bookkeeping); and a change in the manager's lifestyle (thieves are not Robinhoods; they spend their ill-gotten gains on themselves, on gambling, booze, drugs, jewelry, clothes, or cars). Keep an eye on them. No, keep two eyes on them.

Terminating

Sometimes a management arrangement just doesn't work out, and you find yourself faced with the unpleasant task of terminating managers, something rendered all the more awkward because they live on the premises as a condition of employment. You are terminating them, and you are evicting them at the same time. Until they go, you don't even have a place for the new managers to live.

Under these circumstances, time is of the essence. You want them to vacate as quickly as possible. To get them to vacate quickly, offer them some incentive to leave within twenty-four hours, perhaps a hundred or two-hundred dollars, perhaps a rental truck and two months' rent of a self-storage unit. Reclaim the keys, bookkeeping records, equipment, and supplies immediately. Ask a trusted tenant to look after things for the time being, but do not divulge to anyone the particulars of the termination. If any announcement is in order, it might center around the transfer of managerial responsibilities and nothing more.

Believe it or not, I have acquired good properties at below-market prices from owners who sold them to me because they were unwilling or unable to terminate their incompetent managers, admittedly an unpleasant task, but definitely doable.

When you have to do it, do it.

Giving References

From time to time, you will be called upon by other employers to furnish information about former or even current employees who are looking around for other employment. You'll want to give good employees a good recommendation, and giving them a good recommendation presents no problem at all. On the other hand, you'll want to give bad employees a bad recommendation, but doing so presents a definite problem. You leave yourself open to a lawsuit whenever you say anything negative about an employee which you couldn't prove conclusively in a court of law.

Go ahead and give concrete details about salary and length of employment whenever you're asked for that information legitimately. It can't be disputed and won't get you into any trouble. But whenever you're asked to give information which is subject to interpretation and which might be construed as negative, say, "No comment!" It speaks volumes and won't get you into any trouble at all.

Some Last Words

In spite of all the complications involved in hiring help, you will find that your landlording business will prosper so much more with help than without it and that you will feel liberated enough to enjoy some of the advantages of the business. You cannot do all the work yourself. Don't die trying!

15
Participating in the Section 8 Housing Choice Voucher Program

Every inveterate M*A*S*H rerun watcher has heard the term "Section 8" often enough. Corporal Max Klinger keeps dressing up in outrageous female garb and concocting outlandish schemes to get out of the U.S. Army on a Section 8. That Section 8, a release for psychological reasons, bears scant resemblance to the Section 8 of this chapter. They just happen to share the same section numbers in their respective government documents. That's all.

The Section 8 of this chapter does bear a remarkable resemblance to something else which has the stamp of GOVERNMENT all over it, however, and that is the food stamp program.

The Section 8 housing program is to rental housing what food stamps are to groceries. Both are federal government assistance programs, and both enable the poor to live better than their incomes would otherwise allow them to. Through these programs, they get to enjoy meat, potatoes, milk, and indoor plumbing on a gruel, bread, water, and shantytown pocketbook.

Section 8 differs markedly from the other types of government housing programs which I maligned in the introduction to this book. Those are essentially *housing*-based assistance programs. Tenants must live in a particular place to get their assistance under those programs. Section 8 is a *tenant*-based program. It requires that tenants qualify financially just as the other programs do, but it doesn't restrict them to living in housing which is government-owned, government-financed, or government-operated. They could be living in rental housing belonging to anybody, even to you or me. When they move from one rental dwelling to another, their assistance goes with them.

Whereas other government housing programs operate outside the competitive marketplace, Section 8 operates inside it. In fact, Section 8 includes a monitoring of the competitive rental housing market which is designed to make its local administrators better informed about what's happening in the market than many landlords and property managers. Its administrators need to know the current market rents in their areas so they can attract landlords and property managers to the program by offering them fair market rents and certain program benefits in exchange for renting to tenants who themselves don't have enough income to qualify as renters under normal circumstances.

The program's full official title is the "Section 8 Tenant-Based Assistance Housing Choice Voucher Program." Bureaucrats within the U.S. Department of Housing and Urban Development (HUD), which manages the program at the federal level, call it the "voucher program" for short. Here we'll simply call it what the po' folks call it, "Section 8."

Established by the 1974 Housing and Community Development Act, Section 8 is now a major federal program involving billions of dollars and thousands upon thousands of people. So far, it has had a salutary effect upon the rental housing business, and though changes lie ahead for the program as legislators tinker with it, it likely will continue to have a salutary effect on the business for years to come.

As a free-enterprising landlord, you may be one of the three key local elements in the program if you want to be, but you certainly don't have to be. Unlike poor, frustrated Klinger, who wanted desperately to become a Section 8 soldier and failed, you have a choice about whether to become a Section 8 landlord.

Interested or not, you really ought to know something about this government program and how it operates. Knowing something about it will help you respond to those loonies who propose rent control in your community as the perfect solution to the high cost of housing for the poor, when what they really want to do is bash landlords and transfer the burden of providing inexpensive housing for the poor from the public sector, where it belongs, to the private sector, where it doesn't.

Our government has programs to help the poor live cheaply in decent housing, and well it should, because the poor *are* the government's responsibility. They are not the responsibility of any one segment of the population. Surely, they are not the responsibility of landlords alone, in spite of what some people think, those same people who don't mind giving away property, so long as it's other people's property.

Section 8 is just one of our government's housing programs, and it seems to be working as well as any government program can work. Unlike rent control, it is not a scattergun approach to making rental housing affordable. It does not help everybody, rich and poor alike, who happens to live in rental housing in a particular jurisdiction. It is a targeted approach. It helps those who need help. It helps the poor, and it helps them by allowing them to live in housing where anybody might live rather than isolating them in overcrowded, poorly maintained housing projects too frequently dominated by criminal elements.

The "Right Kind" of Housing

Just as there are no special "food stamp groceries" in the supermarket, there is no such thing as special Section 8 housing.

Yet there is a "right kind." It may take many forms, from tract houses to townhouses, from mobilehomes to apartments.

The right kind of housing must meet minimal size, amenity, and condition requirements. At the very least, it must have a separate and private bathroom, a living room, and a separate kitchen or a

kitchen area in the living room. In other words, a studio or efficiency apartment would do nicely. A hotel room without a private bath and without facilities for food preparation would not.

As a general rule, Section 8 housing must have one bedroom for every two people. It must have walls, floors, ceilings, windows, roof, wiring, plumbing, heating, and locks, all in good condition, and there must be no lead-based paint anywhere about. That's one thing the government is adamant about in any residential housing it subsidizes. Simply put, it should be what Section 8 materials repeatedly call "decent, safe, and sanitary" housing.

Abe Lincoln's log cabin would not qualify as the "right kind" of housing for Section 8 tenants today. HUD expects better, and HUD gets better.

HUD'S Role

HUD bankrolls the entire cost of the program, from the cost of administering it at every level to the funds allocated for the housing assistance payments made to those landlords who elect to participate.

In addition, HUD acts as a watchdog of the program's local administrators to ensure that they follow the rules adopted at the federal level for implementing the program at the local level.

Roles of the Three Local Parties

Three parties make Section 8 work at the local level, and they are all key parties. Without any one of them, there would be no program. The three are tenants, landlords, and local public housing agencies.

Tenants qualify to participate according to income and family size. Landlords qualify by having the right kind of rental housing available and by being willing to participate. Local public housing agencies "qualify" by having the necessary funds funneled through to them by the federal government and by having the personnel available to run the program.

Qualified tenants may be young or old, normal or handicapped, active or lethargic, single or multiple, bright or dull, married or not, but they may not be rich or poor. They may only be poor, not necessarily penniless, mind you, just poor enough according to the federal government's poverty level definition.

The "very low income" people who qualify for Section 8 assistance must have incomes amounting to less than 50% of the median income for their given family size located in their particular part of the country.

The "extremely low income" people who qualify, who make up 75% of those in the program, must have incomes amounting to less than 30% of the median income for their given family size located in their particular part of the country.

Incidentally, a "family" for Section 8 qualification purposes consists of two or more persons who have established a stable relationship and have lived together for a minimum of ninety consecutive days.

As you might imagine, there are more people applying for Section 8 assistance who qualify as "truly needy" than there is assistance available, so the local housing agency has to put qualified applicants on waiting lists until funds become available. It gives preference on these lists to applicants according to various criteria which it determines. Generally, preference goes to those whose income falls below 30% of the area's median income, those who are paying more than 50% of their income in rent, those who are homeless or living in substandard housing, those who are veterans, those who already reside in the area, those who are single and pregnant, those who are disabled or handicapped, those who are at least 62 years old, and those who are being displaced from their homes through governmental action.

For landlords to qualify to participate in Section 8, they must have the right kind of housing available. They must be willing to accept tenants who are poor enough to qualify. They must be willing to sign a year's lease with the tenants and a year's assistance payments contract with the local public housing agency. They must be willing to have the property inspected by the housing agency. They must be willing to maintain the property according to minimal standards, and they must be willing to set the rent at or below the fair market value as determined by HUD for that county or metropolitan area.

The third key party, the local public housing agency, identified as the "PHA" in HUD documents, is the local administrator of the program. It acts as the liaison with HUD, as the conduit for the funds, and as the "inspector general." It is directly responsible to the federal government and takes care of all the paperwork involved in making the program work at the local level. It qualifies the tenant-applicants, inspects the housing, negotiates the rent, signs the assistance payments contract, calculates the tenants' contributions, collects the federal monies, pays the landlords, and polices the abuses. As you might imagine, it has plenty to do.

How the Program Works

All three parties have to be involved for Section 8 to work, but they don't all have to begin their involvement at the same time. The housing agency is the first to become involved because it has to work together with HUD to set up the program at the local level and secure the monies. Once that's done, it solicits tenants to apply.

Tenants apply for admission to the program by proving that they're poor enough to participate. They submit information on family income, assets, and family composition. If that information proves they qualify, either they receive an assistance voucher which entitles them to the assistance right away or they receive a place on a waiting list with others who qualify for Section 8 assistance but can't get it just yet because there's none available.

For those lucky enough to receive a voucher, there's still more to do before they can move in somewhere and start living a better life. They have to go scouting for rental housing on the open market like everyone else. When they find something they like which would seem to fit the Section 8 guidelines for their family size, they must ask you as the landlord whether you would be willing to participate in the Section 8 program yourself and whether you would be willing to accept them as tenants, even though they do not qualify to rent from you on economic grounds. If you respond positively to both questions, you and the tenants sign a request for tenancy approval form provided by the agency.

**Housing Assistance Payments Contract
(HAP Contract)
Section 8 Tenant-Based Assistance
Housing Choice Voucher Program**

Part C of HAP Contract: Tenancy Addendum

1. **Section 8 Voucher Program**

   a. The owner is leasing the contract unit to the tenant for occupancy by the tenant's family with assistance for a tenancy under the Section 8 housing choice voucher program (voucher program) of the United States Department of Housing and Urban Development (HUD).

   b. The owner has entered into a Housing Assistance Payments Contract (HAP contract) with the PHA under the voucher program. Under the HAP contract, the PHA will make housing assistance payments to the owner to assist the tenant in leasing the unit from the owner.

2. **Lease**

   a. The owner has given the PHA a copy of the lease, including any revisions agreed by the owner and the tenant. The owner certifies that the terms of the lease are in accordance with all provisions of the HAP contract and that the lease includes the tenancy addendum.

   b. The tenant shall have the right to enforce the tenancy addendum against the owner. If there is any conflict between the tenancy addendum and any other provisions of the lease, the language of the tenancy addendum shall control.

3. **Use of Contract Unit**

   a. During the lease term, the family will reside in the contract unit with assistance under the voucher program.

   b. The composition of the household must be approved by the PHA. The family must promptly inform the PHA of the birth, adoption or court-awarded custody of a child. Other persons may not be added to the household without prior written approval of the owner and the PHA.

   c. The contract unit may only be used for residence by the PHA-approved household members. The unit must be the family's only residence. Members of the household may engage in legal profit making activities incidental to primary use of the unit for residence by members of the family.

   d. The tenant may not sublease or let the unit.

   e. The tenant may not assign the lease or transfer the unit.

4. **Rent to Owner**

   a. The initial rent to owner may not exceed the amount approved by the PHA in accordance with HUD requirements.

   b. Changes in the rent to owner shall be determined by the provisions of the lease. However, the owner may not raise the rent during the initial term of the lease.

   c. During the term of the lease (including the initial term of the lease and any extension term), the rent to owner may at no time exceed:

      (1) The reasonable rent for the unit as most recently determined or redetermined by the PHA in accordance with HUD requirements, or

      (2) Rent charged by the owner for comparable unassisted units in the premises.

5. **Family Payment to Owner**

   a. The family is responsible for paying the owner any portion of the rent to owner that is not covered by the PHA housing assistance payment.

   b. Each month, the PHA will make a housing assistance payment to the owner on behalf of the family in accordance with the HAP contract. The amount of the monthly housing assistance payment will be determined by the PHA in accordance with HUD requirements for a tenancy under the Section 8 voucher program.

   c. The monthly housing assistance payment shall be credited against the monthly rent to owner for the contract unit.

   d. The tenant is not responsible for paying the portion of rent to owner covered by the PHA housing assistance payment under the HAP contract between the owner and the PHA. A PHA failure to pay the housing assistance payment to the owner is not a violation of the lease. The owner may not terminate the tenancy for nonpayment of the PHA housing assistance payment.

   e. The owner may not charge or accept, from the family or from any other source, any payment for rent of the unit in addition to the rent to owner. Rent to owner includes all housing services, maintenance, utilities and appliances to be provided and paid by the owner in accordance with the lease.

   f. The owner must immediately return any excess rent payment to the tenant.

6. **Other Fees and Charges**

   a. Rent to owner does not include cost of any meals or supportive services or furniture which may be provided by the owner.

   b. The owner may not require the tenant or family members to pay charges for any meals or supportive services or furniture which may be provided by the owner. Nonpayment of any such charges is not grounds for termination of tenancy.

   c. The owner may not charge the tenant extra amounts for items customarily included in rent to owner in the locality, or provided at no additional cost to unsubsidized tenants in the premises.

7. **Maintenance, Utilities, and Other Services**

   a. **Maintenance**

Acting on the request, the housing agency dispatches an inspector to look the place over and negotiate lease terms. If the housing qualifies and you can agree on terms, you and the tenants sign a lease, which may be your own so long as it conforms with certain guidelines provided in HUD's tenancy addendum. Where it doesn't conform, the HUD addendum takes precedence.

The addendum's first page appears here. You may examine the complete addendum by searching the internet using "Section 8 Tenancy Addendum" as your search words.

As an alternative to using your own lease, you may use one provided by the housing agency for this purpose.

Then you and the housing agency sign a Housing Assistance Payments Contract, known to bureaucrats as the HAP Contract. Part A of the contract appears on the next page. To examine the complete contract, search for it on the internet using "HAP Contract" as your search words.

Finally, you collect the advance monies, the tenants move in, and you all live happily ever after, well, presumably for a year at least.

If your housing does not pass inspection, you may make the repairs and improvements to remedy its deficiencies and try again, or you may refuse to try again. That's up to you. No Section 8 tenants may move into any rental dwelling until it does pass inspection, though, and they aren't allowed to fix it up themselves so that it will comply. You must do the work.

As a landlord-participant, you will receive directly from the tenants that portion of the rent which they are responsible for and directly from the housing agency that portion of the rent which it has promised to pay. Should your Section 8 tenants fail to pay you their share of the rent when it's due, you may still assess them late penalties and evict them if necessary, just as you would any other tenant. That doesn't change. You also receive the security/cleaning deposit directly from the tenant, and you handle that just as you would a deposit from any other tenant.

If you as a landlord wish to participate in the Section 8 housing program and you don't have a qualified tenant already lined up, you may contact your local housing agency and request that your name be placed on the referral list of available dwellings. Tenants who are looking for housing under Section 8 will know in advance that you are familiar with the program and are willing to participate, and they will contact you directly about your vacancy.

Advantages and Disadvantages

There are certain advantages and certain disadvantages to participating in Section 8, and you'll have to weigh them against one another yourself as you decide whether to participate.

The primary advantage is that you get to enjoy the benefits of having a strong co-signer, the federal government, on the hook for the tenants' financial obligations to you. This co-signer seldom has to step in and pay for the tenants' obligations, however, because Section 8 tenants are more motivated to pay whatever they owe you than the average low-income tenant is. They know that they're getting something for nothing, and they want to hold onto a good thing. They also know that "big government" is involved now. If they break their lease, not only is their landlord going to become provoked and evict them, but big government is going to become aware of what's going on, and they're going to have to explain themselves all the more thoroughly when they next try to qualify for financial assistance from a government agency.

If Section 8 tenants don't pay and you have to evict them, the program will continue to pay its share of the rent during eviction proceedings. It will pay a portion of the entire rent for a period of up to thirty days following the last time the rent was paid under the program. The same holds true if the tenants break their lease and vacate without notice. You'll still get something from Section 8 for a short time after they leave.

There's another advantage, a major advantage, for landlords who own rent-controlled property and choose to participate in the program. Because Section 8 housing is exempt from most rent control laws, a dwelling renting for a ridiculously low rent under rent control will rent for market rent under Section 8.

In addition to those advantages, the program has the potential to reduce your vacancy losses because you'll be able to rent to a greater number of tenants.

As for disadvantages, the primary one is that you're hampered more than otherwise. You're hampered because you have to commit your property to the program for at least a year. You're hampered because you have to handle more paperwork and take the time to deal with a third

**Housing Assistance Payments Contract
(HAP Contract)
Section 8 Tenant-Based Assistance
Housing Choice Voucher Program**

**U.S. Department of Housing
and Urban Development**
Office of Public and Indian Housing

Part A of the HAP Contract: Contract Information

(To prepare the contract, fill out all contract information in Part A.)

1. **Contents of Contract**
    This HAP contract has three parts:
    - Part A: Contract Information
    - Part B: Body of Contract
    - Part C: Tenancy Addendum

2. **Tenant**

    Martin C. McDougal
    Sharon B. McDougal

3. **Contract Unit**

    1533 Oak Street
    Scawind, KY 41702

4. **Household**

    The following persons may reside in the unit. Other persons may not be added to the household without prior written approval of the owner and the PHA.

    Martin C. McDougal
    Sharon B. McDougal
    Bertie B. McDougal
    Shelly F. McDougal
    Mary Alice McDougal

5. **Initial Lease Term**

    The initial lease term begins on (mm/dd/yyyy): 11/16/2020

    The initial lease term ends on (mm/dd/yyyy): 11/15/2021

6. **Initial Rent to Owner**

    The initial rent to owner is: $ 1,200.00
    During the initial lease term, the owner may not raise the rent to owner.

7. **Initial Housing Assistance Payment**

    The HAP contract term commences on the first day of the initial lease term. At the beginning of the HAP contract term, the amount of the housing assistance payment by the PHA to the owner is $ 823.00 per month.
    The amount of the monthly housing assistance payment by the PHA to the owner is subject to change during the HAP contract term in accordance with HUD requirements.

party which isn't known for being swift to act or having much common sense, and you're hampered because you have to rent to low-income people who tend to be more ignorant and less responsible than tenants who can afford to pay the entire rent themselves.

You won't notice these disadvantages at all if you'd normally be plagued with vacancies, evictions, artificially low rents, and damage losses, but you might notice them a lot if such woes have never bothered you before.

An Important Distinction

In whatever rental agreement you sign with Section 8 tenants, make sure you distinguish between the rent paid by the tenants and the housing assistance payments paid by Section 8. In other words, do not label the funds paid by Section 8 as "rent." Label it "housing assistance payments." You might even want to mention specifically that the housing assistance payments are *not* rent. This seemingly unimportant distinction may become an important distinction later should you ever have to evict your Section 8 tenants.

Let's say that you give a proper notice-to-terminate-tenancy to some Section 8 tenants because they won't keep their dog under control. You have warned them and warned them, but their dog continues to bark at all hours and escape regularly from its backyard pen to terrorize neighborhood children. Your other tenants in the duplex are fed up, and so are you. You decide to evict the dog's owners. Upon giving them their notice, they stop paying their rent, but the housing authority continues making the Section 8 housing assistance payments on their behalf, and you accept the payments.

The tenants decide to fight their eviction in court. They argue that you continued accepting rent from Section 8 after the notice period expired, so the notice you gave them is meaningless. They claim that you waived your right to evict them.

You argue that you did indeed stop accepting rent from them. You continued to accept only the housing assistance payments. They're not rent at all. The Housing Assistance Payments Contract, which is between the housing agency and you, even says that the housing agency agrees only to make assistance payments. It does not agree to pay rent. Besides, neither HUD nor the housing agency administering the local Section 8 program is a party to the rental agreement. They have no right of possession, and because they have no right of possession, they cannot be making any *rent* payments. Rent payments are paid by *tenants* for the purpose of using and possessing a property.

You cannot be absolutely certain that this argument will sway a judge, but you stand a much better chance of prevailing if you make the distinction between rent and housing assistance payments in whatever rental agreement you sign with Section 8 tenants.

Some Misunderstandings

Landlords often misunderstand two aspects of the Section 8 program. They tend to think that a tenant needs no further screening after being qualified as acceptable by the public housing agency, and they tend to think that the "published" fair market rent figures are the actual rents which they can charge. Neither happens to be the case.

The housing agency screens tenants according to need primarily, and it may screen them according to other criteria, too, such as prior their tenancy history and their landlord references, but its screening procedures and yours may be very different. You cannot rely upon the agency to do your screening. You must do it.

You must qualify Section 8 tenants in exactly the same way you qualify any other tenant on every criterion except financial capability. That's only good management, and good management goes hand in hand with the whole Section 8 program.

The other common misunderstanding involves the fair market rent figures which you may see in an article published in your local newspaper. Don't get all excited when you see that Section 8 will pay $75 more per month for two-bedroom places than what you're currently charging for your two-bedroom places. The figures are misleading.

For one thing, they include a utility allowance for water, garbage, electricity, and gas. When you eliminate payment for these items, the "fair-market rent" which you as the landlord stand to receive, declines accordingly.

For another thing, the published rents are the top rents approved for dwellings with that number of bedrooms. The housing agency's inspector will negotiate with you to determine what rent you may charge a Section 8 tenant for your particular dwelling. You are not automatically assured that you will get the top rent allowed.

Fair Market Value

The primary bone of contention most landlord-participants have with the program is the tendency of the housing agency to undervalue the market rent for a given dwelling. The agency has an obligation to set the rent at fair market value, but even with lots of data and professional guidance available, they may still come up with what you consider to be a low number for your dwelling.

You as a landlord-participant need to be prepared to justify your own determination of fair market rent for your particular rental dwelling. In order to do that, you need to do your homework. You need to be able to show the agency some proof that the rent you are charging is indeed fair market rent and not some number you arbitrarily decided upon in order to take advantage of the same government which pays high dollars for hammers and toilet seats included in defense contracts.

For the single-family dwelling, you need to identify every feature, big and not so big, including things such as a double-car garage with an automatic door opener, laundry hookups, spacious kitchen, and convenient public transportation, so that you can factor in the value of such features when making comparisons with other properties currently listed for rent. Show the agency's property inspector how you arrived at your valuation.

For the multi-family dwelling, you need to identify the unit with the highest rent which is most similar to the one you want to make available under Section 8. That rented unit in the same building will provide perfect justification for the current market rent.

If you and the agency don't agree that your rent is reasonable, the Section 8 tenant may still decide to rent from you and pay the difference between what you want to charge and what the agency will subsidize.

The Future

As a landlord, you might be hesitant about participating in Section 8 because of its uncertain future as a federal government welfare program. Don't be. Future administrations, no matter how conservative, are not going to succeed in cutting back Section 8 funding anytime soon. Its future is probably more assured than that of some of our businesses and industries. Do expect the program to change, though. Presumably it will become more like the food stamp program in that it will provide subsidies to tenants which they may spend on housing pretty much as they see fit. That prospect bodes well for landlords.

Some Last Words

Face it. This is a welfare program, one of those government giveaway programs which some taxpayers resent and rail against. If you personally feel that welfare programs are wrong and that welfare recipients are lazy, good-for-nothing chiselers, then don't participate. Your attitude would surface eventually, and you'd probably find yourself saying or doing something which would put you behind the Section 8 eightball before long.

If you're either ambivalent about or supportive of government welfare programs, consider participating, but don't commit yourself initially to more than one Section 8 tenant. Try one and get a feel for the operation of the program first. Then if you find you like the way it all works, commit yourself to more. Otherwise, limit your participation to that one tenant or stop participating altogether.

Whether you participate or not is up to you. Whether you continue to participate or not is up to you as well.

By the way, for a very practical and irreverent approach to Section 8, read the *Section 8 Bible*, written by two fellows in Pennsylvania who learned the hard way how to prosper when renting to Section 8 tenants. You'll find the book (published in two volumes) available on their website (section8bible.com) along with sample paragraphs from each of the chapters.

16
Fattening The Bottom Line

Fattening your own bottom is a whole lot easier than fattening your bottom line in the landlording business. 'Tis true. 'Tis also true that you can indeed fatten your bottom line in landlording. All you have to do is increase your income and decrease your expenses. It's that simple.

Simple, eh? What a joke! Ha, ha! Only a simpleton would call it simple. It's simple to say but not quite so simple to do. It's like a stock market advisor saying that you should buy low and sell high. Duh! It's like a presidential candidate saying he's going to balance the budget by lowering taxes and increasing the spending on the latest fashionable government enterprise. Hey, wait a minute! That sounds simple all right, but it also sounds suspiciously like "voodoo economics," doesn't it? We all know what has happened as a result of many years of that kind of economic thinking. The federal budget has gone further out of whack than it's ever been, and future generations are now stuck with an enormous national debt.

Well, you don't have to practice any voodoo economics to fatten your bottom line in landlording, but you should be aware that fattening the bottom line in the landlording business is not only a matter of increasing income and decreasing expenses. That improves the cash flow all right, but it's just one of the ways to fatten the bottom line. There are four all told, each tied to one of the four ways to make money in this business. Remember them? They were mentioned in chapter 7.

Let's see, besides the cash flow which results from your income exceeding your expenses, the other three are making your property worth more (appreciation), saving more money on your income taxes (tax shelter), and paying off your mortgage with more dollars going to principal (equity buildup) and less to interest.

Each one of them has a bottom line of sorts, and all of them together contribute to the big bottom line, which is the sum of the differences between the following—net sales price and net purchase price, income tax savings and income tax liabilities, positive cash flow and negative cash flow, original loan amount and payoff loan balance—over the entire period of ownership. That's the overall bottom line. That's the big picture.

Keep all of these bottom lines in mind. You can hardly do otherwise because they're so inter-related that you can scarcely do something about any one of them without affecting the others. Try to fatten all of them whenever you can, but recognize that in this chapter we're referring to one bottom line primarily, the cash-flow bottom line. That means increasing income and decreasing expenses.

Increasing Income

Other *Landlording* chapters mention only incidentally a variety of things you can do to increase a rental property's income, from raising rents to lowering rents (amazing but true), to outfitting the laundry room with your own machines, marketing illusions by installing dazzlers, setting up interest-bearing checking accounts, shortening turnover time by not trying to do everything yourself, adding furniture, infilling your property with another dwelling or two, and so forth.

These are all good ways to fatten the bottom line, but they aren't the only ways to fatten it.

This chapter introduces a number of additional ways. Some of them require a certain expertise to make them pay off best. Some of them require additional capital investment. Some of them require certain existing facilities or extra unused space to work. Some of them require extra labor and attention. All of them yield a good

STORAGE AGREEMENT

THIS CONTRACT LIMITS OWNER'S LIABILITY--READ IT

PARTIES--THIS AGREEMENT, dated ___*June 16, XXXX*___, is by and between

___*Brian Nunn*___, "Owner," and

___*Sophie Sorenson*___, "Occupant,"

for storage of a vehicle, boat, trailer, or other personal property located at the following address:

___*2232 Thornbird Avenue, Buffalo, IA 52000*___.

OCCUPANT'S ADDRESS: ___*16 Tradeway St., Muscatine, IA 52111*___

OCCUPANT'S ALTERNATIVE ADDRESS: ___*3506 Scotts Blvd., Jimtown, IA 52666*___

[X]   INDOOR STORAGE--Unit: ___*6*___

[ ]   OUTDOOR STORAGE--Personal Property to be Stored--

   Type: _____

   Description (Color, etc.): _____

   Dimensions: _____

   Identification Number: _____

   License Number (State, too): _____

   Legal Owner (Name, Address, Phone): _____

   _____

   Registered Owner (Name, Address, Phone): _____

   _____

TERM--Occupant agrees to rent the space for storage on a month-to-month basis beginning ___*June 16, XXXX*___.

RENT--Occupant agrees to pay Owner, without deduction, the sum of $_*110*_ per month, payable in advance, on the first (1st) day of each month of the term hereof. Rent paid more than _*10*_ days following the due date is subject to a late fee of ten percent (10%) of the month's rent. Under no circumstances will prepaid rents be refunded.

CONSIDERATION FOR EXECUTION OF AGREEMENT--Owner hereby acknowledges receipt of $_*165*_ from Occupant which covers the first full month's rent under this agreement and any prorations necessary to pay rent to the first of the following month, plus any other sums here identified ___*None*___. Payment pays rent through ___*July 31, XXXX*___.

TERMINATION--Either party may terminate this agreement by giving the other party thirty days' written notice, and the rent shall be paid through that date.

return under the right circumstances.

If you're running on empty for ideas, think about these.

■ **Don't give away the space you might be charging for**—As a landlord, you're renting out living space primarily, but you probably own other space which you consider so incidental to your primary business that you may be giving it away. This other space I'm referring to is parking and storage space.

Are you giving away parking and storage space to those who rent living space from you whether they have any need for it or not? Parking and storage space has value no matter where it is. It's just more valuable in some places than it is in others, and it's more valuable to some people than it is to others.

Tenants with cars need garages more than tenants without them. Pack rats need storage space more than clutterbusters.

Look carefully at the allocation of the parking and storage space on your rental property. Try to determine how much rent you're getting from it now, even if it is bundled together with the rent you're charging for living space. Then try to determine how much you could be getting for it if you were to separate it out and rent it to either the same tenant who's using it now or to somebody else.

You might find that you can increase your income by charging separately for your parking and storage space, for this is one of those instances where the whole is worth less than the sum of its parts. If you think you might charge separately for your parking and storage space and that it might bring in more income, why not do just that?

Lest you be reluctant to wrest space away from a tenant who's been "paying" you for it all along and isn't using it, consider reducing the tenant's overall rent somewhat. Then rent the space out to somebody else who's ready to pay you what it's worth on the open market.

Wondering what it's worth on the open market? Check the Craigslist listings under "parking/storage." They'll give you a good indication of what it's worth.

■ **Convert carports into garages**—Most tenants will pay more for a carport than they will for a mere parking space, and they will pay more for a garage than they will for a carport. Take advantage of this potential for increasing your income. Convert parking spaces into carports or garages. Convert carports into garages.

Whereas converting parking spaces into garages can be pricey unless you can do the work yourself and it can be time-consuming unless you can do the work without the involvement of your local planning and building departments, it still may be worth the money and time. Do the math before you begin.

On the other hand, converting a carport into a garage requires little money and little time. All that the conversion requires is three walls and a garage door forming the fourth wall. The roof's already in place, and so is the floor. For less than $1,500 in most cases, you can hire someone to do the converting and in the process create an income of around $95 or more per month. That's a twenty-month payback and an increase in the value of your property of around $6,300!

Wow! That's better than a fourfold return on your investment!

■ **Create your own self-storage facility on vacant land at your multi-family property**—Your tenants are big renters of self-storage units, and you might want to consider satisfying their demand for storage by creating some storage units yourself directly adjacent to your rental dwellings on land otherwise sitting vacant in a back corner of your property.

Before you pooh-pooh this idea as being somehow beneath you because you think of yourself strictly as an owner of residential rental property, consider the phenomenal success of the self-storage facilities which have sprung up everywhere around the country.

Yes, I'll grant you that they're overbuilt today and that they're offering all kinds of incentives to new customers, incentives such as the first month's rent for $1, three months rent at half off when paid in advance, a free movein truck, a free dolly, a free movein helper, a free disk lock, and discount upon discount just for being a warm body.

But, but, but in spite of these discounts and giveaways at the storage facilities with hundreds of units competing fiercely for business against other storage facilities with hundreds of units, you have one big competitive advantage over them. You happen to be closer to where the people live who need storage. Your tenants are your storage customers, and they would rather

USE OF SPACE--Occupant agrees to use the space only for the storage of property wholly owned by Occupant and to store said property under his/her own supervision and control. Occupant shall not store or use or produce on the premises any materials which are classified as hazardous or toxic under any local, state, or federal law or regulation. Occupant shall not store illegal substances, perishables, food items, explosives, paint, varnish, thinner, gasoline, and/or other highly flammable materials. Occupant shall not use the space for any business or for manufacturing or production, nor for human or animal occupancy. Occupant shall not create a nuisance or permit creation of a nuisance on or near the storage premises. Occupant shall remove all trash brought onto the space. Occupant shall not use any electricity in the space for any purpose whatsoever other than for lighting and then only while Occupant is present. Occupant shall turn off lights when leaving space.

OCCUPANT'S AFFIRMATIVE COVENANTS--Occupant agrees to the following:
1) To lock the personal property and keep it secure,
2) To drain all water lines during the wintertime in order to prevent any damage that may be caused to same due to low winter temperatures, and
3) To obtain insurance to cover the property and contents thereof as Occupant is hereby informed that Owner does not carry such insurance. To the extent that Occupant does not maintain insurance, Occupant shall be completely "self-insured" and shall bear all risk of loss or damage.

WAIVER OF LIABILITY--Occupant, as a material part of the consideration under this agreement, hereby waives all claims against Owner for any damage or loss from any cause, other than the negligence of Owner, arising at any time, including but not limited to fire, theft, acts of God, vandalism or any physical damage while the Occupant's personal property remains in the storage area. Occupant does hereby agree to indemnify and hold Owner harmless from and on account of any damage or injury to any person, equipment, or personal property arising from any cause, other than the negligence of Owner, or from the negligence of Occupant, Occupant's family, or Occupant's guests.

SELF-SERVICE STORAGE FACILITY LAWS--This storage agreement is governed by the laws applied to self-service storage facilities in this locality.

ILLEGAL PROVISIONS NOT AFFECTING LEGAL PROVISIONS--Whatever item in this Agreement is found to be contrary to any local, state, or federal law shall be considered null and void, just as if it had never appeared in the Agreement, and it shall not affect the validity of any other item in the Agreement.

ACKNOWLEDGEMENT--Occupant hereby acknowledges that he or she has read this agreement, understands it, agrees to it, and has been given a copy.

_____   _____
              Owner   Occupant

_____   _____
BY Person authorized to represent Owner or Occupant

STORAGE AGREEMENT--Page 2 of 2

rent storage close to where they live than rent it miles or even blocks away from where they live. That's your competitive advantage.

You don't need to compete against the big storage facilities by offering discounts and give-aways. No, you merely need to be aware of their rents and then undercut them by a few dollars.

Where I live, the going rate for a 5'x5' unit is $50 per month, and for the most popular size, 10'x10', it's $95. Your single-car garage, at about 10'x20' would rent for $155, but even producing a rent of only $95 a month, it would be doing well. Check the storage rents in your area. Take the hint! Get with it! There's more money to be made here than you might think.

You know that you have a built-in customer base, and you know that self-storage units make money, so why not make units available to your tenants near where they live? Sound enticing? Ready to give it a try? Where do you start?

From personal experience, I can tell you one place not to start, and that is with a set of plans which you submit to your city or county building department, thereby setting in motion the bureaucratic machinery which grinds down developers with red tape and fees and time delays. Start there only if you have lots of land and want to build a permanent self-storage structure with lots of units anchored to a concrete-slab floor.

I once tried to build such a structure, consisting of twenty-five self-storage units, on some unused land at one of my multi-family properties. I had plans drawn up. I paid the application fees. I notified the neighbors. I attended the hearings. I took the plans to the various departments which needed to approve them. I did everything I was supposed to do in the proper sequence and according to schedule.

Then, just before everything came together, the fire marshal demanded that I install a new fire hydrant within fifty feet of the units. The cost for that one hydrant alone amounted to a third of the cost of the entire project!

I argued that the units were all steel and concrete. They wouldn't need a fire hydrant nearby. I cried foul, and I tried a political end run. Nothing worked. The fire marshal prevailed, and the project was snuffed out.

Months later, I came across those plans and thought about alternatives for building self-storage units in that same location. The best alternative I could think of happened to be portable

steel sheds built in a factory, trucked to the site, and set up on a level dirt pad made more solid with a layer of road base. I bought twenty of them.

Even without a foundation, these sturdy metal sheds become rooted in place. They have 26-gauge steel siding which is galvanized and then painted and cured, inch-and-an-eighth tongue-and-groove plywood floors, pitched roofs, and substantial I-beam steel skids. A tornado might pick them up and set them down somewhere on a farm in Kansas, but otherwise they're not going anywhere unless you want to pick them up and move them elsewhere yourself with a fork lift.

I checked with the building department and found that these portable sheds were perfectly legal in my area. So long as they weren't bolted to a foundation, they could be brought in as personal property, and nobody, not even the fire marshal, could object to them, nor could he demand that we put a fire hydrant nearby.

I did the numbers and determined that these 8'x15' sheds could pay for themselves in two years, and they did. My tenants rented them as soon as they became available for rent.

The sheds also increased the value of my entire property by more than three times their cost.

Incidentally, you should always use a separate storage agreement, something like the one shown here whenever you rent out storage space. Understandings about the rents, insurance, use of the space, applicable laws, refunds, and liability need to be in writing.

When buying sheds, avoid the temptation to buy the cheap sheds you see set up in the parking lots of the big box stores. They may be good enough for the homeowner who wants a back-yard shed to store the kids' toys, the BBQ, the lawn furniture, the pool equipment, and the gardening tools, but they're not good enough to rent out. They're too flimsy, and they're ugly. If they're made of steel, they rust and fall apart in a year or two. If they're made of wood, they need painting in a year or two.

Avoid the temptation to buy shipping containers. They're sturdy all right, but they're ugly. You don't want ugly storage containers making your rental property look bad. Ugh! Not only do they make your property look bad, they make it worth less because they lower the property's desirability, and that affects its capitalization rate.

Avoid the temptation to buy wooden sheds

even if they are well-built. They require more maintenance than metal sheds, and they're susceptible to fire.

The sheds you buy to rent out to your tenants as storage units should be metal, and they should be sturdy, attractive, and low maintenance. In short, they should be commercial or industrial quality, not homeowner quality.

To locate a supplier in your area, search the internet using "portable steel sheds commercial [your state or local area]" as your search words.

■ **Make unproductive space productive—** Have you ever stopped to consider just how much rent you could be charging for those three garages you've reserved for yourself at your rental property? At $95 per month for each of them, you could be getting $3,420 per year for all three or $2,280 for two.

Don't hog all of that storage space yourself. People are willing to pay you for it. Consolidate in one garage all the things you've been hoarding in those three garages. Hold a garage sale to dispose of the stuff you don't really need. Better still, call the Salvation Army to pick up the items they might be able to sell and get them to give you a receipt for your donation. Get the junk out of there. Get some heavy-duty storage racks from Grainger and organize the tools and supplies of your trade better so they require less floor space. One garage is plenty big enough for storing what you really need.

At the very least, realize how much those extra garages are costing you. Is that old bulky stuff you've been saving for years really worth all that much? Sure, you might have some need for it someday, but remember that every month you keep it, you're adding onto its cost to you. You might think that your garage full of the stuff which tenants have left behind doesn't cost you

anything. Well, it may not have cost you anything to begin with, but now it's probably costing you $95 every month, and that mounts up in a hurry. The stuff had had better be worth a pretty penny because it's free no longer.

Garages aren't the only unproductive space you could make productive. Offices and storage rooms have potential as well.

I'm always amazed at how many relatively small apartment complexes have large offices which an architect with no apartment management experience thought would be a good idea to include back when the building was still on the drawing board. Nobody questioned the space then, and nobody questioned it for years afterward.

Ask yourself whether you really need an office at your complex? What are you using the office for? Document storage? Tool and equipment storage? Might it be rented out as office space to an insurance agent, a bookkeeper, an eBay seller, a computer programmer, or someone else, or might it be turned back into an apartment if that's what it once was? Do you really want employees of yours spending time in an office when they could be on call in their own home on the premises?

Just remember that office space is not free even to you as the owner, not when it could be generating income. As one room in a manager's apartment, an office makes sense, but as a totally separate space, and especially if it's an entire apartment which has been converted into an office, it may not make any sense at all.

Is there any other spare room or space on the premises of your rental property which isn't getting the use it should? Might it be converted into rentable, productive space? That's your business, remember, renting out space.

■ **Keep looking for other income possibilities**—Vending machines, arcade games, amusement machines, and coin-operated car washing facilities all offer the apartment house owner other income possibilities, as does renting otherwise unused space for billboards and cellular telephone towers.

Unfortunately, many times these possibilities promise more than they deliver for many different reasons, from unfavorable contracts and increased utility costs to technological changes and demands on your time. Ask advice of others who have had experience with these ventures in similar situations before you commit yourself.

Other than storage sheds and coin-operated laundry machines, soda vending machines have been my own best income producers. A soda machine is like having your own automated lemonade stand. You don't have to be a great math or financial genius to understand that buying sodas for 25¢ and selling them for 75¢ or $1 holds profit potential, big profit potential. Why, after all, are the soda companies so anxious to place their vending machines on your property?

You do need to do some careful estimating before you buy your own soda machine because you might not sell enough soda to make the machine pay for itself. Like a coin-operated laundry machine, it ought to pay for itself in less than three years.

By the way, if you do decide to buy a soda machine, buy a new one. Used ones are headaches. Also, make sure that you factor in the cost of the electricity to run a soda machine when you're doing the numbers. To keep the electricity bill low, place the machine in a cool location, certainly not where it will be in direct sunlight.

My own worst income producer was a satellite television system. After working the numbers and installing a system at considerable expense, I had to compete with the falling prices of the small satellite dishes and their broader range of program offerings. Not only did I lose customers to the small dishes, but I had to continue paying on a three-year contract for a larger customer base than my satellite system was serving.

Expect to win some. Expect to lose some. Keep trying to put more dollars on that bottom line than you lose from it and you'll be a happier landlord.

Decreasing Expenses

Trying to fatten your bottom line by increasing income holds greater potential than trying to fatten it by decreasing expenses. There aren't that many things you can do to decrease expenses, and there's a limit beyond which you cannot go. That limit is zero. You cannot save more than $22,213 in expenses on any property where the expenses are $22,213 per year. You'd be hard pressed to come anywhere near that, of course.

Nevertheless, you should never overlook what opportunities there are to decrease expenses. There are almost always some.

Besides questioning your insurance coverage and its cost, picking the right things to do yourself while hiring out the others, converting master-metered buildings to separate meters, paying the manager according to some realistic measure of the work involved, watching advertising costs, and decreasing expenses in other ways mentioned elsewhere in this book, you still ought to look at some other possibilities. Here are a few.

■ **Monitor your mortgage interest**—Look at your expenses for any property you own and rank them, biggest ones first. Unless you're making extra-large down payments or paying cash for your property, near the top of your list of expenses will be mortgage interest. It's a major expense, right up there with your property taxes. It's one you need to monitor regularly in order to keep it as low as possible.

Lenders don't call their borrowers to offer better loan terms when interest rates decline. You as a borrower have to take the initiative. You have to monitor current rates yourself and compare your rate to them, and you are the one who has to shop around for new financing which will lower your interest expense. Nobody else is going to do it for you.

Before you even begin shopping around for a new loan to lower your mortgage interest, examine your loan documents to see whether the existing mortgage contains a prepayment penalty which still applies to a mortgage as old as yours. If it does, factor the penalty into your cost calculations. You'll trigger the penalty when you pay off the existing loan, and that can make a substantial difference in the calculations.

Once you know the existing loan's prepayment penalty, you need to know the costs you'll incur in obtaining the new loan, from the appraisal fee to the points, right on down to the notary and courier fees.

Finally, you need to consider how long you intend to keep the property. In most cases, the costs involved in obtaining a new loan at a lower interest rate make it unattractive unless you plan to keep the property longer than a year. If you intend to sell the property in less than a year, you may find that the advantages of a new loan at a lower interest rate will evaporate when it's paid off.

If you're currently borrowing $200,000 at 10%, a new loan for that same amount at 8% will reduce your interest expense the first year by $4,000 (assuming for the sake of simplicity that there's no amortization). If the costs involved in obtaining that new loan at the lower interest rate amount to $4,000, and you expect to keep the property longer than a year, you will definitely fatten your bottom line by obtaining the new loan.

Do the numbers before you commit yourself to a new loan at an attractive interest rate.

■ **Reduce your mortgage payment**—Let's say that you've been making monthly mortgage payments of $3,668.82 for 20 years on a $500,000 loan at a fixed interest rate of 8% with an amortization period of 30 years, and you'd like to fatten your bottom line by reducing your payments. You could take money out of the property, but you don't want to. You merely want to reduce your monthly payments. Lucky you, you can because you've paid the principal down by almost $200,000. Your banker says that she'd be glad to write you a new loan for what you owe on the old loan, $302,389.81.

Okay, let's do the numbers. Let's say that the interest rate available to you hasn't changed. It's still 8% fixed, and you're looking at loan costs of $3,000 and an amortization period of 30 years. What's the payment? It's $2,240.84. In other words, you've just fattened your bottom line by a whopping $1,427.98 per month! Not bad, eh?

■ **Fool yourself into thinking your cash flow is negative**—Ordinarily you shouldn't be trying to fool yourself. Fooling oneself carries bad connotations. People say that you're only fooling yourself if you think you can keep up with the Joneses on half their income, if you think a movie star on location in your hometown is going to fall in love with you, if you think money buys happiness, if you think you're going to beat the odds in Las Vegas, if you think your no-name dot.com stocks will rise from their ashes, or if you think that your next cigarette is going to be

your last. Those don't sound like good ways to fool yourself, do they?

They're not. They're not realistic. They're not productive.

There is at least one good way to fool yourself that I know of, one which helps you watch your rental property expenses more carefully. Fool yourself into thinking that you're suffering from a negative cash flow. What? You don't have to fool yourself because you already have a negative cash flow and you'd be delighted just to break even? I'm sorry for you and sorry that this method for decreasing your expenses won't help you in the least, but you will surely understand from first-hand experience how it works.

If you have an honest-to-goodness negative-cash-flow property, you know how closely you watch your expenses. They're supremely important to you because you have to dip into your own pocket every month to support the property. You're depriving yourself of the opportunity to use those funds for other purposes. On the other hand, if your property is generating a positive cash flow, you don't pay nearly as much attention to the expenses. You simply pay them out of the available income and pocket the balance.

You can see how this attitudinal difference works whenever you buy a rental property which in the previous owners' hands was either completely paid off or mostly paid off. You'll notice that they were lax in raising their rents and lax in controlling their expenses. "Easy come, easy go!" was their attitude. With a big new mortgage payment facing you every month, you'll be looking for all kinds of ways to make the property pay, and you'll discover them.

To keep yourself from becoming inattentive to your own expenses, fool yourself into thinking that your positive-cash-flow property is poorer than it actually is. How? Here's how.

Merely transfer the property's excess funds out of its operations account once a month so that the balance is never very high. That's all. You'll be fooling yourself into thinking that the property has little money available to pay its bills, and as a consequence, you'll be watching the expenses more closely.

It's a simple trick, but it works for this old fool.

■ **Question your property tax bill**—Perhaps you have seen one of those "QUESTION AU-

THORITY" bumper stickers on an ancient, beat-up Volkswagen bus. You shake your head and lament the further decline of the old-fashioned values you grew up with. Yet your own attitude toward authority could be costing you some big bucks.

You may be questioning all of your other landlording expenses and trying every which way to control them, but you may not even have thought about questioning your property taxes, and they're always a major expense.

You may have thought your tax bill was sacrosanct because it comes to you on an official computer-printed form and appears to be based on a "Higher Authority" or at the very least upon some mandated formulas.

Whoa now, don't get carried away! That tax bill of yours may have some very exact figures on it, and it may be printed on an official form, but it is definitely open to question. Go ahead and question it. Take the time once a year to examine your tax bill for each property. Make sure that the bill is for the property you own, first of all, and not for some other property which the county has mistakenly linked to your name. Make sure that you understand the bill, and then see whether you agree with the figures. You want to be certain that the law is being applied to you fairly, that the formulas for calculating the value of your property are correct and that the tax rate has been applied to your property correctly.

If anything appears to be out of line, question the authorities.

If you see the error of their ways but you can't quite convince them of their errors yourself, consider whether the sums involved warrant your hiring an "authority" of your own to represent you. There are knowledgeable people who specialize in challenging property tax assessments. They expect to be paid well, of course, but what they expect for their efforts is a portion of your tax savings. They profit only if you profit.

■ **Transfer costs**—When you rent out residences, you are furnishing your tenants with more than a roof over their heads. You are providing them with certain services, too, services which cost you money. Some of these services, such as maintenance and repairs, you absolutely have to provide and you have to pay for them because laws require you to, but that doesn't mean you have to provide and pay for maintenance and repairs when tenants are negligent or destructive.

You don't. You may want to provide the service so the work gets done promptly, but you shouldn't be paying for it as well.

When a tenant shoots a shotgun through the ceiling and blows a hole right through the roof, you go ahead and repair the damage, but you expect the tenant to pay for it, don't you? Sure, the tenant has damaged the building. Who cares whether it happened accidentally or on purpose? The tenant caused the damage. The tenant should have to pay.

If that roof had started to leak as a result of weathering or a windstorm, you would have paid for the repairs. That leak wouldn't be the tenant's fault, and repairing it is your responsibility under the "warranty of habitability" which you provide as a landlord.

When a tenant plugs up a toilet or breaks a window, do you get it fixed and pay for the damage yourself, or do you get it fixed and make the tenant pay? Are plugged-up toilets and broken windows your responsibility or are they your tenant's responsibility?

In my book, they're the tenant's responsibility, and the tenant should have to pay. You didn't plug up the toilet. You didn't break the window. No defect, no normal wear and tear caused the damage, and it certainly didn't happen through an act of God. I'll grant you that it doesn't always happen through an act of your tenants. It could have been a neighbor's kid who put a rock through the window. But if you tell your tenants that they must pay for only those windows which they break and that you will pay for all the others, then you can be sure that no window broken in their place will ever be their fault, and they won't know who broke it. You'll be paying for every broken window.

Why should you pay automatically? Why should you in effect let them charge every plugged-up toilet and every broken window on your MasterCard?

Sure, if there are some special circumstances, you might want to make a deal with your tenants. Get them to pay a portion and you pay the rest. That's reasonable. Just don't pay every time. Make your tenants responsible. Transfer the costs of dealing with these problems to them.

The rental agreements in this book do just that, and you should do the same. If you and your tenants have an existing agreement which fails to mention payment for broken windows and

[Every state sets its own time frame for this notice. If you don't know your state's time frame, call your local rental housing association, check the landlord-tenant laws on your state's website, or check the landlord-tenant law summary in the guest subject area of rhol.org.]

Notice of Change
in Terms of Tenancy

TO   *Sam and Barbara Brooks*   , Tenant in Possession

       3104 Dogwood Drive

       Bigtown, CA 09601

     YOU ARE HEREBY NOTIFIED that the terms of tenancy under which you occupy the above-described premises are to be changed.

     Effective _____ *August 5* _____, *XXXX*, there will be the following changes:

- *Tenants must pay for repairs of all damage, including drain stoppages, which they or their guests have caused.*
- *Tenants must pay for any windows broken in their dwelling while they live there.*

     Dated this *2nd* day of _____ *July* _____, *XXXX* .

                         Clyde Woodard, Manager
                              Owner/Manager

This Notice was served by the Owner/Manager in the following manner (check those which apply):

     (X) by personal delivery to the tenant,
     ( ) by leaving a copy with someone on the premises other than
         the tenant,
     ( ) by mailing,
     ( ) by posting.

plugged drains, you don't have to switch rental agreements to make this change. All you have to do is give your tenants a Notice of Change in Terms of Tenancy which shifts the responsibility from you to them in thirty days (could be longer if you want to play Mr. Niceguy), provided, of course, that your existing agreement and the landlord-tenant laws in your area allow you to do so.

Transferring these costs to your tenants will definitely decrease your expenses.

Look around. Ask yourself whether there are any other services which cost you money but which you are providing free of charge to your tenants? Might you get them to pay for these services? Once they are, you've eliminated another expense and fattened your bottom line a trifle more. Those trifles add up to real money.

■ **Practice sensible energy conservation—** You're a lucky landlord if you happen to own a building where you pay none of the utilities, where everything is on separate meters, and there are no common areas requiring heat, cooling, lighting, or water.

I had such a building once, the first rental property I ever owned. It was a fourplex with a stucco exterior which never needed painting, a pitched roof which shed water like a doorman's umbrella, a concrete yard area which never needed mowing, four separate meters for electricity, four separate meters for gas, four separate meters for water, and four separate cans for garbage. I still think of the place and its minimal expenses. I bought it from the contractor who built it and owned it for fifteen years until he finally decided to retire and move out of the area. He built it to be inexpensive to manage because he planned to keep it himself as a rental property. He was right on the mark. It was inexpensive to manage. The owner paid nothing for electricity, gas, water, or garbage.

Unfortunately, such buildings are about as scarce as modesty among film stars. Most rental buildings generate utility bills for their owners, and those bills can be whoppers, terribly damaging to their owners' financial well-being. As the owner of such a building, you can't expect much relief from the people who contribute to those bills, your tenants, but you can expect to find some relief from the people who send you the bills every month, the utility companies. Seek their advice.

Most utility companies have conservation advisors who specialize in helping customers reduce their energy consumption. At the very least, they will give you booklets on energy conservation. Many offer much more help than that, though. They may give you conservation devices like shower flow restrictors and toilet tank water displacement bags. They may subsidize the cost of low-flush toilets. They may come out and conduct an energy audit of your building and make suggestions for conservation. They may even offer you low-interest loans so you can make building modifications designed to conserve energy, modifications such as installing efficient space and water heaters, thermal windows, fluorescent lighting, and extra insulation.

Take advantage of these programs. Become better informed about energy conservation, and make the changes which offer you a good payback and will fatten your building's bottom line.

■ **Foster conservation, recycling, and reuse of "trash"—**Not only do conservation (using less of anything), recycling (reprocessing used products into new products), and reuse (using something over rather than throwing it away) make good sense ecologically, they make good sense economically, especially for landlords. The more you do to reduce the trash which your tenants throw into the garbage, the more you do to reduce your garbage bills.

Encourage your tenants to recycle their newspapers, magazines, cardboard, glass, aluminum, beverage containers, and plastics. Make it easy for them to do so by providing a place where they can sort their recyclables and by providing separate bins where they can deposit their sorted items. You might even be able to make your recycling effort pay for itself by giving a tenant who's passionate about recycling the responsibility of looking after your building's "recycling center" in exchange for getting to keep whatever monies the recyclables bring.

A conscientious recycling effort will reduce the garbage your tenants generate by at least one-half. Think of how much fatter your building's bottom line would be with its garbage bill cut in half!

■ **Investigate trash-handling alternatives—** Trash disposal is big business. It's expensive business. It has become especially expensive because trash is no longer so easy to dispose of. You can't just burn it in an incinerator, bury it in a hole in the ground, ditch it in an empty lot, or throw it in the ocean. You have to dispose of it properly in accordance with myriad governmental regulations. As a result, dumps nowadays are expensive to open, maintain, and shut down, and because few people want to have a dump in their backyard, new dump sites are further than ever from populated areas. New York City's trash leaves the city on barges and in railcars destined for dumping grounds hundreds of miles away.

Trash charges vary dramatically from place to place for any number of reasons. My most expensive trash bill averages twice what the lowest one averages per dwelling, even though I've made every effort to reduce it. Had I not been careful, it would be higher still. Watch carefully how much you're paying for trash and investigate various trash-handling alternatives when you notice your trash bill growing.

Here are some cost-saving alternatives you might want to investigate—switching from one hauler to another (most haulers have community monopolies and you may have no choice); installing a compactor for an entire complex (compacted trash qualifies for a cheaper rate per yard than loose trash); switching to smaller cans (some households produce less than 20 gallons of trash per week; why should you provide a more expensive 30 gallon can?); switching from individual cans to a dumpster (do the calculations); switching from a dumpster to individual cans (do the calculations again); and hauling your own trash (where local regulations allow residents to haul their own trash to the dump, we do; my staff use a covered utility trailer of a certain size to qualify for a commercial rate; my trash bill is cut in half; they get half the savings; I get half the savings, and we're both happy).

Some Last Words

Take neither your income nor your expenses for granted. Be alert to the opportunities which exist all around you for increasing your income and decreasing your expenses, but don't forget that your primary objective is to fatten your bottom line. It is not merely to increase your income or decrease your expenses, not when the one will have an adverse effect on the other. Increasing your monthly income by $5 while at the same time increasing your monthly expenses by $6 isn't any way to fatten your bottom line, not even when you multiply those numbers many times.

Remember the old joke about the fellow who lost money on every sale but made it up on volume? Don't follow suit.

17
Insurance

Astute blackjack (the card game also known as twenty-one or Pontoon) players know better than to buy insurance when a dealer's upcard is an ace (insurance pays 2:1 if the dealer has a hole card equal to ten) because the odds are with the house. The odds are greater than 2:1 that the dealer's hole card is a ten or a face card. If the house matched those odds in its payouts, the insurance would be a good buy. It doesn't. It expects to make easy money from players who don't know the math, and it does.

The math for the insurance we landlords buy to protect our properties and ourselves is harder to do. Who can predict the risk of a fire, a flood, an earthquake, employee dishonesty, or even a dog bite with any certainty? Nobody can, but insurance company actuaries try. They study past occurrences to predict future events and base insurance premiums upon their findings.

We landlords face any number of risks which we can neither calculate nor afford to bear all by ourselves. Insurance companies serve a useful function in spreading that risk for a fee.

In a society overrun by people who pursue their fortunes through litigation, people who are quick to place a highly inflated dollar value on stubbed toes and kinked necks, we landlords must protect our assets. We need insurance companies. We need insurance.

We become increasingly vulnerable to losses as we build our property assets. We have a lot to lose if a building of ours burns to the ground when it's half paid for. We have a lot to lose if someone files a lawsuit against us just when we've taken early retirement to live off our rental income. Litigants and their legal counsel don't care how hard or how long we've worked to gather our assets. That's of no consequence to them. They show no mercy when they're fighting to get their hands on our assets. They just want everything they can get out of us, and, of course,

they know that we're wealthy because, after all, we own income property. We're landlords.

Because we do own income property, we have special insurance needs above and beyond those of people who don't. We should know something about the many kinds of insurance available to serve those needs. We should know something about exercising prudence whenever we're thinking about insurance, and we should know something about selecting a solid company.

In addition, we should know something about getting a fair settlement, responding to accidents, settling claims ourselves, and helping our tenants understand renters' insurance. These are the subjects of this chapter.

Becoming Acquainted with the Many Kinds of Insurance Available

In the not too distant past, there was only one kind of insurance landlords bought. That was fire insurance. We still buy fire insurance, at least as much as ever, but because we're exposed to so many more types of liability and all sorts of dangers, we need more kinds of insurance, lots more.

Here are nineteen kinds of insurance you should know something about if you want to protect your assets from vanishing like a magician's comely assistant.

■ **Fire**—Kids shouldn't play with fire, and landlords shouldn't play with fire insurance. Fire insurance is serious business. Even lenders know that.

Lenders require you to protect their interest in your building with a fire insurance policy at the very least because they figure that they cannot afford to risk a loss should their collateral go up in smoke and flames. Were that to happen, they'd lose the collateral for their loan and the income as well because they would expect you to

311

stop making payments on a loan which had been backed up by income-producing real estate that is no longer producing income.

Protecting a lender's share of your building with fire insurance is understandable, but what about that share of the building you put up as collateral? Shouldn't you buy fire insurance to cover it, too?

Absolutely! You should be even more cautious than your lender because your equity in a building represents a much greater proportion of your total assets than what the loan on one building represents of a lender's assets.

In addition, your interest in that building keeps growing as appreciation pushes the value up and your equity payments push the loan balance down. With more to protect virtually every month, you should be so cautious about your fire insurance that whenever your premium comes due, you make certain that your building is covered with a policy adequate enough to pay current replacement costs. Anything less, and you're playing with fire. Anything more, and you're wasting your money, for $250,000 worth of coverage on a building which costs $200,000 to replace will pay only $200,000, no matter what.

Note that you should insure only your building, its contents, and the other improvements on the property which might be damaged by fire. Do not insure the land. Fire doesn't damage land. It'll still be there when the fire dies down and the smoke clears, ready for reconstruction.

Being the conservative folks that they are, lenders may tell you that you have to carry enough fire insurance to cover the entire amount of their loan, even when the loan amount exceeds the replacement cost of everything a fire could possibly damage. They don't seem to understand that some of their loan might be secured by land. Enlighten them. Don't pay for an expensive policy with higher than necessary coverage just to appease a nervous, hidebound lender.

I once had a lender demand that I secure a $300,000 fire insurance policy to protect a first mortgage for that amount on a little trailer park. Only after I produced evidence showing that no fire could possibly do more than $75,000 worth of damage to the park did the lender relent and allow me to reduce the policy to $75,000. As you might imagine, my premium for a quarter of the original coverage took a significant drop, and the savings were mine to keep.

Just as you should avoid being forced into buying too much insurance by an ignorant lender, you should avoid buying too little insurance in order to save yourself a few dollars on the premiums.

There are two drawbacks to having too little fire insurance, one obvious and one not so obvious.

Here's the obvious drawback. With $165,000 worth of coverage on a $200,000 building which burned to the ground, you wouldn't be able to collect enough insurance money to replace the building. You'd be $35,000 short.

Here's the less obvious drawback. With too little fire insurance, you're likely to run afoul of the *co-insurance clause* in your policy. Also known as the *average clause* or the *reduced-rate-contribution clause*, the co-insurance clause restricts the payoff to the same percentage of risk you're taking as the owner.

Here's how it works. Suppose you decide to insure your $200,000 building for $100,000 because you read somewhere that firefighters put out the fires in most burning buildings long before they turn to ashes. You figure that you'll get the insurance company to assume the risk for the first $100,000 worth of damage and you'll assume the risk for the second $100,000. Sounds reasonable, don't you think?

You stand to save a fair amount of money on premiums by assuming a risk for the same amount of money as the insurance company, but the truth is that you're not. You're actually taking a much smaller risk, for the first half of a building always burns before the second half.

You're assuming that the insurance company is insuring the first half, the first $100,000 of your building, and you'd be right except for one thing. Insurers ain't stupid. They know that some people think this way, so they include a co-insurance clause in their policies, requiring you as policy holder to insure your building for at least 80% of its replacement cost in order to collect the entire amount of any loss up to your policy limits. If your $200,000 building is insured for $100,000, and you have a loss of $50,000, the policy will pay only $25,000 (50% of the loss) even though you have $100,000 worth of coverage.

Under the co-insurance clause, the *percentage* of coverage you have, not the amount, applies to losses. $100,000 of coverage on a $200,000 building translates into 50%. By insuring your

$200,000 building for at least 80% of its replacement cost, or $160,000 in this case, you'd avoid being caught by the clause, and you'd receive a full $100,000 in the event of a $100,000 loss.

Don't get caught with your coverage down! You could become a big loser by trying to save a few dollars on your premiums.

■ **Extended Coverage**—Most insurance companies offer what they call "extended coverage" (sometimes called "comprehensive coverage" or a "package policy") along with their standard fire insurance policies, and they price this coverage at very attractive rates. It may include damage caused by hail, explosions, windstorms, aircraft, vehicles, smoke, burst pipes, rioting, vandalism, falling trees, freezing, collapse, landslides, or accidental water discharge.

Look into it. It's good coverage to have when a hard freeze breaks water pipes in a rental house you own and as soon as the thaw comes, water squirts everywhere through those burst pipes, ruining the flooring throughout the house.

■ **Earthquake**—Extended coverage policies do not extend far enough to include earthquake coverage. It's always a separate policy. Even with a high deductible and lots of exclusions, it's not cheap, but you shouldn't be without it in any area prone to earthquakes where you own improved property. One earthquake, just seconds-long, could destroy your lifelong work as a landlord.

On the other hand, an insurance consultant told me that he is wary about earthquake coverage because he believes that insurance companies' exposure is too great. They could be wiped out by a major earthquake and be unable to pay their policyholders' claims even after having accepted hefty premiums for years. He advises certain of his clients to take whatever physical precautions they can take to minimize earthquake damage to their property and then self-insure ("self-insuring" and "insuring yourself" mean that you act as your own insurer; you don't buy coverage from anyone else; you assume the risk). He advises other clients to select a company which has abundant assets and little exposure itself to earthquake claims in a single area.

You might want to discuss the subject in detail with your insurance agent or with an independent insurance consultant before you commit yourself to spending any money on an earthquake policy.

■ **Flood**—Water damage is water damage, isn't it? Yes it is, but water damage has many causes, and as far as water damage and insurance coverage are concerned, what's most important is what causes the damage. You could find yourself "high and dry" one of these days upon discovering that your insurance policy covers only water damage caused by accidental leakage and not water damage caused by flooding, high water, or sewage backups.

Ask for the coverage you want according to the likelihood of these calamities' occurring at your property, and don't assume that you have flood insurance unless you see it written in your policy. Like earthquake insurance, flood insurance does not come packaged with other coverage. It's separate.

Many owners of rental property in New Orleans discovered only after Hurricane Katrina that they didn't have flood insurance when they thought they did. That's the wrong time to find out. Find out for yourself whether you need it and whether you have it before Noah's Ark comes floating down your street.

Lenders are certainly aware of flood hazards and flood insurance. They require flood insurance on any property securing a loan if that property is located in a "special flood hazard area subject to inundation by the 1% annual chance flood event." In other words, if you want to obtain financing on a property located in a 100-year flood plain, you must obtain flood insurance. You have no choice.

Before you acquire any property, check FEMA's Map Service Center (msc.fema.gov) to see whether it is located in a 100-year flood plain. If it is, check into the cost of flood insurance and include the cost in your calculation of expenses for the property before you make an offer to purchase.

■ **Other Improvements**—Property improvements other than buildings, including such things as swimming pools, parking lots, walks, fences, and signs, may sustain direct damage from a flood, fire, ice storm, or other disaster, too, but they won't be covered by your standard building policy unless you include them specifically under extended coverage. Examine what your insurer offers for coverage and decide whether the peace of mind is worth the premiums.

Many owners insure themselves for damage to their non-building property improvements because they regard the potential risk of damage, the potential extent of damage, and the potential consequences of damage to be minimal in relation to the other exposure they have.

■ **Vandalism and Malicious Mischief**—Should anyone damage your property, say, by tearing your laundry machines apart to get at the coins or by laying waste a vacant apartment, your vandalism and malicious mischief insurance would pay to repair the damage. You hope you'll never have occasion to use such coverage because damage like this is pretty demoralizing to a conscientious landlord, but if it should happen, you must have the right insurance to pay for the repairs. When included in a package policy, it can be quite inexpensive.

■ **Liability**—Some years ago, few landlords bothered to obtain liability coverage because few people filed liability claims and even fewer collected. Today that's all changed. Today you can't afford to be without liability insurance any more than obstetricians can afford to be without malpractice insurance.

No longer does the age-old maxim, "Caveat emptor!" ("Let the buyer beware!") apply to business dealings. Now it's "Caveat venditor!" ("Let the seller beware!")

You as a landlord are one of these so-called "sellers" who must beware when doing business. You must beware of being anything less than the perfect landlord to your tenants, and you must beware of supplying anything less than the perfect rental property to your tenants all the time. Stumble in your role, and your tenants say "gotcha" with a liability lawsuit.

Both the number of liability cases and the types of cases have increased, as have the awards. It's not just the personal injury case caused by your supposed negligence that you have to worry about nowadays. It's the discrimination case, the wrongful eviction case, the invasion-of-privacy case, the crime-committed-by-a-felon-on-your-property case, the strict liability case, the failure-to-maintain case, the failure-to-keep-me-happy case. Those are ever-present worries.

The worries keep growing, too. "Strict liability" applied to landlording is something new. In case you haven't heard, courts are beginning to rule that tenants need prove only that your "product" was defective and that as a result of the defect they were hurt. They do not have to prove that you were negligent in the least.

This policy of strict liability has been applied to manufactured products for some years here in the U.S. It has caused some companies to go out of business entirely and others to stop making certain products. Cessna Aircraft, for example, stopped manufacturing the popular 152 trainer when its product liability insurance reached $17,000 for each one of these little $40,000 airplanes, the smallest of any they made and one of the safest airplanes ever built.

At that rate (42.5%), your insurance bill on a $600-a-month apartment would be $255 a month, pretty steep for only one type of coverage, wouldn't you say? We can only guess how the application of strict liability is going to affect the landlording business.

Don't go the self-insurance route for this risk. Buy insurance which will cover every liability you can think of, and while you're at it, buy enough. Buy the highest limits available, and add to your liability policy's limits with an umbrella policy. You will find that a million dollars' worth of coverage costs little more than a hundred thousand dollars' worth, and it could save you from the poorhouse, for the awards people manage to get in liability cases, especially when they involve a personal injury, tend to be high.

Expect your liability premiums to become a more noticeable expense than they have been in the past. Complain all you want about the rising rates, but don't neglect paying them.

■ **Loss of Rents**—If a fire or some other mishap renders your rentals uninhabitable, your tenants will stop paying you their rent immediately and you won't have any income to use to pay those many fixed expenses which keep piling up no matter what. You'll have to pay those continuing bills out of your own savings unless you have loss-of-rents insurance coverage. In that case, your insurance company will compensate you for the loss of rental income over a reasonable period of time while your building is being repaired.

With all the other problems you're likely to have if a major mishap occurs at your property, you don't need financial problems, too, not when you can protect yourself for a small premium.

■ **Contents**—The belongings which you own and keep at your rental property, belongings such as mowers, tools, laundry machines, furniture, appliances, supplies, and the like, would be covered against a variety of losses by most comprehensive rental property owners' insurance policies (check yours to make sure), but your tenants' belongings would not be covered at all.

■ **Workers' Compensation**—Even though you hire only casual help or deduct just a few dollars from a tenant's rent in exchange for minor management or maintenance services, you are an "employer" and you *must* have workers' compensation insurance. If that worker of yours were to require medical attention or become incapacitated while on the job, even while driving to the bank to deposit rent monies, you would be held liable. You would have to pay those medical bills, no matter how large or how small.

You don't have to be the least bit at fault to be held liable. In fact, your clumsy worker could be totally at fault for throwing out his back after tripping over a paint bucket which he had carelessly left lying around and you'd still be liable for his medical bills. Fault doesn't matter. Workers' compensation insurance is "no-fault" coverage.

While he was doing some yard work, one of my managers was bitten by a brown recluse spider and nearly died from the resulting complications. Neither he nor I was at fault. We couldn't have done anything to prevent the spider bite. It just happened. I was sick at heart about the whole thing, but I'd have been a lot sicker if I hadn't had a workers' compensation policy to pay for his care. It cost some big bucks.

Don't assume this risk yourself. You know what medical bills can run nowadays, and you probably know what awards juries are making to people who become disabled on the job, even when the disability is only 10%. Whatever the medical bills, whatever the disability, you cannot afford to pay for these things directly yourself. You need workers' compensation insurance to pay them for you.

Don't assume that any all-inclusive insurance policy you buy for your rental property also includes workers' compensation. It doesn't. Workers' compensation insurance is a separate policy altogether.

Most states require every employer to have workers' compensation insurance, and because it's required, the risk pool is large and the rates are reasonable. They're based upon how much your workers earn and upon the type of work they do. The rates are a percentage of earnings, and the percentage increases as the riskiness of the work increases. The rate for somebody who does office work is around 1.2%, while the rate for somebody who does deep sea diving is over 100%.

Rather than letting an insurer arbitrarily classify your workers, make sure you classify them correctly yourself according to the kind of work they do most often. For a manager who does little more than clerical work, you should be paying around 1.2%. For a manager who does a little bit of everything, including both sedentary work and maintenance work, you should be paying around 12%. Don't pay too much or too little by classifying your workers incorrectly.

By the way, workers' compensation insurers conduct audits periodically to ensure that you are paying the correct premiums. Don't think you'll be able to get away with something by classifying your handyman as a clerical worker just to pay a cheaper rate. Besides, if your handyman is classified as a clerical worker and he gets injured using an electric drain auger, you'd better be prepared to do some fast talking. Cheating doesn't pay.

Rates do vary. You will find that you can save on your premiums by buying coverage through a group. Groups get better rates than individuals do. Check to see whether your rental housing association offers a group plan. Many do.

Another way to save on premiums is to buy a single policy to cover all of the workers at all of your properties, and divide up the costs among the properties when you pay the bill.

■ **Mortgage**—Two completely different types of insurance coverage have come to be known as "mortgage insurance." The objective of both types is the same, to pay off the balance of an outstanding mortgage when trouble strikes, but the beneficiaries are definitely not the same.

The first type benefits the property owner. It's pretty much the same as decreasing term life insurance, the decreasing sum being the mortgage balance. It's especially popular with homeowners because they want to protect themselves in case death or disability puts an end to some or all of the income used to make their house payments. The mortgage would then be paid in full. Such insurance is available to cover rental property mortgages as well, and it may be just as important for some rental property owners to have as it is for homeowners, especially when a rental property is running a negative cash flow and one person is contributing income from a job to support it.

When determining whether you should buy this insurance coverage, consider both the salary and the time contributions of each person involved with the property because you may find that the survivor would need to hire help to do the work done by whoever died, and that, of course, would increase the negative cash flow still more. If you do choose to buy this type of mortgage insurance for your income property, consult your tax adviser for advice on whether it is tax-deductible as a business expense. It may or may not be.

The other type of mortgage insurance will pay off the mortgage all right, but it won't benefit you as the property owner in the least. It protects your lender should you default on the mortgage, and should the property be sold off for less than the balance owing, the policy would pay the lender the difference between the two.

Although your lender may require that you pay the premium on such a policy, don't suppose that you're getting the same coverage as the other type of mortgage insurance. You're not. When the first one pays off, you or your heirs wind up with assistance in making your loan payments or with a property which is free and clear. When the second one pays off, neither you nor your heirs get a thing. The lender gets the policy's proceeds.

■ **Fidelity**—In those businesses where dishonest employees have the opportunity to steal cash and/or goods, wary employers buy fidelity insurance, that is, they "bond" their employees to protect themselves from theft, pilferage, embezzlement, forgery, and computer fraud.

The employees you hire to manage and maintain your rental property have an opportunity to steal from you. Of that there is no doubt. They might forge your name on checks. They might appropriate your tools or supplies for their own use. They might under-report occupancies. They might charge higher rents than they report to you. They might withhold more from tenants' security deposits than they tell you about. They might find more than a few coins on the floor after they've counted the laundry money. They might even be more audacious and abscond with an entire month's rent receipts. All of these things

have been known to happen to suspecting and unsuspecting owners alike. They could happen to you.

If you are inclined to put your properties on "automatic pilot," to let your manager run everything for months at a time, checking only now and then to see whether there's any money in the property account down at the bank, you need fidelity insurance. You need it desperately.

If you are looking over your manager's shoulder on either a random or a frequent basis and you believe that you have a pretty good handle on your income, don't bother. The premiums for this kind of insurance are really much too high for the limited amount of exposure you have.

Rather than pay fidelity insurance premiums for a policy which will pay careless employers for their carelessness, save the money and insure yourself by being careful. Reduce the opportunities managers have to steal from you. See that they handle little or no cash. See that they provide you with weekly income and occupancy reports, and see that you select your managers carefully in the first place.

Note that fidelity insurance covers losses you sustain as a result of your own employees' dishonesty. It does not cover losses caused by a manager working at your property if that manager is responsible to a property management company rather than to you. To protect yourself from that kind of loss, insist that any property management company you hire supplies a bond of its own.

■ **Auto**—To protect your property assets, you should obtain the highest liability limits available for your own vehicles. Minimum liability insurance may be quite sufficient for your tenants. If they're hit with a $500,000 judgment, their insurance carrier would pay the limits of the policy, their few assets would be liquidated, and they would declare bankruptcy. That scenario plays out every day. But what if you, a person of property, get hit with a $500,000 judgment, and you have only $100,000 in coverage? Kiss $400,000 of your assets goodbye. Caveat, dear landlord!

■ **Non-Owned Auto**—Non-owned auto liability insurance does not protect you from liability when you're driving a car other than your own. Your regular automobile policy does that.

No, non-owned auto protects you in case anyone you hire, even temporarily, is driving his own automobile and running errands for you when he becomes involved in an automobile accident. When the injured's attorney learns that your employee, while driving to the hardware store to pick up some towel bars for you, caused the accident which injured his client, you will be added to the list of those being sued. Insurance to protect you under such circumstances is reasonably inexpensive and well worth the cost.

■ **Umbrella**—Umbrella insurance coverage has nothing at all to do with those umbrellas we hold up to keep raindrops from falling on our heads. No, umbrella insurance, also known as blanket or excess insurance, keeps covering us when we reach the limits of our other liability policies. Those other policies cost more per dollar of coverage than an umbrella policy does because they pay off more often. They pay the smaller claims. Umbrella policies pay only the larger claims and only the higher amounts of the larger claims. On a $465,000 claim, for example, the primary policy might pay the first $300,000, while the umbrella policy might pay the rest, the $165,000.

Investigate the possibility of keeping the limits of your individual liability policies around $300,000 for each property and then buying an umbrella policy for $300,000 to a million or more. Structuring your policies that way will be less expensive than buying individual policies for a million dollars or more each.

To be effective, your umbrella policy should leave no gaps between the upper limits of your various primary liability policies and the lower limit of the umbrella policy itself. It should also cover you for at least double the value of your personal assets.

To avoid squabbling between two companies with different ideas for settling a single lawsuit, buy your umbrella policy from the same company that writes your primary liability policies.

■ **Boiler and Machinery**—You can imagine how horrendous the explosion of a boiler could be. The deaths, injuries, and property damage could result in some very costly claims, but the risk of claims isn't the only reason you should consider this type of insurance if you have the kind of equipment it covers: boilers, heavy machinery, pressure tanks, large air conditioners, or large compressors. You should consider it because the insurer becomes a partner with you in keeping losses to a minimum by inspecting the equipment regularly and making sure that it is well maintained and safe to operate.

Other insurers ought to spend as much of their premium dollars on loss prevention as boiler and machinery insurers do. They'd have fewer claims to pay.

■ **Waterbed**—Your tenants with waterbeds are the ones who ought to provide waterbed insurance, but face it, they're not going to remember to keep it in force unless you keep reminding them. You'd be wise to charge them enough extra rent to pay for the policy, and then pay the premiums yourself if you want the coverage.

■ **Dog-Bite**—Don't confuse pet insurance with dog-bite insurance. Pet insurance is health insurance for pets. Dog-bite insurance is liability insurance to compensate dog bite victims.

Like waterbed insurance, dog-bite insurance is a tenant's responsibility, but you are the one who must insist that any tenant whom you approve to keep an aggressive dog must buy dog-bite insurance and keep it current. That's your responsibility.

More than that, you may find that you cannot get a liability policy to cover your rental property unless the dog owners renting from you purchase dog-bite insurance. Make your insurance requirements part of the process of allowing a tenant to have a dog, and you won't be taken aback when your insurer cancels your liability policy because an inspector for the insurance company noticed a potentially dangerous dog on the property.

■ **Title**—When you learn that title insurance companies pay less than ten cents in claims out of every dollar they collect in premiums, you're inclined to think that you ought to stop whatever you're doing and become a title insurer yourself, whatever it is that title insurers do. After all, the house take in Vegas doesn't approach ninety cents out of every dollar bet. If it did, gamblers wouldn't return to the tables.

Well, then, should you buy title insurance yourself on your newly acquired properties? Why does title insurance pay out so little? What is title insurance anyway?

First of all, title insurance protects buyers against other people's claims to a property which might result from any number of unexpected occurrences, such as forgeries, identical names, and undisclosed heirs. Title insurance guarantees that nothing out of a property's past will catch up with you and deny you ownership now or in the future. It guarantees that you have clear title, that you and no one else truly owns the property.

Title insurance companies pay out so little in claims because they go to great lengths to discover problems with the title, and these protective measures are included in the price of the policy. If fire insurance companies operated similarly, they'd install an automatic sprinkler system in every building they cover and include the cost of the system in the price of the policy.

As to whether you should buy title insurance or not, you may not have a choice. Institutional lenders require you to buy enough title insurance to cover their loan, but the policy they require is strictly a lender's policy, not a buyer's policy. It's like the mortgage insurance which some lenders require borrowers to buy to protect the lenders. It doesn't pay off for you, although it does benefit you somewhat because it pays for the insurer's exhaustive title search, and consequently, the buyer's title insurance premium, which you may choose to buy or not, is less expensive than it would be otherwise.

When you're trying to decide whether to buy a buyer's title insurance policy, you should remember that you pay for it only once, when you first acquire the property, and then both you and your heirs are covered for as long as you or they own the property. You never pay another premium after that.

Whatever you do, don't acquire any property without having someone search the title at the very least, even if no lender's involved and you're paying for it in cash, yes, even if you win it in a poker game. That title search is an absolute must. It could reveal mechanics' liens, attachments, and old loans which the owner told you nothing about and which could trouble you for years to come.

Exercising Prudence

Insurance companies play the odds just as casinos do, just as you do when you gamble on renting to a certain applicant or on buying a particular property. You should play the odds when you buy insurance, too. Although there is some kind of insurance available for every conceivable risk connected with landlording, if you want to pay for it, and there are a great many insurance agents around who would be delighted to sell it to you, you don't want insurance to become your number-one expense. Seize the opportunity to save money every time you review your insurance needs.

Naturally you might be prudent in trying to save or you might be imprudent.

Here's how to be prudent—

• Select only the kinds of coverage you need for your location and situation. ("Are there all that many hurricanes in Billings, Montana?")

• Calculate carefully the amount of coverage you need. ("Do you really need $320,000 worth of fire insurance for your $160,000 duplex?")

• Shop around for coverage two months before the renewal date on your policy, and do it every time. ("$285? Why, Gerry wants $450 for the very same thing!")

• Price package policies. ("You mean that fire, vandalism, liability, loss of rents, and contents coverage all together are only $80 more than fire insurance alone?")

• Consider policies with deductibles you can live with. ("Does earthquake insurance with a $25,000 deductible clause really have a premium $222 lower? Does liability insurance with a $500 deductible really cost $93 less every year?")

• Hire an insurance consultant (to find one, search the internet using "insurance consultants & advisors [your state or local area]" as your search words) who sells no insurance himself to review your properties and coverage and make suggestions for reducing your insurance costs. ("Will adding two more fire extinguishers really save me $65 in premiums?")

Here's how to be imprudent—

- Buy only the kinds and amounts of coverage your lender and the law require. ("The tenant in Apt. 112 wants how much for tripping on that broken step?")
- Buy whatever coverage your agent sells you. ("You think I need glacier coverage? OK, if you say so. The winters have been getting colder around here. Write it up.")
- Buy only from your bridge partner who sells insurance on the side. ("Can you get me a good deal, Gerry?")
- Buy separate policies for each kind of peril. ("Is it $85 more for contents and $18 for loss of rents or vice versa?")
- Buy non-deductible coverage. ("You want to settle my claim about the dent in my commercial washing machine for $52?")
- Trust insurance agents to give you money-saving suggestions. ("Did you say that you drove by the property and everything looked all right?")

Selecting a Solid Insurance Company

Not so long ago we needn't have concerned ourselves with the ability of our insurance company to pay a claim. We simply shopped for the best price and took for granted that the company we selected would be sound enough to pay whatever claims we might have.

Today, some companies, having put their hoarded premiums into failed investments and having had to pay numerous unexpected settlements, are finding themselves on ground shakier than a southern California earthquake fault, unable to pay claims without digging deep into their assets. Even the venerable Lloyd's of London has been in trouble and many of the "names" who back the Lloyd's policies with their personal fortunes have suffered their own Dust Bowl Depression and lost everything.

Lucky for us, we don't have to depend upon flacks and advertising agencies for information about insurance companies. Their assets and their history are not cloaked in secrecy. They're public information. Insurance companies are rated by an independent company, A.M. Best, and you may consult their ratings online by going to A.M. Best's Consumer Insurance Information Center (ambest.com/consumers). There you will find "quick and dirty" financial strength ratings for free, and for a few bucks, you may purchase a comprehensive report providing a company's rating history, its market share, and a list of its competitors.

Understand that the ratings change as the companies' fortunes change. What was a solid company two years ago may be jelly today.

Getting a Fair Settlement

Some insurance companies don't pay claims very willingly or very fairly. They make you jump through their flaming hoops before they will pay you even a pittance. Should you feel that your insurance company isn't treating you fairly when handling your claim, secure the services of a public insurance adjuster. Their business is to represent policyholders. They know how much claims are worth because they're involved with them all the time. For a percentage of your claim, they get bids, do the paperwork, make the phone calls, and argue on your behalf.

They make sure that you get every cent your insurance company owes you and that you get it promptly.

Responding to an Accident

Whenever an accident on your property results in an injury, see that the injured party receives proper medical attention right away. Immediately after that, contact your insurance agent and complete an accident report. As time goes by, the witnesses and the injured party tend to forget what actually happened, and you can be sure that their muddled memories are not going to favor their landlord as they struggle to reconstruct the mishap.

Settling Tenants' Claims Yourself

Because they don't want their premiums raised or their coverage canceled, motorists will sometimes try to settle "fender-bender" claims themselves rather than turn them over to their insurance companies.

For these same reasons and a few others, I have settled tenants' claims myself at times. The re-

February 25, XXXX

Dear *Richard and Rose Renter,*

    As we do every year when the premiums come due, we have been reviewing our insurance policies, and we thought that you might like to know how you are affected by the insurance we carry.

    Basically, our policies cover only the building itself where you live. They do not cover any of your belongings against damage or disappearance, nor do they cover you for negligence should you, for example, leave a burner going under a pan and start a fire which damages the kitchen.

    To protect yourself against these calamities, you should get a tenant's insurance policy. Most insurance companies and agents will write such a policy for you, and we would strongly urge that you inquire about getting one.

    For the peace of mind that it gives, a tenant's insurance policy is reasonable indeed.

                Sincerely,

                Leslie Landlady

sults have been mixed. In most cases, the tenants took what I offered and went away pleased. In one case I well remember, the tenant took what I offered and acted pleased. Then, without any warning or attempt to discuss the matter further, she went to an attorney and filed suit. I was not pleased.

Just as greed among heirs surfaces when estates are being settled, greed among tenants surfaces when damage claims are being settled. Greed, you must recognize, feeds upon itself in some people. No matter how much you offer to settle a claim, it won't be enough. They expect a lifetime annuity for a hangnail, but if you offer them a lifetime annuity straightaway, they'll hold out for a life-after-death annuity, too, and expect you to deliver it wherever they happen to be.

If you are inclined to settle a claim yourself, be cautious every step of the way, but do act fast and do document everything. Determine, first of all, whether you are at fault for what has happened. Listen to what everybody has to say. Get statements from witnesses if possible, and decide whether you ought to bother making an offer at all. Sometimes the best thing you can do is ask the tenants what they think is fair for you to do under the circumstances. Take your cues from them. They might surprise you and say something reasonable.

Tailor your offer to the type of tenants you're dealing with (do not even bother approaching "difficult" tenants; let an insurance adjustor deal with them), the type of incident (stick with property damage cases and cases involving minor medical expenses), and the severity of the incident (do not bother with any "serious" cases; turn them over to your insurance company immediately).

Be aware that if you do turn a claim over to your insurance company after you have given your tenants some compensation, the insurance company will not reimburse you for whatever you gave the tenants.

Whenever you give your tenants some compensation, get a statement from them in writing, whether it will stand up under close scrutiny or not, stating that they have been fully compensated for whatever has happened.

Although a wily attorney can poke holes in any statement you ask your tenants to sign, most tenants feel inclined to abide by what they sign, and they feel disinclined to take the matter any further. They consider the matter settled, and they will thank you for treating them fairly and quickly in a time of need.

Helping Your Tenants Understand the Benefits of Having Renters' Insurance

Only a third of all tenants have renters' insurance to protect themselves from calamity in case their possessions go up in smoke or they're flooded out when the creek rises or their child burns down their rental house while playing with matches. Your owners' policy would pay to repair or replace the building if something were to happen to it, but your policy would not cover the tenants' possessions nor the tenants' liability if they were found to have caused damage to the property.

This state of affairs raises any number of questions, and you should have some answers so you can help your tenants understand renters' insurance and encourage them to buy it.

Why do so few tenants purchase renters insurance?
- They erroneously believe that their landlord carries insurance covering them and their belongings.
- They have never given it a thought because nobody has ever made them aware of it.
- They think they can't afford it.
- They think their belongings are too worthless to be concerned about.
- They'd rather gamble that the premiums they'd pay over time would exceed whatever benefits they'd receive.

Why should you as a landlord be concerned about whether your tenants have a renters' insurance policy?
- Tenants who have insurance are less likely to sue their landlords after a calamity than tenants who don't have insurance. Tenants who have insurance don't have to turn to you for compensation. They turn to their own insurance company for compensation.
- You should show a positive, caring attitude toward your tenants whenever you can. After all, you are a scrupulous landlord, aren't you?

What does a renters' policy cover?
- It may cover fire damage only or fire damage plus lots more.
- It may cover tenants' personal goods which

are damaged or stolen on the premises.

- It may cover losses to their goods when they are off the premises, such as golf clubs or a camera stolen out of their locked car.
- It may cover them in case someone mugs them on or off the premises where they live, forges their checks, or steals their credit cards.
- It may cover personal liability in case they are negligent as tenants and cause damage to the dwelling.
- It may cover personal liability for non-auto bodily injury claims brought by others.

Where can tenants buy a renters' policy?

- Almost all the big general insurance companies offer it—Allstate, Farmers, GEICO, Nationwide, Safeco, State Farm, Travelers.
- Tenants might start their search by asking their auto insurance agent. Chances are that the agent can bundle tenants' insurance with their auto insurance at an attractive rate.
- Tenants who know how to use the internet need only search on "renters insurance" to find the websites of companies that write it.

How much does it cost?

- Rates vary by regions. One company has different rates for nine different regions in a single state.
- Typically, renters' insurance will cost between $8 and $25 per month for $25,000 worth of coverage with a $250 deductible. Personal liability on such a policy is $300,000.
- Policies with minimal coverage cost as little as $96 per year and go up from there.

Can tenants pay in installments?

- Most insurers offer a variety of payment plans—monthly, quarterly, semiannually, and annually. Ask. Of course, there is a service charge for the extra bookkeeping required to handle installment payments.

What discounts are available?

- Discounts are available for those who have any combination of the following–a deadbolt lock, a smoke alarm, a fire alarm, a sprinklered dwelling, or a fire extinguisher.

How can you make your tenants aware of the benefits of a renters' policy?

- Mention when you first rent to them that they

should secure a renters' insurance policy if they want coverage.

- Remind them of their exposure every so often in a note included with their rent receipt. Use a letter like the one shown in this chapter.

How can you convince them that they ought to have renters' insurance?

- Include a clause in the rental agreement which either requires them to secure renters' insurance or informs them that they are otherwise self-insured.
- Make them aware that their possessions are indeed worth something, probably more than they think.
- Tell them that they would be liable if they caused a fire at the property, and the place burned down. A renters' policy would cover them.
- Tell them that a renters' policy includes much broader coverage than they might think.

Are there any ways you can help them get a renters' policy?

- You may buy a policy for them in their name and include its cost in their rent, but do recognize that it becomes their policy. Should they move out six months after you paid the annual premium and should you then ask the company for a refund, the tenants will get the refund, not you, because the policy must be in their name.

Will the insurance company notify the landlord when a renters' policy lapses?

- If you ask to be notified, you will be notified. Have yourself listed as an "additionally insured" party, and you'll be notified automatically via email when there's any change in the status of the policy, including cancellation for lack of payment.

Some Last Words

Be prudent whenever you buy insurance affecting your income property business. You'll save on the premiums and you'll protect your assets so that someday you'll be able to enjoy those assets yourself.

Also, make your tenants aware of the benefits of having a renters' policy and then help them get one.

18
Providing for
Safety & Security

Absolute safety and true security are utterly impossible to guarantee in this world. They always have been and they always will be.

Metal detectors, X-ray machines, CT scanners, bomb-sniffing dogs, and sharp-eyed security people at airline passenger terminals around the world have helped reduce, but not eliminate, in-flight crises.

Mandatory fire sprinkling systems installed at great expense in gleaming high rises usually prevent small fires from becoming big fires, but not always.

Even the most sophisticated electronic alarm systems and well-trained, round-the-clock Secret Service agents cannot protect the President of the United States from the maniacs bent on doing him harm.

All we landlords can hope to do is provide a modicum of safety and security for our tenants and ourselves by taking reasonable precautions. That's what this chapter is about, taking reasonable safety and security precautions to provide as much safety and security as we can for our tenants and ourselves at a reasonable cost.

Learning About Fire Safety

As a landlord, you need to know the basics of fire safety because you are directly resonsible for the habitability of your rental property, and you are indirectly responsible for the lives of your tenants. Take these responsibilities seriously. Learn what you can about fire safety and pass what you know along to your tenants.

Ignorance about fire safety is not bliss. It's death. Every day in the United States at least eight people die horrible deaths in home fires. Knowledge about fire safety might have prevented those deaths.

With 99.9% of all human knowledge now available on the internet, it's an exhaustive and readily accessible source of fire safety information, but your tenants are unlikely to spend any time searching it for fire safety information. You should, and you should make the results of your search readily available to them.

On the following page is a compilation of fire safety tips taken from a number of websites, including that of America's most famous fire department, the New York City Fire Department (FDNY). In addition, there's a list of search words and websites anybody may use to gather more fire safety information both in word and video form.

Put this fire safety information in the hands of your tenants and encourage them to digest it.

Consider hosting a gathering of your tenants to help them understand the importance of fire safety. Invite a fire marshal to speak on the subject, and make the gathering all the more dramatic and memorable by demonstrating the correct way to use a fire extinguisher, one exactly like those you provide, to put out a raging wastebasket fire (conduct the demonstation outdoors in a safe location). Entice your tenants to come by providing finger food, treats, and non-alcoholic drinks. They'll come, and they'll learn. Some of them may even thank you for making them more aware of fire safety.

Selecting and
Placing Fire Extinguishers

Why don't all insurance companies require fire extinguishers for all of the buildings they insure? I certainly don't know. I do know that no rental building I have ever purchased has had them installed when I assumed ownership. As soon as I take possession, the first thing I do is place extinguishers where they're conspicuous and within easy reach of every tenant. Whether your insurance company is concerned enough about fire safety to require that you supply extinguishers

Fire Safety Tips

Use Care When Cooking
Keep cooking areas clear of combustibles, and don't leave your cooking unattended. Keep the handles of your pots turned inward so nobody is likely to knock them over the edge of the stove. If grease catches fire, turn off the burner immediately. Then slide a lid over the pan to smother the flames or else put them out with a fire extinguisher or ordinary baking soda.

Keep Matches and Lighters Hidden
Keep matches and lighters hidden out of youngsters' reach. Teach them early that matches and lighters are tools for grownups, not toys for youngsters, and that they should tell a grownup immediately if they find any matches or lighters.

Use Electricity Safely
If an appliance smokes or smells strange, unplug it immediately and have it checked. Check your electrical cords periodically, including extension cords, and replace any that are cracked or frayed. Also, don't run extension cords under carpets or overload them with high-energy devices such as irons, space heaters, toasters, hot plates, and microwaves. Remember that fuses and circuit breakers protect you from fire. Don't tamper with the fuse box or use fuses too large for the circuit.

Practice Candle Safety
Never leave a lit candle unattended. Never leave candles burning when you go to sleep. Never use candles near combustible materials such as curtains, drapes, bedding, and cabinets.

Give Space to Space Heaters
Keep portable space heaters at least 3 feet (1 meter) away from curtains, furniture, clothing, bedding, and anything else that burns. Never leave heaters turned on when you leave home or go to sleep, and keep children and pets well away from them.

Plan and Practice Your Escape
With your housemates, plan two ways to escape from every room. Your escape route must not require taking an elevator because it might stop and trap you inside or take you to where the fire is the worst. Include in your plan a meeting place outside where everyone should gather. Practice your escape plan once or twice a year.

Stop, Drop, and Roll
If your clothing catches fire, slowly get clear of any surrounding fire which could re-ignite your clothing. Then stop, drop to the ground, and roll over and over to smother the flames. Cover your face with your hands to protect your face and lungs.

Get Out and Stay Out of a Burning Building
If you find yourself in a burning building, get out fast. Once you leave, stay out. Do not go back to rescue a person, animal, or thing you suspect may still be inside. Leave the rescue operations to firefighters who have the right training and equipment.

Crawl Low Under Smoke
If smoke is clogging your primary exit route, look for a better exit route through clean air. If you must exit through smoke, get down to where you'll find clean air several inches off the floor and crawl to the nearest safe exit.

Cool a Burn
If you notice a burn on your skin, place it in cool water immediately for 10 to 15 minutes to ease the pain. Do not use butter on a burn, as this can prolong the heat and further damage the skin. If the burn chars or turns into a nasty blister, seek emergency medical care to help eliminate the pain and reduce the infection.

Keep and Maintain Fire Extinguishers
Keep a sodium bicarbonate dry chemical fire extinguisher in your kitchen. Keep an ammonium phosphate dry chemical fire extinguisher in your car or garage. Keep a clean agent gas fire extinguisher alongside your computer. Check the gauges on the extinguishers twice a year, and shake the dry chemical extinguishers once a year to keep the chemical from caking.

Check Smoke Detectors
Make sure you have smoke detectors on every level of your dwelling and next to every sleeping area. Test regularly, and replace batteries yearly or when you hear chirps signaling that a battery is dying.

Learn More
There's more to learn about fire safety, and you'll find plenty of fire safety information on the internet. Use the following search words to find at least some of it:
    fire fighting misconceptions
    evacuating a burning building
    trapped in a burning building
    fire extinguisher identification
    fire extinguisher use
    flashover

Check the following websites for sound information about fire safety:
    en.wikipedia.org/wiki/fire_safety
    firesafety.gov
    nfpa.org
    osha.gov/SLTC/firesafety/
    sparky.org
    usfa.dhs.gov/citizens/

shouldn't matter. You need them. Your tenants need them, and you need to provide them.

You are undoubtedly violating local fire ordinances if you do not have extinguishers available at your multi-family rental properties, but enforcement of the ordinances is so lax that chances are good you won't be fined or even warned if you fail to supply them.

Why wait for your insurance company or a fire marshal to tell you to install extinguishers before you do? They are so important that you should rush out to buy and install them as soon as you read about them here. Remember that your property and your tenants' lives and their property are all in jeopardy if there's no extinguisher available when needed.

Also, remember that if anybody should perish or become injured in a fire on your property, you would face a charge of negligence in a court of law for having failed to provide legally required extinguishers. Even a hard-drinking, incompetent plaintiff's attorney could nail you on that one. What's more, you'd be chastising yourself until the end of your days because it was your oversight that led to somebody's horrible death or injury by fire.

You need witness only one fire at your rental property to become convinced that you need fire extinguishers. If you haven't witnessed any fires at your rental property and you're not convinced yet, consider the following scenario.

After cooking a big breakfast for her family, your tenant is cleaning up the kitchen when she hears familiar music introducing her favorite morning television program. In her haste to watch, she inadvertently turns the electric burner beneath the pan of bacon grease to high heat, one click from off, and hurries into the living room. Ten minutes later, all of a sudden, the grease ignites into flames high enough to scorch the kitchen cabinets and set the walls on fire. The tenant notices the fire and springs into action. She rushes about looking for an extinguisher nearby, and finding none, she tries dousing the flames with water. The water only feeds the flames. Finally realizing her plight, she grabs her portable TV, scrambles out, and screams "FIRE!" Someone calls the fire department, but by the time the fire trucks arrive and the fire fighters can put out the blaze, the entire apartment and the one next to it have sustained so much damage that they're uninhabitable. The tenants salvage what they can and move out.

Then what happens? The insurance adjuster surveys the damage. You get estimates for repairs, and sometime later the work begins. Three months after the fire, you're looking around for new tenants to move into the two repaired apartments. You have lost three months' rent on the two apartments, you've spent hours of your own time planning and supervising, and you've gone through the uncertainties again of selecting more new tenants. In other words, you're out of pocket a considerable amount of money for expenses, and you've wasted a considerable amount of time coordinating everything.

Even if your fire insurance policy does cover every dollar of the repairs and every dollar of lost rent, you still suffer a loss because your insurance won't compensate you for your time.

As a landlord, you need fire extinguishers. There's no doubt about that. They're every bit as essential as the lock on a bank vault.

Before you start looking around to buy fire extinguishers, you should know the meaning of the letters and numbers used to determine the class and size of fire each can effectively extinguish so you can match the extinguishers you buy to their applications, and you should know the parameters affecting your choice.

The letters stand for classes of fire. "A" firefighting agents will put out fires fed by wood, paper, cloth, rubbish, and some plastics. "B" firefighting agents will put out fires fed by flammable liquids and gases such as gasoline, diesel fuel, propane, oil-based paint, grease, and cooking oil. "C" firefighting agents will put out live-wire electrical fires without endangering the firefighter. "D" firefighting agents will put out fires fed by combustible metals, such as titanium, magnesium, and lithium, and "K" firefighting agents will put out fires fed by cooking oils.

The number appearing before each class indicates the size of the fire in that class which the extinguisher will put out. The larger the number, the larger the fire it will put out, and hence the greater is the extinguisher's effectiveness. A "1A" extinguisher, for example, will put out 50 burning pieces of wood which are 2"x2"x20"; a "2A" extinguisher will put out a fire twice that size, and so on. A "1B" extinguisher will put out a fire fed by 3.25 gallons of naphtha (a solvent) blazing away in a 2.5 square-foot pan, and, likewise, a "2B" extinguisher will extinguish a blaze twice that size. The "C" class has no numerical rating nor do the "D" and "K" classes.

Now consider these five parameters affecting your choice of extinguisher here expressed as questions:

1) Is it effective in fighting all kinds of fires?
2) Is it light enough for anybody to carry?
3) Is it easy to use?
4) Is its residue easy to clean up?
5) Is it modestly priced.

No extinguisher fits all of these parameters, but several come close. Before I mention them, I want to warn you about two that you should avoid as if they were incendiary bombs.

The two are soda-acid extinguishers and pressurized water extinguishers, both of which have been around since the 19th century. They're easy to recognize because they look like "real fire extinguishers." They're shiny stainless steel or brass cylinders about two feet tall and eight inches in diameter. They're quite impressive to somebody who knows nothing about fire extinguishers.

You'll find them in use in some older apartment buildings and find them for sale in antique shops. I suppose they're still in use at all because grandpa and grandma once used them, and I suppose they're still adequate if you happen to have a stationery store, a lumber yard, or a yardage shop because they're good for putting out paper, wood, and natural fiber fires, but they're as messy as a litter of untrained puppies to clean up after. They're also heavy, and they only aggravate other types of fires because their extinguishing agent is water, not the best fluid for putting out an electrical or grease fire.

Around your rental properties, you should use ammonium phosphate dry chemical extinguishers for general-purpose use, sodium bicarbonate dry chemical extinguishers for use in kitchens, and Halotron gas extinguishers for use around electronics such as computers and televisions.

Dry chemical extinguishers filled with ammonium phosphate as an extinguishing agent are the most commonly available extinguishers on the market today for domestic use. They satisfy four of the five parameters you want in a fire extinguisher. The one parameter they don't satisfy is number 4. Their residue is not easy to clean up.

Their residue is not easy to clean up because ammonium phosphate is corrosive and sticky, and it spoils food. In other words, after you use an extinguisher filled with ammonium phosphate to put out a kitchen fire, you'll have to scrub and scrub to clean up the mess, and you'll have to throw away any food it touches. After you use one to put out a fire in your computer workspace, you'll likely have to throw away your computer.

Dry chemical extinguishers filled with sodium bicarbonate as an entinguishing agent satisfy parameter number 4 all right, but they don't satisfy parameter number 1. They are not effective in fighting all kinds of fires. They don't warrant even a "1" rating to extinguish class "A" fires. What good are they then? They're good in the kitchen. They extinguish the most common household fire of all, the grease fire, and they leave behind nothing but an edible biodegradable residue which is easy to wipe up. After all, sodium bicarbonate is baking soda!

Kidde's FX10K Kitchen Fire Extinguisher is a good example of a sodium bicarbonate extinguisher which looks and works like the extinguishers you're used to seeing.

Fire extinguishers filled with Halotron are called "clean agent" extinguishers because they use a fire-smothering gas rather than a liquid or powder and the gas leaves no mess behind once it extinguishes a fire. Halotron extinguishers satisfy all the parameters you look for in an extinguisher except for number 5. They aren't cheap, but they need less maintenance during storage, never clog during use, and require no cleanup after use.

As for prices, you'll find that the most common type, ammonium phosphate, range from $20 for a two-pounder with a rating of "1A:10BC" to $60 for a ten-pounder with a rating of "4A:60BC." The sodium bicarbonate kitchen extinguishers range from $12 to $20, and the small Halotron extinguishers are just shy of $100. These prices are for a single extinguisher. Buy them in quantity and the prices drop.

Having selected an extinguisher suitable in type and size to your application, you still must decide where to place it. The word for placement is "conspicuous." Your tenants must know where it is within seconds of when they need it, for a fire can double in size in thirty seconds, and they cannot afford to waste time looking for an extinguisher. It must be in a conspicuous place.

You are the best person to judge what is a conspicuous place for extinguishers located indoors.

Outdoors, when you're placing a medium-sized (5-pound) extinguisher for multiple tenants to use, you should place it in a conspicuous place within thirty feet of the furthest dwelling entrance and with its carrying handle five feet above ground level at most.

You should also place it in a fire extinguisher cabinet. Both Amazon and HD Supply carry my favorite, the Kidde 468041 Potter Roemer Surface-Mount 5-Pound Fire Extinguisher Cabinet. It's made of galvanized steel painted ivory, and it's fitted with tempered safety glass, which eliminates the dangerous glass shards resulting from breaking plate glass, and a non-removable BreakRite™ handle, which eliminates the need for a heavy tool to break the glass. It sells for around $40.

CAUTIONS AHEAD—The following cautions have all resulted from costly or painful experiences I have had with fire extinguishers myself. I hope you learn the lessons I had to learn through experience without having to repeat the experiences yourself.

✔ **Caution ONE**—You would think that extinguishers labeled "rechargeable" would, in fact, be rechargeable. Well, technically they may be, but in the real world they may not be. They may be able to hold only their original charge but not one they get in the field, at least not for any reasonable period of time. When their charge has been spent on a fire or they have lost their charge spontaneously over time, you might try to have them recharged at an extinguisher service shop only to learn that they are really disposable extinguishers rather than rechargeable ones because the service shop won't recharge them for you. The shop won't recharge them because it doesn't want you blaming them when the charge soon fails, and the fault lies not with them but with the manufacturer's cheap materials.

If you expect your extinguishers to last a long time and take recharging, ask for buying advice of somebody trustworthy who recharges extinguishers for a living, preferably somebody who does not also sell extinguishers. Lacking the advice of an expert, select an extinguisher which has an all-metal head rather than one made of plastic. I have yet to encounter an extinguisher with an all-metal head which couldn't be recharged, while I have encountered many extinguishers with plastic heads which couldn't be.

✔ **Caution TWO**—If you buy the smaller extinguishers, be wary about placing them in exposed areas, including shared laundry facilities. They're perfect for use in cars, trucks, boats, planes, and recreational vehicles, and they sometimes mysteriously develop legs. To discourage people from taking them, engrave them with your name or your property's name and address, and also paint them with a colored marking of some sort, perhaps a few blue dots or a pink band. Then, if they do disappear, you will be able to make a positive identification if you should happen to see them later in a tenant's possession.

✔ **Caution THREE**—Heads, bare fists, and feet were not made to break plate glass, filmed barroom brawls notwithstanding. Instruct your tenants to use a shod foot or any hard object that doesn't bleed when they have to break an extinguisher cabinet's plate glass pane in an emergency to get at an extinguisher. Tempered safety glass like that used in the Potter Roemer cabinet is another matter entirely. Break it with anything, and it turns into harmless pebble-like pieces.

✔ **Caution FOUR**—No extinguisher lasts long during use. Nine to twelve seconds is all that a five-pound dry chemical extinguisher will last in a sustained blast. Extinguishers last longer and work more effectively when used in short blasts, and though they certainly will not extinguish a burning house, they can extinguish any small fire your tenants are apt to have if they discover and fight it early.

✔ **Caution FIVE**—Most extinguishers carry instructions warning users to stand back a certain distance from a burning target while attempting to put it out. One reason for this warning is obvious. The closer you are to the flames, the greater are the chances that you'll get burned. The other reason is not so obvious. The pressure of the extinguisher's stream can act like a blast of air and actually blow away some of whatever's burning, thereby spreading the fire to another area. If an extinguisher says, "Stand back 6 feet and aim at base of fire," do so. Don't doubt the wisdom of that advice. You can be sure that some lab technicians have tested the extinguisher under controlled conditions and have determined that six feet is the optimum distance for effectiveness. Don't think that you know better and that the extinguisher would be more effective up close. It won't be.

✔ **Caution SIX**—Fire extinguishers which use a powder as their extinguishing agent should be shook by hand or struck on the bottom with a rubber mallet at least once a year to "fluff" the powder so it doesn't "cake" in the bottom of the cannister. When caking occurs, the extinguisher is worse than useless because it will shoot its propellant at the fire and cause it to spread.

Keeping a Firefighter on Duty In the Kitchen 24 Hours a Day

Most residential fires start in the kitchen when an unattended burner on the stove becomes too hot and ignites something flammable on or near the burner. To put out such fires in restaurant kitchens, fire codes require that their stove hoods have fire extinguishing systems which activate automatically when the temperature rises to a dangerous level. Until recently, anyone wanting an automatic extinguishing system in a residential kitchen would have had to install the same kind of expensive system used in restaurants.

Now there's an extinguisher on the market designed specifically for residential kitchens. Although not nearly as powerful as a restaurant's system, the FireStop Automatic Fire Extinguisher works well enough to extinguish stovetop fires soon after they start, and it works without human intervention. It works automatically.

Either a direct flame or a temperature above 277° Fahrenheit (136° Celsius) will activate the extinguisher. It then does two things. It makes a very loud (146 dB) popping sound to alert anybody within earshot that something has gone terribly wrong in the kitchen, and it releases its full load of siliconized bicarbonate of soda (yep, it's baking soda) directly onto the fire by gravity.

As you might imagine, fires start small and grow large quickly, doubling every thirty seconds. The sooner you try to extinguish them, the better are your chances of putting them out. Because these extinguishers attack the fire as soon as they sense that there is a fire danger, and because they work automatically, like an automobile's airbag, they are effective. They're almost like keeping a firefighter on duty in the kitchen 24 hours a day.

These extinguishers are especially easy to install. They come with a built-in magnet which clings to the underside of the vent hood and keeps them mostly, if not completely, out of sight. There's no drilling or sawing required. There are no bolts and no screws, just magnets. What could be easier to install than that?

They are a little pricey at $28.50 each (quantity one), especially when you need two of them for a four burner stove, and they must be replaced every five years, so that adds to their overall cost as well, but with the average kitchen fire causing $3,000-$4,000 worth of damage and with fire insurance premium discounts available on buildings which have them, they may not "cost" anything at all in the long run.

Look into the quantity discounts, and you'll find that they bring the unit price down by as much as 40%. With that big of a discount available on quantity purchases, you should offer to pool people's orders at the next meeting of your rental housing association so that all of you will get these firefighters-in-a-can at a wholesale price.

The extinguishers are available directly from the manufacturer Williams-Pyro (stovetop-firestop.com) and from dealers such as HD Supply (hdsupplysolutions.com) and Fire Extinguisher Depot (fire-extinguisher-depot.com).

If you're inclined to be skeptical about purchasing these extinguishers for all of your properties, try a set of them in your own kitchen, and also try them in your rental dwellings occupied by the disabled, by anyone who has had a kitchen fire in the past, and by the elderly who live alone. They are most at risk.

These extinguishers will make a believer out of you when they save a life or a building. They're the best kind of "fire insurance" you can buy because they put out fires before there's any damage to life, limb, or property.

Providing Smoke Detectors

Surely some landlord must have invented paint rollers. Who else besides a professional painter has to paint so often? Who else benefits so much from rolling paint instead of brushing it? Likewise, some landlord must have invented smoke detectors because they provide the rental property owner the great benefit of minimizing exposure to fire danger and damage in even the most klutzy and irresponsible tenant's dwelling.

Because tenants tend to be more careless about handling fire-causing agents than you are in your own home and because you can't possibly keep watch over them constantly, smoke detectors are ideal watchdogs to warn everyone within earshot of fire danger. They aren't fire sprinklers or extinguishers, mind you. They can't put out fires, but they do a good job of warning the living that there is fire danger.

Now that so many manufacturers make them, perfectly adequate smoke detectors are available for as little as $10 and as much as $35. At such prices, there's no good reason for any rental dwelling to be without them, and there's no good reason for a landlord not to replace them quickly when they malfunction or reach the end of their lifespan, which is ten years following their date of installation.

There are two fire detection techniques used in the smoke detectors readily available today, ionization and photocell. Each has distinct advantages. Ionization detectors, which sound an alarm when smoke interferes with an electric current flowing constantly through an ionization chamber, are better at detecting rapidly burning, flaming fires. Photocell detectors, which sound their alarm when smoke deflects a beam of light to a photocell, are better at sensing slow, smoldering fires.

In order to detect both types of fires in their earliest stages, you need both types of smoke detection. A detector which combines both ionization and photocell detection in a single unit is my first choice in smoke detectors.

My second choice is two different types of detectors mounted in two different locations. The photocell detector might be located near the bedrooms because that's where smoky fires tend to start, and the ionization type might be located near the kitchen because that's where blazing fires tend to start.

My third choice is a photocell detector alone. Photocell detectors, it is true, are slower in detecting rapidly burning fires, but only by mere seconds, whereas ionization detectors are slower by minutes in detecting smoldering fires.

My fourth choice is an ionization detector alone. Ionization detectors work satisfactorily and are the least expensive detectors on the market.

Though they're not the best detectors available, they're better than no detector at all.

As for location, if you're installing only one detector, mount it near the bedrooms where it will awaken the sleepiest of sleepyheads. They're the ones who really need the warning so they can get out alive. Avoid locating any detector in a kitchen because anybody's cooking is bound to cause nuisance alarms, and you don't want your tenants disarming a detector altogether in order to stop the inevitable nuisance alarms.

Detectors all require an electrical power source. Some run on batteries alone, and some run on batteries and house current. Those running on batteries and house current are preferable because they have a backup electrical power source, but unless your building is just now being built or rewired, you might as well forget about installing detectors which run on batteries and house current. Retrofitting a dwelling with new electrical outlets in the locations best suited for detectors is simply too expensive.

You needn't worry about the locations of electrical outlets when you're installing battery-operated detectors. They're so adaptable that airlines install them in their aircrafts' restrooms so flight attendants can catch smokers who are so desperate for a cigarette that they'll light up in flight at the risk of a heavy fine.

Use only alkaline batteries in your battery-operated detectors, batteries like Duracell or the Energizer, not the cheap carbon ones which fail without warning. Alkaline batteries last longer and discharge slowly enough to send proper warnings when they need replacing.

Don't use rechargeable batteries. They die too quickly at the end of their charge and cannot send warning chirps long enough so you can be certain that somebody will hear them.

Detectors using long-lasting lithium batteries,

which are supposed to last ten years, are now available. They work no better than other detectors. They simply have longer lasting batteries and higher price tags.

Unless you are a super-conscientious "Smokey the Bear" type and you take the time to monitor the batteries in your smoke detectors frequently, schedule the batteries for testing and replacement, if called for, once every year. Put a label on the outside of each detector and write on it when the battery is next scheduled for testing. Put this date in your maintenance records, too, where you can't miss it.

Before you buy any detector, familiarize yourself with your community's recommendations and regulations. Contact your fire department for guidance. Some require a certain type and some require a certain number of detectors to be installed in certain locations. Find out what those regulations are and comply.

Every time you conduct orientations for new tenants, give instructions in smoke detector care. Show them where each detector is, tell them why each was located there, show them how to conduct a functional test, explain to them how to shut off the detector when it's sounding a nuisance alarm, and demonstrate how to replace the battery. Make sure that each detector is in working order when they move in, and have them initial the smoke detector paragraph on the Condition & Inventory Checksheet, but don't rely on them to check the functioning of each detector. Do it yourself periodically.

Protecting Tenants Against Carbon Monoxide Poisoning

The *Journal of the American Medical Association* has reported that carbon monoxide poisoning is the leading cause of accidental poisoning deaths in the United States.

Carbon monoxide itself is a colorless, odorless, and tasteless gas resulting from the incomplete burning of fuels such as wood, coal, charcoal, propane, natural gas, oil, kerosene, and gasoline. Because it's ever so slightly lighter than air, it rises toward the top of any confined space and remains there.

In vehicles, people die of carbon monoxide poisoning when exhaust enters the passenger compartment and can't get out. In dwellings, people die of carbon monoxide poisoning when flame-fueled devices, such as fireplaces, space heaters, grills, ranges, ovens, furnaces, and water heaters, are not vented properly and when attached garages allow exhaust fumes to enter the dwelling.

The "fix" is simply to vent the carbon monoxide to the outside, but the problem is detection. Since nobody can sense the presence of carbon monoxide, it can build up to dangerous levels without warning and starve those affected of oxygen, leading to nausea, confusion, unconsciousness, and death.

A detector, located at least five feet up on a wall or on a ceiling near a sleeping area, will warn people to seek fresh air before the symptoms of carbon monoxide poisoning begin.

Absent any regulation requiring you to install carbon monoxide detectors in your rental dwellings, consider whether there are any sources of the gas in the dwellings themselves before you bother installing detectors. An "all-electric" house with a detached garage has no source, that is, unless it has a working fireplace or the tenants are using a kerosene space heater. An apartment heated by a gas-fired wall heater has a source, as does a steam-heated apartment with a gas range and oven.

Detectors made to detect carbon monoxide alone sell for around $25. Detectors made to detect both carbon monoxide and smoke sell for around $40.

Setting Water Heater Temperature

Here's the scenario—A groggy tenant steps into her shower and inadvertently turns the hot water to high. You have a good recirculating hot water system in your apartment building, so the shower immediately blasts the tenant with scalding water. Before she can think clearly enough to do anything about it, she has sustained skin burns and requires a trip to the emergency room. She looks to you to cover her medical bills and compensate her for her pain and suffering and for the time she misses from work. Your insurance company settles for $25,000 and cancels your policy.

The simple act of turning down the thermostat on the building's hot water heater would have changed this scenario. The tenant would not have been burned, and your insurance policy would not have been canceled. Moreover, you would have saved money on your energy bill every month.

Water heaters have thermostats just as space

heaters do, and you may set the temperature yourself according to the manufacturer's recommendation, which is 120° Fahrenheit (49° Celsius). You should. That's less than the 150° Fahrenheit (65° Celsius) dishwashers require, but it's more than the 100° Fahrenheit (38° Celsius) people require for their baths and showers.

Dishwashers have their own internal heaters to boost water temperature, so lowering the water temperature to the water heater manufacturer's recommendation presents no problem in cleaning dishes hygienically and thoroughly.

Some clothes washers have internal heaters, too, to bring the water temperature up to 140° Fahrenheit (60° Celsius), but they still wash satisfactorily at 120° Fahrenheit (49° Celsius). Again, there's no problem.

There is one little problem you'll need to be aware of before you set the thermostat to the recommended temperature. You'll likely find that the markings on the water heater's thermostat will be the words, "Warm," "Hot," and "Very Hot," rather than actual temperature numbers in Fahrenheit or Celsius. These relative designations are subjective. What's warm to one person may be hot to another. You want as precise a setting as you can get, and for that you'll need a thermometer to insert directly into a stream of water flowing from a faucet which is attached to or close by the water heater.

The first time you check the water temperature, you'll know whether to turn the thermostat up or down, but once you do, you won't know exactly how close the setting is to the desired temperature. Because of the volume of water already in the tank, any change you make in the setting will take time to show up in the reading. You'll need to return later to recheck the temperature and reset the thermostat as necessary. Set it as close to the manufacturer's recommendation as you can even if it requires more than two visits. This job is worth doing right.

Should you be skeptical about how reducing the water temperature will save you money, consider that there will be less heat loss as the water sits in the tank and as it circulates through the pipes. That alone translates into lower energy costs for heating the water. During periods of minimal use, which is, after all, most of the time, the heater won't turn on as often. During periods of maximum use, it will stay on longer because more water will be flowing through the heater as users mix a larger amount of hot water to achieve the temperature they prefer for washing themselves, but the heater still won't have to raise the temperature as much.

Talk about a winning combination! This is a good one. You provide for the safety of your tenants, and you save money at the same time.

Changing Locks

Give your new tenants the assurance that the locks on their dwellings have been changed so that previous tenants couldn't possibly use old keys for access. You needn't hire a locksmith for this job. You can do it yourself. If you can turn a screwdriver, you can change locks. You can, can't you?

The simplest way to make this change, if you lack the expertise and equipment to rekey lock cylinders, is to keep several spare locksets on hand. They should be exactly like the old ones if possible (locks from the same manufacturer shouldn't require changing either the spring-loaded latches or the striker plates, nor should you have to worry about adjusting the door cutout sizes). In most cases, you can change locks simply by zipping out two screws with a screwdriver, removing the old lock, putting a new one in its place, and securing it by zipping the two screws back in again. That's all there is to it.

To keep dust and water from settling inside the pin chambers and gumming up the works, always install locks so that the flat edge of the keyway is on the bottom. In other words, the key cuts should point up whenever a key is inserted. To reverse their keyways, Kwikset locks, America's most popular doorlocks, require a special cylinder removing tool, an inexpensive item available from a hardware store or locksmith shop. Buy one if you use Kwikset locks.

What do you do with the old locks? Why, you play "musical locks" with them, of course. No one need know where they went. If anybody asks, say they went to "Lock Heaven."

Whether you install new or resurrected locks doesn't seem to matter at all to tenants. What is most important to their feeling of security is knowing that former tenants of that particular dwelling no longer have ready access.

While you're changing the locks on their doors, you might want to inform your tenants exactly who does have access to their dwelling. You may be the only one, or you may have a resident manager and a maintenance person who have full sets of keys or master keys. Tell the tenants. They have a right to know.

Using "Landlord Locks"

Landlords who have more than a rental house or two should know about Landlord Locks (landlordlocks.com), a unique lock replacement system which is quick, inexpensive, secure, simple, and convenient. Landlord Locks are a "Why didn't I think of that?" idea.

Once installed, they enable a landlord to rekey a lock in seconds while still maintaining access to any number of locks with a single master key. In other words, they help landlords in two different ways. They reduce the time needed to rekey locks, and they offer the convenience of master keying.

To work their magic, Landlord Locks use six-pin (six-pin locks offer greater security than commonly used five-pin locks because they're harder to pick and offer a greater number of key code combinations) UltraMax-brand locks manufactured by Kwikset. Their design enables anybody to release the cylinder through the front of the lock body in such a way that what normally requires removal of the entire lock from a door can all be done with the lock in place.

In order to understand how Landlord Locks work, you need to know the meanings of several locksmithing terms applicable to pin tumbler locks—plug, pins, cylinder, master key, and change key.

A lock plug is a rotating rod the size of a wine cork. It sits in the center of a pin-tumbler lock. Its keyway accepts the key, and it rotates only when the correct key is inserted into the keyway.

Lock pins determine whether any one key will open a lock. They're about a sixteenth of an inch

PLUG FOLLOWER

KEY CUTS UP

PUSH CYLINDER PLUG OUT WITH PLUG FOLLOWER.

The conventional way to rekey a lock requires removal of the lock from the door to gain access to its backside.

in diameter and come in varying lengths. Their lengths vary according to the cuts on the key shaped to open the lock. In most locks, every pin chamber has an upper and a lower pin and a top spring holding them in place, and the pins move up and down in their chambers when a key is inserted. The correct key will line up the lower pins to form a sheer line on the surface of the plug and enable the plug to rotate and open the lock.

A lock cylinder is the essence of a pin-tumbler lock. It consists of a plug and pins and their casing.

A master key will open locks with many different pin combinations so long as they've been set up in advance to open with that master key.

A change key will open only those locks with a certain pin combination. Locks keyed alike all have the same pin combination and open with the same change key.

To rekey a lock the conventional way, you remove the lock from the door to gain access to its backside. If the cylinder detaches from the lock body as most do, you may exchange it with another one or else disassemble the cylinder and change the lower pins to match a new key. Time required for the job: a minimum of fifteen minutes.

To rekey a Landlord Lock, you simply insert its master key into the keyway, turn the key a quarter turn to the nine o'clock position, and slowly remove the cylinder. You exchange the cylinder with another one which will open with that same master key and a change key different from the one the lock opened with previously, and you complete the installation by reversing the removal steps. Time required for the job: a maximum of one minute.

Both entry and deadbolt Landlord Locks sell for approximately $20 each, depending upon the finish. Spare cylinders sell for a little less than $10 each. Master-keyed padlocks sell for approximately $16 each.

When you consider that Landlord Locks supply you with a quick-change lock replacement system that anybody can use and a master key system as well, all for the same money, you realize that they give good value for money.

By the way, Kwikset now offers a unique SmartKey™ lock with BumpGuard™ protection, which makes re-keying locks quick and easy and also defeats "lock bumping," but users have reported just enough problems with these new locks that you might want to take a "wait and see" approach before switching to them entirely.

Selecting Padlocks

To gain access with just one key to all the padlocked garages and storage enclosures where you keep your landlording equipment and supplies, buy padlocks which are keyed alike. All padlock manufacturers make them and most regular hardware stores carry them in stock.

If you decide to order doorlocks from Landlord Locks, check out their padlocks, too. They come keyed alike, keyed separatedly, keyed for master keys, and keyed for contractor access.

Don't use keyed-alike padlocks for those applications at multiple-family dwellings where every tenant needs access, applications such as gates and common storage areas. You don't want to have to issue still another key to each of your tenants. For those applications, use a combination padlock called the Sesamee Keyless Padlock (Master Lock makes a version as well). You may set its four dials to any of ten thousand combinations and reset them very simply at any time. Set them to an easily remembered number, like a building address or the current year, and your tenants will all have access when they need it without having to fumble for keys.

Do note this about any padlock used by more than one tenant: It will soon disappear unless you attach a chain to its shackle. Ask at your hardware store for a special padlock chain restraint made by the Master Lock Company which fits most padlocks and eliminates this problem.

Installing Peepscopes

Some entrances to dwellings are blind, that is, there's no way for the occupants to see who's at the door. Occupants have to either talk through the door or open it a crack to answer. Sometimes people attach security chains to their doors and door jambs to limit the door's movement and restrict access, but these chains provide more psychological than physical security because they pull loose from their flimsy mountings in response to the slightest blow and expose the occupants immediately to outside danger.

A far better way to solve this problem is to install a peepscope right in the door itself so that occupants can see who's out there knocking on the door without jeopardizing their own safety. Peepscopes cost less than $5 each and take less than ten minutes to install. Take care to install yours low enough, say around four and a half feet from the door bottom, so little people will be able to peep through without having to use a stepstool and big people will be able to peep through without getting a backache.

Tenants need peepscopes. Tenants use peepscopes. Tenants appreciate peepscopes.

Helping to Deter Criminal Activity

You will want to try what you can to prevent criminal activity from occurring at your rental property because every crime committed there reflects negatively on the property itself and scares off the better tenants, but you hardly have unlimited funds to spend for prevention, and you must recognize that no measure you take will be 100% effective, no matter how much it costs.

Before you spend big bucks to hire an around-the-clock security service or install decorative iron grillwork on the outside of your building, try taking other much less expensive measures which your tenants will surely appreciate, measures like installing closet safes, installing strategically located outside lighting, installing video surveillance, and adopting "Operation Identification" procedures.

■ **Closet Safe**—The closet safe is a damage-control measure designed to lessen the magnitude of burglaries. It does nothing to prevent them from occurring. A closet safe is merely a closet with a lock on its door where tenants may keep their valuables. It delays burglars, compelling them to spend more time and make more noise than they would like, many times frustrating them completely and causing them to leave with far less than what they came for. The lock on a closet safe might be a doorknob or a deadbolt lock keyed like the entrance locks, or it might be a padlock which the tenants supply themselves.

Having tenants supply their own padlocks is preferable because it relieves you of the responsibility of looking after still another lock and key. The usual padlock hardware is unsightly, I know, and you might shake your head at the thought of installing it on an inside door, but the Master No. 60 Padlock Eyes (see illustration next page), which attach to the door edge and the door jamb so they can be locked together with a padlock, are almost unnoticeable. Yet they, together with a good door and a good padlock, create a reasonably secure closet safe, one which is quite capable of providing some extra protection for tenants' valuables.

Whatever else you can do to thwart burglars and give your tenants a sense of security will help you keep your good tenants longer, and that's good business.

■ **Outside Lighting**—When the sun goes down, criminals come to life. They use darkness as a shield to protect themselves from being noticed while doing their dastardly deeds. Because burglars, robbers, muggers, rapists, and vandals all tend to avoid well-lit areas, you have to provide good lighting to keep them at bay. If you don't and a crime should occur on your rental property in a location where some attorney tells a sympathetic jury that you, you penny-pinching landlord, "should have installed adequate lighting," you will be held responsible for the crime just as surely as if you had slipped on your black nylon windbreaker, your rubber gloves, and your panty hose (over your head, of course) and taken up your Saturday night special to go out and do wrong.

You're left with no choice but to provide good lighting. Provide it.

As for the lighting itself, you have many choices. When making your choices, consider the following—location, vandalism resistance, operating cost, initial cost of the installation, lumen output, and availability of replacement bulbs.

Location is of primary importance for every kind of real estate. It's also important for outside security lights. Ask the tenants who would be most affected by the installation of a new outside light just where they would locate it to do the most good. They'll usually make good suggestions because they're the ones who walk the area at night. Go with them at night yourself and examine the area. You'll be showing them you care, and you'll be getting some good ideas.

Be practical when selecting the location. It should have readily available electricity, and it should be far enough out of reach to frustrate the garden variety bulb-snatcher. (Do you know how the New York Transportation Authority (MTA) frustrates bulb-snatchers in its subways? Its screw-in lightbulbs have left-handed threads. They won't fit ordinary light fixtures.)

Keeping a light fixture out of the reach of bulb-snatchers will go a long way toward eliminating vandalism, but you may have to go a step further. You may have to install a fixture with a polycarbonate (Lexan) lens so kids playing "sharpshooter" can't break the bulb with their pellet guns. Lexan-lens fixtures are more expensive than fixtures with ordinary plastic or glass lenses, so you may want to try an ordinary fixture first to see how long it lasts before you buy an expensive Lexan-lens fixture. An ordinary fixture may be good enough.

These are the most common lamp types, together with their lumen output per watt—incandescent (15-20 lumens per watt), tungsten-halogen (18-25 lpw), mercury-vapor (40-60 lpw), fluorescent (55-100 lpw), high-pressure sodium (75-140 lpw), metal halide (80-125 lpw), and low-pressure sodium (around 200 lpw).

The higher the lumens per watt, the more efficient is the source, and the lower is the operating cost. Incandescent lamps have the highest operating cost, and sodium-vapor lamps have the lowest. In fact, a 60-watt high-pressure sodium vapor produces five to seven times more lumens than the 60-watt incandescent. It's that much more efficient.

One day soon LED (light-emitting diode) lamps will surpass even low-pressure sodium lamps in efficiency, but they're not there yet. Currently, the two are nearly tied, but the promise of much greater efficiency in LED lamps is spurring research around the world.

Efficiency has its price, naturally, so you'll want to do some calculations to determine whether you can save enough over three years to justify the higher cost of more energy-efficient fixtures. Factor into your calculations the cost of the fixtures themselves, the bulb life-expectancy, and the price you pay for electricity. Where electricity is expensive, the extra efficiency of sodium-vapor lighting easily pays for the higher cost of the fixtures.

Any one of the commonly available lamp types, from incandescents to sodiums, is available in a size which will provide the lumen output you need to illuminate areas adequately. Match the output to a particular application carefully, and make sure that you can get enough lumens to illuminate what you want to illuminate when you mount the light source at a certain height. The higher the light source is, the fewer the lumens on a given area. Don't mount your light fixtures so high that they light more of the sky than they do of the ground.

As you know, the lightbulbs you use around your house all have the same screw-type bases, whether the bulbs are 60-watt or 150-watt, whether they're floodlamps or reading lamps. You can install either low- or high-wattage bulbs in the same socket interchangeably. In the case of most other lamp types, the bulb is matched to the fixture. When you buy a fixture, that fixture will accommodate only one particular bulb and no other. So don't try to put a 70-watt sodium-vapor bulb in a 50-watt sodium-vapor fixture. It won't work. The ballast differs and the base may differ as well.

W.W. Grainger offers an extensive selection of light fixtures and lamps in its regular catalog and also publishes a special lamp and ballast ordering guide. Don't even consider buying any fixture unless Grainger carries the replacement lamp. In-cidentally, Grainger's catalogs are full of useful information about lamps and fixtures.

Light as much outside area as you can with energy-efficient lighting, and you'll be marking your property as a poor target for nighttime burglars, as well as assisting your tenants in their nocturnal perambulations.

■ **Video Surveillance**—Security-conscious owners of apartment complexes, banks, casinos, hospitals, hotels, mansions, office buildings, retail stores, schools, and warehouses have all been installing video surveillance systems for years because they're effective in deterring criminal activity before it happens, helpful in mitigating criminal activity as it happens, and useful in analyzing criminal activity after it happens.

Until recently, these systems have had one major drawback. They've been expensive, expensive to purchase, install, monitor, and maintain. No longer.

The prices of electronics, surveillance systems included, have dropped precipitously over the past several years. You can now purchase a sophisticated video surveillance system with cameras, monitor, and digital video recorder (DVR) for less than $1,000, and anybody who is the least bit handy can install it and operate it.

When you go to purchase a surveillance system, you might find that a videocassette recorder (VCR) is available and is dollars cheaper than a DVR, but I want to caution you not to incorporate a VCR into your system. There are two important reasons: 1) somebody will have to remember to change the videocassettes on a scheduled basis, and you know what that means, and 2) searching through a videocassette or two or three for something that happened during a particular timeframe is a tedious and time-consuming task.

Specify that you want your system to include a DVR. A DVR is really a computer in a "black box." It records video on a hard drive which needs no human intervention to keep working 24/7/365. Depending upon the amount of activity it's recording and the size of its hard drive, it will store about a month's worth of video, and you can search through that video quickly to find something recorded weeks before.

Besides being easy to search through, today's video surveillance systems can be monitored remotely on a computer or even on a cell phone. In other words, you could be anywhere in the world where there's internet access or a cell phone tower, and you could look through the eyes of your security system cameras to see what's happening on your property.

Install those cameras in places such as entrances, hallways, parking areas, managers' offices, and trashbin corrals, and then put up signs saying something like this: "SECURITY NOTICE— This area is under 24-hour video surveillance."

Some sly landlords install dummy cameras and put up video surveillance signs, hoping that miscreants will think that the dummy cameras are working cameras. These landlords may outsmart some miscreants, those who pay heed to signage, but they won't outsmart all miscreants. Plus, they're giving their tenants a false sense of security which may backfire should things go wrong.

Should a tenant who took the signage at its face value ever tell a jury that he blames his landlord for lying about having a video surveillance system and that his landlord is therefore at least partly responsible for certain injuries and losses he sustained because he thought he was safer than he really was, the landlord would be hard-pressed to prove otherwise.

Don't bother with dummy cameras and fake signs, not now when real cameras and good working surveillance systems are within every landlord's budget.

■ **Operation Identification**—"Operation Identification" is a nationwide burglary prevention program. It involves engraving every item of value with the owner's name and driver's license number to prevent burglars from selling the item easily. Whether they keep their marked booty or sell it, they have good cause to worry that they will be linked to their crime and arrested. They can try to eradicate the engraved markings by grinding them off, but that's too much like work, and it damages the item, diminishing its value. Whenever they come upon an engraved item, burglars tend to leave it behind because there's plenty of other stuff around for the taking that won't cause them a bit of trouble.

Many urban police departments keep a supply of engravers on hand to lend out, and they give away warning decals to "Operation Identification" participants so that burglars will know what to expect inside when they're casing a property.

Consider buying an engraver yourself (they're less than $20), identifying all of your own tools and valuables, and then lending it to your tenants to use. They'll appreciate it, and you'll all find that it works.

Incidentally, for less laborious, better-looking engraving, use cursive script rather than printing each letter separately. Try both on paper with a pen or pencil first, and you'll notice how much smoother cursive writing is. That smoothness translates into good-looking engraving.

Hiring a Security Service

Even though "rent-a-cops" earn low wages, a security service can cost a landlord plenty as an on-going monthly expense. Having had several experiences with such services over the years, I have come to understand when and how to use them.

Use them when there's a drug problem in your complex or when so-called "criminal" elements are at work there. Then hire a security service to position a guard on your site during nighttime hours to record people's comings and goings and report them to the police. Before long, likely within a week, you should find that the drug problem and the criminal elements have vanished, and you can have the security service remove the guard. The cost to you for the service during that period won't amount to much, and it will be a one-time expense rather than an on-going monthly expense.

Avoid signing up for a regular security patrol service. It's nothing more than a drive-by every few hours and is a waste of money for a residential complex. It's something which might be useful for an office complex where there are no people about during the night, but residential complexes are full of people at night, and the many eyes of those people who may be awake at any given time are far better for noticing and reporting criminal activity than are the two eyes of one guard who happens to drive by every few hours.

"Neighborhood Watch" works better than a security patrol service, and its price is better, too. Use whatever influence you have with your tenants to get one started and then support it.

Neutering Tenant Identification

To thwart the criminal elements who prey on single women, identify your tenants on their mail boxes, bell buttons, and tenant directories with their last names only or with their last names and first initials only.

Do not give would-be intruders a single clue as to the sex or number of people living in any one dwelling.

Selecting "Harmless" Employees and Tenants

Whenever you're selecting employees and tenants, be especially cautious in determining whether they might pose a physical threat to others. Whether they appear to be harmless or suspicious on the surface, investigate them as thoroughly as you can before you hire them or rent to them because once you begin doing business with them on a regular basis, you assume a certain amount of responsibility for their behavior.

If they should ever harm a tenant physically during an argument or run down a tenant's child while driving drunk or use their master key to waylay a tenant, and if there happened to have been something in their past which you should have discovered, something which would have indicated that they might indeed hurt somebody, and you didn't even attempt to discover it, you will be held responsible for having hired them or rented to them in the first place, and you will be called upon to compensate their victims.

When you check out their applications, look for missteps in their past. If you find anything suspicious, reject them. Don't take pity on people who have checkered pasts, thinking that you're the one who ought to give them a second or a tenth chance. You're not in the business of rehabilitating people who've gone wrong. You're in the business of providing secure, safe housing to good people.

If you find no missteps while checking into your applicants' backgrounds, but they go sour anyway while they're working for you or renting from you, at least you can't be faulted for having failed to investigate them to begin with. You tried.

Let's suppose that you did try, but you still made a mistake. You hired a handyman who drinks too much and drives recklessly, or you rented to a tenant who is showing signs of pedophilia. Don't wait for something bad to happen. Deal with the situation immediately. Learn the details, ascertain the truth, and act quickly. Do whatever you have to do to get rid of them legally. Don't put your good tenants in any kind of jeopardy because of something you did or failed to do. Keep your tenants out of harm's way. That's your responsibility.

Taking Safety Precautions When Handling Rent

You are a wise landlord indeed to insist on cash, a money order, or a cashier's check for a tenant's move-in monies. You have to be absolutely certain that you're not giving a new tenant the keys to a dwelling worth $100,000 or more in exchange for a worthless piece of paper.

After that, you should be concerned about the risk in handling cash, for you could lose your property's entire monthly income all too easily if you happen to misplace the cash or get robbed, and since there's no affordable insurance policy to protect you from the loss, it would be yours alone to bear. Take the precaution, therefore, of refusing to accept cash for rent payments.

Some tenants will want to pay you their rent money in cash because they transact all of their business dealings in cash, and since cash is legal tender for all money transactions, you will have to take it unless you stipulate with adequate notice in advance that you won't. State in your rental agreement or takeover letter that you do not accept cash as payment for rent, and you don't have to accept it.

Some contrary tenants who deal strictly in cash may wave a fistful of greenbacks in your face and say, "Take it or leave it," and you'll have to weigh all the factors of the situation before deciding what to do. If you accept it, they will continue trying to pay you in cash month after month, and if you decline it, you may never collect their rent at all.

I usually accept their cash and patiently explain each time why I prefer rents to be paid by check or money order until they finally tire of hearing my repeated explanations and give in.

Even though you are resolute about not accepting cash, you may face a loss if someone robs you and gets away with your rent checks and money orders, because even stolen checks and money orders can be negotiated by a thief who knows how. To foil the thief, add one extra safety precaution—the "Little Old Rubber Stamp Trick."

Invest a few dollars in deposit stamps for yourself and any manager who handles rent for you so that stolen checks and money orders cannot be negotiated easily, if at all. As soon as a tenant hands you a check or a money order, stamp the back with a rubber stamp which might read something like one of these—

FOR DEPOSIT ONLY
to the account of
Lester Landlord
Leslie Landlord

—or—

PAY TO THE ORDER OF
BIG BANK
Lester Landlord
Leslie Landlord
011-123456
FOR DEPOSIT ONLY

Stamped on the backs of your checks and money orders, such a deposit stamp renders them worthless except as deposits to your own bank account. No one can cash them by trying to impersonate you at the corner liquor store. They can only be put into your account.

These same deposit stamps are also handy for marking the coin wrappers you use for rolling all those quarters, dimes, and nickels generated by your coin-operated laundry machines. Banks usually insist that rolls of coins be identified, just in case they happen to be short a coin or two.

If using the "Little Old Rubber Stamp Trick" saves you just one unauthorized check cashing, it's well worth the minimal cost.

Taking Personal Safety Precautions

We landlords tend to neglect our own personal safety because we're so conditioned to thinking about the safety of our tenants first and foremost. We also think that we can take care of ourselves no matter what happens. We've been "around the block" once or twice, and we think we've seen everything. Why should we be concerned?

Wake up. Bad things do happen to good people nowadays because there are all too many drugs, guns, gangs, hoodlums, loonies, and no-accounts loose in our society. There are so many opportunities for weak-willed people to get into trouble that they yield to temptation sooner rather than later, and the chances that a miscreant will be apprehended and then punished for a single criminal act are so slim that they can expect to get away with many such acts before anything happens to them.

We landlords are more vulnerable to "bad

things" than most people because we're more exposed. We sometimes alienate people who have short fuses, people who think nothing of venting their frustrations upon us directly because they have nothing to lose. We sometimes find ourselves alone with people who have just come off the street, strangers we know nothing about. We also sometimes have tempting amounts of cash on hand, and we're not the only ones who know we have it.

Pay heed to the news accounts of the landlord who was attacked by an irate tenant and the landlady who was assaulted by someone posing as a prospective tenant. Take personal safety precautions, and if you have people working for you, help them do likewise. Don't become a chalk outline on the pavement.

Here are some precautions you might want to take to reduce the risk of becoming a crime statistic—

✔ Whenever you go to show a vacancy to a prospective tenant, day or night, tell somebody else exactly where you're going and when you'll be returning. If there's nobody to tell, at the very least leave a note somewhere in plain sight.

✔ Whenever you're working in a vacant dwelling at night, hang something on the windows so you can't be seen by passersby, and keep the doors locked so you won't be surprised by somebody who walks in on you.

✔ Work together with a second person if possible. Criminals who work alone and are bent upon committing robbery or assault tend to be intimidated by the presence of more than one person. They're afraid of being overwhelmed by that extra person and losing control of the situation while they're victimizing you. They're also afraid of being identified by a corroborating witness should they ever be hauled into court for their crimes.

✔ Keep a personal security device with you at all times so you can startle, disable, or mark a person who is threatening you. My favorite is a noise maker about half the size of a deck of playing cards. Pull its pin, and it lets out a shrill 110-decibel wail which demands immediate attention. It startles the criminal and attracts the attention of anybody in the vicinity who might give or summon help.

✔ Keep your cell phone with you, charged up

and turned on, whenever you go out on land-lording business so you can summon help immediately should you need it.

✔ Whenever you have to confront a tenant with something unpleasant and you suspect that things could get nasty, rehearse what you're going to say in advance. Choose your words carefully, recognizing that the very words you use could get you hurt or even killed but that they could also have the opposite effect. They could disarm the tenant and defuse the situation.

Go meet the tenant in a public place or else take someone with you as a witness if you're meeting in a not-so-public place, preferably someone of the opposite sex (instruct your witness to be attentive but keep quiet, no matter how intense things become). Be friendly and personal in your approach. State your business briefly, mentioning only the important reasons why the tenant should be cooperative. Then let the tenant talk and talk and talk. Remain calm. Do not raise your voice or make any threats, even though the tenant is shouting threats at you at an ear-damaging volume.

If things get intense, say something disarmingly crazy, something like this, "Maybe we're both getting a little too worked up over all this. Why don't we just stop for a minute and take three deep breaths? Come on now. One, two, three. That's good. How about three more? One, two, three. Okay, now where were we?"

Sure, this sounds crazy. It is crazy, but so are loud arguments, and they never help matters. They just get people upset, perhaps upset enough to reach for their weaponry and harm somebody they had no intention of harming. Doing something as idiotic as taking six deep breaths together with an irate tenant may be enough for you and the tenant to smile at one another and recognize how idiotic your disagreement is. It might be enough for the two of you to begin seeking common ground for settling your disagreement.

Maybe you'll succeed, and maybe you won't.

As soon as you realize that words and ploys won't help and that the tenant is going to be obstinate no matter what you do, leave the scene. You've tried all you could. The time has come for you to make everything impersonal. The time has come for you to get somebody else to deliver, within hours, a written notice appropriate to the situation. Pursue the matter through intermediaries. Keep out of it yourself.

✔ Whenever you do anything at your rental property, ask yourself whether you're taking needless personal risks and whether you can do something, anything, to reduce those risks.

Coping with Lead-Based Paint Worries

Lead is good for many things. It's good for paints because it makes them last longer. It's good for gasolines because it makes them burn evenly and longer instead of simply exploding quickly. It's good for plastics because it gives them stability. It's good for crystal because it adds brilliance and weight. It's good for shielding because it stops X-rays and radiation. It's good for batteries because it reacts with acid to store an electrical charge efficiently. It's good for solder because it connects electronic components reliably. It's good for wine bottle foils because it keeps rodents from gnawing the corks. It's good for roofing, even flat roofing, because it lasts almost indefinitely when exposed to the elements.

Lead is good for many, many things, but it is not good for humans. Lead in humans, whether ingested by mouth, inhaled through the nose, or absorbed through the skin, can be just as damaging as a lead bullet. It simply acts more slowly. It can cause neurological damage, high blood pressure, headaches, joint pain, and all kinds of other medical problems.

Children are especially vulnerable to lead poisoning because their little bodies tend to absorb it readily and because they are more sensitive to it than adults are.

Many dwellings built prior to 1978, the year when the federal government banned lead paint for use in housing (some states banned it even earlier, and some paint companies, knowing the hazards, stopped manufacturing it even earlier), have lead-based paint in them, and we landlords who own any of these older dwellings must comply with the federal regulations requiring us to disclose to our tenants whatever we know about lead hazards on the property.

The mandated disclosure form for this purpose appears in chapter 4. You must give a copy of the form and a copy of the EPA booklet, "Protect Your Family from Lead in Your Home," to everyone who rents a pre-1978 dwelling from you (give new tenants the form and booklet when they move in; give existing tenants the form and booklet as soon as possible if you haven't done so already, but no later than when the terms of their tenancy change) unless any of the following apply—

• The units have zero bedrooms, such as studios and lofts;
• The occupancy is expected to last less than 100 days;
• The housing is for the elderly (unless children also live there);
• The housing is for the handicapped (unless children also live there); or
• The housing has been found by a certified inspector to be free of lead-based paint.

More than that, the question we need to be asking ourselves is this: "What should we as landlords be doing to minimize our own and our tenants' exposure to whatever lead-based paint hazards might be on any property we own which was built prior to 1978?"

First, we should assume that all of the existing gloss and semi-gloss paint is lead-based, whether it is or it isn't. The truth is that we don't want to know for sure because if we know, we have to disclose what we know. If we know nothing, we simply state that we know nothing.

Second, we should make no effort to remove any of the existing paint unless we absolutely have to. Hiring experts to remove it properly is expensive and adds no value to the property. Hiring just anybody to remove it exposes them to danger and us to liability. Removing it ourselves exposes us to contaminated fumes and dust and may expose others as well. Don't gamble that removing lead paint from your pre-1978 property will go well. It won't. It's bound to be expensive and bound to bring you and your property under the scrutiny of bureaucrats who may mean well but lack common sense.

Third, we should maintain all of the existing paint according to the highest standards, that is, we should keep it clean, and we should repair any surfaces where the paint is peeling, chipping, chalking, or cracking. Repairing might involve repainting the surface with an unleaded paint or covering the surface with wallpaper, paneling, sheetrock, or siding.

By being aware of the possible presence of lead-based paint, by being careful not to disturb it, and by complying with the federal guidelines, we are acting responsibly in coping with whatever lead-based paint hazards there might be on our property.

Coping with Asbestos Worries

Like lead, asbestos used to show up in all kinds of products, more than 5,000 of them all told, because of its desirable properties. It is very durable, very poor as a conductor of electricity, and very resistant to heat, chemicals, and water. It's inexpensive and indestructible. When it became regulated for being especially dangerous to humans, it disappeared from most of those products.

Around dwellings, those products include adhesives, acoustical plaster, caulk, ceiling tile, ceramic tile, electrical insulation, floor tile, linoleum, patching plaster, roofing felt, sheetrock, shingles, siding, and thermal insulation. You won't find asbestos in any of those products today, but you will find it in them if they were manufactured before asbestos became regulated in the 1980s.

If your rental property was built after 1980, chances are good that it contains no asbestos. Prior to that, it may or it may not.

Let's say that your rental property built in the 1970s has asbestos in its acoustical ceiling, its floor tiles, and its heating system's insulation. That's bad news, but it's not a catastrophe. Just remember that short of spending more than the property is worth on removing it, you cannot rid the property of asbestos entirely. You shouldn't try. You needn't try.

What you want to do is make the asbestos safe to be around. That's neither particularly difficult nor particularly expensive. It does require knowledge of the danger, periodic inspections, and a careful repair when necessary.

The danger in asbestos lies partly in its near invisibility and partly in its great durability. When asbestos fibers are visible to the naked eye, they are bound together, stable, and safe to be around. When they're disturbed, they become dangerous. They become "friable," that is, they separate like a windblown dandelion seed puff into tiny individual fibers and escape into the air. So tiny are they that you'd have to bundle 1,200 of them together to equal the thickness of one strand of human hair! Being that tiny, they tend to float in the air for a long, long time before they settle somewhere or get sucked into something like a human lung, where they remain forever and begin causing health problems. That's the danger they pose to us humans.

Compounding that danger is the long period of time (typically 10 to 30 years) between exposure to friable asbestos and the appearance of the symptoms of diseases caused by asbestos. In other words, you could be removing the stuff from your property without observing proper safety techniques and you could be breathing enough of it into your lungs to cause you health problems twenty years later.

The Twin Towers, which were built in the late 1960s, contained between 400 and 2,000 tons, yes, TONS, of asbestos when they collapsed. That asbestos became an invisible airborne killer on 9/11, affecting the first responders and the people of New York City alike almost immediately and causing what came to be known as "The World Trade Center Cough." So prevalent was the friable asbestos in the air around the towers after they collapsed that people who were exposed to it and weren't wearing respirators began having symptoms of severe lung disease within little more than ONE YEAR and dying in little more than FOUR YEARS, far sooner than is typical.

The people who were anywhere close to the Twin Towers during the aftermath of the collapse weren't aware of the grave danger of breathing the contaminated air, and they continue to suffer the cosequences.

You have no excuse. You know that asbestos can be a killer, and you know that you need to take its presence in and around your property seriously.

Periodic inspection of your property's suspecious areas is the best course to take to keep asbestos under control. Check to see that any material containing asbestos is solid in appearance and solid to the touch and that it appears to be in good condition. If it is, then it presents no danger, for it is not releasing any of its tiny fibers into the air.

Should you find deterioration in any material containing asbestos, chances are good that it can be repaired. In fact, you will want to repair it rather than remove it because removal will only disturb the material and release more fibers into the air. Repair may involve something as simple as coating it with paint to seal the fibers or filling the damaged areas with a commercial product designed for containment.

For information about coping with asbestos, read the Environmental Protection Agency (EPA) publications, "Guidance for Controlling Asbestos-Containing Materials in Buildings," otherwise known as the "Purple Book," and "Managing Asbestos in Place: A Building Owner's Guide to Operations and Maintenance Programs," otherwise known as the "Green Book." You may obtain them through the EPA website (epa.gov/asbestos).

Coping with Mold Worries

Whereas lead and asbestos are dangerous to all humans, some mold is dangerous to some humans. Mold is in the same category as peanuts. It makes some people deathly ill, that is, unless an infestation has grown so large that its spores fill the air and it makes everybody ill.

Mold is everywhere. There's no escaping it. Outdoors it serves as a recycling mechanism, breaking down organic matter so that it becomes useful in another capacity. Indoors, it works the same way, except that it breaks down what we don't want broken down, the components and furnishings of a structure. Outdoors, in nature, it's useful. Indoors, in structures, it's damaging. You might say that mold is a flower when it occurs in a natural environment, and it's a weed when it occurs in a man-made environment.

Over the years, we landlords have been level-headed about managing mold. Managing it has been part of the ongoing maintenance of our rental properties. Only recently has mold grabbed headlines with horror stories and highly charged terminology. We read stories about "killer mold" and big court settlements, and we cringe at the thought of being sued because our rental dwellings have so much mold in them that it makes our tenants ill.

In spite of these scary stories and the fear that we must retain professionals to keep mold problems at bay, good maintenance is still the best form of mold management. Good maintenance, combined with a greater awareness of mold's presence in a structure and its potential as a health hazard and destructive force, will keep you as a landlord out of trouble.

To increase your mold awareness, avail yourself of the good information available from the EPA (epa.gov/mold), beginning with the publication, "Key to Mold Control." Here's a quote: "The key to mold control is moisture control. If mold is a problem in your home, you should clean up the mold promptly *and* fix the water problem. It is important to dry water-damaged areas and items within 24-48 hours to prevent mold growth."

Take that advice, and you needn't worry about mold in your rentals. Also, read the two EPA publications, "A Brief Guide to Mold, Moisture, and Your Home" and "Mold Remediation in Schools and Commercial Buildings" and give your tenants a copy of the brief guide so that they, too, will know more about the tell-tale signs of mold and know what to do about it.

Here are some do's and don'ts to help you cope better with your mold worries.

Don't be frightened whenever tenants mention the word "mold" while talking about their dwelling.

Don't suppose that your tenants are out to get you if they report a mold problem.

Don't rely solely upon your tenants to inform you of the presence of mold in their dwelling. Be constantly on the alert for it yourself.

Don't be complacent about your property's potential for mold problems. Even new properties can have mold.

Do respond immediately to any tenant complaint about mold.

Do use the "Notice and Release Agreement Mold and Radon" (introduced in chapter 4) to minimize your legal exposure to mold claims.

Do give your tenants copies of appropriate EPA publications on mold.

Coping with Radon Worries

Radon is a colorless, odorless, and tasteless radioactive gas, and as such, it is impossible to detect with human senses. It occurs everywhere in soil, water, and air, produced by the decay of naturally occurring uranium. It is a proven carcinogen and, after cigarette smoking, is thought to be the primary cause of lung cancer.

Although there is no known safe level of radon, the EPA (epa.gov/radon) strongly recommends that indoor air with a radon level of 4 or more picocuries per liter (pCi/L) be reduced to a lower level and even recommends reducing levels of 2-4 pCi/L to lower levels. The average radon level for American dwellings is 1.3 pCi/L, and the average radon level for outdoor air is .4 pCi/L.

Radon levels are not the same throughout a neighborhood or even throughout a building. They vary on a dwelling-by-dwelling basis and on a room-by-room basis, too, and tend to be higher in dwellings with basements, dwellings on slabs, and dwellings with multiple floors.

The EPA estimates that one in fifteen dwellings in the United States exceeds its "national action level" of 4 pCi/L.

If you as a landlord know that elevated radon levels occur in the neighborhood where you own rental property, you should at the very least advise your tenants of this fact or you could be held liable for failure to disclose. Unless obligated by law to test for radon, you don't have to test, but you cannot keep your tenants from testing. If you or your tenants do test for radon and find elevated levels, then you must take measures to reduce those levels.

Here are some do's and don'ts to help you cope better with your radon worries.

Don't be frightened whenever tenants mention the word "radon" while talking about their dwelling.

Don't suppose that your tenants are out to get you if they decide to test for radon.

Don't rely solely upon your tenants' radon testing before you hire a contractor to install a radon reduction system. Confirm the tenants' testing with your own.

Don't be complacent about your property's potential for radon problems. Even new properties can have elevated levels of radon.

Do respond immediately to any tenant complaint about radon.

Do use the "Notice and Release Agreement Mold and Radon" (introduced in chapter 4) to minimize your legal exposure to radon claims.

Do give your tenants copies of appropriate EPA publications on radon. You will find them in the radon section of the EPA website.

Some Last Words

Go ahead and provide every available safety measure and every available security precaution which appears reasonable and appropriate for the kind of property you have and for where it's located, but don't advertise your property's safety and security. Don't even mention safety and security features when you're showing prospective tenants around the premises. Let them make up their own minds about the safety and security of the property.

You don't want to be sued by a tenant who becomes the victim of a crime or some medical malady and claims to have developed a false sense of safety and security after having been misled by your advertising or your verbal remarks.

19
Keeping Records

For some people the most onerous chore of landlording is keeping records. They'll care for their properties with vigor. They'll look after their tenants with delight. They'll show their properties with pride. Ah, but speak to them about keeping records, and they'll laugh nervously, perhaps they'll point to an old dog-eared rent receipt book and a stack of shoeboxes stuffed with miscellaneous slips of paper, and they'll say that they just don't have time to sit down and shuffle papers. They have more important work to do. Besides, they have an accountant who does all of that stuff for them.

Sound familiar? How about you? Have any more excuses to add?

Unfortunately, people who neglect recordkeeping don't seem to understand what's truly important in this business. Since they keep their records haphazardly, they don't know what's really happening at all and they can't possibly make good decisions because their decisions aren't informed decisions.

They don't know whether their rents are covering their expenses, so they haven't a clue whether a rent raise is warranted. They don't know how much they're spending on utilities compared to previous periods, so they have yet to consider conserving utilities as a cost-saving measure. They don't keep any figures on their coin-operated laundry machines, so they're still charging 25¢ to wash and 10¢ to dry. They don't even know when they'll be making the final payment on a second mortgage. Consequently, they can't know when to expect an increase in cash flow. When can they afford to buy that new Cadillac? They can't say. They don't know.

These things are truly important in this business. Sure, you have to do a great many other important things, but few are ever quite so important as recordkeeping, and none will assist you in both managing your property day by day and satisfying the requirements of the IRS. You cannot afford to neglect it. Don't.

Landlording without recordkeeping is like playing baseball without keeping score. Nobody would know what was going on. If the teams didn't know their scores and the number of innings remaining, they couldn't adjust their strategies, and the fans wouldn't know whether to get excited or go home. Batting, fielding, and pitching are only parts of the game. Recordkeeping *is* the game. Sports almanacs have more baseball statistics than *The Wall Street Journal* has financial statistics. Baseball fans study those statistics and compare players, teams, stadiums, leagues, and years one with another. You ought to be at least one-tenth that diligent with the recordkeeping and statistics for your landlording business because they affect you much more directly than baseball statistics could ever affect a fan.

To do your own recordkeeping, you may use a quill pen, an ink pot, an eye shade, sleeve garters, and a leather-bound ledger if you want to. You may use a cutting-edge computer with a speedy processor, a capacious hard disk, more RAM than ewes ever see, and the best software available, or you may use some combination of low-tech and high-tech bookkeeping. How you do your recordkeeping doesn't matter. What does matter is that you have a recordkeeping system, preferably one which you can understand yourself, and that you use it diligently.

The one outlined in this chapter might be considered rudimentary by some standards, but it is wholly sufficient for landlords who do their own recordkeeping. Some people have used it for just one rental house, and others have used it for more than three hundred rentals. It's a flexible system, simple to follow, easy to crosscheck, and exhaustive enough to lead into tax preparations. It's based on forms which are designed to be read vertically and to fit into a standard 8.5"x11" binder. Best of all, it's all right here in your hands. You can get started using it right away by making copies of the forms included in the back of this book or by making equivalents of these forms on your computer.

Before we get to the forms themselves, though, let's consider a way to keep those miscellaneous slips of paper out of your old shoeboxes.

Filing

You handle so many important written records in your landlording business that you must organize them so they are readily accessible when needed or you will become hopelessly bogged down in futile searches for lost records again and again. A simple filing system will help.

For each of your properties, make up three file folders (use folders of a different color for each property so they're readily distinguishable). Label each folder with the property's address or some other designation plus descriptive words for the contents of the folder— "RECORDS," "TENANT RECORDS," and "RECEIPTS."

In the RECORDS folder, keep the property's insur-

ance policies, title papers, termite reports, tax information, deeds, notes, loan records, and anything else pertaining to the property as a whole that you're not already keeping in your safety deposit box.

In the TENANT RECORDS folder, keep completed Rental Applications, Rental Agreements, Leases, Condition & Inventory Checksheets, and any other papers pertaining to the property's tenants, including those tenants who have moved out.

In the RECEIPTS folder, keep the paid receipts for expenses related to the property. As soon as you receive a receipt, circle the amount paid, the date of payment, and the name of the vendor. Mark it with the method of payment (a "$" for cash, a "✓" mark and a number for a check, and a "CC" for credit cards) and a property ID, so you'll be able to identify it easily if it happens to become mislaid. If the receipt does not already include a description of the item or service paid for, write a description right on it.

Prorate on an itemized or percentage basis those receipts which cover expenses for more than one property so that each property pays its share. If two properties are involved, make a duplicate receipt for one property's share and reference it to the original bill, which should be adjusted and then inserted into the other property's file. For unreceipted expenses, such as casual labor, make up your own receipt with the important information, get a signature if you can, and file it with the other expense receipts.

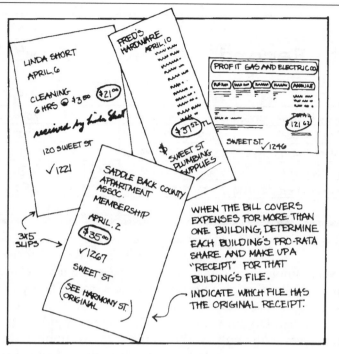

Arrange all receipts chronologically in the file folder so they will be easier to post. Arranging them is easy unless you get behind in arranging them and your receipts become mixed up. Just put the receipts face up in the back of the folder, oldest first and most recent last, and you won't have to bother sorting them later. They'll be in proper sequence already. Keep all the receipts for one month together and slip them into a folded sheet of paper which is identified with the month and the year. When you finish recording the receipts for the month, staple them together inside the folded sheet and leave them in the folder.

At the end of the year, empty the RECEIPTS folder of that year's receipts and put them, along with the year's income and expense sheets referred to later, into a large envelope for storage.

Because you never can tell when the IRS will want to audit your tax returns and you'll be called upon to produce evidence in support of your numbers, you would be wise to keep them for years (ever since some seven-year-old records helped to net me a $20,000 income tax refund windfall, I recommend keeping them seven years at least).

If you begin accumulating more and more properties, you will want to add more folders to your filing system to accommodate the greater volume of paperwork and to keep it more narrowly divided. The following folders might prove useful—INCOMING, UNPAID BILLS, BANKING, LOANS, PAYROLL, and RENTAL APPLICATIONS (all except those of your current tenants, which should remain with the tenants' other papers). You'll surely find plenty of stray items to keep safely and neatly tucked away inside these folders.

That's all there is to keeping your written records organized. Read on to learn how to use these records to do your bookkeeping.

Bookkeeping

The loose-leaf binder kept for recording purposes has the following five sections—TENANTS, INCOME, EXPENSES, SUMMARIES, and LOANS/INSURANCE.

Properly filled out and kept up to date, the forms in these sections will give you quick access to most of the

Tenant Record   Property _456-64 Sweet Street_

	Unit	Tenant	Phone	Date Moved In	Moved Out	Rent Date	Rent	Deposit	Bank/Chkg. Acct. Nos.
1	456	Richard + Rose RENTER	555-2207	1/xx		1st	750-	610-	BIG BANK 570-66-301
2	458	Lu MELANDER	555-4137	3/xx		✓	700-	550-	MAIN BANK 151193-461
3	460	Kathy + Rick BODEN	555-6916	10/xx		✓	700-	623-	BIG BANK 6397810-2
4	462	Nelly BUNN	555-0812	7/xx	3/xx	✓	650-	350-	
5	464	Jan + Jennifer BROWN	555-3771	4/xx		✓	750	650-	SAFE BANK 0210-006.89
6									

information you need as you look after your rental property.

Form blanks for every sample form shown in these sections appear in the back of this book. Use the form blanks as originals and copy them for your own loose-leaf binder. Do not write on the original forms themselves. Write only on the copies.

■ Tenants—Tenant Record

The first section, the one for tenant information, has only one form. It's called the Tenant Record. Record information on it which you expect to refer to occasionally, information such as rent due dates and tenants' telephone numbers.

Nowadays so many people have unlisted phones and cell phones that you may not be able to get your tenants' numbers from a directory or an operator. Having the numbers handy will save you lots of fumbling, frustration, and wasted trips.

Although you hope you won't ever have to take advantage of such information, you may use the Tenant Record form to keep track of your tenants' current checking and savings account numbers, too. Then you'll know exactly where to go to attach their assets if you ever have to collect a money judgment against them. The savings account number should be on the Rental Application, and the checking account number will be written in those funny-looking magnetic numbers at the bottom of the tenant's rent check. Be prepared!

Because you will be referring to the Tenant Record repeatedly and because these sheets should last for years, you may wish to keep them pristine with a transparent page protector which slips on and off easily and is available in stationery stores. When tenants move, cross them off the Tenant Record using a squiggly line or a yellow highlighter felt pen. Both still give you access to the old information if you need it. The highlighting just looks neater.

Monthly Rental Income   Page _1_

Property _SWEET ST. & NEAT ST._

Period _XXXX_

	Unit	January	February	March	April	May	
1	456 SWEET STREET	750-	750-	750-	750-	750-	1
2	458 " "	700-	700-	700-	700-	700-	2
3	460 " "	700-	700-	700-	700-	700-	3
4	462 " "	650-	650-	650-	750-	750-	4
5	464 " "	750-	750-	750-	750-	750-	5
6	TOTAL	3550-	3550-	3550-	3650-	3650-	6
7							7
8							8
9	125 NEAT STREET	875-	875-	875-	875-	875-	9
10							10
11	TOTAL BOTH BLDGS	4425-	4425-	4425-	4525-	4525-	11

Add new tenants to the bottom of the list. Even though they won't be in sequence according to their dwelling number or letter designation, their information will be readily accessible.

Use a separate Tenant Record sheet for every multiple-family property, and use a separate one for a small collection of rental houses.

■ Income—Monthly Rental Income Record

The second bookkeeping section, INCOME, includes three different forms—Monthly Rental Income Record, Laundry Income, and Other Receipts and Income.

Unless you have many properties, one of each form should suffice. For example, if you are Lester Landlord and you have one duplex, half of which you occupy yourself, and one fiveplex, you can easily list both properties on a single Monthly Rental Income Record.

If you do enter more than one property on a form, use a highlighter pen to highlight the "TOTAL" lines all the way across both sheets, and you'll be able to spot the totals more easily.

If you have room, you might even use the same record sheets for subsequent years by listing the properties again further down the sheets and indicating on each "TOTAL" line which year you're recording. One advantage of recording your rental income in this way is that you have instant access to past years' rental income for comparison purposes. You'll know when you last raised rents and how much of a vacancy factor you created by doing so, and you can use this information to help you prepare for the next rent increase.

After using these sheets to record rental income for a full year, calculate the total year's income for each dwelling and enter it in the "Year's Totals" column. Total that column so you can crosscheck the monthly totals for all buildings on the sheets. If your figures don't match, find out why they don't and correct your error.

This kind of crosschecking is easy work with an electronic calculator. Get yourself a printing calculator which produces a paper tape record of its entries. Sometimes just one slightly incorrect entry will cause an error and you'll be able to find it without painstakingly adding each item again merely by comparing the tape, item for item, with the Monthly Rental Income Record figures.

■ Income—Other Receipts & Income

Like the Monthly Rental Income Record, the form called Other Receipts & Income requires two sheets to span a full year. It records miscellaneous income, or income considered incidental to the primary business. In the residential landlording business, that's anything other than rental income from dwellings.

Other income items which may be included are added appliances or furniture, deposit forfeits, interest on deposits, late charges (unless you use the discounted rent policy, in which case both gross and net rents could be recorded as regular rental income), laundry collections, laundry commissions, soda machine revenues, garage rent, storage rent, etc.

Those income items normally included in the

Other Receipts & Income

Added Appliances or Furniture, Deposit Forfeits, Interest, Late Charges, Laundry, Garages, etc.

Page ___1___

Property _SWEET ST. + NEAT ST._

Period _XXXX_

	Description of Income	January	February	March	April	May	
1	SWEET STREET						1
2	Laundry	8 6 75	8 5 50	9 2 25	7 8 75	8 6 75	2
3	Garage(s)	45 -	45 -	3 0 -	45 -	45 -	3
4	INTEREST on deposit account				1 8 86		4
5							5
6	TOTAL	1 3 1 75	1 3 0 50	1 2 2 25	1 4 2 61	1 3 1 75	6
7							7
8	NEAT STREET						8
9	Late Rents						9
10	INTEREST on deposit accounts				3 90		10

Laundry Income

Property _SWEET STREET_
Period _KKKK_

	Date	Washer	Dryer	Both	Cumulative Totals	Monthly Totals
1	1/05	22 50	21 25	43 75	43 75	
2	1/24	19 50	23 50	43 00	86 75	86 75
3	2/05	18 25	14 75	33 00	119 75	
4	2/21	24 00	28 50	52 50	172 25	85 50
5	3/09	22 75	25 25	48 00	220 25	
6	3/23	26 75	17 50	44 25	264 50	92 25

rent should be recorded as rental income and not here. Rents for furnished apartments, for example, need not be itemized separately, nor should a garage rent be recorded separately if it's normally included in the dwelling's rent. If you bill tenants separately for their garage, refrigerator, or anything else, then you may wish to include those separate amounts here.

` Still, don't worry yourself much about where to include an item. Worry instead about whether you've inadvertently recorded any income on both the Monthly Rental Income Record and the Other Receipts & Income record. Do avoid that! Only the laundry income should be recorded in two places, the Laundry Income sheet and the Other Receipts & Income sheets.

Although tenants' deposits may seem like some kind of income when you receive them, they're not. They're deposits to be held by you for insuring the tenants' compliance with the Rental Agreement. Upon receiving them, do not record them here or anywhere else as income. Instead, record them as deposits on the Tenant Record form. When the tenants move out and you have to use part or all of the deposits to pay for back rent, cleaning, or damages, that's when you list as income the portion you keep. After all, that's when deposit monies do become income, not before.

Last month's rent and any other rents paid in advance are another story. The IRS tells us that they must be considered income when received. There's no choice.

Since that's the official word, take the hint and don't ask incoming tenants for a last month's rent. Increase their deposits by the equivalent of what you'd otherwise be charging them for last month's rent. The move-in costs remain the same, but you need list as income right then only what you label as rent.

A single Other Receipts & Income form may last you a year or it may last you several, depending upon the number of properties you have. Fill it out pretty much the same way you fill out the Monthly Rental Income Record, grouping all the items for one building together.

■ Income—Laundry Income

Owners of coin-operated laundry machines may use the Laundry Income form as an interim record or as a basis for a more detailed analysis of what's happening in the laundry room.

To use it strictly as an interim record, make only a "Date" entry and a "Both" entry for every time you empty the coin boxes. Then post the monthly totals to the more permanent Other Receipts & Income sheets once a month. The "Both" entry, of course, would be your total for each collection from both the washer(s) and the dryer(s).

If you don't use something like the Laundry Income form, you'll have to save little scraps of paper, each representing one collection, until you have a full month's worth of collections and can make the monthly entry. Those scraps may very well get lost in the wash if they remain too long in your pockets.

To use the form as the basis for a more detailed analysis, complete more of the form's seven columns. The other columns provide information useful to anyone who bothers to take the time to complete them. The separate washer and dryer columns tell you how much each machine is used. From these figures, you can calculate each machine's exact number of loads. You can then use this information to check on a machine's reliability whenever it needs repair and to decide whether you ought to change brands of machines when they need replacement or when you purchase a set for another location.

The separate washer-dryer columns also provide a revealing ratio of use for the machines. If a tenant claims that the dryer is requiring twice as many coins to dry each load as it used to, you can calculate whether it is or it isn't by checking for a change in the income ratio between the machines. You'll have a quick clue whether the machine really does need a good cleaning or maintenance or repair or whether the tenant is foaming at the mouth.

The "Cumulative Totals" column tells you at a glance whether your investment is paying off. Let's say that your machines cost you $1,000 and you take in a minimal $200 in the first six months. At that rate, recouping your capital investment would take two and a half years, but that's not including the utilities needed to run them or the cost of the repairs. Still, that's a decent return. Anything that pays for itself in three years or less is a good investment.

If the machines last ten years and on a projected basis take in $70 a month or $8,400 in all, $2,500 of which goes for utilities and $800 for repairs, you'll make a tidy return of 51% per year on your investment. That's a spectacular return! I'll take that kind of return anytime. Wouldn't you? That's the kind of return a casino owner might hope to get out of the one-armed bandits in the casino's best locations.

The "Monthly Totals" column is a convenience especially for the purpose of entering the necessary figures on the Other Receipts & Income sheets, but these figures will also let you compare month-by-month laundry receipts if your collection dates are fairly consistent and frequent. Remember that not every line requires a monthly entry in this column. Only those which represent the last collection for the month require an entry.

■ Expenses—Expense and Payment Record

There are three forms in the expense section of the loose-leaf record binder—the Expense and Payment Record, the Depreciation Record, and the Payroll Record.

The first one, the Expense and Payment Record, is undoubtedly the most used of all the forms in the binder. Remember all those receipts you moved from your shoeboxes and shopping bags into a neat file folder labeled "RECEIPTS," which you then organized by date of payment? Well, here's where you record them all.

The entries are made chronologically and should include all the expense receipts in the RECEIPTS folder, plus the payroll expenses from the Payroll Record and the loan payments recorded on the Loan & Note Record sheets.

Besides being chronological, the entries are separated into eleven different categories so you can refer easily to certain kinds of expenses whenever you want to find out where all your money's going. You may find some surprises when you examine the categories, surprises that appear only when you examine a series of similar bills rather than just one. Might you, for example, have inadvertently paid your property taxes or your insurance twice? Don't laugh. It happens. Here's where you can check on your own absentmindedness.

Filling out these expense sheets can cause drowsiness, and you might not want to operate heavy machinery afterwards, that is, unless you make a conscious effort to concentrate on what you're doing. Tell yourself that these numbers you're working with are important stuff and that they have to be accurate. Mistaking one number for another here, transposing two numbers there, adding an extra digit somewhere else will all skew the outcome of your hard work. You cannot afford to make mistakes while posting.

Posting the loan payments requires even more concentration than other entries. Loan payment entries are a little tricky because one payment might have to be distributed to three columns, column 2 for interest, column 11 for mortgage principal, and column 12 for nondeductible impounds. Column 2 is the only one of the three which is deductible as an expense. Column 11, which is the amount you pay on the principal of your loan, represents an increase in your net worth rather than an expense. Yet, since it is definitely money paid out, it should be recorded as such. Likewise, an impound amount, which should be posted to column 12 as a nondeductible item, goes into a "savings" account. It's called an impound account, and it's forced savings, to be sure, but it's still a savings account. The mortgagor uses an impound account to pay taxes and insurance, and the funds you pay into an impound account are not an expense, strictly speaking, until they're actually used.

When the mortgagor uses your impounded funds to pay taxes or insurance, you then record the payment like any other and stipulate in the

"How Paid" column that funds for payment came out of the impound account.

I know. I know what you're thinking. You're thinking this means that the amount in the "Total Paid Out" column is actually more than what you will have paid out. Trust me, though, and I'll show you on the Summary of Business and Statement of Income form how everything evens out again. Just don't worry about it for now, and don't worry about the matter at all if you're not paying into an impound account with a portion of your mortgage payment.

Now let's take a look at the procedure for ordinary entries. After you complete the information called for in the first five columns, you come to the columns with the eleven different headings. Choose whichever one best fits each expense and put the amount in that column. Be sure, however, that it's all on the same horizontal line. Even though the lines are numbered four times on the two sheets, sometimes your eyes will play tricks on you and you may inadvertently post some figures on the wrong line. Use a straight edge if you have trouble finding the right places to put your figures. Even a piece of paper will work as a straight edge.

Don't deliberate too much about the proper categories for ambiguous expenses. If you can't easily decide whether something should be called a "service" or not, then it can't matter much, and since you identify each item in the "For" column anyway, you always have backup information in case you want to change categories later for some reason or other.

If you find that you have no use for a certain column heading, if, for example, you have no payroll to enter, change the heading to something more useful to you. Other possibilities are travel/telephone, advertising/rental fees, and non-employee labor.

Now look again at the sample Expense and Payment Record for Lester Landlord's fiveplex. Note that the distribution of the mortgage payments is broken into three categories—interest, mortgage payment, and nondeductible (impounds). Note also that the first line of these sample sheets has the totals brought forward from the previous sheets. You must do this on every page except the first one for the year (corresponding left and right sheets should have the same page numbers).

After you have entered your final expenditure for the year, total the last sheet and you'll have your annual expenditures for the property.

Let me caution you here, though, about two important no-no's related to your Expense and Payment Record sheets.

No-No Number One...Never include as a regular deductible expense the items which the government considers "depreciable."

No-No Number Two...Never include as a regular deductible expense the money you pay yourself.

"Depreciable items" are property used in your landlording business (a utility trailer, for example) or property replacements (new roof) or property improvements (new patio), all of which have long useful lives and cost more than $750. Unless these

Expense & Payment Record

Page 3
Property SWEET STREET
Period APRIL XXXX

	Date Paid	How Paid	To Whom Paid	For	1 Total Paid Out	2 Interest	3 Taxes, Licenses	4 Insurance		
1			BAL FWD		4956 29	1949 96	24 80			1
2	4/02	267	BIG BANK	1ST. MORT.	879 00	521 20				2
3	✓	268	S. MONEY BAGS	2nd. MORT.	250 00	135 12				3
4	4/06	269	LITTLETOWN HDWE	ELEC SAW, EXT. CORD	48 59					4
5	4/07	270	SADDLEBACK CNTY	PROR TAX 2nd PYMT	674 31		674 31			5
6	4/07	271	MONOPOLY GAS + ELEC	3/1-31	86 12					6
7	4/11	272	KMART	SHADES	12 26					7
8	4/12	273	LITTLETOWN WTR. DIST.	3/1-31	58 20					8
9	✓	274	CARTEL GARBAGE	3/1-31	102 00					9
10	4/15	275	PHONEY PAINT	PAINT + SUP.	32 64					10
11	4/15	276	BIG BANK	1st QTR PAYROLL TAXES	31 10					11

items qualify as "Section 179" property (check a current tax book for details because there are any number of restrictions) and can be expensed in the year they were purchased, you have to "depreciate" them, that is, you have to write them off little by little over a period of years (the IRS specifies the period according to the item's type).

You might think that a new fence and some new appliances are items which you should be able to charge off against this year's income. After all, you had to pay for them this year, didn't you? Shouldn't you be able to write them off this year? Normally you can't, but whether you can or can't, whether they qualify for first-year expensing or they don't, you should still enter these expenditures in column 10 so you can keep track of them in a special way as depreciable items. You'll see in a moment how they're treated.

By the way, there's no difference as far as depreciation is concerned between items which you bought and paid for completely this year and items which you bought this year and are paying for over any number of years, having borrowed the money to pay for them. Depreciables bought entirely with cash and depreciables bought entirely or partly with borrowed money are treated in exactly the same way.

Whereas the money you pay anybody other than yourself is called payroll or casual labor and is an expense, the money you pay yourself from your property's income is called a personal draw. It is definitely not an expense, and it is not the least bit deductible. It's personal income withdrawn from the business. If you wish to keep track of any money you pay yourself out of your property account, and you would be wise to do so, enter it on the Expense and Payment Record, but be sure to list it as a nondeductible item in column 12. It is not deductible in the least by any stretch of a landlord's vivid imagination.

■ **Expenses—Depreciation Record**

The Depreciation Record is a worksheet which enables you to keep track of the amount of depreciation available to you for every year you own a depreciable item. It serves to remind you years after you have paid for something depreciable whether you still have any depreciation coming to you and precisely how much it is. It also helps you calculate your adjusted basis and the amount of depreciation which must be recaptured when you dispose of a property.

As mentioned already, depreciable items are the various kinds of costlier and longer lasting items used in your landlording business, as well as the improvements made to your real property and the replacements. They include everything except the land itself. Land is not depreciable.

Here are some examples of depreciable items—big buildings, little buildings, portable storage buildings, mobilehomes, equipment, appliances, air conditioners, roof replacements, carpeting, linoleum, grading, swimming pools, laundry machines, vending machines, replumbing, rewiring, remodeling, and draperies.

With these depreciable items in mind, do you think that either an $80 sander or a $30 kitchen faucet replacement would be depreciable? No, they wouldn't. They do have long useful lives,

Expense & Payment Distribution   Page 3

	5 Utilities	6 Services, Rep., Maint.	7 Merch., Supplies	8 Payroll	9 Misc.	10 Depreciable	11 Mortgage Principal	12 Non-deduct.	
1	549 40	399 39	153 70	197 60	16 90		1417 04	247 50	1
2							357 80		2
3							114 88		3
4		48 59							4
5									5
6	86 12								6
7		12 26							7
8	58 20								8
9		102 00							9
10			32 64						10
11					31 10				11

Depreciation Record

Property or Capital Improvement
Location and Description   SWEET ST. CARPET, DRAPES, LINO

Date Acquired or Converted to Business JUNE, XXXX   New or Used NEW

Method of Depreciation ACCELERATED   Useful Life 5 YEARS

Cost or Other Basis $ 1,683.55

minus (-) Land Value or 1st Year Expensing $ Ø

equals (=) Depreciable Basis $ 1,683.55

	Tax Year	Prior Depreciation	Depreciable Balance	% Year Held	% Bus. Use	Rate	Depreciation This Year
1	XX		1,683.55		100	.20	336.70
2	XX	336.70	1,346.85			.32	538.73
3	XX	875.43	808.12			.192	323.24
4	XX	1,198.67	484.88			.1152	193.94
5	XX	1,392.61	290.94			.1152	193.94
6	XX	1,586.55	97.00			.0576	96.97
7							
8							
9							
10							
11							
12							
13							
14							
15							

Depreciation Record

Property or Capital Improvement
Location and Description   OAK STREET

Date Acquired or Converted to Business 10/1/XX   New or Used USED

Method of Depreciation STRAIGHT LINE   Useful Life 40 YEARS

Cost or Other Basis $ 382,000

minus (-) Land Value or 1st Year Expensing $ 114,600

equals (=) Depreciable Basis $ 267,400

	Tax Year	Prior Depreciation	Depreciable Balance	% Year Held	% Bus. Use	Rate	Depreciation This Year
1	XX		267,400.00	.25	100		1,671.25
2	XX	1,671.25	265,728.75	100	✓		6,685.00
3	XX	8,356.25	259,043.75	✓	✓		✓
4	XX	15,041.25	252,358.75	✓	✓		✓
5	XX	21,726.25	245,673.75	✓	✓		✓
6	XX	28,411.25	238,988.75	✓	✓		✓
7	XX	35,096.25	232,303.75	✓	✓		✓
8	XX	41,781.25	225,618.75	✓	✓		✓
9	XX	48,466.25	218,933.75	✓	✓		✓
10	XX	55,151.25	212,248.75	✓	✓		✓
11	XX	61,836.25	205,563.75	✓	✓		✓
12	XX	68,521.25	198,878.75	✓	✓		✓
13	XX	75,206.25	192,193.75	✓	✓		✓
14	XX	81,891.25	185,508.75	✓	✓		✓
15	XX	88,576.25	178,823.75	✓	✓		✓

but they're not costly enough to bother with. In general, you should depreciate an item only if it costs more than seven-hundred-and-fifty dollars and has a useful life of more than two or three years. Painting is an exception. Even if an exterior paint job costs $3,500, improves the appearance of your rental property 100%, and lasts nine years, you can and should expense it.

Remember that expensing is better than depreciating because it allows you an immediate deduction from income instead of your having to wait for it. You don't get any bigger deduction by depreciating, so if you have some doubt about whether to expense or depreciate an item because of its cost or useful life, go ahead and expense it. For example, carpet that cost you $739 ought to be expensed, as should some $596 worth of replacement draperies.

On the other hand, $739 worth of carpet which is part of a larger carpet replacement order totaling $1,863 ought to be depreciated.

Before you fill out a Depreciation Record for anything depreciable, you need to know its particulars—its description, its purchase price, its date of acquisition, and its percentage of business use. You also need to know the IRS classification it falls under. Then you will have to decide which depreciation method to use.

At present, there are five primary classifications of interest to rental property owners—5-year property (computers, light trucks, appliances, water heaters, carpets, draperies, furniture), 7-year property (office furniture and equipment), 15-year property (land improvements such as landscaping, paving, and site lighting), 27.5-year property (residential rental property), and 39-year property (non-residential real property). The first two of these classifications correspond roughly to what you might expect their items' useful lives to be. The last four are flights of fancy. They don't correspond to anything within reason. After all, who can say that a mobilehome has a useful life of ten years or that landscaping will last fifteen?

As for methods, there are really only two you should know something about, accelerated and straight line.

Accelerated depreciation uses percentages which change every year according to a set schedule. Were you to depreciate 7-year property using an accelerated schedule, for example, you would get 14.28% of the full purchase price as your depreciation for the first year, 24.49% for

the second, 17.49% for the third, 12.49% for the fourth, 8.93% for the fifth through the seventh years, and 4.46% for the eighth year.

Were you to add up the percentages, you would find that the first four years provide more than 68% of all the depreciation available over the entire eight years. That's how "accelerated" depreciation works. It allocates more depreciation to the early years, so you get a greater benefit earlier than you would with straight-line depreciation. You would also find by adding up all the percentages that they total 100%. Accelerated depreciation doesn't offer you any more or any less than straight-line depreciation. It merely enables you to take more depreciation in the early years.

The depreciation allowable for each property classification is simple to calculate from prescribed percentages. Use the tables provided for this purpose in IRS Publication 946 or in current editions of any general-interest tax book.

The sample Depreciation Record for carpet, draperies, and linoleum illustrates how accelerated depreciation works for 5-year property. Note that all of the 5-year depreciable expenditures made during the year for the one rental property are lumped together on one Depreciation Record sheet. You needn't fill out a separate sheet for each item and then do separate calculations. That would be a major waste of your time.

The "straight line" method lets you write off a depreciable at a constant rate and, if you prefer, over a longer period of time than accelerated depreciation provides. The sample Depreciation Record for the Oak Street apartment house illustrates how straight line works when applied to a property being depreciated over forty years, something an owner would do only in certain tax situations where smaller amounts of depreciation spread over many years would prove beneficial.

The Oak Street owners deducted the presumed land value from the acquisition cost and got their depreciable basis. Then they divided their basis by 40, the useful life they selected, and multiplied that by 25%, the percentage of the first year they held the property, and they came up with their depreciation for the first year. For the next year and all successive years, except the final one, their depreciation equals 1/40th or 5% of the original basis. The final year (the 41st) picks up the balance for those months they didn't own the property during the first year.

Payroll Record

Property __456-64 Sweet Street__
Employee __Alfred Good__   Social Sec.No. __100-00-000__
Pay Rate __$6⁰⁰/HR__   Exemptions __2__   Married ☒ Single ☐

	Period	Base Wages	Lodging	Fed Whldg	Employee FICA	Employee Medcare	Employer FICA	Employer Medcare	State Disblty	State Whldg	Other	Net	Chk No	
1	1/01-31	300.00	∅	∅	18.60	4.35	—	—	1.50	∅	∅	275.55	218	1
2	2/01-28	294.50	∅	∅	18.26	4.27	—	—	1.47	∅	∅	270.50	243	2
3	3/01-31	312.00	∅	∅	19.34	4.52	—	—	1.56	∅	∅	286.58	271	3
4														4
5	1ST QTR	906.50	∅	∅	56.20	13.14	—	—	4.53	∅	∅	832.63		5
6	TAX DEP.				56.20	13.14	56.20	13.14				138.68	287	6
7														7
8														8
9														9
10														10
11	4/01-30	332.00	∅	∅	20.58	4.81	—	—	1.66	∅	∅	304.95	295	11

That's pretty easy, isn't it?

Once you begin filling out a Depreciation Record, you should complete it for the item's entire useful life so you will know exactly how much depreciation you can expect to take for every year you own the property.

■ Expenses—Payroll Record

For each employee you hire, you will have to keep some sort of a Payroll Record. It's absolutely essential because it shows a complete breakdown of the various categories of payroll deductions, as well as the employer's contributions. Fortunately, it's a relatively simple form to use.

Once you have calculated the employee's various payroll deductions and have prepared the statement-of-earnings-and-deductions form to accompany each payroll check (see chapter 14), post those figures onto the Payroll Record, and then add to all that the employer's contribution to Social Security and Medicare. Remember that you do not deduct the employer's contributions from the employee's gross. It's an expense item for you, not for your employee. You merely keep track of it here so that you will know how much you need to pay out of your own pocket every quarter.

Refer to this form whenever you have to prepare monthly, quarterly, or annual reports for the government agencies involved.

■ Summaries—Annual Summary of Expenses and Payments

The summaries section includes two different forms. The first one closely parallels the Expense and Payment Record and is solely for the purpose of gathering together the expenditures for several properties. If you have only one property, you would already have figured your expenditures for the year on the final Expense and Payment Record page, and you would not need to use this form.

Expense & Payment Record

Annual Summary   Property __Sweet St & Neat Street__   Page __1__
Period __XXXX__

	Units	1 Total Paid Out (2-12)	2 Interest	3 Taxes, Licences	4 Insurance	5 Utilities	
1	456-64 Sweet St.	21576.73	6496.72	2930.71	1348.62	648.12	1
2							2
3	125 Neat St.	4915.68	1358.69	1002.48	593.87	261.74	3
4							4
5	TOTAL	26492.41	7855.41	3933.19	1348.62	909.86	5
6							6

The only difference between the regular Expense and Payment Record form and this Annual Summary of Expenses and Payments form is that "Unit(s)" takes the place of the first four columns, "Date," "How Paid," "To Whom Paid," and "For," and there's a thirteenth column for recording both regular and supplemental depreciation.

List each property's location on the form first and then record the total expenses just as you have calculated them on the final Expense and Payment Record sheets for each property. That accomplished, you will be prepared with the figures needed for the next form.

■ Summaries—Summary of Business and Statement of Income

The Summary of Business and Statement of Income form brings together all income and all expenses for a final reckoning. Use them monthly if you want to and you'll be exceedingly well informed about the financial status of your property. Though desirable, monthly summaries are hardly indispensable, however, and most landlords use them just once a year unless they're using a computer bookkeeping system such as the one shown in the previous chapter. It gives

Summary of Business & Statement of Income

Property __SWEET STREET__ Period __XXXX / APRIL__

1						
2						
3	INCOME					
4	Rental		3	6 5 0	00	
5	Other			1 4 2	61	
6	TOTAL INCOME		3	7 9 2	61	
7						
8						
9						
10						
11						
12	EXPENSES & PAYMENTS					
13	Interest			6 5 6	32	
14	Taxes, Licenses			6 7 4	31	
15	Insurance			8 8 6	54	
16	Utilities			1 4 4	32	
17	Services, Repairs, Maintenance			1 7 1	08	
18	Merchandise, Supplies			3 9	70	
19	Payroll			1 1 3	18	
20	Miscellaneous Expenses			1 6	38	
21	Depreciable			1 5 9	74	
22	Mortgage Principal			4 7 2	68	
23	Non-deductible			2 0 0	00	
24						
25						
26	TOTAL EXPENSES & PAYMENTS		3	5 3 4	25	
27	minus Non-deductible (line 23)			2 0 0	00	
28	TOTAL		3	3 3 4	25	
29	minus Depreciable (line 21)			1 5 9	74	
30	TOTAL		3	1 7 4	51	
31	minus Mortgage Prin. (line 22)			4 7 2	68	

monthly and year-to-date totals automatically.

Whether you use this summary form on an annual or a monthly basis, you will make some important calculations using it. Here's where you subtract from your expense totals the depreciable items you paid for this year, the amounts credited to your loan principals, as well as your sundry non-deductibles (including impounds). In addition, if you haven't done so already, here's where you have the opportunity to deduct as business expenses your telephone, the office space used in your home (use discretion with this one; be ready with proof), and your mileage (log your

landlording trips for substantiation). When you have completed all of these calculations, you'll have a net expense figure ready for your income tax return.

What's more, when you take the difference between your total expenditures and your non-deductibles and you subtract this figure from your total income, you will know what your actual cash flow is, that is, what you actually took in minus what you actually paid out.

Note that this cash flow figure includes as "expenses" what you paid out for both mortgage principal and depreciable items. Even though

Loan & Note Record

Property 456-64 SWEET STREET

Noteholder BIG BANK, P.O. Box 678, LITTLETOWN Loan Number 01-2345

Original Loan 214,114 Interest Rate 10% Payment 1,879.00 Due Date 8/01/xx

	Date Paid/Ck.#/New Payment if Changed	Interest	Principal	Impounds & (Imp.Disb.)	Impound Balance	Principal Balance	
1	BAL FWD					209770 26	1
2	3/01/xx ✓ 567	1748 09	130 91			209639 35	2
3	4/01/xx ✓ 631	1746 99	132 01			209507 34	3
4	5/02/xx ✓ 672	1745 89	133 11			209374 23	4
5	6/01/xx ✓ 694	1744 79	134 21			209240 02	5
6	7/01/xx ✓ 716	1743 67	135 33			209104 69	6
7	8/01/xx ✓ 729	1742 54	136 46			208968 23	7
8	9/01/xx ✓ 747	1741 40	137 60			208830 63	8
9	10/03/xx ✓ 762	1740 26	138 74			208691 89	9
10	11/01/xx ✓ 788	1739 10	139 90			208551 99	10
11	12/01/xx ✓ 797	1737 93	141 07			208410 92	11
12	1/02/xx ✓ 811	1736 76	142 24			208268 68	12
13	2/01/xx ✓ 832	1735 57	143 43			208125 25	13
14	3/01/xx ✓ 847	1734 38	144 62			207980 63	14
15	4/03/xx ✓ 860	1733 17	145 83			207834 80	15
16	5/01/xx ✓ 879	1731 96	147 04			207687 76	16
17	6/01/xx - 893	1730 73	148 27			207539 49	17
18	7/02/xx ✓ 914	1729 50	149 50			207389 99	18
19	8/03/xx ✓ 930	1728 25	150 75			207239 24	19
20	9/01/xx ✓ 943	1726 99	152 01			207087 23	20
21	9/30/xx ✓ 959	1725 73	153 27			206933 96	21
22	11/02/xx ✓ 975	1724 45	154 55			206779 41	22
23	12/02/xx ✓ 987	1723 16	155 84			206623 57	23
24	1/03/xx ✓ 1012	1721 86	157 14			206466 43	24
25	2/01/xx ✓ 1020	1720 55	158 45			206307 98	25
26	3/03/xx ✓ 1031	1719 23	159 77			206148 21	26
27	4/01/xx ✓ 1053	1717 90	161 10			205987 11	27
28	5/01/xx ✓ 1062	1716 56	162 44			205824 67	28
29	6/01/xx ✓ 1071	1715 21	163 79			205660 88	29
30	7/02/xx ✓ 1090	1713 84	165 16			205495 72	30
31	8/01/xx ✓ 1106	1712 46	166 54			205329 18	31
32	8/30/xx ✓ 1115	1711 08	167 92			205161 26	32

what you paid toward mortgage principal represents a kind of forced savings account and what you paid for depreciable items will be deducted for tax purposes over a number of years, you still had to pay out that money this year. What's left over for spending, saving, or investing after you've paid all your expenses is in one sense the true cash flow produced by the property. But it's not the same as the "cash flow" which has been referred to elsewhere in this book along with the other three ways to make money in the landlording business. If you want to calculate that cash flow, you include neither the mortgage principal payments (they're really contributing to your "equity buildup," remember) nor the cost of the depreciable items. You include among the ordinary expenses only the amount of this year's depreciation on the depreciable items you paid for during this year and prior years.

That's the classic way to calculate cash flow, but it results in an unreal figure. It's not really the money you get to pocket. Personally, I think the other figure makes more sense.

Use whichever one makes more sense to you.

■ Loans/Insurance—Loan & Note Record

The Loan & Note Record form enables you to keep tabs on your loans, an activity some might say is akin to the miser's counting his stacks of gold and silver coins. It ain't necessarily so. Actually, this form provides you with information which is very useful when you're renegotiating a loan, when you're double-checking a lender's interest calculations, or when your payment receipt is lost in the mail. Everything's here, the original amount of the loan, the interest rate, the payment, the principal balance, etc., and filling it out takes just a moment after you receive your payment receipt from the lender.

Come to think of it, filling out this record is a pleasure, too, because you get to watch the equity in your property gradually building up every time you fill another line with figures. Maybe misers do have more fun. In this business you have to take your fun when and where you can get it.

■ Loans/Insurance—Insurance Record

This last form keeps track of the insurance policies for your properties, all of your properties. It's not an absolutely essential part of your records, and you won't get any jollies out of keeping it up to date or reading it when you have nothing else to do, but you will find that having all of your insurance information in this one place is convenient when you begin wondering how soon a policy is due or what coverage you still have on a certain property. Insurance policies

Insurance Record   Property __456-64 Sweet Street__

Company and/or Agent	Type of Policy	Policy Number	Limits	Premium	Expiration Date
COMFY INSUR. 555-2845	WORKERS' COMP.	00479	—	# 136 - 5/10/xx '1063	6/01/xx
DRIVER FRIENDLY GLENDA LACY 555-1181	AUTO	2YA-30454	1,000,000 liability	# 483 - 10/20/xx '1149	11/12/xx
WHOLESALE INSUR. VERNAGAE LEE 555-1068	APT. OWNERS	F1-778 1101	1,000,000 liability	# 886.54 4/20/xx '1279	4/30/xx
DRIVER FRIENDLY GLENDA LACY 555-1181	(Pick-up) AUTO	2Y.A.30864	1,000,000 liability	# 321 - 3/26/xx '1212	11/12/xx
MAJOR CARRIER VICTOR WONG 555-3050	EARTHQUAKE	099837L	37,000 Deduct.	# 867 5/11/xx '1292	6/01/xx

themselves don't yield that kind of information quickly. Typically you have to read through lots of fine print before you discover the information you're looking for. Read the fine print only once and record the pertinent information here. Then you'll have it handy when you need it.

Some Last Words

Do your recordkeeping regularly at least once a month, and you'll find that it's practically tolerable. It will also give you the current information you need when you're merely curious about how well your properties are doing or when you're preparing the numbers a banker wants to see before she'll give you a new loan.

Better still, get yourself a computer and follow the suggestions in chapter 21 for computerizing your operations. Even a homegrown computer bookkeeping system will save you lots of drudgery and time, and it should motivate you enough to keep on top of all your recordkeeping instead of sinking beneath it.

20
Doing Taxes

During the first two weeks of April every year, many adults seem to suffer from the same malady, the dreaded DT's. They wobble a little and complain a lot, and their eyes grow bug-eyed and red. They start imagining all sorts of devils and demons and beastly beasties, and it isn't until after the fifteenth of the month that the symptoms finally disappear, because not until then do they finish DOING TAXES.

Landlord, if you're among these seasonal sufferers, you should be ashamed of yourself! Income tax time is an especially good time for you, and you should enjoy the opportunity to snicker a little over your good fortune. Don't wait until April 15th to file your return. Do it as soon as you can, so you'll have your income tax refund check in hand when everyone else is suffering those dreaded DT's. Besides, you need that check early to help you pay your property taxes.

You get to snicker over your income taxes because at tax time you get to take advantage of one of the four ways to make money in landlording—depreciation. (If you don't remember the other three, look back at the beginning of chapter 7.)

Here's how depreciation works for rental property owners. Every year, little by little, you get to deduct from your property's income a portion of the value of the capital improvements just as if they were honest-to-goodness, out-of-purse expenses incurred during the year. "Capital improvements" include everything but the raw land where the property is located. Many times, even though the property is producing a positive cash flow, these extra deductions will shelter that cash flow and create a paper loss on the property besides. You as owner may then apply this loss to your other income (within legal limits naturally) in order to reduce your overall income tax burden. When you finally sell the property, you then pay income taxes on the "depreciation recapture" (the amount of depreciation you took while you owned the property) and the "capital gain" (the difference between the net sales price and the net purchase price).

Here's a straightforward example. Let's say that you bought a fourplex for $125,000 (this sum would be your purchase price) and you depreciated it down to $75,000 (this sum would be your depreciable balance) over the years you owned the property. During that time, you avoided paying taxes on $50,000 of your income. If you now sell the property for $300,000 (to learn about the impending tax consequences every time you plan to acquire or dispose of income property, spend a few bucks and consult a knowledgeable, aggressive accountant or tax attorney), you'll have a depreciation recapture total of $50,000 and a capital gain total of $175,000.

Neither of these sums is earned income. Depreciation recapture and capital gain fall under tax classifications which are treated more favorably than earned income. In other words, even though you were sheltering earned income with depreciation and you profited handsomely from the capital gain you received when you sold the property, you pay less in taxes on those sums than you would have if they had been earned income.

That in itself is an advantage, but the real advantage you enjoyed in depreciating this property for tax purposes is that you didn't have to pay taxes on the $50,000 you took as depreciation during the years you owned the property. If the property generated that amount or more in cash flow while you owned it, then you paid no income taxes whatsoever on $50,000 of its cash flow. If it generated less than that amount in cash flow, then it enabled you to pay no taxes on the cash flow the property did generate, and the excess depreciation sheltered some of your regular income as well, provided, of course, that you qualified to use it according to the IRS income and activity requirements.

Remember that a dollar in your pocket today is worth more than a dollar in your pocket next year and every year after that. If you can postpone paying a bill today and pay it with the same amount of money years hence, that is, without having to pay any interest on the amount you owe, then you get to put that money to use for your own benefit, and it costs you nothing to do so. What a deal! You are essentially borrowing money from a bank which doesn't charge any interest!

Consider how much money you'd have if you could somehow retrieve every dollar you ever paid in income taxes and you could use that money to buy more rental property if you chose to. You'd be worth a lot more money than you're worth today, wouldn't you?

Well, the situation is similar when you consider that depreciation for tax purposes enables you to keep a portion of your income from being taxed. You get to keep the tax money you would otherwise be paying to Uncle Sam. It becomes part of your net worth. What a deal!

Here's an even better deal. What if you could save some or all of the money you pay in income taxes every year and not just postpone paying those taxes until some later date but never pay them at all? Yes, yes, you read that right–*never pay them at all*. You can. You can indeed!

You can if you exchange your property. Exchanging is the best way available to avoid depreciation recapture and capital gains taxes altogether when you want to get rid of one property and acquire another like-kind property. In fact, exchanges are easier to arrange now than ever before because they don't have to be simultaneous as they did years ago.

Non-simultaneous exchanges first became known as "Starker exchanges" when the IRS had to allow them as a result of a court case back in 1979 involving the Starker family. After that, the IRS had to give non-simultaneous exchanges its full blessing, and it set out the rules for them in Section 1031 of the Internal Revenue Code. Hence the name by which they are known today–1031 exchanges.

Here's how they work. You sell your property and put the proceeds into an exchange account which requires your signature plus the signature of another qualified person for withdrawal. You then have forty-five days to identify as many as three properties to purchase. You may purchase one or more of the three, but what you do purchase must have an equal or greater value than the property you sold in order for you to pay no taxes at all. Having identified the property, you then have six months from the date when you sold your property to consummate the acquisition using the exchange account funds. Each transaction merely needs to have the proper verbiage to indicate that it is part of an interdependent sale and reinvestment.

For practical information about doing 1031 exchanges with or without pricey assistance, see "How to Do a Delayed Exchange." It's a 58-page special report written by John Reed, the author of *John T. Reed's Real Estate Investor's Monthly* (johntreed.com). He calls them "the granddaddy of all real estate tax breaks." He's right. They certainly are.

In the case of the fourplex which you sold for $300,000, you would get to reinvest all of the proceeds from that sale in another property without paying any taxes on your considerable capital gain or on the recapture of the depreciation so long as you set up the transaction as a 1031 exchange! If the loan balance on the old property were $70,000, and the sales commission and costs were $16,000, you'd have $214,000 in untaxed cash to reinvest, and you should be able to purchase a new property selling for $650,000 to $1,000,000.

Had you not exchanged, you'd have had to pay something like $73,000 of your proceeds in state and federal taxes. Consequently, you'd have had only $141,000 to reinvest, and you'd have been limited to smaller properties in the $425,000 to $700,000 range. A 1031 exchange would have saved you $73,000!

Invested in good income-producing real estate with a cap rate of 9 (remember now—"cap rate" is the return generated by a property exclusive of debt service; it's really a percentage figure derived from dividing the net operating income by the value of a property; higher numbers are better), that $73,000 should be making you an extra $547 per month, month after month after month for the rest of your life!

Where does all this end?

If you continue exchanging and exchanging, you may defer the payment of taxes until you finally sell off your properties, or you may keep exchanging property after property and keep avoiding the payment of taxes on the capital gains forever.

When your heirs assume ownership of your property, they do so at its then current value, not at its old basis or depreciable balance. By exchanging, you avoid paying the capital gains taxes while you're alive, and your heirs pay no capital gains taxes when they acquire it upon your death.

Tax-deferred exchanges can be true tax-free exchanges!

Is your mind boggled? It should be. Think about this. You can be increasing your net worth year after year every time you depreciate your property for tax purposes while at the same time the property itself actually appreciates in value. Yet you are not liable for income taxes on the resulting increase in your net worth, not even when you sell one property and use the proceeds to buy another! That's more amazing than any pickled two-headed billy goat I've ever seen and a heck of a lot more important to you and me as real estate investors.

Ah, but you say, "I've only got a fourplex, and I just want to learn how to prepare the tax forms I need to submit along with my income tax return. I can't be wasting my time dreaming about exchanging my property and becoming wealthy while I sleep. I have all the rental property I can handle right now. One place is plenty. Heck, most of the time it's more than plenty!"

Okay, okay. Here's how to do your return, and here are some sample tax form sheets completed for Lester Landlord (he's no millionaire either). He has a duplex and a fiveplex.

To begin with, we'll assume that you're old-fashioned and still doing your taxes by hand and calculator, but even if you aren't old-fashioned and you plan to do your taxes using a computer program, a review of the basics behind tax preparation for landlords will do you good.

After that, we'll look at doing your taxes using a computer program.

Doing Your Own Taxes by Hand and Calculator

Begin preparing your taxes by completing a Depreciation Record sheet (see chapter 19) for every building you own and for the various expenditures you have to depreciate, including those which qualify for first-year expensing as Section 179 property.

Consult IRS Publication 946, "How to Depreciate Property," for guidance in determining what useful life is appropriate, whether a depreciable item may be expensed in its first year, and how much depreciation you may take for every year you own a property.

Use a Depreciation Record for all of your buildings and depreciable expenditures, but use one sheet for each building and one sheet for each classification of depreciable expenditures made for a particular building. For example, Lester should have one sheet for the new roof he put on his duplex and another one for the new roof he put on his fiveplex several years later. He should have one sheet for all the five-year items he bought for his duplex in one year and another sheet for all the seven-year items he bought for his fiveplex that same year. All of these Depreciation Records should remain in his three-hole recordkeeping binder for reference whenever the time to do taxes arrives.

Next comes the biggest job of all for procrastinators, completion of the annual summary reports for all rental property held. You may do them manually with the forms provided in chapter 19. You may do them with a spreadsheet template like the one shown in chapter 21. You may

Form E-3	RENTAL INCOME AND EXPENSE						YEAR KXXX	

NAME(S) OF TAXPAYERS: LESTER LANDLORD **SOC. SEC. NUMBER:** 123 45 6789

PROPERTY LOCATION & DESCRIPTION		GROSS INCOME
Property A	123 NEAT ST. LITTLETOWN	10,500.00
Property B	456-464 SWEET ST. ✓	42,600.00
Property C		
Property D		
Property E		
Property F		
Property G		
	TOTAL GROSS INCOME	53,100.00

EXPENSES	A	B	C	D	E	F	G	Totals
Interest	3,643.06	7,312.78						
Taxes, Licenses	1,648.62	1,374.42						
Insurance	741.80	886.54						
Utilities	490.07	2,177.60						
Serv, Rep, Maint.	232.31	1407.90						
Merch., Supplies	387.91	489.27						
Payroll	⊖	790.60						
Misc. Expenses	248.72	92.79						
Other: Tel	138.48	⊖						
Travel	149.70	⊖						
Subtotal	7,680.67							
% Business Use	50%							
Subtotals	3,840.33	14,540.90						18,381.23
Deprec. (D-1)	1,426.08	3,465.00						4,891.08 *
Deprec. (SD)		412.30						412.30
Totals	5,266.41	18,418.20						23,684.61

*Sum of D-1 and SD Depreciation Totals   5,303.38 *

Form D-1	DEPRECIATION WORKSHEET		YEAR XXXX

NAME(S) OF TAXPAYERS LESTER LANDLORD **SOC. SEC. NUMBER** 123 45 6789

PROPERTY LOCATION & DESCRIPTION

Property A 123 NEAT ST., LITTLETOWN

Property B 456-464 SWEET ST.,

Property C

Property D

Property E

Property F

Property G

	A	B	C	D	E	F	G	Totals
Date Acqd. or Conv. to Bus.	2/XX	10/XX						
New or Used	USED	USED						
Cost or Other Basis	112,356	198,000						
Land Value	34,000	59,400						
Salvage Value	0	0						
1st Year Special Depreciation	0	0						0
Depreciable Basis	78,356	138,600						
Prior Depreciation	25,669.43	18,191.25						
Depreciable Balance	52,686.51	120,408.75						
Method of Depreciation	ACCEL	SL						
Useful Life	27.5	40						
Full Year Depreciation	2852.16	3465.00						
Percentage of Year Held	100	100						
Percentage of Business Use	50	100						
Depreciation This Year	1426.08	3465.00						4,891.08

PAGE TOTAL 4,891.08

Form SD	**SUPPLEMENTAL DEPRECIATION**							YEAR **XXXX**

NAME(S) OF TAXPAYERS   *LESTER LANDLORD*   SOC. SEC. NUMBER   123 45 6789

CAPITAL IMPROVEMENT LOCATION & DESCRIPTION

1 456-464 SWEET ST., CARPETING, DRAPERIES, LINOLEUM

2

3

4

5

6

7

	1	2	3	4	5	6	7	Totals
Date Acqd. or Conv. to Bus.	6/xx							
New or Used	NEW							
Cost or Other Basis	1683.55							
Salvage Value	⊖							
1st Year Special Depreciation	⊖							
Depreciable Basis	1,683.55							
Prior Depreciation	240.41							
Depreciable Balance	1,443.14							
Method of Depreciation	ACCEL							
Useful Life	7							
Full Year Depreciation	412.30							
Percentage of Year Held	100							
Percentage for Business Use	100							
Depreciation This Year	412.30							412.30

PAGE TOTAL 412.30

do them with a computer checkwriting program like Quicken or a computer bookkeeping program like QuickBooks. How you arrive at the summaries doesn't matter so long as they're accurate. Once you complete the summaries, keep them close at hand. Together with the depreciation sheets, they comprise the primary source of data essential from here on.

Now make blank copies of tax forms E-3, D-1, and SD in the FORMS section of this book (these forms, by the way, could be made into computer spreadsheet templates as well; in fact, Landlording on Disk (The Forms) includes several such templates), and using applicable information from your Depreciation Record sheets, fill out D-1 and SD. Use D-1 for buildings only and SD for anything else depreciable, from furnaces to roofs.

Enter the appropriate property location and description information on form E-3 and post each building's depreciation for the year from form D-1 to E-3. Add all the supplemental depreciation as noted on SD for each property and post the figures onto E-3 in the space marked "Deprec. (SD)." Remember that you must add up all of the supplemental depreciation for each building before you post it.

After you post both regular and supplemental depreciation for your properties onto E-3, enter the gross income as calculated on the Summary of Business and Statement of Income form. Then post the expenses from the summary sheet to E-3 (you'll notice that the categories are the same on both forms) and calculate the totals. Remember to add the two asterisked boxes and post their sum in the bottommost box on the form.

Using all of this information, you can easily fill out Form 1040, Schedule E, otherwise known as the "Supplemental Income and Loss Schedule."

In Part I of Schedule E, simply write "SEE ATTACHED FORM E-3" where it's most obvious, perhaps where you might otherwise identify the location of "Property A." Then post the TOTALS from E-3 to the corresponding lines of Schedule E. Post the total income (rents received) where indicated and the total expenses where indicated.

You needn't go to all the trouble of itemizing the expenses again on Schedule E. Just post the total expenses. Use the "Property A" column for these figures, and make sure that you post an in-come figure and an expenses figure separately. Do not combine them before posting them on Schedule E.

By all means, do remember to post your depreciation total on its proper line.

Then follow the instructions printed right on Schedule E for adding the expenses and the depreciation together and subtracting them from the rents received.

Also at this time, write "SEE FORMS E-3 AND SD FOR DEPRECIATION CALCULATIONS" across the bottom of the form to advise the reviewer of your return where to look for your depreciation information.

If the other parts on page 2 apply to you, include their totals with your Part I total in the summary section under the final part. If they don't, merely transfer the total from Part I to the designated line on Form 1040.

Should you show a loss from your rentals, check the tax booklet's instructions for Schedule E to determine whether you're eligible to apply the loss to your other income. The rules for eligibility keep changing, so even though you might not have been eligible before, you might be now. Keep checking the rules, and take whatever losses you can. Hey, they're a gift! Gifts from the IRS are almost as scarce as winning tickets in a lottery. Take 'em when you can get 'em.

From this point on, just go ahead and finish your tax computations as you normally do, snickering as you go, and remember to attach forms E-3, D-1, and SD to your Schedule E when you submit your return.

Doing Your Own Taxes by Computer

Ever since tax preparation software first appeared back in the 1980's, it has become more sophisticated, more reliable, more complete, and more functional while still remaining inexpensive.

Even a first look at a computer-assisted tax preparation program will make you put manual tax preparation in the same category as washboard laundering. It's stunning! It may even convince you that you ought to try doing your own taxes for once.

No longer do you have to concentrate so intently on making sure that you do every calculation on your return correctly, that you post the right total from one box on one form to a corresponding box on another form, and that you be

```
===========================================================================
DEPRECIATION STATEMENT
===========================================================================
    YEAR: XXXX                                   NAME: Lester Landlord
PROPERTY: 456-464 Sweet St., Tarrytown        SOC SEC NO: 123-45-6789
```

Description of Property	Date Acq	Cost/Basis (less land)	Sec. 179 Election This Yr	Prior Dep (Fed)	Prior Dep (State)	Remaining Cost (Fed)	Remaining Cost (State)	Mthd	Life in Yrs	Fed Rate	State Rate	Prtn Yr Held	Fed Dep This Yr	St Dep This Yr
5-Plex Bldg	10/1/XX	138,600		18,191	18,191	120,409	120,409	SL	40			1	3,465	3,465
Cpt, lino	6/2/XX	1,684		240	240	1,444	1,444	A	7	0.2449	0.2449	1	412	412
						0	0						0	0
						0	0						0	0
						0	0						0	0
						0	0						0	0
						0	0						0	0
						0	0						0	0
TOTALS		140,284		18,431	18,431	121,853	121,853						3,877	3,877

Methods:
  SL, straight line; A, accelerated

consistent with the names and Social Security numbers on every form you submit. No longer do you have to redo your return when you discover belatedly that you forgot to include the second payment you made on the property taxes for one of your rental houses. Add that figure into the expenses for the house, and these programs take care of all the necessary recalculations right on down the line.

They remove most of the grunt work from tax preparation and give you the opportunity to analyze your return to see whether you might save on your taxes by readjusting your investments. They let you play "what if?" with the numbers, something real estate investors ought to do now and then.

Typically, you have the option of entering data directly onto computer versions of the IRS forms themselves or submitting answers to plain-English questions which result in numbers on the forms, whichever you prefer.

Not only do they produce your federal return, they produce your state return as well. They transfer the appropriate data from your federal return to your state return and help you fill it out correctly.

The only thing they don't do is sign the return. You still have to do that.

The two most widely used software programs are Intuit's TurboTax and H&R Block's At Home, with the simpler, faster, cheaper TaxAct not far behind. All three also have their own tax preparation websites where you can do your taxes online rather than doing them offline, but they aren't the only ones offering online tax preparation. Others such as CompleteTax compete with them in that arena.

Tax preparation programs vary enough in price and features that you should compare them yourself by visiting their websites and by using a search engine to search on the words "tax preparation software comparison" and "tax preparation online comparison." You may find that any one of them will do what you want a tax preparation program to do for you but that one of them charges much less to do the three different state returns you're obliged to do because you live in one state, have an inherited family farm in another, and own an apartment house in still another.

You may find that tax preparation software loaded on your own computer and used independently of the internet will let you do any number of tax returns at no extra charge, while a commercial online tax preparation service may let you do only one return for the price charged, although that price is apt to be only half as much as the offline tax preparation software offered by the same company.

You may find that offline software will import prior-year data from other tax preparation programs and import current-year data from personal finance programs, whereas online software may not, that is, unless you're using the same service you used for your prior-year return. You may have to re-enter the data which would otherwise be imported.

When deciding whether to do your taxes with any tax-preparation program offline or online, consider especially how many returns you plan to do (returns you do for your parents and your children will cost you extra if you do them online), whether you have a high-speed internet connection (a dial-up connection will make doing taxes online all the more painful), and whether the program will import data from other programs (re-entering data is both time-consuming and prone to errors).

Tax Collectors' Websites

The IRS itself maintains a website (irs.gov) (do not confuse irs.gov with irs.com, which is a commercial website connected to banks.com) where you will find all of its latest forms and publications and a host of resources.

There's an alternative minimum tax (AMT) worksheet which tests information you enter anonymously and determines whether you're subject to the troublesome AMT.

There's information about eligibility requirements, payment options, phishing, and tax scams, such as those promoting frivolous legal positions, hiding income offshore, and outright fraud. There are where-to-file addresses and taxpayer-assistance-center addresses.

There are frequently asked questions covering all kinds of topics related to income taxes, organized by category, subcategory, and keywords. Some examples of the questions you'll find are these: "I purchased a rental property last year. What closing costs can I deduct?" "Can you deduct private mortgage insurance premiums on rental property? If so, which line item should I use for reporting it on Schedule E?" "We have incurred substantial repairs to our rental property: new roof, gutters, windows, furnace, and outside paint. What are the IRS rules concerning depreciation?" "I am renting a house to my son and daughter-in-law. Can I claim rental expenses?"

There are links to every state's official website, where you will find a link to your state's office of taxation which may itself have a website as useful as the IRS website.

In addition, it includes two free programs which may be of help to you, "Free File" and "e-file."

Free File offers two different methods to help taxpayers prepare their tax returns for free. The first method, "traditional Free File," works in conjunction with commercial software companies which offer free tax preparation software. It provides users with step-by-step help, does the math, checks for accuracy, and files the return, but it does have its limitations, starting with the size of the adjusted gross income (check irs.com for the current limit).

The second method, "fillable forms," provides users with electronic versions of the most commonly filed IRS forms. Users choose and prepare the applicable forms themselves just as if they were using the IRS paper forms except that the program does the basic calculations and then files the return. "Free File Fillable Forms" has no adjusted gross income limits, but it does have limitations of its own, all related to the complexity of the return.

"e-file" is an electronic alternative to filing paper returns. It enables you to bypass the copy machine, the stationery store, and the post office, and it gives you assurance that the IRS has received your return milliseconds after you send it.

The IRS website has heaps of information you can rely upon. Check it out for yourself.

Another Way

Another way to enlist the aid of a computer, virtually any computer, for doing your taxes is to use a spreadsheet program to create your own spreadsheets according to the patterns of the forms shown in this chapter. Once you have them set up to your liking, you can use them year after year with little alteration. They won't automate your income tax preparation nearly as much as one of the tax preparation programs will, but they will be useful.

The printout on the previous page shows how the forms D-1 and SD might look as a computer spreadsheet. Here they're combined and arranged horizontally to show all the depreciation on one property for a single year. The spreadsheet includes formulas which calculate the federal and the state depreciation, if they're different, and then they add the totals at the bottom.

Some Last Words

There are those naysayers you'll encounter in this world who will say you're a pig-headed fool for doing your own taxes. They'll say you should have a sorcerer in tax matters do them for you, someone who's thoroughly experienced in doing income taxes for propertied folk, someone who knows all the latest loopholes applicable to your situation, and those naysayers may be right. It all depends on your ability and your inclination.

Some people have the good sense to invest in rental property, but they lack the capacity to deal with numerical data and somewhat complicated instructions. People like that should leave their taxes to the experts.

Some people have the good sense to invest in rental property and are good with numbers, but they find tax preparation too tedious to do themselves. They'd rather spend their time looking after their properties, looking for more properties to acquire, and learning more about the landlording business. People like that should leave their taxes to the experts, too.

If you happen to be a landlord who has the ability and the inclination to prepare your own taxes, you ought to do them yourself, by all means, but once you finish them, you may want to get a second opinion from a specialist by buying an hour or two of professional advice. You cannot possibly keep abreast of the volumes of current tax laws, and you could unknowingly be throwing money away by overlooking perfectly legitimate tax angles.

At the very least, have your self-prepared returns reviewed by a professional preparer every three years, when you can still amend any of your returns and can change items reported in error or omitted from the original.

Whether you have your taxes prepared for you or whether you do them yourself, try to get a feel for the tax principles which affect the landlording business. Read about taxes in periodicals whenever you can, and get a copy of John T. Reed's *Aggressive Tax Avoidance for Real Estate Investors*, a book you should read from cover to cover.

21
Using a Computer

If you have a computer already, you may find in this chapter several ways to put it to better use.

If you don't have a computer yet, you may find in this chapter some very good reasons why you ought to begin using one because computers have become essential for 21st century landlords. They're as essential in landlording today as they were back when Neil Armstrong and Buzz Aldrin landed safely on the moon.

When the first edition of this book appeared in 1975, which was the same year, believe it or not, that Volkswagen stopped selling the original "Beetle" in the U.S. and America got out of Vietnam, there was no such thing as a computer for "everyman." Computers were monstrosities which cost a small fortune to acquire, a small staff to operate, a small priesthood to program, a small utility company to power, and a small throne room to house. They weren't available to mere mortals. The closest thing then to today's ubiquitous computers were dedicated word processing machines which cost $15,000 apiece and were little more than electronic typewriters with monitors attached.

In the years since, a lot has happened in the computer world. Fortunes have been made and lost, companies have come and gone, innovators have surfaced and vanished, and reputations have waxed and waned, but now we can enjoy the fruits of many, many creative people's hard labor. We have available to us today some very powerful, very compact, very useful, and very inexpensive computers, computers which are now also very easy to use compared to their predecessors.

Whereas the average person today buys a computer strictly for personal reasons, in order to send emails to friends, pay bills, play games, download podcasts, catch the latest news, check on their kids' progress at school, book flights, and doctor their digital photographs, you are more fortunate. You have both personal and business reasons for acquiring one. A computer is a business expenditure for you as a landlord because it has many landlording applications and enables you to look after your landlording business like never before, and with greater accuracy and more ease, just as if you were a Fortune 500 company.

No longer does a computer merely save a landlord time by performing certain tasks quickly. Now it handles tasks which nothing else can.

Should you have any fears or doubts, should you wonder how a computer might help you, read on.

Fear Not

Computers are stupid. They are so stupid, so obedient, that they will do exactly what you tell them to do every time and they'll do it in exactly the same way every time! Be honest now. When was the last time you got a tenant to do that?

Computers are passive, too. In spite of what you may have seen in some science-fiction film or other, computers have never been known to attack people. Why be afraid of them? There's nothing they can do to hurt you or you to hurt them.

You can hit every key on a computer's keyboard all day and all night long and in every conceivable combination, and you won't get executed, you won't start a nuclear war, you won't even break into American Airline's reservation system or a Citibank payroll file, not accidentally you won't. Have no fear of that.

Ordinary people did have something to fear about computers only a few years ago, before the graphical user interface (GUI) became the norm. Computers were different then. They were primitive beasts. They were tough to tame, requiring lots of patience, technical knowledge, concentration, and logical thinking out of the user. They could do a lot of work for you, but as often as not, they would make work for you.

All that's changed now. Now they come pretty much tamed and housebroken, and you have nothing to fear from having them around. What's more, you don't have to spend all that much time learning how to use one anymore.

If you're embarrassed to learn anything about computers because you don't want to appear ignorant around little kids who seem to grasp how to use these perplexing machines so quickly, don't be. Most kids and most adults, too, who are computer "junkies," love to show others what they can make their computers do, and they love to show others how neophytes can work wonders with a computer. They show and tell and teach with joy, and they hope that they will awaken the computer nerd in everybody.

Remember that everybody's been a computer beginner sometime. If you don't know diddlysquat about computers right now, so what! Now's the time to get started, no matter how young or how old you are.

I have helped people in their eighties and nineties learn how to use a computer and become more productive as a result. One of these days I'm sure I'll come across some intrepid souls in their nineties who want to learn how to use a computer. I'll show them what they need to know, and they'll be so delighted by all they can do that they'll want to extend their lease on life for at least another decade.

But What Can You Really Do with One?

What can you, dear landlord, really do with a computer?

For starters, you can write checks with it. When you write your checks using a computer, you enter the figures only once rather than two or three times. You eliminate the inevitable errors which creep in when you transcribe check amounts to the check register by hand and later when you post them by hand to a spreadsheet. Computer checkwriting programs automatically post the original amounts entered on the checks themselves. Reconciling your monthly statement becomes a pleasant task instead of a frustrating one, and preparing the expense reports for your properties is a snap.

You can analyze your expenses using percentages and graphs, and you will know, for example, whether you're spending too great a percentage of your expenses on insurance. You can't tell that without using a computer unless you take a lot of extra time to produce comparable figures. A computer can do it for you in a jiffy.

You can analyze the occupancy rates of your various-sized dwellings so you can tell whether the rents for your one-bedroom units are too high or too low. If they're showing an 80% occupancy rate over the same period of time that your two-bedroom units are showing a 96% occupancy rate, your one-bedroom rents are probably set too high and should be adjusted. The rental market is always speaking to you. All you have to do is listen and interpret what it's saying.

You can create professional-looking rental agreements and pay-rent-or-quit notices to suit your particular needs, and then you can change them whenever you choose.

You can keep track of your tenants' addresses, phone numbers, email addresses, bank account numbers, birthdays, rents, deposits, payment history, and rent-raise anniversaries. You can create rent statements and receipts and maintenance requests and work orders.

You can create letters as readily and as perfectly as the best legal secretary could ever type them on an electric typewriter.

You can set up a year's budget in advance and try to stay within it. When have you ever been able to do that before?

You can analyze the potential of a property which is being offered for sale and calculate a fair offer. When you get ready to sell your own property, you can calculate a fair sales price based upon the detailed operational figures you've assembled.

You can run the numbers applicable to any number of different IRS Section 1031 delayed exchange scenarios so you can select the best one. Once you've run the numbers, you can also determine the depreciable basis for your new property without having to hire an accountant to do it for you.

You can complete your own tax return almost painlessly, and you won't need an eraser or a calculator or any midnight oil to help you do it.

You can produce loan payment schedules for all your loans, including those held by private parties, those with variable interest rates, those with irregular payments, and those with balloon payments.

You can update your financial statements regularly so you'll understand fully how well you're doing in your financial dealings and know when you've joined the Millionaire Club of America.

You can access the internet and verify information on rental applications, order credit and eviction reports, locate former tenants who skipped out owing you money, check out the latest in fair housing laws, download and read the current state codes applicable to rental properties, research market rents in your area, retrieve an unusual IRS form you didn't know you needed until late on April 15th, search for hard-to-find parts, shop for more rental properties, advertise your vacancies, and even chat with other landlords.

That's pretty heady stuff, isn't it? Believe it or not, you can do all of these tasks with the various programs mentioned in this chapter and with internet access.

A Little Jargon

Before you start thinking much about using a computer in landlording, you really ought to learn a little computer jargon, some "tech talk."

Jargon helps people engaged in similar pursuits understand each other quickly. As a real estate investor, you unwittingly use jargon sometimes, and few outsiders would understand what in the world you're talking about. "COE" (close of escrow), "REO" (real estate owned by note holders who have foreclosed), "paper" (mortgages or notes in lieu of cash), "points" (percentage points charged by lenders to make a loan), "boot" (difference between equities involved in a trade), "DOS" (due on sale), "recording" (placing a document on file with the county for all to see), "wrap" (a combination of existing loans and a new one carried by the seller), and "title" (evidence of someone's right to a property) are all terms which mean something special to you, something quite different from what they mean

to John and Jane Doe.

Computer people use jargon just as you unwittingly do. They use so much of it that one group of computer people using one type of computer frequently cannot understand their colleagues who use another type of computer. Four words they all understand, though, are "hardware," "software," "programs," and "files," and you should know what they mean, too. They're essential terms.

"Hardware" in computer jargon is anything you can see and touch. That includes the computer which sits on your desk, the central processing unit (CPU) and the random access memory (RAM) inside, the screen you stare at, the keyboard your fingers tap on, the mouse you use to move your pointer around the screen and execute commands, the printer which gives you hard copy on paper, and the device which connects you to the internet. "Hardware" also includes the hard drives, flash drives, and disks which store your data and programs.

"Software" in computer jargon is anything you can't see or touch. The computer programs which do word and number processing are "software" as are the instructions which tell the computer where to find what's stored in its memory. Software is essential to making hardware work the way you want it to work.

A movie stored on a DVD is software. You can't see it unless the DVD player interprets it for you, and you can't touch it. Yet you know the movie is there. The same is true with computer software. You know that something is in there interpreting your commands. You just can't see it. That's the software at work.

"Programs" are software. You can't see them or touch them. They're stored on disks, CD-ROMs (compact disks, read-only memory), flash drives, and computer memory "chips." They are very detailed instructions written by computer programmers to make computers act in certain ways in response to user commands.

Programs turn computers into many different things. There are programs that make personal computers act like office calculators, flight simulators, electronic typewriters, typesetters, speed reading machines, filing cabinets, telephone dialers, fax machines, video arcade machines, drawing boards, musical instruments, utility usage monitors, photograph retouchers, animation editors, et cetera. The list goes on and on.

"Files" are software, too. They're what you, the computer user, save on disk. When you write a letter using a computer or enter a whole series of numbers that you want to save, you save them on a disk as a file. Once they're stored, you can retrieve and use them whenever you wish, so long as you have a program which can open them.

Whew, that's enough jargon for now! Don't you agree?

The Programs

Let's take a look at how you might use computer programs for word processing, number handling, data management, and sundry specialized uses.

■ **Word Processing**—Word processing programs enable you to manipulate words easily and quickly. With a word processor, you may type away on your computer's keyboard to your imagination's content and then move those words around to suit your second and third thoughts.

The two primary uses for word processing in landlording are correspondence and forms creation.

Correspondence is obvious enough. Whenever you "feel a letter coming on," you sit down at your computer and bang away on the keyboard. When the letter looks pretty good to you on the screen, you tell the program to print it out on paper. If it looks good to you on paper, you send it. If it doesn't, you go back to the same letter on the computer screen and change it to your liking without having to type it all over again or use correction fluid. You add a comma here, move a paragraph there, delete a word in paragraph two, and change an abbreviation in paragraph six. Then you print the letter-perfect version. That done, you save the letter on your computer if you think you might want to use parts or all of it again sometime or else you go ahead and trash it.

Forms creation isn't that much different from correspondence. It involves either making up your own forms from scratch or using someone else's like the ones in this book. All you do is create a word processing "template" for each form you want to use repeatedly. You may take a "standard rental application" and a "standard rental contract" and adapt them to fit your locale, the type of tenant you cater to, the type of rental dwelling you own, and the times, and then print copies whenever you need them.

You may also personalize your agreements for each of your tenants if you want to, using a form you set up with what are called "fields" in place of the variable data, shown otherwise as underlined blanks to be filled in. These fields accept data from another file when the two are "merge-printed." The data file contains only such things as the tenants' names, their address, the amount of the rent, and anything else specific to the tenancy. The result is a beautiful looking personalized document with no blanks to fill in except for the signature blanks. The computer program "fills in" all the other blanks with data.

Learn how to merge-print using your word processor, and you'll find many uses for this technique.

■ **Spreadsheet Programs**—Spreadsheet programs are not the only computer programs that process numbers, but they're the easiest for ordinary people like us to learn and use. Usually the second business application program mastered by the personal computer user, they do more to justify the use of a computer by landlords than any other program because they're so versatile and powerful. They can do so much.

What's surprising is that the computer spreadsheet program is such a recent innovation that even my unabridged edition of *The Random House Dictionary of the English Language*, copyrighted in 1971, lacks an entry for the word "spreadsheet."

The granddaddy spreadsheet program of them all, VisiCalc, first appeared on the scene in 1977 and worked only on the Apple II computer. Because so many businesspeople recognized its potential immediately, that program alone sold thousands upon thousands of Apple II's and helped establish Apple as a credible computer company.

Today, many people consider the computer spreadsheet program one of the most innovative ideas of the 20th century. I readily agree. Spreadsheet programs now run on every computer, and they are so much improved that they make the first version of VisiCalc seem as crude as a crystal set.

A computer spreadsheet program consists of what resembles a large piece of graph paper inside the computer. Each one of the graph paper's little boxes, or "cells," as they're called, may be addressed individually with a column and a row designation, like every good seat in a college football stadium. The very first cell in the upper left-hand corner of a spreadsheet is A1 ("A" is the column and "1" is the row). The very last one in the bottom right-hand corner, depending on how many cells your spreadsheet program contains, might be BK63 ("BK" is the column and "63" is the row).

Now, if these carefully identified cells could hold only numbers, they'd be about as useful as a curl of calculator tape in a wastebasket. We'd have to keep asking ourselves what the numbers meant, just as we'd be asking ourselves what a radio sportscaster meant in announcing, "We have two great basketball scores for you, folks, 89 to 88 and 106 to 104!" You'd have to admit that those were great scores indicating close games, exciting games, but they wouldn't mean anything to anybody without team names attached to them.

So, spreadsheet programs allow you to put words into their cells as well as numbers, but what's more important, they allow you to put formulas (add up what's in cells C6 through C42 and put the sum in cell C47) and cell references (look at another cell and put its value or formula in this one) there, too. These formulas and cell references are what make spreadsheet programs so versatile and powerful.

Because a blank computer spreadsheet has so many cells waiting to be filled and so many capabilities waiting to be used, it has tremendous potential in and of itself, but you won't see the true measure of that potential until you fill some of those cells with a carefully prepared layout which you can use over and over again. These cell layouts are called "templates," just like their word processing counterparts. They're actually nothing more than frequently used words and formulas.

Rather than begin each computer spreadsheet session with a blank spreadsheet and put into it the same words and formulas you've used before

and know you'll use again, you use a template, one you make up yourself or one you buy from someone else (ExPress sells them; see "Landlording on Disk (The Forms)" in SOURCES & RESOURCES).

Except for one essential difference, a spreadsheet template is much like any of the bookkeeping forms in this book. The big difference is that the spreadsheet template has a "calculator" built right into it, and you can tell this calculator to perform its mathematical calculations automatically or upon command.

Were you manually posting a series of numbers on a paper bookkeeping form, you'd first have to enter the numbers on the form and then you'd have to run a calculator tape to total them. You'd be entering every number twice, once on the paper form and once on the calculator, and doubling your odds for making errors. Using a spreadsheet program and a template, you enter the numbers only once. The built-in calculator takes over from there, so you have fewer opportunities to make mistakes.

Is it any wonder, then, that accounting firms today, which have to be extremely accurate in their calculations, cannot be without their computers, spreadsheet programs, and templates?

You could create all sorts of these templates yourself if you wanted to. You could create them for loan tables, property analysis, tax schedules, financial statements, bookkeeping, and anything else involving numbers.

The expense-and-payments-record template shown on the next pages is a good example of a useful template which you could use with any spreadsheet program. The first two pages include a month's worth of data so you can visualize what it looks like when it's in use. The two pages after that show what the template looks like with its formulas exposed.

To create this template yourself, you'd enter into your spreadsheet program what appears in the cells on the second two pages. Doing so is not nearly as hard as it may first appear because many of the cell entries are repeated with only slight modifications. The program itself will sense what you're trying to do and make the cell address adjustments automatically. Enter a formula and command your spreadsheet genie to copy that one to other cells. G56, for example, is copied with adjustments into all the cells from H56 through AG56.

Income and Expense Spreadsheet with Dummy Data

	A	B	C	D	E	F	G	H	I	J	K	L	M	N	O	P	Q	R	S	T
2	PROPERTY NAME: SWEET ST			INCOME AND EXPENSES -					MONTH: April						SWST	PAGE 2				
4	Date	Ck #		Paid To		For	Total	Adverts	BnkChg	Car Exp	Dues&Pub	Garbage	Insurance	Interest	Lgl&Prof	Lic/Perm	OfcSupls	OutSrvs	Pstg&Frt	Promo
6	4/2	267		Big Bank		1st mortgage	579.03							311.42						
7	"	268		S. Moneybags		2d mortgage	122.00							53.34						
8	4/6	269		Littletown Hdw		hdw account	43.29													
9	4/7	270		Saddlebk Cnty		prop taxes	674.31													
10	4/10	271		Monopoly Util		3/1-4/1	57.12													
11	4/11	272		K-Mart		shades	24.42													
12	4/12	273		Lttletwn Water		April water	41.30													
13	"	274		Monopoly Garb		April service	22.50					22.50								
14	4/15	275		Phoenix Paints		paint & suppl	8.23													
15	"	276		Lester Landlord		pers draw	280.00													
16	"	277		C. Goodfolks		payroll	30.00													
17	4/19	278		" " P/C		plumbsupp	20.52												4.40	
18	4/20	279		USA Insurance		annual prem	286.54						286.54							
19	4/21	280		LittltwnOffSup		copying	5.47										5.47			
20	4/25	281		Seeres Co.		water heater	443.64													
21	4/31	282		C. Goodfolks		payroll	74.13													
22							0.00													
23	4/15	$$$		Mtn Oaks Hdw		pnt brushes,	17.40													
24	4/22	$$$		Littletown Rag		ad to rent apt	6.50	6.50												
25							0.00													
26							0.00													
27							0.00													
28							0.00													
29							0.00													
30							0.00													
31							0.00													
32							0.00													
33							0.00													
34							0.00													
35							0.00													
36							0.00													
37							0.00													
38							0.00													
39							0.00													
40							0.00													
41							0.00													
42							0.00													
43							0.00													
44							0.00													
45							0.00													
46							0.00													
47							0.00													
48							0.00													
49							0.00													
50							0.00													
51							0.00													
52							0.00													
53							0.00													
54							0.00													
56				THIS MONTH'S TOTALS			2736.40	6.50	0.00	0.00	0.00	22.50	286.54	364.76	0.00	0.00	5.47	0.00	4.40	0.00

NOTES:

These facing pages show what an income and expense spreadsheet looks like when completed for a single month.

Designed to print on three 8.5"x11" pages, this spreadsheet has been condensed here to fit onto two pages. The page breaks should come where you see the solid black vertical lines.

This sample includes row and column headings for easy reference. For better looking results, don't print the headings on your final copy.

Column G, you'll be happy to note, requires no user input. It adds whatever you enter in columns H through AG and puts that total where it belongs.

Columns AE through AG include expenditures which are not, strictly speaking, expenses, at least not for tax purposes. Nonetheless, because they do come out of the property's checking account and do relate to the property, you have to keep track of them somewhere. This is the place.

Column AJ starts with zeros in January. Other months show the year-to-date figures from the previous month's spreadsheet.

Column AK automatically picks up the current month's totals for each category of expenditures. You have to enter the income figures for the month here.

Journal columns (U–AG)

Row	U Repairs	V Sewer	W Supplies	X Txs,EPT	Y Txs,Pay	Z Txs,Prop	AA Tel	AB Trv&Ent	AC Util	AD Wages	AE Deprec	AF Princpl	AG Non-Ded
								SW ST PAGE 3				
7												267.61	
8	43.29											68.66	
9						674.31							
11			24.42						57.12				
13									41.30				
14	8.23												
15													280.00
16										30.00			
17			16.12										
20											443.64		
21									74.13				
23			17.40										
56	51.52	0.00	57.94	0.00	0.00	674.31	0.00	0.00	98.42	104.13	443.64	336.27	280.00

SUMMARY

	Prior Month	This Month	Yr to Date	% Ttls
Income:				
Rental	6,398.00	2,314.00	8,712.00	94%
Laundry	264.50	78.75	343.25	4%
Storage	120.00	45.00	165.00	2%
Other	0.00	18.86	18.86	0%
TOTAL INCOME	6,782.50	2,456.61	9,239.11	100%
Expenditures:				
Advertising	12.50	6.50	19.00	0%
Bank Charges	0.00	0.00	0.00	0%
Car Expenses	0.00	0.00	0.00	0%
Dues&Publications	0.00	0.00	0.00	0%
Garbage	90.00	22.50	112.50	2%
Insurance	0.00	286.54	286.54	5%
Interest	1,104.39	364.76	1,469.15	28%
Legal&Professional	0.00	0.00	0.00	0%
Licenses&Permits	10.00	0.00	10.00	0%
Office Supplies	1.37	5.47	6.84	0%
Outside Services	35.00	0.00	35.00	1%
Postage&Freight	4.40	4.40	8.80	0%
Promotion	0.00	0.00	0.00	0%
Repairs	74.39	51.52	125.91	2%
Sewer	0.00	0.00	0.00	0%
Supplies	152.33	57.94	210.27	4%
Taxes, Employer'sPay	7.40	0.00	7.40	0%
Taxes,Payroll	7.40	0.00	7.40	0%
Taxes,Property	0.00	674.31	674.31	13%
Telephone	25.67	0.00	25.67	0%
Travel&Entertainment	0.00	0.00	0.00	0%
Utilities	193.73	98.42	292.15	6%
Wages	97.60	104.13	201.73	4%
Depreciable	0.00	443.64	443.64	8%
Mortgage Principal	990.64	336.27	1,326.91	25%
Non-Deductible	247.50	280.00	527.50	
TOTAL	3,054.32	2,736.40	5,790.72	
Less Non-Deduct	247.50	280.00	527.50	
TOTAL EXPENDITURES	2,806.82	2,456.40	5,263.22	100%
Income	6,782.50	2,456.61	9,239.11	
Less Expenditures	2,806.82	2,456.40	5,263.22	
CASH FLOW	3,975.68	0.21	3,975.89	
Tot Exp less Debt Serv & Deprec as % of Tot Income	10%	53%	22%	
Checkbook Balance		359.14		

Column AL adds columns AJ and AK to get figures reflecting the entire year through the current month.

Column AM calculates some important percentages. Examine them to see in relative terms where the property's money is coming from and where it's going. If one appears to be out of proportion to the others, find out why.

Row 50 is the actual cash flow from the property after the total expenditures have been deducted from the income. This figure is not the same as the net income for tax purposes. To get that figure, you'd have to add back what was paid for depreciable items and what was paid on the mortgage principal.

Row 53, like column AM, calculates a percentage. This time the percentage excludes debt service and depreciable items and shows what proportion of the income the expenses are. Use these percentages to compare one month with another and one property with another. This percentage is useful because it strips properties of their debt service so you can compare them on an equal basis. By the way, can you tell why the percentage for April is so high when compared with the previous months?

The checkbook balance, cell AK56, is strictly a reference figure which you enter from your checkbook register at the end of the month. It puts everything into perspective so you know whether to add money to the property account, whether to take money out as a personal draw, or whether to leave it alone.

Income and Expense Spreadsheet Template

	A	B	C	D	E	F	G	H	I	J	K
1	=	=	=	=	=	=	=	=	=	=	=
2	PROPERTY NAME:					INCOME AND EXPENSES				MONTH:	
3	=	=	=	=	=	=	=	=	=	=	=
4	Date	Ck #		Paid To		For	Total	Adverts	BnkChgs	Car Exp	Dues&Pub
5	-		-	-	-	-	-		-	-	-
6							=SUM(H6:AG6)				
7							=SUM(H7:AG7)				
8							=SUM(H8:AG8)				
9							=SUM(H9:AG9)				
10							=SUM(H10:AG10)				
11							=SUM(H11:AG11)				
12							=SUM(H12:AG12)				
13							=SUM(H13:AG13)				
14							=SUM(H14:AG14)				
15							=SUM(H15:AG15)				
16							=SUM(H16:AG16)				
17							=SUM(H17:AG17)				
18							=SUM(H18:AG18)				
19							=SUM(H19:AG19)				
20							=SUM(H20:AG20)				
21							=SUM(H21:AG21)				
22							=SUM(H22:AG22)				
23							=SUM(H23:AG23)				
24							=SUM(H24:AG24)				
25							=SUM(H25:AG25)				
26							=SUM(H26:AG26)				
27							=SUM(H27:AG27)				
28							=SUM(H28:AG28)				
29							=SUM(H29:AG29)				
30							=SUM(H30:AG30)				
31							=SUM(H31:AG31)				
32							=SUM(H32:AG32)				
33							=SUM(H33:AG33)				
34							=SUM(H34:AG34)				
35							=SUM(H35:AG35)				
36							=SUM(H36:AG36)				
37							=SUM(H37:AG37)				
38							=SUM(H38:AG38)				
39							=SUM(H39:AG39)				
40							=SUM(H40:AG40)				
41							=SUM(H41:AG41)				
42							=SUM(H42:AG42)				
43							=SUM(H43:AG43)				
44							=SUM(H44:AG44)				
45							=SUM(H45:AG45)				
46							=SUM(H46:AG46)				
47							=SUM(H47:AG47)				
48							=SUM(H48:AG48)				
49							=SUM(H49:AG49)				
50							=SUM(H50:AG50)				
51							=SUM(H51:AG51)				
52							=SUM(H52:AG52)				
53							=SUM(H53:AG53)				
54							=SUM(H54:AG54)				
55	-			-	-	-	-	-	-	-	-
56				THIS MONTH'S TOTALS			=SUM(G6:G54)	=SUM(H6:H54)	=SUM(I6:I54)	=SUM(J6:J54)	=SUM(K6:K54)

NOTES:

These pages show the words and formulas used to create the template which forms the basis for what you see on the previous two pages.

Because of space limitations, columns L through AG have been omitted. Except for their "totals" cells in row 56, which reflect a particular column letter designation, they look just like columns H-K shown here.

Rows 1, 3, 5, and 55 all have symbols which repeat across the pages. The symbols look like single or double lines when they're set to fill out their cells.

Columns C, E, and AH are narrow spacer columns. They separate entries to prevent confusion in the final printout.

The "=" sign in this particular spreadsheet program, which happens to be Excel™, identifies a cell as a formula cell. Cell G6, for example, totals everything in cells H6 through AG6. Cell H56 totals everything in cells H6 through H54.

To get the prior month's figures for column AJ, copy the figures, NOT THE FORMULAS, from the previous month's column AL and paste them into column AJ for the current month.

	AH	AI	AJ	AK	AL	AM
1	=	=	=	=	=	=
2			SUMMARY			
3	=	=	=	=	=	
4			Prior Months	This Month	Yr to Date	% Ttls
5	-		-	-	-	-
6		Income:				
7		Rental			=SUM(AJ7:AK7)	=AL7/AL12
8		Laundry			=SUM(AJ8:AK8)	=AL8/AL12
9		Storage			=SUM(AJ9:AK9)	=AL9/AL12
10		Other			=SUM(AJ10:AK10)	=AL10/AL12
11	-		-		-	-
12		TOTAL INCOME	=SUM(AJ7:AJ10)	=SUM(AK7:AK10)	=SUM(AL7:AL10)	=SUM(AM7:AM10)
13						
14		Expenditures:				
15		Advertising	0	=H56	=AJ15+AK15	=AL15/AL45
16		Bank Charges	0	=I56	=AJ16+AK16	=AL16/AL45
17		Car Expenses	0	=J56	=AJ17+AK17	=AL17/AL45
18		Dues&Publications	0	=K56	=AJ18+AK18	=AL18/AL45
19		Garbage	0	=L56	=AJ19+AK19	=AL19/AL45
20		Insurance	0	=M56	=AJ20+AK20	=AL20/AL45
21		Interest	0	=N56	=AJ21+AK21	=AL21/AL45
22		Legal&Professional	0	=O56	=AJ22+AK22	=AL22/AL45
23		Licenses&Permits	0	=P56	=AJ23+AK23	=AL23/AL45
24		Office Supplies	0	=Q56	=AJ24+AK24	=AL24/AL45
25		Outside Services	0	=R56	=AJ25+AK25	=AL25/AL45
26		Postage&Freight	0	=S56	=AJ26+AK26	=AL26/AL45
27		Promotion	0	=T56	=AJ27+AK27	=AL27/AL45
28		Repairs	0	=U56	=AJ28+AK28	=AL28/AL45
29		Sewer	0	=V56	=AJ29+AK29	=AL29/AL45
30		Supplies	0	=W56	=AJ30+AK30	=AL30/AL45
31		Taxes, Employer'sPayroll	0	=X56	=AJ31+AK31	=AL31/AL45
32		Taxes,Payroll	0	=Y56	=AJ32+AK32	=AL32/AL45
33		Taxes,Property	0	=Z56	=AJ33+AK33	=AL33/AL45
34		Telephone	0	=AA56	=AJ34+AK34	=AL34/AL45
35		Travel&Entertainment	0	=AB56	=AJ35+AK35	=AL35/AL45
36		Utilities	0	=AC56	=AJ36+AK36	=AL36/AL45
37		Wages	0	=AD56	=AJ37+AK37	=AL37/AL45
38		Depreciable	0	=AE56	=AJ38+AK38	=AL38/AL45
39		Mortgage Principal	0	=AF56	=AJ39+AK39	=AL39/AL45
40		Non-Deductible	0	=AG56	=AJ40+AK40	
41	-		-		-	-
42		TOTAL	=SUM(AJ15:AJ40)	=SUM(AK15:AK40)	=SUM(AL15:AL40)	
43		Less Non-Deduct	=AJ40	=AK40	=AL40	
44	-		-	-	-	-
45		TOTAL EXPENDITURES	=AJ42-AJ43	=AK42-AK43	=AL42-AL43	=SUM(AM15:AM39)
46						
47		Income	=AJ12	=AK12	=AJ47+AK47	
48		Less Expenditures	=AJ45	=AK45	=AL45	
49	-		-	-	-	-
50		* * CASH FLOW * *	=AJ47-AJ48	=AK47-AK48	=AL47-AL48	
51	-		-	-	-	-
52		Tot Exp less Debt				
53		Serv & Deprec as	=(AJ45-(AJ21+AJ38+AJ39))/AJ12	=(AK45-(AK21+AK38+AK39))/AK12	=(AL45-(AL21+AL38+AL39))/AL12	
54		% of Tot Income				
55	-		-		-	-
56		Checkbook Balance		0		

Column AK requires original input for the income figures, cells AK7 through AK10, but it takes its expenditure figures from row 56 across the spreadsheet. Cell AK15, for example, picks up the total spent for advertising during the month. It appears as "=H56," which means repeat here exactly what appears in cell H56.

Column AL merely adds columns AJ and AK to produce the year-to-date figures.

Column AM divides each category of expenditure except Non-Deductible by the total amount of expenditures so far this year to get a percentage.

The percentages in row 53 are different from those in column AM. Look at the formula in cell AL53 to see what I mean. It lumps all the expenditures together except Non-Deductible, cell AL45, deducts the total paid for debt service and depreciable items, cells AL21, AL38, and AL39, and divides that by the total income, cell AL12, to show what percentage of total income the property's expenses are.

Once you set up an expense and payment record template, you don't have to do it again. That's the beauty of it. All you do after that is call up the template, enter the appropriate property designation and dates in row 2, and go to cell A6 to enter the date for the first expenditure. Follow across the row and enter the check number, the payee, and a description of the expense or payment item itself. Then you select the column heading which best describes the item you're posting and enter the dollar amount there. As you do that for each of the month's entries, the spreadsheet program will insert the total for the line into column "G," total the columns, and place the column totals into the proper positions for the cumulative summary over in the "This Month" column (AK), all automatically.

But wait, there are several more steps you ought to take to get full advantage of the really important information the template can provide. After you've posted all the expenditure entries as outlined, enter the income for the current month in cells AK7 through AK10. Then load the "Year to Date" column from the previous month's spreadsheet into the "Prior Months" column (AJ) on this month's spreadsheet, and the program will figure everything else out for you, right down to cash flow and percentages. That's useful information, easily produced!

Now let's take a look at another spreadsheet template. This one helps a buyer analyze the numbers for a property under consideration for purchase.

The entire upper section calls for pertinent information readily available to the buyer or else predicted from experience. The purchase price, down payment, total annual payments, scheduled gross income, and square footage are all readily available to the buyer, and the anticipated vacancy factor and anticipated annual expenses are reasonable predictions.

Once the user enters those figures, the spreadsheet calculates ten numbers every investor wants to know before buying a property—cost per square foot, effective gross income, net operating income, cash flow, gross rent multipliers (two different), capitalization rate, cash-on-cash return, operating expense ratio, and debt coverage ratio.

Directly adjacent to the calculated numbers on the spreadsheet sample, you see the formulas entered into column E, where all of the numbers and resultant calculations reside.

One by one, here are the formulas.

The formula for "cost per square foot" is a simple one. It's E6 divided by E22. That's the purchase price divided by the square footage.

The "effective gross income" is E13 times 1 minus E16. That's the scheduled gross income times one minus the vacancy factor. One minus the vacancy factor yields the percentage of occupancy. That's the number we need to multiply by the gross income to get the effective gross income. Make sense?

The "net operating income" is the effective gross income we just calculated minus the anticipated annual expenses, or E13 times 1 minus E16 minus E19. Often referred to as the NOI, the net operating income is one of those important numbers we like to know about any income-producing property, the ones we own and the ones we'd like to own, because it's an essential ingredient in the capitalization rate and the debt coverage ratio.

"Cash flow" is on every investor's mind because it's the amount of money which goes into or comes out of the investor's pocket every month. The spreadsheet adds E19, the anticipated annual expenses, and E10, the total annual loan payments, and subtracts them from the effective gross income, E13 times 1 minus E16, to get the cash flow.

The two "gross rent multipliers" differ only slightly, with the first one using the scheduled gross income, E13, as its multiplier and the second one using the effective gross income, E13 times 1 minus E16, as its multiplier. The first resembles a proforma. It's more optimistic than the second, but it's the one most commonly used to compare one rental property with another.

The "capitalization rate" AKA the "cap rate" is another yardstick investors want to know. Higher numbers indicate a higher return. The spreadsheet comes up with the cap rate by dividing the NOI, E13 times 1 minus E16 minus E19, by the purchase price, E6.

The "cash-on-cash return" calculation takes the cash flow formula, (E13*(1-E16))-(E19+E10), and divides it by the amount of the down payment, E8. It shows the investor's percentage return on the down payment.

The "operating expense ratio" is another good property comparison number, revealing management efficiency. Our spreadsheet divides E19, the anticipated annual expenses, by E13 times 1 mi-

```
=======================================================================
ACQUISITION ANALYSIS OF PROPERTY KNOWN AS:      Bonnie Brae Court
=======================================================================
Input the following PERTINENT INFORMATION:
```

PURCHASE PRICE:	250,000	<< E6
DOWN PAYMENT:	35,000	<< E8
TOTAL ANNUAL LOAN PAYMENT(S): (principal and interest; also known as debt service)	18,036	<< E10
SCHEDULED GROSS INCOME: (not including vacancy factor)	19,200	<< E13
ANTICIPATED VACANCY FACTOR: (including uncollectable rents)	2%	<< E16
ANTICIPATED ANNUAL EXPENSES: (everything except debt service)	3,000	<< E19
SIZE (SQUARE FOOTAGE):	2,200	<< E22

```
=======================================================================
Worksheet calculates the following INFORMATION:
```

COST PER SQUARE FOOT: (cost divided by total square footage)	$113.64	=E6/E22
EFFECTIVE GROSS INCOME: (scheduled gross income minus vacancy factor)	18,816	=(E13*(1-E16))
NET OPERATING INCOME: (effective gross income minus annual expenses)	15,816	=(E13*(1-E16))-E19
CASH FLOW: (net operating income minus debt service)	(2,220)	=(E13*(1-E16))-(E19+E10)
GROSS RENT MULTIPLIER ONE: (purchase price divided by scheduled gross income)	13.021	=E6/E13
GROSS RENT MULTIPLIER TWO: (purchase price divided by effective gross income)	13.287	=E6/(E13*(1-E16))
CAPITALIZATION RATE: (net operating income divided by purchase price)	6.33%	=((E13*(1-E16))-E19)/E6
CASH-ON-CASH RETURN: (cash flow divided by down payment)	-6.34%	=((E13*(1-E16))- (E19+E10))/E8
OPERATING EXPENSE RATIO: (annual expenses divided by effective gross income)	15.94%	=E19/(E13*(1-E16))
DEBT COVERAGE RATIO: (net operating income divided by debt service)	0.877	=((E13*(1-E16))-E19)/E10

Exercise the utmost discretion when acquiring any rental property. This spreadsheet analysis is no substitute for a detailed analysis. There are many other factors to consider.

nus E16, the effective gross income, to get the operating expense ratio.

Bankers always want to know a property's "debt coverage ratio." They like to see a ratio of 1.15 or more, sometimes even 1.25 or more. If the ratio is less than 1, the property isn't generating enough income to make the loan payments, and they want the borrower to increase the down payment or show enough other income to make the monthly payments. The formula divides the NOI, E13 times 1 minus E16 minus E19, by the total annual payments, E10, to come up with the ratio.

Using a spreadsheet program, you can create this very spreadsheet yourself or else create a variation more suited to the properties of interest to you, and you can use it again and again to help you analyze properties easily. As you might imagine, calculating all of these figures without using a computer is never easy.

I would like to caution you here to examine closely every spreadsheet template you create. Once you've created a template and are using it, you needn't worry much about data entry errors because they'll be noticeable. Ah, but a simple formula error in one cell will be magnified whenever that formula affects another cell. The error will just keep being repeated. Neither the computer nor the program knows any better. If, for example, you inadvertently tell the program to put the sum of every cell from H7 through H54 into cell H56, when you meant to include cell H6, too, you're going to have a problem. The problem may not surface for a while if you seldom enter a number in cell H6, and even when you do enter a number in H6, you may not notice what's wrong in H56 right away. There won't be any bells tolling or error messages appearing on your viewing screen. The error will just creep in quietly, on little rat feet.

If that ever happens, you'll know why computer people are so mindful of their oft repeated saying, "Garbage in, garbage out!" Do be careful. Spreadsheets are powerful, but they're also unforgiving. Check and double-check your work.

■ **Database Management Programs**—Database management programs are essentially filing programs with search, sort, and math functions added.

Your telephone book is a large database, and all the names in it are filed alphabetically according to last names. If you wanted a list of all the people who have a certain telephone prefix and live on a certain street and you weren't using a database management program, you'd have to sit down and laboriously make a list of them one by one. Ah, but if you had your whole telephone book entered into a database management program, all you'd have to do to get a list of the people who live on Tewkesbury Street and have a 555 telephone prefix is ask for it. The program would find everyone with those two things in common, and it would list them in any order you specify, that is, by last name, street address, or telephone number.

Database management programs are powerful, but in times past they were difficult to master. Without attending intense seminars or lengthy classes or pouring over some very technical material and learning a host of cryptic commands, you could never become proficient in using a database management program.

Fortunately, the database management programs of today, such as FileMaker, are much easier to learn and use, and they're far more versatile. With FileMaker, you as a non-programmer could design an entire recordkeeping system to keep track of just about everything for your rental properties. Ultimately, it would be even easier to use on a monthly basis than a spreadsheet template, though it would take more time to design. I know that from experience.

■ **Software Suites**—Sometimes likened to Swiss Army knives because they're capable of handling many different tasks, software suites can do word processing, spreadsheets, databases, presentations, graphics, and more.

Although the early versions of these programs were anemic, the current ones are powerful, very powerful. You needn't buy copies of Word and Excel for your ordinary landlording chores. They're overkill. They have far more features than you'd ever use. Software suites can do everything you as a landlord need to do with a computer, and they're practically "road kill" in cost. MicrosoftWorks and iWorks, each of which sells for less than $100, are both good examples of capable software suites, but there's one which is even more capable, and it's free. It's called OpenOffice, and it's the result of more than twenty years of development.

OpenOffice is completely cross-platform, that is, it runs under all the major computer operating systems, including Windows, Mac, and Linux, and it saves its files in many different formats. It even creates pdf (portable document format) files readable on virtually any computer. Download it from openoffice.org, and give it a try before you spend a dollar on any other software suite.

■ **Web-Authoring Programs**—In the chapter on advertising, you read about the web-authoring programs I have used to create websites of my own to promote my rental properties without having to learn and write cryptic HTML (HyperText Markup Language) coding.

There are so many web-authoring programs on the market now that a book like this cannot keep up with them all. Search them out yourself on the internet, looking for the features you want and the price you want to pay. You will find many, many choices, from rudimentary to cutting-edge, from free to spendy.

■ **Single-Purpose Programs**—Single-purpose programs are different from word processing, spreadsheet, database management, and suites programs. Single-purpose programs are not nearly as flexible as other programs. They are not written to be flexible. They're written to perform specific tasks. Single-purpose programs for handlings business matters might be said to resemble the combination of a spreadsheet program and a certain spreadsheet template linked inextricably together and working together.

Good examples of such single-purpose programs are Quicken, QuickBooks, InnQuest, and SiteLink. They have very specific applications and cannot do anything else. InnQuest, for example, is a front desk program for managing hotels and motels. It won't work for managing self-storage facilities. SiteLink is a site-based program for managing self-storage facilities. It won't work for

managing apartment houses.

If you're inclined to purchase any single-purpose program to help you manage your rental property, be wary. You want to buy software which will work as advertised and make your life easier, not harder. If possible, download a trial version, and give it a try before you buy.

Internet Access

With so much useful landlording and real estate investor information readily available over the internet these days, you must have a means of accessing it yourself. Not only should you be accessing it yourself, you should be using it in a hundred different ways.

Below are a number of recommendations related to your use of the internet as a landlord—

✔ Even if you have high-speed internet access, set up a dialup account, too. It can be a lifesaver when your high-speed service is malfunctioning or when you're traveling and have only a laptop and a phone line available to you. You'll be glad to know that Juno (juno.com) has a free dialup service for anybody who needs ten or fewer hours of access per month.

✔ Sign up for a web-based email account with HotMail, YahooMail, or Gmail. They're free, and they're accessible through any computer with internet access anywhere in the world. If you already have an established email account using a POP3 (Post Office Protocol v3) service and you retrieve your email at home using an email client such as Outlook Express, you can always set that account to forward your email to your web-based email account whenever you're traveling.

✔ Be aware that Windows is especially susceptible to viruses because hackers enjoy attacking what they call the "evil empire." To them, that's Microsoft. Because your Windows computer could inadvertently contract a virus through an internet connection when you're downloading and because that virus could bring your system to a halt as well as destroy your files, be alert and cautious. Run Microsoft Security Essentials (it's a free download) whenever you start Windows, do not open unsolicited email or their attachments, and back up your most precious files onto an external storage device at least once a day. You won't be sorry you did. You could be very sorry you didn't.

✔ Internet browsers keep adding features and getting better all the time. Microsoft's Internet Explorer and Apple's Safari are excellent browsers, but they're not the only ones. The best alternative is one called Firefox. It's a free download from mozilla.org. It's compact, fast, open-source, and easily customizable. It installs quickly and it can import any other resident browser's settings. It works with Windows, Linux, and Macs. It has good security and privacy tools built-in, and it has many competent and dedicated supporters who volunteer their time to improve the program and root out its bugs. Try it.

✔ Google may be the world's most popular search engine, but it does have its rivals, and you might want to search for them and give them a try. My current favorite is one called Nibbo (nibbo.com) because its search-results layout isn't cluttered with advertising and it's readable at a glance.

General Computer Recommendations

Here are a number of general computer recommendations related to landlording—

✔ Do not buy any computer hardware or software until you can see an immediate need for it. There's not one computer or computer-related purchase I have ever made, whether it's been on sale or not when I bought it, which I couldn't buy today for less money than what I originally paid for it. Because you have to spend some time learning how to use each new piece of software for your computer, buying a whole lot of it which you can't use right away is foolish. By the time you get around to using all you bought, there

will be newer, improved versions available, and you'll have to pay extra for the updates.

✔ Consider buying a used computer. Even the newer models appear for sale used, sold presumably by those who have to try the latest of everything without thinking about how much it costs. Look for them on Craigslist and eBay.

When buying a used computer, be especially wary about whether the price is right, whether it has been stolen, whether it is free of viruses and spyware, and whether any software included is legitimately yours or is pirated.

Know your prices before you go shopping. The prices of new computers keep falling so much that even though you might think a computer which cost $1,500 two years ago is a good deal at $750, it might not be at all if you can now buy a new one with a faster clock speed, more RAM, a larger hard drive, and built-in WI-FI for $450. That older computer ought to be selling for $50-200.

Be wary about whether the used computer you want to buy has been stolen. A used computer ought to come with the manufacturer's serial number intact. If you can't find one, the computer is probably stolen, and you will have to do some mighty fast talking whenever you take it in for repair. You may have to do that fast talking down at the police station, and you may even have the computer confiscated as stolen property if you're not careful. The first thing a computer repairer looks for is that serial number, so it should be one of the first things you look for when you're contemplating the purchase of a used computer. No serial number, no purchase!

Be wary about whether the used computer you want to buy is infected with viruses and spyware which can cause you almost as much grief as a problem tenant. If it is infected, you may need to disinfect it by restoring the operating system from the original backup disks. If you can do the job youself, fine; if not, it may cost you as much to do as you pay for the computer itself.

Another thing to be wary about when buying a used computer is the software included with the machine. Because of software piracy (unauthorized copying), so-called "used" software doesn't have much market value. Yet, new software costs plenty if you have to go out and buy it. With a used machine, you generally get valuable software for little or nothing. If you do acquire any used software, make sure that the seller gives you all the original CD's and documentation and agrees to help you get the software license transferred into your name. Sometimes sellers will give you the original CD's and manuals from an early version of software which they have upgraded and intend to continue using themselves in the later version. In that case, the early version is the same as pirated software in the eyes of the software publisher. Ask for a clarification of what you're getting.

✔ If you already have a computer, so long as it can run a word processing program, a spreadsheet program, a check writing program, and an internet browser, and so long as you feel comfortable with it, use it. Don't run out every year or two to buy something which is new and improved and just a little bit faster. Every time you change computers, you face the daunting task of transferring the files and upgrading the software.

On the other hand, if you're still using MS-DOS, Windows 3.1, or a pre-PowerPC Mac, you ought to upgrade to a more current computer. You'll notice a dramatic increase in speed.

✔ Always "back up" your work, that is, make duplicate copies. Power outages, magnetic fields, defective drives, operator error, disk drive problems, software viruses, software bugs, static electricity, and coffee spills all conspire now and then to cause you to lose the precious work you labored over. The loony bins are full of people who didn't back up their work. Don't join them. Back up your work regularly.

✔ Check for competitive upgrades when buying software, especially any software selling for hundreds of dollars. "Competitive upgrades" are complete programs made available to users of competing programs. Let's say that you've been using one database management program for years, but you've heard many good things about another one and you'd like to acquire a copy. Whereas the best price you can find after shopping around is $250, you may find that the competitive upgrade price is only $100 or even less. Why pay more when you can legitimately pay less?

My Own Biased Personal Computer Recommendations

Seasoned computer users tend to be biased in favor of one system over another and in favor of one kind of software over another. These biases can lead to intolerance and belligerence among otherwise intelligent and tolerant adults. I admit to being biased myself, but I don't get fighting mad when people I know buy precisely the system I've advised them not to buy. I just shake my head. I'm a landlord. I'm used to having people do precisely the opposite of what I say.

Although I use both Windows machines and Macs, I prefer the Mac. Macs don't crash or get viruses the way Windows machines do, and unlike Windows machines, because the Mac was designed for a graphical user interface from the silicon up, you never have to revert to old line-oriented commands.

Were you to compare the Windows and Mac operating systems in terms of the time required for learning and manipulating, you'd find that Windows users typically spend more time on learning the basics and on file management, data communications, and virus issues.

Whereas there used to be a big price differential between the two, today there is little if any for comparably equipped systems.

If you don't have some compelling reason to buy one computer over another and you want to use a computer to help you with your landlording chores without your having to spend much time learning how to use a computer, consider the following recommendations. They are my own biased personal hardware and software recommendations made by a long-time user of all kinds of computers and software in both education and business.

Buy a Macintosh. *Consumer Reports* consistently gives Apple high marks for technical support and reliability.

Lest you worry that Mac users are isolated, you should know that Intel Macs can run Windows software while even older Macs can share files with Windows machines. The Mac you have at home for your kids' schoolwork and your landlording business can read the word processing and spreadsheet files you bring home from the office. Using equivalent programs, you can work on the files at home on your Mac and return to work the next day with your office work completed.

Buy an inexpensive laser printer. The print quality is outstanding, and the cost for supplies is much less than it is for ink-jet printers.

For software, use OpenOffice. It has more than everything you're ever likely to need for everyday landlording tasks. Use Quicken for writing checks and keeping track of your expenses.

Finally, use Landlording on Disk (The Forms)™, my own collection of word processing forms and spreadsheet templates.

Pushbutton Landlording

In an often rued weak moment back in 1992 after having already paid thousands of dollars to programmers to write a stand-alone landlording program and getting no usable results, I decided to write a stand-alone landlording program myself. I knew what I wanted, and I knew what I didn't want.

I didn't want the program to deal with expenses. I didn't want it to write checks. I was already using Quicken for those tasks and knew that I couldn't improve on it. I wanted my landlording program to handle the tenant and income side of rental property management. I wanted it to keep track of my properties, my units, and my tenants. I wanted it to produce rental applications, rental agreements, statements, receipts, notices, and maintenance requests. I wanted it to crank out income and occupancy reports. I wanted it to produce a list of late tenants at the push of a button and to produce late notices at the push of another button. I wanted it to be easy to use and attractive to look at. I wanted it to run on Windows machines and Macs.

Little did I know then that I would be spending two years of my life cooped up in a room filled with computers and computer peripherals. Little did I know then that there would be so many details and problems to deal with that I would be thinking about them every hour of the day and night, every day of the week.

The first version of Pushbutton Landlording emerged from all of this activity and did what it was supposed to do, but it wasn't very attractive to look at. In fact, it was downright ugly.

Some years later, I took this ugly program and turned it into a thing of beauty. We use it ourselves for all of our rental properties, half of them on a Windows machine and half on a Macintosh. The program looks the same and works the same on both platforms.

It's all written in FileMaker, the most popular database management program on Macs and likewise on Windows machines when users are purchasing an unbundled database management program (Microsoft Access is the most popular bundled database management program on Windows machines), and it comes with a run-time version of FileMaker so that it truly is a stand-alone program.

It accommodates an unlimited number of properties and units and tenants, and it exports its income data to checkwriting programs.

Pushbutton Landlording works through a primary menu which directs the user to any number of tasks, from just getting started with the program to exiting and being reminded to back up the data. Everything works with the colorful pushbuttons designed so that they indicate what they do when pushed.

Throughout the program there are explanations to guide the user along, and there's always a "Help" button which takes the user to specific help.

For the novice user, there's a "step-through" procedure for entering tenants which includes copious notes. For the experienced user, there's a "fly-through" procedure which has minimal notes.

Elsewhere in this book you have seen printouts from Pushbutton Landlording. The statement, the receipt, and the maintenance request all come from the program.

The program isn't perfect (no software is), and it isn't for everybody (some people can make any program fail), but it's pretty good as it is, it's pretty useful as it is, and it will only get better as users make suggestions for improvement.

You will find a screen shot of the primary menu on the landlording.com website.

If you'd like to experiment with a trial version, be my guest. Download it from the landlording.com website and put it through its paces. You may find that it's just what you've been looking for. If so, go ahead and order it from the website. If not, keep looking.

Some Last Words

Some day there will be computers available which will repair leaky roofs, collect rents, do all your bookkeeping chores, discipline your tenants, draw your bathwater, bake you an apple pie while you're unplugging a toilet, and read you a favorite bedtime story in any language you choose. While you're waiting for that day to arrive, consider using a computer to assist you in handling some of the more mundane of your landlording chores. That kind of computer and the programs to run it are available right now, today.

22 Potpourri

This final chapter addresses certain subjects which are very different from one another; hence the title, "Potpourri." That they should share a single chapter here is almost as unthinkable as a hard-drinking, cigar-puffing communist's happily sharing his living quarters with a teetotaling, antismoking capitalist, but here they are nonetheless, these strange chapterfellows. They don't really fit anywhere else.

The first three subjects are awkward or difficult situations which you may encounter at some time or another in your career as a landlord. You ought to have some clue how to handle them when they do occur because making the wrong move in these situations could provoke some disgruntled person to drag you into court. You know you don't want to go there. Courts tend not to be level playing fields for landlords.

The fourth subject is a serious matter which you need to keep in mind all the time. It's illegal discrimination during tenancy. An awareness of the subject will make you less likely to commit some innocent, but costly, blunders.

The fifth subject is lease termination. Who's supposed to do what when a lease is about to end?

The sixth subject is house rules. Most landlords don't bother spelling out their house rules even though most tenants need them. You should spell out yours.

The seventh subject should allow you to step back and look at your landlording efforts in a detached way and assess them realistically using a common yardstick, money. Too few of us landlords step back now and then to evaluate what we're doing and where we're headed. Instead, we simply keep our heads down and plow forward through one difficulty after another, never knowing whether we're really getting anywhere.

The eighth subject, incorporation, beckons seductively to many landlords with promises of special dispensations. After the seduction comes the realization that Oz and Kansas are quite different. Here we look at some of the differences.

The ninth subject is vacation time, something you need to give yourself at least once a year to get your mind off your landlording troubles and put everything in a different perspective.

The tenth subject offers some alternatives to paying a heap of capital gains taxes when you want to retire from landlording and live some of your dreams.

The eleventh subject summarizes this whole book in ten commandments, just in case you need to be reminded periodically whether you're doing the right thing.

We start with a subject which would seem to be a landlord's dream, having two qualified tenants who want to live in the same dwelling.

A stranger to this business might liken the situation to a marriageable young person's having two good-looking suitors who are loving, kind, handy, talented, intelligent, well-educated, well-read, entertaining, sophisticated, generous, and wealthy.

Wrong! Wrong! Wrong!

The situation is simply another landlording headache.

Two Tenants— One Rental Dwelling

Because you want to keep your vacancy losses to a minimum, you will likely begin trying to attract a new tenant to fill an upcoming vacancy shortly after your existing tenant gives you notice that he is leaving. You may advertise, interview prospects, show the place, select a desirable prospect, and sign a rental agreement all before the vacating tenant has packed so much as a toothbrush.

Good for you! That's the way to run a landlording business!

Ah, but what happens if you and the new tenant are both waiting anxiously for the old tenant to vacate so you can make the transition smoothly, and then you learn that the old tenant has decided not to move out after all?

Arrgh! What a revolting development!

Besides strangling the old tenant, praying for an unexpected vacancy in another rental, doubling the tenants up, moving the new tenant temporarily into your recreational vehicle, or hammering together a prefabricated rental overnight, how can you extricate yourself from this predicament which you couldn't have predicted and you didn't cause?

Let's try.

Although you have an agreement with only one of the two tenants at this time, unfortunately it's not with the one who is occupying your rental. His agreement terminated on the date he gave you for moving out, and he is now "holding over." You now have an agreement with the new tenant alone, but you, through no fault of your own, cannot perform according to the agreement. Arrgh! Arrgh!

You could sue the existing tenant for possession and damages if you wanted to, but you could be sued as well by the new tenant, and, of course, since you probably have real assets to tap, you could still lose on balance even if you won the suit involving the existing tenant and lost the suit involving the new tenant.

There's another problem, too.

Although you would have little trouble bringing a case against your old tenant for eviction (if you were proceeding with an eviction in a situation like this, you need give no notice before filing; the written notice the tenant gave you that he was going to move on a certain date is the necessary notice; always make certain that tenants who are moving out give you notice in writing, and if they don't, you should provide a notice form for them to fill out and sign; otherwise, should complications such as these arise, it's your word against his, and you should assume that he can tell lies better than you can tell the truth), by the time you pursued the case to a successful conclusion several weeks later, the other tenant might no longer want to move in.

To forestall your legal liability for this kind of problem, always put the clause, "occupancy is contingent upon the existing tenant's vacating the premises," in any rental agreement you sign with someone who is renting a dwelling from you which has yet to become vacant. The problem of having two tenants and only one rental dwelling could still arise, but at least then you could go about solving the problem without fearing that you might be sued successfully by the new tenant.

In addition to including the clause, maintain regular contact with both tenants so you can let the new tenant know immediately if any complications arise which might prevent the change in tenancy from occurring on time. If the departing tenant tells you there's going to be a delay, let the new tenant know immediately. Tenants like to know so they can make plans, and you want to let them know so they will understand that you're trying your best to facilitate the transition.

Should you encounter the "two tenants–one rental dwelling" problem unexpectedly and when you had not prepared in advance to deal with it, determine as nearly as you can why the holdover tenant isn't leaving and whether his plight is permanent or temporary. With definite information concerning the nature of his problem and when it will be resolved, you can proceed to resolve your own problems and that of the new tenant with all the finesse of a career diplomat.

If, after explaining to the holdover tenant that he is residing there wrongfully and that the new tenant is rightfully entitled to possession, you cannot resolve the matter to everyone's satisfaction and if you expect to be sued yourself by the new tenant, you will want to coerce the holdover tenant to leave or else you could sue for possession. Before resorting to the courts, however, try to settle the matter by helping the new tenant find suitable housing elsewhere.

Be sensible and helpful in trying to resolve the problem, and avoid confrontations which will only exacerbate it and result in lawsuits flying back and forth among the three of you.

By the way, avoid taking any rent from the holdover tenant while you're still trying to settle this matter because your acceptance of rent automatically entitles him to possession even though the old rental agreement was terminated by his notice of intention to vacate. If you do accept rent from him and you have a binding agreement with the new tenant, then you're in real trouble.

You would have "agreements" with both tenants and room for only one.

Divorce or Separation

When two of your tenants decide to separate or get a divorce, they seldom remain under the same roof together. This situation presents several unique problems to you as the landlord who rented to them when they were a happy couple.

There is the problem of access to the dwelling, especially if their parting is acrimonious, and the remaining partner wants to keep the other one out.

There is the problem of responsibility for the dwelling and the rent—past, present, and future.

There is the problem of creating a new tenancy and ending the old one.

To deal with these problems before they become critical, you must move quickly. Visit the remaining tenant as soon as possible to learn what you can about the intentions of both parties.

After hearing the tenant out, you will want to explain your position as a landlord who wants to help the surviving tenant insure her privacy and start a new life, regardless of your personal feelings about their breakup.

Explain that you and the tenants, both surviving and departing, are all still bound by the original rental agreement which everybody signed.

Explain that so long as the current rental agreement remains in force, both tenants are legally obligated for all of the rent when it comes due, whether they are living there or not.

Explain that you as landlord must give both of them access to the dwelling unless the surviving tenant has secured a temporary restraining order specifically excluding the other one. (You may change the locks on the doors for the surviving tenant even without a restraining order,

but you would have to give access to the other tenant if it were requested of you.)

Explain that you want to try to resolve the matters of dwelling access and rent responsibility by drawing up a new agreement to take the place of the old one, so long as everyone concerned is agreeable, but that because you rented the place to a couple with a combined income sufficient to pay the rent and because you must protect your own interest in the property, you will need the tenant who signs the new rental agreement to submit an application specifically for determining financial ability.

If the surviving tenant does not qualify financially (gross monthly income should be at least three times the rent), require a co-signer other than the departing tenant. Any reliable and financially capable person would be a better co-signer than the departing tenant because the question of access would not be an issue nor would other acrimonious matters surface later. In a pinch, the departing tenant could be the co-signer, but that person must understand that the co-signer obligation comes with no access privileges.

Whatever you do when you learn that your tenants are separating or divorcing, do not take a "wait and see" position. The tenants don't have a clue how their situation will affect their tenancy. You do. Act quickly to solve the tenancy problems, and you may avoid creating still more problems.

You may avoid becoming the target of a lawsuit brought by one of the tenants for favoring one tenant over the other or for violating the agreement binding on all of you.

You may avoid damage done to your property by an irate ex-spouse or "significant other."

You may avoid loss of rent because the surviving tenant couldn't afford to live there.

You may avoid creating another vacancy because you failed to help out.

Deal with the situation as soon as it arises, and you may succeed in avoiding unwelcome and unforeseen trouble later.

Death of a Tenant

Whenever a tenant who has lived alone in one of your rental dwellings dies, you may be besieged by relatives and other strangers, all claiming to be entitled to certain of the deceased tenant's possessions. At a time like this, when there are certain to be attorneys and courts and public agencies involved, you should be careful about complying strictly with the law, even though you want to clear the personal property out as soon as possible and re-rent the place. Be patient and cautious, and you will stay out of trouble.

Here's the chronological sequence of what you should do—

1) Call the fire department as soon as you or anyone else discovers what is believed to be a corpse. Fire department rescue squads are trained and equipped to examine the body for signs of life and foul play, and they will try to save the life if at all possible. They will then contact either the appropriate law enforcement agency or the county coroner, and they will direct you as to what to do next.

2) Keep everyone out of the dwelling. "Everyone" includes friends, neighbors, former roommates, bill collectors, handymen, the curious, even relatives. Consider the place "sealed" just as if it were a crime scene. Be firm in keeping everyone out, but don't be nasty. Later, you'll be asking one of those people you're keeping out now to pay you the rent owed on the place. You don't want to alienate them too much. If asked, explain why you're keeping everyone out. Say,

—You know, Mabel, I sure hate to see old Simpson go. He was a fixture around here so long that I thought he'd live forever. I always knew they'd have to carry him out of here.

—I'm surprised to hear you say anything nice about him. I thought you two never got along.
—Sure, we had our differences, but he was the only tenant I had who always paid his rent on time.

"It's the law, and I have to follow the law so that everything is handled correctly according to the law and the wishes of the deceased."

3) Notify the next of kin, and allow them to remove only the body and the personal effects needed for the funeral, nothing more.

4) Release the deceased's personal property only to the county's public administrator or to a court-appointed administrator or to an executor of the estate who can produce either Letters Testamentary or Letters of Administration, documents giving that person possession of the personal property. If the deceased's estate is worth little or nothing, close relatives may qualify to take possession of the personal property without having to get involved in formal proceedings. In that case, make sure that they sign a receipt for whatever items they remove.

5) Submit a claim for unpaid rent (you are entitled to rent covering the full period that the deceased's personal property remains in the dwelling and makes it unavailable for re-renting) to the probate court clerk. If there is no probate of the deceased's estate, submit a written claim for rent to the heirs or next of kin and request payment, but do not hold any of the deceased's personal goods until they're ransomed with a rent payment. If the heirs or next of kin claim that there's no money in the estate to compensate you for the rent owed, make a deal with them, a deal which might include your receiving some of the deceased's belongings in exchange for what is owed. Put the deal in writing.

Illegal Discrimination During the Tenancy

You already know that you must not discriminate illegally when you're selecting tenants. You must treat every applicant alike. You must discard your personal prejudices and judge every applicant according to the same selection criteria. That's the law.

You also know that you must not discriminate illegally when you're evicting tenants, either.

You may not know that you must treat every tenant alike during the tenancy as well. You must not discriminate against your tenants because of their race, color, religion, sex, national origin, age, familial status, or handicap and whatever other categories apply in your area.

You probably never gave the matter much thought. You probably just assumed that you wouldn't encounter any discrimination problems once you selected your tenants according to the proper procedures and went about the business of landlording in a businesslike manner.

Well, you should give the matter some thought, for you could wind up being accused of discriminating illegally when you never meant to at all, and you simply didn't know that what you were doing really was discriminatory.

We're going to assume here that you do know better than to discriminate against your tenants overtly. You know that you can't call them derogatory names because they're handicapped or come from Timbuktu. You know that you can't extend special privileges to all of your black tenants gratuitously and require all of your brown tenants to jump through hoops to obtain the same privileges. You must treat all your tenants alike, no matter what. When your Cambodian tenants are late with their rent, you must follow the same collection procedures you'd follow for your Russian tenants. When your blind tenants are having a loud party, you must approach them with warnings to quiet down in the same way you'd approach your sighted square-dancing tenants. Those situations are pretty obvious.

What's not so obvious is the discrimination you may be practicing against people in two of HUD's protected categories, age and handicap.

Let's take "age" first. Simply put, you may not discriminate against your younger tenants any more than you may discriminate against your older tenants.

Nowhere is age discrimination more apparent during a tenancy than it is in the house rules we landlords draft to supplement our rental agreements. Frequently they restrict certain times, activities, and areas to adults only. Adults may be in the laundry room whereas children may not be. Adults may be in the swimming pool whereas children may not be. Adults may be in the parking area playing whereas children may not be.

Be very careful in drafting your rules. For example, do not draft a pool rule which sets aside one period of time for family swimming and another period for adult swimming. That would be discriminating against children and would make you vulnerable to a HUD complaint.

You might include a pool rule which limits the pool to lap swimming at certain times and opens it to all kinds of swimming at other times, but even then you should be careful not to allocate too much time to lap swimmers. Although lap swimmers of all ages would be allowed to use the pool during lap swimming time, somebody might argue that you're really trying to set the pool aside for adults during that period.

To test your rules for age discrimination, substitute a racial group for "child[ren]" every time the word appears and see how the rule sounds. If it sounds discriminating against the racial group, then it would be discriminating against children.

Handicapped tenants require special consideration as well, consideration you may never have thought about giving them before they became a protected category. Here the discrimination would not be apparent in rules. It would be apparent in the direct relationship between landlord and tenant. It would be apparent in what you say to your handicapped tenants and in what you do for them.

Don't offer your handicapped tenants anything they don't ask for. Approaching them and offering to do something special for them, like setting aside a particular parking place, might be considered patronizing and might subject you to a discrimination complaint. Let them come to you with their requests.

When they do come to you with a special request, listen to them carefully, and ask only those questions whose answers you need to know to accommodate them. Do not ask about the severity or nature of their handicap, for example. Just assume that they are handicapped enough to need the accommodation they are requesting or they wouldn't be requesting it in the first place.

Whatever they request, you must provide so long as the request satisfies these three requirements—

1) They must make an actual request;

LEASE   TERMINATION   ARRANGEMENTS

Date ___1/31/xxxx___

Dear ___DENISE BERGER___ :

We want you to be aware that the lease under which you occupy
the premises located at ___1220 DOGWOOD DRIVE, JIMTOWN___
will terminate on ___3/31/xxxx___ .

When the lease terminates...

[ ] you will need to vacate the premises.

[X] you may continue to occupy the premises...

    [ ] upon signing another fixed-term lease for _____ months

       at a new rent of $_____ per month.

    [X] on a month-to-month basis at a new rent of $_1,250_

       per month and...

        [X] all other provisions of your original lease will

           continue to apply to your tenancy.

        [ ] you will need to sign a new agreement, in this

           case a month-to-month agreement.

In order for us to begin making plans, we need to know what
you plan to do when your lease terminates. Please let us know by
completing the information below and returning it to us within
three days. Thank you.

Sincerely,

Robert Hardy

Manager/Owner

* * * * * * * * * * * * * * * * * * * *

[ ] I plan to vacate the premises when the lease terminates.

[ ] If given the choice, I plan to continue occupying the premises
when the lease terminates.

_____   _____
Date   Tenant

2) The accommodation requested must give the handicapped tenants an equal opportunity to use and enjoy their dwelling; and

3) The accommodation must be considered reasonable.

Generally, they will ask for reasonable accommodations, such as whether they can modify the entrance to accommodate a wheelchair; whether they can add an alert light to the doorbell; whether they can add grab bars to the bathtub surround; or whether they can have a reserved parking place close to the entrance of their dwelling.

These requests meet the requirements above and should be granted. If you have any doubts about a particular request or situation, stall the tenants, and call HUD's "Housing Discrimination Hotline" at 800.669.9777 to ask for some help in determining how to handle the tenants' request.

Just remember that handicapped people make excellent tenants, and you'd be wise to accommodate them even if there were no laws compelling you to do so. That they are willing to make modifications to their rental dwelling shows that they want to be long-term tenants. What could possibly be better? Accommodating them is definitely as much in your interest as it is in theirs.

Lease Termination

When their lease term is about to end, tenants are at a loss as to what their landlord expects of them. Are they supposed to tell their landlord whether they plan to stay where they are or move out? Are they supposed to wait for their landlord to say something to them about moving? Are they supposed to wait until the very last day of their lease and then move out without saying anything to their landlord in advance? If they do stay, will they have to sign a new lease on new terms or will they become month-to-month tenants on new terms? They need to know what you as their landlord expect of them, and you need to know what they expect of you.

The best thing you can do to clarify matters is provide them with a letter like the one shown here, a letter which tells them what you expect of them and also gives them a chance to reply.

Send them this letter at least sixty days before their lease term ends so that each of you will know what the other one plans to do and so that each of you will have plenty of time to prepare.

House Rules

The rental agreement you use, whether it's one page or fifty, tends to be something you and your tenants review only when they move in. After that, you file your copy away with your other important papers for that dwelling, and your tenants file their copy away with their important papers. When the tenants are ready to move out, they look for their copy and try to figure out what they need to do to get their deposits back, and you retrieve your copy to see what all it says about the move-out.

Rental agreements tend not to be words to live by on a day-to-day basis, even though they may contain words aplenty. House rules, on the other hand, *are* words to live by on a day-to-day basis. They are just as legitimate and just as authoritative as rental agreements, but they address practical tenancy concerns in a less formal and less intimidating way. They're useful.

Rental agreements are specific to a particular tenant and a particular dwelling. An agreement for tenants occupying one dwelling does not apply to tenants occupying another dwelling. Their agreements were filled out differently at different times and may even use completely different forms.

On the other hand, house rules are uniform and egalitarian. They are all the same for a single property, and they apply equally to everyone who lives there.

Whereas you are not absolutely required to have house rules for your rental property, you may find that having them helps your landlord-tenant relationship be more consistent. Your tenants know what's expected of them on a day-to-day basis because they have everything circumscribed in writing, and they know that it applies to everybody. They can judge you on your enforcement of the rules, and you can judge them on their compliance with the rules.

I recommend that you create house rules for every one of your rental properties and that you examine them periodically and change them as needed.

When you set about creating house rules for a property, you'll find that there's no particular form or verbiage sufficient for the job. You have to create them yourself in order to cover the unique characteristics of a property and what it is you consider important for your tenants to follow there.

Sure, creating house rules is another tiresome task, but it's hardly a daunting task. They're not all that hard to create so long as you keep a few things in mind.

Keeping in mind what you already know about illegal discrimination, make certain that your house rules do not discriminate against anybody in the protected classes, especially children.

Make certain that your house rules are understandable. Use words that any sixth-grader would understand, and when you finish writing your rules, reread them yourself four or five times over during the space of a week to see whether they make good sense to you. Then ask your tenants whether any of them would like to read your "draft" of the new house rules and comment on them. Some tenants may be eager to read and comment, but even if nobody responds, at least you will have asked for their input, and they can't accuse you of acting like a tyrant. What's more, some of them may pass along good ideas you hadn't thought of yourself, ideas you'd want to incorporate in the final version.

Make certain that your house rules are both reasonable and enforceable. "Reasonable" means that your quiet hours, for example, ought to be from 10 p.m. to 8 a.m. rather than from 6 p.m. to 10 a.m. "Enforceable" means that you can and will do something when tenants call you to tattle on their neighbors for breaking the rules.

Make certain that your rules are dated on every page so that the most recent rules won't be mistaken for earlier ones. That's important. Tenants sometimes claim that they don't have to do such-and-such because it's not in the rules. It may not have been in the old rules which were in effect when they moved in, the ones they were referring to, whereas it is most definitely in the new rules they neglected to read and save. Dating the rules helps to differentiate the versions, and it also helps to remind you how old they are, so you will think about reviewing and revising them periodically.

Don't worry about whether your house rules repeat what appears in your rental agreement. They may be repetitious in places. So what! Certain things are important enough in landlord-tenant relations that they should be repeated.

Draft a letter explaining why you have created new house rules and asking for everyone's cooperation in following them. It needn't be a long letter. It might say simply that you felt new rules were needed and that you considered each one of them carefully while you were writing them. Say that you would appreciate feedback, especially if anybody feels strongly about certain ones. Distribute this letter along with the new rules themselves.

As for tenants' signatures, they're somewhat important as an acknowledgment that tenants have received the rules, but because many tenants balk at signing anything you give them to sign after they move in, don't bother trying to secure signatures. Getting signatures from existing tenants is just too much trouble. I don't even put a blank for the tenant's signature anywhere on the rules. I merely leave blank space somewhere near the bottom where new tenants may sign the rules when they get their copies.

Here are some subjects you may want to address in your rules. They're arranged here alphabetically—

- *Alterations*—alterations requiring landlord's permission; alterations not requiring permission
- *Appliances*—responsibility for maintaining landlord-owned appliances; tenant-owned major appliances allowed; care in moving tenant-owned major appliances
- *Deposits*—requirements for return of deposits; handling of deposits when one tenant who has contributed to the deposits moves out and everybody else remains
- *Garbage*—acceptable items; non-acceptable items; recycling possibilities; suitable trash containers; preparation for collection; collection schedule
- *Guests*—length of stay allowed; number allowed; use of common facilities
- *Insurance*—extent of coverage for tenant-caused calamities and tenants' possessions
- *Landscaping and gardening care*—front yard; back yard; changes in plantings; watering; trimming; mowing
- *Laundry room*—hours of operation; accessibility if kept locked; use of the room by non-residents and guests; handling of non-attended laundry; responsibility for lost laundry
- *Locks and lockouts*—changing locks; lockout charges
- *Parking*—resident parking areas; guest parking areas; towing of wrongly parked vehicles
- *Patios and decks*—items acceptable for storage on patios and decks

- *Pest control*—scheduled service; as-needed service; responsibility for particular kinds of infestations, such as ants, cockroaches, fleas, mice, and spiders
- *Pets*—pets allowed; pet approval procedure; number of pets; separate pet agreement; pet care; pet replacement
- *Playground*—hours; noise; guest usage; play restrictions
- *Quiet hours*—hours when all should be especially quiet in consideration of others
- *Rent*—collection procedure; form of payment; return check charges and consequences; receipt policy; late payment consequences; partial payment
- *Repairs*—making repair and maintenance requests; charges for tenants' failure to report promptly a malfunction or breakage requiring repair; entering the tenants' dwelling for repairs
- *Responsible parties*—determination of tenant responsible for dwelling; procedure when that person leaves
- *Sewer stoppages*—reporting; handling; conditions for determining the landlord's responsibility and conditions for determining the tenants' responsibility
- *Storage space*—availability; location; cost
- *Swimming pool*—hours; times set aside for lap swimming; attire; minimum and maximum number of swimmers allowed; guest usage; poolside activities; swim toys; swimming proficiency requirements
- *Utilities*—changing utilities to tenants' names; responsibility for payment
- *Vehicles and parking*—types and number of vehicles allowed; towing of inoperable and unlicensed vehicles; responsibility for oil-leak damage to paving; repairs permitted on the premises; changing of oil; disposal of used crankcase oil; time limitations for repairs; storage of boats and recreational vehicles; vehicle washing
- *Waterbeds*—acceptance according to applicable laws; acceptance according to property's characteristics; separate waterbed agreement
- *Window breakage*—reporting; handling; conditions for determining the landlord's responsibility and conditions for determining the tenants' responsibility

Once you create and implement your first set of rules, you'll find after a while that you want to change something. Go ahead. Change the rules. Changing them is a simpler matter than changing rental agreements because you don't have to individualize every copy as you do with rental agreements. When you want to change your rules, you simply crank out an original and copy it for everybody. Everybody gets a copy of the same original.

Please note that house rules go into effect sometime after you distribute them. They do not go into effect the very day you distribute them. Generally the lag time is the same as it is for other notices which announce changes in terms of tenancy, that is, unless there's another notice period specifically mentioned in the rental agreement. It would be a week for those tenants who pay their rent weekly, two weeks for those tenants who pay their rent bi-weekly, and a month for those tenants who pay their rent monthly. The "kitchen-sink" agreement introduced in chapter 5 states that new rules take effect upon at least two weeks' notice.

Regardless of what their agreement says or how frequently they pay rent, make new house rules effective on the same date for everybody living in a complex. Set the effective date at the conclusion of as generous a lag time as anybody gets, and announce the date in an accompanying letter.

Your Score

You already know that there are four ways to make money in this business, but you won't know whether you're actually making any money at any of them unless you sharpen your pencil, uncover your calculator, grab your abacus, or power up your computer and have a session with the numbers now and then.

Naturally, you need only keep up with your regular bookkeeping to know whether you're getting any cash flow or equity buildup, and you need only do your income taxes every year to know whether you're getting any tax shelter, but you won't know whether you're getting any appreciation on your properties and you won't know whether you're getting any closer to becoming independently wealthy unless you complete a financial statement. It alone can tell you whether you've really "made it." It's your score.

If you haven't been keeping track of your financial health with a financial statement, shame on you. It's one of the more agreeable undertakings in this entire business. Some landlords say it's the best part by far.

You're in good company if you don't have a clue about the state of your financial health. While being escorted around the newly opened Disneyland by Walt Disney, one foreign potentate, suitably impressed, remarked that Disney must be a very wealthy man, whereupon Disney replied, "I guess I am. They tell me I owe ten million dollars." He honestly had no idea what he was worth! He never realized he could walk into an automobile showroom and drive out in a snazzy little sportscar until he did just that on a whim sometime later. Fortunately for him, Walt Disney had a brother who kept track of the finances, and he had a banker, A.P. Giannini himself (founder of Bank of America), who kept an eye on the company's fortunes.

Lacking a devoted brother and an astute banker to look after your financial health, you're left to do the job yourself. There's nothing wrong with that. It's not something you ought to have somebody else do for you anyway. Nobody else is going to find the special pleasure in preparing your financial statement that you are. It's more fun than watching the Olympics or the Super Bowl. It's more like participating in them and winning.

What you may not realize is that you have probably been doing financial statements for years without even thinking much about them, certainly without enjoying them. That's right! Every time you've applied for a loan and filled out a loan application, you've actually completed a financial statement. That's mostly what loan applications are, you see. They're a picture of your financial health. They tell the lender how much you're worth and whether you have enough income to repay the loan. You haven't been enjoy-

ing them because you were forced into doing them. Isn't that right? They were "assignments," required "homework." Ugh!

Go on. Go to your files and get the last loan application form you filled out. See. You had to list your assets and your liabilities, your income and your expenses, and somewhere on that form you had to calculate what your net worth was at the time. That's all a financial statement is. It's two basic parts—a *balance sheet*, which is comprised of your assets and liabilities, and an *income and expense statement*, which is comprised of your annual income and your annual expenses. Subtract your liabilities from your assets and you can tell whether you're independently wealthy. Subtract your annual expenses from your annual income and you can tell whether you're going to be independently wealthy for very long.

If you don't particularly care what you're worth or you just don't want to know, then continue doing what you've been doing all along. Complete your latest "financial statement" only when you're applying for a loan to buy some more rental property. Don't think much about it, and above all, don't enjoy doing it. In-between-times, go about your business oblivious of your financial health. Press your nose to the window of that Cadillac, BMW, or Lexus showroom and keep on dreaming of the day when you can afford to walk in there and buy the biggest, fanciest model with cash.

Oh, come on! Let a little joy into your life while you can still enjoy it! There's more to life as a landlord than terrible tenants and temperamental toilets. There's no delight in all of that. Is there? You don't really want to be oblivious to your financial health and spend your time dreaming about a rosy future while you're out there taking flak from tenants and fixing their plugged toilets. Do you?

That sort of plodding, mindless approach to one's lot in life may work for those people who juggle their income and expenses one week at a time and buy lottery tickets with their every spare dollar, but that's not a good approach for anyone who's regularly accumulating assets. That's not a good approach for you. It's chancy and unbusinesslike, and it's terribly shortsighted. You cannot make informed business decisions unless you are informed about your own affairs, and your financial statement is a large part of what makes you informed.

Convinced? Good, good, good! Go to the head of the class, and we'll start calculating what your assets are.

As far as your personal financial statement is concerned, your assets are your rental properties, your house, vehicles, airplanes, boats, stocks, bonds, mutual funds, cash accounts, precious metals, livestock, raw land, partnerships, business interests, personal goods, vested pensions, notes receivable, trusts, and the cash surrender value of your life insurance. They all have a value. They're all worth something if they have to be liquidated. Perhaps they're worth what you have in them, perhaps less, perhaps a lot more.

You may think you have other assets, too, such as straight teeth, a good golf swing, a winning personality, a college degree, and a trim figure, but they're figurative assets as opposed to hard, literal assets. Like family photo albums and bronzed baby shoes, they have personal value but no market value. They can't be converted into ready cash. No one would pay you anything for them. Don't list them on your financial statement.

Establishing the value of all your assets which do have a market value does take some doing, especially since you own real estate. Whenever possible, professional appraisers base their income property appraisals on several approaches, most commonly, *replacement cost* (how much the property improvements would cost to build today, plus a certain market value for the land), *income* (how much the property produces in income times an accepted multiplier which would depend upon property type and whether the income were net or gross), and *comparable sales* (how much other similar properties have sold for recently). Not one of these three can yield an exact figure. Each is merely an approximation, and the final appraisal figure is merely a composite of these approxima-tions.

When you're just trying to figure out approximately what your real estate is worth so you can include it among your assets, you needn't go to all the trouble that professional appraisers do. You're going to be reasonably accurate most of the time with just a cursory appraisal using any one of the approaches they use. You won't be right on the money, but then, neither would they. It'll be close enough.

When you're appraising your own property for your financial statement, try to detach yourself from it if you can. Think of yourself as a potential buyer of the property, not as the owner. Look the numbers over, perform some calculations, check some websites, close your eyes, and ask yourself what you'd pay for the property realistically yourself if it belonged to somebody else. Be honest. Cheating doesn't pay. Base your appraisal on something you can justify.

If it's multiple-family rental property you're appraising, some sort of income formula like a gross rent multiplier will do, whatever applies to your type of rental property. Don't go overboard and value it at ten or twelve times the annual gross income when it ought to be seven. That will make a substantial difference in the property's value and will distort your balance sheet and resultant net worth. Find out what the commonly used yardstick is for your type of multiple-family rental property and use it.

If it's a single-family rental property or the house you occupy, try eppraisal.com and zillow.com first. They offer free, instant valuations based on public records. If you don't like their numbers, check county records for comparable sales figures. Remember that sales figures are different from listing figures. Sellers may list their properties at whatever price they want to list them for. They don't sell their properties at whatever price they want to sell them for. Properties sell for whatever a buyer is willing to pay and a seller is willing to take. You want sales figures to help you establish the fair market value of your property.

The trouble is that even if you were able to peg the price of your property correctly and a buyer were to give you that price, you wouldn't net that amount in bankable money. You'd net something less. Commissions, prepayment penalties, transaction fees, transfer taxes, legal fees, and other costs would reduce the net proceeds you'd realize from the sale. Be that as it may, don't discount your holdings to reflect these costs. A lender might do that upon looking at your figures, and you don't want it deducted twice. You're not looking for a liquidated cash value for your holdings. You're not holding a fire sale. All you want is a market value.

You might want to do a little research to learn the market value of your other assets, but that'll be easy compared to putting a value on your multiple-family rental properties. Just don't forget anything, not even that timeshare in Orlando you bought during a weak moment.

Whereas your assets may take a little time to calculate, your liabilities won't, so long as there's a semblance of order in your recordkeeping system. The mortgages, loans, and credit card balances you owe are all liabilities, and they have definite dollar figures attached to them. They're solid figures, but you must remember that they change every day because the interest on your liabilities is accruing daily, and the loan balances are changing as well. Also remember that there may be some liabilities you tend to overlook, such as taxes you owe but haven't paid yet, a mechanics lien on your property, an old student loan, or an interest-free loan from a trusting family member. They're liabilities, too. They reduce your assets. Estimate what they are and include them among your liabilities.

Calculating your net worth is the easiest part of all, once you know what your assets and liabilities are. Simply subtract your liabilities from your assets and presto, you have the all-important telltale figure. That's it. That's your momentous net worth figure. That's your score. Now you know what everybody else would like to know about you—how much you're worth in dollars and cents.

If it's seven figures or more, then you're a millionaire. Congratulations! You've arrived at an important milestone in your life! You've learned a lot from playing Monopoly all those years, haven't you? Now you ought to read *The Millionaire Next Door* to see how you measure up to the other millionaires who live in your neighborhood. Their life-styles may surprise you.

If your net worth is four, five, or even six figures, you're still a lowly thousandaire. Keep working. If it's in three figures and you've been landlording for more than a year, you'd better think about raising your rents and reading Nickerson's classic book on making money with rental properties, *How I Turned $1,000 into Five Million in Real Estate in My Spare Time*. You need all the help you can get!

Once you've calculated your net worth, you're nearly finished with your financial statement, but you still need to indicate how much you're taking in and how much you're shelling out. That's the income-and-expense portion of your financial statement. Its end result will show whether the cash flow in your life is coming or going, whether it's positive or negative.

You might have a substantial net worth and think that you've done pretty well for yourself until you find out that you actually have more money going out every month than you have coming in. Negative-cash-flow properties can put you in that position, you know. They're a slippery business, much like trying to twirl around an ice skating rink on roller skates. One or two such properties may not affect you much if you have substantial earned income that you want to protect from taxes and if you feel that the properties have good upside potential, but more than that and you could begin to have problems. Watch those properties. They can be more voracious than a Little League baseball team at a pizza parlor after an exhausting game. They can eat their owners out of houses and homes.

Well, how do your income and expenses look? Are you going to be holding onto your net worth? Let's hope so.

At least you now have a clue as to how you're doing. You have a score to keep in mind when you're cleaning toilets and painting vacant apartments at 3 a.m., and you can make your plans for the future accordingly.

Incorporation

Some people believe that owning a corporation catapults them into the major leagues. Owners of corporations draw big salaries, fly in private jets or at the very least in first class, smoke the best cigars, maintain several palatial residences, ride everywhere in chauffeured limos, keep their yacht in the Bahamas, watch every home game of their favorite sports team from their own luxury suite, follow their favorite sports team to all of its away games, mingle with the rich and famous at charity events, and sleep soundly at night because they cannot be sued for something relating to the corporation's business. Dream on, big shot!

Owning a big corporation has its perks and advantages, some of which appear in the paragraph above. Owning a little corporation has no perks and no advantages which appear in the paragraph above.

The biggest carrot dangled in front of anybody who has a few rental properties and a few hundred thousand dollars in assets and is thinking about incorporating is asset protection. Advocates of incorporating say that you should incorporate so that the liabilities you incur as a corporation will not affect your personal wealth. That argument appears sound until you become involved in a Robinhood lawsuit and the attorney suing your closely held corporation convinces the court that the corporation is nothing but a sham, designed strictly to protect you from liability. The attorney pierces your so-called corporate veil, and you and your personal assets are laid bare for the vultures to devour.

Incorporating may succeed in protecting you from liability and then again it may not. Why bother incorporating at all? Wouldn't you be better off keeping your life simple than you would be in complicating it by forming a corporation just to protect your assets?

We're talking major complications here. A corporation compounds your legal work (you must abide by the latest corporate laws) and your paperwork (you must have officers, hold meetings, and keep minutes) and your bookkeeping (you must keep a separate set of books for the corporation) and your tax preparation (you must submit a state tax return and a federal tax return for the corporation), and it prevents you from representing yourself in court even for the simplest eviction. You must hire an attorney.

The "keep it simple, stupid" admonition applies here. A corporation simply ain't simple.

If you're worried about your assets, buy enough insurance to protect them from predators. That's what umbrella insurance policies are for.

If you're still unconvinced, still romanced by the notion of incorporating, seek out some people whose assets are similar to yours in extent and substance and who have incorporated themselves and ask them about the advantages of incorporating versus the disadvantages. Ask them whether they would choose to incorporate again if they could. They're more inclined to give you straight answers than someone who stands to profit from your decision to incorporate.

Incorporating is much like declaring bankruptcy for the protection bankruptcy provides. There's a time and a circumstance for bankruptcy, and as many tenants have discovered after declaring bankruptcy during an eviction, the extra month or two they gained during their eviction wasn't enough of a benefit to warrant declaring bankruptcy. Naturally, they didn't know that at the time. They suffered later when they needed credit to buy a car or a house and couldn't get it or had to pay more in interest and fees than otherwise.

There's a time and a circumstance for incorporating, too. Make absolutely sure that the time and circumstances are right for you to be taking this step. Make absolutely sure that the rewards are greater than the consequences, for incorporating is a very big step into a very different world, and once you take that step, you cannot easily retreat.

Vacation Time

Landlording can be all-consuming work, sucking up as much of your time as you are willing to give it. There's always something you can do to make your tenants happier or your properties better, and you know that there's nobody who can do all of that better than you can.

Don't succumb to the temptation to manage and maintain your properties every hour of every day of every year yourself. Succumb to the temptation to get away from them now and then. Take a vacation.

There are plenty of excuses you might offer for staying on the job and not taking a vacation, but there are also plenty of reasons why you should get away. Not only might you discover some landlording "pearls" when you aren't tending to business and distracted by minutiae, you will definitely find yourself refreshed when you return. You will approach your work with a spring in your step, a smile on your face, a clarity in your mind, and maybe a new tool in your hand.

Of course, you will need to arrange for somebody to look after your properties while you're away. That's easy. Find another landlord who's willing, able, and trustworthy, and arrange for that person to look after your properties during your much deserved vacations in exchange for your doing the same during that landlord's vacations.

Take some vacation time. It will make you a better landlord.

Retirement

Eventually you may conclude that you no longer want to own residential rental properties, and you're going to be looking for ways to reduce or eliminate your personal involvement.

You want to retire and kick back, do some serious traveling, write a chronicle about the black sheep in your family, take up the piano, polish your Russian, follow in the footsteps of Julia Child and study at a French cooking school, circumnavigate the globe in a comfortable sloop, attend film festivals around the world, concentrate on your golf game, build a kitplane and learn to fly it, earn an advanced degree, participate in a year-long archeological dig in Turkey, become a *Ring* nut and see every complete production on earth every year, clean Mt. Everest of climbers' debris, volunteer to teach reading to dyslexics at a neighborhood school, join a Habitat for Humanity crew, chase rainbows, or catch falling stars. In short, after spending years accumulating your fortune, you have decided you want to start enjoying life more. You want to enjoy the fruits of your labors at long last.

You'd like to sell your holdings, but there's one thing stopping you, one major thing. You don't want to pay the capital gains taxes on a good portion of your personal wealth.

Let's say that you own $2 million worth of rental properties free and clear, and your basis in them is $200,000. If you sell, you will owe federal and state income taxes on a gain of $1.8 million. Were the combined (state and federal) tax rate on capital gains 35%, you would be writing checks to the IRS and to your state income tax collector totaling $630,000. With a few strokes of your pen, your $2 million worth of rental properties would drop precipitously to $1,370,000 in cash, and you and your heirs would lose the income-generating potential of that $630,000 forever.

You don't have to lose the income-generating potential of that money forever. You can reduce or eliminate your personal involvement in your rental properties in a number of ways without incurring a huge tax bill.

One way is to keep the properties you have and hire somebody else to manage them for you. Whether you hire a trusted relative, a faithful friend, or a professional management company, you know that they will not manage your properties as efficiently as you have. The return on investment will decline, but it won't decline as much as it would if you sold the properties, gave the government its tax money, and put what's left into safe investments.

Another way is to set up a charitable remainder trust. You put your free-and-clear properties (they must be free-and-clear) into the trust, naming one or more of your favorite charities as the beneficiaries of the trust when you die. After putting the properties into the trust, you sell them and put the cash, all of it, into any income-generating vehicle you select. You maintain control of the trust and collect its income as long as you live (whatever money you withdraw from the trust is taxable to you personally), and the charities take over the trust when you die. To protect your heirs' inheritance, you may use a portion of your income from the trust to buy as much term life insurance as you want them to receive when you die.

Still another way, my very favorite way, to get out from under the burdens of owning residential rental properties which claim too much of my time is the tax-free exchange. Some people call it a tax-deferred exchange. Call it what you want, a tax-free or a tax-deferred exchange, it's the same thing. You pay no tax at all when you consummate an IRS Section 1031 exchange and put the entire proceeds from the property you sell into a property you purchase. In other words, when you take no money out of the exchange (money taken out of an exchange is called "boot"), it's entirely tax free. You may choose to sell outright later and pay taxes then if you wish, but that's your choice. You'll find a brief explanation of the 1031 exchange in the "Doing Taxes" chapter.

In order to achieve your retirement objective in an exchange, you sell your management-intensive property and use the proceeds to buy another property which requires less management. You look for properties which require less management and have good cap (capitalization) rates.

A property's "cap rate" is its net operating income (NOI) divided by its sales price, loan costs excluded. Cap rates are expressed in percentages with higher figures indicating a higher return.

Calculate the cap rate for your own properties first, so you know how they compare with other properties, and when you do, make sure you include something for off-site management when making your calculations. You may not have been paying anything for off-site management, but it's a standard cost included in cap rate calculations.

You could trade out of an apartment house with a cap rate of seven and trade into a triple-net-leased (triple-net, or NNN, leases require the tenant to pay for property taxes, insurance, maintenance, and utilities) property with a cap rate of seven leased to a Fortune 500 company, and you'd be moving closer to Easy Street. You'd also be preserving your capital, and you'd be benefitting from whatever escalation clauses there are in the lease.

Where do you find triple-net-leased properties and other minimal-management commercial properties for sale? Try a local brokerage firm which specializes in commercial properties, and also look through the listings on the Loopnet (loopnet.com) website.

Loopnet enables you to search for properties by area, type, and price. If you want to find all of Loopnet's listings of net-leased office buildings in your state selling for $2m-$5m, enter those parameters, and see what results. To enlarge the list, enlarge your parameters.

You'll notice that Loopnet includes cap rates in its listings. Be wary about those figures. Because you don't know whether they're based upon current or proforma data, you should consider them little more than starting points for your property comparisons.

Yes, you can retire from landlording. When you're ready, you should, but you should plan your retirement carefully in order to preserve the capital you have worked so hard to accumulate. Look at the alternatives to selling out and paying the capital gains taxes.

Landlording's Ten Commandments

No, these commandments were not handed down by God to Moses. They were handed down by many wise and successful landlords who had to make them up as they went along to suit the realities of life as a landlord.

Heed them, and you, too, will be successful. Ignore them, and you will perish many times over.

1) Thou shalt investigate and qualify every applicant thoroughly, being mindful of discrimination laws and intent upon finding people who will make good neighbors and good tenants.
2) Thou shalt permit no tenants to move in until they have paid every bit of their move-in monies in greenbacks, gold pieces, silver bars, money orders, or verified cashier's checks.
3) Thou shalt be friendly with all tenants but friends with none.
4) Thou shalt listen to thy tenants, that is, "l-i-s-t-e-n," as in open thine ears and close thy mouth.
5) Thou shalt not kill thy tenants in a fit of anger or at any other time, nor shalt thou vent thine anger or frustrations around thy tenants, no matter how angry or frustrated they make thee.
6) Thou shalt stay current with the local market for rents and adjust thine own rents accordingly.
7) Thou shalt consider the payment of rent a mandatory ritual and brook no excuses for ignoring it, hounding those who try to ignore it until they leave in ignominy and with ruined credit.
8) Thou shalt keep thy property in good repair as if thou wert living there thyself.
9) Thou shalt make thy tenants no promise thou canst not keep.
10) Thou shalt commit consequential landlording matters to writing rather than committing them to memory.

Some Last Words

Surely the primary purpose of landlording is to become independently wealthy, and even though many things and many people may conspire to frustrate you from reaching that goal, do not despair. Walk through landlording's "valley of the shadow of death," its perilous minefields, heeding landlording's ten commandments as best you can, and you won't have to fear becoming independently poor.

Words in Edgewise

Yours is a thankless job, dear landlord and landlady. Just remember that landlording is a business. People are not going to commend you for your efforts, but neither are they going to stop depending on you. People who are too timid, too transient, too insolvent, too young, too feeble, too smart, too stupid, or otherwise too indisposed to own their own housing are all depending on you to provide them with housing. Do just that, and do it as best you can.

There will be times when you will feel distraught over your landlording troubles and trials, times when you will have tried your best and yet you find yourself on the short end. Don't show your anger. Keep a punching bag at home for that. But if you cannot get along with a tenant or a tenant with you, get the tenant out. You know how to do it. Run your business yourself. Don't let your tenants run it for you.

Forms

The forms in this section have been introduced in the text, all, that is, except for the bulk of the rent reminders (only two of the twelve reminders appear in the text). Blank forms are included here so you may reproduce them on any copier according to your needs.*

If you do plan to copy them, keep them clean and free of marks. These are your originals, remember. Any marks you make on them will show up on your copies.

To assist you in finding the blank forms you seek, we put small page numbers in the upper corners. When you go to copy these forms, either white-out the page numbers, cut them off, or fold over the corners of the pages so the numbers will not appear your copies.

The Forms

(Forms appear here alphabetically; bracketed numbers refer to samples in text.)

NOTA BENE

The author assumes no responsibility for the legality or currency of these forms. Before using them, check with your local housing authorities, your local rental housing association, and/or an attorney knowledgeable about real estate law to determine whether they are appropriate for your use.

The author hereby grants permission to the purchaser of this book to copy any of these forms for personal use. Their reproduction for sale or distribution shall constitute an infringement of copyright.

AGREEMENT FOR TENANT ALTERATIONS

Agreement between _____, Tenants, who occupy a dwelling located at _____ and _____, Owners, who are the owners of this dwelling.

Owners hereby give permission for Tenants to make the following alterations to their dwelling (identify location, describe alteration, and indicate whether the alteration is to be removed or left behind when tenants vacate; also indicate date when final alteration was inspected and approved):

1) Location _____ Alteration _____
[ ] To be removed when Tenants vacate -- [ ] To be left when Tenants vacate
Alteration inspected and approved by Owner [date, initials] _____

2) Location _____ Alteration _____
[ ] To be removed when Tenants vacate -- [ ] To be left when Tenants vacate
Alteration inspected and approved by Owner [date, initials] _____

3) Location _____ Alteration _____
[ ] To be removed when Tenants vacate -- [ ] To be left when Tenants vacate
Alteration inspected and approved by Owner [date, initials] _____

Tenants acknowledge that they are responsible for payment of all costs incurred for alterations, including materials, labor, and permits.

Tenants agree to hire workers, if any, who are licensed contractors and have appropriate insurance, including workers compensation.

If an alteration is removed when Tenants vacate, they acknowledge that they are responsible for restoring the altered area to its original condition.

Tenants agree to put up a deposit of $_____ solely to insure that they will restore their dwelling to its original condition when they vacate.

If an alteration is to be left when Tenants vacate, they agree that it will become the Owners' property and that they will not be reimbursed for it.

_____   _____
Date   Tenant(s)

_____   _____
Date   Owner

Agreement to Hold Dwelling Off the Market

RECEIVED FROM _____, Approved Applicant,

the sum of _____ $_____.

$_____ of this sum is <u>nonrefundable</u>. It shall be used for the purpose of holding off the market the rental dwelling commonly known as

_____

for the period from _____ through _____ only.

$_____ of this sum is <u>refundable</u> if approved applicant does not move in. If applicant moves in, it shall be applied to move-in monies.

The applicant whose name appears above has been approved to rent the dwelling identified above but for one reason or another cannot take possession now.

The applicant has read and approved the rental agreement but has not paid all of the sums required to move in. The applicant has no right to receive keys or take possession of the dwelling until all of the sums required to take possession have been paid in full.

The owner/manager retains possession of the dwelling under this agreement and is obligated to safeguard it and maintain its condition so that it does not deteriorate during the term of this agreement. If it is materially damaged, applicant shall receive a refund of all monies paid.

At least twenty-four hours prior to the termination of this agreement, the applicant must notify the owner/manager of his/her intentions to take possession or not take possession of the dwelling. Notice must be made in writing and delivered to the owner/manager during normal business hours (9am-5pm) at the owner/manager's address shown below.

Should the applicant fail to notify the owner/manager of his/her intentions to take possession as outlined above, owner/manager will put the dwelling back on the market upon the termination of this agreement.

Should the applicant take possession of the dwelling prior to the termination of this agreement, the applicant will be credited as having paid rent through the termination date of this agreement, and this agreement will then be superseded by the rental agreement.

Should the applicant not take possession of the dwelling prior to or upon the expiration of this agreement, the owner/manager will keep the entire nonrefundable sum paid as consideration for having held the rental dwelling off the market for the time period specified above and will refund the applicant's refundable sum within forty-eight hours.

_____   _____
Date/Time   Approved Applicant--Name / Signature

                             _____
                             Address / Phone

_____   _____
Date/Time   Owner/Manager--Name / Signature

                             _____
                             Address / Phone

Agreement to Vacate   Dated_____

    Agreement between _____, Tenants, who occupy a dwelling located at _____ and _____, Owners, who are the owners of this dwelling.

    Tenants acknowledge that no one other than those listed above currently occupies the dwelling.

    Tenants occupy this dwelling under a rental agreement dated _____. This agreement is ( ) month to month; ( ) a lease expiring _____.

    The current rent for this dwelling is $_____. The current late fee is $_____.

    As of this date, tenants have paid rent through the following date: _____. They owe owners a total of $_____, itemized as follows: _____.

    Tenants agree that they have no excuses or defenses for failing to pay what they owe.

    Tenants agree to vacate the dwelling on or before _____ at _____ pm/am.

    If tenants DO vacate as agreed above, owners agree to the following:

(1) to apply the tenants' security/cleaning deposit to the amount owed and to waive the balance of any amount owed; any excess remaining from the security/cleaning deposit after the full amount owed has been paid in full shall be returned to the tenants after they have moved out completely, provided that they leave the dwelling reasonably clean and undamaged;

(2) to release tenants of any further obligation to pay rent under the lease (if any);

(3) to make no report to any credit reporting agency regarding tenants' credit;

(4) to make no report to any eviction reporting agency regarding tenants' tenancy.

    If tenants DO NOT vacate as agreed above, this agreement shall be null and void, and owners may begin eviction proceedings immediately.

    Tenants agree to keep this agreement confidential between the parties involved. If tenants fail to keep this agreement confidential, this agreement shall be null and void.

Owner_____ Tenant_____

By_____ Tenant_____

APPLICANT QUALIFIER

Name_____ Date/Time_____

Dwelling_____

Disqualifiers
Any ONE of the following conditions automatically disqualifies the applicant.

1) Applicant has failed to provide essential information, that is, information about current or previous tenancies, employment, identification (drivers license or Social Security Number), or finances.
2) Applicant has falsified essential information.
3) Applicant was evicted through court action within the previous 24 months.
4) Applicant has gross income less than three times the prospective rent.
5) Applicant cannot pay all move-in monies prior to move-in.
6) Applicant is not prepared to move in when unit is available or not prepared to pay rent as of that date.
7) Applicant has no verifiable source of income.
8) Applicant has been convicted of a felony which is drug-related, violent, or sexual in nature.
9) Applicant and fellow residents exceed the maximum number of people legally permitted to occupy the dwelling.
10) Applicant refuses to sign notice and release agreement regarding mold and radon.
11) Applicant's current dwelling fails scrutiny during inspection visit.
12) CONDITIONAL: Applicant smokes (if dwelling is non-smoking).
13) CONDITIONAL: Applicant has a dog or cat (if pets are forbidden).
14) CONDITIONAL: Applicant has a waterbed (if waterbeds are forbidden).
15) CONDITIONAL: Applicant has too many vehicles (if parking is limited).

Qualifiers
Give ZERO points if no choice applies in a category.
Numbers in parentheses are points suggested for that choice.

_____ ADEQUACY OF INCOME
Applicant has gross income 21-100% higher than three times the monthly rent. (20)
Applicant and others in the household have gross income 21-100% higher than three times the monthly rent. (15)
Applicant has gross income 10-20% higher than three times the monthly rent. (15)
Applicant and others in the household have gross income 10-20% higher than three times the monthly rent. (10)

_____ STABILITY OF INCOME
Applicant has had same sources of income for two years or more. (20)
Applicant has had same sources of income for one to two years. (15)
Applicant has had same sources of income for less than one year. (10)

_____ CREDIT STANDING
Applicant has a FICO score of 690 or greater. (20)
Applicant has a FICO score of 620 to 689. (15)
Applicant has a FICO score of 560 to 619. (10)
Applicant has a FICO score below 560. (5)
Applicant has no credit information available. (0)

_____ BANKRUPTCY (Previous 48 Months)
Applicant has never declared bankruptcy. (0)
Applicant has declared bankruptcy due primarily to divorce or medical expenses. (-5)
Applicant has declared bankruptcy for reasons other than divorce or medical expenses. (-15)

Applicant Qualifier (Page 2)

_____ RENT PAYMENT HISTORY (Previous 24 Months)
Applicant has never been late in paying rent. (10)
Applicant has never been more than five days late in paying rent. (0)
Applicant has received one or more notices to pay rent or quit and has paid the rent
   within the time limit and satisfied the late payment consequences. (-10)
Applicant habitually pays late within ten days after the due date. (-10)

_____ EVICTION HISTORY (Previous 24 Months)
Applicant has never been evicted or been given a "notice to comply" for any reason.
   (15)
Applicant received a "notice to comply" for a reason other than nonpayment and
   complied fully. (-5)
Applicant received a notice to pay rent or quit, vacated voluntarily in the time
   allowed, and paid landlord the entire amount owed. (-5)
Applicant received a notice to pay rent or quit, vacated voluntarily in the time
   allowed, but did not pay landlord the amount owed. (-15)

_____ RENTAL HISTORY
Applicant has lived in the same dwelling for the past 24 months. (15)
Applicant has lived in two different dwellings in the past 24 months. (10)
Applicant has lived in more than two different dwellings in the past 24 months. (5)
Applicant lives with roommates and is a responsible party on the rental agreement.
   (5)
Applicant lives with roommates and is not a responsible party on the rental
   agreement. (0)
Applicant has never lived away from home before. (0)

_____ LANDLORD RECOMMENDATIONS
Previous landlord would rent to the applicant again. (20)
Previous landlord is unavailable. Current landlord would rent to the applicant
   again. (5)
Neither previous nor current landlord is available to give a recommendation. (0)
Applicant has no previous tenancy. (0)
Previous landlord would not rent to the applicant again. (-15)
Previous landlord is unavailable. Current landlord would not rent to the applicant
   again. (-20)

_____ RENT COMPARISON
Current rent is equal to, or greater than, prospective rent (10).
Current rent is 10% below prospective rent (5).
Current rent is 11-20% below prospective rent (0).
Current rent is more than 20% below prospective rent (-10).

_____ CO-SIGNER (Make-Up Points)
Applicant agrees to secure a co-signer who has a FICO score of 700 or greater and
   owns local real estate. (10)

_____ ADDITIONAL DEPOSIT (Make-Up Points)
Applicant agrees to put up an additional deposit equal to one-half of the
   prospective rent. (10)

Total Points

_____ TOTAL POINTS (90 or more is acceptable; 80 to 89 is marginal; below 80 is
   unacceptable.)

Availability of Information Regarding Registered Sex Offenders

(Addendum to Rental Agreement)

This disclosure is attached to and forms a part of the Rental Agreement dated _____ between _____, Owners, and _____, Tenants.

The following text applies in California only:
Notice: Pursuant to Section 290.46 of the Penal Code, information about specified registered sex offenders is made available to the public via an Internet Web site maintained by the Department of Justice at www.meganslaw.ca.gov. Depending on an offender's criminal history, this information will include either the address at which the offender resides or the community of residence and ZIP Code in which he or she resides.

The following text applies in states other than California:
Notice: The state justice department, sheriff's departments, police departments serving jurisdictions of 200,000 or more and many other local law enforcement authorities maintain for public access a data base of the locations of persons required to register pursuant to "Megan's Law" or a similar statute. The data base is updated on a regular basis and is a source of information about the presence of these individuals in any neighborhood. Contact the state justice department to determine whether it also maintains a telephone service through which inquiries about individuals may be made.

The following acknowledge that the Owner or Owner's Agent whose signature appears below has provided a copy of this Rental Agreement Addendum to the Tenant(s) whose signature(s) appear(s) below.

Date_____ Tenant _____

Date_____ Tenant _____

Date_____ Owner or Manager_____

Co-Signer Agreement Dated _____
(Addendum to Rental Agreement)

This agreement is attached to and forms a part of the Rental

Agreement dated _____ between _____,

Owners, and _____, Tenants.

My name is _____.

I have completed a Rental Application for the express purpose of enabling the Owners to check my credit. I have no intention of occupying the dwelling referred to in the Rental Agreement above.

I have read the Rental Agreement, and I promise to guarantee the Tenants' compliance with the financial obligations of this Agreement.

I understand that I may be required to pay for rent, cleaning charges, or damage assessments in such amounts as are incurred by the Tenants under the terms of this Agreement if, and only if, the Tenants themselves fail to pay.

I also understand that this Co-Signer Agreement will remain in force throughout the entire term of the Tenants' tenancy, even if their tenancy is extended and/or changed in its terms.

I am paying the sum of ten dollars ($10) as a consideration of acceptance of this Co-Signer Agreement by all parties concerned.

_____
Co-Signer

_____
Accepted by Owner/Manager

COMPLAINT

We understand that every so often you may have a complaint which you want to make known to the management. We want to hear about it so we can take care of it or if we already know about it, so we can tell you what we're doing about it. Please use this form to register your complaint with us.

Type of complaint: [ ]   Against management

                             [ ]   Against another tenant

                             [ ]   Regarding general conditions

If your complaint is against a particular person, please give that person's name and address.

Name_____

Address_____

Give details about the incident, complaint, or problem (include date, time, and place as applicable):

_____

_____

_____

_____

_____

_____

What action do you suggest that management should take?

_____

_____

_____

Please note that management cannot promise complete confidentiality if this complaint is raised against another tenant.

Submitted by_____ Date_____

* *

Received by_____ Date_____

Action taken _____

_____

_____

410

Condition & Inventory Checksheet

Tenants: _____ Dated: _____

Address: _____

Date Moved In: _____ Notice Given: _____ Moved Out: _____

Abbreviations:

Air Cond, AC	Clean, Cl	Drape, Drp	Hood, Hd	OK, OK	Table, Tbl
Bed, Bd	Cracked, Cr	Dryer, Dry	Just Painted, JP	Poor, P	Tile, Tl
Broken, Brk	Curtain, Ctn	Fair, F	Lamp, Lmp	Refrigerator, Rf	Venet'n Blind, VB
Carpet, Cpt	Dinette, Din	Good, G	Lightbulb, LtB	Shade, Sh	Washer, Wsh
Chair, Ch	Dishwasher, Dsh	Heater, Htr	Linoleum, Lino	Sofa, Sfa	Waxed, Wxd
Chest, Chst	Disposer, Dsp	Hole, H	Nightstand, Ntst	Stove, Stv	Wood, Wd

Circle rooms; enter abbre-viations	Walls, Doors		Floors		Windows		Lt. Fixtures		Inventory: Appliances, Furniture		
	cond.	chgs.	cond.	chgs.	cond.	chgs.	cond.	chgs.	Item	cond.	chgs.
Living Rm											
Dining Rm											
Kitchen											
Bath 1											
Bath 2											
Bedroom 1											
Bedroom 2											
Bedroom 3											
Other											
Itemized Charges											

TOTAL ITEMIZED CHARGES _____

Other Charges Not Itemized
(Dirty garage, etc.
Explained on Backside) _____

Deduction for Improper Notice _____

Deduction for Missing Keys _____

TOTAL DEDUCTIONS _____

TOTAL DEPOSITS _____

minus (-) TOTAL DEDUCTIONS _____

equals (=) DEPOSIT REFUND
or (Amount Owed) _____

☐ Tenants acknowledge that the smoke detector was tested in their presence and found to be in working order and that its operation was explained to them. Tenants agree to test the detector at least every other week and to report any problems to Owners in writing. If the detector is battery operated, Tenants agree to replace the battery as necessary with a new ALKALINE battery (unless applicable laws require otherwise).

Tenants hereby acknowledge that they have read this Checksheet, agree that the condition and contents of the above-mentioned rental dwelling are without exception as represented herein, understand that they are liable for any damage done to this dwelling as outlined in their Lease or Rental Agreement, and have received a copy of this Checksheet.

_____
Owner

BY Person authorized to represent Owners

_____
Tenant

_____
Tenant

Credit Check & Screening Receipt

RECEIVED FROM _____, Applicant,

the sum of _____ $_____

for the purpose of verifying the information submitted on the
application to rent that dwelling commonly known as

_____.

Sum received will be used as follows:
1) Cost to obtain credit report, eviction $_____
   report, and/or other screening reports

2) Cost to process and verify information $_____
   (time and associated costs)

It is understood that this sum received is in no way to be considered
a deposit to hold the dwelling. The Owner/Manager may take other
applications to rent the dwelling and indeed may already have done
so.

The sum received is refundable only if the Owner/Manager selects
another applicant to rent the dwelling BEFORE checking Applicant's
credit history. Otherwise, this sum is entirely non-refundable.

Date:_____   _____
                                          Owner/Manager
Time:_____

                                  _____
                                           Applicant

                                  _____
                                           Applicant

Deposit Receipt & Agreement

RECEIVED FROM _____, Applicant,

the sum of _____ $_____

for the purpose of verifying information submitted on the application and for holding the rental dwelling commonly known as

_____

until _____ or such earlier time as the undersigned Owner/Manager is able to complete a verification of the information submitted on Applicant's rental application.

This dwelling will be rented to the Applicant provided that:
1) The Applicant's rental application and credit history satisfy the Owner/Manager;
2) Within 24 hours of being approved, the Applicant signs the rental agreement offered by the Owner/Manager, a copy of which the Applicant has received, read, and approved; and
3) Within 24 hours of being approved, the Applicant pays all of the sums necessary to move in.

Should the Applicant be approved to rent this dwelling and meet all three conditions above, all monies received will be refunded except for the sum of $_____, used to process Applicant's rental application, here itemized as follows:
1) Cost to obtain credit report, eviction $_____
   report, and/or other screening reports
2) Cost to process and verify information $_____
   (time and associated costs)

Should the Applicant be approved to rent this dwelling and not do so, none of the monies received will be refunded.

Should the Applicant not be approved to rent this dwelling, the Owner/Manager will refund all monies received except for the sum used to process Applicant's rental application (itemized above).

Date: _____   _____
                                                Owner/Manager
Time: _____

                                        _____
                                                Applicant

                                        _____
                                                Applicant

Depreciation Record

Property or Capital Improvement
Location and Description _____

Date Acquired or Converted to Business _____ New or Used _____

Method of Depreciation _____ Useful Life _____

Cost or Other Basis $_____

minus (-) Land Value or 1st Year Expensing $_____

equals (=) Depreciable Basis $_____

Tax Year	Prior Depreciation	Depreciable Balance	% Year Held	% Bus. Use	Rate	Depreciation This Year
1						
2						
3						
4						
5						
6						
7						
8						
9						
10						
11						
12						
13						
14						
15						
16						
17						
18						
19						
20						
21						
22						
23						
24						
25						
26						
27						
28						
29						
30						
31						
32						
33						
34						
35						
36						
37						
38						
39						
40						
41						

DEPRECIATION WORKSHEET

Form D-1

YEAR

NAME(S) OF TAXPAYERS

SOC. SEC. NUMBER

PROPERTY LOCATION & DESCRIPTION

Property A

Property B

Property C

Property D

Property E

Property F

Property G

	A	B	C	D	E	F	G	Totals
Date Acqd. or Conv. to Bus.								
New or Used								
Cost or Other Basis								
Land Value								
Salvage Value								
1st Year Special Depreciation								
Depreciable Basis								
Prior Depreciation								
Depreciable Balance								
Method of Depreciation								
Useful Life								
Full Year Depreciation								
Percentage of Year Held								
Percentage of Business Use								
Depreciation This Year								

PAGE TOTAL

Disclosure of Information on Lead-Based Paint and/or Lead-Based Paint Hazards

Lead Warning Statement

Housing built before 1978 may contain lead-based paint. Lead from paint, paint chips, and dust can pose health hazards if not managed properly. Lead exposure is especially harmful to young children and pregnant women. Before renting pre-1978 housing, lessors must disclose the presence of known lead-based paint and/or lead-based paint hazards in the dwelling. Lessees must also receive a federally approved pamphlet on lead poisoning prevention.

Lessor's Disclosure

(a) Presence of lead-based paint and/or lead-based paint hazards (check (i) or (ii) below):

    (i) _____ Known lead-based paint and/or lead-based paint hazards are present in the housing (explain).

    _____

    _____

    (ii) _____ Lessor has no knowledge of lead-based paint and/or lead-based paint hazards in the housing.

(b) Records and reports available to the lessor (check (i) or (ii) below):

    (i) _____ Lessor has provided the lessee with all available records and reports pertaining to lead-based paint and/or lead-based paint hazards in the housing (list documents below).

    _____

    _____

    (ii) _____ Lessor has no reports or records pertaining to lead-based paint and/or lead-based paint hazards in the housing.

Lessee's Acknowledgment (initial)

(c) _____ Lessee has received copies of all information listed above.

(d) _____ Lessee has received the pamphlet *Protect Your Family from Lead in Your Home.*

Agent's Acknowledgment (initial)

(e) _____ Agent has informed the lessor of the lessor's obligations under 42 U.S.C. 4852(d) and is aware of his/her responsibility to ensure compliance.

Certification of Accuracy

The following parties have reviewed the information above and certify, to the best of their knowledge, that the information they have provided is true and accurate.

Lessor	Date	Lessor	Date
Lessee	Date	Lessee	Date
Agent	Date	Agent	Date

Employment Application

>>APPLICANT<<

Name_____ Home Phone_____ Work Phone_____

Social Security No._____ Driver's License No._____

Own _____ How long at
Present Address_____ Rent_____ this address?_____

Present/Last How long with
Occupation_____ Employer_____ this employer?_____

Reason for   Monthly   Name of   May we
Leaving?_____ Gross_____ Supervisor_____ contact?_____Phone_____

Previous How long with
Occupation_____ Employer_____ this employer?_____

Reason for   Monthly   Name of   May we
Leaving?_____ Gross_____ Supervisor_____ contact?_____Phone_____

How many years of   Course of   What languages do you
schooling have you had?_____ study_____ speak fluently?_____

>>SPOUSE/PARTNER<<

Name_____ Social Security No._____ Driver's License No._____

Present/Last How long with
Occupation_____ Employer_____ this employer?_____

Reason for   Monthly   Name of   May we
Leaving?_____ Gross_____ Supervisor_____ contact?_____Phone_____

Previous How long with
Occupation_____ Employer_____ this employer?_____

Reason for   Monthly   Name of   May we
Leaving?_____ Gross_____ Supervisor_____ contact?_____Phone_____

How many years of schooling   Course of   What languages does spouse/partner
has spouse/partner had?_____ study_____ speak fluently?_____

>>APPLICANT AND SPOUSE/PARTNER<<

What are your skills related to this job?_____

What experience have you and your
spouse/partner had related to this job?_____

What tools do you and your spouse/partner
have which might be useful on this job?_____

What transportation do you and your spouse/partner
have which might be useful on this job?_____

How many dependents do you   What do you and your spouse/partner receive
and your spouse/partner have?_____ monthly from pensions, alimony, etc.?_____

What health insurance   What do you and your spouse/partner pay monthly for
do you have?_____ debts, alimony, child support, etc.?_____

Are you and your
spouse/partner bondable?_____ Previous bonding?_____

Savings or Checking Account   Account
Bank Name_____ Branch_____ Number_____

Credit   Account   Balance   Monthly
Reference_____ Number_____ Owed_____ Payment_____

Personal
Reference_____ Address_____ Phone (   )_____

Personal
Reference_____ Address_____ Phone (   )_____

Contact in
Emergency_____ Address_____ Phone (   )_____

Have you ever been convicted of   Will you take   When are you available
a felony or serious misdemeanor?_____ a drug test?_____ for this job?_____

I/we declare that the information above is true and correct, and I/we hereby authorize
verification of this information and a thorough background check.

Date_____ Signed_____

Employment Verification

TO: EMPLOYER _____

_____

_____

RE: EMPLOYEE _____

We are in the process of checking out a rental application submitted by the person named above as "EMPLOYEE."

This person claims to be working for you currently as a _____ earning $_____ per _____.

This person also claims to have started working for you as of _____.

Because time is a factor in our approving this employee to rent from us, we would appreciate your PHONING us as soon as possible with a verification of this information. Our telephone number is _____, and we are generally available at the following times: _____.

If you cannot phone us, please complete the section below and mail this entire letter back to us at your earliest convenience.

Thank you.   Signed _____

Address _____

- -

The above information is correct with the following exceptions:

_____ (if none, write "none.")

Is this employment part-time?   or full-time?

Is this employment temporary?   or permanent?

INFORMATION PROVIDED BY

Name_____ Title_____ Date_____

Expense & Payment Record

Page _____

Property _____

Period _____

	How Date Paid		To Whom Paid	For	1 Total Paid Out	2 Interest	3 Taxes, Licenses	4 Insurance	
1									1
2									2
3									3
4									4
5									5
6									6
7									7
8									8
9									9
10									10
11									11
12									12
13									13
14									14
15									15
16									16
17									17
18									18
19									19
20									20
21									21
22									22
23									23
24									24
25									25
26									26
27									27
28									28
29									29
30									30
31									31
32									32
33									33
34									34
35									35
36									36
37									37
38									38
39									39
40									40
41									41

Expense & Payment Distribution Page _____

	5 Utilities	6 Services, Rep., Maint.	7 Merch., Supplies	8 Payroll	9 Misc.	10 Depreciable	11 Mortgage Principal	12 Non-deduct.	
1									1
2									2
3									3
4									4
5									5
6									6
7									7
8									8
9									9
10									10
11									11
12									12
13									13
14									14
15									15
16									16
17									17
18									18
19									19
20									20
21									21
22									22
23									23
24									24
25									25
26									26
27									27
28									28
29									29
30									30
31									31
32									32
33									33
34									34
35									35
36									36
37									37
38									38
39									39
40									40
41									41

Expense & Payment Record

Annual Summary

Page _____

Property _____

Period _____

Units	1 Total Paid Out (2-12)	2 Interest	3 Taxes, Licences	4 Insurance	5 Utilities	
1						1
2						2
3						3
4						4
5						5
6						6
7						7
8						8
9						9
10						10
11						11
12						12
13						13
14						14
15						15
16						16
17						17
18						18
19						19
20						20
21						21
22						22
23						23
24						24
25						25
26						26
27						27
28						28
29						29
30						30
31						31
32						32
33						33
34						34
35						35
36						36
37						37
38						38
39						39
40						40
41						41

Expense & Payment Distribution Page _____

Annual Summary

6 Services, Rep., Maint.	7 Merch., Supplies	8 Payroll	9 Misc.	10 Depreciable	11 Mortgage Principal	12 Non-Deduct.	13 All Depreciation

Date: _____

To: _____

Your application to rent from us has been rejected either partly or solely because of information provided by the following sources:

CREDIT REPORT

[ ] Equifax Credit Information Service, P. O. Box 740241, Atlanta, GA 30374-2041; 800.685.1111

[ ] Experian Consumer Assistance, P. O. Box 949, Allen, TX 75002; 800.682.7654

[ ] Trans Union Consumer Relations, P. O. Box 1000, 2 Baldwin Place, Chester, PA 19022; 800.888.4213

[ ] _____

COURT RECORDS REPORT

[ ] American Tenant Screen, 131 N. Narberth Ave., Narberth, PA 19072; 610.664.2323

[ ] _____

BAD CHECK REPORT

[ ] Telecheck Services, P.O. Box 4513, Houston, TX 77210-4513; 800.366.2425

[ ] _____

The federal Fair Credit Reporting Act requires us to reveal the source of whatever credit reports figured in the decision to reject you as an applicant. Please note that the agencies checked above only provided information about you. They did not make the decision, nor can they explain the decision.

Under federal law, you have the right to obtain a free copy of your credit report within sixty days from the date when we inquired about your credit. That was _____/_____/_____.

To secure the report, you must provide the following: your full name, your complete mailing address, your residential address if different from your mailing address, your daytime phone number, your employer's name, your Social Security number, your driver's license number and the state where issued (bad checks only), and the name of the company which rejected you. Our company name is _____.

If you believe your report is inaccurate or incomplete, you may contact the agency to dispute its accuracy and insert a 100-word consumer statement of explanation. Assistance is available at the credit reporting agency to help you with the statement.

You may have additional rights under the credit reporting or consumer protection laws of your state. To find out what they are, you may contact your state or local consumer protection agency or the office of your state attorney general. See the government listings in the white pages of your telephone book.

Sincerely,

Fellow Landlord:

_____ has applied to rent from us and has identified you as a current or former landlord or rental property manager having first-hand experience with him/her as a tenant.

We are trying to determine what this person was like when living at _____ as your tenant and would appreciate your answering the following questions about him/her:

How long was this person your tenant?
Less than six months [ ] Six months to a year [ ]
One to two years [ ] More than two years [ ]

When did this tenant move out? _____

How much was the rent when he/she moved out? $_____

How many other people were living with this tenant?
None [ ] One [ ] Two [ ] Three [ ] Four [ ] Five [ ] Six [ ]

Did the tenant have any pets?
Yes [ ] No [ ] If so, what kind? _____

How many times did the tenant fail to pay the rent on time?
Once [ ] Twice [ ] Three times [ ] More than three times [ ]

Did you ever have to serve the tenant with a notice to pay rent or quit? Yes [ ] No [ ]

Did you ever have to serve the tenant with any other notice?
Yes [ ] No [ ] If so, what kind? _____

Was this tenant reasonably quiet? Yes [ ] No [ ]

Was this tenant reasonably clean? Yes [ ] No [ ]

Did the tenant give enough notice that he/she was moving?
Yes [ ] No [ ]

Did the tenant leave the premises clean and undamaged?
Yes [ ] No [ ]

If you withheld any of the tenant's cleaning/security deposit, why did you withhold it? _____

Did the tenant leave owing you any money?
Yes [ ] No [ ] If so, how much? $_____

On a scale of one to ten, with ten being the most cooperative and zero being the least cooperative, how would you rate this tenant in terms of his/her cooperating with you?
10 9 8 7 6 5 4 3 2 1 (Circle only one number.)

If you had the opportunity, would you rent to this tenant again?
Yes [ ] No [ ]

Thank you very much for answering these questions.

Sincerely,

FINANCIAL QUALIFIER
(all figures monthly)

APPLICANT NAME _____
Number of Adults _____
Ages of Children _____
Adults all work? _____
Health plan through work? _____
Child care? _____
Pets? _____

G R O S S   V E R I F I A B L E   I N C O M E
(amounts)   (notes)

Wages _____
Wages _____
Wages _____
Wages _____
Social Security _____
Pension _____
Alimony _____
Child Support _____
Interest _____
Dividends _____
Other _____

_____
TOTAL INCOME _____ (+)

E X P E N S E S   &   D E D U C T I O N S
(amounts)   (notes)

Income Taxes _____ 20% if state inc tax; 17% if none
Credit Card Payments _____
Vehicle Payments _____
Loan Payments _____
Vehicle Expenses _____ $100/fin; $75/not; add $30 hi risk
Gas & Electricity _____ check local utility for sq ft avg
Telephone _____ ask re avg bill; otherwise $25
Cable TV _____
Food _____ $140/person
Health Care _____ $85/person wo paid plan; $25 with
Alimony _____
Child Care _____ $450/child full day; $200 partial
Child Support _____
Pet Care _____ $35/dog; $25/cat
Other _____ $200/adult; $100/child

_____
TOTAL EXPENSES & DEDUCTIONS _____ (−)

SAVINGS ACCOUNT BALANCE _____ add 5% bal to "available for rent"

AVAILABLE FOR RENT _____ (=) ADJUSTED _____
(total income minus total expenses & deductions)

Fire Safety Tips

Use Care When Cooking
Keep cooking areas clear of combustibles, and don't leave your cooking unattended. Keep the handles of your pots turned inward so nobody is likely to knock them over the edge of the stove. If grease catches fire, turn off the burner immediately. Then slide a lid over the pan to smother the flames or else put them out with a fire extinguisher or ordinary baking soda.

Keep Matches and Lighters Hidden
Keep matches and lighters hidden out of youngsters' reach. Teach them early that matches and lighters are tools for grownups, not toys for youngsters, and that they should tell a grownup immediately if they find any matches or lighters.

Use Electricity Safely
If an appliance smokes or smells strange, unplug it immediately and have it checked. Check your electrical cords periodically, including extension cords, and replace any that are cracked or frayed. Also, don't run extension cords under carpets or overload them with high-energy devices such as irons, space heaters, toasters, hot plates, and microwaves. Remember that fuses and circuit breakers protect you from fire. Don't tamper with the fuse box or use fuses too large for the circuit.

Practice Candle Safety
Never leave a lit candle unattended. Never leave candles burning when you go to sleep. Never use candles near combustible materials such as curtains, drapes, bedding, and cabinets.

Give Space to Space Heaters
Keep portable space heaters at least 3 feet (1 meter) away from curtains, furniture, clothing, bedding, and anything else that burns. Never leave heaters turned on when you leave home or go to sleep, and keep children and pets well away from them.

Plan and Practice Your Escape
With your housemates, plan two ways to escape from every room. Your escape route must not require taking an elevator because it might stop and trap you inside or take you to where the fire is the worst. Include in your plan a meeting place outside where everyone should gather. Practice your escape plan once or twice a year.

Stop, Drop, and Roll
If your clothing catches fire, slowly get clear of any surrounding fire which could re-ignite your clothing. Then stop, drop to the ground, and roll over and over to smother the flames. Cover your face with your hands to protect your face and lungs.

Get Out and Stay Out of a Burning Building
If you find yourself in a burning building, get out fast. Once you leave, stay out. Do not go back to rescue a person, animal, or thing you suspect may still be inside. Leave the rescue operations to firefighters who have the right training and equipment.

Crawl Low Under Smoke
If smoke is clogging your primary exit route, look for a better exit route through clean air. If you must exit through smoke, get down to where you'll find clean air several inches off the floor and crawl to the nearest safe exit.

Cool a Burn
If you notice a burn on your skin, place it in cool water immediately for 10 to 15 minutes to ease the pain. Do not use butter on a burn, as this can prolong the heat and further damage the skin. If the burn chars or turns into a nasty blister, seek emergency medical care to help eliminate the pain and reduce the infection.

Keep and Maintain Fire Extinguishers
Keep a sodium bicarbonate dry chemical fire extinguisher in your kitchen. Keep an ammonium phosphate dry chemical fire extinguisher in your car or garage. Keep a clean agent gas fire extinguisher alongside your computer. Check the gauges on the extinguishers twice a year, and shake the dry chemical extinguishers once a year to keep the chemical from caking.

Check Smoke Detectors
Make sure you have smoke detectors on every level of your dwelling and next to every sleeping area. Test regularly, and replace batteries yearly or when you hear chirps signaling that a battery is dying.

Learn More
There's more to learn about fire safety, and you'll find plenty of fire safety information on the internet. Use the following search words to find at least some of it:
    fire fighting misconceptions
    evacuating a burning building
    trapped in a burning building
    fire extinguisher identification
    fire extinguisher use
    flashover

Check the following websites for sound information about fire safety:
    en.wikipedia.org/wiki/fire_safety
    firesafety.gov
    nfpa.org
    osha.gov/SLTC/firesafety/
    sparky.org
    usfa.dhs.gov/citizens/

For Your Information:

Important Numbers

Police_____   Telephone Co._____

Fire_____   Gas Co._____

Ambulance_____   Electric Co._____

Paramedic_____   Water Co._____

Doctor_____   Manager_____

The best time to contact the manager is _____.

In an emergency, when you cannot get hold of the manager, call

_____.

Helpful Hints

　　　1) A fire extinguisher is located _____.
Use short bursts aimed at the base of the fire. Never use water on
a grease fire; either use the extinguisher provided or throw
baking soda on it.

　　　2) The main electrical shutoff for your dwelling is located
_____.
Check there to see whether a fuse has blown (have an extra on
hand) or a circuit breaker has tripped. Restore service by
replacing any fuse which appears to be blown (use one with the
same number on it) or by flipping the circuit breaker switch back
and forth once.

　　　3) The main gas shutoff for your dwelling is located
_____,
but there may be an individual valve on the line supplying each
appliance as well. Shut off the gas by turning the valve 90
degrees, that is, so it crosses the direction of the supply line.

　　　4) The main water shutoff for your dwelling is located
_____,
but you may be able to shut off the water to an individual faucet
by turning off the supply valve below your sink or toilet (not
your tub or shower). If hot water is leaking anywhere, shut off
the valve on top of the hot water heater.

　　　5) Whenever you defrost the refrigerator, turn it off or set
the control knob to defrost. Place a pan to catch the water and
empty it when necessary. Do not try to break up the ice with any
implement like a knife or an ice pick. Let it melt on its own or
speed it up by placing a pot of hot water in the freezing
compartment. Dry the floor thoroughly when you have finished.

FOR YOUR INFORMATION - Page 2

6) Whenever you use the garbage disposer, if you have one, feed garbage in gradually along with lots of cold water, and let the water run for half a minute after you turn off the switch. Use the disposer only for those things which are edible, but don't put either cooking oil or grease down it; put them and everything else except toxic liquids in the trash. Keep metal objects out of the sink while using the disposer and turn off the switch immediately if you hear any loud metallic noises. Do not put your hand into the disposer (use tongs to retrieve objects) and do not use any chemical drain openers. If the disposer stops running on its own and you haven't heard it make any strange noises, something may have gotten stuck. Try turning the blades with a disposer wrench. Then push the reset button. After you have tried all this and you find that it still doesn't work, call the manager.

7) Whenever you want to dispose of any liquids which aren't edible, please see the manager. Many liquids are toxic and should not be put down the drain or into the trash. They must be disposed of carefully so they will not contaminate the soil or the water supply in this area. Included in this list of hazardous household wastes are the following: oven cleaners, ammonia-based cleaners, drain cleaners, floor wax, furniture polish, deodorizers, spot removers, medicines, paint, thinners, paint removers, wood preservatives, art supplies, photographic chemicals, antifreeze, car waxes, crankcase oil, fuels, radiator flushes, rust inhibitors, engine cleaners, insect sprays, weed killers, and swimming pool chemicals.

8) Whenever water rises in the toilet bowl, do not try flushing the toilet again. The bowl can hold just one tank of water at a time. More water from the tank will only cause the bowl to flow over. Use a plunger first, and then try flushing it again. Do not try to flush feminine napkins or paper diapers down the toilet. They may disappear from the toilet bowl, but that's no guarantee they'll clear the sewer pipes completely. They could require a plumber's visit, and that'll cost you money.

9) Whenever you have showered or bathed, please take a moment to mop up the excess water on the bathroom floor. A dry floor is a safe floor.

10) Whenever you want to hang anything from, or stick anything to, the walls or ceilings in your dwelling, please ask the manager to explain how to do it acceptably.

11) Whenever you want to remove the screens from your windows, please ask the manager how to do it properly. Some screens have to be removed from the inside and some from the outside. The manager will show you how.

Dear

    As we do every year when the premiums come due, we have been reviewing our insurance policies, and we thought that you might like to know how you are affected by the insurance we carry.

    Basically, our policies cover only the building itself where you live. They do not cover any of your belongings against damage or disappearance, nor do they cover you for negligence should you, for example, leave a burner going under a pan and start a fire which damages the kitchen.

    To protect yourself against these calamities, you should get a tenant's insurance policy. Most insurance companies and agents will write such a policy for you, and we would strongly urge that you inquire about getting one.

    For the peace of mind that it gives, a tenant's insurance policy is reasonable indeed.

              Sincerely,

Insurance Record   Property _____

Company and/or Agent	Type of Policy	Policy Number	Limits	Premium	Expiration Date

Laundry Income

Property _____

Period _____

Date	Washer	Dryer	Both	Cumulative Totals	Monthly Totals
1					
2					
3					
4					
5					
6					
7					
8					
9					
10					
11					
12					
13					
14					
15					
16					
17					
18					
19					
20					
21					
22					
23					
24					
25					
26					
27					
28					
29					
30					
31					
32					
33					
34					
35					
36					
37					
38					
39					
40					
41					

Lease

Dated_____

    Agreement between_____, Owners, and _____, Tenants, for a dwelling located at _____. Tenants agree to lease this dwelling for a term of _____, beginning _____ and ending _____ for $_____ per month, payable in advance on the ____ day of every calendar month to Owners or their Agent*, _____, whose address is _____. When rent is paid on or before the _____ day of the calendar month, Owners will give Tenants a (discount) (rebate) of $_____.

    The first month's rent is $_____.

    The security/cleaning deposit on this dwelling is $_____. It is refundable if Tenants leave the dwelling reasonably clean and undamaged.

    Upon expiration, this Agreement shall become a month-to-month agreement AUTOMATICALLY, UNLESS either Tenants or Owners notify the other party in writing at least thirty days prior to expiration that they do not wish this Agreement to continue on any basis.

    Should Tenants move before this Agreement expires, they will be responsible for paying rent through the end of the term or until another tenant approved by the Owners has moved in, whichever comes first.

    Owners will refund all deposits due within ____ days after Tenants have moved out completely and returned their keys.

    Only the following ____ persons and ____ pets are to live in this dwelling:
_____

Without Owners' prior written permission, no other persons may live there, and no other pets may stay there, even temporarily, nor may the dwelling be sublet or used for business purposes.

    Use of the following is included in the rent: _____
_____

    Remarks: _____
_____

TENANTS AGREE TO THE FOLLOWING:
1) to accept the dwelling "as is," having already inspected it.
2) to keep yards and garbage areas clean.
3) to keep from making loud or bothersome noises and disturbances and to play music and broadcast programs at all times so as not to disturb other people's peace and quiet.
4) not to paint or alter the dwelling without first getting Owners' written permission.
5) to park their motor vehicle in assigned space and to keep that space clean of oil drippings and grease.
6) not to repair their motor vehicle on the premises (unless it is in an enclosed garage) if such repairs will take longer than a single day.
7) to allow Owners to inspect the dwelling, work on it, or show it to prospective tenants at any and all reasonable times.
8) not to keep any liquid-filled furniture in this dwelling.
9) to pay rent by check or money order made out to Owners. (Checks must be good when paid or applicable late-payment consequences will apply.)
10) to pay for repairs of all damage, including drain stoppages, they or their guests have caused.
11) to pay for any windows broken in their dwelling while they live there.

    Violation of any part of this Agreement or nonpayment of rent when due shall be cause for eviction under applicable code sections. The prevailing party (shall) (shall not) recover reasonable legal services fees involved.

    Tenants hereby acknowledge that they have read this Agreement, understand it, agree to it, and have been given a copy.

Owner_____ Tenant_____
*By_____ Tenant_____
*Person authorized to accept legal service on Owners' behalf

LEASE TERMINATION ARRANGEMENTS

Date _____

Dear _____ :

    We want you to be aware that the lease under which you occupy the premises located at _____ will terminate on _____ .

    When the lease terminates...

[ ] you will need to vacate the premises.

[ ] you may continue to occupy the premises...

    [ ] upon signing another fixed-term lease for _____ months at a new rent of $_____ per month.

    [ ] on a month-to-month basis at a new rent of $_____ per month and...

        [ ] all other provisions of your original lease will continue to apply to your tenancy.

        [ ] you will need to sign a new agreement, in this case a month-to-month agreement.

    In order for us to begin making plans, we need to know what you plan to do when your lease terminates. Please let us know by completing the information below and returning it to us within three days. Thank you.

            Sincerely,

            _____
            Manager/Owner

* *

[ ] I plan to vacate the premises when the lease terminates.

[ ] If given the choice, I plan to continue occupying the premises when the lease terminates.

_____   _____
Date   Tenant

Dear

     We want to make the place where you live as safe as it can be. We are constantly on the lookout for anything around your home which might prove hazardous to life, limb, or property. But hard as we try, we cannot uncover every potential danger all by ourselves. We need your help.

     Because you are around your home much more than we are, you have a greater opportunity to notice hazards. Please report to us anything you notice which you think might prove hazardous to you or anyone else. We promise that we will investigate the hazardous condition and remedy it if we possibly can.

     Please complete the bottom section of this letter and return it to us with your next rent payment.

     Thank you for your cooperation in making your home a safer place to live.

            Sincerely,

= =

[ ] We know of nothing which appears to be unsafe in or around our home, but we will alert you whenever we do notice something.

[ ] We would like to call your attention to the following unsafe conditions in or around our home:

_____

_____

_____

_____

We suggest that you take the following corrective action:

_____

_____

_____

_____

Signed   Dated

Loan & Note Record

Property _____

Noteholder _____ Loan Number _____

Original Loan _____ Interest Rate _____ Payment _____ Due Date _____

	Date Paid/Ck.#/New Payment if Changed	Interest	Principal	Impounds & (Imp.Disb.)	Impound Balance	Principal Balance	
1							1
2							2
3							3
4							4
5							5
6							6
7							7
8							8
9							9
10							10
11							11
12							12
13							13
14							14
15							15
16							16
17							17
18							18
19							19
20							20
21							21
22							22
23							23
24							24
25							25
26							26
27							27
28							28
29							29
30							30
31							31
32							32
33							33
34							34
35							35
36							36
37							37
38							38
39							39
40							40
41							41

Lodger Rental Agreement

Dated _____

Agreement between _____, Landlord, and
_____, Lodger, for a room located
at _____. Lodger agrees
to rent this room on a (week-to-week) (month-to-month) basis, beginning
_____, 20___, for $_____ per _____, payable in advance on or
before the first day of every rental period to Landlord. Rent is due on the
first day of the rental period. It is late if not paid on or before the
_____ day of the rental period and is then subject to a late fee of $_____.

The security/cleaning deposit is $_____. If Lodger leaves the room
reasonably clean and undamaged, it is refundable within ___ days after Lodger
has moved out completely and returned the keys.

The amount to be applied to the last rental period's rent is $_____.

Lodger will give ___ days' notice in writing before he/she moves and will
be responsible for paying rent through the end of this notice period.
Use of the following is included in the rent: _____
_____

Remarks: _____
_____

LODGER UNDERSTANDS THE FOLLOWING:
1) that state laws, if any, relating to lodgers/roomers govern this
   occupancy. If there are no such laws, landlord-tenant laws apply.
2) that Landlord does not grant possession of the room to the Lodger.
3) that Landlord may enter Lodger's room without notice or good cause.
4) that Landlord shares the use of this/these room(s) with the Lodger:
   _____
5) that Lodger may not have overnight guests without written permission.
6) that Lodger (is) (is not) responsible for periodic cleaning of the room
   he/she is renting under this agreement.
7) that Lodger is responsible for the security of his/her personal property.
8) that Lodger, whether in residence or not in residence, (is) (is not)
   responsible for paying a share of the utilities (gas, fuel oil,
   electricity, water, sewer, garbage, cable TV, and internet) as follows:
   _____

LODGER AGREES TO THE FOLLOWING:
1) to accept the Lodger's room "as is," having already inspected it.
2) not to paint or alter the room without first getting Landlord's written
   permission.
3) to keep from making loud or bothersome noises and disturbances and to
   play music and broadcast programs at all times so as not to disturb other
   people's peace and quiet.
4) to keep yards and garbage areas clean.
5) to park his/her motor vehicle in assigned space and to keep that space
   clean of oil drippings and grease.
6) not to repair his/her motor vehicle on the premises (unless it is in an
   enclosed garage) if such repairs will take longer than a single day.
7) to pay rent by check or money order made out to Landlord. (Checks must be
   good when paid or applicable late-payment consequences will apply.)
8) to show Landlord evidence of a current renters' insurance policy.
9) to pay for repairs of all damage, including drain stoppages, he/she or
   his/her guests have caused.
10) to do the following household chores: _____
    Violation of any part of this Agreement, incompatibility of the Lodger
and the Landlord as determined by the Landlord, or nonpayment of rent when
due shall be cause for eviction under applicable code sections.
    Lodger hereby acknowledges that he/she has read this Agreement,
understands it, agrees to it, and has been given a copy.

Landlord_____ Lodger_____

Maintenance Request

Tenant _____

Unit _____

Home Phone _____ Work _____

Date of Request _____ Time _____

Maintenance Request _____

_____

_____

_____

_____

Permission to Enter _____

Best Time _____

Request Submitted By _____

Work Order

Work Order No _____ Status _____

Work Authorized By _____

Date Work Attempted _____ Time Begun _____ Ended _____

Date Work Completed _____ Time Begun _____ Ended _____

Work Completed _____

_____

_____

_____

_____

Materials Used _____

COST	
Labor _____	_____
Materials _____	_____
Services _____	_____
TOTAL _____	_____

Percentage of Work
Charged to Tenant _____

Work Performed By _____

Tenant Notice

We entered your dwelling today for necessary repairs, maintenance, and/or inspections.

The work is _____

Incomplete work, if any, resulted from a lack of the following:

☐ tools. ☐ parts. ☐ time. ☐ assistance.

We expect to return on or about _____

_____

Thank you for your cooperation.

Date _____   _____

Management Agreement

Dated_____

Agreement between _____, Owner, and _____, Manager, for management and maintenance of property located at _____.

Compensation for Manager shall be in the form of a lodging credit and cash payments. The lodging credit shall be $_____ per _____ (must not exceed credit allowed by state law). The combined rate of compensation shall equal $_____ per hour (must equal or exceed minimum wage). Owner may adjust the lodging credit and hourly rate upon notice to Manager.

In spite of rental property management's irregular and variable hours, Manager is responsible for planning and carrying out assigned duties so as to work no more than eight hours per day and forty hours per week. Overtime hours will be compensated provided that Manager obtains Owner's permission in advance or, in case of an emergency, provided that Owner is notified within 48 hours afterwards. Manager shall take a ten-minute break for every four hours of work and take an unpaid meal break of at least thirty minutes after every five hours of work. Manager shall record working hours on timesheets provided, one timesheet for each person, and shall submit signed timesheets at the close of each pay period to certify that the hours recorded were actually worked and that no unrecorded hours were worked. Paydays will be _____.

Other compensation shall be as follows: _____
Manager shall have days off as follows: _____
Manager shall have vacation time as follows: _____
Manager shall have sick leave as follows: _____
Manager's duties and responsibilities shall be as follows:

_____

(Either party to this Agreement may request a review of compensation, days off, vacation, sick leave, duties, responsibilities, etc. Any changes superseding the Agreement must be in writing and must be signed by all parties.)

Manager shall receipt all monies collected on the Owner's behalf and shall deposit or transfer them within _____ of collection as follows:

_____

Manager shall spend, or commit to spend, no more than $_____ on the Owner's behalf without first obtaining permission.

Manager agrees to reside on the premises of the property as an employee and not as a tenant. Manager is an at-will employee who may be terminated at any time. Either Manager or Owner may terminate this Agreement upon _____ written notice. Immediately upon termination, Manager shall surrender all keys, records, supplies, equipment, and other items related to the position and shall vacate whatever lodging Owner supplies as a condition of employment. In no event shall Manager vacate later than 72 hours following termination.

(THIS PARAGRAPH APPLIES ONLY IF INITIALED BY BOTH PARTIES. Initials: Owner_____; Manager_____.) Manager and Owner agree to submit all disputes that cannot be resolved between them, except failure to vacate, to arbitration. The party seeking to arbitrate a dispute shall begin arbitration by serving a written demand to arbitrate on the other party and on the Judicial Arbitration and Mediation Services (JAMS). Arbitration costs shall be shared equally by both parties, and the costs shall be estimated in advance.

Any item in this Agreement found to be illegal, invalid, or unenforceable shall be considered null and void, and it shall not affect the validity of any other item in the Agreement.

As written, this Agreement constitutes the entire agreement between Owner and Manager. They have made no further promises of any kind to one another, nor have they reached any other understandings, either verbal or written.

Manager hereby acknowledges that he/she has read this Agreement, understands it, agrees to it voluntarily, and has been given a copy.

Owner _____   Manager _____

By _____   Manager _____

Monthly Rental Income

Page _____

Property _____

Period _____

Unit	January	February	March	April	May	
1						1
2						2
3						3
4						4
5						5
6						6
7						7
8						8
9						9
10						10
11						11
12						12
13						13
14						14
15						15
16						16
17						17
18						18
19						19
20						20
21						21
22						22
23						23
24						24
25						25
26						26
27						27
28						28
29						29
30						30
31						31
32						32
33						33
34						34
35						35
36						36
37						37
38						38
39						39
40						40
41						41

Monthly Rental Income Record

Page _____

	June	July	August	September	October	November	December	Year's Totals	
1									1
2									2
3									3
4									4
5									5
6									6
7									7
8									8
9									9
10									10
11									11
12									12
13									13
14									14
15									15
16									16
17									17
18									18
19									19
20									20
21									21
22									22
23									23
24									24
25									25
26									26
27									27
28									28
29									29
30									30
31									31
32									32
33									33
34									34
35									35
36									36
37									37
38									38
39									39
40									40
41									41

Move-Out Charges

Here's what we charge for most of the things we have to do when tenants move out and leave their dwelling in need of something or other. Please note that these charges are averages. Sometimes the actual charges are higher; sometimes they're lower. But most of the time they are exactly as shown. We give allowances for normal wear and tear, of course, and for the length of time something has been in use. Replacement charges include parts and labor.

Cleaning

Clean refrigerator _____
Clean stove top _____
Clean oven _____
Clean stove hood _____
Clean kitchen cabinets _____
Clean kitchen floor _____
Clean tub/shower and surround _____
Clean toilet and sink _____
Clean bathroom cabinets & floor _____
Vacuum throughout dwelling _____
Clean greasy parking space _____

Flooring

Remove carpet stains _____
Deodorize carpet _____
Repair carpet _____
Repair hardwood floor _____
Refinish hardwood floor _____
Repair linoleum _____
Replace kitchen linoleum _____
Replace bathroom linoleum _____
Repair floor tile _____
Replace kitchen floor tile _____
Replace bathroom floor tile _____

Walls

Remove mildew and treat surface _____
Cover crayon marks _____
Repair hole in wall _____
Remove wallpaper _____
Repaint (per wall/ceiling) _____

Doors

Repair hole in hollow-core door _____
Repair forced door damage _____
Replace door (inside) _____
Replace door (outside) _____
Replace sliding glass door (sgl) _____
Replace sliding glass door (dbl) _____
Rescreen sliding door screen _____
Replace sliding door screen _____

Electrical

Replace light bulb _____
Replace light fixture globe _____
Replace light fixture _____
Replace electrical outlet/switch _____
Replace electrical cover plate _____

Plumbing

Replace kitchen faucet _____
Replace bathroom faucet _____
Replace faucet handle _____
Replace faucet aerator _____
Replace shower head _____
Replace toilet tank lid _____
Replace toilet _____
Replace garbage disposer _____

Locks

Replace key (door or mailbox) _____
Replace cylindrical doorlock _____
Replace passage doorlock _____
Replace deadbolt lock _____
Replace mailbox lock _____

Windows & Window Coverings

Replace window pane (sgl) _____
Replace window pane (dbl) _____
Replace Venetian blind _____
Replace window shade _____
Replace drapery rod _____
Replace drapery (sill length) _____
Replace drapery (floor length) _____
Rescreen window screen _____
Replace window screen _____

Miscellaneous

Replace refrigerator shelf _____
Paint refrigerator _____
Replace stove/oven knob _____
Repair ceramic tile _____
Replace ceramic tile countertop _____
Repair plastic countertop _____
Replace plastic countertop _____
Replace cutting board _____
Replace mirror _____
Replace medicine cabinet _____
Replace towel bar _____
Replace shower curtain rod _____
Replace shower/tub enclosure _____
Repair porcelain _____
Replace thermostat _____
Recharge fire extinguisher _____
Replace fire extinguisher _____
Fumigate for fleas _____
Remove junk and debris _____

MOVE-OUT CONFIRMATION

We confirm that we have moved out of the dwelling located at the following address:

_____

We have returned our keys to the owner/manager and have returned possession to the owner/manager as of this date.

KEYS

[ ] To the best of our knowledge, there are no keys to the dwelling in anyone's possession other than those keys we have returned.

[ ] We will retrieve the _____ duplicate keys which are now in the possession of _____ and give them to the owner/manager within _____ days.

ITEMS LEFT BEHIND

[ ] We have left no items of value to us on the premises.

[ ] We have left certain items of no value to us on the premises and authorize management to dispose of them and charge us for doing so.

[ ] We have left certain items of value to us on the premises and will return to pick them up by _____ after arranging a pickup time with management at least twenty-four hours in advance of pickup. If we do not return to pick them up by this date, we authorize management to dispose of them and charge us for doing so.

[ ] We have left certain items of value to us on the premises and will return to pick them up by _____ after arranging a pickup time with management at least twenty-four hours in advance of pickup. If we do not return to pick them up by this date, we authorize management to move them to another location and store them for pickup and to charge us for both moving and storage. If we do not return to pick them up within _____ of the date when this acknowledgment was received by the owner/manager, we authorize management to dispose of them and charge us for doing so.

RETURN OF DEPOSIT

We understand that our deposit will be accounted for and refunded to us within _____ days. We prefer that both the accounting and the deposit be given to us in the following way:

[ ] Held for us to pick up on or after _____. (PLEASE NOTE: Pickup time must be arranged at least twenty-four hours in advance.)

[ ] Sent to us at the following address _____.

_____   _____
Date/Time   Tenant / New Address / Best Phone Number for Contact

_____   _____
Date/Time   Tenant / New Address / Best Phone Number for Contact

_____   _____
Date/Time   Received by Owner/Manager / Address / Phone

Dear

Moving time is always a busy time, and you will have lots of things on your mind now that you have given notice you are moving. One of those things undoubtedly is how to get your deposits back promptly. In your case, they amount to $_____.

Contrary to what some tenants believe, we WANT to return your deposits, and we WILL return them to you so long as you leave your place "reasonably clean and undamaged." That's what your rental agreement says and that's what we will do. You're probably wondering, however, what "reasonably clean and undamaged" means, so we'd like to tell you how we interpret it and tell you also what you should do to get your deposits back.

"Reasonably clean" to us means as clean as you would leave your dwelling if you knew your best friend or your favorite aunt were going to move in after you. To get it that clean, we expect you to clean the appliances, stove hood, and cabinets (under sinks, too) both inside and out; remove all non-adhesive shelf paper; use an appropriate cleanser on the showers, tubs, toilets, sinks, mirrors, and medicine cabinets (inside as well); dust the ceilings (for cobwebs), baseboards, window sills, and closet shelving; wash the kitchen and bathroom walls and spot-clean the walls in the other rooms; wash the light fixtures and windows inside and out; vacuum the floors; scrub the floor tile or linoleum; sweep the entry, patio, storage enclosure, and garage; remove all personal belongings (including clothes hangers and cleaning supplies); and dispose of all trash. PLEASE DO NOT CLEAN THE DRAPERIES, SHAMPOO THE CARPETS, OR WAX THE FLOORS. We prefer to do those cleaning chores ourselves, and we will not deduct anything from your deposits for our doing them.

"Reasonably undamaged" to us means that items which we have supplied should not be missing (including light bulbs) or broken; that there should be no new burns, cracks, chips, or holes in the dwelling or its furnishings; and that the paint on the walls should be sufficient to last at least two years from the time they were last painted. PLEASE DO NOT REMOVE ANYTHING YOU HAVE ATTACHED TO THE WALLS OR CEILING WITHOUT FIRST TALKING TO US, and please try to avoid nicking the paint in the halls and doorways as you move things out.

Please note that until you have returned your keys, you have not "officially" moved out, and you are still liable for paying rent. Make sure that you give us your keys as soon as you move out.

After you have moved out, we would like to inspect your dwelling with you to check it for cleanliness and damage. We will refund all deposits owed to you within seven days thereafter.

We expect you to have moved out completely by _____. Because we are making arrangements for new tenants to move in after you move, we would appreciate hearing from you immediately if your moving plans should change.

We hope your moving goes smoothly, and we wish you happiness in your new home.

                        Sincerely,

Notice and Release Agreement--Mold and Radon

Property Address: _____

Mold is a general term for the visible growth of fungus, whether it is plainly visible or whether it is visible only when barriers like building components, such as walls, or furnishings, such as carpets, are removed.

Radon is an invisible, odorless, radioactive gas.

TENANTS ARE HEREBY NOTIFIED, AND UNDERSTAND, THAT CERTAIN MOLDS AND RADON HAVE THE POTENTIAL TO CAUSE SERIOUS HEALTH PROBLEMS.

TENANTS ARE ENCOURAGED TO OBTAIN THE SERVICES OF A QUALIFIED AND EXPERIENCED PROFESSIONAL TO CONDUCT INSPECTIONS AND TESTS REGARDING MOLD AND RADON PRIOR TO THEIR COMMITTING TO RENT.

Tenants acknowledge and accept that the property described above is being offered for rent with no representations as to its condition regarding mold or radon. The owners of the property have no knowledge of mold or radon in, on, or around the property other than the following:

_____.

Tenants represent and warrant that they have not relied on the accuracy or completeness of any representations that have been made by the owners as to the presence of mold or radon and that the tenants have not relied on the owners' failure to provide information regarding the presence or effects of any mold or radon found on the property.

Tenants are hereby notified and agree that they are solely responsible for any required remediation and/or resulting damages, including, but not limited to, any effects on health, due to mold or radon in, on, or around the property.

In consideration of the rental of the property to the undersigned tenants, they do hereby release, indemnify, hold harmless and forever discharge the owners of the property from any and all claims, liabilities, or causes of action of any kind that the tenants may have now or at any time in the future against the owners from the presence of mold or radon in, on, or around the property.

Tenants have been given the opportunity to review this release agreement with their attorney or other advisors of their own choosing, and hereby acknowledge reading and understanding this release. Tenants also understand that the promises, representations, and warranties made in this release are a material inducement for the owners to enter into the agreement to rent the property to tenants.

Date: _____

_____   _____
Tenant's Signature   Tenant's Signature

_____   _____
Tenant's Printed Name   Tenant's Printed Name

Notice of Change
in Terms of Tenancy

TO _____, Tenant in Possession

_____

_____

     YOU ARE HEREBY NOTIFIED that the terms of tenancy under which you occupy the above-described premises are to be changed.

     Effective _____, _____, there will be the following changes:

_____

_____

_____

_____

     Dated this _____ day of _____, _____.

_____
                        Owner/Manager

This Notice was served by the Owner/Manager in the following manner (check those which apply):

    ( ) by personal delivery to the tenant,
    ( ) by leaving a copy with someone on the premises other than the tenant,
    ( ) by mailing,
    ( ) by posting.

Notice of Change
in Terms of Tenancy

(Rent)

TO _____, Tenant in Possession

_____

_____

YOU ARE HEREBY NOTIFIED that the terms of tenancy under which you occupy the above-described premises are to be changed.

Effective _____, _____, your rent will be increased by _____ per month, from _____ per month to _____ per month, payable in advance.

Dated this _____ day of _____, _____.

_____
Owner/Manager

This Notice was served by the Owner/Manager in the following manner (check those which apply):

( ) by personal delivery to the tenant,
( ) by leaving a copy with someone on the premises other than the tenant,
( ) by mailing,
( ) by posting.

Notice of Intention to Enter

TO _____, Tenant in Possession

_____

_____

YOU ARE HEREBY NOTIFIED that at or about _____ (a.m.) (p.m.)
on _____, _____, the Owner, Manager, Owner's
agent, or Owner's employees intend to enter the premises
identified above which you hold and occupy. They should need to
stay approximately _____ hour(s).

The purpose for entry is as follows:

_____

_____

You are not required to be on the premises to provide access.
Whoever comes to enter will first knock and after determining that
no one is available to answer, will enter using a passkey.

If the lock has been changed without proper notice and you
have not given management a duplicate key, a locksmith will be
called upon to open the door and rekey the locks. Your account
will be charged for these services, and you will be provided with
a new key.

This is intended to be a reasonable notice of at least twenty-
four (24) hours.

This Notice was personally served by the Owner/Manager at the
following time: _____(a.m.) (p.m.) and date: _____.

_____
Owner/Manager

Notice of Intention to Vacate

TO: _____

FROM: _____

Dated _____

    Please be advised that on _____ we intend to move from our residence at _____.

    We understand that our Rental Agreement calls for _____ days' notice before we move and that this is _____ days' notice. We understand that we are responsible for paying rent through the end of the notice period called for in the rental agreement or until another tenant approved by the management has moved in, whichever comes first.

    We understand that our deposits will be refunded within _____ days after we have moved out completely and returned our keys to the management, so long as we leave our dwelling reasonably clean and undamaged.

    Reasons for leaving: _____

_____

    Forwarding address: _____

    In accordance with our Rental Agreement, we agree to allow the management to show our dwelling to prospective tenants at any and all reasonable times.

                  Tenant _____

                  Tenant _____

Received by _____

Date _____

Notice to Pay Rent or Quit

TO: _____

_____

and all other tenants in possession of the premises described as:

_____

PLEASE TAKE NOTICE that the rent is now due and payable on the above-described premises which you currently hold and occupy.

Your rental account is delinquent in the amount itemized as follows:

Rental Period: _____ Rent due $_____

less partial payment of $_____

equals TOTAL BALANCE DUE of $_____

YOU ARE HEREBY REQUIRED to pay said rent in full within_____ days or to remove from and deliver up possession of the above-described premises, or legal proceedings will be instituted against you to recover possession of said premises, to declare the forfeiture of the Lease or Rental Agreement under which you occupy said premises and to recover rents and damages, together with court costs and attorney's fees, according to the terms of your Lease or Rental Agreement.

RENT MUST BE PAID IN FULL AND IN PERSON TO THE FOLLOWING PERSON OR ENTITY:

Name _____ Phone _____

Address where rent is to be paid _____

Usual days and times for payment of rent_____
Please phone in advance to make sure that someone will be available to accept payment.

OTHER REQUIRED WORDING, IF ANY:

Dated: _____   _____
                                                                    Owner/Manager

PROOF OF SERVICE (Complete this proof of service only AFTER tenants have been served.)
   I, the undersigned, being at least 18 years of age, declare under penalty of perjury that I served the above notice, of which this is a true copy, on the above-mentioned tenant(s) in possession in the manner(s) indicated below (NOTE: Methods two and three below may also require mailing):

☐ On _____, I handed the notice to the tenant(s).

☐ On _____, after attempting personal service, I handed the notice to a person of suitable age and discretion at the residence/business of the tenant(s).

☐ On _____, after attempting service in both manners indicated above, I posted the notice in a conspicuous place at the residence of the tenant(s).

☐ On _____, I sent a true copy of the notice in a sealed envelope via
   ☐ first-class   ☐ certified   ☐ registered mail with U.S.P.S. postage fully prepaid, addressed to the tenant(s) at his/her/their place of residence.

Executed on _____, at the City of _____,

County of _____, State of _____.

                                Served by _____

Notice to Perform Covenant

TO: _____

_____

and all other tenants in possession of the premises described as:

_____

PLEASE TAKE NOTICE that you have violated the following covenant(s) in your Lease or Rental Agreement:

_____

_____

_____

YOU ARE HEREBY REQUIRED within _____ days to perform the aforesaid covenant(s) or to deliver up possession of the above-described premises which you currently hold and occupy.

If you fail to do so, legal proceedings will be instituted against you to recover said premises and such damages as the law allows.

This notice is intended to be a _____ day notice to perform the aforesaid covenant(s). It is not intended to terminate or forfeit the Lease or Rental Agreement under which you occupy said premises. If, after legal proceedings, said premises are recovered from you, the owners will try to rent the premises for the best possible rent, giving you credit for sums received and holding you liable for any deficiencies arising during the term of your Lease or Rental Agreement.

Dated: _____   _____

Owner/Manager

PROOF OF SERVICE (Complete this proof of service only AFTER tenants have been served.)
  I, the undersigned, being at least 18 years of age, declare under penalty of perjury that I served the above notice, of which this is a true copy, on the above-mentioned tenant(s) in possession in the manner(s) indicated below (NOTE: Methods two and three below may also require mailing):

☐ On _____, I handed the notice to the tenant(s).

☐ On _____, after attempting personal service, I handed the notice to a person of suitable age and discretion at the residence/business of the tenant(s).

☐ On _____, after attempting service in both manners indicated above, I posted the notice in a conspicuous place at the residence of the tenant(s).

☐ On _____, I sent a true copy of the notice in a sealed envelope via
  ☐ first-class ☐ certified ☐ registered mail with U.S.P.S. postage fully prepaid, addressed to the tenant(s) at his/her/their place of residence.

Executed on _____, at the City of _____,

County of _____, State of _____.

Served by _____

Notice to Terminate Tenancy

TO: _____

_____

and all other tenants in possession of the premises described as:

_____

PLEASE TAKE NOTICE that you are hereby required within _____ days to remove from and deliver up possession of the above-described premises, which you currently hold and occupy.

This notice is intended for the purpose of terminating the Rental Agreement by which you now hold possession of the above-described premises, and should you fail to comply, legal proceedings will be instituted against you to recover possession, to declare said Rental Agreement forfeited, and to recover rents and damages for the period of the unlawful detention.

Dated: _____   _____

                                                                Owner/Manager

---

PROOF OF SERVICE (Complete this proof of service only AFTER tenants have been served.)
   I, the undersigned, being at least 18 years of age, declare under penalty of perjury that I served the above notice, of which this is a true copy, on the above-mentioned tenant(s) in possession in the manner(s) indicated below (NOTE: Methods two and three below may also require mailing):

☐ On _____, I handed the notice to the tenant(s).

☐ On _____, after attempting personal service, I handed the notice to a person of suitable age and discretion at the residence/business of the tenant(s).

☐ On _____, after attempting service in both manners indicated above, I posted the notice in a conspicuous place at the residence of the tenant(s).

☐ On _____, I sent a true copy of the notice in a sealed envelope via
   ☐ first-class ☐ certified ☐ registered mail with U.S.P.S. postage fully prepaid, addressed to the tenant(s) at his/her/their place of residence.

Executed on _____, at the City of _____,

County of _____, State of _____.

Served by _____

Other Receipts & Income

Added Appliances or Furniture, Deposit
Forfeits, Interest, Late Charges, Laundry,
Garages, etc.

Page _____

Property _____

Period _____

	Description of Income	January	February	March	April	May	
1							1
2							2
3							3
4							4
5							5
6							6
7							7
8							8
9							9
10							10
11							11
12							12
13							13
14							14
15							15
16							16
17							17
18							18
19							19
20							20
21							21
22							22
23							23
24							24
25							25
26							26
27							27
28							28
29							29
30							30
31							31
32							32
33							33
34							34
35							35
36							36
37							37
38							38
39							39
40							40
41							41

Other Receipts & Income

Page _____

	June	July	August	September	October	November	December	Year's Totals	
1									1
2									2
3									3
4									4
5									5
6									6
7									7
8									8
9									9
10									10
11									11
12									12
13									13
14									14
15									15
16									16
17									17
18									18
19									19
20									20
21									21
22									22
23									23
24									24
25									25
26									26
27									27
28									28
29									29
30									30
31									31
32									32
33									33
34									34
35									35
36									36
37									37
38									38
39									39
40									40
41									41

Payment Pledge

Dear Landlord/Landlady:

    On or before _____, I promise to pay you $_____ for rent and other charges now owing on the dwelling which I rent from you located at _____.

    I expect to be receiving sufficient funds to pay you from the following sources:

Name	Address	Phone	Amount Expected

    Should you wish to, you have my authorization to verify these sources.

    If I fail to honor this pledge, I understand that I will be evicted and that this pledge will be used against me as evidence of my bad faith in paying what I owe.

    ____ I acknowledge receipt of a Notice to Pay Rent or Quit as required by law to begin eviction proceedings. I understand that the Notice may show a balance owed which is different from that given above because a Notice to Pay Rent or Quit can demand only delinquent rent. I also understand that the period mentioned in this Notice is being extended to the date given above, at which time I promise to pay you what I owe. If I fail to pay on or before that date, you have the right to continue the legal eviction procedure against me without having to serve me another Notice to Pay Rent or Quit. I have already been served. I am being given the extra time to pay only as a courtesy and only this once.

Signed _____

Dated _____

Payroll Record

Property _____

Employee _____ Social Sec.No. _____

Pay Rate _____ Exemptions _____ Married ☐ Single ☐

Period	Base Wages	Lod-ging	Fed Whldg	Employee FICA	Medcare	Employer FICA	Medcare	State Disblty	State Whldg	Other	Net	Chk No
1												1
2												2
3												3
4												4
5												5
6												6
7												7
8												8
9												9
10												10
11												11
12												12
13												13
14												14
15												15
16												16
17												17
18												18
19												19
20												20
21												21
22												22
23												23
24												24
25												25
26												26
27												27
28												28
29												29
30												30
31												31
32												32
33												33
34												34
35												35
36												36
37												37
38												38
39												39
40												40
41												41

Pet Agreement

Dated _____

(Addendum to Rental Agreement)

   This agreement is attached to and forms a part of the Rental Agreement dated _____ between _____, Owners, and _____, Tenants.

   Tenants desire to keep a pet named _____ and described as _____ in the dwelling they occupy under the Rental Agreement referred to above, and because this Agreement specifically prohibits keeping pets without the Owners' permission, Tenants agree to the following terms and conditions in exchange for this permission:

1) Tenants agree to keep their pet under control at all times.
2) Tenants agree to keep their pet restrained, but not tethered, when it is outside their dwelling.
3) Tenants agree to adhere to local ordinances, including leash and licensing requirements.
4) Tenants agree not to leave their pet unattended for any unreasonable periods.
5) Tenants agree to clean up after their pet and to dispose of their pet's waste properly and quickly.
6) Tenants agree not to leave food or water for their pet or any other animal outside their dwelling where it will attract other animals.
7) Tenants agree to keep their pet from being unnecessarily noisy or aggressive and causing any annoyance or discomfort to others and will remedy immediately any complaints made through the Owners or Manager.
8) Tenants agree to provide their pet with regular health care, to include inoculations as recommended.
9) Tenants agree to provide their pet with an identification tag.
10) Tenants agree to get rid of their pet's offspring within eight weeks of birth.
11) Tenants agree to pay immediately for any damage, loss, or expense caused by their pet, and in addition, they will add $_____ to their security/cleaning deposit, any of which may be used for cleaning, repairs, or delinquent rent when Tenants vacate. This added deposit, or what remains of it when pet damages have been assessed, will be returned to Tenants within _____ days after they have proved that they no longer keep this pet.
12) Tenants agree that this Agreement applies only to the specific pet described above and that no other pet may be substituted.
13) Tenants agree to furnish Owners with a picture of their pet.
14) Tenants agree that Owners reserve the right to revoke permission to keep the pet should Tenants break this Agreement.
15) Tenants agree to purchase a dog-bite insurance policy if required by Owners and to supply Owners evidence of a current policy.

Owner _____   Tenant _____

By _____   Tenant _____

Page _____ of _____

Property Viewing
& Keys Agreement

With my signature below, I hereby acknowledge receipt of the key(s) to the dwelling located at _____

_____ .

I intend to use the key(s) for the express purpose of viewing the dwelling to consider whether it is suitable for me to rent, and I will neither disturb nor remove anything found there.

As a courtesy, I will report to the owner/manager whatever appears to be amiss at the dwelling.

I have given the owner/manager, whose acknowledgment appears below, a deposit of $_____, and also a valuable personal item consisting of _____,
both of which will be returned to me when I return the key(s).

I promise to return the key(s) by _____ (a.m.) (p.m.) TODAY to the owner/manager at EITHER--

     ( ) the same place where I picked them up OR

     ( ) the following place _____.

Should I fail to do so, the owner/manager is entitled to keep the deposit to pay for changing the locks on the dwelling but will return my valuable personal item to me when asked.

I understand that this agreement gives me no occupancy rights whatsoever and that I must complete a rental application if I want to be considered as an applicant to rent this dwelling.

Signed _____

Current Address _____

Current Telephone Number _____

Date & Time _____

Acknowledged by _____
                               Owner/Manager

Date: _____

To: _____

We appreciate your applying to rent a dwelling from us. We regret to inform you that you will need to continue looking for a place to live somewhere else for the following reasons:

CIRCUMSTANCES

[ ] Dwelling rented to previously approved applicant

[ ] Unsigned application   [ ] Incomplete application

[ ] Discrepancies on application

CREDIT REPORT (If items here are checked, see attachment.)

[ ] Credit not verifiable   [ ] Bankruptcy filed

[ ] Judgments, garnishments, liens   [ ] Slow pay

[ ] Account(s) sent for collection   [ ] Low credit score

INCOME/ASSETS

[ ] Income not verifiable   [ ] Insufficient income

[ ] Assets not verifiable   [ ] Insufficient assets

EMPLOYMENT HISTORY

[ ] Employment not verifiable   [ ] Unsteady employment

[ ] Temporary employment

TENANCY HISTORY

[ ] Tenancy not verifiable   [ ] Eviction on record

[ ] Late payments   [ ] Insufficient funds checks

[ ] Agreement violation(s)   [ ] Lack of cooperation

PERSONAL REFERENCES

[ ] References not verifiable   [ ] Negative reference

OTHER REASONS

_____

Your application will remain in our files for a minimum of two years. If you would like to discuss it or our reasons above, please contact us for an appointment.

We wish you good luck in finding an even better place to live.

Sincerely,

RENT PAYMENT DETAILS

These rent payment details apply to the tenancy formalized in the Rental Agreement dated _____ between _____, Owners, and _____, Tenants, who occupy the rental dwelling located at _____.

Rent Payment Dates: Due date _____; late date _____

Prompt Payment Policy
[ ] Fee of $_____ charged when payment NOT RECEIVED by LATE DATE
[ ] Discount of $_____ given when payment RECEIVED by LATE DATE
[ ] Rebate of $_____ given when payment RECEIVED by LATE DATE

Rent Statement Delivery
[ ] Statement mailed to address above or to this alternative
    address _____
[ ] Statement sent to Tenants' email address below
[ ] Statement faxed to Tenants' fax number below
[ ] Statement not provided
[ ] Other _____

Rent Collection
Rent payment shall be made in the following way:
[ ] Delivered to Owner's office or office of Owner's Agent
[ ] Picked up by Owner or Owner's Agent at Tenants' dwelling
[ ] Mailed to Owner's office
[ ] Electronic transfer from Tenants' account
[ ] Electronic transfer via payment processor _____
[ ] Other _____

Rent Payment
Rent payment shall be made in the following form:
[ ] Cash [ ] Personal check [ ] Money order [ ] Cashiers check
[ ] Electronic funds transfer to Owner's account (nine-digit routing
    number) _____

Rent Receipt Delivery
Owners shall acknowledge receipt of payment in the following way(s):
[ ] Receipt held for pickup at _____
[ ] Receipt mailed to address above or to this alternative
    address _____
[ ] Receipt sent to Tenants' email address below
[ ] Receipt faxed to Tenants' fax number below
[ ] Receipt not provided
[ ] Other _____

Notice of Nonpayment of Rent
Owners shall notify Tenants of missed rent due date as follows:
[ ] Notice sent to Tenants' email address below (courtesy)
[ ] Notice mailed to address above (courtesy)
[ ] Notice delivered to Tenants (begins eviction proceedings)

Best ways to contact Tenants (priority number in brackets)
[ ] Email _____
[ ] Cell phone _____   [ ] Home phone _____
[ ] Work phone _____   [ ] Fax number _____

Best ways to contact Owner (priority number in brackets)
[ ] Email _____
[ ] Cell phone _____   [ ] Home phone _____
[ ] Office phone _____   [ ] Fax number _____

We acknowledge a familiarity with the rent payment details given above.

_____   _____
Date   Tenant(s)

_____   _____
Date   Owner

461

Rental Agreement

Dated: _____

Agreement between Owners: _____
and Tenants: _____
for a dwelling located at: _____

[Initial ONE of the boxes below to indicate whether this Agreement is month-to-month or fixed term.]

☐ **Month-to-Month Agreement**—Tenants agree to rent this dwelling on a month-to-month basis beginning _____.

☐ **Fixed-Term Agreement (Lease)**—Tenants agree to lease this dwelling for a fixed term of _____, beginning _____ and ending _____.
Upon expiration, this Agreement shall become a month-to-month agreement AUTOMATICALLY, UNLESS either Tenants or Owners notify the other party in writing at least thirty days prior to expiration that they do not wish this Agreement to continue on any basis.

Rent—Tenants agree to rent this dwelling for $_____ per _____, payable in advance. The first month's rent is $_____.

Rent Due/Late Consequences—Rent is due on the _____. It is late on the _____. Owners expect to RECEIVE the rent BEFORE the late date. Should exceptional circumstances prevent prompt payment, _____.

Returned Checks—If, FOR ANY REASON, a check used by Tenants to pay Owners is returned without having been paid, Tenants will pay a returned check charge of $_____ AND take whatever other consequences there might be in making a late payment. After the second time that a Tenants' check is returned, Tenants must thereafter secure a cashier's check or money order for payment of rent.

Form of Payment—Tenants agree to pay rent in the form of a personal check, a cashier's check, or a money order made out to _____.

Rent Payment Procedure—Tenants agree to pay their rent in the following way:
_____

Deposits—Tenants agree to deposit with the Owners the sum of $_____, payable before they occupy the premises. Owners may withhold from these deposits only what is reasonably necessary to cover the following tenant defaults: 1) damages to the dwelling; 2) certain cleaning costs following Tenants' departure; and 3) unpaid rent and various other accrued and unpaid charges. Tenants may not apply any part of these deposits to their last month's rent.

Refund of Tenants' Deposits—Within _____ days after Tenants have moved out completely, Owners shall provide a written accounting of the disposition of the Tenants' deposits and shall at the same time return all deposits remaining.

Utilities/Services—Tenants agree to pay all utilities and services with the exception of the following which Owners agree to pay:_____

Occupants—In addition to the Tenants mentioned above, only the following persons may live in this dwelling:
_____
No one else may live there, even temporarily, without Owners' prior written permission.

Guests—Tenants may house any single guest for a maximum period of fourteen days every six months or for whatever other period of time the law allows. Provided that they maintain a separate residence, nurses or maids required to care for Tenants during an illness are excepted from this provision.

Subletting and Assignment—Tenants shall not sublet the entire premises or any part of the premises, nor shall they assign this Agreement to anyone else without first obtaining the Owners' written permission. Owners shall not withhold permission unreasonably.

Pets—Tenants have received permission to house the following pet(s) on the premises:

_____

Tenants may house no other pet of any kind on the premises, even temporarily, without first obtaining Owners' written permission. "Pets" includes, but is not limited to, both warm- and cold-blooded animals, such as dogs, cats, fish, hamsters, rats, birds, snakes, lizards, and insects. "Pets" does not include animals trained to serve the handicapped, such as seeing-eye dogs, hearing dogs, or service dogs. These animals may be housed on the premises so long as they are in the direct service of those they were trained to serve and so long as Owners are notified in advance in writing of the circumstances.

Liquid-filled Furniture—Tenants agree not to keep any liquid-filled furniture in this dwelling without first obtaining Owners' written permission.

Vehicles—Tenants agree to park their vehicles in assigned spaces and to keep those spaces clean of oil drippings. Tenants agree to keep no more than _____ vehicle(s) on the premises. Vehicle(s) must be both operable and currently licensed. Tenants agree to advise their visitors about parking and to take responsibility for where their visitors park. Only those motorcycles which have exhaust muffling comparable to that of a passenger car are allowed. Only those self-propelled recreational vehicles which are used for regular personal transportation are allowed. Tenants agree not to park boats, recreational trailers, utility trailers, and the like on the premises without first obtaining Owners' written permission. Tenants agree not to repair their vehicle(s) on the premises if such repairs will take longer than a single day unless the vehicle is kept in an enclosed garage.

Appliances—Although the following appliances are presently in the dwelling:

_____

the use of these appliances is not included in the rent. If Tenants wish to use these appliances, they agree to assume all responsibility for care and maintenance. If Tenants wish to use their own appliances, they may request that the owner's appliances be removed from the premises.

Tenant Inspection—Tenants have inspected the dwelling and its contents and agree that they are in satisfactory order, as are the electrical, plumbing, and heating systems.

Notification of Serious Building Problems—Tenants agree to notify the Owners immediately upon first discovering any signs of serious building problems such as a crack in the foundation, a tilting porch, a crack in the plaster or stucco, moisture in the ceiling, buckling sheetrock or siding, a leaky roof, a spongy floor, a leaky water heater, or termite activity.

Reasonable Time for Repairs—Upon being notified by Tenants that there is some building defect which is hazardous to life, health, or safety, Owners shall undertake repairs as soon as possible. Should there be a delay of more than seventy-two (72) hours in making the repairs, due to a difficulty in scheduling the work or obtaining parts or for any other reason beyond the Owners' control, Owners agree to keep Tenants informed about the progress of the work.

Windows—Except for those windows which are noted in writing as being cracked or broken when Tenants move in, Tenants agree to be responsible for any windows which become cracked or broken in their dwelling while they live there. Tenants may repair the windows themselves if they can do the work in a professional manner. Otherwise, they may hire a glazier or submit a maintenance request to Owners. If they submit a maintenance request, Owners will charge them no more for the work than the least expensive written bid for the work which Tenants can obtain.

Drain Stoppages—As of the date of this Agreement, Owners warrant that the dwelling's sewage drains are in good working order and that they will accept the normal household waste for which they were designed. They will not accept things such as paper diapers, sanitary napkins, tampons, children's toys, wads of toilet paper, balls of hair, grease, oil, table scraps, clothing, rags, sand, dirt, rocks, or newspapers. Tenants agree to pay for clearing the drains of any and all stoppages except those which the plumber who is called to clear the stoppage will attest in writing were caused by defective plumbing, tree roots, or acts of God.

Trash—Tenants agree to dispose of their ordinary household trash by placing it into a receptacle for periodic collection. They agree to dispose of their extraordinary household trash, such as Christmas trees, damaged furniture, broken appliances, and the like, by compacting it so that it will fit inside their trash receptacle or by hauling it to the dump themselves or by paying someone else to haul it away.

Outside Placement—Owners reserve the right to place trash receptacles, portable storage units, and the like wherever convenient on the premises. Owners further reserve the right to construct property improvements above or below the ground anywhere on the premises so long as they conform to all building codes.

Damage—Tenants agree to pay for repairs of all damage which they or their guests have caused.

Locks—Tenants agree that they will not change the locks on any door or mailbox without first obtaining Owners' written permission. Having obtained permission, they agree to pay for changing the locks themselves and to provide the Owners with one duplicate key per lock.

Lockouts—Should Tenants lock themselves out of their dwelling and be unable to gain access through their own resources, they may call upon a professional locksmith or the manager to let them in. In either case, they are responsible for payment of the charges and/or damages involved. Management charges a fee of $15 for providing this service between the hours of 8 a.m. and 6 p.m., Monday through Saturday, excepting holidays, and a fee of $25 at other times. This fee is due and payable when the service is provided.

Landscaping—[*This paragraph applies only if it is initialed by both parties.*] Tenants agree to maintain the existing landscaping by watering, weeding, fertilizing, mowing, and shaping it as necessary.

Alterations, Decorations, and Repairs—Except as provided by law, Tenants agree not to alter or decorate their dwelling without first obtaining Owners' written permission. Decorations include painting and wallpapering. Further, Tenants agree not to repair their dwelling or anything belonging to the Owners without first obtaining Owners' written permission unless such repairs cost less than one hundred dollars ($100), and Tenants agree to pay for them. Tenants shall hold Owners harmless for any mechanics liens or proceedings which Tenants cause. When approved by Owners, Tenants' plans for alterations and decorations shall bear a determination regarding ownership. If Tenants are able to convince Owners that Tenants can remove the alterations or decorations and restore that part of their dwelling to its original condition, then Owners may grant Tenants the right to remove them. Otherwise, any alterations or decorations made by Tenants become the property of Owners when Tenants vacate.

Painting—Owners reserve the right to determine when the dwelling will be painted unless there is any law to the contrary.

Access—Owners recognize that Tenants have a right to privacy and wish to observe that right scrupulously. At certain times, however, Owners, their employees, or agents may have to gain access to the Tenants' dwelling for purposes of showing it to prospective Tenants, purchasers, lenders, or others or for repairs, inspection, or maintenance. When seeking access under ordinary circumstances, Owners will schedule entry between the hours of 8 a.m. and 8 p.m., Monday through Saturday, excepting holidays, and Owners will provide Tenants reasonable notice of twenty-four hours, or less than twenty-four hours notice with Tenants' concurrence. In emergencies, there will be no notice.

Peace and Quiet—Tenants are entitled to the quiet enjoyment of their own dwelling, and their neighbors are entitled to the same. Tenants agree that they will refrain from making loud noises and disturbances, that they will keep down the volume of their music and broadcast programs at all times so as not to disturb other people's peace and quiet, and that they will not install wind chimes.

Telephone—If and when Tenants install a telephone in their dwelling, they will furnish Owners with the number within five calendar days. When divulging the number, Tenants shall advise Owners whether the number is listed or unlisted. If it is unlisted, Owners agree to take reasonable precautions to keep it from falling into the hands of third parties.

Prolonged Absences—Tenants agree that they will notify Owners whenever they plan to be absent from their dwelling for more than ten days.

Business Use—Tenants agree to use this dwelling as their personal residence. They agree to conduct no business on the premises without first obtaining Owners' written permission.

Lawful Use—Tenants agree that they will not themselves engage in any illegal activities on the premises nor will they allow others to engage in any illegal activities on the premises insofar as they have the power to stop such activities.

Insurance—Owners have obtained insurance to cover fire damage to the building itself and liability insurance to cover certain personal injuries occurring as a result of property defects or owner negligence. Owners' insurance does not cover Tenants' possessions or Tenants' negligence. Tenants shall obtain a Tenants' insurance policy to cover damage to or loss of their own possessions, as well as losses resulting from their negligence. Tenants agree to show Owners evidence of such a policy within one month from the date of this Agreement.

Insurance Considerations—Tenants agree that they will do nothing to the premises nor keep anything on the premises which will result in an increase in the Owners' insurance policy or an endangering of the premises. Neither will they allow anyone else to do so.

Fire or Casualty Damage—During any time when the dwelling cannot be used because of fire or casualty damage, Tenants are not responsible for payment of rent. Should a portion of the dwelling become unusable due to fire or casualty damage, Tenants are not responsible for payment of rent on that portion. In either case, Owners reserve the right to decide whether the dwelling is usable and what portions are usable. Owners are not responsible for repairing or replacing any improvements made by Tenants if those improvements are damaged. Should the fire or casualty damage have been caused by Tenants' own action or neglect, they shall have not be relieved of the responsibility for payment of rent, and they shall also bear the full responsibility for repair of the damage.

Rules and Regulations—Owners' existing rules and regulations, if any, shall be signed by Tenants, attached to this Agreement, and incorporated into it. Owners may adopt other rules and regulations at a later time provided that they have a legitimate purpose, not modify Tenants' rights substantially, and not become effective without notice of at least two (2) weeks.

Service of Process—Every Tenant who signs this Agreement agrees to be the agent of the other Tenants and occupants of this dwelling and is both authorized and required to accept, on behalf of the other Tenants and occupants, service of summons and other notices relative to the tenancy.

Identity of Manager—The person who is responsible for managing this dwelling and is authorized to accept legal service on Owners' behalf is _____ whose address is

_____.

Changes in Terms of Tenancy—[*This paragraph applies only when this Agreement is or has become a month-to-month agreement.*] Owners shall advise Tenants of any changes in terms of tenancy with advance notice of at least _____ days. Changes may include notices of termination, rent adjustments, or other reasonable changes in the terms of this Agreement.

Notice of Intention to Vacate—[*This paragraph applies only when this Agreement is or has become a month-to-month agreement.*] When Tenants have decided to vacate the premises, they will give Owners written notice of their intentions at least _____ days prior to their departure, and they will give an exact date when they expect to be moved out completely.

Holding Over—If Tenants remain on the premises following the date of their termination of tenancy, they are "holding over" and become liable for "rental damages" equaling one/thirtieth of the amount of their then current monthly rent for every day they hold over.

Possession—Owners shall endeavor to deliver possession to Tenants by the commencement date of this Agreement. Should Owners be unable to do so, they shall not be held liable for any damages Tenants suffer as a consequence, nor shall this Agreement be considered void unless Owners are unable to deliver possession within ten (10) days following the commencement date. Tenants' responsibility to pay rent shall begin when they receive possession.

Sale of the Dwelling—If Owners sell this dwelling or otherwise transfer its Ownership to another party, they shall have the right to terminate this Agreement by giving Tenants written notice of at least sixty days, notwithstanding any conflicting occupancy rights Tenants might have under a fixed-term agreement. Should Tenants have conflicting occupancy rights guaranteed them by law, however, those legal rights shall prevail.

Illegal Provisions Not Affecting Legal Provisions—Whatever item in this Agreement is found to be contrary to any local, state, or federal law shall be considered null and void, just as if it had never appeared in the Agreement, and it shall not affect the validity of any other item in the Agreement.

Non-Waiver—Should either Owners or Tenants waive their rights to enforce any breach of this Agreement, that waiver shall be considered temporary and not a continuing waiver of any later breach. Although Owners may know when accepting rent that Tenants are violating one or more of this Agreement's conditions, Owners in accepting the rent are in no way waiving their rights to enforce the breach. Neither Owners nor Tenants shall have waived their rights to enforce any breach unless they agree to a waiver in writing.

References in Wording—Plural references made to the parties involved in this Agreement may also be singular, and singular references may be plural. These references also apply to Owners' and Tenants' heirs, executors, administrators, or successors, as the case may be.

Application Part of Agreement—The rental application Tenants submitted to rent this dwelling forms a part of this Agreement. Falsified information on the application shall be considered a breach of this Agreement.

Entire Agreement—As written, this Agreement constitutes the entire agreement between the Tenants and Owners. They have made no further promises of any kind to one another, nor have they reached any other understandings, either verbal or written.

Consequences—Violation of any part of this Agreement or nonpayment of rent when due shall be cause for eviction under appropriate sections of the applicable code.

Trial by Judge—[*This paragraph applies only if it is initialed by both parties.*] Should any aspect of this Agreement or tenancy be litigated in civil court, Owners and Tenants agree to waive their rights to a trial by jury and have the matter tried by a judge.

Legal Service's Fees—If either party to this Agreement shall bring a cause of action against the other party for enforcement of the Agreement, the prevailing party [*cross out the alternative which does not apply and initial the beginning of this paragraph*] (shall) (shall not) recover reasonable legal service's fees involved.

Other—_____

_____

Acknowledgment—Tenants hereby acknowledge that they have read this Agreement, understand it, agree to it, and have been given a copy.

_____   _____
Owner   Tenant

_____   _____
BY Person authorized to represent Owners   Tenant

Rental Agreement—Page 5 of ___

Rental Agreement

Dated_____

(Month-to-Month)

Agreement between_____, Owners, and _____, Tenants, for a dwelling located at _____.
Tenants agree to rent this dwelling on a month-to-month basis for $_____ per month, payable in advance on the _____ day of every calendar month to Owners or their Agent*, _____, whose address is

_____
When rent is paid on or before the _____ day of the calendar month, Owners will give Tenants a (discount) (rebate) of $_____.
    The first month's rent for this dwelling is $_____.
    The security/cleaning deposit on this dwelling is $_____. It is refundable if Tenants leave the dwelling reasonably clean and undamaged.
    Tenants will give ___ days' notice in writing before they move and will be responsible for paying rent through the end of this notice period or until another tenant approved by the Owners has moved in, whichever comes first.
    Owners will refund all deposits due within ___ days after Tenants have moved out completely and returned their keys.
    Only the following ___ persons and ___ pets are to live in this dwelling:
_____
Without Owners' prior written permission, no other persons may live there, and no other pets may stay there, even temporarily, nor may the dwelling be sublet or used for business purposes.
    Use of the following is included in the rent: _____
_____
    Remarks: _____
_____
TENANTS AGREE TO THE FOLLOWING:
 1) to accept the dwelling "as is," having already inspected it.
 2) to keep yards and garbage areas clean.
 3) to keep from making loud or bothersome noises and disturbances and to play music and broadcast programs at all times so as not to disturb other people's peace and quiet.
 4) not to paint or alter the dwelling without first getting Owners' written permission.
 5) to park their motor vehicle in assigned space and to keep that space clean of oil drippings and grease.
 6) not to repair their motor vehicle on the premises (unless it is in an enclosed garage) if such repairs will take longer than a single day.
 7) to allow Owners to inspect the dwelling, work on it, or show it to prospective tenants at any and all reasonable times.
 8) not to keep any liquid-filled furniture in this dwelling.
 9) to pay rent by check or money order made out to Owners. (Checks must be good when paid or applicable late-payment consequences will apply.)
10) to pay for repairs of all damage, including drain stoppages, they or their guests have caused.
11) to pay for any windows broken in their dwelling while they live there.

    Violation of any part of this Agreement or nonpayment of rent when due shall be cause for eviction under applicable code sections. The prevailing party (shall) (shall not) recover reasonable legal services fees involved.
    Tenants hereby acknowledge that they have read this Agreement, understand it, agree to it, and have been given a copy.

Owner_____ Tenant_____

*By_____ Tenant_____
*Person authorized to accept legal service on Owners' behalf

Rental Application for (address)_____

	Home	Cell
Name_____	Phone_____	Phone_____
Email	Social Security	Driver License
Address_____	No._____	No._____

Present Address_____

How long at   Reason for

this address?_____ Rent $_____ moving_____

Owner/Manager_____ Phone_____

Previous Address_____

How long at   Reason for

this address?_____ Rent $_____ moving_____

Owner/Manager_____ Phone_____

Name of every person to live with you, even if only temporarily:

_____

_____

Any pets?_____ Describe_____ Waterbed?_____

Present
Employer_____ Phone_____

How long with this

employer?_____ Supervisor_____ Phone_____

Previous
Employer_____ Phone_____

How long with this

employer?_____ Supervisor_____ Phone_____

Current Gross Income Per Month (before deductions) $_____

Sources and amounts of other income (other than present employment income above):

_____

_____

Amount of alimony and/or child support you receive $_____ or pay $_____

Savings		Account No.
Account: Bank_____ Branch_____		(Last 4 Digits)_____
Checking		Account No.
Account: Bank_____ Branch_____		(Last 4 Digits)_____

Major Credit	Account No.	Balance	Monthly
Card_____	(Last 4 Digits)_____	Owed_____	Pmt._____
Credit	Account No.	Balance	Monthly
Reference_____	(Last 4 Digits)_____	Owed_____	Pmt._____
Credit	Account No.	Balance	Monthly
Reference_____	(Last 4 Digits)_____	Owed_____	Pmt._____

(Use back to explain any "yes" answers to questions below.) HAVE YOU..ever filed
bankruptcy?_____ ever been evicted?_____ ever been convicted of a felony?_____

Vehicle(s)
Make(s)_____ Model(s)_____ Year(s)_____ License(s)_____

Personal
Reference_____ Address_____ Phone_____

Contact in
Emergency_____ Address_____ Phone_____

I declare that the statements above are true and correct. I authorize verification of
my references and credit as they relate to my tenancy and to future rent collections.

Date_____ Signed_____

Verified: SSN___ DL/ID___ CurTenancy___ Prev___ Credit___ Inc___ PersRefs___ By_____

RENTAL APPLICATION INSTRUCTIONS

We appreciate your interest in the rental dwelling we currently have available. Because we want to rent this dwelling to people who are considerate of their neighbors, clean in their living habits, capable of paying the rent, and prompt in paying their bills, we use a rental application to help us determine whether our applicants meet these qualifications.

In order for you to rent from us, you must complete a rental application. We want you to know how to complete the application we use, and we also want you to know what our company does with your application.

When filling out the application, put something in every blank, even if you have to put "None" or "N.A." in some blanks. Try to write so that your entries fit in the spaces provided. If they don't, continue them on the back side. Take your time and look up any information called for on the application which you're at all uncertain about. Don't guess.

Make sure that you read the declaration just above the signature line and agree to it before you sign your name to the application. It states that the information on your application is true and correct, and it authorizes us to verify your references and your credit as they relate to your tenancy now and to your paying rent in the future.

When you have completed your application, read it over carefully to make sure that it is accurate, complete, and legible. Look especially for misspellings and transposed numbers.

Once we receive your application, we verify as much of it as we can. If you look at the last line on the application itself, you will notice all of the things we verify. We verify your Social Security number (SSN), your driver's license (DL) or personal identification number (ID), your current tenancy (CurTenancy), your previous tenancy (Prev), your credit (Credit), your income (Inc), and your personal references (PersRefs). When we have verified each of these items, we put a check mark next to its abbreviation.

We verify this information in a variety of ways. We look at your Social Security card or some other evidence of your Social Security number. We look at your actual driver's license or some other official picture identification which you use whenever you cash a check. We call your current landlord or manager to ask whether the information you put on your application is correct about how long you've been at your current address, how much you've been paying in rent, and why you are moving. Then we call your previous landlord or manager and ask the same questions about your previous tenancy.

At the same time that we order a credit report, we also order an eviction report and a bad check report. The credit report tells us whether you pay your bills on time. The eviction report tells us whether you have ever been evicted and why. The bad check report tells us whether you write bad checks.

Next, we call whoever can verify your source of income to determine how much you generally receive from that source every month and how long you have been receiving it.

Finally, we call your personal references to verify that they know you and that we have their correct addresses and phone numbers so that we can contact them should anything happen to you.

That's the procedure we follow when we check applications.

Now, if you suspect we might discover a "skeleton in your closet" when we check your application and you want to tell us about it before we go to all the trouble of checking you out, please feel free to do so. We'd be glad to talk with you about it. Otherwise, we will expect no surprises when we're checking you out and hope that we will soon be doing business together as landlord and tenant.

Form E-3	RENTAL INCOME AND EXPENSE		YEAR

NAME(S) OF TAXPAYERS		SOC. SEC. NUMBER	

PROPERTY LOCATION & DESCRIPTION	GROSS INCOME
Property A	
Property B	
Property C	
Property D	
Property E	
Property F	
Property G	
TOTAL GROSS INCOME	

EXPENSES	A	B	C	D	E	F	G	Totals
Interest								
Taxes, Licenses								
Insurance								
Utilities								
Serv,Rep,Maint.								
Merch., Supplies								
Payroll								
Misc. Expenses								
Other:								
Subtotal								
% Business Use								
Subtotals								
Deprec. (D-1)								*
Deprec. (SD)								*
Totals								

*Sum of D-1 and SD Depreciation Totals *

Request for Verification of Deposit

Instructions: Landlord—Complete items 1 through 7. Have applicant(s) complete item 8. Forward directly to depository named in item 1. Depository—Please complete items 9 through 15 and return DIRECTLY to landlord named in item 2.

Part I—Request

1. To (Name and Address of Depository)	2. From (Name and Address of Landlord)

3. Signature of Landlord/Manager	4. Title	5. Date

6. INFORMATION TO BE VERIFIED

Type of Account	Account in Name of	Account Number	Balance
			$
			$
			$
			$

To Depository: I/We have applied to rent a dwelling and stated in the rental application that the balance on deposit with you is as shown above. You are authorized to verify this information and to supply the landlord identified above with the information requested in items 9 through 12. Your response is solely a matter of courtesy for which no responsibility is attached to your institution or any of your officers.

7. Name and Address of Applicant(s)	8. Signature of Applicant(s)

To Be Completed by Depository

Part II–Verification of Depository

9. Deposit Accounts of Applicant(s)

Type of Account	Account Number	Current Balance	Average Balance for Previous Two Months	Date Opened
		$	$	
		$	$	
		$	$	
		$	$	

10. Bank Card Accounts of Applicant(s)

Type of Bank Card	Account Number	Current Balance	Average Monthly Payment	Expiration Date
		$	$	
		$	$	

11. Loans Outstanding to Applicant(s)

Loan Number	Date of Loan	Original Amount	Current Balance	Installments		Secured by	No. Late Pmts.
		$	$	$	per		
		$	$	$	per		

12. Please include any additional information which may be of assistance in determination of credit worthiness. (Please include information on loans paid-in-full in item 11 above.)

13. Signature of Depository	14. Title	15. Date

The confidentiality of the information you have furnished will be preserved except where disclosure of this information is required by applicable law. The form is to be transmitted directly to the landlord and is not to be transmitted through the applicant(s) or any other party.

Roommate Agreement   Dated _____

(Addendum to Rental Agreement)

   This Agreement amends, is incorporated into, and forms a part of the Rental Agreement dated _____ between _____, Owners, and _____, Tenants.

   Tenants, also known here as "Roommates," desire to rent the premises on a "roommates arrangement." Owners agree to this arrangement under the following terms and conditions:

ROOMMATE APPROVAL AND SUBSTITUTION--Every person who wishes to become a Roommate under this Agreement, whether as an original Roommate or as a substituted Roommate, must first submit a Rental Application and be approved by Owners in writing. Owners, at their option, may require substituted Roommates to sign the existing Rental Agreement or may require an entirely new agreement to be signed by the substituted Roommates and the remaining Roommates. Upon substitution of Roommates, Owners may elect to increase the deposit.

FINANCIAL RESPONSIBILITY--Each Roommate agrees to be jointly and severally liable to the Owners for the entire rent and the entire amount of any other charges incurred under the Rental Agreement.

DEPOSITS--Roommates agree to pay deposits to Owners in the form of a single certified check or money order. Owners will hold all deposits until the entire dwelling has been vacated completely. Owners may make deposit refunds in the form of a single check made payable jointly to all Roommates with rights to the deposits. This check and the itemized accounting of deposit deductions may be sent to any one of the Roommates with rights to the deposits.

DEPARTING ROOMMATES--Roommates who move out while this Agreement is in effect continue to have financial responsibility under this Agreement unless Owners release them from this responsibility in writing or unless they are replaced by substituted Roommates approved by Owners. Upon being relieved of financial liability, departing Roommates relinquish all rights to the deposits.

MAXIMUM NUMBER OF ROOMMATES ALLOWED--Without the prior written approval of Owners, Roommates may at no time exceed ____ in number.

GUESTS--Tenants may house any single guest for a maximum period of fourteen days every six months or for whatever other period of time the law allows. Guests may at no time exceed ____ in number.

COMMUNICATIONS--Whenever Owners give a notice to one Roommate, it shall be considered as having been communicated to all Roommates. Whenever one Roommate gives a notice to the Owners, it shall be considered as having been communicated from all Roommates.

Owner _____   Roommate _____

By _____   Roommate _____

                                    Roommate _____

Page _____ of _____

SITE VISIT   Property Name:_____ Date:_____

Needs Attention:_____

_____

_____

_____

Safety Concerns:_____

_____

_____

_____

Comments:_____

_____

_____

_____

Paperwork/Logbook:_____

_____

Looks Good:_____

_____

_____

Vacancies (circle if ready to rent):_____

_____

Visitor's Followup:_____

_____

_____

Visited by:_____ Time:_____ Expenses:_____

STORAGE AGREEMENT
THIS CONTRACT LIMITS OWNER'S LIABILITY--READ IT

PARTIES--THIS AGREEMENT, dated _____, is by and between

_____, "Owner," and

_____, "Occupant,"

for storage of a vehicle, boat, trailer, or other personal property located at the following address:

_____.

OCCUPANT'S ADDRESS: _____

OCCUPANT'S ALTERNATIVE ADDRESS: _____

[ ]   INDOOR STORAGE--Unit: _____

[ ]   OUTDOOR STORAGE--Personal Property to be Stored--

Type: _____

Description (Color, etc.): _____

Dimensions: _____

Identification Number: _____

License Number (State, too): _____

Legal Owner (Name, Address, Phone): _____

_____

Registered Owner (Name, Address, Phone): _____

_____

TERM--Occupant agrees to rent the space for storage on a month-to-month basis beginning _____.

RENT--Occupant agrees to pay Owner, without deduction, the sum of $_____ per month, payable in advance, on the first (1st) day of each month of the term hereof. Rent paid more than ___ days following the due date is subject to a late fee of ten percent (10%) of the month's rent. Under no circumstances will prepaid rents be refunded.

CONSIDERATION FOR EXECUTION OF AGREEMENT--Owner hereby acknowledges receipt of $_____ from Occupant which covers the first full month's rent under this agreement and any prorations necessary to pay rent to the first of the following month, plus any other sums here identified _____. Payment pays rent through _____.

TERMINATION--Either party may terminate this agreement by giving the other party thirty days' written notice, and the rent shall be paid through that date.

USE OF SPACE--Occupant agrees to use the space only for the storage of property wholly owned by Occupant and to store said property under his/her own supervision and control. Occupant shall not store or use or produce on the premises any materials which are classified as hazardous or toxic under any local, state, or federal law or regulation. Occupant shall not store illegal substances, perishables, food items, explosives, paint, varnish, thinner, gasoline, and/or other highly flammable materials. Occupant shall not use the space for any business or for manufacturing or production, nor for human or animal occupancy. Occupant shall not create a nuisance or permit creation of a nuisance on or near the storage premises. Occupant shall remove all trash brought onto the space. Occupant shall not use any electricity in the space for any purpose whatsoever other than for lighting and then only while Occupant is present. Occupant shall turn off lights when leaving space.

OCCUPANT'S AFFIRMATIVE COVENANTS--Occupant agrees to the following:
1) To lock the personal property and keep it secure,
2) To drain all water lines during the wintertime in order to prevent any damage that may be caused to same due to low winter temperatures, and
3) To obtain insurance to cover the property and contents thereof as Occupant is hereby informed that Owner does not carry such insurance. To the extent that Occupant does not maintain insurance, Occupant shall be completely "self-insured" and shall bear all risk of loss or damage.

WAIVER OF LIABILITY--Occupant, as a material part of the consideration under this agreement, hereby waives all claims against Owner for any damage or loss from any cause, other than the negligence of Owner, arising at any time, including but not limited to fire, theft, acts of God, vandalism or any physical damage while the Occupant's personal property remains in the storage area. Occupant does hereby agree to indemnify and hold Owner harmless from and on account of any damage or injury to any person, equipment, or personal property arising from any cause, other than the negligence of Owner, or from the negligence of Occupant, Occupant's family, or Occupant's guests.

SELF-SERVICE STORAGE FACILITY LAWS--This storage agreement is governed by the laws applied to self-service storage facilities in this locality.

ILLEGAL PROVISIONS NOT AFFECTING LEGAL PROVISIONS--Whatever item in this Agreement is found to be contrary to any local, state, or federal law shall be considered null and void, just as if it had never appeared in the Agreement, and it shall not affect the validity of any other item in the Agreement.

ACKNOWLEDGEMENT--Occupant hereby acknowledges that he or she has read this agreement, understands it, agrees to it, and has been given a copy.

_____   _____
            Owner   Occupant

_____   _____
BY Person authorized to represent Owner or Occupant

STORAGE AGREEMENT--Page 2 of 2

Summary of Business & Statement of Income

Property _____ Period _____

1								
2								
3	INCOME							
4	Rental							
5	Other							
6	TOTAL INCOME							
7								
8								
9								
10								
11								
12	EXPENSES & PAYMENTS							
13	Interest							
14	Taxes, Licenses							
15	Insurance							
16	Utilities							
17	Services, Repairs, Maintenance							
18	Merchandise, Supplies							
19	Payroll							
20	Miscellaneous Expenses							
21	Depreciable							
22	Mortgage Principal							
23	Non-deductible							
24								
25								
26	TOTAL EXPENSES & PAYMENTS							
27	minus Non-deductible (line 23)							
28	TOTAL							
29	minus Depreciable (line 21)							
30	TOTAL							
31	minus Mortgage Prin. (line 22)							
32	TOTAL NET EXPENSES (for tax purp.)							
33								
34	TOTAL INCOME (line 6)							
35	minus line 28							
36	CASH FLOW							
37								
38								
39								
40								
41								

480

Form SD	SUPPLEMENTAL DEPRECIATION		YEAR	

NAME(S) OF TAXPAYERS		SOC. SEC. NUMBER			

CAPITAL IMPROVEMENT LOCATION & DESCRIPTION

1

2

3

4

5

6

7

	1	2	3	4	5	6	7	Totals
Date Acqd. or Conv. to Bus.								
New or Used								
Cost or Other Basis								
Salvage Value								
1st Year Special Depreciation								
Depreciable Basis								
Prior Depreciation								
Depreciable Balance								
Method of Depreciation								
Useful Life								
Full Year Depreciation								
Percentage of Year Held								
Percentage for Business Use								
Depreciation This Year								

PAGE TOTAL

Dear

    You probably know already that the building where you live has changed hands. Because tenants usually feel some apprehension every time such a changeover occurs, we would like to take this opportunity to clear the air by letting you know just what you can expect in the future about a few things.

    DEPOSITS...One special concern you must have is your deposits. We are concerned, too, and we want to make absolutely certain that all of your deposits are credited to you. To avoid any misunderstandings about your deposits and other matters related to your living here, we would like you to answer the questions on the sheet attached. They are questions which you should be able to answer quickly from memory or by referring to information readily available to you. Please do so as soon as possible and return your answers to us in the envelope provided.

    PAYMENT BY CHECK OR MONEY ORDER...Since it is unwise for anyone to keep or carry cash around in quantities, we request that you pay your rent by check or money order (made payable to us exactly as underlined below). You will be protected and so will we.

    PROMPT PAYMENT...You are expected to pay your rent within three days after the due date. For example, rent due on the first must be paid by the fourth at the very latest. If you anticipate being late beyond that for any reason whatsoever, please let us know beforehand. If you don't, we will assume that you are deliberately avoiding payment, and we will immediately serve you with the notice which starts eviction proceedings.

    MAINTENANCE...We expect you to pay your rent promptly, and you can expect us to respond promptly to maintenance problems. Sometime within the next week, we will visit you to inspect for any building maintenance work that should be taken care of. You can help by starting now to make a list of such work which you notice around the house.

    RENTAL AGREEMENT...We will also stop by soon to explain to you the standard rental agreement we use, and we will leave you with a copy of your own.

    We are reasonable people and we will try anything within reason to make living here enjoyable for you, but naturally we need your cooperation. If we have it, we will get along well together and we can all take pride in this place that you call home.

              Sincerely,

Tenant Information:

Your Name_____

Your Address_____

Your Home Phone_____ Cell Phone_____

Your Email Address_____

Your Soc. Sec. No._____ Driver's License_____

Who lives with you? (Include ages of children, please)_____
_____

What pet(s) do you have?_____

Do you have a waterbed?_____

What vehicle(s) do you have? Make(s)_____ License(s)_____

Where do you work? (Company name)_____

What is your phone number at work?_____

Where does your co-tenant work? (Company name)_____

What is your co-tenant's phone number at work?_____

When did you move in?_____

What is your current rent per month?_____

What date is your rent paid up to right now?_____

When is your rent due each month?_____

What refundable deposits have you paid? Keys $_____ Security $_____

   Cleaning $_____ Other (please explain) $_____

   When you moved in, you paid your first month's rent. Did you also
   then pay your last month's rent?_____ If so, how much did you
   pay? $_____ Does what you paid as last month's rent now equal
   your current rent?_____

Which of the following furnishings in your dwelling belong to the
   owners of the building? (Please give room locations where
   appropriate.)

   Carpets_____ Drapes_____

   Shades_____ Blinds_____

   Stove_____ Refrigerator_____

   Other appliances? (Please list)_____

   Other furniture? (Please list)_____

Do you have a rental agreement or lease in writing?_____

   If so, what is the date of the latest one?_____

In case of an emergency, what friend or relative should we contact?

   Name_____ Phone Number_____

Date _____ Your Signature_____

Tenant Record Property _____

Unit	Tenant	Phone	Date In	Moved Out	Rent Date	Rent	Deposit	Bank/Chkg. Acct. Nos.
1								
2								
3								
4								
5								
6								
7								
8								
9								
10								
11								
12								
13								
14								
15								
16								
17								
18								
19								
20								
21								
22								
23								
24								
25								
26								
27								
28								
29								
30								
31								
32								
33								
34								
35								

484

Time Sheet

Employee's Name _____   Property _____

Employee's Signature _____   Pay Period _____ to _____

Date	Times		Hours	Description of Work Performed	Contract Amount

Total Hours _____

Rate _____

Hourly Gross _____

Contract _____

Total Gross _____

Total Contract _____

Approved by _____   Date

TIMELY MAINTENANCE GUARANTEE

The management responsible for maintaining the dwelling located at the address given below hereby guarantees to repair any defects discovered in the dwelling which are hazardous to life, health, or safety within seventy-two hours (three days) following notification by the tenants who occupy the dwelling. Tenants' notice may be either verbal or written, but it must be *acknowledged* in writing by someone whom management has authorized to accept such notice.

Should management fail to repair the defects, either temporarily or permanently, within seventy-two hours (three days), tenants shall be relieved of the responsibility for paying rent for every day or portion thereof during which the defects go unrepaired following the initial seventy-two-hour (three-day) period allotted for completing this work in a timely manner. Tenants' responsibility for paying rent shall begin again once the defects have been repaired.

To receive the benefit of any rent abatement owed to them under this guarantee, tenants must be current in their rent payments and must pay their next rent in full when due. Whatever rent abatement is owed will then be paid to them in the form of a rebate within forty-eight hours following receipt of their rent payment.

This guarantee applies only to those defects which are the responsibility of management to maintain as mandated by law and/or as outlined in the applicable lease or rental agreement.

This guarantee does not apply when a portion of the dwelling becomes uninhabitable as a result of flooding, fire, earthquake, or an act of God, and the tenants choose to remain in residence during reconstruction. In such cases, management and tenants will negotiate a fair rent covering the reconstruction period.

This guarantee shall remain in effect so long as there is a valid lease or rental agreement between the parties below covering the dwelling located at the address given below.

Dated _____ Address _____

Tenants _____

Owner/Manager _____

Waterbed Agreement

Dated _____

(Addendum to Rental Agreement)

This agreement is attached to and forms a part of the Rental Agreement dated _____ between _____, Owners, and _____, Tenants.
Tenants desire to keep a waterbed described as _____
_____ in the dwelling they occupy under the Rental Agreement referred to above, and because this agreement specifically prohibits keeping waterbeds without the Owners' permission, Tenants agree to the following terms and conditions in exchange for this permission:

1) Tenants agree to keep one waterbed approved by Owners for this dwelling. Waterbed shall consist of a mattress at least 20 mil thick with lap seams, a safety liner at least 8 mil, and a sturdy frame enclosure made of plywood or solid natural wood only, no particle board.

2) Tenants agree to consult with the Owners about the location of the waterbed. They agree to hire qualified professionals to install and dismantle the bed according to the manufacturer's specifications and further agree not to relocate it without the Owners' consent.

3) Tenants agree to allow Owners to inspect the waterbed installation at any and all reasonable times, and Tenants agree to remedy any problems or potential problems immediately.

4) Tenants agree to furnish Owners with a copy of a valid liability insurance policy for at least $100,000 covering this waterbed installation and agree to renew the policy as necessary for continuous coverage.

5) Tenants agree to pay immediately for any damage caused by their waterbed, and in addition, they will add $_____ to their security/cleaning deposit, any of which may be used for cleaning, repairs, or delinquent rent when Tenants vacate. This added deposit, or what remains of it when waterbed damages have been assessed, will be returned to Tenants within _____ days after they prove that they no longer keep this waterbed.

6) In consideration of the additional time, effort, costs, and risks involved in this waterbed installation, Tenants agree to pay additional rent of $_____, which /includes/does not include/ the premium for the waterbed liability insurance policy referred to in item 4.

7) Tenants agree that the Owners reserve the right to revoke this permission to keep a waterbed should the Tenants break this agreement.

Owner _____ Tenant _____

By _____ Tenant _____

Page_____ of _____

"WEAR AND TEAR" OR "DAMAGES"?

"Normal wear and tear" caused by ordinary comings and goings	"Damage" caused by carelessness, abuse, thievery, mysterious disappearance, accident, rules violation, or special request
Well-worn keys	Missing keys
"Sticky" key	Key broken off inside lock
Balky door lock	Door lock replaced by tenant without management's permission
Depressurized fire extinguisher with unbroken seal	Depressurized fire extinguisher with broken seal (not used to put out fire)
Worn pattern in plastic countertop	Burn in plastic countertop
Rust stain under sink faucet	Sink discolored by clothing dye
Loose, inoperable faucet handle	Missing faucet handle
Rusty refrigerator shelf	Missing refrigerator shelf
Discolored ceramic tile	Painted ceramic tile
Loose grout around ceramic tile	Chipped or cracked ceramic tile
Carpet seam unraveling	Carpet burn
Threadbare carpet in hallway	Rust marks on carpet from indoor plant container
Scuffing on wooden floor	Gouge in wooden floor
Linoleum with the back showing through	Tear in linoleum
Wobbly toilet	Broken toilet tank lid
Rusty shower curtain rod	Kinked shower curtain rod
Rust stain under bathtub spout	Chip in bathtub enamel
Tracks on doorjamb where door rubs	Hole in hollow-core door
Door off its hinges and stored in garage	Missing door
Plant hanger left in ceiling	Two-inch-diameter hole in ceiling
Stain on ceiling caused by leaky roof	Stain on ceiling caused by popping champagne or beer bottles
Cracked paint	Crayon marks on wall
Chipped paint (minor)	Walls painted by tenant in dark color necessitating repainting
Pleasing, professional tenant wallpapering	Amateurish tenant wallpapering
Mildew around shower or tub	Mildew where tenant kept aquarium
Urine odor around toilet	Urine odor in carpet
Discolored light fixture globe	Missing light fixture globe
Odd-wattage lightbulbs which work	Burned out or missing lightbulbs
Light fixture installed by tenant which fits its location	Light fixture installed by tenant which must be replaced
Window cracked by settling or high wind	Window cracked by movers
Faded shade	Torn shade
Paint-blistered Venetian blinds	Venetian blinds with bent slats
Sun-damaged drapes	Pet-damaged drapes
Drapery rod which won't close properly	Drapery rod with missing parts
Dirty window screen	Missing, bent, or torn window screen
Ants inside after rain storm	Fleas left behind by tenant's pet
Scrawny landscaping which was sparingly watered due to drought conditions	Neglected landscaping which must be replaced with similar plantings
Grease stains on parking space	Caked grease on parking space

WHAT DO YOU KNOW ABOUT LANDLORDING MAINTENANCE?

1. How do you repair a toilet which cycles on and off all by itself every twenty minutes or so?

2. How do you repair a burn in a kitchen counter made of Formica® laminate?

3. How do you repair a four-inch hole in a hollow-core door?

4. How do you remove a bathtub spout without putting any permanent marks on it?

5. A new tenant calls to report that half of an electrical outlet doesn't work. How do you fix it?

6. What's the difference between fuses and circuit breakers?

7. Describe the function of each of the following: closet auger, drum auger, Teflon® tape, hack saw, saber saw.

8. What determines whether a doorknob lock is installed right-side up or upside down?

9. Where should you be sure to install a smoke detector?

10. Prioritize the following maintenance tasks: sweep the parking area, unclog a garbage disposer, replace an outside light, paint a bathroom in a vacant apartment, change locks for a tenant whose boyfriend moved out yesterday.

WHAT DO YOU KNOW ABOUT RENTAL PROPERTY MANAGEMENT?

1. How do you determine the market rent for a vacant apartment?

2. If an applicant must have a gross income of three and a half times the rent, how much of an income does the applicant need in order to qualify to rent a house which rents for $1,250 per month?

3. We always collect an entire month's rent and all the deposits whenever a tenant moves in, and we prorate the rent for the second month when it comes due. Let's say that some tenants move in on the twentieth of August. Their rent is $900 and their deposits are $975. How much do you collect from them before they move in, and how much do you collect from them when their September rent comes due?

4. Give several legal reasons you might use for refusing to rent to someone.

5. Under what three circumstances may you enter a tenant's dwelling when the tenant is not at home?

6. Our rental agreement states that the rent must be paid by check or money order, not in cash. How do you respond to a late-paying tenant who offers to pay everything up in cash on a Friday afternoon?

7. What's a realistic late fee for an apartment which rents for $750 per month?

8. How do you begin an eviction for nonpayment of rent?

9. When a tenant calls to give you notice that she's moving, what should you do above all?

10. Prioritize the following tasks which need to be done before a certain vacant apartment can be re-rented: "steam" clean the carpets, dry-clean the draperies, re-key the locks, patch a doorknob hole in a bedroom wall, advertise, replace a broken window, paint the rooms which need painting.

Your Pet and You

Please provide us with a photograph of your pet, plus some specifics about your pet and you. This information will help us make an informed decision when we are considering both of you as tenants for our rental dwelling.

Your name_____ Date_____

Description...pet's name, breed, age, weight, size (give height and length), activity level, and traits

_____

Training...obedience school or other training (give dates, too)

_____

Background...aggressiveness (ever bitten someone or exhibited aggressive behavior? if so, give particulars and indicate measures taken to curb aggressiveness since last episode)

_____

Activities...exercise (give type and frequency)

_____

Health...spayed or neutered; vaccinations; health exams (give schedule); veterinarian (give name and phone number)

_____

Grooming...schedule of grooming; groomer (give name and phone number)

_____

Care arrangements...caretaker during absences (give name and phone number)

_____

Commitment...duration of relationship with this pet; pet license particulars; membership in animal protection organizations such as the S.P.C.A.; willingness to put up an additional deposit

_____

Insurance...pet health and/or dog-bite (describe policy)

_____

References...people who know your pet and you (give particulars)

_____

Sources & Resources

The information given here was checked for accuracy when this edition of *Landlording* went to press. Surely some of it was already outdated when the book came off the press. If you have trouble locating any of these sources or resources, log onto the internet and go directly to their websites or else search on their names.

For your information, I have no financial relationship with any organization or company mentioned here and stand to profit nothing from your contributions to the organizations or from your purchases of these companies' products, that is, with the notable exception of any purchases you might make of my own books and software, all of which I recommend here shamelessly.

Associations & Organizations

HALT. 1612 K Street, NW, Suite 510, Washington, DC 20006. (halt.org) 202.887.8255.

HALT stands for "Help Abolish Legal Tyranny." It's a non-partisan membership organization founded in 1977 to reduce the cost and improve the quality of legal services in America. Such modest goals! Methinks that researchers will find cures for cancer and heart trouble long before legal services improve in this country. We have to start sometime somewhere, however, and HALT is a very good start. HALT also publishes a series called Citizens Legal Manuals, one of which is *Using a Lawyer: And What To Do If Things Go Wrong*. The manuals are useful and so is the organization.

National Apartment Association. 4300 Wilson Blvd., Suite 400, Arlington, VA 22203. (naahq.org) 703.518.6141.

Most state and local rental housing associations are affiliated with the National Apartment Association, which is headquartered near the nation's capitol and acts as lobbyist, trade association, and information repository for rental property owners. Anyone who wants to know what Washington is doing to help or hinder our business at a national level would do well to read NAA's monthly *Units* magazine, available in an electronic version on their website. Anyone who wants to find an affiliate association need only go to the NAA affiliate directory on their website.

Pacific Legal Foundation. 3900 Lennane Drive, Suite 200, Sacramento, CA 95834. (pacificlegal.org) 916.419.7111.

This nonprofit organization should not be necessary in a free, self-governing society. People living in a free society ought to have enough sense to realize that private property rights are sacrosanct and absolutely vital to the workings of such a society. Unfortunately, they don't, not even here in the United States, where private property rights are guaranteed by the Constitution. Every day zealous government officials and government agencies appropriate people's property rights through a variety of legitimate and quasi-legitimate means such as rent control, zoning, and environmental regulations. Every day property owners choose not to fight the "taking" of their property because fighting is so costly. They cannot afford to "fight city hall" for years and years. Enter the Pacific Legal Foundation. Its attorneys take on cases involving property rights and personal rights where government has overstepped the boundaries of fairness. They will take cases all the way to the U.S. Supreme Court if they have to, just as they did when they helped a widow fight eight years for the right to build a house on a lot she owned in a built-out subdivision. If you are concerned about your property rights, if you want to help champion a just cause, if you want to keep abreast of what's happening with legal challenges to rent control, support this organization. It's a good one. What it's doing is right up every landlord's alley.

Books—Investment

When you notice the publication dates for some of the books in this and the following four sections, you might wonder why books more than twenty years old, some of which are out of print, are listed here. They're here because they're good. They're here because they're not as dated as you might think. They're here because they're readily available in libraries and through internet searches. They're here because new print technology enables publishers to reprint out-of-print books in small quantities profitably. Your interest in these books will awaken publishers to this possibility.

Bruss, Robert. *The Smart Investor's Guide to Real Estate: Big Profits from Small Investments*. New York: Crown, 1989.

Real estate's "Answer Man," the syndicated columnist who answered everybody's real estate questions in his "Real Estate Mailbag" column, gathers all of his sound advice together here in this one place. To make the book especially understandable, he spices his advice with numerous practical examples showing how real estate ideas apply to real-world situations. He also includes selected answers to the many questions asked of him over the years.

de Heer, Robert. *Realty Bluebook*. Chicago: Dearborn (dearbornre.com), 2003.

Written primarily for real estate salespeople, it includes some stuff you might not be interested in, such as sales techniques, but it does have some most helpful tax, financing, and risk management information, plus sales checklists and explanations of real estate contract clauses. The financial tables, part of the original *Realty Bluebook*, now appear in a separate volume called *Realty Bluebook Financial Tables*.

Gardner, Scott. *Live Rent-Free for Life and Other Incredible Revelations About NYC Rent Control*. New York: Free-Rent Press, 1990.

This book doesn't belong in the category of "Investment Books," not really. It deserves a category all its own. That category should be "Anti-Investment Books," for this is the sad tale of someone who tangled with New York City's rent control establishment and lost bigtime. The tale is uneven, but it's heartfelt and full of clever black humor. You have to sympathize with the poor author who barely escaped with the shirt on his back after enduring ten years as the owner of six units in New York City, all tenanted by profes-sional people making good money and less in need of rent control than he was in need of a fair return on his investment. Yes, New York City landlords do have some scary stories to tell, and we all ought to be listening. There but for the grace of God go we!

Hare, Patrick; Jolene Osler. *Creating an Accessory Apartment*. New York: McGraw-Hill, 1987.

The in-law apartment has come a long way, baby! Variously known as an "outlawed in-law" and a "bootlegged apartment" because its very existence so often violated building and zoning codes, the "accessory apartment," as it's called in this book, is seeing a resurgence in popularity. Partly, this popularity is a result of the demand for inexpensive housing, and partly it's a result of a change in laws. Many communities now permit homeowners to modify their homes and create accessory apartments legally. If you can visualize the possibility of creating an accessory apartment in, under, on, or beside any house you own, read this book before you take the first step. It's written by two land-use planners who have guided homeowners through the process every step of the way. It'll surely save you grief.

Lowry, Albert. *How You Can Become Financially Independent by Investing in Real Estate*. New York: Simon & Schuster, 1982.

The Lowry-Nickerson Real Estate Investors Seminar was a fixture on the American scene for years. I'd be willing to bet that it produced more graduates who went on to become millionaires than the nation's leading school of business produced since the year it was founded. Because Lowry was involved so long with this successful teaching program, you might suspect that he has a lot to say about the subject matter. You also might suspect that the subject matter is going to be well organized. You'd be right on both counts. Lowry's book summarizes on half a page his tested, foolproof formula for becoming financially independent. Then it goes on to detail the many do's and don'ts involved in making that formula work. It's one of those "oldy but goody" real estate investment books, still worth reading.

Maloney, Roy. *Real Estate Quick & Easy*. San Francisco: Dropzone Press, 1999.

Ever have somebody sit down with you and explain patiently and concisely just what "cap rate," "internal rate of return," "gross rent multiplier," "mechanic's liens," "prescriptive easement," "riparian rights," and the "Rule of 72" are? That's what this book does. It explains hundreds of real estate terms and concepts in the simplest way possible, through illustrations, graphs, and a highly condensed text. Use it as you would a real estate dictionary. It has an ample index useful for this very purpose.

Nickerson, William. *How I Turned $1,000 into Five Million in Real Estate in My Spare Time.* New York: Simon & Schuster, 1984.

This book is classic enough so that most buyers of rental property know what a "Nickerson" is (it's a fixer-upper with potential for forced appreciation, yielding at least two dollars of added value for every dollar spent on fixing it up). The book is loaded with sage advice and good information about purchasing, improving, managing, and exchanging rental properties. Sure, it's an old book, even the 1984 revision, but the techniques it espouses for pyramiding your real estate wealth remain the same today as they did when it was first published in 1959, when you could buy rental properties any day of the month for $5,000 a unit. Anyone who bought the book back then and bought properties according to Nickerson's twenty-year plan couldn't fail to have become a millionaire by 1979. Any edition of the book will do. Just roll your eyes at the numbers in the early editions and pay attention to the formulas. They're still valid today.

Randel, Jim. *The Skinny on Real Estate Investing.* Westport, CT: RAND Publishing (randpublishing.com), 2009.

Interested in real estate investing? Got a few minutes and only a few minutes to learn the basics? This "Skinny" book is for you. The first of Jim Randel's Skinny books, *The Skinny on the Housing Crisis,* won "gold" in the 2d Annual Robert Bruss Real Estate Book Awards contest conducted by the National Association of Real Estate Editors. It wowed the judges. This Skinny book on real estate investing has the same graphic format, stick figures with a minimum of dialogue and text on every page to illustrate and develop key points. It begins by debunking the gurus who prey on the gullible with their get-rich-quick pitches, and it goes on to show readers how to determine whether they're cut out to be real estate investors, how to analyze real estate investments, how to buy properties at the right price, how to improve them to increase their value, and

how to sell them at a profit. Twitter junkies especially will love the whole Skinny series.

Reed, John. *How to Increase the Value of Real Estate.* Alamo, CA: Reed Publishing (johntreed.com), published on demand.

Most people wait around for the value of their real estate to go up, and sooner or later it usually does. That's the slow track. If you'd rather be on the fast track to real estate wealth, you need to know as many ways as possible to force the value of your real estate to go up. Here's a book which examines all kinds of ways, from the obvious to the obscure. Not only does it examine the ways, it provides the mathematics to show you how the ways work.

Scher, Les; Carol Scher. *Finding and Buying Your Place in the Country.* Chicago: Dearborn (dearborntrade.com), 2000.

This book does cover country property, but there's so much that urban and suburban properties have in common with country property that you'll want to examine a copy of this book even though you never plan to leave West 89th Street. It's very thorough. It tells about dealing with insurance agents, lawyers, lenders, neighbors, partners, real estate agents, sellers, and tax assessors, not so that you can take advantage of them, but so that they won't take advantage of you, whether you're a city hick or a country slicker.

Books—Law & Eviction

The second book mentioned here is intended for use only in California.

Portman, Janet, and Marcia Stewart. *Renters' Rights: The Basics.* Berkeley, CA: Nolo (nolo.com), 2009.

Some landlords might think that this is the enemy's battle plan and might even think of it as offensive. Some of it is. But it is primarily defensive. After all, there are a few unscrupulous landlords lurking about, and tenants do need help in dealing with them. Your reading the book will give you a chance to consider the tenant's point of view for a change. You might even want to give your tenants a copy after reading it yourself.

Robinson, Leigh. *The Eviction Book for California.* El Cerrito, CA: ExPress (expresspublishing.com), 2010.

It details every step of the entire legal eviction process in California and includes the forms necessary to do an eviction yourself. When you've exhausted every possible method for getting problem tenants to move without resorting to the courts, find a copy of this book and get them out by going into court. It also covers certain other matters related to evictions, such as how to handle tenants who declare bankruptcy, how to handle tenants who stop paying rent for a garage or self-storage unit, how to evict a former owner from a foreclosure property, how to handle squatters, how to handle nonpayment and noncompliance in a mobilehome or RV park, and how to collect a money judgment.

Stewart, Marcia; Ralph Warner; and Janet Portman. *Every Landlord's Legal Guide.* Berkeley, CA: Nolo (nolo.com), 2010.

This is not one of those impressively bound tomes which line the walls of attorneys' offices and are dusted more often than they're consulted. This is a frank and friendly law book written by attorneys who are committed to making accurate legal information available to the uninitiated. Go to Nolo's website and read the sample chapter. Included with the book is a CD-ROM with forms.

Books—Maintenance

Ebeling, Walter. *Urban Entomology.* Berkeley, CA: University of California, Division of Agricultural Sciences, Publications Office. 1978.

More than a big book about the bugs plaguing city dwellers, it's over six hundred pages of detailed, factual information about all kinds of cosmopolitan pests, from cockroaches to snakes. It explains where they come from, how they live, and how they die. It may save you from having to hire a professional exterminator when your tenants are demanding that you eradicate an "infestation" of an unfamiliar bug, two of which they saw sauntering across their kitchen counter on a Sunday morning.

Though this book is out of print, it is available in libraries and now online free-of-charge on the website of the University of California at Riverside, Department of Entomology at the following URL, entomology.ucr.edu/ebeling.

How Things Work in Your Home (and What to Do When They Don't). New York: Holt Paperbacks, 1987.

In clear illustrations and tight prose, this book outlines how plumbing, electrical, heating, and cooling systems work. It explains how the various components of these systems operate, and it details ways to troubleshoot malfunctioning heaters, appliances, septic tanks, faucets, and the like.

Phillips, Bill. *The Complete Book of Locks and Locksmithing.* New York: McGraw-Hill Professional. 2005.

This exhaustive training manual for professionals more than suffices as a source book for landlords who want to learn only enough about locksmithing practices to duplicate keys, rekey locks, repair locks, master-key locks, and even pick locks.

Reader's Digest New Complete Do-It-Yourself Manual. Pleasantville, NY: The Reader's Digest Association, 2005.

It's a valuable book full of good illustrations and photographs. If you have a job to do, like pouring a cement walkway or repairing a decayed threshold, you can look the subject up in the index and then turn to practical hints for doing the job right the very first time you do it.

Reader's Digest New Fix-It-Yourself Manual. Pleasantville, NY: The Reader's Digest Association, 1996.

Shhh, don't tell anybody, but the "complete" manual above wasn't 100% complete. Here's more of the same, just as good.

Books—Management

Bierbrier, Doreen. *Living with Tenants: How to Happily Share Your House with Tenants for Profit and Security.* New York: McGraw-Hill. 1986.

Anyone who contemplates sharing a house with a lodger should learn how this specialized kind of landlording works. After sharing her house with lodgers, Bierbrier made most of the mistakes and most of the discoveries. You ought to make the most of what she's written on the subject. She also wrote *Managing Your Rental House for Increased Income,* published by Bantam in 1991, in which she writes about tenanting rental houses with single people whose aggregate rent is greater than what a single family would pay. Because Bierbrier writes from practical experience in both of her books, you know she knows her subjects well.

Bramson, Robert M. *Coping with Difficult People.* New York: Dell. 1988.

Strictly speaking, this is not a rental property management book as are the other books under this heading, but it belongs here anyway because it clearly identifies the various types of difficult tenants we landlords encounter, and it describes various ways of coping with them. Difficult tenants can make your life as a landlord miserable if you let them. They tend to bring out the worst in you and make you do things which you come to regret later. This book helps you understand what's really happening when somebody is being difficult so that you will be able to respond sensibly and solve problems rather than exacerbate them. There's nothing quite like this book. It's a seminal work. Reading it will make you a better landlord.

Edwards, Brian F.; Casey Edwards; and Susannah Craig. *The Complete Idiot's Guide to Making Money with Rental Properties.* Indianapolis, IN: Alpha Books (idiotsguides.com), 2004.

One of the "Idiot's Guides" series, this book follows the series formula with lots of graphics and lists. If you like the series, you'll like this book. It makes a commendable effort to include landlord-tenant statutes for each state, but you may want to use the internet to check the current statutes for your state before you bet the farm on them. It includes blank forms, although they're in a poor format dictated by the book's physical dimensions.

Griswold, Robert. *Property Management Kit for Dummies.* New York: Wiley (wiley.com). 2008.

Another in the "Dummies" series, this is as good a starting place as any for somebody who knows absolutely nothing about landlording. It makes the reader hungry for more. If you buy either the "dummy" or the "idiot" book, put a brown paper wrapper over its cover. You don't want to give your tenants any wrong ideas about your intelligence.

Hrib-Karpinski, Christine. *How to Rent Vacation Properties by Owner: The Complete Guide to Buy, Manage, Furnish, Rent, Maintain and Advertise your Vacation Rental Investment.* Woodstock, GA: Kinney Pollack Press (howtorentby-owner.com). 2007.

For anyone who rents out a vacation home by the week or weekend and wants help in making it pay, this book is a treasure-trove of good ideas written in great detail. In addition to covering the tasks mentioned in the title, the book has ideas on taking photos and creating an attractive website, taking inquiries, screening renters, hiring cleaning people, handling keys, dealing with emergencies from a distance, and keeping people

coming back year after year. Be forewarned that if you use all of this book's good ideas, your vacation home will be so booked up that you won't be able to find accommodations there for yourself. You'll have to rent someone else's. That, I suppose, is the epitome of success in the vacation home rental business.

Kelley, Edward. *Practical Apartment Management.* Chicago (irem.org): Institute of Real Estate Management. 2009.

This is a somewhat pedantic, but competent, treatment of the subject, written primarily for the managers of large apartment complexes who aren't owners themselves but need to learn to think like owners.

Lowry, Albert. *How to Manage Real Estate Successfully in Your Spare Time.* New York: Simon & Schuster. 1980.

This book's strong suit is sales, finding warm bodies and getting them to rent empty apartments. It should be particularly helpful to anyone who's trying to fill a new apartment building in an area where others are trying to do the same.

Perry, Greg. *Managing Rental Properties for Maximum Profit.* New York: Crown. 2000.

This book has ideas all its own. They're not ones I readily agree with. For example, I don't agree that landlords should omit their telephone numbers from classified ads and rely strictly on open houses. I don't agree that landlords should bother to record tenants' lease agreements at the county courthouse. I don't agree that widely separated rental properties ought to have their locks keyed alike for the landlord's benefit. I do agree that landlords ought to open escrow accounts for deposits. I could go on. Let's just say that this book describes a unique approach to landlording, one you might want to acquaint yourself with and draw ideas from.

Reed, John. *How to Manage Residential Property for Maximum Cash Flow and Resale Value.* Alamo, CA: Reed Publishing (johntreed.com). 2010.

Should you suspect that you're becoming soft in the heart, read this book. It's written by someone who's hard-hearted, hard-headed, and hard-nosed about rental properties. He's the kind whose heart is eagerly sought after for transplants. It's been so little used. Contrary to what you might think, the book does not come with a black cape, glue-on handlebar mustache, and braided cowhide whip. They're extras.

Robinson, Leigh. *What's a Landlord to Do?* El Cerrito, CA: ExPress (expresspublishing.com). 2005.

The title of this book is a question because the book itself consists of questions, questions, and more questions. They are questions submitted by many landlords and a few tenants through the landlording.com website. My answers follow every question. Many of the questions I never could have imagined myself, such as the one about coping with the strong odors of East Indian cooking at a duplex. Even though I couldn't have imagined the questions, I could imagine the answers. They're here for you to read.

Taylor, Jeffrey. *The Landlord's Kit: A Complete Set of Ready-to-Use Forms, Letters, and Notices to Increase Profits, Take Control, and Eliminate the Hassle.* Chicago: Dearborn (dearborntrade.com). 2007.

Good forms make the good landlord a better landlord, but they require a lifetime of writing and refining. Now comes Mr. Landlord, Jeffrey Taylor, to share his many good landlording forms, developed over his lifetime, with all of us. Bless him!

Books—Tax

Bernstein, Peter W. (ed.). *The Ernst & Young Tax Guide.* Auburn Heights, MI: PublishNow (publishnow.net). Published annually.

There is a book within this book. It's the official IRS tax guide called *Your Income Tax*, and it's reproduced here in its entirety. Ernst & Young's (one of the country's leading accounting firms) experts expand upon the official IRS guide with examples, comments, explanations, and tips. The book includes a special section for real estate investors, just what we landlords need when we're preparing our income tax returns.

Reed, John. *Aggressive Tax Avoidance for Real Estate Investors.* Alamo, CA: Reed Publishing (johntreed.com). Published on demand.

This "English-language translation" of income tax laws affecting real estate investors minces no words. With mathematical proof, it explains why you should be aggressive in those many gray areas of tax law, and then it shows you how to be aggressive. The book's rules for understanding income taxes may surprise you, but unless you follow them, you're paying more taxes than the law requires. It explains depreciation and IRS 1031 exchanges clearly and also tells how to find a good, aggressive tax adviser. It's revised continually to reflect changes in the tax laws themselves and in their interpretation.

Internet and Catalog Vendors

Shopping via the internet and catalogs has become more and more popular ever since the price of gasoline started ratcheting up. It is still growing in popularity, and no wonder. It's fun. It's convenient. It saves time. It saves fuel. It offers wide variety. It offers value, and it allows for easy comparison shopping.

Each of the companies listed here publishes a printed or virtual catalog and maintains a website which you may use no matter where you or your rental properties happen to be. Some of them also have stores here and there around the country. Except as noted, the addresses listed here are for the companies' main offices. If you want to shop in person, contact that office to learn whether there is a store near you.

American Blinds and Draperies. 1168 San Luis Obispo Avenue, Hayward, CA 94544. (americandrapery.com) 800.972.0660; in northern California, call 510.487.3500.

American has become one of the largest apartment drapery, mini-blind, and vertical blind manufacturers in the country by offering landlords long-lasting window coverings at factory-direct wholesale prices. They maintain a large inventory, so they can ship most standard sizes the same day they get your order, provided you call before 10:30 a.m. Contact them before you need window coverings in a hurry, and ask them to send you a free information kit with samples, prices, and a credit application. Mention this book when you call to order and ask for a special discount.

Grainger. 14441 W. Illinois Route 60, Lake Forest, IL 60045. (grainger.com) 800.323.0620.

This thick (more than 4,000 pages, more than five pounds), informative catalog lists thousands upon thousands of products, including almost every known electric motor for both general and specialized applications. It also lists compressors, pumps, light fixtures, carpet steam cleaners, electric drain augers, hand tools, testing devices, and so on and so on. The listings include ample information and descriptions to help you select the right item for your application. In addition, it has many pages of technical data and terminology, including a decimal equivalent chart and the codes and standards for plumbing products. Grainger's many branch locations stock lots of catalog items and offer same-day pickup. Call their toll-free number and ask them to send you one of their catalogs. It doubles as a dumbbell or a doorstop. Take your pick.

HD Supply Facilities Maintenance. P.O. Box 509055, San Diego, CA 92150. (hdsupplysolutions.com) 800.431.3000.

HD Supply Facilities Maintenance specializes in providing most of the tools, equipment, materials, and supplies we landlords use in our maintenance rounds. Were you to make a list of the many things you use most often and replace most often around your rental property, chances are good that you'd find them all in this catalog. It has faucet parts, stove parts, locksmithing supplies, ganged mailboxes, paint, appliance dollies, cleaning supplies, stove top fire extinguishers, and more, lots more. Need only a toilet tank lid to replace the one a tenant broke with a karate chop? They've got 'em. Need a "shoe" for a toilet? They've got 'em. Uh, what's a toilet shoe? It's something designed to hide the ruined or unsightly floor covering surrounding a toilet base. Who else but landlords would ever need a toilet shoe? To guarantee speedy shipment, they direct orders automatically to the warehouse nearest you. Shipping is included on orders totaling more than $50, that is, except for some heavy or bulky items, and orders reach 95% of the U.S. population the day after they're placed. Get one of their wonderful catalogs. Their bulky full-line catalog is a must, and it's free for the asking. HD Supply Facilities Maintenance offers a truly unique service, one-stop shopping for landlording necessities, plus, they now offer customer training classes (most are free) on a wide variety of maintenance subjects, such as air conditioning, conservation maintenance, electrical problems, heating systems, kitchen appliance repair, laundry appliance repair, locks and rekeying, plumbing, pool care & maintenance, and safety on site. Go to their website for information on these classes which are held nationwide.

Peachtree. P.O. Box 13290, Atlanta, GA 30324. (pbp1.com) 800.241.4623.

Peachtree carries a full line of rental property management forms and other related products, including rent payment systems, door tags, parking control supplies, pet permit stickers, pool safety products, door tags, flags, banners, and signs. They offer free shipping, too.

Recreonics, Inc. 4200 Schmitt Ave., Louisville, KY 40213. (recreonics.com) 800.428.3254.

Looking for something which goes in, on, under, over, or near a swimming pool? You'll find it in this company's extensive catalog listing everything remotely connected with swimming pools, both big and small.

Safe-Hit Corporation. 35 East Wacker Drive, Suite 1100, Chicago, IL 60601. (safe-hit.com) 800.537.8958.

This company makes all kinds of parking and traffic-control signs, as well as traffic guideposts. What's unique about the signs is their flexibility. Bad drivers can run into them and damage neither the signs nor their own cars.

Sears, Roebuck and Co. Contract Sales. (contractsales.sears.com) 800.359.2000.

Sears, Roebuck and Company is an American institution, but the Sears of today is a very different company from the Sears of yesteryear. It no longer dominates retailing, and it no longer publishes the famous Sears catalog. Nonetheless, it is still very much in business. One of its divisions, which you may not have encountered before and which you as a landlord ought to know something about, is Sears Contract Sales. Its virtual online catalog lists items such as refrigerators, stoves, and coin-operated laundry machines, and it sells them for less than Sears in-store prices.

Seton Identification Products. P.O. Box 819, Branford, CT 06405-0819. (seton.com) 800.571.2596.

Seton is a good source for safety, labeling, and signage products. It sells in-stock and custom signs, stickers, labels, markers, tags, name plates, badges, and decals of all kinds. Need a fire extinguisher sign, an OSHA sign, or a "NO PARKING ANY TIME" sign? Seton has 'em. Need a custom sign? Seton has an online sign designing tool which enables you to create your own custom sign without incurring any setup charges.

USA Bluebook, a division of HD Supply. 3781 Bur Wood Drive, Waukegan IL 60073. (usabluebook.com) 800.548.1234.

Have your own well or wastewater treatment system (a septic tank qualifies)? Then you need to have a look at USA Bluebook's massive virtual or printed catalog. It lists all kinds of equipment and supplies used in water and wastewater treatment systems, such as pumps of every description, blower silencers, water meters, wastewater meters, flushing machines, chemical feeders, safety equipment, and handbooks, plus testing and troubleshooting equipment like underground leak detectors, plastic pipe locators, sewer pipe videocameras, and chart recorders.

Wilmar Industries. 200 East Park Drive, Suite 200, Mt. Laurel, NJ 08054. (wilmar.com) 800.345.3000.

This company bought out the long-established Pier-Angelli Company. It continues in the Pier-Angelli mold as one of the best sources for hard-to-find plumbing parts and hardware. Their large catalog has lots of technical illustrations which make the positive identification of parts as easy as it can be. Orders above their minimum order requirements are shipped free of charge from their many warehouses scattered throughout the country.

Computer Software

Some of these programs are cross-platform (work on both Macs and Windows computers). Some are not. Before you buy any software, make sure it will run on your computer.

iWork®. Apple Computer (apple.com). Mac only.

This integrated software program has everything most landlords need to do their word and number processing. iWork can import and export files in a variety of formats, and it can mix capabilities within documents. In other words, you can put a spreadsheet directly into a letter you're writing and use both word processor and spreadsheet functions on the same page. It works so smoothly that you'd swear you were driving a computer with an automatic transmission.

Eviction Forms Creator™ (California only). ExPress (expresspublishing.com). Windows only.

"Tedious" is the word for the task of filling out all the forms required to evict a tenant through California courts. They require a lot of very repetitive typing. I wrote Eviction Forms Creator to make the task easier and less time-consuming. Enter the name and address of the tenant you're evicting and the same information relevant to yourself and the court, and the program puts those particulars on all the forms in just the right places. Then it prints the forms for you, including the state-mandated Judicial Council forms and many of the locally mandated forms as well, all on plain paper.

FileMaker®. FileMaker (filemaker.com). Cross-platform.

Anyone who has ever attempted to learn how to use a computerized database management system such as dBASE® will recognize with even a cursory glance just how well-designed FileMaker is. It's especially easy for a non-programmer to learn, set up, and use, and it stores and sorts graphic images as well as alphanumeric data. You could use it for keeping track of your bookkeeping, your buildings (including pictures), your various types of units (including floor plans), your vacancy statistics, your tenants, your loan schedules, your paint cans, your rental furniture, your competition, your ships as they come in, or your cows as they come home. I used FileMaker myself to write both Pushbutton Landlording and Eviction Forms Creator. It's an awesome program. It's the biggest selling database for the Macintosh and the biggest selling database for Windows, that is, when purchased as simply a database and not as part of a larger collection of programs.

Landlording on Disk (The Forms)®. ExPress (expresspublishing.com). Cross-platform.

There's nothing awesome here, but you could go a long way toward automating your entire landlording empire with a word processing program and a spreadsheet program and what's on this disk. I have. The disk consists of two major components—all the wordy forms from the *Landlording* book, more than thirty in all, those which can be "word processed" sensibly, and more than a dozen spreadsheet templates, including the two shown in chapter 21, and others which calculate loan payments, create loan tables, figure depreciation, and keep track of income. Do keep in mind that the word processing forms have to be used with a program capable of reading word processing files, and the templates have to be used with a program capable of reading spreadsheet files. They cannot be used by themselves. This is not a "stand-alone program." You could enter everything which comes on this disk into your computer yourself if you were so inclined, but you'd have to spend many hours doing so. This disk is an inexpensive alternative.

Microsoft Works®. Microsoft. (microsoft.com). Cross-platform.

Microsoft Works is a powerhouse. Like iWorks, it may be all the software you need for handling documents and numbers. Its various components will enable you to create documents, spreadsheets, and databases plus keep a personal calendar and an address book and handle your email. Its file formats are exactly the same as those of MS Word and MS Excel. Give it a chance before you lay out bigger bucks for Microsoft Office®.

Open Office®. Oracle (openoffice.org). Cross-platform.

Don't be deceived into thinking that this office suite is somehow less than excellent because it's free. It isn't. It is five excellent programs in one. One creates word documents. One creates spreadsheets. One creates presentations. One creates drawings, and one creates databases. It outputs its files in an international open standard format and also in other more common formats, including those used by Microsoft Office. What's more, it even outputs its files in the Adobe pdf format.

Pushbutton Landlording®. ExPress (expresspublishing.com). Cross-platform.

Like the book you are holding in your hands, this program is my own creation. It does virtually everything a computer can do to help the landlord run a landlording business except write checks. It doesn't write checks because Quicken handles that task better than any single component of a landlording software package ever could. Pushbutton Landlording handles the income and tenant side of the business. You enter information about yourself, your rental property, and your tenants, and it will produce rental agreements, condition and inventory checksheets, rent receipts, monthly statements, maintenance work orders, notices to pay rent or quit, tenant lists, tenant mailing labels, and a variety of reports. It all works with pushbuttons, hence the name. You push a few buttons, and it will tell you whose rent is one day or more late. You push another button, and it will create late-rent notices for those late tenants. It's a marvel, even if I do have to say so myself.

QuickBooks®. Intuit (intuit.com). Cross-platform.

This remarkable program is inexpensive, readily available, and widely used, and it seems simple enough at first glance, but it will either work wonders for you or cause you grief. Don't start using it right out of the box without first taking the time to learn how to use it correctly either by studying the user guide, by watching instructive videotapes, by hiring a tutor who knows the program intimately, or by taking a class at your local adult school. It's much more than it seems. It's not just a checkwriting program. It's an accounting program, a double-entry accounting program at that, and you must know at least the rudiments of accounting to take advantage of its many capabilities and benefits. It writes checks. It lists payables. It tracks expenses. It handles payroll. It produces balance sheets. It doesn't sing or dance, but it does reward the knowledgeable user many times over with useful reports and graphs. My own knowledgeable office manager uses it in all of our accounting operations. She knows it. Shes loves it.

Quicken®. Intuit (intuit.com). Cross-platform.

Writing checks and reconciling your bank statement were never easier. This program handles your bookkeeping through your checkbook. Write a check and the amount is automatically deducted from your checking account register at the same time the expenditure is posted to the proper category. It stores information for recurring transactions like the loan payments you make every month. It prints checks with the payee's address so they can be inserted into window envelopes, and it produces any number of reports. It can also export data easily into a spreadsheet program. I recommend Quicken highly.

Quicken® Rental Property Manager. Intuit (intuit.com). Windows only.

Quicken's Rental Property Manager includes Quicken itself and expands upon it to focus directly on the financial side of the landlording business, so you might say that it can handle both your personal finances and your landlording finances. It writes rent receipts and tracks rental income tenant by tenant. It writes checks and tracks expenses category by category. Because it records both income and expenses, it can easily provide you with a profit and loss report, so you can tell immediately whether you're making any money as a landlord. It's easy to use for anybody familiar with Quicken, and it exports its data directly to Intuit's other great product, TurboTax.

TurboTax®. Intuit (intuit.com). Cross-platform.

Seeing TurboTax for the first time is like seeing color TV after a lifetime of viewing black-and-white. Right on the computer's screen are facsimiles of the familiar IRS forms themselves. You enter the appropriate figures once in the same boxes you'd be using if you were filling out the forms manually, and the program does all the calculations for you. All of the forms are linked, too. Complete Schedule E, and the appropriate figures are posted automatically to your 1040. Change something on Schedule E, and everything related to it throughout your return will change as well. Do "what if" calculations on any part of your return and you'll know instantly how they affect the results. In addition, the entire IRS instruction booklet is part of the program and available for retrieval on demand. Want information about a particular item on an IRS form? Point to that line and click. Presto, the IRS helps appear. No IRS agent could possibly be any faster! Want to print out your return? No problem! Put blank paper in your printer and print. There's no need to shuffle through the IRS preprinted forms. If the IRS were sending U.S. taxpayers a manual version and a computer version of its 1040 tax reporting package, this would be the computer version. I can't imagine a better one. It reduces the onerous tax-preparation chore from days to hours, and it's totally accurate. What's more, it's inexpensive, and you needn't spend a week studying a New-York-City-telephone-directory-sized manual learning how to run the program. It uses standard commands, so if you know how to run other programs in a graphical environment, you already know how to use TurboTax. The program will do any number of federal returns plus any number of state returns for a single state. If you need to do returns for additional states, you'll have to pay extra for them.

Forms

Professional Publishing (profpub.com).

Printed versions of Professional Publishing's Plain Language™ real estate forms are no longer available. Computerized versions are. Go to Professional Publishing's website, and you'll be directed to another website where you may preview and purchase the forms. They're still as good as they ever were.

Periodicals

These periodicals carry no advertising and hence have no biases except those of their writers, editors, and publishers, which may in themselves be considerable.

Consumer Reports. Consumer Reports, P.O. Box 2109, Harlan, IA 51593. (consumerreports.org) 12 issues a year, plus an annual buyer's guide, no advertising.

This trustworthy magazine publishes the results of the tests and studies conducted in its own fiercely independent laboratories. Although it is obviously pro-consumer, supposing that *Consumer Reports* is therefore anti-business would be a true non-sequitur. Expect it to publish articles written from a tenant's perspective (they're the "consumers" in our business, remember) from time to time, but also remember that you in your role as a landlord are a consumer of various goods and services, too. Look to it for forthright evaluations of fire extinguishers, smoke alarms, ladders, paints, cleaning agents, carpets, computers, appliances, locks, telephones, and tools. You'll even find informative articles on mortgages, wills, banks, and insurance companies. The annual buying guide, published in December, summarizes earlier articles and runs to many pages. It's available separately at newsstands and bookstores.

John T. Reed's Real Estate Investor's Monthly. Reed Publishing, 342 Bryan Dr., Alamo, CA 94507. (johntreed.com) 925.820.6292. 12 issues a year, no advertising.

Well ahead of the real estate investing herd, this eight-page newsletter, written by the prolific John Reed, divulges real estate investment ideas which make sense and make money. It's newsy, it's current, it's practical, it's lively, it's analytical, and what's more, it's bottom-line oriented, just as you'd expect from a Harvard Business School MBA who's spent almost a lifetime inhaling and exhaling real estate.

Mr. Landlord. MrLandlord.com, P.O. Box 64442, Virginia Beach, VA 23467. (mrlandlord.com) 800.950.2250. 12 issues a year, some advertising.

The expression "down-to-earth" best characterizes this eight-page newsletter which bills itself as "the survival newsletter for landlords and landladies." That it is. It's written by landlords who scramble around in the trenches for landlords who scramble around in the trenches. You can't help but pick up at least one practical idea from each issue. Maybe you'll even see something of yourself in the landlord interview feature; it profiles a different landlord from around the country every month.

Strategies and Solutions. Pro Serve Corp., 2677 S. Tamiami Trail, Suite 4, Sarasota, FL 34239. (johnschaub.com) 800.237.9222. 6 issues a year, no advertising.

For years, John Schaub has been the voice of the rental house investor. Still an active rental house investor himself, he knows the subject better than anybody and shares what he knows freely at his seminars and conferences and in his books and newsletter. Recent newsletters have focused on lowering insurance bills, tax-free exchanging, the down market, lead paint problems, and con artists, all subjects we can't know enough about.

Websites

Websites of use to landlords keep popping up all the time as people keep coming up with new ideas. The websites listed here are not the only ones useful to landlords even now. They're only the ones I'm familiar with as of now. You might want to become familiar with them, too, and keep searching for new ones whenever you have the urge.

craigslist.org—If you own rental property where Craigslist offers localized listings, consider yourself fortunate because you get to list your vacancies for little or nothing. Check out the site and use it. Everybody else does, both landlords and tenants.

e-renter.com—Inexpensive tenant screening packages in full compliance with the Fair Credit Reporting Act are this website's forte. Have a look at their sample reports, and you'll see how easy they are to understand.

getrentcheck.com—Cloud computing, which enables you to access your files and applications remotely over the internet as opposed to accessing them locally on a stand-alone computer, has come to the landlording business. Go to this website, watch the video, sign up for a free 30-day trial, and give it a try, but understand that there is an ongoing charge for using RentCheck after the free trial.

inman.com—Updated daily by a staff who take pride in being accurate and being first, it has the very latest in real estate news and information. It calls itself "the leading source of independent real estate news, information, advice, research, opin-

ion and commentary for industry professionals and consumers alike," and that's no puffery. It has won numerous awards, including the National Association of Real Estate Editor's "Best Website" award. Read "Brad's Blog" once, and you'll keep coming back for more.

johntreed.com—Besides listing all of Mr. Reed's materials, this site includes choice morsels of his writings, such as his "Real Estate B.S. Artist Detection Checklist." He doesn't mince his words.

mrlandlord.com—Like Alice's Restaurant in Arlo Guthrie's song, you can get anything you want at mrlandlord.com. It's a busy place, and it serves up a big menu, everything from a free reminder service to a tip of the week to a chat room. It offers instant, low-cost tenant credit reports and explains why you should submit to an on-site inspection to become authorized as a legitimate business permitted to request credit report information on tenant applicants. Visit the website and you'll surely find something there that will fill you with delight.

landlording.com—This is my own website, where you will find information about my books and software. You will also find a page called "What's New?" where I comment on subjects of current interest to landlords and a Q&A page where I answer questions submitted via email.

landlording.tv—Yes, there is a golf channel. There is a food channel. There is a cartoon channel. There is a travel channel. There is a sci fi channel. Why shouldn't there be a landlording channel? Uh, there probably should be, but there isn't one. The landlording.tv website is close enough, and it's good enough for me. It's a well-designed website run by avid landlord Justin Palma, who puts his landlording expertise and his video production talents and web authoring skills to good use. His videos show "how to organize and run a profitable rental empire" whether you're working in the office or in the trenches. Have a look.

landlordlocks.com—Seeing is more believing than reading is. In Chapter 18 of this book, I describe how Landlord Locks work. Now see how they work in photographs showing the three-step lock change. Next, read the questions people commonly ask about Landlord Locks and the corresponding answers. Finally, place an order.

landlord-success.com—Ever wonder how another landlord solved a problem you're having? Go here to "The Successful Landlord Blog," and you'll find out. If you find nothing about your problem, post a blog about it yourself, and don't be surprised when dozens of other landlords offer you their good advice.

loopnet.com—Buyers and sellers of commercial, industrial, and multi-family residential properties will find listings here organized by location, type, and price. Check the listings in your price range of exactly the type of property you're looking to buy or sell in your area. Then broaden or narrow your criteria to come up with a more useful list. Whether you're in the market to find an exchange property to identify by tomorrow or just browsing to get an idea what your property might be worth were you to put it on the market today, Loopnet will save you hours and hours of trying to locate properties which meet your criteria.

mybackgroundcheck.com—The good news about this unique service is that it enables an applicant to purchase his own background check and then give you access to the unalterable results online via a certificate with an ID and password. The onus of the background check is on the applicant and not on the landlord. That's all good. The bad news is that it's expensive. Compare this service's prices on its menu of background checks with those available elsewhere, and you'll find that they're roughly twice the price. Yes, I know that the applicant pays these expenses, and the landlord pays nothing to access the results, but if I were a tenant, I'd balk at paying around $100 for the background checks most commonly requested by landlords.

nibbo.com—Nibbo has come late to the search-engine party, but it's so attractive that it cannot be ignored. You must try it. Try searching something, anything, using Google and Yahoo first, and then search the same thing using Nibbo. Nibbo's list will be at least as pertinent and comprehensive, but it will be easier to sort through and more pleasing to the eye. You may customize the list layout to show what you want it to show, too. I like mine to show images related to the search, positioned directly beside the list itself so I have visual clues for searching further. Go ahead. Try it! You're apt to like it and make it your default search engine just as I have.

nolo.com—Nolo has long been a publisher of legal books and software oriented toward the layperson. It maintains an excellent website with all kinds of information about its products, including sample chapters from its books, plus a law dictionary, downloadable forms, and a lawyer directory. Please note that Nolo gives legal information, not legal advice.

rentals.com—Check out this website and its counterparts, "apartments.com," "move.com," "vacancynet.com," etc., to see how they work and whether they would work well for you. Evaluate them the same way you'd evaluate any other kind of advertising, by the cost per suitable prospect they produce.

rhol.org—Rental Housing On Line is a cornucopia of landlording "stuff." The site is stuffed full of information, forms, forums, association listings, laws, a vacancy listing service called "vacancylist.net," and more. Nonmembers may access hundreds of its web pages. Members may access everything. They get credit reports, including credit scoring, for a nominal $9.95. They can get other tenant-screening reports at nominal prices, too. A prior address locator report is $4.95. A sex offender report is $4.95. A state criminal report is $9.95, and an eviction report is $7.95. Membership is $39.95 per year. Quite simply, it's a deal!

xi2010.com—Any number of websites offer tenant screening. This one offers tenant screening and delinquent tenant reporting. As an account holder, you may report your tenants' payment history, both good and bad, just as the credit card companies do, and it will appear on their credit reports. How's that for having the power to give your tenants an extra incentive to pay their rent promptly?

X-Classification

ApplianceSmart. (appliancesmart.com) 800.673.0671.

ApplianceSmart buys truckloads of new appliances directly from manufacturers. These major household appliances may be closeouts or factory overruns, or they may have slight imperfections. As such, they fall outside the normal distribution channels and can be sold at rock-bottom prices, even with a one-year guarantee. Currently, ApplianceSmart has twenty outlets in Georgia, Minnesota, Ohio, and Texas. Check their website for locations. Would that they were everywhere!

Index